...STUDENT TESTED.

First-Year Business Students:

Great book for all levels of business background. This book is not all about the numbers. It is also about the people, the company, and how they will work together to make a successful business (company).

—Amanda Lewis

This textbook provides great insight into the management side of business, from the perspective of students, corporations, and managers. It will provide the foundation for all future business endeavours.

—Yifan Zhou

A very practical and informative textbook. The author really made me feel as if he was talking to me while I was reading it.

—Cole Castellarin

This book kept me interested all through the 15 chapters. It was my only textbook I willingly wanted to read.

—Mrinali Goyal

This textbook is very useful in the way that it explains management strategies, methods, and theory without simply spitting out information to be memorized. This made it a more enjoyable to read and helped me to retain more information.

—Kathryn Hajjar

Upper Year (non-Commerce major) Students:

It is like an entire business degree condensed into one reference manual.

—Rachel Henderson

The textbook provides valuable information regarding an introduction to business. The information within the book is supported by student experience, corporate examples and detailed diagrams which makes the learning process and retention of information more easy and effective.

—Alexandra Marinelli

This textbook provides a fantastic overview of the many key concepts in the study of business, presenting them in a clear and understandable

way. Reading this book can help stimulate an interest in business for readers with little to no prior business knowledge.

—Joel Covert

The text is current and provides real-life applicable examples to nearly all concepts covered, as well as easy-to-read theory and simple visuals that aid in the understanding of complex ideas.

—Emily Meyers

This book covers all the fundamentals of business and is a great place to start your business education.

—Julia Marsala

FIRST EDITION

Business

STRATEGY • DEVELOPMENT • APPLICATION

Gary J. Bissonette
Queen's University

McGraw-Hill Ryerson
Connect. Learn. Succeed.

Statistics Canada information is used with the permission of Statistics Canada. Users are forbidden to copy this material and/or redisseminate the data, in an original or modified form, for commercial purposes, without the expressed permission of Statistics Canada. Information on the availability of the wide range of data from Statistics Canada can be obtained from Statistics Canada's Regional Offices, its World Wide Web site at http://www.statcan.ca and its toll-free access number 1-800-263-1136.

The Internet addresses listed in the text were accurate at the time of publication. The inclusion of a Web site does not indicate an endorsement by the authors or McGraw-Hill Ryerson, and McGraw-Hill Ryerson does not guarantee the accuracy of information presented at these sites.

ISBN 13: 978-0-07-096746-5
ISBN 10: 0-07-096746-6

1 2 3 4 5 6 7 8 9 10 QDB 1 9 8 7 6 5 4 3 2

Printed and bound in the United States of America.

Care has been taken to trace ownership of copyright material contained in this text; however, the publisher will welcome any information that enables them to rectify any reference or credit for subsequent editions.

Executive Sponsoring Editor: *Kim Brewster*
Marketing Manager: *Cathie Lefebvre*
Developmental Editor: *Lori McLellan*
Senior Editorial Associate: *Christine Lomas*
Supervising Editor: *Katie McHale*
Production Coordinator: *Lena Keating*
Copy Editor: *Kelli Howey*
Permissions Researcher: *Tracy Leonard*
Inside Design: *Dave Murphy/Valid Design*
Composition: *Aptara®, Inc.*
Cover Design: *Dave Murphy/Valid Design*
Cover Photo: *ULTRA.F/Getty Images*
Printer: *Quad/Graphics Dubuque (U.S.)*

Library and Archives Canada Cataloguing in Publication Data
Bissonette, Gary J.
    Business : strategy, development, application / Gary Bissonette.—1st ed.

Includes bibliographical references and index.
ISBN 978-0-07-096746-5

    1. Business—Textbooks.   2. Management—Textbooks. I. Title.

HF1008.B57 2012   650   C2011-907758-2

About the Author

Gary Bissonette

is an Assistant Professor at Queen's University School of Business. He has 18 plus years of business teaching experience in Canada and the United States, at both the undergraduate and graduate levels. The author has both private industry and public not-for-profit experience, holding a variety of management positions, including that of C.E.O. of a medium-size NFP for over 14 years. Gary also has SME experience as a business owner and operator. Gary currently provides consulting and advisory services to both the not-for-profit and SME sectors.

Courtesy of Queen's University

Brief Contents

Contents

Chapter 3: The Global Marketplace 58

Chapter 4: The Environment and Sustainable Business Practices 88

PART 2: MANAGING AND GUIDING YOUR TEAM

Chapter 5: Ethics and Corporate Social Responsibility 116

Chapter 6: Developing a Business Strategy 142

Chapter 7: Developing Your Business Structure and Culture 168

Chapter 8: Managing and Leading the Organization's Talent 194

PART 3: MANAGING THE VALUE CHAIN

Chapter 9: Operations and Supply Chain Management 218

Chapter 10: The Marketing Challenge 250

Chapter 11: Understanding the Marketing Effort 276

PART 4: UNDERSTANDING BUSINESS FINANCES

Chapter 12: Cost-Base Analysis and Pricing 314

Chapter 13: Introduction to Capital and Financial Markets 350

Chapter 14: Understanding Financial Statements 384

Chapter 15: Analyzing New Business Ventures 422

Preface

A Blue Ocean Approach to Business Management Fundamentals

In a marketplace full of introductory business textbooks, what makes this one different? Why does it make sense to choose this textbook versus others available to you? The response to these questions can be best described by the analogy of Blue Ocean versus Red Ocean thinking.

In developing this textbook for the Canadian marketplace, the choice that presented itself was the following: create a textbook in a similar vein to the many books that already populate the marketplace and seek to convince you to try an alternate version of already existing products (Red Ocean), or create a new, unique, and exciting approach that supports the teaching of core concepts and models in a manner that generates a true understanding of business and communicates an excitement and appreciation for its role in today's society (Blue Ocean).

Business: Strategy, Development, Application chooses the latter approach. Created indigenously for the Canadian market by an author with considerable senior management expertise and many years of teaching experience at both the university and college levels, this textbook delivers a unique interpretation of the practical application of business in a way that ensures a true understanding of today's complex—yet exciting—business environment. Fundamental to its delivery is the communication of chapter content in a manner that students can easily grasp, and that ensures that core learning takes place. Rich in examples, Web-based interaction, and practical-application illustration, the textbook delivers to the instructor and students a sound base for future business management learning and action.

Yes, this textbook is truly different in its approach—"Blue Ocean" different. It is uniquely positioned: focusing on knowledge and skill development in a usable format that students can immediately transfer to current employment situations, or use to leverage in managerial or self-employment opportunities that will challenge them in the future. It is also significantly more interactive, challenging students to participate in the current global marketplace via active, Web-based searches and references.

Why Choose This Textbook?

Many of us have been challenged throughout our careers with trying to find the perfect textbook that would enable an instructor to deliver an entry-level business management course in a way that was creative, thought provoking, and of interest to students. Essential to this search was the desire to have a textbook that goes beyond the typical template, definition-focused approach common to entry-level textbooks, and deliver content that results in a true understanding of business fundamentals. This textbook responds to this challenge and desired outcome. Specifically, *Business: Strategy, Development, Application* delivers the following:

- chapter content that explains the use of key business concepts and models via a writing style that encourages understanding and generates interest in the topic being discussed;

- extensive use of Canadian-based examples from a wide spectrum of business scenarios within the for-profit, not-for-profit, and SME business environments;
- a full understanding and appreciation of the globalization taking place today and the unique positioning that Canada and its economic base currently have—and will continue to benefit from—due to this globalization process;
- an emphasis on identifying and defining current business trends occurring within the Canadian marketplace, including, but not limited to, multi cultural diversification, sustainable business thinking and practices, and regulatory trends and shifts; and
- delivery of key business concepts and models from the viewpoint of the C level or general manager, thus ensuring not only a base-level understanding of such core business requirements, but also an understanding of how and why such concepts and models are used in managing a business entity.

A Special Note to Students

Regardless of the occupation that you enter into, you will come in direct contact with the world of business and, ultimately, the global marketplace. Whether you enter into the field of marketing, engineering, nursing, programming, or social services, or consider a business opportunity as an entrepreneur, many aspects of your job responsibilities will be framed around the business concepts and models discussed within this textbook. In writing this textbook, it is my hope that you will come to fully understand how businesses and the marketplace operate, and how you can use this information to your advantage as you pursue your chosen career. Also unique to this textbook is the writing style that is focused on defining and describing the role of the general manager in overseeing a business entity and how business fundamentals come into play within his or her decision-making process. The textbook's intent is to deliver a variety of business and management tools illustrated in a manner that will help to ensure easy application in the future.

Organization of the Textbook

Business: Strategy, Development, Application has been designed to be as flexible and modular as possible with each chapter possessing the ability to stand on its own. The textbook is built around four themes:

- Macro Business Environment;
- Managing and Guiding Your Team;
- Managing the Value Chain; and
- Understanding Business Finances

Although presented within the textbook as noted above, each section (theme) has been developed independently of the other sections so that instructors can feel comfortable in rearranging sections to fit their teaching style and/or course emphasis. A special focus has also been placed on ensuring that the textbook responds not only to the operational framework of corporate Canada, but also to the needs of students and instructors interested in SMEs (small and medium-size enterprises) and not-for-profit organizations.

Specific areas of focus within the four theme sections are as follows:

Part		Chapter Topics
Part 1: Macro Business Environment	Chapter 1	What Is Business?
	Chapter 2	The Canadian Economic Environment
	Chapter 3	The Global Marketplace
	Chapter 4	The Environment and Sustainable Business Practices
Part 2: Managing and Guiding Your Team	Chapter 5	Ethics and Corporate Social Responsibility
	Chapter 6	Developing a Business Strategy
	Chapter 7	Developing Your Business Structure and Culture
	Chapter 8	Managing and Leading the Organization's Talent
Part 3: Managing the Value Chain	Chapter 9	Operations and Supply Chain Management
	Chapter 10	The Marketing Challenge
	Chapter 11	Understanding the Marketing Effort
Part 4: Understanding Business Finances	Chapter 12	Cost-Base Analysis and Pricing
	Chapter 13	Introduction to Capital and Financial Markets
	Chapter 14	Understanding Financial Statements
	Chapter 15	Analyzing New Business Ventures

In-Chapter Learning Features

A fundamental feature of this textbook is its turnkey approach to supporting student learning. Each chapter has been carefully crafted in a manner that will ensure that students fully understand the material being presented, and that they are directed to supplemental resource locations to update and enhance their competencies of critical concepts and models. Also unique to this textbook is an opening vignette, titled "From the Student's Perspective," that provides an insight into the focus and importance of the chapter from the perspective of a student. In-chapter learning features include the following:

Learning Objectives
Help students preview what they should know after reading the chapter.

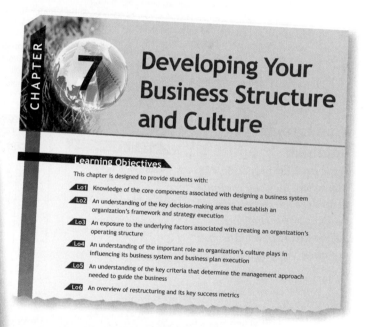

CHAPTER 7

Developing Your Business Structure and Culture

Learning Objectives
This chapter is designed to provide students with:

- **Lo1** Knowledge of the core components associated with designing a business system
- **Lo2** An understanding of the key decision-making areas that establish an organization's framework and strategy execution
- **Lo3** An exposure to the underlying factors associated with creating an organization's operating structure
- **Lo4** An understanding of the important role an organization's culture plays in influencing its business system and business plan execution
- **Lo5** An understanding of the key criteria that determine the management approach needed to guide the business
- **Lo6** An overview of restructuring and its key success metrics

From the Student's Perspective

In the past, managers have followed one rule in making business decisions: make the most money possible. Companies that did things the fastest and the cheapest were the industry leaders. Everyone wanted to be on top, taking nothing into account except for the bottom line. Profit was king.

However, what happens when profit comes at the expense of the environment, social well-being, or even somebody's life? Transparency in the media has shown us the consequence of business without ethics: global warming, impoverished communities, and, just two years ago, the biggest financial crisis in history. When companies like Walmart have sales equal to the GDP of hundreds of countries, they have the responsibility to further the well-being and sustainability of all their stakeholders—not just their shareholders. They have the responsibility to instigate change for the better. In the end, we have to acknowledge the virtuous cycle in which all of us operate: in order to survive, what we take, we must give back.

Further, instead of being a hindrance to profitability, ethical business has actually become *good business*. Consumers today demand socially responsible initiatives from most, if not all, companies—whether it be through fair trade practices or the preservation of human rights. Companies centred on corporate social responsibility are actually thriving in today's business environment. And what has happened to companies like Nortel, Enron, and Lehman Brothers? Society has doled out its justice.

Nevertheless, as with any moral issue, all decisions are based on free will and choice. As future managers, the choice is up to you. What will you do?

Joanna Pleta is a Queen's University BComm'10 who is currently working Assistant Marketing Manager for Ame Express. She is originally from the Ph pines but has also lived in Switzerlar the United Arab Emirates, and the U Kingdom. At Queen's, she was a recip of the Certificate of Corporate Socia Responsibility and the D.I. McLeod's List Scholarship for four consecutive She has also been involved in organiz such as the Queen's Finance Associat Conference, the Principal's Innovatio Fund, and Unilever. In the future, sh aspires to excel in the marketing fie become fluent in French and Spanish work in Europe or Latin America.

From the Student's Perspective
Provides an insight into the focus and importance of the chapter from the perspective of a business student.

Snapshot—What to Expect in This Chapter
This chapter provides students with a broad introductory overview of what a business owner or a senior management team needs to understand to successfully manage a business organization. The content emphasized in this chapter includes the following:

- The Big Picture
- What Is Business?
  - The Fundamental Objectives of Business
- The Business Model and Profitability
  - The Difference between Profit and Profitability
  - Improving Profitability
- Creating a Value Proposition
  - The Impact of Price
  - Understanding Your Cost Base
- The Business Decision-Making Landscape
- Management Reflection—Focus on Business

Snapshot—What to Expect in This Chapter
Outlines the key topics covered within the chapter.

BUSINESS in Action

Canada and Water Consumption

According to statistics released by the Conference Board of Canada (2008), our country ranks 15th out of 16 peer countries in terms of water conservation. Only the United States scored worse than Canada with respect to water consumption. Graded on the basis of A, B, C, and D, Canada received a "D" for its water conservation practices. The Conference Board of Canada study reinforces a prior study conducted by the OECD (Organisation for Economic Co-operation and Development). The OECD, which studied water use in 29 different countries from 1980 to 2000, ranked Canada 28th out of 29 countries. Again, only the residents of the United States, on a per capita basis, use more water than Canadians. Canadians currently use just under an estimated 1500 cubic metres of water per person per year. This is double the 16-country average identified in the Conference Board study, and more than nine times greater than the number-one ranked country, the United Kingdom (est. 155 cubic metres per person per year). Of the 16 countries analyzed, 10 countries had water consumption, on a per capita basis, of less than 641 cubic metres.[1] That is less than 45 percent of Canada's consumption level. Although Canada's largest water consumer is industry (68 percent), Canadian households use more than 300 litres of water per day. So, why is it that Canadians use so much water? The Conference Board of Canada study pointed to two key factors. First, Canada, as a whole, suffers from a lack of widespread water conservation practices. As an example, agriculture, the largest industrial user of water in Canada, is particularly inefficient, recycling less than 30 percent of the water it uses. While many countries in the study have worked toward reducing water consumption over the last two decades, Canadian water consumption has actually increased by 26 percent during this same period (although recently this has decreased slightly). The second reason given for our high water utilization has to do with the price of water in Canada. In many areas in Canada, the price of water

Business in Action Vignettes

Spread throughout each chapter; provide practical, marketplace applications of business situations and business best practices.

Web Integration Sidebars

Refer students to specific Web sites where they can continue to analyze the success of a business or the challenge highlighted within a Business in Action vignette.

WEB INTEGRATION

Want to learn more about Canada's water conservation and water management initiatives? Visit the Conference Board of Canada Web site at **www.conferenceboard.ca**, or Google "Canada's water consumption practices."

warming, population growth, and industry expansion are all working toward depleting this precious resource. In 2001, the federal Commissioner of the Environment and Sustainable Development declared fresh water in southern Canada to be heavily used and overly stressed.[2] As Canadians, our task is to protect and respect this finite resource, through stronger conservation practices and through pricing strategies that ensure our water resource is managed to the benefit of not just current but also future generations.[3]

To truly create a culture of ethical behaviour and financial decision integrity, the board of directors (or owner-representative body) must be active in the ongoing monitoring of the organization and take a leadership role in the tightening of such processes when and where it is required.

Highlighted Key Takeaways

Presented throughout each chapter; reinforce the key learning fundamentals that students should understand as they read through and comprehend the information offered within a chapter's various sections.

The key takeaway from the list above is that the board of directors, as representatives of the stakeholders of an organization, must see itself as the creator and sentinel of the organization's conscience. To ensure this occurs, boards must take a lead role in the development of management compensation policies, the shaping of an organization's personnel policy, the

Management Reflection—It Is All About Trust

Management Reflection

Provides a closing commentary on how managers use the key models and concepts discussed within a chapter and, in some cases, how small businesses or not-for-profits respond to the themes/challenges posed in the material presented.

Business courses worldwide continually reinforce the need for organizations to encourage entrepreneurship, innovation, and risk taking. Managers and executives have hundreds of articles and books at their disposal on how to manage and motivate their employees. Organizations continuously look for ways to empower people to develop new processes and operating efficiencies. So, just what is the common thread that allows for all these things to occur within successful organizations? The common thread is trust. Trust is fundamental to all that we do and to everyone that we interact with. As indicated in this chapter, the best asset you can bring to work, on a day-to-day basis, is your integrity. This means being honest, respecting the dignity of others, listening before you speak, being accountable for your mistakes, doing what you say you are going to do, demonstrating transparency in the decisions you make, not presuming you have all the answers, and thanking people for their feedback. Successful managers are open and authentic. They encourage open discussion, communicate their concerns, actively discuss risk, and don't manipulate people or distort facts.

End-of-Chapter Support: Developing Business Knowledge and Skills

In addition to the above, the end-of-chapter support within *Business: Strategy, Development, Application* has been designed to provide instructors and students with an effective review and with additional learning materials focused on reinforcing the critical takeaways from within each chapter. Key ingredients of this end-of-chapter support include the following:

- Chapter Summary: An overview of the content of a chapter and the key models and concepts that were presented;
- Key Terms: Identification of the key business terms used in a chapter;
- Questions for Discussion: A set of chapter-related questions and points of reflection that ensure that students fully understand the key components of chapter material presented;
- Question for Individual Action: A chapter-specific assignment suitable for assigning to an individual student;
- Team Exercise: A chapter-specific assignment that instructors can assign to groups or teams of students for analytical and/or presentation purposes; and
- Case for Discussion: A pertinent and to-the-point application/illustration of the chapter theme designed to complement both the reading material presented and the in-class discussions that will take place. Case discussions have been designed for use within a single instructional session.

Comprehensive Teaching and Learning Package: The McGraw-Hill Ryerson Advantage

CONNECT

McGraw-Hill Connect™ is a Web-based assignment and assessment platform that gives students the means to better connect with their coursework, with their instructors, and with the important concepts that they will need to know for success now and in the future.

With Connect, instructors can deliver assignments, quizzes, and tests online. Nearly all the questions from the text are presented in an auto-gradeable format and tied to the text's learning objectives. Instructors can edit existing questions and author entirely new problems. Track individual student performance—by question, assignment, or in relation to the class overall—with detailed grade reports. Integrate grade reports easily with Learning Management Systems (LMS) such as WebCT and Blackboard. And much more.

By choosing Connect, instructors are providing their students with a powerful tool for improving academic performance and truly mastering course material. Connect allows students to practise important skills at their own pace and on their own schedule. Importantly, students' assessment results and instructors' feedback are all saved online—so students can continually review their progress and plot their course to success.

Connect also provides 24/7 online access to an eBook—an online edition of the text—to aid them in successfully completing their work, wherever and whenever they choose.

Key Features

SIMPLE ASSIGNMENT MANAGEMENT

With Connect, creating assignments is easier than ever, so you can spend more time teaching and less time managing.

- Create and deliver assignments easily with selectable end-of-chapter questions and test bank material to assign online.
- Streamline lesson planning, student progress reporting, and assignment grading to make classroom management more efficient than ever.
- Go paperless with the eBook and online submission and grading of student assignments.

SMART GRADING

When it comes to studying, time is precious. Connect helps students learn more efficiently by providing feedback and practice material when they need it, where they need it.

- Automatically score assignments, giving students immediate feedback on their work and side-by-side comparisons with correct answers.
- Access and review each response; manually change grades or leave comments for students to review.
- Reinforce classroom concepts with practice tests and instant quizzes.

INSTRUCTOR LIBRARY

The Connect Instructor Library is your course creation hub. It provides all the critical resources you'll need to build your course, just how you want to teach it.

- Assign eBook readings and draw from a rich collection of textbook-specific assignments.
- Access instructor resources, including ready-made PowerPoint presentations and media to use in your lectures.
- View assignments and resources created for past sections.
- Post your own resources for students to use.

eBOOK

Connect reinvents the textbook learning experience for the modern student. Every Connect subject area is seamlessly integrated with Connect eBooks, which are designed to keep students focused on the concepts key to their success.

- Provide students with a Connect eBook, allowing for anytime, anywhere access to the textbook.
- Merge media, animation, and assessments with the text's narrative to engage students and improve learning and retention.
- Pinpoint and connect key concepts in a snap using the powerful eBook search engine.
- Manage notes, highlights, and bookmarks in one place for simple, comprehensive review.

COURSE MANAGEMENT

McGraw-Hill Ryerson offers a range of flexible integration solutions for Blackboard, WebCT, Desire2Learn, Moodle, and other leading learning management platforms. Please contact your local McGraw-Hill Ryerson *i*Learning Sales Specialist for details.

TEGRITY

Tegrity is a service that makes class time available all the time by automatically capturing every lecture in a searchable format for students to review when they study and complete assignments. With a simple one-click start-and-stop process, you capture all computer screens and corresponding audio. Students replay any part of any class with easy-to-use browser-based viewing on a PC or Mac. Educators know that the more students can see, hear, and experience class resources, the better they learn. With Tegrity, students quickly recall key moments by using Tegrity's unique search feature. This search helps students efficiently find what they need, when they need it across an entire semester of class recordings. Help turn all your students' study time into learning moments immediately supported by your lecture. To learn more about Tegrity watch a 2-minute Flash demo at http://tegritycampus.mhhe.com.

INSTRUCTOR RESOURCES

Instructor's Manual: Prepared by the text author, this contains a short topic outline of the chapter and a listing of learning objectives and key terms, a resource checklist with supplements that correspond to each chapter, a detailed lecture outline including marginal notes recommending where to use supplementary cases, lecture enhancers, and critical thinking exercises.

Computerized Test Bank: Written by Jeff Ryan, Grant MacEwan University, the computerized EZ Test version allows instructors to add and edit questions, save and reload multiple test versions, select questions based on type, difficulty, or key word and use password protection. True/False questions test three levels of learning: (1) knowledge of key terms, (2) understanding of concepts and principles, and (3) application of principles.

Microsoft® PowerPoint® Presentation: Prepared by Kim Richter, Kwantlen Polytechnic University, the slideshow for each chapter is based around the learning objectives and includes many of the figures and tables from the textbook, as well as some additional slides that support and expand the text discussions. Slides can be modified by instructors with PowerPoint®.

Videos: Complementary videos are available on DVD and can also be accessed on the password-protected area of Connect. Detailed teaching notes written by the text author are available in the Instructor's Manual and on the instructor area of Connect.

MANAGER'S HOT SEAT VIDEOS

In today's workplace, managers are confronted daily with issues such as ethics, diversity, working in teams, and the virtual workplace. The Manager's Hot Seat is an online resource that allows students to watch as 15 real managers apply their years of experience to confront these issues. These videos are available as a complementary instructor supplement or for bundling with student textbooks.

BUSINESS PLAN PRO

Business Plan Pro is available as a bundled option that includes more than 250 sample business plans and 400 case studies to give you a wide variety of examples as you create your own plan. It helps you set up your business by answering questions that help the software customize your plan. You then enter your financial data to generate financial worksheets and statements.

NEW BUSINESS MENTOR

For instructors who incorporate a business plan project into their class, the New Business Mentor software can be bundled upon request with student textbooks and includes sample business plans, resources to help you as you start your business, business and feasibility planning software, and the "mentor," who will walk you through each step of the business plan. Teaching notes are also available.

E-STAT

E-STAT is an educational resource designed by Statistics Canada and made available to Canadian educational institutions. Using 450 000 current CANSIM (Canadian Socio-economic Information Management Systems) Time Series and the most recent—as well as historical—census data, E-STAT allows you to bring data to life in colourful graphs and maps. Access to E-STAT is made available to purchasers of this book, via Connect, by special arrangement between McGraw-Hill Ryerson and Statistics Canada.

Superior Service

SUPERIOR SERVICE

Service takes on a whole new meaning with McGraw-Hill Ryerson and *Business: Strategy, Development, Application.* More than just bringing you the textbook, we have consistently raised the bar in terms of innovation and educational research—both in business and in education in general. These investments in learning and the education community have helped us to understand the needs of students and educators across the country, and allowed us to foster the growth of truly innovative, integrated learning.

INTEGRATED LEARNING

Your Integrated *i*Learning Sales Specialist is a McGraw-Hill Ryerson representative who has the experience, product knowledge, training, and support to help you assess and integrate any of our products, technology, and services into your course for optimal teaching and learning performance. Whether it's helping your students improve their grades, or putting your entire course online, your *i*Learning Sales Specialist is there to help you do it. Contact your *i*Learning Sales Specialist today to learn how to maximize all of McGraw-Hill Ryerson's resources!

CREATE ONLINE

McGraw-Hill's Create Online places the most abundant resource at your fingertips—literally. With a few mouse clicks, you can create customized learning tools simply and affordably. McGraw-Hill Ryerson has included many of its market-leading textbooks within Create Online for eBook and print customization as well as many licensed readings and cases. For more information, please visit **www.mcgrawhillcreate.com**.

COURSESMART

CourseSmart brings together thousands of textbooks across hundreds of courses in an eTextbook format providing unique benefits to students and faculty. By purchasing an eTextbook, students can save up to 50 percent off the cost of a print textbook, reduce their impact on the environment, and gain access to powerful Web tools for learning, including full text search, notes and highlighting, and e-mail tools for sharing notes among classmates. For faculty, CourseSmart provides instant access to review and compare textbooks and course materials in their discipline area without the time, cost, and environmental impact of mailing print examination copies. For further details, contact your *i*Learning sales specialist or visit www.coursesmart.com.

Acknowledgements

Although the cover of this textbook lists me as the sole author, this is somewhat of a misnomer. The completion of this textbook could not have been accomplished without considerable contribution by many others. First and foremost, I would like to thank my wife, Lynda. Not only was she a supporter of this initiative, but she spent countless hours proofing, editing, and questioning the communication approach within it. It was truly a joint initiative. Her commitment to enabling me to succeed will never be forgotten. She is truly the best life partner one could ever hope for.

Much of what I have learned over the course of my career has been the result of a combination of my own experiences, both positive and negative. Equally as important has been my advantage to work at Queen's University with some of the brightest minds in Canada. The work of Drs. Ken Wong, Peter Richardson, and Elspeth Murray has had a real influence on both my teaching style and conceptual emphasis. David McConomy has been a true mentor, both in reviewing and commenting on this textbook as it unfolded and in demonstrating best practices in the classroom. Additional thanks goes to professors Greg Libitz, Darren McCaugherty, Paul Roman, and Vikram Varma, who used chapters from this textbook in their courses and who offered a number of valuable comments to improve this final product. The School of Business itself has been an invaluable part of my career development, offering an academic environment second to none.

I would also like to thank Michael Portner-Gartke, my research assistant, for his excellent critique of the various chapter drafts, as well as his contributions to the development of both case studies within the textbook and a number of its "Business in Action" vignettes. Equally important is a need to thank the 1000+ students at Queen's University who, over the past two years, used a manuscript version of this textbook within their courses, and who offered tremendous insight and commentary relating to its strengths and weaknesses.

In addition, I would like to thank the editorial and marketing team at McGraw-Hill Ryerson, including Kim Brewster, Executive Sponsoring Editor; Lori McLellan, Developmental Editor; Katie McHale, Supervising Editor; and Kelli Howey, Copy Editor, for their commitment and support to this undertaking. Their guidance and professional interaction is truly appreciated.

Finally, I extend sincere thanks to the reviewers who provided insightful feedback that helped to shape this book:

Carole Bonanni, University College of the Fraser Valley
Elisabeth Carter, Douglas College
John Fakouri, Algonquin College of Applied Arts and Technology
David Fleming, George Brown College
Dwight Heinrichs, University of Regina
Cathie Hurley, University of New Brunswick
Diane Jurkowski, York University
Hugh Lawrence, University of Toronto
Robert Maher, University of New Brunswick
David McConomy, Queen's University
Peter Mombourquette, Mount Saint Vincent University

Paul Myers, St. Clair College
Sang Nam, University of Victoria
Kayrod Niamir, Dawson College
Grace O'Farrell, University of Winnipeg
Mary Oxner, St. Francis Xavier University
Kim Richter, Kwantlen Polytechnic University
Frank Saccucci, Grant MacEwan University
Sheldon Shiewitz, Humber College
Indira Somwaru, Seneca College of Applied Arts and Technology
Alex Stewart, Centennial College

1 What Is Business?

Learning Objectives

This chapter is designed to provide students with:

Lo1 A base-level understanding of what business is

Lo2 Exposure to the four major components of the business model and their impact on an organization's competitive advantage

Lo3 An understanding of how businesses plan

Lo4 An introduction to the difference between profit and profitability

Lo5 Exposure to the importance of creating a well-differentiated value proposition as key to a business's success

Lo6 A cursory overview of the relationship between business strategy and tactics, and the importance of successfully executing both for a business to achieve its identified objectives

Snapshot—What to Expect in This Chapter

This chapter provides students with a broad introductory overview of what a business owner or a senior management team needs to understand to successfully manage a business organization. The content emphasized in this chapter includes the following:

- The Big Picture

- What Is Business?
  - The Fundamental Objectives of Business

- The Business Model and Profitability
  - The Difference between Profit and Profitability
  - Improving Profitability

- Creating a Value Proposition
  - The Impact of Price
  - Understanding Your Cost Base

- The Business Decision-Making Landscape

- Management Reflection—Focus on Business

From the Student's Perspective

Congratulations on your decision to study the world of commerce! It's an interesting, multi-faceted subject that impacts us all each day. My business education has helped me not only professionally, but in everyday life as well.

A business, most simply stated, is an organization that provides goods and services to those (either individuals or other businesses) who want or need them. The goal of most businesses is to make money, known as profit, for the owners of the company, or shareholders. There are, however, many business-related careers in non-profit organizations, such as in government and educational settings. From the clothes you wear, to the school you attend, to this very textbook, the world of business surrounds you. The range of careers in business provides a fantastic opportunity for you to apply your personal skill set in a professional setting. Some business functions include:

> Accounting
> Finance
> Human resource management
> Information systems
> Insurance
> Law
> Marketing
> Operations management

Each area plays a unique role in an organization and provides opportunities for you to apply your distinct skills and interests. I personally chose to pursue a business education because I felt it would lead to professional careers that offer the opportunity to contribute to the greater good of society. The ability to move laterally across business functions lends itself to continuous personal and professional learning, and most business careers offer ample opportunity for promotion. It's the breadth and depth of the subject—and its relevance to everyday life—that make it most appealing to me.

Best wishes as you begin your study of business!

David Waugh graduated in 2008 with a Bachelor of Commerce (Honours) degree, focusing on strategic management and organizational behaviour. While at university, David was the president of the undergraduate business student government (Commerce Society), and was a teaching assistant for professors in marketing, business ethics, and introductory business courses. With international study experience at the HEC School of Management in Paris, France, David has travelled to 25 countries. After spending two summers in commercial finance at RBC, he has opted to attend Queen's University for graduate study.

The Big Picture

Perhaps the best way to think about business, in its broadest context, is to view it as a system of integrated actions designed to ensure that an organization develops and grows a market for its goods and/or services in a manner that creates organizational value (wealth) on behalf of its stakeholders. To accomplish both facets of this definition, organizations must succeed in properly identifying solutions to needs that the marketplace desires, and creating a mechanism for delivering such solutions to the right customer, at the right place, at the right time, for the right price. These integrated actions are categorized into areas such as technology application, product engineering and design, manufacturing and operations, marketing and sales, distribution, and service. An efficient and effective operating platform can be assessed against three fundamental characteristics: its commercial endeavours, its employee interaction model, and its organizational efficiency and structure (see Figure 1.1).

Commercial Endeavours refers to the markets the organization serves, the products and services it offers, and the needs it professes to meet in the marketplace.

Employee Interaction refers to the value-creating skills an organization's employees bring to the marketplace. The success of many businesses lies with the specialized skills that exist within its labour force.

Organizational Efficiency and Structure is a reflection of the complexities of the business activities that circulate within an organization.

Commercial endeavours refers to the markets the organization serves, the products and services it offers, and the needs it professes to meet in the marketplace. It reflects the results of understanding the demand/supply relationships that exist in the marketplace and the capacity and capability of each competitor within such a market to deliver products/services to its buyers. Understanding this relationship, coupled with an understanding of the price/cost requirements needed to produce goods and services, is what enables the creation of a business system that delivers a profitable outcome to the organization. **Employee interaction** refers to the value-creating skills that an organization's employees bring to the marketplace. The success of many businesses lies with the specialized skills that exist within its labour force. The leveraging of these skills in the production of goods and/or the delivery of services is what enables a business to create value and enables transactions to occur that will allow the firm to make a profit. **Organizational efficiency and structure** is a reflection of the complexities of the business activities that circulate within an organization. It is reflective of the development of the infrastructure and its related culture, which an organization creates, and the transaction processes that it develops to service the marketplace it targets. These three characteristics, when assessed jointly, result in an understanding of a business system whose objective is the design, production, distribution, and communication of goods and services that are sought after by the marketplace and valued by the customers being targeted.

FIGURE 1.1   Business: The Big Picture

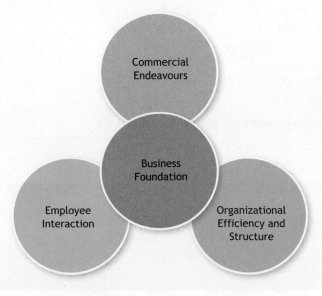

As an example of this assessment process, think of the industry-leading search engine company Google. Google's business system can be assessed against the three characteristics identified above. For Google, the "commercial endeavour" objective is the generation of revenue and profits resulting from such market offerings as its "point and click" advertising services, its acquisitions of YouTube and DoubleClick, and its entry into mobile phone services (voice, applications, and software, known as Android). Its "employee interaction" relates to the many developers, engineers, and system designers with specialized skills whom Google employs to develop and support the products and services the company offers. Google's "organizational efficiency and structure" refers to the formal framework it has put into place to manage and deliver its products and services. It refers to Google's server farms and related infrastructure, managerial hierarchy, operating processes, and decision-making and communication processes.

> An efficient and effective operating platform (business system) will also possess three fundamental characteristics against which it can be assessed: its commercial endeavours, its human resource (employee) interaction model, and its organizational efficiency and structure.

What Is Business?

"Business" is a challenging word to define and understand because it has several different but related meanings. For some, it is simply a mechanism from which to drive profit via the sales of goods/services. For others, it is the ability to create and develop an organization whose primary mission is to satisfy an identified customer or society-based need. Recognizing that the definition will be personalized by each of us involved in a business operation, let's try to provide a broad-based definition of what business is all about.

Business can most easily be thought of as mission-focused activities aimed at identifying the needs of a particular market, or markets, and the development of a solution to such needs through the acquisition or transformation of goods and services that can be delivered to the marketplace at a profit. Through the development of a business model or system, managers will attempt to initiate and control these activities in a manner that results in the most efficient and effective approach to the marketplace. To accomplish this, an organization will build its business model or system around four core fundamental resource areas—*assets, labour, capital,* and *managerial acumen.* **Assets**, in simplistic terms, represent the infrastructure and resource base of the organization. This includes (but is not limited to) an organization's land, buildings, process and infrastructure base (bricks and mortar, e-commerce, etc.), equipment and technology framework, raw materials, and brand power. **Labour** refers to the human resource requirements of the business, while **capital** refers to the money needed by an organization to support asset-based expenditures, meet operating cash requirements, and invest in the development of the new products or services that the organization desires to introduce into the marketplace. **Managerial acumen** refers to the foresight, drive, knowledge, ability, decision-making competency, and ingenuity of the organization's key individuals—its owners or top-level managers.[1] A key component of managerial acumen is the visionary leadership that a senior management team or business owner provides to the organization. Visionary leadership refers to the ability of managers to establish a direction for the organization based on the needs identified in the marketplace and the mission (reason for being) of the organization. This is then translated into a strategic plan designed to guide the organization to fulfilling such needs while meeting its mission. Combined, the application of these four resource areas, in support of the transformation and sale of goods and services, determines a company's cost base and overall operating platform, or what is called its **business model or system**. This is illustrated in Figure 1.2.

The role of the business owner or management team is to anticipate, recognize, or sense an opportunity to create a product, and to deliver a service that is felt to be unique, important, and of value (meaningful) to a targeted customer or customers. This vision of market opportunity is

Business refers to the mission-focused activities aimed at identifying the needs of a particular market or markets, and the development of a solution to such needs through the acquisition and transformation of resources into goods and services that can be delivered to the marketplace at a profit.

Assets refers to the infrastructure and resource base of the organization.

Labour refers to the human resource requirements of the business.

Capital refers to the money needed by an organization to support asset-based expenditures, meet operating cash requirements, and invest in the development of new products and/or services which the organization desires to introduce into the marketplace.

Managerial Acumen refers to the foresight, drive, knowledge, ability, decision-making competency, and ingenuity of the organization's key individuals—its owners or top-level managers.

Business Model (System) is the operational platform or structure that a business uses to generate revenue and profit.

FIGURE 1.2   Relationship between Productive Resources and the Business System

realized via the efficient and effective application of the other productive resources the organization possesses (assets, labour, and capital). Fundamental to this challenge is for the business owner and his/her management team to conduct a "strategy and 3C assessment" (capabilities, competencies, capacity). By *strategy*, we are referring to the specific objectives an organization hopes to achieve during the planning cycle. A *3C assessment* means analyzing the resources available to the organization and the capabilities and competencies it possesses. This defines the capacity of what the organization can and cannot do, which then enables the management team to define how and to what extent it can capitalize on its identified strategic opportunities in a manner that is superior to the competition it competes against on a day-to-day basis.

Understanding its strategic opportunities and its capabilities, competencies, and overall capacity, the business management team develops a business plan via a process called the business planning cycle (see Figure 1.3), which outlines its focus and methodology for using its resources to create valuable products and services that will create a unique position in the marketplace.[2] In an ideal situation, this unique position would be built around a competitive advantage. A company has a **competitive advantage** when it can offer customers a product or service that has more value to them than similar products offered by other companies. If the business plan is competitive and executed properly, and customers are attracted to the company's product/service offering(s), the company generates money, or revenue, from the sale of the product. Assuming that the plan is executed in an efficient and effective manner, this revenue will exceed the expenses associated with producing or delivering the product/service, thereby generating a profit for the firm. This then enables the company to grow through

Competitive Advantage is an advantage an organization has over its competitors that enables it to generate more sales, achieve greater margins, achieve a lower cost base, or attract and retain more customers.

FIGURE 1.3   Business Planning Cycle

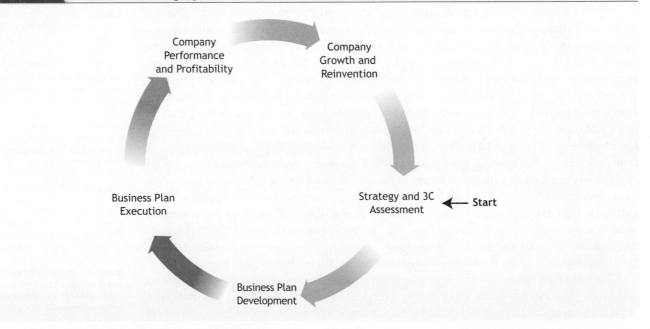

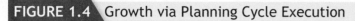

FIGURE 1.4   Growth via Planning Cycle Execution

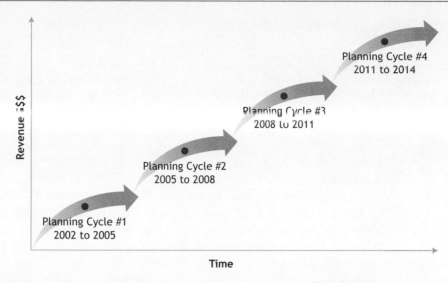

reinvestment of these profits (along with capital from other sources, if required) into the business and the expansion of the business opportunities that the organization undertakes.

> The role of the business owner or management team is to anticipate, recognize, or sense an opportunity to create a product or to deliver a service that is felt to be unique, important, and of value (meaningful) to a targeted customer or customers.

In fact, businesses grow by executing a series of planning cycles over time (see Figure 1.4). Each planning cycle is designed to direct the positioning of the company within the marketplace, orchestrate the creation of a business plan that will achieve the objectives formulated for the planning period, ensure linkage with the vision and mission of the organization, and develop the required operational tactics that will ensure the plan is executed in a fashion that leads to growth and profitability. Businesses need to identify and set objectives that will enable them to achieve a defined position in the marketplace, and detail an implementation strategy that will enable them to achieve this desired position. Such objectives should be specific, measurable, actionable, and controllable (SMAC) by the firm's management team. They should also be achievable within the given time frame that defines the planning cycle. The management team must then allocate the resources and leverage the company's capabilities in a manner that ensures the tactics designed to achieve the objective actually work and produce the desired results. Finally, the management team needs to assess the success of the company in achieving the desired objectives, and determine adjustments required in order to further grow the company within upcoming planning cycles (see Figure 1.5). If an organization does not achieve its objectives as a result of either poor positioning or poor execution of the strategies initiated, then the company will most likely not achieve the results anticipated and will need to redirect the current organizational effort in order to get back on track and achieve its revenue and profitability targets. A flattening, or declining, of revenue or a reduction in overall profitability are key identifiers as to whether a given plan is working. Figure 1.6 illustrates a failure to grow the company to the desired position and meet its objectives during a planning cycle. It should be noted that this failure to meet the objectives of a planning cycle can be the result of poor positioning, poor operational execution, or a combination of the two.

> The failure to meet the objectives of a planning cycle can be the result of poor positioning, poor operational execution, or a combination of the two.

FIGURE 1.5   Planning Cycle Staging

Planning Cycle Staging

Direction/Positioning	Implementation	Assessment
• What do we want to do? • Why do we want to do it? • Can we do it?	• How will we do it? • What needs to be changed in order for us to succeed? • Where will resources be allocated?	• Did we meet our goal? • What needs to be changed or improved? • What systems require fine-tuning? • What further capacity adjustments are required?

FIGURE 1.6   Planning Cycle Outcome

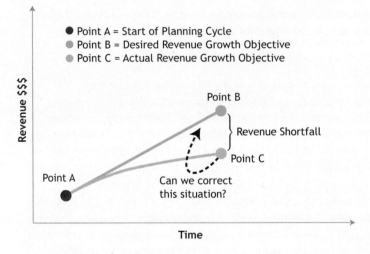

The following example illustrates the planning cycle concept. The author was CEO of the YMCA of Kingston, Ontario, from January 1995 to August 2008. During this period, the management team and the board of directors initiated a series of planning cycles with the intent to first stabilize this not-for-profit organization and then grow it. The series of planning cycles, initiated from 2000 to 2008, resulted in the charity-based organization growing its membership base from 2500 to 8500; realizing revenue growth from $1.2 million to $4.5 million annually; opening a second recreational facility in partnership with St. Lawrence College in Kingston; and undertaking a $5.8-million expansion of the YMCA of Kingston's main facility. With its facilities updated and its membership base stabilizing, the current planning cycle of the YMCA has shifted its attention to increasing its reach, both in the local community and internationally, through YMCA-based current program enhancement and new program expansion. Planning cycles and business growth strategies will be covered in more detail in later chapters. For now, it is just important for you to understand this concept at the macro level provided.

Before we go on, we should recognize that while **for-profit companies** need competitive business models, so do *not-for-profit* organizations, such as hospitals, school boards, YMCAs, social service agencies, educational institutions, and registered charities. By definition,

For-Profit Companies are organizations whose overarching objective is profitability and wealth creation on behalf of their shareholders and stakeholders.

not-for-profit organizations are those that are not in business to make a profit, but rather seek to deliver services to the people, groups, and communities they serve. Nevertheless, not-for-profits still need a business plan, operating model, and business system that will enable them to cover their operating costs and to employ strategies to fund the ongoing delivery of meaningful services. Small businesses, as well, need to recognize the need for a well-thought-out business plan in order to determine just how, where, and when to compete.

Not-For-Profit Organizations (NFPs) are organizations whose overarching objective is not profitability and wealth creation but to deliver services to the people, groups, and communities that they serve via a model of collective interest and social goal achievement.

BUSINESS *in Action*

Research In Motion: Business Planning Cycle in Action

Research In Motion® (RIM), based in Waterloo, Ontario, was founded in 1984. RIM is engaged in the design, manufacturing, distribution, and marketing of handheld wireless devices, with a predominant focus on the global mobile communications market. RIM's initial business plan recognized a niche in the marketplace that was not being served by other competitors. This niche involved the wireless communication of data. While other competitors, such as Nokia and Ericsson, concentrated on wireless voice (cell phone) models, RIM focused on the ability to transmit email and other data-based information requirements on behalf of its customers. This focus enabled it to develop an initial, significant customer base in the business and government market sectors. With this different market focus, RIM has been able to develop significant competitive advantages that have enabled its co-founders and management team to further grow the organization's product offerings and overall market reach. Today, RIM, with annual sales in excess of $14.9 billion (February 2010), is a market leader in handheld mobile communication (voice and data) products and services, anchored by its well-known BlackBerry® Smartphones brand. RIM's success has stemmed from its ability to recognize its resource and competency capabilities and develop a business plan that enabled it to leverage such capabilities in the marketplace in a manner that was of value to its target customers and that has been delivered to those customers via a business model (system) that has been considered superior to its competitors. The challenge for RIM in the face of increasing competition and changing consumer trends is how to continue to maintain and grow its market position. Successful initially as a focused player, RIM's expansion into the broader marketplace has not met with the same level of success that it has had in the business and government market segments. Yes, its customer base continues to grow, but both Apple and Android-based system providers are growing their customer bases at a faster rate. RIM's proprietary data encryption system, historically a core component of its competitive advantage, is being challenged by governments in developing economies that are demanding greater accessibility to the information being transmitted by their citizens. RIM's

encryption platform is developed around the attribute of information transfer privacy and security, not open monitoring. For RIM, much of its future growth lies in building its customer base in these countries, so responding to the needs of these governments while respecting and supporting the confidentiality of its customers (a key selling feature for RIM) is becoming a real balancing act. Its recently launched PlayBook tablet has been received with mixed reviews and comes after the release of Apple's iPad 2. With an expected increase in the number of tablet options in the marketplace (with as many as 60 models available by the end of 2011), RIM will be challenged to effectively penetrate this market. For RIM's management team, maintaining its market share and gaining access to new markets remain high priorities within its current business planning cycle. The key will be planning, positioning, timing, and execution. The outcomes will determine whether RIM continues to be a major market challenger in these markets or faces a slow relegation to a market position of that of a marginal player. For RIM, this current planning cycle is crucial. The technology and the market segments within which it competes are moving very quickly.[3]

WEB INTEGRATION

Want to learn more about RIM's products, services, and future plans? Visit **www.rim.com**.

The Fundamental Objectives of Business

As discussed above, businesses utilize resources with the idea of transforming them into products and services. These products and services are then sold to other businesses or to consumers (such as you and me) to achieve a *profit* for the firm. Profit is necessary in the immediate term for the business to pay its bills and reinvest in the future. Making a profit on a monthly, quarterly, and annual basis is fundamental to ensuring the immediate survival of the firm. This, however, is just one of three fundamental objectives that business owners and their management teams must seek to achieve (see Figure 1.7).

As managers consider current and future business direction, an equally important objective to short-term profit must be considered. This second objective is to set in motion the ability of the organization to achieve *long-term growth and profitability*. Businesses recognize that the demand for the products and services they currently offer will change, and could, in fact, disappear over time. Given this, businesses are constantly searching for new markets and new opportunities to further grow the scope and focus of their organizations. Although immediate-term operating performance is based on the products and services a business offers today, new products and services will need to be developed to ensure the organization remains healthy and continues to grow. Apple Inc. has driven significant profits over the past several years from its iPod products and iTunes store. It recognizes, however, that it must continue to look beyond this current success and seek new opportunities for future growth, thus ensuring its ongoing profitability. The launch of the iPhone in 2007, Apple's App Store in 2008, and the iPad in 2010 are examples of Apple's desire to broaden its scope and lines of business by entering into new markets. Innovations to the iMac, including the Mac Mini and Mac Pro, are other examples of Apple's focus on continuous growth via product innovation.[4]

The third objective, and one that is becoming increasingly important as part of the business decision-making process, is that of *social and environmental responsibility*. On a global basis, consumers are encouraging—and, in some industries, demanding—that businesses operate and act in a manner that demonstrates social responsibility with respect to product development, resource consumption, and operating processes. Green initiatives, truth in advertising, environmentally sustainable resource practices, and other environmental and social

---

FIGURE 1.7   Fundamental Objectives of Business Managers

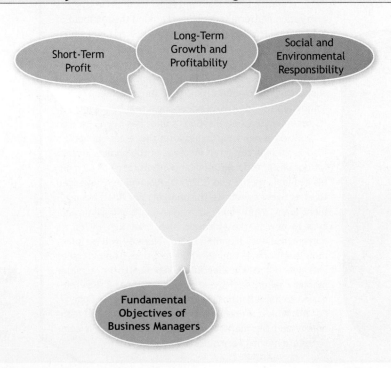

Short-Term Profit

Long-Term Growth and Profitability

Social and Environmental Responsibility

Fundamental Objectives of Business Managers

codes of conduct are challenging businesses to position themselves as good corporate citizens in order to acquire and retain customers. Individual managers are also challenged to make decisions and implement actions that conform to the highest ethical standards. Managers are expected to place society, the organization, and the organization's **stakeholders** ahead of personal gain when making decisions and when interacting with the marketplace. Social responsibility, including ethics and environmentally sustainable business concepts and practices, is discussed more fully in chapters 4 and 5.

Stakeholders refers to individuals, groups, or organizations that have a direct or indirect relationship with an organization, and that can be impacted by its policies, actions, and decisions. Stakeholders could include customers, suppliers, government, employees, and so on.

These same fundamentals also hold true for the not-for-profit sector. Although not-for-profit organizations (NFPs) do not strive for a profit, they do need to create operational surpluses and/or acquire external capital funding commitments that enable reinvestment in the organization to ensure it remains vibrant and responsive to community needs. NFPs also need to assess their services on a regular basis to ensure they remain meaningful to the customers they serve and to expand such services where demand exists and where they have the capabilities to do so. Also, NFPs are held to a high level of social responsibility in that their core existence is based on their ability to meet societal needs that are not responded to by the for-profit sector. Referring back to our example of the Kingston YMCA, a registered charity, a fundamental requirement of its planning is that the association earns an operating surplus on an annual basis to ensure that future building, equipment, technology, and programming financial needs are met for both today and tomorrow. It also needs to continually review the programs and services it offers to ensure they remain meaningful to members and facility users. Add to this the need to develop new programs and services that respond to new, emerging community needs. Finally, it must do all of these things in accordance with its charitable mission, and be willing to accept responsibility for the delivery of socially required programs and services that for-profit entities would choose not to deliver due to an absence of a profit opportunity.

In closing, organizations and their management teams must learn to make decisions that enable all three of these responsibilities to be considered equally. Too much emphasis on short-term profitability, for example, may result in decisions that are detrimental to long-term market opportunities and fall short of social responsibility expectations. Many analysts have concluded that the overemphasis on short-term profits was fundamental to the collapse of the financial services sector in 2008. Investment banks and other financial services companies overleveraged their organizations in high-risk investments, which provided some very positive short-term results (pre 2008) but exposed the organizations to significant losses and asset devaluation when the global marketplace found itself in a recession in 2008–09. Likewise, too much emphasis on developing future products or services—versus responding to customer needs today—may result in liquidity issues for the business if it is unable to cover its expenses in the short term. Managers and management teams therefore must, as part of their planning process, manage the balance between short-term profit requirements and aspirations with longer-term objectives and risk management techniques in a manner that ensures optimal market position and sustainable operating performance.

> Too much emphasis on short-term profitability may result in decisions that are detrimental to long-term market opportunities and fall short of social responsibility expectations.

BUSINESS *in Action*

Toyota Builds for a Greener Future

Toyota's commitment to the environment, and its status as one of the greenest automakers, is symbolized by its famous Prius—to date, the world's best-selling hybrid vehicle. While the Prius is the most visible symbol of Toyota's approach to protecting the environment, the company continues to seek approaches to meeting the world's growing transportation needs in ways that are less harmful to the planet. To achieve this balance, Toyota continually re-examines its products, business strategies, and daily operations, and sets goals for environmental improvement. It is all part of Toyota's Earth Charter and 2010 Global Vision, a commitment by Toyota to the environment and to the communities where it does business. Environmental initiatives and programs are core to the Toyota organization and its Canadian operations. These programs range from the development of the Hybrid Synergy Drive systems, to partnerships in Canada with organizations such as Evergreen and Earth Day, as well as a conscious effort to reduce its environmental footprint from manufacturing operations. Toyota's Earth Charter consists of four pillars: growth in harmony with the environment with the challenge to achieve zero carbon emissions through all areas of business activity; pursuit of all possible environmental technologies and the development of those technologies; the creation of a voluntary improvement plan based on preventive measures and compliance with laws to address environmental issues; and the building of close relationships with individuals and organizations involved in environmental preservation.

WEB INTEGRATION
Want to know more about Toyota's sustainability initiatives? Visit **www.toyota.com** and type *sustainability initiatives* or *Toyota's Earth Charter* in the search browser.

For Toyota, the integration of its commitment to the environment is a conscious part of its business decision and implementation process. This commitment has resulted in the development of one of the most comprehensive waste-reduction and recycling programs in North America, significant energy reduction initiatives, and global leader status in its efforts to achieve an optimal balance between fuel consumption and emissions reduction.[5]

LO4 The Business Model and Profitability

As discussed earlier, a successful business model (system) is one that enables a company to meet the needs of the marketplace in a manner which is superior to that of its competitors. Such a model could be built around cost advantages, service advantages, sales and marketing advantages, technological advantages, or human resource competency advantages. To determine how well a company is performing in a particular industry, it makes sense to look at the company's performance relative to that of its competitors. Looking back on our initial discussion of Research In Motion (RIM), direct industry competitors for RIM would be Nokia, Ericsson, Motorola, HP (via acquisition of Palm Inc.), and Apple. Essentially, these companies are competing for the same broad set of customers. Each company will look to differentiate itself from its competitors and target the customers who it believes will be most receptive to its product/service offering. The most common way of comparing how well a specific company is performing is by measuring its profitability over a period of time, and in direct comparison with its industry competitors.

The Difference between Profit and Profitability

Profit is the "bottom line" result an organization has realized for an identified, immediate period of time. In simple terms, Total Revenue − Total Expenses = Profit.

Profitability measures how well a company is using its resources over a specific period of time to generate earnings relative to its competitors.

Individuals often confuse the concepts of profit and profitability. **Profit** is strictly the "bottom line" results that an organization has realized for a given period of time. In simple terms, Total Revenue − Total Expenses = Profit. If a firm had total current-year revenue from the sale of its products and services of $10 million, and the organization had total current-year expenses of $7 million (costs of developing, manufacturing, and selling such products and services), then it would realize a current-year profit (excluding tax considerations) of $3 million ($10 million − $7 million = $3 million). **Profitability**, on the other hand, corresponds to the efficiency and effectiveness of an organization to use its assets and its capital to generate profits for the organization over a period of time. Profitability analysis takes into consideration such factors as return on the capital invested, return on equity, the financial leverage the organization undertook to finance its assets and operations, the level of pre-tax income it earned, and so on. Profitability analysis is generally assessed over a period of time so that efficiency and effectiveness results, as noted above, can be compared on a period-over-period basis. This enables a management team to determine whether the operation has improved in its effective utilization of its assets and capital. Profitability analysis also focuses on comparisons among competitors within an industry to determine which organizations are the most effective in their utilization of resources. Competitors who are the most profitable over a period of time are generally the most attractive to investors for investment purposes. The benefit of profitability analysis is that it levels the playing field between competitors, recognizing that some may be significantly larger than others.

Let's look at an example to illustrate the importance of profitability analysis as one metric for assessing the overall value of a company. Assume that we have three companies within a given industry, companies X, Y, and Z. For the current year, Company X achieved a profit of $60 million. Company Y achieved a profit of $15 million, and Company Z's current-year profit was $7.5 million. On the surface, without any additional information, one could conclude that Company X was the most profitable company. Profitability analysis, however, goes beyond the absolute monetary value of the current-year profit. Referring to the data in Table 1.1, let's draw additional conclusions relating to the performance of these three companies. In other words, let's conduct a simplified profitability analysis. Table 1.1 provides us with the level of sales that occurred in the current year, as well as identifying the size of the asset base of each company and the value of the equity stake that **stockholders** have within each firm. Table 1.2 takes this information and, based on the profit earned by each company, calculates the return on each of the categories noted (sales, assets, and equity). As you can see from the results identified in Table 1.2, Company Y is the most profitable company, earning a healthy 15-percent return on sales, a 50-percent return on the assets utilized to drive these sales, and $1.50 in profit for each $1.00 of equity invested in the company. The profitability analysis shows that Company X, despite having the largest absolute profit, would rank second in profitability, followed by Company Z in a distant third position. Let's further extend this analysis to Figure 1.8, as a company's profitability is usually assessed over time, and this historical track record can be thought of as a good baseline reflection of its ability to generate future profits and raise additional capital. Assume that this chart reflects the profitability level of each company over the past several years. As you can see, Company Y has consistently outperformed both companies X and Z for the period shown. For an investor, the returns being realized from Company Y are superior to those of X and Z—and, therefore, all other things being equal, Company Y would be the preferred company to invest in.

> **Stockholders** refers to any person, company, or organization that owns at least one share of stock in a specific company.

TABLE 1.1

	Company X	Company Y	Company Z
Profit	$60 million	$15 million	$7.5 million
Sales	$600 million	$100 million	$250 million
Assets (total)	$240 million	$30 million	$200 million
Equity (total)	$100 million	$10 million	$140 million

TABLE 1.2

	Company X	Company Y	Company Z
Return on Sales (profit/sales)	10%	15%	3%
Return on Assets (profit/assets)	25%	50%	4%
Return on Equity (profit/equity)	60%	150%	5%

FIGURE 1.8 Profitability Analysis: Return on Sales

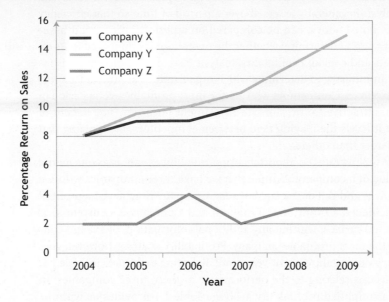

Although Company X is making a decent return, its management team will be challenged to further improve its efficiencies and processes to drive profitability more closely in line with the profitability growth of Company Y. Company Z's performance clearly is significantly below that of X and Y. Its lower returns would be cause for concern—particularly if the demand for its goods and services softens, as this could cause further erosion to its earnings and, therefore, its return on sales, assets, and equity. Further erosion of its sales levels or its cost base could result in it moving from a position of a small profit to that of an operating loss. At this point, it is important just to understand the value of assessing companies in terms of profitability versus absolute profits. The analytical process associated with assessing an organization's financial capacity and profitability is covered in more detail in chapters 12 through 14.

Improving Profitability

Like Company X above, companies in the marketplace are continually being challenged to develop new product opportunities, meet evolving needs in emerging markets, and streamline operations, all in an effort to improve immediate and longer-term profitability. Competition from Walmart and other U.S.-based retailers, as well as up-and-coming Canadian players—for example, Simons Inc.—has challenged NRDC Equity Partners, the owners of the Hudson's Bay Company and its banner stores of Zellers and The Bay, to try to find better ways to use their assets, human resources, and capital in order to improve current profitability levels or attract additional capital to fund their operations. The Bay is investing heavily into renovating and repositioning its stores, as well as installing new kinds of information technology to lower overall operating costs. The intent of these investments is to position The Bay as more of an upscale retailer, using high-end designers, such as Chanel and Juicy Couture, to attract a wealthier and more "trendy" customer base. The anticipated outcome of these investments and business strategy adjustments will be a stronger profitability position going forward. Although satisfied with the progress it is seeing with The Bay, NRDC Equity Partners has not experienced the same results from its efforts to reposition Zellers. NRDC initially focused its investments into Zellers on enhancing the shopping experience for Zellers customers and improving the quality of the products being offered, hoping to win customers' shopping loyalty even though Zellers may be unable to match Walmart's lower price points.

NRDC realized, however, that the size of the investment and the length of time required to turn Zellers around, combined with doubts over the probability of success of this strategy, was too much of a business risk. It simply did not see Zellers meeting the long-term profitability objectives needed to remain part of its portfolio. NRDC therefore decided, in 2010, to place Zellers up for sale. In January 2011, it was announced that Minneapolis, MN-based Target Corporation would purchase the assets of Zellers for $1.85 billion.[6]

The challenge to improve profitability faces companies large and small. Assume that Backyard Pools is a small business specializing in the installation and servicing of residential pools. The operation includes a retail location that sells the chemicals necessary for ongoing swimming pool maintenance and use, and also sells related summer seasonal products such as patio furniture, BBQ grills, and pool toys. Backyard Pools is very busy during the months of April through September, and enjoys an annual operating profit. However, there is not tremendous demand for swimming-pool products and related services in Canada from October to March. In an effort to improve its overall profitability and keep its assets (building, employees, etc.) functional and revenue-producing during the off-season, Backyard Pools could look to broaden its offerings. This could include (as many similar operations have found) expanding their product line to include spas (which have year-round demand) and branching out into opposite-season lines, such as fitness equipment, billiard tables, and products whose demand and sales peak during the winter months.

WEB INTEGRATION

Visit the Web site of a local swimming pool retailer in your town, and see what products they have added to maximize the use of their asset base during the swimming pool off-season. Need an example? Visit **www.stlawrencepools.ca** to see what this company has done.

Creating a Value Proposition

LO5

Up to this point, we have discussed the overall definition of what a business is and the overarching objectives that guide a business's decision making. Within this context, we have commented on the need for business organizations to design, produce, distribute, and communicate to the marketplace the products and services they offer. The management team accomplishes this through the development of a **value proposition**.

A value proposition is a statement that summarizes whom a product or service is geared toward and the benefits the purchaser will realize as a result of using the product or service (see Figure 1.9). It also communicates to the purchaser how the product or service differs from competing products or services offered in the marketplace. For example, suppose you decide to purchase an MP3 player. The question for you is which product to purchase; the marketplace offers a number of competing choices. You could purchase an Apple iPod, Microsoft Zune, or one of the models offered by other companies, such as Creative Technology, SanDisk, Panasonic, Samsung, or Sony. Your decision will be influenced by the benefits the products offer. In order to position themselves in the marketplace, companies develop value propositions for the purpose of communicating to customers how their products or services are different and the important benefits they offer. It is important to understand that value propositions are not driven strictly by tangible or functional product benefits. In fact, many of the reasons why products or services are purchased have little to do with the actual product itself, but more with the perceived benefits the product or service offers. The following equation is often used to describe what needs to be included in a value proposition.

Value Proposition is a statement that summarizes whom a product/service is geared toward and the benefits the purchaser will realize as a result of using the product.

Value Proposition = Service Benefits + Product Benefits + Brand Benefits + Cost Benefits + Emotional Benefits

> Companies develop value propositions for the purpose of communicating to customers how their products/services are different and the important benefits which they offer.

The strength of the value proposition is the perceived sum of your company's ability to deliver in each area noted within the value proposition equation versus the strength of your competitors' value propositions measured across these same benefit areas.

FIGURE 1.9   Value Proposition Composition

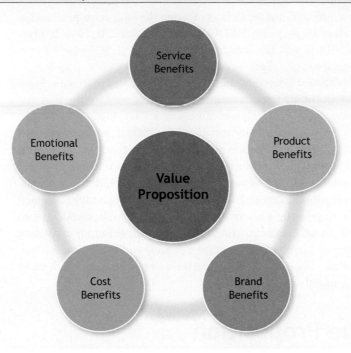

Figure 1.10 illustrates the fundamental questions to which a value proposition must respond.[7] Successful value propositions are geared toward highlighting the key decision criteria purchasers believe to be most important, and communicate how the product or service best responds to these needs. Going back to our MP3 example, the current market leader in this marketplace is the Apple iPod. Why? Because customers have concluded that the tangible product features (touch screen and other interfaces, video capabilities) along with the brand benefits (Apple's brand strength), the support services (such as iTunes), the overall ease of use, and the peer affiliation of owning an iPod make it the preferred choice. Simply stated, for the major portion of the market segment interested in MP3 players, Apple's value proposition is deemed to be the best choice for the greatest number of customers. We will discuss, in more detail, the development of the value proposition and the methodology used to communicate it to the marketplace in later chapters.

FIGURE 1.10   Sample Positioning Statement Template

PART 1 OF THE STATEMENT

For . . . . (the target market)

Who want . . . . (the consumer need)

Our products or services are . . . . (demonstration of the solution)

Which feature . . . . (key benefits provided)

PART 2 OF THE STATEMENT

Unlike. . . . . (our main competitors)

Our products(s) provide . . . . (key points of differences)

As supported by . . . . (what makes our differences possible)

And protected by . . . . (why the competition cannot easily overcome it)

Source: Courtesy of K. Wong, Queen's University

The Impact of Price

One thing we did not focus on in our discussion of the development of the value proposition is the impact of price. As noted in the formula above, price is also a key component in a potential purchaser's assessment of an organization's value proposition. Purchasers will assess the price/quality relationship of one business's value proposition and measure it against those of its competitors. For businesses, it is important to offer the most attractive price/quality relationship for the target market segment. The price/quality relationship is the relationship between what consumers are being asked to pay for a product and what they expect to receive (benefits). Again, keep in mind that the benefits may be both tangible (product features) and intangible (emotional benefits, status, image). In general, the more unique, important, and value-driven your product is, the greater the opportunity to communicate to the potential purchaser a value proposition that has a positive price/quality relationship and that is considered superior to those of your competitors. Figure 1.11 provides an illustration of the relationship of price and quality (benefits) from the perspective of a potential purchaser. What this buyer is looking for is a purchase that results in the benefits obtained exceeding the price paid. This differential can be viewed as the value the consumer places on the purchase of this product/service.

> In general, the more unique, important, and value-driven your product is, the greater the opportunity to communicate to the potential purchaser a value proposition which has a positive price/quality relationship, and which can be considered to be superior to those of your competitors.

The reason for this discussion about value propositions is that being in business is not always about having the lowest price. It is more about understanding the needs and desires of the marketplace and offering a product/service that responds to those needs. It is also about recognizing that segments within the market will have different feelings as to how these needs can be met. Think about the potential purchase of a handbag, for example. A budget-minded person may be inclined to visit Sears Canada and purchase a Jessica handbag for approximately

FIGURE 1.11   Price/Quality Relationship

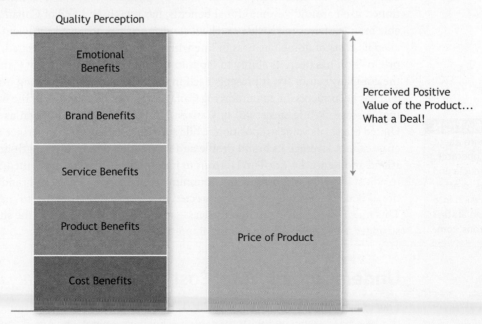

$35 to $90. This bag is perfectly functional and meets the needs of this individual. Another individual, desiring a higher level of quality and allowing the influence of emotional and brand benefits to drive the purchase decision, may choose to purchase a Coach Leatherware handbag, costing typically in the $300 to $500 range. A third person, with greater monetary capacity and desiring even greater quality, brand, and emotional benefit distinction, may purchase a Gucci or Prada handbag with a price tag typically exceeding $1000. The key is to recognize the qualities of the product/service you are offering and to match them against the segment of the market that will best respond, and then deliver the value proposition in a manner superior to the competition that is seeking the same market position and set of customers as you are.

In developing your value proposition, five fundamental questions need to be assessed and will ultimately assist the management team of a business in determining how and where to compete in the marketplace. These questions are as follows:

- What is my *cost base* for producing and/or delivering this product/service to the marketplace, and how does this compare to that of my main competitor(s)?

- Do I have a strong *brand profile* in the marketplace that I can leverage as part of the benefit to the customer when purchasing this product?

- Are there *emotional benefits* that the customer will attach to this product/service offering? If so, how can I use this to assist me in strengthening my value proposition?

- Are there unique *service benefits* I can incorporate into this value proposition that will assist me in supporting potential and existing customers?

In analyzing the above-mentioned questions, can I create a strong enough value proposition to enable me to successfully compete against other competitors in the **market segment** in which I choose to compete?

A discussion of Tim Hortons, with respect to these questions, will provide some insight regarding value proposition development and assessment. Tim Hortons is a market leader in Canada in the quick-service restaurant category. Its main revenue driver is its legendary Tim Hortons coffee, but the organization is also well known for its donut and Timbit line, as well as its growing sandwich options and recently-introduced breakfast entrées. Over 40 years old, Tim Hortons has more than 3000 stores in Canada, and over 560 stores in the United States.[8] Why is it that more Canadians choose Tim Hortons for their morning java fix than any other competitor? It comes down to their value proposition. Tim Hortons has successfully positioned itself around key emotional benefits, has established one of Canada's most recognizable brands, strives to provide excellent service, and has achieved sufficient size and scope to keep its costs of doing business in line with the competition. As indicated, a key to its value proposition has been its ability to tap into the emotional affiliation of Canadians with what the company stands for. It presents itself in its communications as being uniquely Canadian, and has been successful in reinforcing Canadian values and our way of life within its positioning message. While successful in Canada, Tim Hortons has not been as successful in the United States. Its value proposition, while still solid, with respect to service and product benefits, cannot leverage its brand profile and its emotional benefit strength in areas like Rhode Island and Kentucky. For Tim Hortons to improve its success in the United States, it will need to adjust its value proposition and communication emphasis until its brand profile and emotional benefit messaging can be redirected in a way that is attractive to the U.S. population. This may include having to lower prices—and accept lower profits in the short term—until a stronger message of uniqueness and importance can be delivered.

Market Segment is a portion of the market that is deemed to possess unique characteristics businesses can target in order to generate a preference for their products and/or services.

WEB INTEGRATION

Want to learn more about how Tim Hortons operates, what new products and services it plans to offer, and its expansion into the United States? Visit **www.timhortons.com.**

Understanding Your Cost Base

Like our discussion on pricing, it makes sense to have an initial discussion on understanding the cost base associated with managing a business operation. Again, our focus here will simply be to introduce the topic, with the understanding that a more thorough discussion will be provided later in this book (see chapter 12).

A key component of managing any business is in understanding the expenses that must be considered when setting the price of a product or service offering. Expenses can take the form of either asset-based expenditures (capital asset expenditures) or operating expenses. **Asset-based expenditures** are those expenditures incurred in commencing a business operation or expanding its capacity. Examples of such expenses could be the purchase of equipment or building(s). **Operating expenditures** are expenses incurred as a result of the normal business operations. Examples of such expenses are the salaries/wages of employees, the purchase of raw materials for the fabrication of products, the costs of shipping products from point A to point B, or the costs of advertising campaigns. Managers and business owners need to understand the costs they will incur in setting up, expanding, and operating their businesses. These costs must be recognized within their business plans and pricing strategies to ensure the costs of the operation and other related financial obligations are fully offset by the revenue generated by the business and that acceptable levels of profit are realized. An example of getting a feel for the costs associated with a business operation are provided in the Business in Action feature "So, You Want to Start a Booster Juice."

Asset-Based Expenditures are expenditures for the purchase of assets required by a firm in order to support the company's business operations, and which contribute to the firm's ability to earn a profit.

Operating Expenditures are expenses incurred as a result of a company performing its normal business operations.

A key component of managing any business is in understanding the expenses that must be considered when setting the price of a product/service offering.

BUSINESS *in Action*

So, You Want to Start a Booster Juice

Booster Juice is an example of a great Canadian small business success story. The brainchild of two young entrepreneurs, Dale Wishewan and Jon Amack, Booster Juice has grown from its humble beginning in 1999 to an international business with operations as far away as Dubai. Through solid business planning and execution of its franchise-based operations strategy, Booster Juice now has more than 100 stores across Canada (over 170 stores worldwide). Although the product line was originally based on smoothies, the menu has grown to include juices, hot drinks, shakes, and food offerings such as paninis and grilled chicken quesadillas.

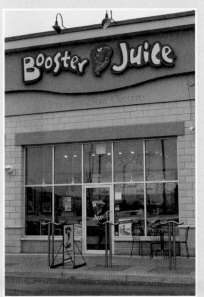

Interested in opening a Booster Juice franchise? In doing so, you need to consider the two types of costs (expenses) we have discussed in this chapter. First, you will need to understand your asset-based expenditures. In this particular situation, these can be thought of as the costs of starting the business. You will need to pay an initial franchise fee to Booster Juice for the rights to use their name and for their involvement in assisting you in establishing your business. You will also need to purchase the equipment to set up the business, and fund the additional one-time start-up expenses, such as beginning inventory, pre-opening business expenses, professional fees (accounting and legal fees, etc.), and leasehold-improvement expenses. Overall, depending on the site chosen, the style of store you have agreed to set up, and the geographic location of your operation, these expenses could total between $175 000 and $285 000.

Once set up, you now have to run the business on a day-to-day basis. This means that you need to sell your smoothies and the related menu items at a level sufficient to cover expenses. You also need to purchase the food and beverage items to create the smoothies and other menu offerings, and the packaging required to serve them. Add to this the labour required to serve your customers, as well as the business costs associated with running your operation—utilities, insurance, debt interest repayment (assuming you borrowed part of the money needed to set up the business), advertising, royalties to Booster Juice, and other miscellaneous operating expenses. Suppose these are estimated to run $350 000 on an annual basis.

This means that your Booster Juice business needs to generate at least $350 000 of revenue per year just to cover its cost base (excluding any desired return on investment by the owner). These costs need to be incorporated into your pricing strategy to ensure that the prices you set cover the costs of being in business. In looking at your menu, if the average amount a customer spends when visiting your Booster Juice is $7, then you need to have at least 50 000 customers per year to achieve the revenue stream of $350 000 that is necessary to cover your operating expenses and make your debt interest payments. This means that you need 4167 customers per month, or just over 1000 per week, or 148 customers per day.[9]

WEB INTEGRATION
Want to learn more about Booster Juice and its operations? Visit www.boosterjuice.com.

LO6 The Business Decision-Making Landscape

Being in business goes beyond simply developing your value proposition and understanding its asset base and cost structure. It is about being able to understand the macro environment around you; the resources, capability, and capacity that you possess; and the ability to communicate to the marketplace the uniqueness and importance of the products/services you offer. At its core base, developing and managing a business requires its owners/managers to:

- create a vision of the opportunity in the marketplace

- confirm that the market size of customers is large enough that, once commercialized, the opportunity can enable the organization to make a profit and sustain this profitability for the anticipated planning cycle and beyond

- confirm that a position within the market is feasible, which will enable the company to compete in a manner that is superior to its direct competition

- confirm that the market situation will stay constant long enough for the business plan to be developed and executed

- confirm that the business has the resource base and the capability to execute the strategy

- execute the strategy in an efficient and effective manner, achieving the objectives set forth within the business plan created

Strategy refers to the development of plans and decisions that will guide the direction of the firm and determine its long-term performance.

Tactics refers to the immediate-term actions which a firm executes in order to meet the short-term objectives set forth in the current planning cycle.

As this process demonstrates (see Figure 1.12), being in business is really a question of developing strategy and executing tactics. **Strategy** is the development of plans and decisions that will guide the direction of the firm and determine its long-term performance. Strategy focuses on the vision of the firm and the opportunity it believes exists in the marketplace. It also checks that the life expectancy of the product or service is long enough to ensure that the initial investment can be recovered and that the firm can make a profit. Finally, strategy development assesses whether the firm has the competencies and resources to compete in this targeted market. **Tactics** are the immediate-term actions that a firm executes to meet the short-term objectives set forth in the current planning cycle. Tactics can be thought of as the action items a firm undertakes to ensure that it is successful in achieving its strategic objectives. Tactics could involve the expenditure of money for new equipment, the hiring of new staff with specialized skills, or the manufacturing processes undertaken to develop a product or service. To successfully grow a company, the management team has to be successful in both planning strategy and executing tactics (see Figure 1.13). Strategically, managers need to

FIGURE 1.12   Business Decision-Making Model

| Visualize and Assess the Business Opportunity | Confirm Market Size and Profitability Potential | Determine Market Position, Approach, and Continuity | Assess Company Resources and Capabilities | Determine the Tactics Required to Achieve Objectives |

FIGURE 1.13   Interdependency of Strategy and Tactics

Well-Directed and Positioned Strategy **+** Efficient and Effective Tactics Execution **=** Business Growth and Profitability

understand where the market is going and how their products and services will fit into the market and meet customer needs. Tactically, they need to ensure that the right product reaches the right customer at the right time, and at the right place for the right price. Chapter 6 outlines in more detail the strategic planning process and the relationship between strategy and tactics. The intent here is just to introduce these concepts so that you get a sense as to their overall importance in managing a business. Their introduction now also will make them easier for you to understand as you move through this course and textbook.

BUSINESS *in Action*

Airbus A380: Strategy and Tactics

The interdependency of strategy and tactics can be fully illustrated by looking at the development of the Airbus A380, the largest passenger plane in the world, by EADS and its subsidiary Airbus. Strategically, the idea by EADS in developing the Airbus A380 was to build a plane that could deliver more passengers than ever before to a destination, at a cost that was 15 percent to 20 percent below that of its nearest competitor—Boeing and its Boeing 747. The A380 would hold approximately 555 passengers, enabling airline companies to maximize the number of passengers moving from point A to point B. Incorporating the latest technology, the plan was for the Airbus A380 to be one of the most efficient planes ever built. Unique to its design, the Airbus A380 had 49 percent more floor area than the Boeing 747, but was installing only 35 percent more seats. This enabled Airbus to provide significantly better passenger amenities, such as bars, gymnasiums, private cabins, and duty-free shops, all geared toward making the Airbus A380 a unique flying experience. Strategically, the idea was well directed and, once executed, was intended to further secure Airbus as the dominant player in the large-plane market segment. The first plane was scheduled to be delivered to Singapore Airlines in March 2006; Singapore Airlines finally received its first plane in October

EADS

2007. So, what happened? Building this sophisticated plane is no easy task. It is especially more complicated for EADS, whose primary contractors are spread across Europe and whose ownership and decision making is fragmented across both private partners and publicly traded companies. EADS's manufacturing assembly partners are located in France, the United Kingdom, Germany, and Spain. Parts are also being manufactured in Belgium, South Korea, Malaysia, Italy, Japan, and Finland (to name a few). The decentralized manufacturing processes and convoluted decision making resulted in the poor initial execution of the tactics and processes required to get the plane built. Engineers working in different countries were not aware of design changes being made. Electrical wiring, which was fabricated and installed at different locations, was incompatible, and software incompatibilities resulted in a need for significant manual intervention during manufacturing and assembly processes. These complications and poor execution of the tactics needed to build the plane on budget and on time have resulted in what could be as much as a $6 billion cost overrun to the project, and deliveries of planes to customers are being pushed back from 2007 to 2010 and beyond. For EADS, the challenge now is to appease customers who may have

to wait as long as five additional years before receiving their planes. Penalties in the hundreds of millions of dollars may be incurred due to delivery dates not being met, and customers are considering cancelling their orders and shifting to Boeing and its fleet of planes (747, 757, 777, 787), whose production schedules can beat those of the Airbus A380 and the forthcoming A350.[10]

WEB INTEGRATION
Want to read the latest on the development of the Airbus A380? Go to **www.airbus.com.**

Management Reflection—Focus on Business

Business is not about producing and distributing goods and services. It is about delivering value to customers in a manner that meets their wants and desires. With few exceptions, the marketplace provides customers with significant choice. The key is to ensure that the value you deliver to the customers you target via the products and services you offer exceeds that of your competitors. As managers, in conducting business we need to avoid the temptation to become predominantly focused on short-term results. Managers need to make decisions in recognition of both immediate needs and longer-term requirements in order to protect and grow the general health of the organization. A key aspect of this process is to understand that business (and the marketplace) is not static, but dynamic. It is changing all the time. What has worked in the past may not necessarily work in the future. As an example, Blockbuster Inc. built its market leader position in the movie rental marketplace on the basis of a bricks-and-mortar (physical store locations) business model. Successful in the 1970s, 80s, and 90s, this model is giving way to video streaming, downloading, and competitive intensity from new market entrants such as Netflix and cable companies. We can expect Apple and Google also to become more significant players in this market segment. This means that managers must continually assess and reassess market conditions and their own business's position in the markets they serve. Innovation and reinvention of how they do business and where to compete are becoming more fundamental to business planning than ever before. Visionary leadership and the ability to anticipate new market space and new market opportunities are necessary skills of today's managers. Managers must also recognize that the decisions they make impact both internal and external stakeholders. These stakeholders expect managers to conduct business in a manner that is ethical, socially responsible, and mindful of the sustainability requirements of our world. Having said all of this, building, growing, and managing a company is one of the most rewarding experiences an individual will ever have. The feeling of accomplishment of a job well done is second to none.

> Business is not only about producing and distributing goods and services; it is about delivering value to customers in a manner that meets their needs and desires.

Chapter Summary

In this chapter, we have described the nature of business and discussed the ways in which businesses create profits and interact with the marketplace in order to meet the needs, wants, and desires of targeted customers. Our discussion focused on the interaction of business as a commercial endeavour, guided by employee interaction and supported by organizational efficiency and structure, which results in the development of a business system and, ultimately, a business model designed to deliver desired goods and services to the marketplace. Utilizing productive resources at their disposal (assets, labour, capital, and managerial acumen), businesses seek to drive a profit from the sale of such goods and services and ensure long-term profitability and growth by continually seeking to make the most efficient use of their resources. While striving for profitability, businesses are being increasingly challenged by customers, and the marketplace at large, to be good corporate citizens, acknowledging their responsibility to act in a socially acceptable manner and respecting the finite nature and scarcity of resources. This new requirement of businesses is resulting in a significant emphasis on resource sustainability and environmental initiatives. To help you to understand why some companies are more successful than others, a significant portion of this chapter's focus emphasizes the importance of developing and communicating a value proposition to the customer group that a business is trying to attract in a manner that differentiates the business's products and services from those of its direct competitors, and that attempts to develop and sustain a competitive advantage in the marketplace. The creation of this value proposition takes into consideration both tangible and intangible benefits that the product or service offers, and looks to determine the extent at which price will become a key decision criterion within the customer's purchase decision. The chapter closes with a discussion associated with the importance and interrelationship between strategy and tactics and the need for managers to recognize that in order to be successful, businesses not only have to properly develop a plan for attacking the marketplace, but also must be effective in the implementation of this plan.

Developing Business Knowledge and Skills

KEY TERMS

commercial endeavours *p. 4*

employee interaction *p. 4*

organizational efficiency and structure *p. 4*

business *p. 5*

assets *p. 5*

labour *p. 5*

capital *p. 5*

managerial acumen *p. 5*

business model or system *p. 5*

competitive advantage *p. 6*

for-profit companies *p. 8*

not-for-profit organizations (NFPs) *p. 9*

stakeholders *p. 11*

profit *p. 12*

profitability *p. 12*

stockholder(s) *p. 13*

value proposition *p. 15*

market segment *p. 18*

asset-based expenditures *p. 19*

operating expenditures *p. 19*

strategy *p. 20*

tactic(s) *p. 20*

QUESTIONS FOR DISCUSSION

1. In your opinion, based on the concepts presented within this chapter, what key fundamentals do managers need to understand to successfully manage a business?

2. Define what is meant by a business planning cycle. What are its key components?

3. What are the three fundamental objectives of a business? How are they interconnected? Why is each so important in ensuring the long-term viability of a business entity?

4. What is the difference between profit and profitability? How are the two interrelated?

5. Why is developing a value proposition for the products/services offered so important for a business? How much impact do you think a well-developed value proposition has on the success of a product or service?

6. Which is more important in ensuring a successful planning cycle for a business, the direction in which its strategy is moving the organization toward, or the tactics the organization must employ to get there?

QUESTION FOR INDIVIDUAL ACTION

Using the sample positioning template illustrated in Figure 1.10, write a positioning statement for one of the following products or operations: Apple iPad, WestJet, Walmart, Ford Focus, Game Stop.

TEAM EXERCISE

MySpace and Facebook are two of the largest social networking engines in today's Internet-based marketplace. A key to their long-term survival and success will be their ability to shift from solely providing social networking services to incorporating revenue generation and profitable business opportunities into their sites. At this stage of their evolution, what have each of these sites recently done to evolve their Web services to more of a revenue-generating and profitable business model?

Case for Discussion

Sylvie DeShane, CEO of Cruiser Laptops Inc., has just returned from the annual Computer and Electronics Show held in Las Vegas, Nevada. This one-week show provides computer and electronics companies with the opportunity to showcase new and upcoming products and services. It also provides CEOs and other senior managers of global suppliers an opportunity to discuss and assess the status of the marketplace and trends occurring within it. Sylvie spent a great deal of time with a number of CEOs discussing the increasing trend by buyers to determine which laptop they were going to purchase predominantly on the basis of price. As one customer put it, "What difference does it make which brand I buy? All manufacturers use the same components anyway." With razor-thin margins to begin with, Sylvie and others are concerned that this continual emphasis on pushing the price down will cause serious profitability problems down the road. Sylvie's dilemma: To determine just how manufacturers like Cruiser Laptops Inc. allowed price to become such an important part of the decision-making process.

QUESTIONS

1. What does this trend in the laptop industry imply about the way manufacturers have been marketing their products to customers? What have they failed to do?

2. If Sylvie decided to position Cruiser Laptops Inc. as a premium-price laptop manufacturer, what sort of things must she do to be successful?

3. If positioning as a premium-price manufacturer is not possible, what other options does Sylvie have? What sort of things must she do in order to be successful with this alternate position?

4. If you were Sylvie, what type of analysis would you conduct prior to determining a strategic direction? What key questions would you ask?

Practise and learn online with Connect. Connect resources include additional and interactive study exercises, videos, and practice quizzing, as well as additional material you won't find in the printed text.

2

The Canadian Economic Environment

Learning Objectives

This chapter is designed to provide students with:

Lo1 The ability to identify the major contributing factors that impact overall economic development

Lo2 Exposure to the core economic model that shapes Canada's economic growth and development

Lo3 A base-level understanding of what constitutes economic activity and how economies grow and contract

Lo4 The ability to recognize trends that will influence the future composition of economic development in Canada

Lo5 Guidance on how managers use information on economic trends in today's marketplace to better manage their organizations and respond to the competitive challenges confronting them

Snapshot—What to Expect in This Chapter

This chapter provides students with a broad introductory overview of the fundamentals behind how our economy works and how we as managers can use our understanding of it to better manage our organizations. The content emphasized in this chapter includes the following:

- Canada and Its Economic System

- Key Economic Influencers
  - Contributing Factors to Economic Development
  - The Underlying Economic Model
  - Canada: A Mixed Economic System

- The Economy in Simple Terms

- The Economic Growth Cycle

- Managing the Movement in the Economy

- Trends Impacting the Canadian Market

- Managing in Challenging Times
  - Understanding Competitive Models
  - Sensing Market Change

- Management Reflection—Analyzing Market Trends

From the Student's Perspective

Mention "the economy," and a chorus of grunts and moans tends to follow. Economic study—or the Dismal Science, as it is commonly nicknamed—is notorious for its arcane graphs, complex equations, and contrived theories. With so many opposing views and opinions on the economy, it's easy to wonder whether economists really understand it themselves.

Then why should we study the economy? That's simple—behind the equations, diagrams, and one-dimensional concepts that seem to undermine real life, the economy is an area that affects each and every one of us. From why gas prices inch up every other day, to why the government promises to cut taxes, the economy has a bearing on almost every facet of our lives.

But there is value beyond enabling you to better understand what appears in the major stories on your nightly news program—the study of the economy has a prophetic feature. Just as history repeats itself, so does the economy. For example, economic analysis suggests that a recession occurs every five years or so (we've seen nine official U.S. recessions since 1958). By analyzing past economic events, students and managers alike can make informed business decisions and can better understand the ever-changing economic environment.

Okay, you've made it this far—now read on. The study of the economy doesn't demand intricate math or confusing models, just an open mind and a desire to understand what's happening in the world. You may even like it!

Jay Oduwole received his MIL in Management in 2009. In addition, he possesses an undergraduate degree in Applied Economics with a special interest in financial markets and risk management. Jay played on the varsity football team at Queen's University and enjoys music and international travel. He is originally from Lagos, Nigeria, and was raised in Vancouver.

BUSINESS *in Action*

Canada: A "Petro Economy"

Over the past several years, more and more has been written about Canada's growing dependency on its energy and commodity (mining, natural resources, agriculture) sectors to drive overall economic growth. One just has to look at the "market watch" section of any of our major newspapers or business-focused Web sites to recognize that movements in the price of crude oil and commodities will be largely mimicked by the TSX composite (Toronto Stock Exchange) and the value of the Canadian dollar (as compared to the U.S. dollar and other major currencies). As the price of crude oil and commodities goes up, so too does the value of the TSX and the value of the Canadian dollar. Should the price of oil fall, this change often negatively impacts the value of the TSX and the Canadian dollar. This growing dependency on the energy sector to drive our economy forward results in Canada being referred to as a "petro economy." Energy is becoming one of our largest export sectors and continues to grow in overall economic value. Given the current strength of our dollar when compared to the U.S. dollar, it is now recognized to be one of the major reasons why we should, in the long run, continue to realize a balance of trade surplus—the difference between the value of imports (goods flowing into the country) versus exports (goods flowing out of the country). A surplus results when exports exceed imports. During this course, take the time to visit the "market watch" section of a business newspaper or business-focused Web site and track the movement of the TSX and the Canadian dollar based on the price changes occurring in the price of a barrel of oil or base commodities such as gold, copper, zinc, and potash.

WEB INTEGRATION

Want a great place to track the movement in the TSX, the value of the Canadian dollar, and the price changes to oil and commodities? Visit **www.financialpost.com.** Click on "Business," and then click on "Markets."

Canada and Its Economic System

G7/8 is a quasi-organization comprising the world's major fully developed economies. The G7 consists of the United States, Japan, Germany, Great Britain, France, Italy, and Canada. In 2006, the G7 transitioned to the G7/8 with the inclusion of Russia into its membership. Heads of the G7/8 countries meet at least once annually to discuss major economic, political, and societal issues challenging the global marketplace. Recent meeting trends have also resulted in representatives of major developing economies (such as China) attending at least part or all of such summit meetings.

As a current member of the **G7/8**,[1] Canada possesses one of the most fully developed economic systems in the world. Our abundance of natural resources, the skills of our labour force, and the sophistication of our technology-based businesses have enabled our economy to grow and prosper over the past 200-plus years. During this time, we have seen our economy move from being primarily agricultural to a diversified system with products and services sought by consumers and businesses around the world. Productivity gains, strong business investment, technological innovation, moderate wage increases, and a favourable currency exchange rate are all key factors that are deemed critical to ensuring our economy remains resilient and competitive now and in the future. Specific products driving Canada's current economic and trade performance include crude oil and other petroleum gases; wheat, canola, and other agricultural-based products; metals, such as gold and nickel; and minerals, such as sulphur and potash. On the manufacturing side, although hard-hit by the economic downturn of 2008–09, areas such as telecommunications, aerospace, energy support products (e.g., gas turbines), forestry-related products, and the automotive sector continue to demonstrate Canada's ability to develop world-class competitive products.[2]

> Productivity gains, strong business investment, technological innovation, moderate wage increases, and a favourable currency exchange rate are all key factors that are deemed to be critical in ensuring that our economy remains resilient and competitive now and in the future.

Key Economic Influencers

What enables some economies and nations to prosper, while others struggle? The response to this question is twofold. The first part has to do with the contributing factors for economic development that are in place within a particular economy. The second part focuses on the economic model that governs overall activity.

Contributing Factors to Economic Development

A core requirement to the stability and growth of any economic system lies in its ability to support and promote both the current and future economic activity taking place. This encompasses both the ability to provide a stable environment for economic growth and to ensure that the required business and economic management systems are in place to support an organized approach to economic development. In assessing the potential for current and future economic growth, the factors identified in Figure 2.1, although not all-inclusive, are generally viewed as being essential to economic vitality.[3]

In assessing Canada with regard to these factors, it can be quickly determined that Canada is fortunate to possess, within its economic fabric, the elements critical to supporting and growing an economic system. Our political system is stable. Our economy contains the necessary factors of production, such as roads, ports, utility systems, educated workforce, and technology-based business management systems that are essential to the efficient and effective development and delivery of goods and services throughout our economy. Our national and provincial debt levels are within acceptable limits, with both our federal and provincial governments working to reduce such debt loads (although additional debt has been added due to the financial sector and economic recovery programs put into place in 2008–09). Our

---

FIGURE 2.1 Contributing Factors to Economic Development

banking system is considered to be one of the most efficient and techno-savvy in the world, and our inflation levels have been well managed in recent years by the monetary policies and actions put in place by our central bank, the Bank of Canada. Our country is considered to possess a strong, fair, and equitable legal system, and the existence of corruption is viewed as being minimal in both our public and private sectors. In addition, our possession of a strong natural resource base results in our having a **comparative advantage** when it comes to the commodities and energy market sectors. The end result is that many domestic and foreign companies and investors view Canada as a safe and lucrative place to do business. In 2008, as an example, **foreign direct investment (FDI)** into Canada topped $500 billion, a 2.8-percent increase over 2007, and up 17.5 percent over 2006 inflows. Approximately 53 percent of the FDI flowing into Canada comes from the United States, although investment and acquisitions from countries other than the United States, particularly with respect to corporate acquisitions, continue to rise. In fact, almost all of the increases in FDI in 2008 were from non-U.S. sources.[4] Recent acquisitions by foreign entities of Inco, Falconbridge, Newbridge Networks, and BioChem Pharma are examples. Outright acquisitions of Canadian companies are not the only investment road being taken by international-based companies and country-based sovereign wealth funds. Minority interests in Canadian companies by foreign entities, particularly in the energy and commodity sectors, are also becoming more common. These global moves by a variety of international players are discussed in more detail in chapter 3.

Comparative Advantage refers to the ability of a country to produce or supply goods or services at a lower cost than other countries or to possess resources or unique services that are unavailable elsewhere.

Foreign Direct Investment (FDI) occurs when a company or individual from one country makes an investment into a business within another country. This investment can reflect the physical ownership of productive assets or the purchase of a significant interest in the operations of a business.

> A core requirement to the stability and growth of any economic system lies in its ability to service and promote both the current and future economic activity taking place.

The Underlying Economic Model

In addition to these contributing factors to economic development, in order for an economic system to develop and grow and to encourage and foster a climate that promotes and rewards economic risk, a balanced relationship also needs to be established among three fundamental market composition principles:

1. The law of supply and demand
2. Allowance for private ownership, entrepreneurship, and wealth creation
3. Extent of government involvement in influencing economic activity and direction

LAW OF SUPPLY AND DEMAND

Law of Supply and Demand refers to the ability of the market, independent of external influences, to determine the price for which a product or service will be bought and sold.

A core fundamental of an open economic environment, the **law of supply and demand** refers to the ability of the market, independent of external influences, to determine the price for which a product or service will be bought and sold. Demand reflects the number of purchasers who are willing to pay for a product or service at various price points. Demand can be perceived to be elastic or inelastic, depending on the movement in the quantity demanded for the various price points at which producers are considering offering a product or service to the marketplace. Inelastic demand results when movement in price does not result in significant changes in demand. As an example, Figure 2.2 illustrates an inelastic demand situation; the demand for gasoline changes little even though the price of gasoline rises. This is due to purchasers' need for gasoline to operate their vehicles and the lack of substitutes for gasoline in the marketplace. As an example, gasoline prices in Ontario rose from a low of $0.67 per litre to over $1.30 per litre from December 2007 to May 2011.[5] Despite this dramatic increase in price, the overall demand for gasoline remained relatively stable during this period (allowing for some seasonal fluctuation).

Elastic demand, however, reflects a situation where the quantity demanded does change significantly due to a change in price. Assume that buyers are interested in purchasing an electronic reader such as the Amazon Kindle. Offered at an initial price point of $699, demand for this electronic reader may be relatively low. As the price drops, however, more and more buyers become attracted to the opportunity of owning an electronic reader (see Figure 2.3).

FIGURE 2.2   Inelastic Demand: Gasoline

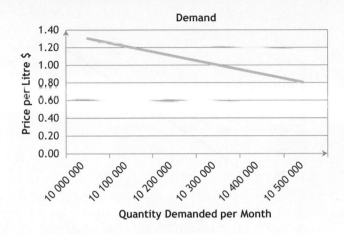

Demand

FIGURE 2.3   Elastic Demand: Electronic Reader

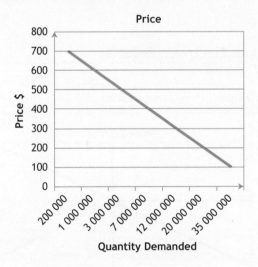

Price

While "demand" reflects the buyer's position toward a product, "supply" reflects how much of a product or service producers are willing to provide the market at various price points. The easiest way to think of this is as a supply schedule (see Figure 2.4) representing the amount of product or service a producer is willing to offer at a particular price point. Suppliers need to think about the cost of production versus the revenue that will be received from selling their product, and the change in profit that will be realized at different points on the schedule. Using our electronic reader example, suppliers may be willing to offer only a limited number of readers at $99, as their ability to make a profit at this price point is very suspect. Conversely, they are willing to provide a large quantity of readers at the price of $699, as this would maximize their profit potential.

Together, these concepts (demand and supply) form the basis for the law of supply and demand, which, again, defines the relationship between quantity demanded and quantity supplied. In pure economic terms, it refers to the point where the quantity supplied equals the quantity demanded, with the price point set by this equalization (see Figure 2.5). At this point, the market is in perfect equilibrium with there being no shortage or surplus of goods at the agreed-upon price point. When prices fall too low, a shortage may occur due to demand exceeding supply or the willingness to supply. When prices move higher, surpluses within the market may occur due to purchasers becoming unwilling to pay the higher price. When such events occur, in the absence of other external factors the market will correct itself back to an equilibrium price.

FIGURE 2.4   Supply Schedule: Electronic Readers

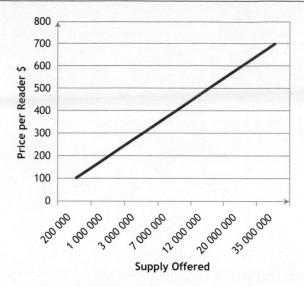

FIGURE 2.5   Supply and Demand: Electronic Readers

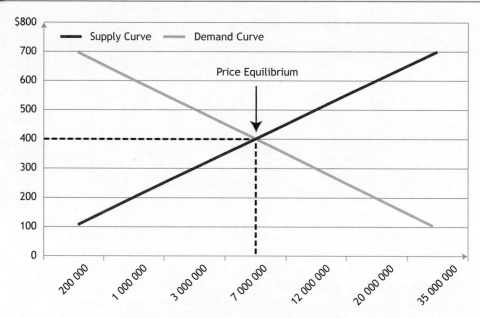

Our focus on this law with respect to economic activity and development looks at the freedom within the market to allow prices to be set in such a fashion. In some situations, price may be influenced or controlled by external mechanisms such as duties, tariffs, subsidies, or regulatory practices. In other economic settings, the law of supply and demand is provided with a much freer rein and, as such, plays a much bigger role in the actual price being charged for a particular product or service. Keep in mind that the example above has been kept simple to illustrate the theory behind the law of supply and demand. Influences such as consumer income, consumer preference, the number of product or service substitutes, and cost base reductions due to technology and productivity improvements have been removed from our analysis. Such factors, when considered, can result in significant influence on the relationship between supply and demand, particularly in the long run.

ALLOWANCE FOR PRIVATE OWNERSHIP, ENTREPRENEURSHIP, AND WEALTH CREATION

This principle refers to the openness of the market to support, encourage, and promote the concepts of private enterprise, personal ownership, entrepreneurship, and wealth creation. To a varying degree, economies around the world allow individuals and corporations these rights. Some economies, such as the United States and Canada, fully support these concepts in a climate of risk versus return. Developing economies such as the People's Republic of China and India are allowing greater access to these fundamentals, whereas others, such as North Korea, are less willing to provide strong support of these capitalistic principles.

GOVERNMENT INVOLVEMENT IN INFLUENCING ECONOMIC ACTIVITY AND DIRECTION

Government involvement in the economy relates to the varying roles government can play within ongoing day-to-day economic activities. Government can act as a customer via the purchasing of goods and services; as a regulator, restricting access or defining competitive protocols within particular economic sectors; as a manager via powers granted to Crown organizations, such as the Bank of Canada; as a taxation agent; as an economic stimulation agent via grant and subsidy programs, infrastructure development programs, and specific industry or company bailout programs; and as a competitor (providing services in direct competition for private-sector businesses), to name a few.

These three market composition principles will come together to provide the overall framework for economic activity within a given nation or economy. With each nation developing its own economic equilibrium, and with government policies shifting on an ongoing basis, it is best to view the relationship between these three market composition principles as being on a continuum. This is illustrated in Figure 2.6. At one end of the continuum is a fully **open system**, which is governed largely by the law of supply and demand, provides full and open access to the principles of private ownership, entrepreneurship and wealth creation, and possesses an absence of regulation on the part of a government. Open systems are also interpreted as being systems where foreign trade and movements in labour and capital are largely unrestricted. At the opposite end of the continuum is an economic system that is considered to be planned or controlled, in that the fundamentals of the law of supply and demand, private ownership, entrepreneurship, and wealth creation are largely restricted or absent, and the government fully controls the economic direction and activity on behalf of all (state authorities making decisions relating to domestic prices, output, and production). **Controlled systems** are also defined as economies that operate without or experience minimal external trade.[6] Within today's global economy no system can be considered completely open, although the

Open System refers to an economic system that adheres to the principles of economic freedom: the law of supply and demand, full and open access to the principles of private ownership, entrepreneurship, and wealth creation, and an absence of regulation on the part of government.

Controlled System refers to an economic system where the fundamentals of the law of supply and demand, private ownership, entrepreneurship, and wealth creation are largely restricted or absent, and the government fully controls the economic direction and activity.

FIGURE 2.6 Market Composition Principles: Economic Continuum

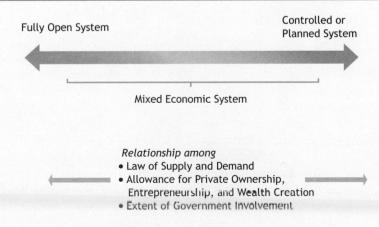

Fully Open System

Controlled or Planned System

Mixed Economic System

Relationship among
- Law of Supply and Demand
- Allowance for Private Ownership, Entrepreneurship, and Wealth Creation
- Extent of Government Involvement

economy of the United States historically has been considered to be the closest example of an open system given its significant emphasis on the law of supply and demand, private ownership, entrepreneurship, and wealth creation. However, given the recent financial services and economic crisis, we have seen a significant economic management role being undertaken by this government, which has moved this economy in the direction of a more **mixed economic system**. As indicated earlier, North Korea is currently one of the most-referred-to planned or controlled economic systems. Again, keep in mind that the openness or restrictiveness of a system can change over time (as noted with the U.S. above) as regulatory policies, development strategies, and external influences will impact overall economic governance. The evolution of the economies of the People's Republic of China and India, along with the variety of actions taken by the central banks and governments of various countries to combat the financial and economic crisis of 2008–09, are good examples of this.

Mixed Economic System refers to an economic system that contains components of both open and controlled systems. It includes the core principles of economic freedom, with some degree of centralized economic planning and government regulation and involvement.

Canada: A Mixed Economic System

Canada, like most fully developed economies, is considered to be a mixed economic system. By this, we mean that our economy allows the law of supply and demand to significantly influence the market. The principles of private ownership, entrepreneurship, and wealth creation, and their corresponding risk and return opportunities, are present and supported within our economic fundamentals. Our government, although an active participant in our economy, attempts to manage and influence economic activity through a cooperative/competitive model, participating where and how it feels it is of benefit to the market as a whole. Our government will become more or less engaged when it believes that, in doing so, it would be in the best interest of our nation in order to protect and regulate industries or guide economic initiatives. It also manages the economy via its powers of taxation, regulation, national debt targets, provincial transfers, and monetary policy control (see Figure 2.7).

> Canada, like most fully developed economies, is considered to be a mixed economic system.

FIGURE 2.7   Canadian Mixed Economic System

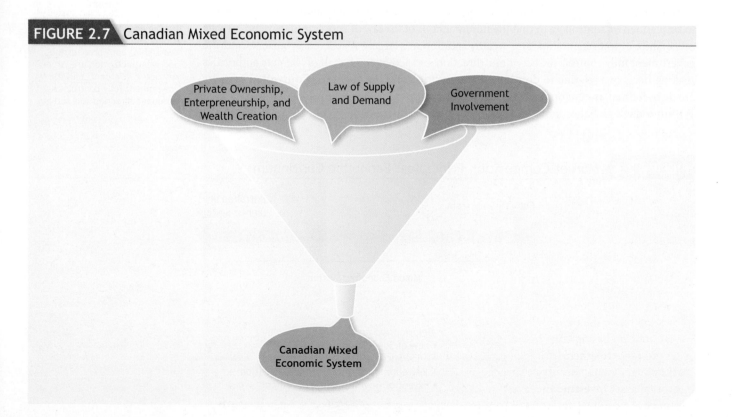

BUSINESS *in Action*

Role of the Bank of Canada

The Bank of Canada is Canada's central bank. Created in 1934, the Bank of Canada became a Crown corporation in 1938. The fundamental responsibility of the Bank of Canada is to develop and manage the monetary policies and financial systems associated with Canada's economic security. Specifically, the Bank of Canada has the following core areas of responsibility: influencing the economic activity within Canada via actions focused on managing inflation and currency supply; developing and managing the financial systems in place within Canada to ensure that sound fundamental practices are followed and safeguards are in place to protect the interest of Canadians; providing fund management services to our chartered banks and other financial institutions; and providing ongoing research and leadership in the development of corporate administration practices focused on ensuring that efficient and effective systems and practices are followed within the financial services sector. Over the past several years, increasing emphasis has been placed by the media on actions taken by the Bank of Canada with respect to its efforts to balance growth in economic activity and the resulting inflationary pressures. This media attention is most often associated with the benchmarks developed with respect to targeted inflation rates and with its setting of the base lending rate (the rate at which money is lent to our chartered banks), which, ultimately, impacts the borrowing and the savings rate you and I experience in the marketplace. Interest rate adjustment is the primary weapon the Bank of Canada uses in controlling inflationary pressures in the short term. Monetary managers and economists within the Bank of Canada typically meet eight times per year to assess the status of our economy and related inflationary pressures, and may or may not take action to influence the growth rate or the direction of economic activity depending on the outcomes derived from their analysis. With the continual evolution of the global economy, their management of this important part of the Bank of Canada's mandate will become increasingly apparent. The current Governor of the Bank of Canada is Mark Carney (appointed in October 2007).[7]

WEB INTEGRATION
Want to learn more about the role of the Bank of Canada and the methods it uses to influence economic activity? Visit **www.bankofcanada.ca**.

The Economy in Simple Terms

Perhaps the easiest way to understand the economy is to look at yourself as a self-contained economic unit. Your individual productivity will generate X number of dollars as a result of the economic activity you engage in. This productivity and its resulting economic activity will be predicated on the basis of four fundamental factors:

1. **Expenditures**: the purchases you make in support of your day-to-day economic activity that are deemed to be of value in meeting sustenance needs and in improving your overall quality of life. Clothing, food, housing, and transportation would be examples of such expenditures.

2. **Savings**: dollars you set aside today that will support economic activity and wealth creation in/for the future. Placing money in an RRSP (Registered Retirement Savings Plan) or purchasing GICs (guaranteed investment certificates) are examples. Your savings are then lent to others with the intent of stimulating their economic activity in the hopes of enhancing their wealth and private ownership levels.

3. **Capital asset investments**: investments you are making today to further expand your capacity to conduct and expand your productivity and overall economic capacity. If your

business requires an additional truck in order to expand, the purchase of this truck would be considered an investment focused on expanding your productivity and economic activity. Investments in real estate with the purpose of building future equity via wealth appreciation are an additional example.

4. **Credit**: the borrowing of dollars to support expenditures or investments being made. You may have needed to borrow money to purchase the above-mentioned truck, which you deem necessary to expand your business's capacity and capabilities, or to finance the real estate purchase you made.

> Economic Activity = Expenditures + Savings + Investment + Credit

The economy, as a whole, operates on these same principles. Economies move and grow as a result of the activities of everyone (consumers, businesses, and government) in these same areas (expenditures, savings, investments, credit). This is done on a continuous basis, quarter after quarter, year after year. As is illustrated above, interdependency among these four areas develops, with each one acting as a pillar in support of the overall economic activity (see Figure 2.8). It should be noted that economic growth relies as well on an equilibrium-based relationship among these factors. Too much credit (debt) will, ultimately, hinder economic growth, as larger and larger amounts of economic productivity must be used to repay this debt versus generating new economic growth opportunities. Savings, while necessary, also cannot be overemphasized, as too much emphasis on savings versus spending will similarly result in a tendency to reduce economic growth due to such expenditure reductions.

FIGURE 2.8   Four Pillars of Economic Activity and Growth

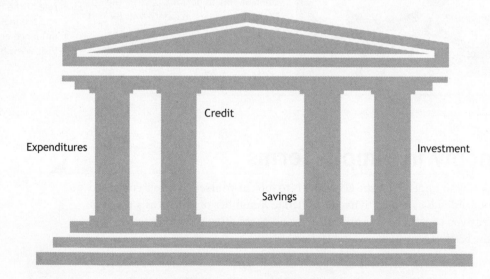

LO3   The Economic Growth Cycle

GDP (Gross Domestic Product) refers to the total market value of the goods and services (economic output) a nation produces domestically over a period of time (generally one calendar year).

So, how do economies grow? The answer to this question varies depending upon the development stage of the economy and what is interpreted as its key GDP driver. The total value of a nation's economy is measured by its **gross domestic product, or GDP**. Think of GDP as being all the economic activity generated by individuals, businesses, and government for the economy as a whole. GDP is the total market value of the goods and services a nation produces domestically over a defined period of time (usually one year). Examples of factors that contribute to economic growth and, therefore, the total value of GDP are:

- goods and services produced and purchased domestically for consumption

- business investments within the economy

- goods produced for export purposes

- government spending

Economists track the movement of GDP (upward or downward) over a period of time to determine whether an economy is growing or contracting. Figure 2.9 shows the overall growth in the Canadian economy between 1998 and 2010.[8] As you can see in Figure 2.9, overall our economy has grown (as measured by GDP) over the last 10-plus years, peaking in 2009 before the full effects of the most recent recession were felt in 2010. Figure 2.10 demonstrates, however, that this growth does not necessarily occur on a linear basis, but that growth does vary from year to year and quarter to quarter. As shown in Figure 2.10,[9] GDP growth during 2008 did taper off significantly versus that of 2007, and we actually experienced a significant contraction in GDP in the final quarter of 2008 and through most of 2009—the impact of a global

FIGURE 2.9 Canada's GDP Growth

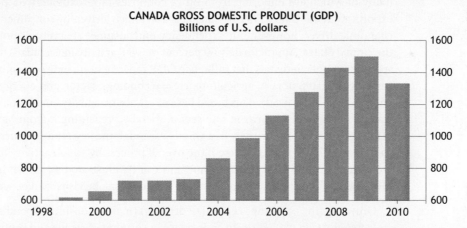

Source: Trading Economics; Gross Domestic Product, Canada, www.google.com/publicdata; The World Bank Group: World Development Indicators; IndexMundi, http://www.indexmundi.com/canada/gdp_real_growth_rate.htm; CIA World Fact Book: https://www.cia.gov/library/publications/the-world-factbook/.

FIGURE 2.10 GDP Movement, 2007 to 2011

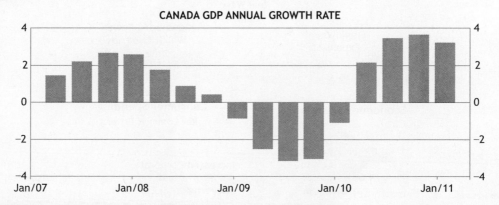

Sources: TradingEconomics.com; STCA Statistics Canada; IndexMundi, http://www.indexmundi.com/canada/gdp_real_growth_rate.html; The World Bank, GDP growth (annual %), http://data.worldbank.org/indicator/NY.GDP.MKTP.KD.ZG.

Recession is a period of time that marks a contraction in the overall economic activity within an economy. A recession is typically believed to occur when an economy experiences two or more quarters of negative GDP movement.

recession and financial services market crisis. This 2009 GDP contraction was in part due to a decline in real domestic demand, which relates to the level of consumer personal spending and business investment, both of which experienced sharp declines during this period as a result of the economic climate impacting individual purchase and business operating decisions.[10]

> Economists track the movement of GDP (upward or downward) over a period of time to determine whether an economy is growing or contracting.

Key economic drivers vary from country to country. Think of the global marketplace as a world full of buyers and sellers. For some economies, for example the People's Republic of China, the current key economic driver lies with the production of goods and services. This production can either be import or export focused. In China's case, a predominant portion of the production activity currently taking place is for the purpose of exporting these products and services to other countries. For others, such as the United States, the key GDP driver is that of consumer spending. The United States is one of the leading purchasers of goods and services. Its US$14.7-trillion-plus economy (2010 estimate) is the largest in the world, and the United States, because of its consumer-purchase-based economy, is considered by many to be the engine that drives the current global economy. More than 70 percent of U.S. economic activity is driven by consumer spending on goods and services, many of which are imported from other countries (approximately 85 percent of Canada's exports go to the United States). Canada is also largely driven by consumer spending as its key economic driver; however, our dependency on consumer spending is not as great as that in the United States. Approximately 60 percent of GDP activity in Canada is driven by consumer spending. Other activities that influence GDP movement include our natural resource sector (mining, forestry, potash, agriculture, etc.), technology sector, and energy-producing industries (oil and natural gas). This broad base of economic activity enables our economy to withstand economic downturns in one sector, thereby preventing it from having a detrimental influence on economic activity as a whole. Although the key economic driver may vary (consumer spending, production, etc.), the overall process by which activity is stimulated within an economic cycle is largely the same and can be illustrated as shown in Figure 2.11. The movement of economic activity within an economy can be visualized or sequenced as follows:

1. Growth in the economy via its GDP driver(s) (mainly consumer spending in the United States and Canada) results in an increase in corporate revenue and profits and government tax revenue (increased tax revenue, GST revenue, provincial tax revenue, etc.).

FIGURE 2.11   Economic Growth Cycle, North America: Economic Expansion

2. As a result of this increase in profits and tax revenue, both business and government will possess increased capacity to invest in new infrastructure and new product/service offerings for consumers. These investments expand the economic infrastructure to meet the growing needs of the economy and the people within it, and add further stimulation to economic activity.

3. Increased business activity requires more employees, resulting in an expansion of employment opportunities. In Canada, as an example, between 2005 and 2008 we realized some of the lowest unemployment numbers ever as a result of strong economic growth and the need for an expanded workforce.

4. With an increase in the need for workers, employers are forced to pay higher wages to attract and retain employees. These higher wages result in additional dollars for workers (consumers) to spend and, therefore, contribute to economic growth (via further spending and/or expanded credit capabilities). As long as this real wage growth outpaces inflationary pressures, true economic growth will occur. With prolonged periods of economic growth, such as that which Canada experienced from 2001 through 2006, the cycle continues to repeat itself and overall economic activity continues to expand. During the period from 2001 through 2006, for example, Canada's GDP growth averaged between 2.5 percent and 3.5 percent annually.[11]

> This broad base of economic activity enables our Canadian economy to withstand an economic downturn in one sector, thereby preventing it from having a detrimental influence on economic activity as a whole.

In periods of economic contraction, the reverse holds true. For example, a softening of consumer spending will place downward pressure on corporate profits and government tax revenues (see Figure 2.12). With this reduction to profits and tax revenue, businesses and government will reduce spending. This in turn will reduce investment in economic expansion–based activities. With this reduced spending and lower levels of consumer spending, fewer workers will be needed because the amount of goods and services being produced will be reduced. This will have a negative impact on employment requirements, resulting in an increasing supply of available workers (due to downsizing, retrenchment, and business closings) that, ultimately, will be reflected in higher unemployment rates. With more workers available, the supply of workers will exceed the demand, which will result in a downward

FIGURE 2.12   Economic Growth Cycle, North America: Economic Contraction

pressure on wages and wage increases. This results in fewer dollars for consumers to spend and therefore contributes to a further slowing of economic activity (the cycle continues). A number of analysts and economists view this as what took place in the global economy commencing in the fall of 2008, and peaking in the fourth quarter of 2009 and into the first half of 2010. This was further accelerated by the financial crisis that was a compounding catalyst to this recessionary period. It should be noted that this recent economic crisis resulted in significant capital infusion by governments and central banks (including the Government of Canada and the Bank of Canada). Much of this infusion was the result of the need to ensure liquidity into the financial services sector, as well as the need to develop mechanisms for job creation. This significant capital infusion should be considered an abnormal response, by governments, to general recessionary periods (not driven by catastrophic events, such as the financial sector meltdown), with this liquidity infusion largely debt-based (money has been borrowed) versus being revenue-driven as a result of economic activity.

BUSINESS *in Action*

GDP: Where Does It Come From?

GDP represents the total market value of the goods and services a specified area (nation, province, etc.) produces domestically over a period of time. It is a reflection of the overall economic output of such a country, or province, or region. What makes up GDP? Well, take the province of Alberta as an example. In 2008, the total value of Alberta's GDP was $291.7 billion. This means the total value of goods and services produced by economic manufacturers, suppliers,

Government of Alberta ▪

and buyers in Alberta equalled this amount. Where did it come from? Figure 2.13 illustrates the various sectors of Alberta's economy whose contribution to economic activity stimulated Alberta's GDP to the $291.7-billion level.[12]

FIGURE 2.13   Alberta's GDP, 2008

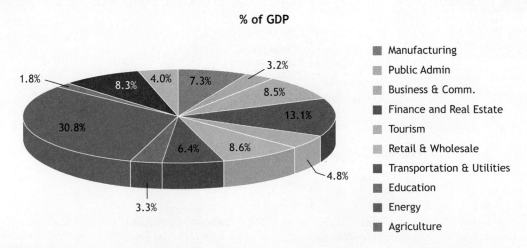

% of GDP

- Manufacturing
- Public Admin
- Business & Comm.
- Finance and Real Estate
- Tourism
- Retail & Wholesale
- Transportation & Utilities
- Education
- Energy
- Agriculture

1.8% 8.3% 4.0% 7.3% 3.2% 8.5% 13.1% 30.8% 6.4% 8.6% 4.8% 3.3%

Source: Government of Alberta, Alberta Finance and Enterprise, Alberta Economic Quick Facts, February 2010, www.finance.alberta.ca and www.albertacanada.com. ISSN: 1718-1410 (PDF).

BUSINESS *in Action*

Canadian Banks: On a Global Buying Spree

What is the advantage of a strong Canadian currency in the global marketplace coupled with strong managerial and financial controls? Well, for Canada's large **chartered banks** (e.g., BMO, CIBC, RBC, Scotiabank, and TD Canada Trust), it represents an opportunity to grow outside of Canada through acquisitions (acquiring other companies). With the current housing market collapse in the United States and the weakness of its regional banking system due to the sub prime mortgage market credit issues that accompanied the slowdown, regional banks in the United States are ripe for acquisition, and our stronger Canadian banks are well positioned to take advantage of this. Both RBC and BMO have incorporated into their business strategies an ongoing acquisition interest in the U.S. market. RBC's focus has been in the southeastern United States buying regional banks such as Centura and AmSouth, which cover the states of Georgia, Florida, and the Carolinas. BMO has focused on the Chicago area, where it already owns Harris Bank and has made a number of other smaller acquisitions. TD Canada Trust has also entered the U.S. market recently, illustrated by its acquisition of New Jersey-based Commerce Bank. Scotiabank, whose focus to date has been on continuing to build its presence in Latin America (purchasing banks in Mexico, Peru, El Salvador, the Dominican Republic, Puerto Rico, Panama, Belize, and Chile) with a purchase of Corporacion Interfin in Costa Rica, is also assessing opportunities in the United States. While acquisitions offer opportunities for growth, there is still risk. Managers need to be sure that these investments live up to their profitability expectations, fit within their current structures, and contribute toward the overall growth and value of our chartered banks to the satisfaction of all their stakeholders.[13]

Chartered Banks are financial institutions regulated under the Canada Bank Act. Their primary responsibility is to bring together borrowers and lenders by accepting deposits and lending out money—all in a manner that safeguards the interests of their customers.

WEB INTEGRATION
Want to learn more about the acquisitions our chartered banks are making? Visit their Web sites.

Managing the Movement in the Economy

Managing the movement in the economy is no easy task. In general, growth in overall economic activity is desired; however, this growth needs to be managed in a way that stimulates investment yet maintains control of **inflation** and other inefficient economic influencers. This balance is critical to ensure the growth that is taking place is real growth and not masked by inflation. The Government of Canada, in conjunction with its affiliated regulatory agencies, provincial governments, and Crown corporations such as the Bank of Canada, seeks to maintain equilibrium between growth and inflation in order to provide an environment that

Inflation is a rise in the level of prices of goods and services within an economy over a period of time.

makes the best use of the capacity and capabilities of our economic platform without allowing it to overheat. It must also take into consideration that, given the geographic distribution of Canada's economic clusters (Halifax, Montreal, Toronto, Winnipeg, Edmonton, Calgary, and Vancouver), regional disparity will exist in terms of growth rates and future economic potential. As an example, the recent hot spot of economic growth within Canada lies within the provinces of Alberta, Saskatchewan, British Columbia, and Newfoundland and Labrador. These provinces have experienced tremendous growth due to increasing demand for natural resources (commodities) and energy products by the developing global economy. Alberta's average annual GDP growth rate for the five-year period from 2003 to 2008 was 3.6 percent, with growth reaching its peak in 2006 when GDP growth hit 6.8 percent. British Columbia, Saskatchewan, and Manitoba also experienced GDP growth rates, from 2003 to 2008, of approximately 3 percent annually. Compare this with annual economic growth rates in Ontario and Quebec of 2 percent or less for the same time period. These softening growth rates in central Canada were the result of a strong Canadian dollar challenging its manufacturing sector in the global marketplace, increasing energy prices, a recession-based U.S. economy (a primary market for central Canada's manufacturing sector), and the emergence of China and other developing countries in the manufacturing and technology sectors. Although the global recession of 2008–09 temporarily halted GDP growth in most provinces (for example, Alberta's GDP contracted by 0.1 percent in 2008 and an estimated 2.5 percent in 2009), 2010 showed positive growth recovery across Canada (see Figure 2.14).[14] The challenge to our government and the Bank of Canada going forward, however, will be to incorporate into its decision-making process actions that will continue to stimulate growth in Central and Eastern Canada without compromising the expected returning higher than average growth rates of our Western provinces. It must also do this in a way that does not cause further inflationary pressures (which will compromise such growth). We must also seek mechanisms to stimulate economic activity in the Maritime provinces, beyond the energy opportunities surfacing in Newfoundland and Labrador, to ensure that economic growth and prosperity occurs in eastern Canada as well.

FIGURE 2.14   GDP Growth, 2010

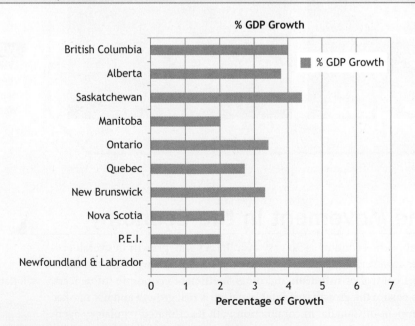

Source: Gordon Isfeld, "Statistics Canada Corrects GDP Figures for 2010," *Financial Post*, May 11, 2011.

> Economic growth needs to be managed in a way that stimulates investment yet maintains control of inflation and other inefficient economic influencers.

Trends Impacting the Canadian Market

LO4

As we have seen in this chapter, the Canadian economic market is a complex entity that continues to change and evolve as internal and external influences impact both its direction and its composition. Looking forward, we continue to view our economic market as being stable and expected to continue in importance within the global community. As managers, it is important that we understand the trends occurring within this economic market, as they pose opportunities and challenges to the livelihood of our individual businesses and for Canadians as a whole. Recognizing that a multitude of factors influence the economy at any given time, the following are some prominent trends we will need to assess in order to plan appropriately for our business operations and for the goods and services that will be demanded by Canadians as a whole.

- inflation

- geographic clustering

- currency exchange rate impact

- branch market impact

- sustainability and green initiatives

- aging workforce, immigration and multi-culturalism

- long-term competitiveness

- small business emphasis

- globalization

INFLATION

As previously discussed, significant inflationary pressures will have a negative impact on the growth of economic activity in Canada. Inflation robs an economy of true growth and psychologically negatively impacts the confidence levels of consumers and business operators alike. With the anticipated increasing demand for energy globally, and the current challenges we face in meeting this growing need, energy and related products and services will continue to escalate in price. With such a heavy reliance on energy for production and transportation needs for the near term, a continued upward pressure on the cost base associated with products and services will result. Such cost increases will need to be transferred to consumers in the form of higher prices. The question will be whether we can offset our significant dependency on fossil fuels with alternate fuel sources quickly enough to minimize, time-wise, a lengthy upward spiral in inflationary tendencies. Similar situations are occurring within the food chain. Prices associated with grains, coffee, and rice, due to an ever-growing demand for these commodities globally, are on the rise. U.S. government-reported price increases between February 2010 and February 2011 indicated that the price of lettuce had risen 289 percent during this period; cucumbers were up by 29 percent, green peppers by 145 percent, and tomatoes by 84 percent. Beef prices during this same period rose 19 percent, with the price of processed turkey up just under 15 percent.[15] While many companies dependent upon these products (fast-food restaurants such as Subway, Tim Hortons, McDonald's, Burger King) shield themselves somewhat through economies of scale and long-term contracts, such cost increases cannot be absorbed forever. McDonald's, for example, sent signals to the marketplace in the first quarter of 2011 that prices at its restaurants would be on the rise.

GEOGRAPHIC CLUSTERING

As already mentioned, the Canadian economy is one that has been transitioning to that predicated on the concept of geographic clustering. Geographic clustering occurs when regional economies develop into what are considered distinct from one another and separated by significant geographic space where interdependency is minimized. In essence, a variety of distinct regional economic platforms occur. Although this occurs frequently at the local level, enough interdependency exists at the regional and national levels to mitigate any negative consequences on the economy. The danger occurs when such distinctness occurs at the broader macro level, resulting in the inability of governments to effectively implement national-based economic management actions to effectively control economic expansion or contraction via monetary policy or inflation control mechanisms. With the current economic distinctness between our western provinces and central and eastern Canada, our management of the economy is being somewhat hampered. Continued emphasis must be placed on the interdependency of the regions to ensure the negative impact of geographic clustering can be minimized.

CURRENCY EXCHANGE RATE IMPACT

The overall appreciation in the value of the Canadian dollar, when benchmarked against the U.S. dollar, has both positive and negative effects for the Canadian economy. On the positive side, the strength of the Canadian dollar has assisted in reducing the price of goods and services being imported into the country from other countries. It has also made trips to the United States less expensive for Canadians. In addition, the overall appreciation has resulted in the revenue received from exports, such as energy (oil and natural gas), natural resources, and other commodities, which are largely traded in U.S. dollars, to grow as well, leading to stronger profits within these sectors. On the negative side, a stronger Canadian dollar has impacted our tourism and manufacturing export sectors, as the price of Canadian goods and services being exported to other countries has risen, making these goods and services more expensive when compared to their domestically produced counterparts, and the cost of visiting Canada by residents of the U.S. (who account for a large percentage of our tourism trade) is now more expensive than before. Think of it this way: in January 2006, the value of the Canadian dollar was US$0.83. In 2007, our dollar rose to a high of US$1.08. In May 2011, it sat at just below US$1.03.[16] This approximate $0.20 to $0.25 increase in the value of the Canadian dollar directly impacts the cost base of Canadian manufacturers and the prices they charge to others in the global market. In general, the Bank of Canada has historically stated that it would ideally like to see our dollar stay around $0.85 to $0.90 USD. This is felt to be an appropriate level to maintain our competitiveness in the global market. Export manufacturers, of course, would like to see this value even lower, as a dollar around the US$0.82 range, for example, would provide them with approximately an $0.18 cost advantage over their U.S. competitors. With our strong energy and natural resource base, and our more diversified economy, analysts anticipate that our dollar will remain near or slightly above **parity** (US$1 range) going forward. Thus, our export manufacturers will need to create other ways to create competitive advantages against their U.S. and global competitors, versus simply hoping for a currency exchange rate advantage.

Parity means being equal or equivalent to; specifically, the value of one currency being equal to that of another.

BRANCH MARKET IMPACT

PPP (Purchasing Power Parity) a measure that takes into account the relative cost of living and the inflation rates of each country, and adjusts the total value of economic activity accordingly.

Although Canada is a $1-trillion-plus economy—**PPP (purchasing power parity)**—the overall size of our economy is small when compared to other countries. This includes both fully developed economies, such as the U.S. ($14-trillion-plus), and developing economies, such as the People's Republic of China ($6.9+ trillion PPP), and India ($2.8+ trillion PPP). In addition, with such strong demand for our natural resources, energy, and commodity-based goods and services, many global organizations have looked to actively purchase Canadian-owned companies. In the past five years, the number of Canadian-owned companies purchased by foreign firms has alarmed a number of analysts and government-sector managers and elected officials. The acquisition of Inco by Vale of Brazil (formerly CVRD), and Falconbridge by Xstrata of Switzerland in 2006 are just two of many examples of the trend occurring within our business sector. For some, the fundamental concern is that Canada, in seeing its major businesses being acquired by foreign entities, is in danger of losing control of its economic base and runs the risk of simply becoming a branch market economy. The Canadian government has been challenged over the past few years to revamp the Investment Canada Act and include a national security test for assessing the impact of foreign ownership in Canadian corporations as a mechanism for controlling the economic and cultural impact of such acquisitions.[17] This issue resurfaced dramatically in the fall of 2010 when Australian-based BHP Billiton attempted a **hostile takeover** of Saskatchewan-based Potash Corporation. This deal was blocked by the Canadian government on the grounds that it was not in the interest of Canada to see this Canadian-based organization become owned by a foreign entity. The first quarter of 2011 saw these concerns arise again when the London Stock Exchange (LSE) announced its intention to acquire the Toronto Stock Exchange (TSX). This proposed acquisition is currently being scrutinized by various government bodies in Canada to determine the impact of allowing such an acquisition to take place. As one can see, the debate associated with foreign ownership is only expected to become louder, and it is anticipated that additional modifications to the Investment Canada Act will occur in the near future.

Hostile Takeover refers to an attempt by a company to take over another company whose management and board of directors are unwilling to agree to the merger or takeover.

WEB INTEGRATION
Want to learn more about changes to Canada's Investment Act and Competition Act? Google "Canada's Investment Act" or "Canada's anti-trust legislation."

SUSTAINABILITY AND GREEN INITIATIVES

Sustainability and green initiatives will have an increasing emphasis across the business spectrum. Companies will seek to achieve both market positioning advantages and cost advantages through the execution of green-based strategies as part of their overall business plan. This will include an increased emphasis on green products, more environmentally friendly packaging, reduced carbon emissions, and greater sensitivity to the use of finite resources in the development, production, and distribution of goods and services to the global community at large. An example of this is Walmart Canada's new Walmart HE stores. Designed to reduce energy consumption by 30 percent, HE stores are projected to deliver, for Walmart, $25 million in energy savings between 2009 and 2014 when compared to stores built in 2005. Walmart will achieve these savings by using initiatives such as rerouting waste energy from refrigerators to help heat stores, reduced lighting costs, and modifying roofing systems to reflect light away from the building thus reducing summer cooling costs. Walmart Canada's long-term focus is the pursuit of three sustainability goals globally: (1) to produce zero waste, (2) to operate with 100 percent renewable energy, and (3) to make available environmentally preferable products.[18]

AGING WORKFORCE, IMMIGRATION AND MULTI-CULTURALISM

Similar to many other fully developed economies, Canada's workforce is aging. As an example, in March 2011 the Petroleum Human Resources Council of Canada issued a report that indicated Canada's aging workforce is poised to impact the employment needs of Canada's energy sector. The report indicates that over 30 percent of this workforce is expected to retire within the next decade, resulting in a need to hire and train at least 39 000 workers.[19] As baby boomers slide into retirement, analysts are becoming increasingly concerned about intellectual capital shortages in fields such as information technology, health care, education, and skilled trades in a number of market sectors, including the petroleum sector as noted above.

With an aging population and one of the lowest birth rates of any fully developed country, Canada's strategy for replacing retiring workers and for continuing to grow our economic base is closely tied to immigration. The need for skilled and well-educated workers will continue to rise, resulting in our need to import such skills due to a shortage domestically. Reliance on immigration brings both challenges and opportunities. The challenges are focused on ensuring that immigrants in Canada find a country that is welcoming to them and respectful of their ethnic backgrounds and traditions. Assimilation into society in a manner that enables them to actively contribute to social and cultural growth is a key to ensuring that Canada remains a preferred choice for the highly technical employee base that a knowledge-based economy will need. Recognition of skill and degrees earned abroad will be a fundamental component of this process in order to ensure that upon their arrival to Canada immigrants are able to positively contribute to Canadian society with minimal barriers. Having said this, a fundamental requirement of this assimilation process will be the challenge of ensuring that this immigrant population possesses, or quickly develops, the required language and critical thinking competency skills necessary for functioning in today's highly technical marketplace. With immigration and multi-culturalism comes the emergence of new ethnic markets that represent business opportunities for the delivery of goods and services to these growing market segments. Toronto and Vancouver, as examples, are two of the most culturally diversified cities in North America. Within these two cities, and across Canada as a whole, we are seeing a growing shift within the retail and service sectors, in particular, to actively market to ethnic neighbourhoods and segments goods and services specific to their cultural and social preferences. This trend will continue to grow stronger as the percentage of our population that is comprised of immigrants to Canada continues to grow.

WEB INTEGRATION

Want to learn more about the impact of immigration and multi-culturalism in Canada? Google "Unlikely Utopia, The Surprising Triumph of Canadian Pluralism," by Michael Adams, or go to **www.michaeladams.ca**.

LONG-TERM COMPETITIVENESS

With the Canadian dollar expected to remain strong against the U.S. dollar for the foreseeable future, and the rise of the developing economies of Asia, Eastern Europe, and South America, Canada will be challenged to maintain its competitive advantages in the marketplace. As one of the world's largest exporters of natural resources, commodities, and energy, these market segments should continue to grow and enable sections of the country to realize ongoing GDP growth. For other parts of Canada, the drive to retain competitive advantages may not be so easy. The challenge to improve productivity levels, the increased cost base associated with our strong currency, and the ability of businesses within developing countries to operate with lower overall costs (largely due to savings in the labour sector) mean that Canadian manufacturers and the economy as a whole will need a shift in emphasis to remain competitive. Where technology advantages have historically been one mechanism for achieving overall competitive advantage, businesses within developing countries now possess the same level of sophistication in this area. For Canada, in addition to our energy and resource sector, our future lies in the ongoing development of knowledge-based industries, where our business acumen will enable us to continue to show global leadership. Education, banking and financial services, and sophisticated operational process development are areas where we must continue to excel in order to ensure our economic platform and our quality of life are protected and enhanced.

SMALL BUSINESS EMPHASIS

Although our larger corporations (e.g., Royal Bank, Manulife, Bombardier, Research In Motion, GM of Canada) tend to dominate the business headlines, it is small business that makes up the most significant portion of the fabric of our marketplace. Companies in Canada that have more than 500 employees make up just 0.1 percent of Canadian businesses. Businesses that are largely owned and operated by sole proprietors and possess no employees make up over 56 percent of our country's businesses. In fact, businesses with fewer than 20 employees represent over 90 percent of our approximately 2.4 million business establishments.[20] Entrepreneurship continues to drive small business creation in Canada and this trend is not anticipated to subside going forward. Domestic ethnic market development, global niche market opportunities, and specialty goods and services offerings are just a few examples of where continuous small business growth will be driven. With technological advances occurring at lightning speed, opportunities for Internet-based companies and techno-savvy start-ups both home and abroad will accelerate in both urban and rural environments.

GLOBALIZATION

Globalization refers to the growing interconnectivity of the world and the heightened interdependence we are seeing among its various economic regions. The advent of social networking tools—Facebook and Twitter, for example—has enabled us to transmit information to as many as 500 million people across the globe with simply the tap of a finger. The Internet has enabled the development of business models that are able to reach potential buyers with few boundaries or restrictions. As the global economy becomes more connected and emerging economies—such as the BRIC countries (Brazil, Russia, India, China) and CIVETS countries (Colombia, Indonesia, Vietnam, Egypt, Turkey, South Africa)—continue to develop their domestic and export-based economies, new business opportunities will arise as never before. At the same time, so will increased competitive pressures. Canadian businesses will need to adapt to remain competitive. Adapting means becoming more efficient and effective in our operational processes, improving the productivity of our workforces, reinventing our businesses as global market needs change, and becoming increasingly innovative and entrepreneurial as product and market life cycles become shorter. Chapter 3 provides a more detailed look at the global marketplace and the concept of globalization.

Managing in Challenging Times
LO5

As managers, it is fundamentally important that we understand what is happening in both our domestic economy and within those global economies that influence our overall economic activity and prosperity. With heightened global activity comes an increased interdependency on national, regional, and even local economies. In this regard, as managers we must be in tune not only with the general directions that are occurring, but also with the opportunities and threats that will develop as a result of such increased economic activity and interdependency. In order to fully understand where the market is going, managers look to generally answer three fundamental questions:

1. What are the general indicators saying about the current economy and about the current relationships among the key variables governing our mixed economic system (law of supply and demand; support for the concepts of entrepreneurship, wealth creation, and private ownership)?
2. What broad-level changes (political, economic, social, technological, environmental, and legal) are occurring within the sectors of the economy that directly impact my organization's future growth and market position?
3. What specific current competitive actions may disrupt the way in which business is done within my organization's particular market sector?

> As managers, it is fundamentally important that we understand what is happening in both our domestic economy and within those global economies that influence our overall economic activity and prosperity.

In terms of the first question, managers will generally look to monitor a number of key economic indicators that reflect the general movement in the economy. Some of the primary economic indicators that we assess on the basis of movement within them are:

— unemployment rate

— inflation rate

— Consumer Price Index (CPI)

— new housing starts

— manufacturing inventory

— Consumer Confidence Index

— price of crude oil (per barrel basis)
— stock market indexes (TSX, S&P 500, Dow Jones)
— currency exchange rate
— monthly retail sales

In addition, many industry-specific indexes can be used to further assess the health and sta-bility of particular market sectors. As an example, manufacturing firms will also look at pro-ductivity indexes, inventory and manufacturing level indexes, and export and producer price indexes. Information relating to each of these indicators can be picked up via government releases, media reports, industry trade and analyst reports, and Web-based searches. Ongoing monitoring of these indicators enables us to assess whether the economy is expanding rapidly, beginning to slow, or moving into a potential market contraction or recession. As an example, during the height of our recent economic expansion (2003 to 2007) unemployment rates in Canada dropped to a record low of 5.8 percent. As the economy began to cool in 2008, this number moved up to 6.5 percent, although in some geographic regions (e.g., Toronto) unem-ployment moved toward 7.1 percent. As the global economy moved into the full recession in late 2008 and 2009, Canada's unemployment figure further increased to 8.7 percent (August 2009), and in the United States unemployment hit 10.1 percent (October 2009).[21] This upward movement in unemployment tells managers that market growth at large remains sluggish and that the movement in the economic growth cycle has been adjusting downward (contracting) for the near future.

In addition to the economic factors discussed above, managers will also assess at the macro level the political, social, technological, environmental, and legal changes that are occurring, commonly referred to as a **PESTEL analysis** (see Figure 2.15). Politically, the as-sessment will be looking for trends in government legislation or activity that may signal a change to the management of the economy and, therefore, the equilibrium relationship within the mixed economic system. This could include mild intervention in the form of interest rate adjustments, or more significant intervention such as direct government investment in par-ticular market segments or consideration of anti-trust legislation or changes to Canada's investment and competition acts in order to protect Canadian companies or market sectors potentially at risk. Increasing tendencies toward **protectionism** could also form part of this high-level political assessment. Socially, managers will look for trends that may fundamen-tally change how consumers want, need, or use products/services, as well as the changing composition of the marketplace. This can include demographic shifts and cultural shifts, as well as behavioural changes. Managers also need to pay attention to changes occurring in the legal sector and its potential impact on the overall business risk. This can include changes to employment law, product liability risk exposure, contract law, and consumer rights, to name

---

WEB INTEGRATION
Want to know Canada's current unemployment rate and get a good under-standing of the "pulse of the economy" at this time? Go to **www.canadianeconomy.gc.ca.**

PESTEL Analysis refers to a macro-level assessment of the political, economic, social, technology, environmental, and legal trends that can or will impact the markets within which an organization competes.

Protectionism is the outcome of the intent of economic policies that are put in place to protect or improve the competitiveness of domestic industries via impeding or restricting the openness of a market or markets to foreign competitors through the use of tariffs, trade restrictions, quotas, artificial control of currency values, or other related activities.

FIGURE 2.15   PESTEL Analysis

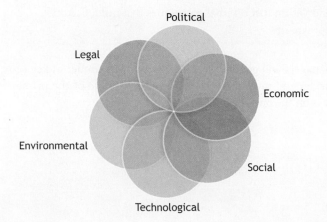

a few. Changes associated with environmental compliance regulations and other environmental sustainability obligations must also be reviewed and brought into the decision-making process. Finally, managers must constantly assess the speed and direction of technology shifts that could potentially render current products, services, and operational processes obsolete. Telecommunications, automation, and ecommerce-based business models are dramatically changing the way in which business is done today, with the rate of change continuing to accelerate as we move forward in the current and upcoming decade.

With respect to the third question posed at the beginning of this section, managers are constantly looking to see where and how their markets are changing in light of competitive influences. In evaluating the current market within which a business is competing, managers need to understand the composition of the competitive model that currently governs the marketplace and the potential for disruption to this model moving forward.

> Managers must constantly look to see where and how their markets are changing in light of competitive influences.

Understanding Competitive Models

An important consideration for any business owner or manager has to do with understanding the nature of competition with respect to the products or services the business is offering and the markets that are being served by these products and services. Understanding the type of competitive environment a business is facing is fundamental to creating a strategy for competing and understanding where and how to allocate resources in support of product/service positioning and overall marketing effort. For simplicity, we tend to categorize markets as fitting into one of four definitive quadrants (see Figure 2.16): purely competitive markets, monopolistic markets, oligopoly-based markets, or a monopoly-controlled market.

> Understanding the type of competitive environment a business is facing is fundamental to creating a strategy for competing and understanding where and how to allocate resources in support of product/service positioning and overall marketing effort.

FIGURE 2.16 Competitive Models

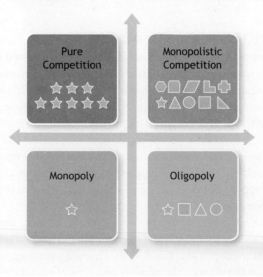

PURELY COMPETITIVE MARKETS

Purely Competitive Markets are markets that are characterized by a number of similar (undifferentiated) products or services, the absence of a dominant market leader, and few barriers to entry.

Purely competitive markets are markets that are characterized by a number of similar products or services and where no single competitor has a dominant market leader position. A key fundamental characteristic of this market is the absence of differentiation among the products or services being offered. These markets generally are characterized as possessing few barriers to new market entrants. Think back to our discussion in chapter 1 regarding value propositions: purely competitive markets are markets where suppliers of products and services are largely unable to create distinctions between the products and services being offered to the target audience. Commodity-based markets and agricultural markets offer a number of good examples of purely competitive markets. Green peppers are green peppers, corn is corn, onions are onions, and so on. In this type of market, the product or service is largely viewed as a commodity, with price being a key component of the overall purchase decision.

MONOPOLISTIC MARKETS

Monopolistic Markets are markets that possess a number of different suppliers of products and services, but the nature of the product or service, along with the marketing effort initiated by businesses within the sector, has enabled true differentiation to set in.

In contrast to purely competitive markets, **monopolistic markets** are markets that possess a number of different suppliers of products and services but where the nature of the product or service, along with the marketing effort initiated by businesses within the sector, has enabled true differentiation to set in. Products and services are viewed by customers as being somewhat different and unique, resulting in a significant shift in the development and marketing of value propositions. The manufacturing of cell phones is a good example of a market that exhibits monopolistic market tendencies. Suppliers such as Nokia, Ericsson, Samsung, Motorola, Apple, and RIM, to name a few, all compete for customers on the basis of product differences, value, and overall price/quality perceptions.

OLIGOPOLY-BASED MARKETS

Oligopoly-based Markets are markets that contain a small number of suppliers that control a large percentage of market share within the market, and that compete on the basis of products and/or services that have achieved success in distinguishing themselves from their competitors.

Oligopoly-based markets are markets that contain a small number of suppliers that control a large percentage of market share within the market and that compete on the basis of products or services that have achieved success in distinguishing themselves from their competitors. The emergence of oligopolies often is the result of the significant capital investment required to enter an industry and the significant economies of scale and scope necessary to be competitive. In addition to the difference in the number of product/service suppliers from that of monopolistic competitive markets, oligopolies will generally have greater control over the price being charged for a product or service due to the limited competition within this marketplace. An example of a current industry where an oligopoly-style marketplace exists is the commercial passenger airline manufacturing business, where Boeing and EADS Airbus are the two major players (with Bombardier Inc. and Embraer existing as smaller-niche marketers).

MONOPOLY-BASED MARKETS

Monopoly-based Markets are markets that are served by a single product/service supplier.

Monopoly-based markets are markets that are served by a single product/service supplier. In monopoly-based markets, many of which are government regulated, the belief is that a single entity can provide the product or service more efficiently and at a better price point than an open-market concept could. Again, similar to oligopolies, the extent of capital investment needed, as well as the infrastructure requirements necessary to maintain the flow of goods or services, makes the monopoly competition model the best solution. The delivery of utilities such as electricity and natural gas is supplied in a monopoly-based market setting in many areas, although we are seeing tendencies in the marketplace today to minimize such a regulated approach to industry and allow alternative mechanisms for product/service delivery to become enabled (i.e., a deregulated market).

As we mentioned in the opening comments to this section (Understanding Competitive Models), a key fundamental in competing in the marketplace is to know which type of market environment you are operating in. This will assist in understanding the role that differentiation plays in the market, the number and type of competitors that are challenging a business, and the emphasis that will be placed on price as a key factor within the delivery of products or services to the marketplace. As an example, purely competitive markets, where there is an absence of product differentiation, tend to experience a market where the product is viewed largely as a commodity and where price is a key determinant in the buying process. Conversely, monopolistic markets (many competitors), where differentiation is a significant weapon of competitive rivalry, can minimize price as a major customer decision criterion and, in fact, attract higher prices by delivering great products or services combined with great marketing.

In addition to recognizing the current status of the competitive market (environment) managers must also recognize that market configuration and composition are not static. Markets change and evolve as new competitors and innovations come into play. One only has to look at the automobile industry as an example of this evolutionary migration. In the 1970s, the North American automobile industry operated in a largely oligopoly-based market environment with three major players: General Motors, Ford Motor Company, and Chrysler Motors (a fourth, American Motors, also existed, but was acquired by Chrysler). As the 1970s progressed into the 80s and 90s, the market configuration changed dramatically, with Japanese and European automobile manufacturers capturing significant market share in North America through the marketing and delivery of quality-based, well-differentiated products. This entry of additional competitors fundamentally shifted the market from one that operated under oligopoly-based strategies, to one that acted significantly more like a monopolistic market. The market continues to shift even more toward one of monopolistic tendencies with the addition of Korean, Chinese, Indian, and Russian producers (see Figure 2.17). In general, the ongoing growth of the global marketplace and the emergence of companies within the world's developing nations will continue to trigger such shifts. Not all shifts will, however, be toward increasingly competitive situations. Some shifts can be in opposite directions. As an example, the current decade has brought about a massive consolidation within the beer industry, as major players have merged in order to take advantage of production and distribution economies of scale and acquire greater market share. Consolidations of this nature have a tendency to reduce the number of competitors, thereby enabling the remaining industry players to stabilize prices and improve their profitability through cost-reduction tactics.

> In addition to recognizing the current status of the competitive market (environment), managers must recognize that market configuration and composition are not static.

FIGURE 2.17 Market Evolution: Competitive Models

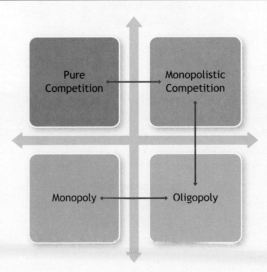

Sensing Market Change

So, how do we sense whether the market within which we are operating is changing? What tools are available to assist in the assessment process? These are two fundamental questions that keep managers up at night as they seek to maintain the competitiveness of their organizations. One of the most-often-used business tools for this purpose is a business model called Porter's Five Forces (see Figure 2.18), created by Michael Porter of the Harvard Business School.[22] Within this model, Michael Porter suggests that managers and business owners can keep their finger on the pulse of the industry within which they operate by assessing changes within five key areas: the intensity of competitive rivalry; the potential for new entrants into the industry; the probability of new products or services that will act as substitutes to the current products and services being offered; the power that suppliers have over manufacturers of goods and services; and the power of buyers within the industry.

In simple terms, by using Porter's Five Forces as a basis for analysis we are trying to ascertain the following:

1. **Rivalry among existing competitors:** How many competitors are currently challenging us for customers in our industry and markets? How strong are they? In general, the more competitors there are, the more intense the rivalry is to acquire customers and grow market share.
2. **Threat of new entrants:** What is the probability that new entrants will enter our industry and markets? Where will they come from? How will their products and services impact our growth and our ability to retain our market share?
3. **Threat of substitute products or services:** What is the probability that our product or service offering could be rendered obsolete, or its overall sales potential significantly impacted by a substitute offering? Do we see such substitute products emerging on the distant horizon?
4. **Bargaining power of suppliers:** What is our relationship with our suppliers? How much control do they have in influencing our operations and our overall cost structure? Are we able to extract concessions from them, if required? Is it easy for them to shift their efforts to supporting one of our competitors? Are we significantly dependent upon them for critical aspects of our product/service offering?

FIGURE 2.18 Porter's Five Forces

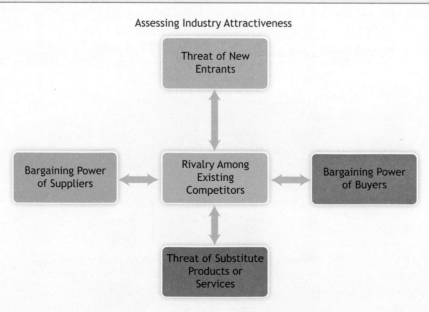

Source: Adapted from *Porter's Five Forces*, Michael Porter

5. **Bargaining power of buyers:** How much choice do buyers have in the purchase of products and services within our industry? Is it easy for them to switch from one product to another? What substitute products/services are currently available to buyers, and what potential substitutes are threatening to attack our industry and market?

WEB INTEGRATION

Want to learn more about Porter's Five Forces? Go to **www.quickmba.com** and search Porter's Five Forces.

Let's use the music industry as an example to illustrate the value of Porter's Five Forces. In the 1980s and even into the 90s, the music industry was largely an oligopoly-based market controlled by the music companies (Sony, Warner, etc.). Music companies would sign artists (suppliers) to a label, and then market that label and the artist's music through bricks and mortar locations, such as HMV, Music World, Sam the Record Man, Walmart, and so on. The music companies also largely managed the price of the music (CDs), suggesting to retailers the price point to be charged to you and me, the buyers. There also existed the requirement to purchase the full CD of an artist's music, regardless of our desire to actually own and listen to all the songs on the CD. With little choice (except location of the purchase), you and I paid the expected price. Artists, as well, found it necessary to be aligned with a music company in order to break into the market and sell their music. For many, a significant portion of the revenue from the sale of their music remained with the music company versus flowing directly to them. What's changed? The answer, of course, is the advent of the Internet and the creation of both new entrants and substitute products. The control the music companies had over the market has largely eroded. With the emergence of Napster and Kazaa in the early years, followed by iTunes and other downloading sites, the delivery of music to you and me, the buyer, has dramatically changed. No longer are we forced to purchase the entire CD. We can now pick and choose the individual songs we desire to purchase. No longer do we need to visit bricks and mortar locations to purchase music. It can simply be purchased (or, in some cases, downloaded free) via Internet-based sites. Artists no longer need recording studios and labels to market their music. Direct sales to customers, via sites such as MySpace, undergroundhiphop.com, and so on, enable artists to reap the full revenue benefits of their work. In essence, the industry has been fundamentally changed forever. Buyers have greater choice on where and how to buy their music, and artists have greater choice on where and how to sell their music. Bricks and mortar locations have to compete not only with each other, but with Internet-based competitors as well. Recording studios must now demonstrate to artists the value of their services, provide greater incentives to artists to maintain their recording studio relations, and communicate to artists the benefits that will accrue by signing with a particular label. For managers, the lesson learned is that we must constantly assess our industry and its markets for potential disruptive changes that will render our products obsolete and/or negatively impact our customer base. This requires continual vigilance and market research and an understanding we must recognize that the status quo is not static and that competitive positions will be, and are, constantly under attack.

> The lesson learned is that we must constantly assess our industry and its markets for potential disruptive changes that will render our products obsolete or negatively impact our customer base.

Management Reflection—Analyzing Market Trends

Managers, regardless of whether they are overseeing a for-profit business or a not-for-profit organization, a large business or a small business, need to recognize the importance of understanding the economic platform that governs our economy. This requires a constant analysis of economic trends through the review and assessment of economic indicators, governmental actions, and shifts that are occurring in global competitiveness. In addition to analyzing economic data, managers need to assess social, cultural, legal, environmental, and technological trends as well, and seek to recognize and respond to disruptive innovations that will impact the specific markets and industries within which they compete. As an example, assume you are in the tourism industry in Canada with a majority of your customers coming from the United States. Your business has been built on significant repeat business by Americans who like to travel north to experience Canada's beautiful scenery and, in particular, your business's outstanding hospitality. You started your business in the 1970s and saw it grow considerably during the 1980s and 1990s. In fact, you realized significant growth right up to 2001. Now, in 2011, the growth has disappeared and your business is down 60 percent from where it was in the 1990s. So, what has changed? Why are the Americans no longer coming to Canada at the same level as before? Two key changes can be recognized as accounting for much of this drop in demand. First, the legacy of the September 11, 2001 terrorist attacks has resulted in political, legal, and behavioural changes within the United States. For example, crossing the border has become more cumbersome due to heightened security requirements. In addition, the United States, as of June 1, 2009, requires all individuals looking to cross the border to have passports. As of January 2011, approximately 37 percent of Americans had passports.[23] This means that two-thirds of Americans are unable to come to Canada. Add to this the fact that the currency exchange relationship between the U.S. and Canada has changed significantly during this same time period. In May 1996, the currency exchange rate was $0.73 CAD for each $1.00 USD. In January 2002, this exchange rate had fallen to $0.619 CAD for each $1.00 USD. In May 2011, the exchange rate had moved to $1.03 CAD for each $1.00 USD.[24] This means that the cost of vacationing in Canada, for Americans, has risen by over 40 percent since 2002. The point of this example is that the marketplace is not static. The situation changes daily. These changes are influenced by both controllable and non-controllable factors. In many cases, these changes can be the result of broader macroeconomic forces beyond a specific industry. As managers, we need to continuously assess what is happening at the macro and industry levels via business models such as a PESTEL analysis and Michael Porter's Five Forces. Our focus is on sensing trends, both positive and negative, which will enable us to redirect our business efforts in order to ensure our long-term business success. For the Canadian tourism industry, dependency on Americans to fill our hotels and fishing lodges and boost our overall economy may be a thing of the past. The need now is to develop new opportunities to support the tourism sector from other parts of the globe and from our population at home.

Chapter Summary

In this chapter, we have described the current composition of the Canadian economy and the key contributing factors that influence its growth and overall direction. In addition to identifying the core fundamentals necessary for economic development, we also focus on describing the market composition principles that govern our economic activity and the nature of Canada's mixed economic system. A considerable emphasis is placed on describing how economic activity is generated and how economies are stimulated or contracted on the basis of movement in their key economic drivers. The discussion associated with the economic growth cycle is fundamental to this overall process. With the basics of the economy having been identified, we shift our focus toward understanding how we attempt to manage our overall economic activity and some of the key trends that will influence our marketplace evolution going forward. We close off our chapter discussing how managers use this information to better understand how changes within the economy and the marketplace in which they operate will impact their organizations. We also provide a brief glimpse as to how the nature of competition within markets can change, and how managers, via such models as Porter's Five Forces, can seek to better understand and respond to trends and market changes through proactive analysis.

Developing Business Knowledge and Skills

KEY TERMS

G7/8 *p. 28*

comparative advantage *p. 30*

foreign direct investment (FDI) *p. 30*

law of supply and demand *p. 30*

open system *p. 33*

controlled system *p. 33*

mixed economic system *p. 34*

GDP (gross domestic product) *p. 36*

recession *p. 38*

chartered banks *p. 41*

inflation *p. 41*

parity *p. 44*

PPP (purchasing power parity) *p. 44*

hostile takeover *p. 45*

PESTEL analysis *p. 48*

protectionism *p. 48*

purely competitive markets *p. 50*

monopolistic markets *p. 50*

oligopoly-based markets *p. 50*

monopoly-based markets *p. 50*

QUESTIONS FOR DISCUSSION

1. Identify the major contributing factors that influence the economic development of a region or nation. Are there any additional factors not mentioned that you feel are significant contributors to whether a country's economy develops?

2. What are the three fundamental principles that influence a mixed economic system? Discuss the differences between the relationship of these three principles with respect to the current structure of the Canadian economy and that of a developing nation such as China or India.

3. Describe the economic growth cycle. How does the cycle change between an expanding and contracting economy?

4. Do you think the Canadian government should modify the Canadian Investment Act and/or the Competition Act to incorporate a national security test to assess the impact a potential acquisition of a Canadian company by a foreign entity could have on our economy? Why?

5. What is meant by a PESTEL analysis? How does it assist managers in better understanding changes that are occurring within the market sector in which their companies compete?

QUESTION FOR INDIVIDUAL ACTION

Conduct an analysis of recent acquisitions of Canadian firms that have occurred over the past few years. Do you think there is legitimate concern that Canada's economy runs the risk of becoming a branch market to other foreign economies, given the dynamics and evolution of today's global market?

TEAM EXERCISE

Can Canada's manufacturing sector survive in today's global economy? Conduct preliminary research on the current status of Canada's manufacturing sector. On the basis of this research, form an opinion as to what Canada's manufacturing sector will need to do to survive in today's global marketplace. Is it possible for our manufacturers to compete with the lower labour costs in Asia and abroad? What about productivity levels—are we as productive as other global manufacturers? Prepare a presentation that formulates the pros and cons of this situation and then look to validate your position on this subject matter.

◢ Case for Discussion

Ed Stelmach, Alberta's premier, has been feeling some pressure. Driven largely by the energy sector, Alberta announced a budgetary surplus of $4.6 billion for fiscal year 2007–08. This comes on the heels of a budgetary surplus of $8.9 billion for fiscal year 2006–07, and marked the sixth straight year of budgetary surpluses for the energy-rich province. Why the heat? Well, if you listen to some of the other provinces, Alberta's surplus has come largely at the expense of the rest of Canada. Unlike Alberta, a number of provinces in central and eastern Canada have been struggling of late, and have seen their debt loads grow thanks to a strong Canadian dollar, high energy prices to fuel their manufacturing sectors, and sluggish consumer demand due to the current global recession and contracting GDP challenges. Alberta's success and cash position is being, and has been, viewed with envy by representatives within both the federal government and the provincial governments of non-energy-rich provinces. The argument being put forward by these governments is that Alberta should share its prosperity with the rest of Canada in the form of transfer payments to its economically weakened provincial cousins. Alberta's reply is that although recent years have ended in a surplus situation, Alberta needs to spend more money than ever in support of its explosive economy. In 2009, Alberta spent a record-breaking $36.4 billion in order to keep up with the needs of its expanding population. This includes a long list of hospitals, roads, and schools, as well as contributions to underfunded pension plans and other capital projects. Simply put, Alberta believes it needs its money to ensure perpetual prosperity for all Albertans. With the global meltdown in 2008, Alberta realized a budget deficit of $1.4 billion for 2008–09, and is projecting deficits for the upcoming three years. Alberta's 2009–10 budget deficit, as an example, was estimated at $4.7 billion (with 2010–11 and 2011–12 calling for an additional $2.4 billion and $1.8 billion, respectively). For Alberta, the $17 billion in its Sustainability Fund (end of 2009)

as a result of the prior surpluses generated is what will enable the province to meet its growth requirements and weather the current global financial downturn. The concern, of course, is that the deficits anticipated will reduce the fund to $2.8 billion by 2012–13, when the government expects its budget to return to a surplus position. Although the rhetoric has subsided due to the current global recession, the discussion is expected to resume once global energy demand picks up and Alberta's coffers begin to swell again.[25]

QUESTIONS

What do you think? Should Alberta be pressured to share its wealth with the other provinces of Canada? If it could, should the federal government assume control of Canada's natural resource base for the benefit of all Canadians? Should the rest of Canada recognize and respect the current position Alberta finds itself in and stop looking for financial subsidy?

Practise and learn online with Connect. Connect resources include additional and interactive study exercises, videos, and practice quizzing, as well as additional material you won't find in the printed text.

3 The Global Marketplace

Learning Objectives

This chapter is designed to provide students with:

Lo1 An overview of the rapidity and extent of change occurring in the global marketplace

Lo2 An understanding of the reasons why businesses expand their operations into international markets

Lo3 Exposure to the interconnectivity of the political and economic influences impacting the global marketplace

Lo4 An understanding of the macro-level trends that will impact the global marketplace going forward

Lo5 An understanding of the fundamental process associated with the development of international trade

Lo6 An understanding of the challenges managers face in considering expansion into the global arena

Snapshot—What to Expect in This Chapter

This chapter provides students with a broad introductory overview of the globalization process currently underway around the world, and the trends and challenges that we as managers will face in guiding our organizations through this economic transformation. The content emphasized in this chapter includes the following:

- Our Changing World

- The Global Marketplace

- Why Go Global?
  - New Market Opportunities
  - Cost Reduction Opportunity
  - Resource Base Control
  - Closeness to Markets
  - Economies of Scale

- Global Market Stability: The Role of Government
  - Ongoing Commitment to International Trade System
  - Market Openness
  - Absence of Protectionism
  - Adherence to the Fundamentals of Fair Trade
  - Balanced Economic Development
  - Responsible Sovereign Debt Management

- Global Market Trends

- The Concept of International Trade
  - Evolution of a Global Presence
  - A Note on Currency Exchange Rates: How Are They Influenced?

- Challenges of Managing in Today's Global Environment

- Management Reflection—The Canadian Challenge

From the Student's Perspective

The global business economy is a topic that floods the news and the classroom every day. As such, it's easy to see the word "globalization" and simply dismiss it as a buzzword rather than thinking about what the term actually means. I believe, however, that it is essential to truly understand the importance of globalization both from a world perspective and also in how it affects our country and our well-being as Canadian consumers.

Today's global economy is changing, with new players rapidly being introduced into the competitive arena. However, these countries not only are sources of competition, but also provide new market and investment opportunities. Consumers have greater choices and lower prices, and people who may have previously been excluded from the global economy, or who were living in poverty, are now able to live better lives.

Many other countries, including Canada's main trading partners, have strategically positioned themselves to compete globally with respect to market share, technology, international value chains, and so on. Canada must follow this example if it wants to remain competitive in the global market. While it's important for us to nurture our trading relationship with the United States, it's also vital that we continue to look beyond our own continent for export opportunities, to attract international talents, and to find new business partnerships. As an example, we can look toward newly enacted bilateral agreements on foreign investment and technology corporations, which are providing steps in the right direction for creating a stronger Canadian presence in the booming Asia-Pacific markets.

The faster the global business economy continues to grow, the more important it will become for Canada to effectively market its advantages in order to remain recognized as a strong player in the global business game. Ultimately, I believe the combination of all of these elements, along with strong management and negotiations of our resources, is what will enhance and enrich the lives of Canadians well into the future.

Gemma Gadher was born in England, grew up in Ottawa, and graduated in 2008 with a Bachelor of Commerce (Honours). She currently works in Toronto for Mars Canada as a Brand Leader in the snack foods division. Her professional interests include marketing and international business, and she looks forward to completing her MBA in the near future. In her spare time, she enjoys watching hockey, attending music festivals, and playing Cranium.

BUSINESS *in Action*

Lululemon Athletica: From a Small Business to a Global Player

Founded by Dennis (Chip) Wilson in 1998, Lululemon Athletica started with an initial store in Vancouver's trendy beach area known as Kitsilano. Following an initial exposure to yoga through classes he was attending, Chip recognized the re-emergence of the practice as a growing trend in the marketplace. Experienced in the retail sector through his many years of work in the skate and snowboard business, and with an understanding of the technical side of athletic fabric

development, Chip set out on his new venture to create not just a retail operation that sold yoga clothing and affiliated products, but a community hub where people could become educated in the physical aspects of healthy living and the mental strength that could be generated from such interaction. Another critical component of Chip's strategy was to create his clothing around feedback received from yoga instructors who were asked to wear it and comment on it. Gone were the days of participating in yoga, dance, running, or general fitness in sweaty and constricting cotton-based athletic wear. Lululemon offered the marketplace an innovative, unique, and distinctive clothing line that enabled participants to stay dry and move freely while keeping in style with the latest in sportswear trends. More than 10 years later, Lululemon has grown into an international business with annual sales in excess of US$711 million as of January 2011. Its product line includes clothing for men and women as well as a full line of fitness-related accessories including bags, socks, underwear, and yoga mats. The company also provides an extensive offering of yoga and lifestyle-related educational DVDs, and prides itself on the education and support it gives its customers concerning fabric care and proper garment size and fitting.

Success did not come all at once for Chip. The transition, from a small, single-location sole proprietor to an international player competing with the likes of Nike, Adidas, and Under Armour, was the result of careful planning and sound financial and market risk management.

IPO (initial public offering) is the sale of a company's stock for the first time in the public marketplace with the intent to raise equity (money) to fund company operations and growth.

WEB INTEGRATION

Want to learn more about Lululemon Athletica? Visit their Web site at **www.lululemon.com**, or go to Google Finance or Yahoo Finance and search LULU.

Expansion initially occurred domestically, followed by entry into the U.S. market, further expansion across Canada, and then international operations (Australia and Japan). It also included both franchise and corporate-owned store approaches to the marketplace. Funding the expansion required the involvement of traditional financing options as well as the use of equity-based cash infusions via venture capital firms. Lululemon went public in July 2007, launching an **IPO (initial public offering)** whose goal was to raise US$200+ million. Analysts estimate that the current value (market capitalization) of Lululemon Athletica, now traded on the NASDAQ stock exchange under the symbol LULU and the TSX (Toronto Stock Exchange) under the symbol LLL, is in excess of US$4.98 billion (see Figure 3.1). As of January 31, 2010, the company had 45 stores in Canada, 70 in the United States, and 9 in Australia (franchised operations). Merchandise is also available for purchase online at www.lululemon.com.[1]

FIGURE 3.1 Lululemon Athletica Growth

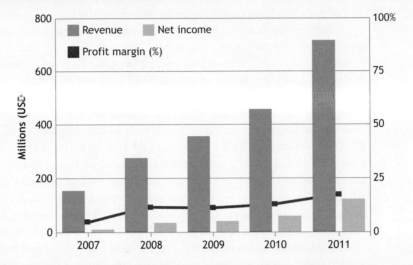

Source: Googlefinance.com; yahoofinance.com; and http://investing.businessweek.com/research/stocks/financials/financials.asp?ticker=LULU:US.

Our Changing World

LO1

What a great time to be studying business! The dynamics of the global marketplace have never been more challenging than they are today. The growth of developing economies in Asia, Eastern Europe, the Middle East, and Central and South America present both opportunities and challenges to Canadian businesses looking to maintain and grow their market share in the global arena. The development of these new markets has resulted in a resurgence of the demand worldwide for Canadian natural resources, resulting in significant new growth within these economic sectors (mining, agriculture, energy). At the same time, manufacturing sectors within Canada continue to be challenged to improve their overall cost competitiveness in the face of new, emerging competitors from China, India, Vietnam, Brazil, and Romania, to name a few. What was once a North America–centric view of the global marketplace, largely resulting from the dominant position the United States economy held globally, is rapidly changing to a more global-centric, interconnective model, as strong, well-capitalized economic growth continues throughout the world. Although today's growth continues to rely on U.S. economic capacity, the next few decades will see a significant shift in this regard as China, India, Brazil, and other economies mature and benefit from the significant foreign direct investment (FDI) currently underway within these countries and from the overall development of their monetary banking systems, legal systems, transportation and production systems, and competitive business models and operating platforms. The end result will be a tremendous growth in these economic regions as 3+ billion people experience an improved standard of living and a heightened desire to buy products and services and benefit from enhanced levels of personal wealth. As the old saying goes, the world is your oyster—view it as an opportunity to experience and benefit from the immense market opportunities that are presenting themselves across its surface.

> Although today's growth continues to rely on significant U.S. economic capacity, the next few decades will see a significant shift in this regard as China, India, Brazil, and other economies mature and benefit from the significant foreign direct investment (FDI) currently underway within these countries, and from the overall development of their monetary banking systems, intermodal transportation facilities, and competitive business models and operating platforms.

The Global Marketplace

Today, the global marketplace is home to some of the largest international-focused business organizations in many sectors. Several of these international companies, such as Royal Dutch Shell (Netherlands), Exxon Mobil (U.S.), Walmart (U.S.), BP (Britain), and Total (France), generate revenues that exceed the total GDP of some countries. For example, Walmart's US$418+ billion in sales in the 12-month period ending January 2011[2] is equal to more than 30 percent of Canada's total GDP. In addition, we are also seeing a number of companies from developing countries compete on the international stage as they seek access to the global marketplace. Sinopec (China), Pemex (Mexico), Gazprom (Russia), PDVSA (Venezuela), PTT (Thailand), and Tata Steel (India) are but a few of these rapidly emerging global players, with a scale and global reach to rival the many North American and European companies whose brands form part of our daily lives. In addition, many small and medium-size businesses are also expanding beyond local, regional, and national borders to become players in the global market. With the ongoing technological revolution these companies are able to actively compete beyond their domestic markets, buying and selling products and services on a worldwide basis. As noted in the Business in Action vignette, the successful Canadian business Lululemon Athletica started out as a small local player and has evolved into an international organization with retail store locations (in addition to Canada) in the U.S. and Australia, and wholesale affiliates in Hong Kong, Mexico, Philippines, Singapore, and Taiwan. Canadian auto parts producer Magna International Inc. is another example of a Canadian international organization: it possesses more than 200 manufacturing locations and over 60 development and engineering centres spread out over more than 20 countries. Magna International is currently involved in a partnership with the Russian company GAZ to build automobiles in Russia.[3] Waterloo, Ontario's RIM (Research In Motion), manufacturer of the world-famous BlackBerry, also operates on an international basis with offices in the United States, Europe, and Asia Pacific. Whether it is through operational growth, strategic alliances, formal partnerships, mergers, or acquisitions, the global marketplace is becoming home to an increasing number of businesses seeking to operate via an international-based business model. With operations becoming increasingly distributed across the globe, managers are more than ever challenged to maintain control and direction over their organizations and to ensure that strategies and operational tactics are being executed in a manner in which the organization's products and services remain relevant and that operational activities continue to meet the growing challenge of an increasingly competitive marketplace.

> Whether it is through operational growth, strategic alliances, formal partnerships, mergers, or acquisitions, the global marketplace is becoming home to an increasing number of businesses seeking to operate via an international-based business model.

BUSINESS in Action

Fortune Global 500

Each year, *Fortune* magazine publishes the Fortune 500 list of the 500 largest (by sales revenue) global companies. Over the past several decades, this list (in particular, the top 100) has been dominated by internationally focused companies whose headquarters are largely located within the G7 nations (United States, Japan, Germany, Great Britain, France, Italy, and Canada). While the G7 nations still make up a sizeable number of top 500 global companies (in 2008, the

U.S. had 140 companies, Japan had 68), developing-nation economies have made great strides in entering this prestigious ranking. As an example, in 1998 there were six Chinese companies listed in the Fortune Global 500. In 2008, this number had grown to 37 and represented 7 percent of total Fortune Global 500 revenues. In fact, a review of the top 100 Fortune Global 500 companies identifies 10 of these companies as having headquarters in developing economies (nations). As these economies continue to grow, it is anticipated that representation on this list will grow as well, with companies from the BRIC countries (Brazil, Russia, India, China) leading the way.[4]

WEB INTEGRATION

Want to learn more about the Fortune 500 Global rankings, which companies made the list, and who is #1? Log on to **www.fortune.com** and search the Fortune Global 500.

Why Go Global?

LO2

Companies look to move beyond their domestic markets for a combination of reasons. For simplicity purposes, these can be categorized around the following (see also Figure 3.2):

- New market opportunities
- Closeness to markets
- Cost reduction opportunity
- Economies of scale
- Resource base control

FIGURE 3.2 Why Go Global?

New Market Opportunities

As explained in Chapter 1, companies need to recognize that markets do mature and that new opportunities for untapped markets for current and future product/service offerings need to form a core part of the strategic planning process. As domestic markets become saturated, organizations will begin to look beyond their current countries and markets in an effort to discover and leverage new markets for the products and services they offer. For many Canadian companies, the natural tendency is to look first to the United States (given its close proximity) for potential growth opportunities and then turn their attention internationally, although this is not always the case. With the rapid growth of the emerging developing economies of the world, tremendous new market potential is being realized by a variety of Canadian and international-based organizations. As noted in Chapter 2, our Canadian banks are rapidly investing in new market opportunities in the United States, Central and South America, and Asia. Educational institutions—such as Queen's University, in Kingston, Ontario—are developing new markets for knowledge-based services in Saudi Arabia, the UAE, and other parts of the world. Magna International is active in Russia, CAE Inc. has flight simulator training facilities worldwide, and Tim Hortons and Canadian Tire have both undertaken ventures into the United States. All of this is in search of new markets and organizational growth. It should be noted that the search for new markets is not a one-way focus, with fully developed economies, such as the United States and Canada, looking for new markets elsewhere around the world. Companies from emerging economies have taken the same approach. China's meteoric economic rise has been largely driven by an export strategy that has found opportunities for Chinese-manufactured products around the world. The same holds true for other Asian nations, South and Central American countries, and the developing economies of Eastern Europe. Although we have focused on organic growth in this discussion, companies can—and do—gain access to new markets via acquisitions as well. The ability to assess global market needs, manufacture products or develop services in response, and then engage in global trade to gain access to these markets has been fundamental to the development of today's global marketplace.

Cost Reduction Opportunity

In terms of global competitiveness, organizations will locate in, and purchase inputs from, countries where the costs of productive resources enable them to generate a competitive advantage. They are attracted to countries where labour costs are relatively low and occupational skills are relatively high. This enables the organization to lower its overall cost base, thereby allowing the organization to maintain a competitive price in today's ever-demanding competitive markets. As an example, technology-based companies are attracted to India, given its well-educated and technology-focused labour pool. Numerous manufacturing processes have been globally shifted to China, given its lower labour costs and productive yields, while the garment industry has seen significant growth in Asia (Thailand, Vietnam, Bangladesh, Mongolia) and in Central America (Costa Rica, Guatemala, Honduras). North American manufacturers, such as the Hershey Company, have also shifted production to Mexico in an effort to take advantage of available lower-priced labour pools and lower their overall cost base. As competition intensifies, and the ability to truly differentiate products and services between one manufacturer and another is becoming more difficult, organizations are sensing an increasing pressure to use price as a weapon of competitive rivalry. In order to be effective with a price-focused strategy, organizations must, in turn, reduce their cost base in order to protect their operating margins and, ultimately, their profit. With labour representing one of the largest cost sectors for many manufacturers, the ability to significantly impact the cost base lies with the ability of firms to reduce such labour costs. This is what makes **offshoring** or **outsourcing** certain elements of the operation to regions where labour costs are lower so attractive. Although labour is used as the primary example, the same rationale holds true for other cost sectors, whether they be raw materials, energy costs, or technology-based costs. As an example, a number of Chinese companies are beginning to establish manufacturing facilities in the United States. Chinese investments in new factory construction and acquisitions in the United States grew from 17 in 2005 to 55 in 2009. Although labour costs are significantly higher (i.e., $10 to $25 per hour versus $2 per hour), the cost of land and utilities in some regional areas within the United States (e.g., South Carolina, Texas) when combined with strong state and municipal tax credits and incentives has made such opportunities very cost-effective

Offshoring is transferring a component (operations, service, support) of a firm's business system to another country for the purpose of reducing costs, improving efficiency or effectiveness, or developing a competitive advantage.

Outsourcing is contracting out a portion of, or a component of, a firm's business system for the purpose of reducing costs, improving efficiency or effectiveness, acquiring expertise, or developing a competitive advantage.

and appealing to Chinese companies. Add to this the reduced transportation costs associated with producing within the market being served, and the end result is that these cost savings can in many cases more than offset the higher labour costs.[5]

> Organizations facing increasingly competitive markets will seek the most efficient and cost-effective product/service delivery systems as a methodology for maintaining cost competitiveness and earning higher margins and profits. An additional side benefit is that by investing in these markets, foreign firms can also diminish concerns relating to protectionism, duties, and other tax levies designed to protect domestic economies.

Resource Base Control

In some business sectors, organizations look globally in an effort to ensure their business portfolios continually add the required resource base necessary for an adequate future supply to support the products and services they offer in the marketplace. This is particularly true of the energy- and commodity-based resource industries. Specific to Canada has been significant interest by foreign firms in acquiring ownership of our natural and energy resource bases. Oil-producing companies, mining companies, and other natural resource–intensive companies have all been active in making direct investments into Canada or obtaining ownership stake in our resource base via business acquisitions. For example, since 2000, over $52 billion has been invested in the Alberta Oil Sands project, with a significant percentage of the investment coming from foreign companies. As mentioned in Chapter 2, significant acquisitions by foreign firms into Canada have occurred, largely for the purpose of obtaining and controlling mineral rights. Xstrata's purchase of Falconbridge and Vale Limited's purchase of Inco are examples of the energy and mining-related acquisitions that have taken place. China has also been quite active in Canada via its sovereign wealth fund, which is called the China Investment Corporation. Two deals this fund has recently been involved in are (1) an $817-million investment for a 45 percent stake in Calgary's Penn West Energy Trust's Peace River oil sands project in Northern Alberta, as well as an additional $435-million investment for a 5 percent stake in Penn West Energy Trust overall (May 2010), and (2) a $1.74-billion investment for a 17 percent stake in Teck Resources Ltd. (July 2009). China Investment Corporation also has holdings in Kinross Gold Corp. and Potash Corp. Sinopec, China's state-owned energy firm, also invested $4.65 billion for a 9 percent stake in Syncrude Canada, and in 2009 PetroChina Co. purchased a 60 percent stake in oil sands projects owned by Athabasca Oil Sands Corp.[6] As was discussed in Chapter 2, Australia's BHP Billiton's attempted takeover of Potash Corporation was largely driven by BHP Billiton's desire to broaden its resource base. This discussion is not meant to imply that Canada is at the mercy of foreign companies. We have also seen significant investment by Canadian firms into foreign markets for the same reasons. For example, Canadian companies have been some of the biggest players in the development of the African mining sector: at the end of 2008, Canadian companies—viewed as a "quiet powerhouse"—had mining assets valued at $21 billion in Africa, spread over 33 countries.[7]

> The key fundamental in resource base acquisition strategies lies in seeking to control supply sources or influence the use of such sources, as well as being able to generate lower costs or better value by having more control over resource-based factors of production.

Closeness to Markets

Companies also look to expand their business operations across the globe for the purpose of being "close to markets." Emerging developing economies in Asia, Eastern Europe, the Middle East, and South America all represent new opportunities for growth for international players.

As was previously mentioned, fully developed economic regions (G7 countries) also represent opportunities for emerging international players. Establishing facilities within developing economic regions enables companies to operate closer to these emerging markets and to react more quickly to market opportunities and trends. Becoming a domestic producer in these areas also enables such companies to create a stronger affiliation for their products and services and overall brands, thereby reinforcing the value of their presence to the local market. For example, resulting from their substantial investments in manufacturing facilities in China—created in partnership with Chinese auto manufacturing companies—both Volkswagen AG and General Motors have generated significant local demand for their vehicles. Their investments have created jobs for local residents, enhanced the spending capabilities of the population via the wages they pay, and generated demand for their products and services as a result of their presence in these areas. Italian carmaker Fiat S.p.A.'s recent acquisition of a controlling interest in North America–based Chrysler is directly related to Fiat's desire to gain immediate access to the North American market via dealer networks and manufacturing facilities. Chinese manufacturer Yuncheng is in the process of opening a production facility in Spartanburg, South Carolina. The plant makes cylinders that are used to print labels for containers, such as plastic soda bottles.[8] And Canada's CAE Inc., which designs, develops, and manufactures flight simulators and related equipment, has expanded its training sites globally in order to bring its product and training service offerings directly to its ever-expanding client base (for more on CAE, see the Business in Action feature).[9] Engaging an organization into new markets often returns the added benefits of identifying new ideas as markets become better understood, developing new products/services in response to those needs, gaining greater market diversification as new markets grow and opportunities are capitalized on, and benefiting from learning new business methods.

BUSINESS *in Action*

CAE

Having developed a network of 29 training centres across the globe, CAE Inc. is the world's leading provider of aviation training and services. Possessing the most advanced flight simulation technology in the world, CAE trains over 75 000 pilots and crew members annually, covering the full spectrum of commercial aircraft, regional jets, and helicopters. Founded in 1947,

this Canadian-based company has clients in more than 100 countries, with 90 percent of its revenue being generated from worldwide exports. Core businesses include sales of simulation products and training services to both civil and military clients. Its close relationships with the military operations of both the United States and the United Kingdom, along with preferred supplier status to military manufacturers such as Lockheed Martin, has enabled CAE Inc. to become an integral part of the training and support of military jet, support craft, and helicopter crews. With annual revenues in excess of US$1.6 billion in April 2009, CAE Inc. has developed flight simulation technology for almost every modern airliner, and has sold its products and services to over 130 airline and aircraft manufacturers worldwide. CAE is a publicly traded company on both the NYSE (New York Stock Exchange) and the TSX (Toronto Stock Exchange).[10]

WEB INTEGRATION
Want to learn more about CAE Inc.? Visit their Web site at **www.cae.com**.

Economies of Scale

In terms of creating competitive advantages, organizations seek to develop, manage, and leverage global production and distribution networks. These **economies of scale** can be realized in the sourcing and production of products; the centralization of services such as marketing; and the sharing of manufacturing and infrastructure facilities to supply products and services to the global market. In industries such as automobiles or computers, for example, internationally focused companies are actively competing for the same customers in numerous global markets. In many cases, the products these companies create are purposely designed for global consumption in order to facilitate operational efficiency and to spread development and production costs across larger volumes. For example, the same car (with perhaps just a few modifications for local markets) can be produced and traded around the world. Toyota, with its TPS (Toyota Production System) process approach, has developed and perfected flexible assembly lines that enable Toyota to quickly change the model being produced in response to shifts in overall demand. Its Yaris and Prius models are examples of vehicles that have been designed for the global (versus a region-specific) marketplace. Ford Motor Company has redesigned its Ford Focus for the global market as well, using a common design, manufacturing platform, and similar components list for production of this vehicle across all of its geographic divisions.

> **Economies of Scale** are reductions in the cost base of an organization as a result of greater size, process standardization, or enhanced operational efficiencies.

Global Market Stability: The Role of Government

LO3

The meltdown of the financial services sector in the fall of 2008 and the accompanying recession of 2009 have brought to the forefront the interdependency and connectivity that exists in the global marketplace. The free flow of debt services and credit facilities, along with an absence of a unified financial regulatory system for the global markets, resulted in a significant domino effect across the global financial services sector, with the end result being severe **liquidity** and **solvency** issues within numerous worldwide banking and financial institutions. In response, the G7/8 and G20 organizations, via their respective forums, are seeking to initiate protocols and regulatory policies that will ensure the situation does not reoccur. Although this will take time, governments across the globe are committed to developing such a regulatory environment with the purpose of managing financial and market risk in a steadily evolving global market.

> **Liquidity** refers to the cash position of a company and its ability to meet its immediate debt and operational obligations. It also refers to the ability of the company to convert existing assets to cash in order to meet such obligations.

> **Solvency** refers to the long-term stability of the company and its ability to meet its ongoing debt and operational obligations, and to fund future growth.

The global economic contraction in 2008–09 (estimated by the World Bank at –2.9 percent) also exposed the disequilibrium that currently exists between buyer and supplier economies.[11] The sharp reduction in spending in the United States, for example, resulted in GDP contraction among a number of nations that rely extensively on exports to the United States as their key GDP driver. What surprised many analysts was the speed with which a recession initially focused in the United States quickly turned into a global recession with economic contraction occurring worldwide. Countries such as Germany, Turkey, and China (to mention a few) felt significant short-term economic repercussions due to the spending reductions and economic slowdown within the United States. With the U.S. economy still the primary purchasing economy in the world, the ability of some nations to weather this economic downturn remains totally reliant on the ability of the United States to pull itself out of this economic slump. As commented on in Chapter 2, Canada—and, in particular, Ontario and Quebec—with more three-quarters of its export trade going to the United States, remains closely linked to the U.S. economy. Although the extent of this dependency does vary by industry, the need for a strong U.S. market is considered critical to the health of our manufacturing sector.

Despite the 2008–09 economic downturn, the long-term economic forecast for the global marketplace remains one of ongoing growth and development. Signs of resilience appeared in 2010 as a number of emerging economies showed remarkable recovery, and fully developed economies such as Canada, the United States, and Germany are also experiencing positive GDP growth. The trend as of this writing continued to show slow but consistent strength into 2011.

The rate and the extent of this growth are, however, dependent upon how countries and regions cooperate with respect to trade development, sovereign debt management, and fiscal regulation and conduct. For such growth to continue, it is essential that governments focus on and support the key fundamental building blocks of global market development (see Figure 3.3). These fundamentals are essential in ensuring the global marketplace grows in a manner that minimizes economic disequilibrium from occurring within singular economies, avoids an overdependency toward protectionist-based marketing practices, and manages financial and market risk in a manner that minimizes the potential for unsustainable growth (i.e., economic bubbles) or counterproductive practices. The six fundamentals (the first five of which have been emphasized by Jeffrey Immelt, CEO of General Electric)[12] that governments globally need to commit to are:

- Ongoing commitment to international trade system

- Market openness

- Absence of protectionism

- Adherence to the fundamentals of fair trade

- Balanced economic development

- Responsible sovereign debt management

Despite the 2008–09 economic downturn and the sluggishness of global trade, the long-term economic forecast for the global marketplace remains one of ongoing growth and development, with emerging economies leading the way.

FIGURE 3.3   Fundamentals of Global Growth

Ongoing Commitment to International Trade System

Ongoing commitment to an international trading system refers to the need for countries to commit (and adhere) to the trade policies and agreements overseen by the WTO (World Trade Organization). Created in 1995, the WTO's main role is to establish the parameters for multilateral trading now and for the future. Constantly evolving, the WTO provides regulatory and policy-based guidance on issues relating to the flow of goods and services, the protection of intellectual property, dispute resolution associated with trade quarrels between countries (e.g., the U.S. versus Canada softwood lumber dispute), and trade policy review associated with the policies individual countries are putting into place. A key purpose of the WTO is to ensure that transparency exists between countries and globally with respect to the manner in which trade is conducted. Its overriding objective is to ensure that trade flows smoothly, fairly, and predictably. This includes creating rules relating to the use and acceptance of tariffs and subsidies by governments as well as anti-dumping measures. In addition to the work noted above, the WTO also provides a variety of support services to developing countries and emerging economies. As of 2009, the WTO had more than 150 members, representing over 97 percent of world trade. Figure 3.4 provides an overview of the services offered by the WTO.[13]

WEB INTEGRATION
Want to learn more about the WTO? Visit **www.wto.org**.

FIGURE 3.4   WTO: Key Services

- Administers trade agreements
- Acts as a forum for trade negotiations
- Settles trade disputes
- Reviews national trade policies
- Assists developing countries in trade policy issues via technical assistance and training
- Links with other international organizations to ensure the smooth flow of trade

Sources: www.wto.org; "Functions of WTO," Mohammad Zaheer, *TRCB.com*, http://www.trcb.com/finance/economics/functions-of-wto-254.htm; "WTO Agreement," *Worldtradelaw.net*, www.worldtradelaw.net/uragreements/wtoagreement.pdf.

BUSINESS *in Action*

Global Spotlight: International Monetary Fund

In addition to the WTO, the IMF (International Monetary Fund) serves a vital role in managing and supporting the international trading system. Focused on strengthening the global financial system, the IMF contributes to the international trade framework by (1) monitoring global economic and financial developments with an emphasis on crisis prevention (and global responses to crises that may occur), exchange rate stability, and balanced economic growth, (2) the issuance of temporary or short-term loans to countries that have balance-of-trade imbalances, thereby eliminating liquidity issues within these countries, and (3) the lending of **credit facilities** to low-income countries for the purpose of poverty reduction and economic development and providing technical support in the development of such poverty-reduction strategies. Most recently, the IMF has expanded its role to include the lending of expertise and financial resources to countries pressured by sovereign debt issues. The IMF played a key role in the development of a solution to the sovereign debt issues challenging the governments of a number of European Union members in 2010 and 2011. IMF loans during this period included $40 billion to Greece, $30 billion to Ireland, and $39 billion to Portugal. IMF loans to emerging markets during the 2008-09 financial crisis totalled an additional $60 billion. Created in 1944, the IMF has grown from its original membership of 29 countries to 187 countries.[14]

Credit Facilities is a general term that describes the variety of loans that could be offered to a business or a country.

WEB INTEGRATION
Want to learn more about the IMF? Visit **www.imf.org**.

BUSINESS *in Action*

Global Spotlight: World Bank

Recognizing the relationship between economic growth and the elimination of poverty in the world's poorest countries, the World Bank provides low-interest loans, interest-free credits, and grants to developing countries for the purpose of funding development projects in areas such as education, health, public administration, infrastructure, financial and private-sector development, agriculture, and environmental and natural resource management. Providing both financial and technical assistance, the World Bank's mission is to work with developing countries to eliminate poverty, enhance growth via sustainable practices, and create individual

opportunity and hope. In undertaking initiatives within countries in need, the World Bank seeks to (1) build capacity through the strengthening of governments via education of government officials, (2) assist in the creation of legal and judicial frameworks within these countries, (3) assist in the development of financial systems to support the development of an economic platform, and (4) combat corruption. Established in 1944, the World Bank has 186 country members and more than 10 000 employees worldwide.[15]

WEB INTEGRATION

Want to learn more about the World Bank? Visit **www.worldbank.org.**

Market Openness

Market openness refers to the need for developing economies to maintain a focus on the core elements of an open economy: the law of supply and demand, the encouragement of entrepreneurship and wealth creation, and the willingness to encourage and support private ownership. It also relates to the willingness of countries to open their borders to competitive goods and services in order to maximize benefits (import and export) to their citizens and residents. This translates into supporting the movement of goods and services, capital, foreign trade, and labour into and out of the country with few to no restrictions. The ongoing development of free-trade agreements; minimization of trade disputes; resistance to the concept of the nationalization of core economic sectors; abolition of the use of tariffs, taxes, and duties to artificially control prices; and elimination of unfair trading practices are all components of an open market system.

Absence of Protectionism

As defined in Chapter 2, protectionism is the intent of economic policies that are put in place to protect or improve the competitiveness of domestic industries via impeding or restricting the openness of a market or markets to foreign competitors through the use of tariffs, trade restrictions, quotas, artificial control of currency values, or other related activities. The need to resist protectionist responses, associated with trade disputes or global market evolution, refers directly to the tendency for governments to initiate policies and practices whose intent is to protect domestic markets, generally to the detriment of the global marketplace. Such responses can spark retaliatory actions on the part of trading partners, resulting in further economic stagnation. Although the perception by governments could be that such actions are necessary for the immediate good of the economy, protectionism largely has detrimental effects on the marketplace in the long run, and often results in economic inefficiencies and higher prices for consumers due to the absence of, or significant restrictions levied against, external competitors.

Adherence to the Fundamentals of Fair Trade

Adherence to the fundamentals of fair trade relates directly to the commitment on the part of governments to support and enforce the intellectual and patent property rights of companies, adhere to generally accepted labour practices, and commit to environmental standards agreed upon by the global marketplace. The expectation associated with fair trade compliance is that governments will seek to eliminate **black market** activities, which violate the intellectual and property rights of developers and manufacturers of products or services. Examples of industries constantly under assault from black market knock-offs range from software and electronic handheld devices to luxury articles such as purses and watches. The motion picture and music industries have both suffered significant revenue and profit degradation due to black market unauthorized reproductions of copyrighted materials. Black market industries and intellectual property infringements are not restricted to developing countries. Although much has been written regarding significant black market activities for electronics, motion picture, and software products in Asia and Mexico, fully developed economies face ongoing battles in this sector as well. For example, for decades Italy has been fighting a piracy culture in the manufacture of handbags.[16] Canada has felt considerable pressure from the motion picture industry to stem black market activities with regard to pirated "bootleg" copies of new film releases. Unauthorized downloading of copyrighted music continues to make the news in the United States.[17] Global fair trade fundamentals also include adherence to anti-dumping regulations, the inappropriate use of subsidies to protect or provide competitive advantage to specific industries, and other difficulties that may arise within a country relating to the ability to adhere to WTO agreements and requirements.

Black Market is the illegal market that arises within economies where goods are scarce, taxation on such goods is high, or the prices of legitimate goods are beyond the capacity of significant segments of the population to buy.

Balanced Economic Development

A key fundamental that governments must work diligently toward is the development of well-balanced economic growth within their respective economies. Governments must look to ensure that the total focus of an economy is not export driven, with the intent of simply supplying products or services to other countries. The development of the domestic side of the economy must be pursued in order to minimize reliance on external buying sources. The development of internal markets for goods and services results in a stronger economic base and expanded economic activity, which is essential to ensuring that nations create stability and growth in the standard of living for their citizens and residents. A core area of the development of the domestic side of the economy lies with the fundamentals of economic market stability first identified in Chapter 2: established factors of production, a national monetary policy and banking system, manageable levels of national debt, low inflation, and a climate of political stability. For economies to experience long-term and sustainable growth, the purchasing power of its residents coupled with the domestic consumption of goods and services must occur in addition to export-driven manufacturing or production considerations. This internal exchange of goods and services drives economic vitality, which creates domestic-based wealth, enabling the emergence of buying power and the ongoing demand for additional goods and services. The current growth within the Chinese economy is a good example. Initially based on manufacturing platforms focused on supplying goods and services to external markets, China's accelerated GDP growth is the result of not only an increased export-based economy, but also one that is generating goods and services domestically for its emerging middle and upper class. The economy also has been the recipient of considerable foreign direct investment (FDI) in addition to domestic (Chinese government) investment that is geared toward developing the infrastructure and capacity to meet this growing domestic-based opportunity.

The development of internal markets for goods and services results in a stronger economic base and expanded economic activity, which is essential to ensuring that nations create stability and growth in the standard of living for their citizens and residents.

Responsible Sovereign Debt Management

Sovereign Debt is debt issued or guaranteed by a national government.

Responsible **sovereign debt** management refers to the obligation that government leaders have to manage their economies in a fiscally prudent manner. In many cases countries will need to develop and carry deficits to effectively manage economic volatility and meet the diverse needs of their citizens. Emerging economies in particular often need significant financial support (World Bank, IMF) to initiate the fundamental changes needed to get economic activity off the ground. The use of debt, however, must be utilized in a manner that recognizes the obligations it will inflict on both current and future generations. Countries must seek to develop stable economic platforms that result in long-term balance of trade positions and that do not jeopardize economic growth due to overburdening deficit obligations. When sovereign debt gets out of hand, the end result can be significant negative pressures on the ability of the economy to grow, loss of control over inflation, political unrest due to the magnitude of taxation, or the reduction in services required to restore fiscal balance. The sovereign debt challenges facing the governments of Greece, Portugal, Ireland, and Spain, its impact on the citizens of these countries, and the impact it is having across the European Union and to the value of the euro are representative of the challenges countries will face when they take on too much debt. Concerns exist, as well, surrounding the amount of debt the United States government has issued as a result of the financial crisis of 2008–09. Canada itself has experienced the harshness of burdening national debt back in the mid-1980s, when high levels of debt significantly impacted economic growth. It was only through prudent government action and restrained fiscal spending that our national debt was brought back under control. Today, thanks to the measures put into place in the 1990s, Canada's national debt position is one of the strongest of the developed economies, with our debt-to-GDP ratio well below that of most other nations. This strength enabled us to initiate the financial stimulus packages needed to prop up our economy as a result of the financial crisis of 2008–09, with fewer concerns than other nations experienced relating to the long-term negative consequences to our economy from taking on this additional debt.

BUSINESS *in Action*

Global Spotlight: People's Republic of China

Balance of Trade is the relationship between imports and exports over a defined period of time. A positive balance (where exports exceed imports) is known as a trade surplus. A negative balance (where imports exceed exports) is known as a trade deficit.

Current Account is a country's net trade in goods and services (balance of trade surplus or deficit), plus net earnings from interest and investments and net transfer payments to and from the rest of the world during the period specified.

The People's Republic of China, over the past decade, has been one of the fastest growing economies of the world. In fact, since 1978, China's economy has grown at a staggering 9.9 percent per year. With a 2008 GDP of approximately US$10.8 trillion based on purchasing power parity (PPP), China now ranks as the second largest economy in the world, and accounts for approximately 11 percent of gross world product. Exports make up approximately 40 percent of China's GDP, with imports representing 27 percent of GDP. China's 2008 **balance of trade** surplus was estimated at US$297 billion. Major exports from China include clothing, toys and games, telecommunications equipment, machinery, and office machines and data processing equipment. Major imports flowing into China, in support of its booming economy, include commodities such as iron, steel, oil, and other minerals; machinery and equipment; plastics; pulp and paperboard; power generation equipment; and medical equipment. While the United States and the European Union are China's largest trading partners, trade with other Asian countries is rapidly growing. China's **current account** balance as of December 2008 was estimated at US$378 billion and represented the largest current account surplus of any country in the world. China's currency exchange and gold reserves were estimated at just over US$2 trillion as of December 31, 2008, and, again, represent the largest reserve position of any country globally.[18]

BUSINESS *in Action*

Global Spotlight: Emergence of the G20

In growing recognition of the influence that emerging economies have had on the global marketplace, in 1999 a broader economic forum was created beyond the original G7 forum and its representative countries. This broader forum is the G20, and its intent is to ensure a consultative process of all major global players relating to matters such as global economic governance, global financial stability, and transparency in fiscal policy. The G20 represents the 20 largest economies in the world. Consisting of both fully developed economies and emerging economies, the G20 represents approximately 90 percent of the world's GDP and an estimated 80 percent of world trade. G20 countries also represent approximately two-thirds of the world's population. Attendees at the G20 forums include the finance ministers and central bank governors of 19 countries, as well as a financial representative from the European Union and a representative from the European Central Bank. In addition to the European Union, the 19 countries that make up the G20 are shown in Figure 3.5.[19]

FIGURE 3.5   G20 Members

Argentina	Japan
Australia	Mexico
Brazil	Russia
Canada	Saudi Arabia
China	South Africa
France	South Korea
Germany	Turkey
India	United Kingdom
Indonesia	United States of America
Italy	European Union

Source: www.G20.org

Global Market Trends

LO4

Recognizing that the global market is a complex entity with all sorts of economic triggers and events happening on an almost daily basis, the following 10 points are offered as an assessment of the key trends and influencers that will most likely impact the global market over the upcoming decade. These are further summarized in Figure 3.6 as a quick reference.

1. The global marketplace will continue to grow, with emerging economies growing at roughly twice the rate of the fully developed economies of the world. Assuming political stability, the BRIC countries of Brazil, Russia, India, and China should continue to lead this emerging-economy impact on the global marketplace. In addition to the BRIC countries, emerging-nation growth will come from other economic players such as Colombia, Indonesia, Vietnam, Egypt, Turkey, and South Africa. Assuming that political instability does not derail the economic progress of the Middle East, we can expect this area of the world to continue to grow as well. Domestic economic growth and high levels of government investment in infrastructure and social benefits will be key drivers of this growth.

2. Economic specialization will continue to be the trend as the ongoing evolution toward the implementation of global free trade continues. The use of technology and supply chain logistics will continue to act as primary drivers of this market approach.

FIGURE 3.6   Forces Shaping the Global Economy

Global Re-balancing	**Improvement or Reinvention**	**Acceleration of Connectivity**
Emerging economies will gain in influence and growth. Developed economies will see reductions in influence and growth.	North American companies will need to continuously improve productivity to remain competitive. Those that cannot will need to reinvent themselves.	The global marketplace will experience ever-increasing connectivity. This will span geography, social groups, and economies.
Managing the Planet	**The State of Nations**	**The Rise of Political Economies**
Changing social attitudes will accelerate the emphasis on sustainability and resource conservation. Regulatory pressures relating to the environment will increase.	Nations will face increasing pressures to maintain social stability in the face of global growth. Immigration, cultural assimilation, employment, and sovereign debt will be key issues.	Governments and businesses will become more interconnected than ever before. Although free trade will be emphasized, protectionism may occur.

Source: "Global Forces: An Introduction," Peter Bisson, Elizabeth Stephenson, S. Patrick Viguerie, *McKinsey Quarterly,* McKinsey & Company, June 2010.

3. The global financial meltdown of 2008, and the related long-term consequences of the sovereign debt incurred by many countries in response to it, will continue to impact the global marketplace in the near term. Greater fiscal and financial regulation will result in tighter credit markets, particularly in the small business sector, and will lead to an overall slower pace of global economic growth than what has been experienced in the past. The European Union, given the current sovereign debt issues challenging a number of its members, could be particularly vulnerable to a drag on growth.

4. Energy prices will continue to have a strong influence on the cost base of many businesses. Oil prices, although not anticipated to return in the near term to the $130+ per barrel prices of 2008, will continue to creep upward as markets recover and the demand for energy shifts upward. This will create new challenges for businesses, particularly where supply chain and distribution costs represent a sizeable portion of their cost base. Alternative energy initiatives will continue to be pressed forward by many governments, particularly within those who are energy dependent on external supply sources. Although still in their infancy, non-fossil-fuel-based business opportunities will continue to grow, particularly in the fields of wind, solar, alternative transportation fuels, and electric battery research. Environmental protection issues—especially in light of the massive explosion of the BP-owned offshore oil rig in the Gulf of Mexico in 2010, and the tsunami-related Fukushima nuclear meltdown in Japan in 2011—will result in a reconsidering of fossil-fuel-based energy exploration policies in highly sensitive environments and the use of nuclear power as a potential energy substitute.

5. The United States and China's political and trade relations will remain critical to global health. As key economic drivers of the global market, the two largest economies of the world will continue to significantly influence the ongoing interaction of global trade. The significant trade imbalances that exist between these countries will need to be closed through a cooperative management process. Concerns relating to the undervaluation of the yuan (Chinese currency) against the U.S. dollar will be a continued point of discussion in the near term. Access and openness to China, the world's fastest-growing major market, will remain a priority for many North American and European-based businesses.

6. Demographics, globally, will continue to influence both trade and political decisions. Aging populations in North America, Europe, and some parts of Asia (China and Japan)

will require broader immigration policies in order to meet the employment, productivity, and social service funding needs of these countries. At the same time, countries with significantly younger populations (Middle East, Turkey), where large percentages of citizens are under age 30, will be challenged to meet the employment needs of their youth.

7. Agricultural subsidy programs will remain a major focal point of global trade discussions. Emerging economies, a number of which rely on agriculture as a core component of their economic development, will continue to lobby for the elimination of agricultural subsidies in fully developed nations, particularly in Europe and North America. These subsidies, from the position of emerging economies, keep prices artificially low in fully developed economies (nations), making it more difficult for developing economies to penetrate these markets and thereby hampering their efforts to grow their economies. In turn, fully developed economies view such subsidies as being necessary to protect their agricultural industries and, thus, are reluctant to reduce or eliminate these programs.

8. Inflation could become a potential drag in the global marketplace in the upcoming years. Although not an immediate issue today in most developed and emerging economies, the significant debt loads that accrued and money supply expansion that occurred as part of the global response to the financial meltdown of 2008 could pose significant pressure on interest rates and market prices going forward. The ability of governments and their central banks to manage monetary and credit policy, individually and jointly, will have significant bearing on inflationary pressures in the years to come.

9. Global warming, carbon cap and trade legislation, the Kyoto Accord, and other macro-level environmental issues and policies will become more and more integrated into the decision-making process of businesses and governments. Developed and emerging nations will need to work together on a global response to growing environmental and sustainable business practices in a way that meets societal concerns and maintains a level playing field for businesses within their respective borders.

10. The global marketplace will become more and more a political economy. The interdependence between countries and companies will continue to grow. Technology, specialization, and the integration of the global financial marketplace will mean that actions and activities in one sector of the world will impact other sectors faster than ever before. Trade infrastructure, depending upon its level of development, will be both a facilitator and inhibitor of trade. As trade growth continues to exceed infrastructure growth, bottlenecks will occur and strain will be placed on the global trading system (ports, transportation, warehousing, etc.). This will require governments to continually spend investment dollars in an attempt to meet the growing trade demands within their country and region. **Free trade agreements** will continue to evolve from country-to-country agreements toward broader free-trade zones. NAFTA could be further expanded into the Agreement of the Americas, encompassing both Central and South America. ASEAN (Association of Southeast Asian Nations) will continue to broaden the number of countries included within this Asian free-trade zone. The European Union, which initially started with six countries (European Economic Community), now includes 27 countries (16 of which use the euro as a common currency), encompassing over 490 million people, with a GDP almost the same size as that of the United States (2008 GDP of US$14+ trillion), the world's largest economy.[20]

Free Trade Agreements facilitate international trade between companies that is not constrained or regulated by governments, and that is not impacted via the use of tariffs, duties, or other monetary restrictions.

Technology, specialization, and the integration of the global financial marketplace will mean that actions and activities in one sector of the world will impact other sectors faster than ever before.

The Concept of International Trade

LO5

There is a common misnomer that trade occurs between countries. In actuality, trade occurs between organizations and individuals. Although countries report movements in GDP and their balance of trade (the relationship between imports and exports) as indicated, such movements are the result of the activities of organizations and individuals who seek to do business within their borders or from within their borders. Sovereign wealth funds, such as the China Investment Corporation, Kuwait Investment Authority, Abu Dhabi Investment Authority, and Singapore's Temasek Holdings, although financed by national account surpluses, are separate organizations that focus on developing investment interests in support of economic activities within their countries. These businesses and individuals could be either domestic residents of the country being assessed, doing business within the country as a result of direct investment or market opportunities that have been developed, or offering opportunities to be developed. As indicated earlier in this chapter, common reasons for seeking opportunities internationally include the appeal of new markets, diversification of operations, closer proximity to key markets, enhanced productivity and supply chain competitiveness, improvement of an organization's overall competitive position, and resource and technology acquisition.

What has allowed trade to flourish is a willingness on the part of the marketplace to engage in the concept of specialization. Specialization is the separation of tasks within a system. From our perspective, it reflects the identification and separation of tasks within a business whose purpose is the development and delivery of goods and services to the marketplace. Specialization recognizes that by having some entities (organizations and/or individuals) provide certain parts of the process, greater efficiencies and productivity will result. Whereas the development of domestic specialization recognizes that certain companies and individuals within a country will be the most efficient and effective at producing particular goods and services, international trade recognizes that the most efficient and effective mechanism for the production of goods and services lies in the development of clusters of specialization across countries. Rather than replicate the development of business systems for the manufacturing and delivery of all goods and services within each country, organizations and individuals have developed international trade, based on specialization, as the framework for meeting the needs of the global marketplace. Combining the concept of trade with capital investment and the desire to seek the most productive and cost-effective systems for the manufacturing and delivery of goods and services is the core component behind the rise of the developing economies of the world and the rapidity of technological advances globally, to the benefit of all. It has also resulted in an overall reduction in the prices of many goods and services, resulting in enhanced purchasing power for consumers.

> What has allowed trade to flourish is a willingness on the part of the marketplace to engage in the concept of specialization.

BUSINESS *in Action*

Canada Goose

When the world thinks about extreme weather clothing, the world thinks about Canada Goose. For more than 50 years, this Canadian-owned apparel manufacturer has been creating high-quality jackets and parkas in Canada. Whether they are going to McMurdo Station in Antarctica, participating in a dogsled race in the Yukon or Alaska, or trekking to one of the most remote locations winter can offer, Canada Goose is the brand people trust to keep them warm. What started as a small Toronto-based business in 1957 under the name Metro Sportswear Ltd. has become a global brand. Their heavy-duty parkas, a main focus of their operations in the 1970s and 1980s, became vital tools of the Canadian Rangers, various municipal police departments, and employees of Corrections Canada. In 1982, David

Reiss (son-in-law of owner Sam Tick), at the time an employee of Metro, purchased the company and re-branded a small collection of jackets as Snow Goose.

In 2001, Dani Reiss (who joined Canada Goose in 1997) took over the company from his father, David. He decided that the future belonged to a small in-house brand named Canada Goose, a brand he had taken to a trade show in Germany where he had received a very positive response. Dani recognized the value of Canadian outerwear being manufactured in Canada and what that could mean in the long term to consumers. He saw an immediate comparison to manufacturing the world's warmest parkas in Canada with making the world's best quality watches in Switzerland. It made sense that real brands be manufactured where they are born.

Today, Dani is President and CEO of Canada Goose, and he continues to steer the company's reach globally with its products, now available in over 40 countries. In 2010, the company opened its European headquarters in Stockholm, Sweden. The European headquarters is responsible for sales of Canada Goose-branded products in Iceland, Norway, Denmark, Sweden, France, and Germany.

For Dani Reiss and Canada Goose, the company is more than just a manufacturer of parkas—it is also about protecting the environment where Canada Goose products are worn. The company is a proud sponsor of Polar Bears International, where Dani also serves as chairman of the board, and a major supporter of the Conservation Alliance, an organization focused on protecting threatened wild places across North America.

Canada Goose has come to represent the true spirit of exploration, quality, authenticity, and great Canadian craftsmanship. The Canada Goose Arctic Disk logo is one of the most easily identifiable logos on parkas and jackets in the world.[21]

WEB INTEGRATION

For more information on Canada Goose products, its business, its partnerships, and plans for the future, visit **www.canada-goose.com**.

Evolution of a Global Presence

Shifting to a global presence for an organization is a strategic decision that requires considerable thought as to where and how to compete. This strategic assessment would include decisions relating to not only the identification of potential foreign buyers, thereby opening up new markets, but also an assessment of the organization's business system to determine if there are parts of the business system that could be made more efficient and cost competitive if they were initiated elsewhere. Also critical to this assessment process is the magnitude of investment that would be required in order to gain access to such new markets or replicate portions of the supply, manufacturing, or distribution logistics processes offshore.

To illustrate some of the considerations required, let's use the XYZ Corporation, a Canadian manufacturer of electronic tracking systems, as an example. Figure 3.7 illustrates XYZ Corporation's current business system. XYZ is a domestically focused organization. Its suppliers (providers of components for its electronic sensors) are Canadian-based companies.

FIGURE 3.7 XYZ Corporation: Domestic Operation

Final assembly of its various sensor products (manufacturing) takes place at its main facility in Moncton, New Brunswick, and buyers of its products are Canadian-based organizations.

In assessing its position in the marketplace, the XYZ Corporation is realizing that its customers are pressuring XYZ to reduce its costs in order to be more competitive with other domestic and foreign competitors who are manufacturing similar products. Reviewing its business system, XYZ Corporation determines that it is able to acquire some of the components necessary for the manufacturing and assembly of its tracking systems from companies based in Asia. These components can be purchased at a lower cost (including shipping costs) than what is being charged by current domestic suppliers. As a result, XYZ Corporation's business system is modified as shown in Figure 3.8.

FIGURE 3.8   XYZ Corporation: International Exposure

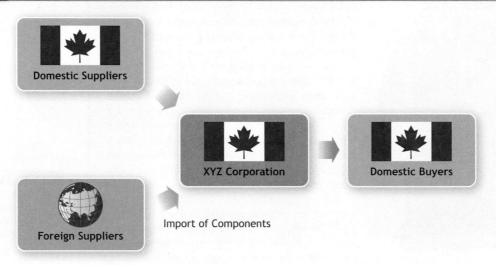

Searching for new opportunities to further grow, and recognizing a demand for its high-quality electronic tracking systems beyond Canada, the marketing and sales team of XYZ Corporation, via work with Export Development Canada, foreign agents, freight forwarding companies, and other industry trade organizations, begins to supply electronic tracking systems to foreign buyers in both the United States and abroad. To achieve initial closeness to its customers, sales offices and sales agent relationships are created in a number of countries when demand for the product warrants such investment. This initial move into the international marketplace shifts XYZ Corporation's business system to that shown in Figure 3.9.

FIGURE 3.9   XYZ Corporation: International Presence

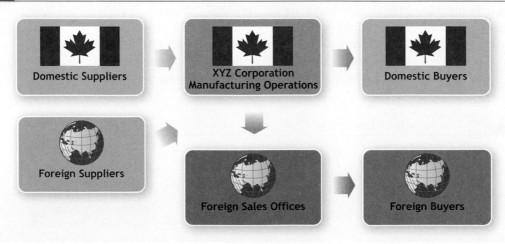

As foreign markets develop and XYZ Corporation's penetration of these market opportunities improves, XYZ Corporation may make the strategic decision to not only have a sales presence in these markets, but also develop a full manufacturing presence. This, of course, would require a significant strategic assessment of current and future market opportunities, as well as an understanding of the capital investment requirements, the operations and logistics requirements of operating a full-fledged manufacturing facility in another country, and legal and risk considerations and concerns with transporting its intellectual and patent properties. In order to minimize some of these risks and to meet the development requirements of the foreign country, this may result in a partnership or strategic alliance with a domestic-based company. In making the decision to go forward, XYZ Corporation's business system is further transformed as shown in Figure 3.10.

Depending on market dynamics, competitive pressures, production efficiencies, and overall cost considerations, a final evolution could be that as shown in Figure 3.11. In this situation, manufacturing has been fully shifted to an offshore location, with support services, head office, and critical intellectual proprietary-based staff positions and responsibilities remaining in Canada.

FIGURE 3.10   XYZ Corporation: International Operation I

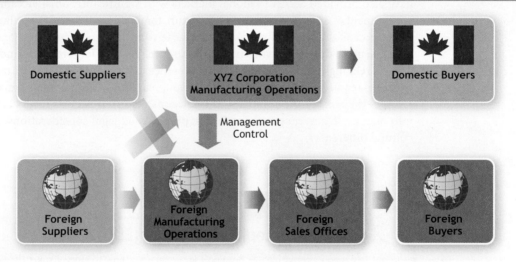

FIGURE 3.11   XYZ Corporation: International Operation II

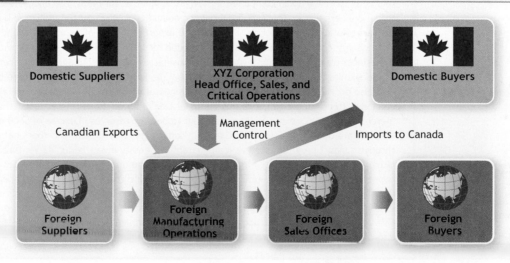

Figure 3.11 does not conclude that all organizations will eventually evolve and choose to move their core manufacturing operations outside of Canada. It should also be understood that a number of entities may not evolve beyond those operating configurations illustrated in Figures 3.7 or 3.8. The overall evolution is dependent upon the opportunities presented, the competitive pressures the company is feeling, the capital available to the company, and the operational efficiencies the organization is aspiring toward in order to develop a sustainable competitive advantage. What is also not fully illustrated in Figures 3.7 to 3.11 is that the size of the organization is also growing, which will result in employment opportunities domestically and abroad. It should also be noted that, while organizations could outsource portions of the manufacturing process and other related operations, a majority may choose to keep their skilled employee requirements (product design and development, engineering, technology support) in house. Keep in mind as well that, as Canadian companies seek to gain an international presence, so too do other organizations worldwide. The figures illustrated above could easily be adjusted to illustrate the expansion of foreign firms into Canada. (The example of Chinese manufacturer Yuncheng earlier in this chapter, which is opening a manufacturing facility in Spartanburg, South Carolina, is a reminder.) Also, although one configuration for the establishment of an international presence is illustrated, the configurations for entry into foreign markets are endless. The Internet and ecommerce models have, in many industries, eliminated the need to replicate full operating structures in foreign countries. They have also provided access to global markets with significantly smaller capital investment requirements—a particularly attractive feature for small businesses. Organizations with significant capital at their disposal may choose to acquire other foreign-based firms as a mechanism to develop an international presence. What is important to understand is that actions relating to developing a foreign presence and in creating a global trading business platform require significant strategic thought, planning, and learning. It also significantly changes the risk for the company, as trade considerations such as tariffs and duties come into play, as do currency exchange rates, political and legal considerations, and social and cultural differences.

BUSINESS *in Action*

Export Development Canada (EDC)

Want to expand internationally, but don't know where or how to start? Export Development Canada is a great place to look for help. EDC provides Canadian companies that are looking to expand internationally with innovative financing, insurance, and risk management and technical and educational support. A Crown corporation wholly owned by the Government of Canada, EDC's primary role is to assist Canadian companies in navigating what is, for many, the uncharted waters of international expansion. This includes providing educational programs to familiarize businesses with trade regulations and protocols; assessing the export readiness of an organization; providing assistance in securing the financial support needed for international expansion; providing guidance in business plan development; and linking businesses with foreign agents and freight-forwarding companies that facilitate trade in the global marketplace. In addition to these core services, EDC also provides internationally focused businesses with critical information relating to global economic trends and changes in international trading laws. Operating as a self-sustaining commercial entity, EDC's expertise has enabled it to develop reserves in excess of $600 million. These reserves are used by EDC to assist Canadian companies in developing international opportunities through support programs such as loan guarantees, equity investments via venture capital practices, and express credit programs, to name a few. The organization also provides access to accounts receivable credit insurance, export protection insurance, contract insurance, political risk insurance, and performance security guarantees. An accomplished leader in Canada's export trade development, EDC has been recognized as one of Canada's top 100 employers for eight consecutive years. EDC provides services annually to more than 8000 Canadian companies, of which approximately 80 percent are identified as small to medium-size businesses.[22]

WEB INTEGRATION

Want to learn more about EDC's programs and services? Visit **www.edc.ca**.

A Note on Currency Exchange Rates: How Are They Influenced?

As the marketplace continues its evolution toward a global playing field, organizations and individuals will become more and more focused on the changes to currency values and the corresponding impact such changes will have on sales and profitability. In Chapter 2, The Canadian Economic Environment, a brief discussion was provided as to how currency exchange rates, particularly when assessed against those of the United States (our largest trading partner), influence our overall competitiveness. And, as mentioned earlier in this chapter, the situation challenging the European Union, predominantly due to the sovereign debt situation associated with some of its members, can result in considerable currency exchange volatility. Figure 3.12 shows the movement in the euro compared to the United States dollar. As the chart illustrates, 2010 saw a substantial devaluation of the euro, as it was during this period that significant concerns over the sovereign debt situations in Greece, Ireland, Spain, and Portugal impacted the stability of these countries and the European Union overall. Key emergency lending packages by the European Union, led by Germany and France and supported by the IMF, resulted in a stabilization of these debt concerns and a recovery of the value of the euro. The euro today continues to remain strong against the U.S. dollar, as the United States is now facing a debt management crisis of its own. Having said this, sovereign debt issues still remain within the European Union, and additional instability in this regard could send the euro tumbling again.

FIGURE 3.12 Euro to U.S. Dollar

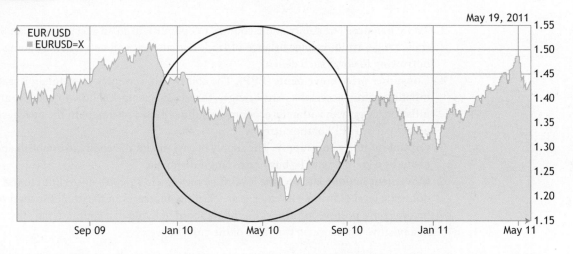

Source: Value of euro to USD, chart analysis, Yahoo Finance, www.yahoofinance.com, May 2011; http://www.xe.com; and www.x-rates.com.

In general, when measured against other currencies (the global benchmark currency remains the U.S. dollar), the value of a nation's currency is influenced by six predominant factors (see Figure 3.13):

1. **GDP movement:** The movement (economic expansion or contraction) in the GDP of the country in question.
2. **Governmental budget deficits/surpluses:** The ability of the country's leaders to develop and adhere to realistic governmental budgets that present to the global community stable and realistic spending patterns and maintain sovereign debt exposure at acceptable levels.

FIGURE 3.13   Foreign Exchange Rates

3. **Trade balance:** The ability of the country to operate within an acceptable balance-of-trade range, avoiding huge balance-of-trade deficits that will necessitate ongoing borrowing to cover such deficits.

4. **Consumer price movements (PPP):** The ability of the country to maintain its rate of inflation within acceptable target ranges, thereby ensuring real growth versus purely inflationary growth within its economy, resulting in improvement in the purchasing power parity (PPP) of the currency.

5. **Capital mobility and supply:** The supply of capital and the ability to establish and utilize credit by a country and its businesses and individuals.

6. **Movement in domestic income level:** The movement (growth or decline) in the domestic level of income its citizens are earning. Increases in the domestic level of income have positive influences on the standard of living of a country's citizens, resulting in a positive influence on the value of the currency.

Strong economic growth, which is balanced domestically and internationally and improves the standard of living of the citizens of a country, and which is developed within a context of prudent government debt and fiscal management policies in an environment of controlled inflation, will result in an upward value of a nation's currency when measured against other countries' currencies. Conversely, nations that see reversals in the areas mentioned above will see an erosion of the value of their currency when measured against other countries' currencies. The Canadian dollar spent a substantial part of the 1990s, and the first part of the current decade, devalued against the U.S. dollar, largely as a result of our sluggish economic growth and our high national debt (when measured against GDP) during that period. As emerging nations increased their demand for the products/services we exported (energy, natural resource commodities), our economy grew. Governmental policies designed to relax trade restrictions, reduce budget deficits, and pay down sovereign debt, coupled with attractive interest rates and low levels of inflation, have all combined to move our Canadian dollar near parity with the U.S. dollar. The United States dollar remains the benchmark currency, largely because of the size of the U.S. economy, its position as the predominant purchaser of goods and services globally, its historical strong economic growth, and its political flexibility. Concerns relating to the U.S. sovereign debt and the potential drag that may result on its economy have caused a number of nations to question whether the U.S. dollar should remain the benchmark going forward. An in-depth discussion of the interrelationship of currency exchange rates on the growth potential and profitability of organizations is beyond the scope of this textbook. Additional references to its influence will be discussed in later chapters relating to understanding business finances. For now, it is enough to recognize that in assessing global market opportunities, currency exchange rates are part of the discussion process.

> Strong economic growth, which is balanced domestically and internationally and improves the standard of living of the citizens of a country, and which is developed within a context of prudent government debt and fiscal management policies in an environment of controlled inflation, will result in an upward value of a nation's currency when measured against other countries' currencies.

Challenges of Managing in Today's Global Environment

LO6

Competing in today's global economy requires a combination of efficient and effective production and manufacturing systems, well-organized and expertly supported trade facilitation processes and distribution logistics, and a solid network of financial intermediation and support. In other words, it's not just about selling products overseas, but it requires organizations and their management teams to view their business system as an integrated trading model. Shifting the organization's focus to that of an international player beyond Canada's boundaries requires a comprehensive review of the financial risks, political risks, legal risks, and reputation risks the organization will face. For managers, this means ensuring a comprehensive strategy is developed that fully outlines the level of capital investment required, the impact the expanded sales channel will have on cash flow and cash operating cycles, and the level of consulting, education, and trade services and expertise that will have to be developed or procured. The global market also challenges managers to look beyond their own local markets to determine where current and future competition will come from, what new products and services are being developed, and what potential disruptors on the horizon could render the organization's products and services less competitive or completely obsolete. In expanding internationally, managers will find that compliance management (trade, customs, security) and risk management (market, financial, intellectual property), along with global technology-based connectivity issues, will demand more and more of their time. Cultural and social issues relating to staffing, customer attitudes, and foreign market needs will present a whole new set of employment and organizational structure requirements and challenges. Add to this the complexity of the impact of currency exchange, protectionist attitudes within some governments, increasingly complex environmental rules within some geographic regions, and growing product liability concerns from globally integrated manufacturing and supply chains, and it is no wonder that a move to becoming a global player can—and will—keep many managers up at night. However, if the risks are managed, then the potential for organizations to successfully grow their companies globally is almost without limit.

> Shifting the organization's focus to that of an international player beyond Canada's boundaries requires a comprehensive review of the financial risks, political risks, legal risks, and reputation risks the organization will face.

Management Reflection—The Canadian Challenge

For Canadian companies, the major challenge will be to reduce our dependency on the U.S. market as the primary "go to" focus of market expansion. The significant recession and financial turmoil of 2008–09 has demonstrated to many Canadian manufacturers and businesses the reality of an overdependency on the United States as the cornerstone of our export strategy. With U.S. demand expected to remain soft for the foreseeable future, as U.S. consumers wrestle with record-high debt loads coupled with a higher propensity for saving versus spending, the market is communicating to our business community that a greater emphasis needs to be placed on emerging markets. It is one thing to say this—but, as noted above, developing a strategy to execute reduced reliance on the U.S. market, given the comfort zone it represents and its strong gravitational pull, is quite another. Our Canadian government is working diligently to assist in opening trade channels with the BRIC nations (Brazil, Russia, India, China) and other emerging players, whose imports have grown over 17 percent annually over the past decade. The growth of the Chinese economy is such that an increase of one-tenth of one percentage point in imports is worth an estimated $20 billion to Canada. Given China's current economic expansion, it is estimated that the value of Canadian imports to China (assuming no greater market share than what we currently have) could reach a quarter of a trillion dollars over the upcoming 20 years. Trade delegations, such as the "China mission" of the summer of 2009, are just the beginning of a renewed focus on exporting beyond North America. What was once the opportunity of an easy living for many of our small and medium-size businesses, simply by expanding our trade south of the border, will now be a much more fierce and competitive global environment. Although the U.S. market will still be there, American consumers can no longer be counted on to be the engine of global economic growth. Canadian imports to the United States, as a percentage of total exports, dropped below 80 percent for the first time in 2007. This number is expected to continue to fall annually. As a nation, our concern should be that Canada is falling behind U.S. and European Union competitors in tapping these precious market opportunities. The downturn in the U.S. market has reawakened a sense of concern surrounding our overdependency on the U.S. economy to carry Canada forward. Coupled with this reawakening is the commencement of efforts to cast our trade nets wider and to seek out new opportunities for growth. The world has gone global—we just have to catch up.

Chapter Summary

Developing economies possess one-third of the world's population. Specialization has enabled many small players to broaden their markets into the global arena by integrating their products and services into the business systems of larger organizations. The use of technology, a key market flattener (in levelling the playing field between large and small organizations), has resulted in much shorter developmental processes, quicker market access, and stronger, immediate competitive positions for organizations seeking to move onto the global stage. In reading this chapter, you have gained a greater understanding of the challenges the global market presents to managers and of the trends managers will have to continue to track going forward. The chapter focused on defining why organizations seek a global presence and the role government will play in developing the rules and facilitating the process of international trade. Highlighted within this chapter were political economy support organizations including the WTO, IMF, World Bank, EDC, and G20. Although "macro" in the breadth of information presented, the commentary applicable to each of these organizations attempted to define just how they fit into the evolving international trade framework. Also offered in this chapter was an overview of the concept of international trade and a brief glimpse of the process associated with the evolution to a global presence by a domestically focused business organization. The chapter closes with a discussion of the challenges of managing within the global marketplace and, in particular, the unique challenges that lie before Canada as our businesses and individuals seek to compete on an international basis.

Developing Business Knowledge and Skills

KEY TERMS

IPO (initial public offering) *p. 60*

offshoring *p. 64*

outsourcing *p. 64*

economies of scale *p. 67*

liquidity *p. 67*

solvency *p. 67*

credit facilities *p. 69*

black market *p. 71*

sovereign debt *p. 72*

balance of trade *p. 72*

current account *p. 72*

free trade agreements *p. 75*

QUESTIONS FOR DISCUSSION

1. What are the five major items companies consider when looking to move beyond their current domestic position and into the global marketplace?

2. What do you believe is the primary role of government with respect to the facilitation of international trade and the support of global trade growth?

3. In your mind, which organizational entity is more important to the stability and growth of global trade, the G8 or the G20? Why?

4. Recognizing that the information provided in this chapter is not all-inclusive, what globalization trends do you feel will most likely impact Canadian companies in the next five to ten years?

5. What do you believe is the overarching challenge that managers of Canadian businesses face in competing in today's global marketplace?

QUESTION FOR INDIVIDUAL ACTION

Conduct a review of Canadian businesses that are actively competing on an international basis. For each of the five reasons why companies go global that are presented in this chapter, identify a Canadian-based company that has chosen to go global for that reason.

TEAM EXERCISE

With nearly US$100 billion to invest abroad, the China Investment Corporation (CIC) is considered by many to be well on its way to becoming one of the most influential investment funds in the world. With US$200 billion in managed assets, CIC, established in 2007, manages approximately 10 percent of China's US$2 trillion reserve. With more than 90 percent of its assets in cash (heading into 2009), CIC has begun to make significant investments abroad. Investments in the United States include a US$3 billion investment in the Blackstone Group, and a US$5.6 billion investment in Morgan Stanley. In July 2009, CIC made its first major investment into Canada, purchasing 17 percent of Teck Resources Ltd. for US$1.74 billion. As a team, research CIC and prepare a presentation on its organizational focus and intended strategy going forward. Include within this presentation your position concerning security concerns that have arisen due to China's increasing global acquisition attempts. Does CIC's current strategy of purchasing minority (non-controlling) stakes in companies abroad concern you?[23]

Case for Discussion

Ford Motor Company, as part of its global repositioning strategy, has announced its intention to sell its Volvo brand. Geely, China's largest automaker, has signalled a possible interest in purchasing Volvo from Ford. Aggressive in its market approach to date, Geely is driven to become one of the largest manufacturers of automobiles in the world. Although sales currently are pegged at approximately 300 000 units, Geely has indicated that, by 2015, its manufacturing capacity will be in the range of 2 million units. As we speak, the company is concurrently developing six model platforms with the intent of offering nine new vehicles to the global market over the upcoming 18 months. In fact, Frank Zhao, Geely's technical director, indicates that it is the company's intent to offer as many as 42 models worldwide by 2015, and predicts annual sales of 1.3 million units outside of China by this date. Geely appears to have no difficulty in funding its expansion. With the combination of private investment, government incentives and tax breaks, and existing partnerships with European-based automotive players, Geely appears to have sufficient reserves and cash flow to complete an acquisition of this size. Geely's founder and chairman, Li Shufu, has publicly committed to Geely entering both the European market and the North American market within the next three to five years. Some analysts, however, question Geely's ability to currently compete in the global marketplace. Concerns are that Geely's expansion plans are simply too aggressive given its current business systems. Questions also exist with regard to the company's ability to meet the quality and emissions standards of a global market. Safety considerations are also a significant concern, as a recent Geely model, the Geely CK Small Saloon, performed badly in a test crash where both the driver and the passenger were given only a 10 percent survival rating at 40 mph. Ford would love to sell Volvo, freeing up significant cash to fund its future market aspirations. It does, however, recognize that Geely is a company that is in a hurry to reach the global stage.[24]

QUESTIONS

A key concern is the intellectual property that would go to Geely should Volvo be sold to this company. What are your thoughts? Should Ford sell Volvo to Geely? What are the pros and cons of this decision?

Practise and learn online with Connect. Connect resources include additional and interactive study exercises, videos, and practice quizzing, as well as additional material you won't find in the printed text.

4 The Environment and Sustainable Business Practices

Learning Objectives

This chapter is designed to provide students with:

Lo1 An overview of the business practices that created the environmental sustainability issues challenging us today

Lo2 An understanding of the major environmental sustainability challenges the global marketplace must respond to

Lo3 An appreciation for the complex factors that affect the ability of governments, organizations, businesses, and individuals to respond to the current environmental sustainability challenge

Lo4 An understanding of the need for organizations to successfully integrate environmental sustainability stewardship into their strategies, operations, and processes

Snapshot—What to Expect in This Chapter

This chapter focuses on the environment and sustainable business practices. The content emphasized in this chapter includes the following:

- The Consumption Journey

- The Sustainability Challenge
  - Climate Change
  - Pollution and Health
  - The Energy Crunch
  - Resource Depletion
  - The Capital Squeeze

- Business's Response to the Sustainability Challenge
  - Trade Management
  - Eco-Efficiency Management
  - Strategic Integration

- Management Reflection—Sustainability Balancing Act

From the Student's Perspective

At Americana 2007, an international environmental technology conference in Montreal, Prime Minister Stephen Harper said that, "Many of the solutions to the environmental challenges we face today will be inspired by the natural energy, creativity and entrepreneurial wisdom of the private sector. Consumption must be balanced with conservation to achieve a sustainable economy. It is all about balance—balancing the roles of the public and private sectors, balancing the responsibilities of the various levels of government, and balancing the economic growth with environmental protection because we will not have one unless we have the other."

It is with this insight that global business leaders of tomorrow must learn to incorporate broader social values into the equation of firm survival. Around the world, companies face stricter regulation, stronger government involvement, and increasingly exigent consumers and stakeholders that force upon our global economy demands for innovation and environmental consideration unparalleled in centuries past. Competitive advantage for corporations and corporate social responsibility are melding into a single focal point at all levels. At this critical juncture, sustainability and shareholder returns are functions of one another; never before have environmental values had such economic relevance in the boardroom and at the front lines. Going forward, modern corporate strategy and vision call for the creation of green products, ideas, and services. Thus, it is with consideration of environmental values that our future, indeed, hangs in the balance.

Kimchi Hoang has an avid interest in politics and the dialogue among business, the global economy, and society. Upon graduation, she began her career with an international strategy consulting firm based out of her home town of Toronto. It is Kimchi's ambition to pursue an international career and contribute to the generation of ideas for a sustainable Earth.

BUSINESS *in Action*

Canada and Water Consumption

According to statistics released by the Conference Board of Canada (2008), our country ranks 15th out of 16 peer countries in terms of water conservation. Only the United States scored worse than Canada with respect to water consumption. Graded on the basis of A, B, C, and D, Canada received a "D" for its water conservation practices. The Conference Board of Canada study reinforces a prior study conducted by the OECD (Organisation for Economic Co-operation and Development). The OECD, which studied water use in 29 different countries from 1980 to 2000, ranked Canada 28th out of 29 countries. Again, only the residents of the United States, on a per capita basis, use more water than Canadians. Canadians currently use just under an estimated 1500 cubic metres of water per person per year. This is double the 16-country average identified in the Conference Board study, and more than nine times greater than the number-one ranked country, the United Kingdom (est. 155 cubic metres per person per year). Of the 16 countries analyzed, 10 countries had water consumption, on a per capita basis, of less than 641 cubic metres.[1] That is less than 45 percent of Canada's consumption level. Although Canada's largest water consumer is industry (68 percent), Canadian households use more than 300 litres of water per day. So, why is it that Canadians use so much water? The Conference Board of Canada study pointed to two key factors. First, Canada, as a whole, suffers from a lack of widespread water conservation practices. As an example, agriculture, the largest industrial user of water in Canada, is particularly inefficient, recycling less than 30 percent of the water it uses. While many countries in the study have worked toward reducing water consumption over the last two decades, Canadian water consumption has actually increased by 26 percent during this same period (although recently this has decreased slightly). The second reason given for our high water utilization has to do with the price of water in Canada. In many areas in Canada, the price of water is significantly less than it should be, with overall revenues falling short of the levels needed to cover operational, repair, upgrading, and water delivery expansion costs. A number of municipalities have not initiated water metering technologies, with many municipalities simply charging a flat rate regardless of the amount used. In fact, according to the Conference Board of Canada study, fewer than 10 percent of Canadians are charged for water on the basis of use, where rates increase in proportion to the amount used. A number of municipalities actually reduce rather than increase the price of water, with the end result being that high users of water receive discounts, not surcharges, for their heavy consumption. This lack of proper pricing has resulted in an aging and seriously deficient water infrastructure system. Experts estimate that Canada will need to spend between $70 billion and $90 billion between now and 2016 in order to meet the future needs of our country. In addition to responding to these aging infrastructure concerns, pricing also aids in the creation and buy-in for conservation practices. As demonstrated by initiatives undertaken by other countries, increasing the cost of water is one of the best incentives for reducing water consumption. We are already seeing a similar pattern in Canada: the Conference Board study indicates that Canadians who are subject to water metering use less water than Canadians who live where metering does not take place. Municipalities that meter and charge on the basis of use have even lower consumption rates. As Canadians, we need to contemplate the inefficiencies that lie within our water consumption practices and build the methodologies and infrastructure that will transition us from a water waster to a water conservationist. Water, much like oil, is a finite resource. The amount of water that exists globally is shrinking. Global warming, population growth, and industry expansion are all working toward depleting this precious resource. In 2001, the federal Commissioner of the Environment and Sustainable Development declared fresh water in southern Canada to be heavily used and overly stressed.[2] As Canadians, our task is to protect and respect this finite resource, through stronger conservation practices and through pricing strategies that ensure our water resource is managed to the benefit of not just current but also future generations.[3]

WEB INTEGRATION

Want to learn more about Canada's water conservation and water management initiatives? Visit the Conference Board of Canada Web site at **www.conferenceboard.ca,** or Google "Canada's water consumption practices."

The Consumption Journey

During the mid-to-late 1700s, the world embarked upon a significant change when the marketplace of Great Britain/Europe began the shift from being a largely agricultural-based society to being one transitioning toward a production-based model. Supported by population growth, an increase in trade and inventiveness, and a growing emphasis on wealth creation, the concept of mercantilism backed by the rise of business systems fundamentally changed the course of economic development and direction forever. This transitioning period, which historically has been referred to as the Industrial Revolution, marked the beginning of a societal shift toward technology and scientific methodologies as mechanisms for economic development. It also marked the change in societal behaviour from self-sustenance to a consumption-inspired marketplace. Driven to meet the needs of this newly emerging society, entrepreneurs and merchants identified and responded to the needs of society in an unprecedented way. This increase in the demand for products and services resulted in the need for greater production, more efficient operations, and a growth in specialization. Technological innovations such as the assembly line, replaceable parts, and factory-based, labour-driven business systems all evolved in response to the growing demand being experienced. The concepts of specialization and outsourcing were both born during this period as organizations sought to create greater efficiency and scale to meet this new demand, as well as capitalizing on the opportunity for wealth and success this "new age" offered.

This societal shift, however, also marked the advent of another defining moment for the global marketplace. This new shift was the dramatic intensification of destructive pressures on our environment. With the Industrial Revolution, and the centuries that followed, businesses and organizations—while focusing on responding to meeting the insatiable appetites of society—pumped billions of kilograms of toxic materials into our air, water, and land. Absent of regulations for governing business behaviour, prosperity was measured by activity and monetary gain, not by long-term legacy and **environmental stewardship**. In many cases, the huge amount of waste that was generated was simply buried, with little concern over its long-term impact on future generations and on the biological species with which we share our planet. Fast-forward to the 20th century, when as humans we begin to sense the environmental degradation that is occurring as developed-nation economies, whose cultures have been largely built around economic performance, become enlightened to the consequences of poor resource management and the toxicity that practices up to this time have allowed to seep into our global environment. In response both to growing scientific evidence and to the occurrence of environmental disasters, governments began to create minimum levels of regulatory environmental compliance for a growing number of business sectors (see Figure 4.1).

Environmental Stewardship is the integration of sustainability values into the managing of environmental resources.

FIGURE 4.1 Societal Response to Environmental Degradation

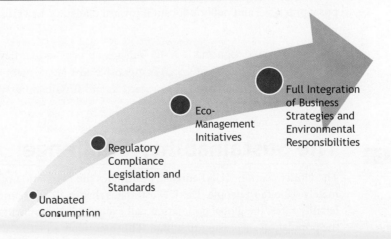

These regulations, for example those associated with pollution and waste, were designed to provide some element of accountability and control with respect to environmental management within the business and public sectors.

Forced to absorb unexpected costs and their corresponding impact to profitability as a result of the legal liability that regulatory compliance mandated (fines, cleanup expenses, injury claims, etc.), a number of organizations began to see the true value in implementing eco-management initiatives and in incorporating environmental policies into their business operations. This need to mitigate risk and organizational exposure to significant economic consequences led organizations to begin to develop environmental policies and environmental management systems in order to reduce, measure, and monitor their risk exposure to enacted legislation directly impacting their industry sector and business operations. These policy initiatives resulted in the base-level development of operational protocols and practices relating to pollution prevention, recycling, and environmental health and safety assessment. The benefit of this risk exposure recognition is that the marketplace began to come to terms with the impact of the unabated consumption practices to date, and the consequences of such activities to our environment.

So, where do we go from here? With the global emergence of economies from developing nations around the world, the acceleration of our consumption of the world's resources continues to increase. The true finite nature of these various resources is truly beginning to be more fully understood in a manner never seen before. Continued unabated **degradation** of our air, land, and water as the accelerated rate of global economic growth continues has the making of a massive environmental and planetary disaster. For businesses and the planet to survive, organizations must make the transition from simply a compliance/eco-management approach to a sustainable business strategy approach. This means we must become fully successful at integrating environmental responsibilities into our business strategies.

The goal is to design and redesign business processes in a way that, while allowing for increased wealth and enhanced competitive advantage, incorporates the principles of human mankind and resource protection and sustainability for the future. This requires organizations to integrate sustainable development and resource management into their core mission, vision, values, codes of conduct, and business systems. This process is much more than just compliance or prevention. Its core fundamental is the integration of the relationship of society, the environment, and economic benefit into every facet of the organization's decision-making process. The successful development of economies and nations can no longer simply be measured in terms of domestic consumption growth, production-based productivity indexes, and GDP growth. To do so simply means the potential disregard for the value of our natural resources, the nature of our planet, and the true well-being of our society. Successful economic development ratings need to go beyond production and consumption indices and include additional measures such as the protection of our biosphere, sustainable use of global resources, energy conservation, environmental restoration, waste reduction, safe waste disposal practices, and public education toward planetary stewardship.[4]

> **Degradation** is the deterioration of the environment through the depletion of resources and the destruction of ecosystems.

> The goal is to design and redesign business processes in a way that, while allowing for increased wealth and enhanced competitive advantage, incorporates the principles of human mankind and resource protection and sustainability for the future.

The Sustainability Challenge

LO2

The United Nations (UN) currently estimates the population of our planet as being approximately 6.8 billion people. The UN estimates that in 2050, assuming no significant changes in fertility rates, the global population will exceed 9.2 billion, with high-end projections seeing the population surpassing 10 billion. This represents an estimated 36 percent increase in residents of Earth over this period. What was initially a trend of declining birth rates in more

FIGURE 4.2   The Challenges Going Forward

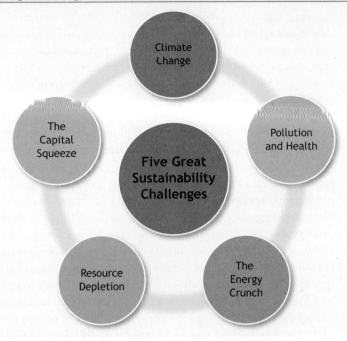

developed economic regions of the world is no longer the case, as birth rates in the developed world (United States and Europe) have actually increased over the five years 2005 to 2010 (from 1.35 to 1.64 children per woman).[5] Although developed countries will not significantly impact the overall population due to this trend reversal, it is important to note that, given this shift and the resulting population stabilization versus decline that it represents, plus the anticipated population increases in emerging and developing regions of the world, the UN's date for world population stabilization has been pushed back even further. Although one could argue the exact numbers associated with this anticipated increase (as statistics from less developed areas of the world may not be fully reliable), one thing is certain: population growth over this period is inevitable, and, given the growth anticipated, significant stress is going to be placed on our planet with respect to resource depletion, climate management, and the health and safety of our global residents.

In assessing the challenges going forward (see Figure 4.2), governments, businesses, and we, as citizens, must respond in ways never thought of before to five critical sustainability challenges: climate change, pollution and health, the energy crunch, resource depletion, and the capital squeeze.

Climate Change

Did you know that a 1°C rise in average temperature can have devastating effects on crop yields? Recent research by David Lobell of Stanford University (published in the periodical *National Climate Change*) has concluded that the rise in global temperatures will reduce corn crop yields across our planet.[6] This is particularly true when the temperature moves above 30°C. Increasing the average temperature a little impacts the number of hot days and, as noted, days above 30°C are particularly damaging. According to Lobell's work, every day the temperature is above 30°C, crop yields can diminish by up to 1 percent. Move up 2°C to 32°C, and the impact is twice that found at 31°C. Given anticipated global temperatures going forward, this could impact corn growing areas, such as Africa, by as much as 20 percent of their yields by the middle of this century (assuming Lobell's data are accurate).

Although the debate on climate degradation is ongoing, for the most part scientists appear to be in agreement that time is running out on our ability to respond to the climate change trends underway and that if we don't act quickly we will be placing our planet at significant risk. Just how much time do we have? The general estimate is probably less than 40 years. Just what do we need to do within this 40-year period? To significantly reverse the downward spiral associated with climate change, we need to cut carbon-based emissions during this period by at least 50 percent from their current levels. Recognizing that the consumption society we have created was built over approximately 200 years, our climate change revolution will need to reverse these trends in 20 percent of the time—a time when our global population, as noted above, is expected to increase by more than 36 percent. Can this result be realized over this period of time? According to a McKinsey Climate Change Special Initiative the answer is yes—*if* we are successful in five key areas (see Figure 4.3).[7]

Although building a reduced-carbon economy will require new capital investments, a number of initiatives can be put into place using existing technologies and little to no new capital. As an example, shifting to low-energy lighting, switching to more fuel-efficient vehicles, and continuing industrial process zero-emission initiatives can significantly reduce the negative impact. Decarbonizing the energy supply by continuing to apply alternate solutions—such as wind, solar, geothermal, biomass, hydro, and even nuclear, where applicable—will further reduce the carbon footprint. If we can successfully employ carbon-capture technologies around carbon-based fuels such as coal, we further reduce the carbon-based emissions flow. This is particularly true in China and the United States, where coal continues to be a major energy source.

Transportation is another key area where a significant improvement can be achieved. The Global Fuel Economy Initiative expects the number of cars worldwide to triple between now and 2050. Unchecked, this rapid growth in vehicles and their carbon-based emissions can have serious climate degradation implications. Having said this, a report titled "50by50: Prospects and Progress," by George C. Eads, Charles River Associates, indicates that with proper action this growth can be managed. Critical to this action is ensuring that governments and manufacturers set fuel economy as a top priority, and that worldwide binding fuel economy targets are set. Creating a regulatory and financial environment that moves manufacturers to stress fuel economy instead of performance could enable us to cut fuel emissions by 50 percent between now and 2030. According to Eads, fuel economy averages in new cars should be able to reach 2.27 litres per 100 kilometres during this period. All of this could be built around

FIGURE 4.3   Building a Reduced-Carbon Economy

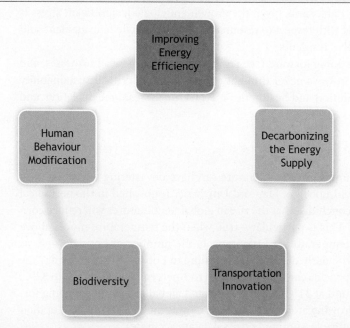

Source: Beinhocker and Oppenheim, "Building a Post-Carbon Economy," McKinsey & Company, February 2009, http://whatmatters.mckinseydigital. com/climate_change/building-a-postcarbon-economy, accessed March 2011.

technologies relating to advancement in internal combustion engine design, hybrids, electric vehicles, and next-generation biofuels.

Protecting our green carpet also needs to remain a top priority. "Green carpet" refers to our forests, trees, and plant life. Farming, logging, and energy consumption have resulted in a serious erosion of our green carpet.[8] Deforestation, which is the massive clearing of the Earth's forest, continues to be a major issue in many developing countries. Honduras, Nigeria, Benin, Ghana, Indonesia, and Nepal have all experienced a huge reduction in their forest areas due to massive clearing of their green carpets. Deforestation largely occurs due to agriculture and logging initiatives as countries seek to create an economic base in order to increase the standard of living of their citizens. In addition to the loss of plant and animal species resulting from deforestation, this process also robs the Earth of its ability to deal with natural carbon dioxide emission absorption. Although the largest contributor to carbon dioxide emissions is the burning of fossil fuels (approximately 77 percent), deforestation accounts for an estimated 22 percent of this problem.[9] In addition to the loss of our ability to offset carbon dioxide emissions with our green carpet, deforestation also contributes to the water cycle and to overall management of Earth's average temperature. Keeping our green carpet is one of the easiest and least expensive ways to combat global warming. Forestry management guidelines—and adherence by all countries—is a needed first step in our fight against global warming. Reforestation education initiatives, particularly in developing nations, are key to successfully maintain and effectively improve our balance between nature and economic growth.

As demonstrated above, our ability to respond to the climate change challenge lies, in large part, in changing current practices and making stronger use of existing technologies. Success lies in our ability to change human behaviour as much as it lies in the development and application of new technologies. This will require a shift in values and lifestyles. Yes, governments and regulatory agencies must enact new policies and create additional incentives (or penalties) in order to kick-start this transition. This can be via stronger use of incentives such as a carbon tax or cap-and-trade system; stronger adoption of compliance methodologies such as those proposed in the **Kyoto protocol** or similar forthcoming global initiatives; and stronger use of tax or investment incentives for transitioning businesses to renewable strategies and making the investments in research and development to spur new technologies.

Kyoto Protocol is the 1997 (effective 2005) international agreement that binds participating nations into stabilizing and reducing greenhouse gas (GHG) emissions.

> Although such governmental and regulatory policies and initiatives will up the compliance scale, it is we as managers and individuals who need to take climate change responsibility into the boardroom and into the business operation to ensure the behaviours exhibited reflect a true integration of environmental sustainability practices into our organizational and corporate strategies.

Pollution and Health

When we look at global mortality rates, we often are reminded of the horrid diseases that take so many lives prematurely. Heart disease, cancer, HIV/AIDS, and malaria may immediately come to mind as possible reasons for premature death. But how many of us think of pollution as a major killer of humans? Recent research by David Pimentel of Cornell University estimates that as many as 62 million deaths per year—representing an estimated 40 percent of deaths globally—may be attributed to environmental factors such as organic and chemical pollutants. Essentially, the cause of death is the air we breathe and the water we drink. According to the World Health Organization (WHO), as many as 1.1 billion people live in areas that do not have access to clean and safe drinking water. Lack of water sanitation alone is a major cause of death worldwide. Unsafe drinking water can be the result of untreated sewage and contaminated surface water. In a number of developing countries, many people simply dump their garbage and waste into the same water they use for drinking and bathing.[10]

Air pollution is another major killer. The WHO estimates that more than 3 million humans die each year from pollution-triggered diseases such as pneumonia, bronchitis, and lung cancer. It comes as a surprise to many of us in fully developed countries such as Canada that indoor pollution from smoke and ash from open indoor stoves is more of a deadly killer than outdoor air pollution.[11]

Our health is also affected by the thousands of toxins released into the air and the environment by businesses and organizations that have operated—or that currently are operating—across the globe. The highly respected Blacksmith Institute, in its 2010 report on the world's worst pollution problems, listed the top six toxic threats to mankind, as shown in Figure 4.4.

The Blacksmith Institute has identified more than 2000 sites that contain these leading toxins (lead, mercury, chromium, arsenic, pesticides, and radionuclides), affecting an estimated 56 million people. According to the Blacksmith Institute, 1000 of these sites are considered toxic hot spots. (In Dzerzhinsk, Russia, for example, the ongoing dumping of chemical waste has contaminated the groundwater to such an extent that the life expectancy for residents has fallen to age 42 for men and age 47 for women.) This identification work, however, is far from complete. Initial estimates, based on work in progress, indicate that the number of sites globally impacted by toxic pollutants could be double the current 2000 sites identified, and the number of people impacted could be more than 100 million, most of whom live in low- and middle-income countries. The Blacksmith Institute is leading an effort to create an international program for addressing the problem of global toxic waste. Preliminary funding estimates for such a program, aimed at tackling the worst of these sites, could run as much as $1 billion or more. The positive news is that, unlike other types of pollution or communicable diseases, in many cases cleaning up these toxic sites is a one-time expense. Once cleaned up, and assuming additional dumping does not take place, the remediation effort involved would most likely be a one-time intervention. To date, involvement in this cleanup process by companies within the industries that have caused the issues has been on an ad hoc basis. Our role, as managers and as planetary citizens, is to move decisively in this area to fund the types of initiatives the Blacksmith Institute is spearheading. This means fully integrating our present and future environmental responsibilities into our business strategies.

FIGURE 4.4   Blacksmith Institute: Top Six Toxic Threats

Toxic Threat	Pollution Location	Estimated Population at Risk at Identified Sites (millions of people)	Estimated Global Impact (millions of people)	Major Health Risks
1. Lead	Air, water, soil, food, dermal contact...metal smelting and mining	10	18-22	Neurological damage, reduced IQ, anemia, nerve disorders, lead poisoning
2. Mercury	Air, water, food, dermal contact...chlorine gas, batteries, electrical switches	8.6	15-19	Damage to brain, kidney, stomach, intestines, lungs
3. Chromium	Air, water, soil, food...metal and steel processing, welding	7.3	13-17	Damage to gastrointestinal, respiratory, immunological systems, reproductive systems
4. Arsenic	Air, water, soil, food... smelting operations	3.7	5-9	Decrease in red and white cell production-arsenic poisoning
5. Pesticides	Ground water and water sources	3.4	5-8	Damage to neurological, reproductive, and dermatological systems
6. Radionuclides	Uranium mining, mine waste, nuclear weapons and energy production	3.3	5-8	Damage to cells, cancer and death (high doses)

Source: McCartor & Becker, "World's Worst Pollution Problems 2010: Top 6 Toxic Threats," Blacksmith Institute, New York, NY, USA.

The Energy Crunch

Without a doubt, our entire global economy is heavily dependent on oil and fossil fuels. Before commercial production of oil began in the mid-1800s, it was estimated that the global supply of oil was approximately 2 trillion barrels. Since commercial production began, our consumption pattern has continued to grow to the point where we have consumed approximately one-half of this amount (1 trillion barrels) and have reached a peak demand of an estimated 30 billion barrels per year.[12] Although the global recession of 2009 and 2010, and the relatively slow recovery beginning to emerge in 2011, has slowed the appetite for oil and energy sources in general, the long-term outlook for energy consumption is considered to be moving upward. Recognizing that energy consumption in fully developed economies such as the United States, Europe, and Japan will remain relatively flat for the long term, the anticipated rebound of energy demand will be driven largely from developing countries. Based on the McKinsey Global Institute's report "Averting the Next Energy Crisis," more than 90 percent of the increase in global energy demand between now and 2020 will come from developing countries. China and India, for example, are anticipated to see growth in energy needs of at least 3.6 percent based on moderate growth forecasts, while the Middle East is anticipated to be one of the fastest growing regions. This growth is distributed relatively equally across both residential and industry-based energy consumption sectors. Growth in energy demand will occur despite the implementation of sustainability initiatives, with sectors such as air transportation, long-haul transportation, infrastructure development, and manufacturing leading the way. For many developing countries, it is all about building the domestic capacity needed to respond to the economic development occurring within their borders and around their regions. Capacity investments are needed in a number of energy-consumption-intensive sectors to enable this economic development to take place.

What also is certain is that the energy supply requirements of these economies are not expected to change over the next couple of decades, with traditional fuel sources being required to support a significant proportion of this new energy need. For example, despite the entry of electric vehicles into the marketplace it is anticipated that the ability of this new product class to significantly impact traditional fossil fuel requirements for transportation will not occur much before 2025. Energy requirements are expected to rise from a level of 495 quadrillion **BTU**s to 622 quadrillion BTUs between now and 2020, with 88 percent of this energy coming from the traditional energy sources of oil, gas, coal, and electric power (see Figure 4.5 and Figure 4.6).

BTU (British thermal unit) is a measure of heat required to raise the temperature of one pound of water by 1°F.

FIGURE 4.5 Long-Term Energy Demand Growth

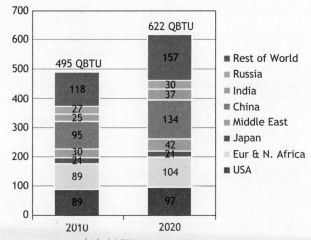

Source: McKinsey Global Institute, Global Energy Demand Model 2009

FIGURE 4.6   The Future Global Fuel Mix

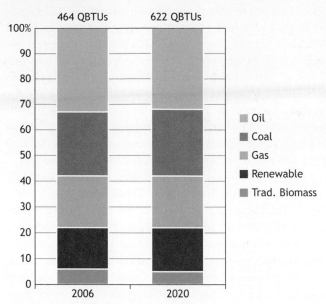

Source: McKinsey Global Institute, Global Energy Demand Model 2009

Recognizing that the global marketplace is going to require 26 percent more energy over the next decade, and that it will need to come from largely existing energy sources, the question becomes whether we have enough supply to deliver on this mandate. The response to this question is that it depends on two core ingredients: (1) resource availability, and (2) improvements in energy productivity from the sources we have available.

RESOURCE AVAILABILITY

Peak Model Theories are based on the belief that resources are finite and that, at some point in time, the availability of such resources will pass their maximum production point and begin to decline.

In terms of resource availability, the possibility of a supply shock is very real given the anticipated tightness between demand and supply. This conclusion is not based primarily on the **peak model theories**, which suggest that the finite supply of these non-renewable sources is coming to an end, but more on the key factors that determine our ability to draw on existing resource availability at this time (see Figure 4.7).

As Figure 4.7 illustrates, the supply side of the demand/supply relationship is influenced by seven key factors. These factors are as follows:

- **Current supply development constraints:** refers to how quickly we can develop the production of existing known resource supplies. This relates to how quickly capital investment in existing sources of energy (i.e., Alberta oil sands opportunities) can result in such energy sources being moved from a state of known, but not developed, to "into the pipeline." This would include the cost/benefit tradeoff of developing such opportunities. It would also include transportation capacity constraints and refining constraints that could bottleneck or impact the delivery of final products to users.

Feed-in Tariffs are government payment subsidy arrangements whereby participants are paid a guaranteed premium for energy developed through the adoption of alternate energy sources.

- **Political impact factors:** refers to political, legislative, or environmental action that constrains the ability of companies and organizations to proceed with supply development. An example is the current disagreement between nations relating to ownership rights for arctic lands that have been found to possess energy reserves. It would also refer to the environmental impact requirements, existing and new-to-come, that will impact costs and time associated with the pre-infrastructure development process. **Feed-in tariff** subsidies

FIGURE 4.7   Key Factors Impacting Energy Supplies

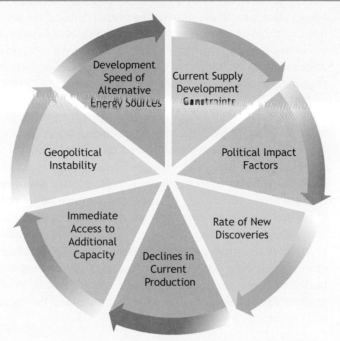

Source: McKinsey Global Institute, "Averting the Next Energy Crisis: The Demand Challenge," McKinsey & Company, March 2009.

and other grant/investment programs developed by governments to support the development of energy alternatives or improvements in energy productivity would also fall under this impact factor. Political impact factors can be viewed as either positive or negative influences on supply.

- **Rate of new discoveries:** refers to the identification of new sources of fossil fuels. New exploration technologies have resulted in the identification of fossil fuel reserves in areas where such reserves were not known to exist.

- **Declines in current production:** refers to the reduction in current supply volume due to energy sources drying up or being taken offline. The closing of a well due to the exhaustion of the oil supply associated with that well is an example of a supply contraction contributor.

- **Immediate access to additional capacity:** refers to the ability of current suppliers to tap into excess capacity to meet the demand needs of the marketplace. The ability of OPEC to increase supply capacity from existing sources is an example. Enhanced production capability in Alberta, resulting in greater resource extraction from existing oil sands sites, is another example of our ability to add capacity to the supply side.

- **Geopolitical instability:** refers to instability in the countries or regions that supply our global energy needs. The instability in the Middle East and in North Africa (Libya) in the first quarter of 2011 is reflective of how supplies can be disrupted due to geopolitical instability.

- **Development speed of alternate energy sources:** refers to the speed at which alternate energy sources can be brought online and achieve the necessary scale and cost structure to be viewed as viable options for energy consumers to consider when looking to meet their current and future energy needs. Political action may or may not be a primary driver of this scale and cost structure development process.

IMPROVEMENTS IN ENERGY PRODUCTIVITY

Energy productivity is all about improving the efficiency of energy production currently taking place, as well as reducing the overall demand for such energy in a manner that does not compromise economic growth. This is where behavioural change and investment in technology come into play. Energy productivity is a measurement of the productivity achieved from each input of energy consumed. Based on the McKinsey Global Institute's research, we, as a global economy, currently consume 12 600 BTUs of energy for each dollar of global GDP output.[13] Although some improvement in energy productivity has been achieved, averting an energy crunch's negative impact to global growth means that we will need to either reduce the amount of energy input per dollar of GDP output, or create more GDP output from the same level of energy input. The approach will, most likely, be a combination of both. Capital investment in new technologies will, hopefully, generate greater output per energy input requirement, and lead to energy savings through reduced consumption. An example of this latter point would be the Energy Star ratings for appliances that require less energy to operate. Behavioural changes will highlight energy conservation in order to reduce the energy input required for each dollar of GDP output. Getting consumers to switch from incandescent lights to fluorescent lights in their homes is an example of a behavioural change. Success in improving energy productivity will need to underscore any global energy policy going forward. Without improvements to energy productivity initiatives, our energy dependency and the tightness of supply that is occurring will continue to magnify.

Resource Depletion

Resource Management is the ability to actively manage existing supplies and regenerate new supplies of materials in such a way that we minimize resource depletion.

Resource management refers to our ability to actively manage existing supplies of materials and regenerate new supplies in a way that minimizes resource depletion. As we have discussed throughout this chapter, our industrial and technology-based society is based on the acquisition and consumption of materials found in, and on, our planet. These materials form the basis for the creation of goods and services designed, in large part, to improve our standard of living. Some of these resources are more renewable than others. What has grown significantly, however, is an overall concern that the replacement rates on renewable resources lag far behind their consumption. This concern is further compounded by the acceleration of non-renewable resource consumption, which in some areas has grown to the point where resources are well past their peak supply points. With the projected population growth for our planet noted above, combined with the tremendous economic growth in emerging economies across the globe, this resource depletion curve continues to accelerate. As indicated in the previous section, much of the discussion around resource depletion has focused on the energy sector. This concern, however, goes well beyond oil and other fossil fuels. Resource depletion is being felt across such areas as mining, fishing, agriculture, and water. The depletion of these supplies is more time-sensitive in some areas than in others. Whereas abundant supplies of some ores may take us well into the centuries to come, total supply levels in other resource areas do not present such leeway. Lithium, for example, may not exist as abundantly as zinc or copper. Mineral depletion could potentially be offset by our capability to make greater use of technology to mine hard-to-reach supplies, or to create synthetic or mineral substitutes. For other categories of resources, however, this is not always the case. Fishing, for example, is an area where very real concern exists relating to the depletion of a fixed stock supply. In a December 2010 report on the fishing sector, The United Nations Environment Program stated that the "clock is ticking" on the sustainability of global fish stocks, and that approximately 80 percent of fish stocks have been depleted.[14] In Canada, one can go back to July 1992 to see the impact of resource depletion of fishing stocks; on this date the government of Canada imposed a moratorium on the northern cod fishery along our country's east coast. This moratorium ended more than 500 years of cod fishing and resulted in an estimated 30 000 jobs being eliminated in

Newfoundland and Labrador (12 percent of the province's workforce).[15] The moratorium was deemed necessary to allow for cod stocks to rebound, and remains in place as of this writing. Equally concerning is the impact that overuse is having on water supplies globally. The replacement rate of fresh water is declining across our planet. According to a UN environmental outlook, it is estimated that by 2025 as many as 1.8 billion people will be living in areas with absolute water scarcity, and two-thirds of the world's population will be living under water stress situations where the availability of water to meet domestic, agriculture, industry, energy, and environmental needs will be compromised.[16] A key problem in this regard is groundwater depletion. Water tables are falling across the globe. An Earth Policy Institute estimate indicates that water tables are down in countries containing more than half the world's population. Groundwater is essential to agriculture (irrigation), industry (hydroelectricity), and domestic use (residential needs). Excessive pumping of groundwater results in the drying up of wells, the lowering of water in lakes, rivers, and streams, the deterioration of water quality, and increased costs as governments, organizations, and businesses strive to gain greater access to this valuable resource. Las Vegas, for example, is in the midst of a water crunch. The city, whose population has doubled over the past two decades, is running out of water. The Lake Mead Reservoir, a major source of water for Las Vegas, Los Angeles, and Phoenix, is currently experiencing its lowest water levels since it was built. Plagued by a lengthy drought and an ongoing drain on the existing water supply, the Southern Nevada Water Authority (SNWA) is proposing to build a 450-km pipeline to bring groundwater from areas in eastern Nevada to Las Vegas and vicinity. The cost of this project—which plans to sink 195 wells as deep as 500 metres to tap deep-water sources—is estimated at $2 billion.[17]

The Capital Squeeze

Over the past two decades, the global marketplace has benefited from an excess supply of capital at very attractive rates. Developing economies driven largely by export-centric practices supplied the fully developed economies of the world with a vast array of goods and services. With most of their trade focused externally, these economies developed considerable capital reserves. As noted in Chapter 3, the People's Republic of China's currency and gold reserves topped US$2 trillion at the close of 2008. These reserves, coupled with the rise of **sovereign wealth funds** within many of these economies and supported by a propensity toward individual savings by their citizens, have resulted in the global marketplace having access to cheap money in volumes never before seen. Fully developed economies, eager to stimulate their own growth, tapped into these dollars to finance their own economic expansion. The end result is that a significant number of nations within the global economy have leveraged their growth via these developing economies' reserves. Add to this the very low rate of savings many of these fully developed economies have experienced among their citizens, and the end result is an overwhelming dependency on emerging economies to meet their capital needs. So, why is this a problem? It is a problem in that, although historically these developing economies have expanded their reserve base through export surpluses and the lending of capital externally, their need for this capital internally is dramatically increasing. The capital needs of the world, given the growth we have seen within these developing economies, will create a need for capital never seen before. A quick look at the growth within Asia, Africa, and Latin America demonstrates the requirement for huge amounts of capital investment that will be needed for infrastructure development such as homes, intermodal transportation systems (ports and highway infrastructure), water systems, hospitals, and public service buildings. Added to this is the need by private domestic and international companies to build factories, plants, and office buildings. According to an analysis compiled by McKinsey & Company via research undertaken by the Economic Intelligence Unit, the global demand for capital, for investment purposes, is expected to top $24 trillion in 2030, assuming that anticipated GDP growth targets are

Sovereign Wealth Funds are country- or state-owned investment funds.

realized. Based on forecasts of GDP growth and anticipated savings rates, this could mean a shortfall of close to $2.5 trillion between what the global marketplace needs and what it can provide.[18] The consequence of this massive capital infusion requirement and the projected capital shortfall will be as follows:

1. Access to capital, particularly by fully developed economies, will become more difficult. This will be due to (a) the low savings rates of their citizens, resulting in little investment capital being generated internally, and (b) the increasing need of developing economies to use their capital reserves for internal, domestic investment, thereby reducing the supply they are able to lend elsewhere.

2. A reduction in savings will most likely occur among citizens in developing economies as their domestic economies grow and as consumption-based practices permeate the lives of their citizens. Simply put, in order to enhance their quality of life, these citizens will save less and spend more obtaining the goods and services that will make their lives easier and more fulfilling. Historically, as economies grow and citizens become wealthier, savings rates decline.

Cost of Capital is the cost of company funds (both debt and equity).

3. The **cost of capital** (interest rates) will increase as the demand for capital for investment purposes exceeds the supply. For governments that financed their current deficits with the low interest rates, their cost of debt will rise as their credit facilities mature and require renewal underwriting.

Financial Protectionism refers to government actions or policies that restrict or restrain the outflow of funds from one economy to another.

4. A form of **financial protectionism** could creep into the global capital marketplace as countries with surpluses seek to keep their capital for internal and external investment in a manner that provides them with a global competitive advantage, offering lower cost of capital to domestic players and higher, risk-laden cost of capital to external borrowers.

The end result of this impending "capital crunch" will be that access to cheap capital will no longer be the large contributor to global growth it has in the past. In fact, the reverse may be true. The inability to gain access to needed funds may result in growth slowing. The scarcity of capital may also increase the gap between countries that have access to capital and those that do not. It also will most likely result in higher taxes and fewer services in those countries forced to pay significantly higher interest rates on existing deficits.[19]

BUSINESS *in Action*

ExxonMobil and Algae Biofuels

In June 2009, ExxonMobil, currently the world's largest publicly traded energy company, announced a $600-million investment in a research and development alliance with Synthetic Genomics Inc. (SGI) for the purpose of developing advanced biofuels from photosynthetic algae. The intent of this investment is to produce a low-net-carbon transportation fuel. With oil prices expected to continue to climb, and with the competing demand

for agricultural products, such as corn, between the food chain and the production of biofuels, the marketplace is actively seeking viable alternate fuel options.

Although some countries, such as Brazil, have been successful in developing significant scale for agriculture-based ethanol production, most experts now agree that the conversion of corn,

sugar cane, and other agricultural-based products to alternate fuels results in three significant benefit offsets: (1) increasing prices to the food products based on the same agricultural source, (2) increasing amounts of land relegated to biofuel-based production, which removes it from producing food to meet global needs (and the corresponding deforestation that may be required to make such land available), and (3) increasing energy required and pollution realized from the ethanol production cycle.

Algae-based fuels, it is hoped, will deliver on the benefits of biofuel while eliminating the offsets noted above. The production of algae-based fuels, for example, does not rely on fresh water or need arable land. The algae-based source for this fuel can be produced using sea water or waste water. Algae are also biodegradable and can be produced with minimal environmental impact. It is also anticipated that the oils produced by the algae can be processed using existing technologies and refineries and would yield a product that can be used as fuel by our current transportation-sector technologies and infrastructure. Algaculture, as the process of farming algae is called, is also being assessed with respect to its ability to produce vegetable oil (among other things), in addition to bioethanol, biogasoline, and biodiesel products. Algaculture is also believed to have a positive impact on global warming, as the photosynthetic process used to grow algae (sunlight and carbon dioxide) offers positive green carpet–based greenhouse gas mitigation benefits. Equally important is the output efficiency that algaculture offers. According to ExxonMobil researchers, algae have the potential of yielding 2000 gallons of fuel for each acre of algae production per year. Current biofuel sources, such as corn (250 gallons per acre per year) and sugar cane (450 gallons per acre per year), produce significantly less biofuel annually. Algae can also be grown more quickly than their land-based alternatives and thereby yield potentially greater efficiencies in the production process.

The strategic research alliance between these two companies unites the synergies of complementary expertise. ExxonMobil brings its engineering, process development, and commercialization expertise. SGI, a leader in biological research, brings to the partnership its expertise in biology-production and bio-oil recovery research and development.

ExxonMobil is not alone in its research into the viability of algaculture-based techniques for the development of algae-based biofuels. A number of competitors have actively entered this market sector. Chevron Corporation, a major competitor to ExxonMobil, for example, has partnered with the U.S. Department of Energy's National Renewable Energy Lab to facilitate the commercialization of algae-based fuels. The actual widespread commercialization of this potentially viable alternate fuel source is still a ways off. If successful, however, it could play a vital role in reducing carbon emissions and in reducing our dependency on fossil fuels for our business and transportation needs.[20]

WEB INTEGRATION
Want to learn more about algae-based fuels? Visit the National Algae Association's Web site at **www.national-algaeassociation.com** or the Algal BioMass Organization's Web site at **www.algalbiomass. org.**

Business's Response to the Sustainability Challenge

LO3, LO4

Businesses alone cannot solve the environmental sustainability challenge that currently confronts us. It will take the combined efforts of governments, organizations, businesses, and individuals to define how we can achieve the level of economic development that will result in an improved standard of living for all global citizens while at the same time protecting this planet we call home. What is important, however, is that businesses, and the people who manage them, take a leadership role in tackling this challenge. The approach to this challenge is not an easy one. It will take an integrated process spanning key tactical decision-making areas, framed by strategic inclusion and broad market support. This process will need to be driven by a top-level management approach that analyzes an organization's current practices, sets sustainable development policies and objectives, and designs and executes an implementation plan that is integrated within an organization's overall strategic plan and supported by key metrics capable of measuring and monitoring success. This commitment will be firmly rooted in the organizational culture and endorsed by members of the stakeholder community who recognize the critical need for environmental sustainability as a core component of the organization's DNA (see Figure 4.8). The more we learn about how our practices impact our environment, the more we need to manage it in order to minimize its degradation. The approach being offered, therefore, is not static but dynamic in that adjustments to it can, and should, take place in order to maximize the effectiveness of the organization's response to the challenges previously noted.

Responding to these challenges will require a definitive and dramatic shift in the way we think about business. Success will require us to rethink our attitude toward trade and the cost/price relationships associated with it. It will also require us to rethink our approach to how we utilize our resources (eco-efficiency management) to develop the products and services we offer to the global marketplace. The process cannot, however, simply stop at the development of tactical initiatives. Management, supported by its stakeholder base and the community at large, must redefine the culture and the thought process of the entire business system. This can be accomplished by creating an approach that contributes positively to the global response to the challenges present today, and to the ones that lie ahead in the years to come. With this in mind, the following discussion is a cursory overview of what is required by businesses in order to effectively respond to the sustainability challenge now upon us.

FIGURE 4.8   Responding to the Sustainability Challenge

Source: BSD, "Business and Sustainability Development: A Global Guide," 2010 International Institute for Sustainable Development, www.isd.org, April 2011.

Trade Management

Trade management involves shifting the impact of trade and economic development away from being the primary driver of environmental harm and planet degradation toward being a process that exists in an arena of environmental sustainability. To achieve success, global market participants must be unanimous in their agreement for the transitioning to, and maintenance of, three critical trading practices:

1. Participation in trade and economic development must agree to pay for the social costs of environmental degradation. It cannot be an option or choice, on an ad hoc basis, as to whether one should participate. Loopholes or lax industry standards that permit inefficient outcomes relating to environmental protection need to be identified and corrected. Retailers and manufacturers must demand that supply chain partners adhere to such practices as well.

2. Participants across markets need to support and accept pricing policies that reflect the full cost of expenses incurred in order to achieve environmental sustainability. This would include charges associated with taxes imposed, emissions fees required, and "cap and trade" mechanisms initiated by various economic sectors. It also recognizes the reality that costs associated with the development and application of new technologies and sustainability processes need to be recovered as part of an organization's pricing strategy.

3. Participants must block the ability of market players to obtain and leverage a competitive advantage as a result of efforts to avoid environmental costs. Global trade participants must develop and adhere to an equal playing field that eliminates practices of non-enforcement or loosening of existing regulations, blockage of the implementation of new, required regulations, and the creation of safe havens for environmental abusers. Recognizing that adherence to environmental sustainability standards and policies currently varies across the globe, the World Trade Organization (WTO) and other such global entities will need to create and manage definitive timetables for compliance.

The movement to a global sustainability model will take time and will be a challenge. This is particularly true when the impact of the costs associated with the transition period needs to be factored in to the prices you and I pay for the products and services we use. The fragility of the global economic recovery, coupled with the significant sovereign debt loads many countries are facing, will add additional hurdles to this initiative. The ability to redefine our trade culture is, however, imperative to the implementation of a successful global sustainability model. Redesigning our trade mentality from that of a consumption model to one that is built around responding to the environmental challenges identified earlier in this chapter is predicated on the ability of businesses to make such investments knowing that costs can be recovered and that, in doing so, such investments do not result in competitive disadvantage.

> Trade management is shifting the impact of trade and economic development away from being the primary driver of environmental harm and planet degradation, to that of a process that exists in an arena of environmental sustainability.

Eco-Efficiency Management

Eco-efficiency management refers to the tactical shifts required within business operations to maximize the efficiency of resource utilization and minimize or eliminate the resulting current degradation of the planet that such operations bring. Eco-efficiency management can be thought of as consisting of two broad categories of operational reassessment: resource management and emissions management.

Eco-efficiency Management is the tactical shift required within our business operations to maximize the efficiency of our resource utilization and minimize or eliminate the resulting current degradation to the planet.

FIGURE 4.9 Consumption Model

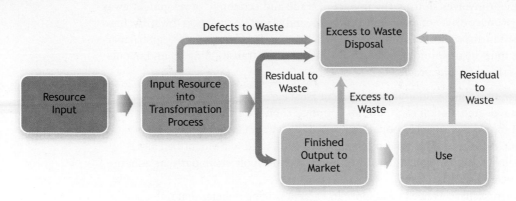

RESOURCE MANAGEMENT

For market participants, resource management focuses on shifting away from the old consumption model whereby resources acquired entered into the transformation process with the end result of producing a product and disposing of waste. What was not sold to the market was simply tossed out. Waste disposal was treated as a "bad and unavoidable cost," so efforts to minimize this expenditure led to minimal efforts to protect the environment (see Figure 4.9).

Although a number of organizations globally still view their existence framed around this consumption model, we are seeing significant strides toward replacing this model with what is called the resource management model (see Figure 4.10). The resource management model has evolved as a result of three fundamental shifts in the thought process associated with waste:

1. The recognition that resources are finite for many market sectors. With increasing global demand, procurement of these resources is resulting in additional "bring to market" costs that are resulting in an upward trend, price-wise, on such commodities and materials.
2. The recognition that resource efficiency, while possibly leading to slightly higher costs in the short run, can lead to lower overall costs in the long run. Investments in 4R initiatives (to reduce, reuse, recycle, and recover) are yielding long-term cost savings to those organizations that effectively undertake 4R programs.
3. Societal pressure. Perhaps one of the most noticeable areas of environmental degradation, the relative strength of a company's waste reduction and waste prevention strategies, is becoming closely linked to company image and brand reputation.

The end result of these three shifts is that more companies are taking a 4R approach to resource management, which has resulted in a more circular approach to the consumption model whereby the emphasis has moved from waste disposal and treatment to that of waste reduction and prevention as shown in Figure 4.10.

The desired outcome of the resource management model is twofold. The first outcome is to achieve the goal of zero waste, which eliminates further degradation of the environment due to the cessation of landfill-based pollution-creating activities. The reduction of waste not only assists in reducing the direct operational costs of the business involved (waste packaging and removal, etc.), but also generates considerable secondary societal benefits and cost savings in terms of lower waste treatment costs, disposal costs, storage costs, energy costs, and cleanup costs (e.g., brownfields remediation).

The second outcome is preservation of resources, which prolongs our ability to tap such resources into the future. This preservation is accomplished through modifications to internal resource and product/service transformation systems via (1) technologies and the use of renewable resource substitutes that reduce the quantity of a finite resource required within

FIGURE 4.10   Resource Management Model

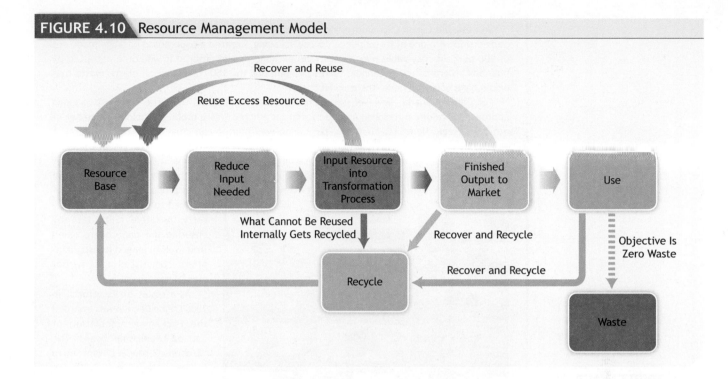

the transformation process, and (2) where finite resources are required, the development of a strong "reusing" of the excess not fully consumed within the initial transformation process. This is further supported by a strong recycling process that maximizes alternate uses of excess resources and resource by-products that cannot be looped back into the internal resource reuse system. Finished output to the marketplace is also accompanied by strong recovery and recycling systems to maximize the reuse potential of product/service by-products, including the final recovery of such products once their use in the marketplace has ended due to consumption practices or obsolescence.

Resource management also includes improving the durability of products to increase their life span, rebuilding or replenishing resources used (e.g., reforestation), reducing the energy consumption used in the associated transformation processes, and reducing or eliminating the use of toxic materials and chemicals within such processes.

> The goal is to create a sustainable resource management model geared toward reducing the material and energy intensity of creating products or services while still being able to produce economically viable products that enhance the lives of global residents.

BUSINESS *in Action*

Canon Canada: Resource Management

Canon Canada Inc. had a problem. Genuinely concerned about the environment, the company was getting ready to launch its new "Ecosense" line of ink for its inkjet printers. So, what was the problem? Canon Canada's "Ecosense" line of ink products was being packaged in plastic containers, which Canon realized would not be accepted for recycling by facilities across Canada. Without changing the packaging, the amount of waste that was going to be generated was estimated to be more than 150 000 pounds of plastic. Such a waste trail would be a tough sell for what was being labelled an "Ecosense" product. More importantly, Canon realized that carrying through with such a launch, given this expected waste trail, was contrary to the organization's overall sustainability strategy.

So, how did Canon Canada respond? The company went back to the drawing board—and, in partnership with one of its suppliers, Jones Packaging, created a paperboard package made out of 100-percent-recyclable paperboard. The package design ensured it would be accepted by blue box programs across Canada, thereby eliminating the 150 000 pounds of plastic waste that would have occurred under the original concept.

For Canon Canada, however, the benefits went well beyond this. The revised packaging approach, in addition to solving the immediate predicted waste problem, yielded a number of other strategic benefits. First, the packaging was lighter and smaller in size (10 percent smaller), thereby enabling Canon to package more units per box, thus cutting down on transportation and related shipping costs and reducing greenhouse emissions in the process. The new packaging was also easier for consumers to open and to work with, thereby adding to its overall convenience for the user. The packaging itself was made from paper products from forests that adhered to the Sustainable Forestry Initiative (SFI), thereby ensuring the paperboard came from well-managed forestry suppliers committed to environmental sustainability.

As a result of its efforts, in 2008 Canon Canada was awarded the Packaging Association of Canada Leadership Award. The "Ecosense" product went on to receive the Eco Excellence Award for Achievement in Packaging at the 2009 Paperboard Packaging Council Carton Competition.[21]

WEB INTEGRATION
To learn more about green initiatives at Canon Canada, see **www.canon.ca.**

EMISSIONS MANAGEMENT

Emissions management is focused on achieving a position of "zero global emissions." The long-term focus should be a global market that produces zero pollution/waste in the air. To accomplish this objective, market participants must do the following:

1. Commit to attacking pollution at the source rather than after it is created. This means looking at the current inputs in an operational process and seeking to develop substitutes for such inputs, or investing in or creating technologies that eliminate such waste prior to it moving into the air. Of critical importance to the achievement of this environmental need is that a timetable for compliance for phasing out hazardous inputs in output processes (i.e., production and manufacturing) is established and adhered to. Where required, education and training, along with financial support in the form of credits or other economic incentives, grants, and/or loans, should be provided to ensure compliance.

2. Prove, prior to implementation, that the processes being employed in new operations will do no harm to the air.

For such an approach to be effective, market participants must be transparent in their operational approaches, and must fully communicate to workers, consumers, and the global community at large the information relating to their environmental performance. As with our discussion surrounding trade management and resource management, the ability for the global marketplace to transition to a "zero emissions" policy will be a challenge to say the least. For many developing economies, it requires not only access to the latest technologies, but also a considerable educational effort. It also means acceptance of the trade-offs required with respect to rapid economic development versus environmental sustainability.

Strategic Integration

Our opening discussion in this chapter focused on the consumption society that has evolved around our current and historical trade practices. We then discussed the impact that such an approach has created with respect to our environment. Although we have transitioned from unabated consumption to a marketplace partially governed by environmental regulatory and legislative compliance, our global society needs to further evolve well beyond our current position. A number of companies have initiated eco-management tactics for resource management and emissions control. In some cases this has been driven by compliance requirements, whereas in others it has evolved as a result of an understanding of the benefits it brings along with a desire to participate in environmental stewardship activities. Societal pressure, often driven by external groups and concerned citizens, has also resulted in a greater awareness and understanding of the environmental challenge we are now facing. For the global marketplace to be truly successful in responding to this challenge, businesses need to completely integrate environmental responsibility into their business strategies. This means balancing what it takes to be a successful business with doing the right thing for society (see Figure 4.11).

Strategic integration means that businesses need to see environmental sustainability as an integral part of value creation and that this creation includes sustaining and enhancing the resources we depend on well into the future. The problem is not that we are unaware of what needs to be done, but rather lies in how to do it. Environmental sustainability is a highly complex challenge that reaches to an organization's core. Integrating it into the organization's long-term strategic plan requires, in many cases, redesigning the business model. Successful execution in this regard requires experience and expertise in an area where many businesses simply do not possess such skills beyond their compliance requirements. It is this gap between

---

FIGURE 4.11 The Sustainability Balancing Act

intent and action that is preventing organizations from moving beyond compliance and eco-management tactics to a position of true strategic integration. So, how do we get businesses to strive for full environmental sustainability integration into their business strategies? First, managers need to recognize the long-term benefits such integration can bring; second, they need to develop the capabilities to successfully conduct a critical self-assessment of how such benefits can be realized within their organization.

> Strategic integration means that businesses need to see environmental sustainability as an integral part of value creation and that this creation includes sustaining and enhancing the resources we depend on well into the future.

LONG-TERM BENEFITS OF ENVIRONMENTAL SUSTAINABILITY STRATEGIC INTEGRATION

For many businesses, environmental sustainability is focused on two short-term outcomes:

- Improved corporate image
- Regulatory compliance

Although these are valid outcomes, integration of environmental sustainability practices into an organization's strategy can yield significantly greater long-term benefits that often are overlooked by organizations and their management teams. Some of these include:

1. **Pricing power:** a stronger brand increases an organization's pricing power.
2. **Enhanced efficiencies:** resource intensity reduction techniques lead to greater long-term operating efficiencies and stronger supply chain management. This can lead to higher margins and an overall lower cost base, which can be leveraged into a competitive advantage.
3. **Customer retention:** improved customer loyalty leads to lower customer desertion rates, resulting in greater opportunity to leverage additional revenue from these customers and lower customer transaction costs.
4. **Stronger employee base:** employee engagement via sustainability initiatives can result in greater employee retention, stronger recruitment positioning, and higher levels of employee motivation and productivity.
5. **Strong environmental management:** leads to lower risk exposure, which can result in lower insurance premiums, lower capital costs, and greater access to capital.
6. **New business options:** can lead to new skill development within the organization, which can lead to the creation of new business opportunities and an enhanced ability to enter into new markets.

CAPABILITIES: CRITICAL SELF-ASSESSMENT

The full immersion of environmental sustainability into the strategic planning process means integrating it throughout our culture, operations, and processes. It also means ensuring the skills necessary for assessing environmental sustainability are embedded within our organization's business acumen. To be successful in such an integrative approach, organizations and their management teams need to recognize where and how their current practices are impacting the environment. Once identified, they need to create a well-organized approach to responding to these issues. Figure 4.12 offers a decision guide to assessing and integrating environmental sustainability into an organization.

Organizations must first understand how environmental sustainability is affecting, or will affect, their businesses. This means developing a clear and succinct understanding of what sustainability is and communicating it across the organization. This initial impact assessment is followed by a comprehensive analysis of the key drivers of environmental

FIGURE 4.12 Integrating Environmental Sustainability

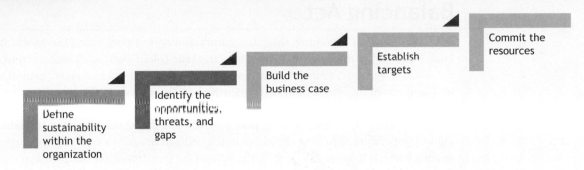

impact and degradation and how each of these identified areas will impact the business system and market positioning. A key outcome of this analysis is the identification of the opportunities such drivers offer, the threats that are present, and a conclusion as to the gaps that exist as well as the risks associated with such gaps. A key aspect of this identification process is also the identifying of channel partners, stakeholders, and external agency partnerships that are considered critical to overall success, as well as the identification of key capabilities that are required but currently do not exist within the organization. Once the gap and risk analyses are completed, the organization will then need to build a thorough business plan that defines how a commitment to environmental sustainability can be integrated into its culture, operations, and processes. This will include both near-term and long-term requirements, impact factors, and a thorough understanding of the cost/benefit tradeoff such commitments will mean. Evolving out of this business plan will be the development of a timetable and the establishment of targets and performance metrics to guide the plan's execution. Also key to this stage of the process is the identification of internal champions designated to ensure committed resources are effectively allocated in pursuit of the organization's sustainability objectives. Resource commitment means ensuring full integration takes place across both the primary activity areas and the supporting activity areas of the value chain.

Strategic integration of environmental sustainability initiatives, for many companies, means rewiring the organization. In many cases, this will require the organization to seek help and support from external parties. It means working both forward and backward with, and through, channel partners. It means reframing the financial models around which a business has been fundamentally built. It also means committing to a long-term plan that, once started, requires revisiting every organizational process.

What generally is not understood is that, for many companies, significant financial investment often is not required to transition to a more environmentally sustainable organization. For example, in examining its footwear design and manufacturing processes Nike realized in hindsight that for every two pairs of shoes it produced it discarded enough waste to have produced a third pair of shoes.[22] Simply by shifting to a more efficient resource management model, Nike is now looping what used to be waste back into its **productivity cycle**. The creation of this closed-loop system, with the goal of zero waste, has saved the company millions of dollars per year. The positive impact of this change benefits both the environment and the organization's bottom line. As has been demonstrated by Nike, in many cases significant progress can be realized through policy changes alone. The key is to build awareness as to how the current practices and processes an organization undertakes impact environmental degradation. Once this awareness and sensitivity is understood the platform for change materializes, and initiatives responding to such degradation are brought into place.

Productivity Cycle includes the processes involved in transforming materials into a product or service available for sale in the marketplace.

Management Reflection—Sustainability Balancing Act

In the U.S. state of Wyoming, there is a natural hot spring pool called the Morning Glory Pool. For decades, this pool—with its distinctive blue colour—attracted visitors from around the world. Over time, visitors began to view the hot spring pool as a giant, natural wishing well, and tossed in coins as they made their wishes. So, what does this have to do with environmental sustainability? Well, what was once a pool of distinctive blue water is now yellow and green. The coins tossed into the pool have blocked its natural heat vents, thereby reducing its temperature. Also, the chemicals in the coins have reacted with the hot spring water, causing bacteria to grow and creating the yellow ring that dominates the outside perimeter of the pool today. What has happened to the Morning Glory Pool reflects the way we have approached our environment. For a number of centuries, actions taking place "one coin toss at a time" have resulted in the planetary conditions that now challenge us. Environmental degradation is real and material. To think that we, as business managers, do not have a role in addressing such issues can no longer be a position by which we operate our companies. The belief that the primary business objective is to maximize return on equity regardless of environmental consequences needs to be shifted to one that is built around the sustainability balancing act illustrated in Figure 4.11. Managers cannot rationalize that sustainability has no impact on their business. Going forward, successful companies will be those that fully integrate environmental sustainability into their strategic planning process and recognize the long-term value creation that will result.[23]

Chapter Summary

The purpose of this chapter is to expose students to the environmental sustainability challenge that is now impacting governments, organizations, businesses, and individuals as we seek to continue to grow and expand the global marketplace. The chapter opens by framing what is termed the "consumption journey," or how our economic evolution has driven the environment degradation to the level that we now face. This is followed by a discussion of the major environmental sustainability issues that lie before us: climate change, pollution and health, the energy crunch, resource depletion, and the capital squeeze. Commentary is offered as to the current and future challenges the global marketplace will need to respond to in each area as we continue to attempt to create and supply the increasing level of products and services desired worldwide. Recognizing that business, on its own, cannot provide solutions to all of these impact factors, the chapter then transitions into discussing the key requirements businesses need to incorporate into their planning processes if we are to reverse the escalating environmental degradation we now face. These include fundamental changes to the way we perceive trade, the need to initiate effective eco-management initiatives, and the need to ensure that environmental sustainability best practices are fully integrated into our strategic planning process. To be successful, managers must identify and understand how the implementation of environmental sustainability practices can benefit their organizations in the long run, and how to identify the gaps that exist within their organizational culture, operations, and processes. This identification and self-assessment process is highlighted as the chapter closes, thereby providing managers with an understanding of the steps organizations need to transition through in order to succeed in integrating environmental sustainability practices into their strategy.

Developing Business Knowledge and Skills

KEY TERMS

environmental stewardship *p. 91*

degradation *p. 92*

Kyoto protocol *p. 95*

BTU (British Thermal Unit) *p. 97*

peak model theories *p. 98*

feed-in tariffs *p. 98*

resource management *p. 100*

sovereign wealth funds *p. 101*

cost of capital *p. 102*

financial protectionism *p. 102*

eco-efficiency management *p. 105*

productivity cycle *p. 111*

QUESTIONS FOR DISCUSSION

1. Identify the five major environmental sustainability challenges going forward. Which one concerns you the most? Why? Is something missing from this list? If so, what is it?

2. What are the key success factors associated with building a reduced carbon-based economy?

3. What are the key factors that will influence the availability of energy supplies over the short term?

4. Which do you feel is the easier response for businesses to enact with respect to environmental sustainability challenges, trade management adjustments or eco-efficiency adjustments? Why?

5. What is the primary difference between the consumption model and the resource management model?

6. Identify what you believe are the primary benefits companies can expect as a result of integrating environmental sustainability practices into their overall strategy.

7. What do you believe is the greatest barrier to organizations fully integrating environmental sustainability initiatives into their business strategies?

QUESTIONS FOR INDIVIDUAL ACTION

Research the Hubbert peak theory of oil production. As part of your research, consider alternate theories and positions. Do you agree with the theory as proposed by Hubbert? Do you feel that advances in technology have rendered the theory obsolete, or will they enable the global marketplace to continue its dependence on fossil fuels for energy well into the future? Prepare a presentation outlining your position. Be prepared to present this to your fellow classmates.

TEAM EXERCISE

Adopted in 1997 and technically in force in 2005, the Kyoto protocol is an international agreement linked to the United Nations Framework Convention on Climate Change. The protocol sets binding targets relating to GHG emissions for participating countries. Since its inception and through its implementation, the Kyoto protocol has been a source of discussion and disagreement, particularly in Canada. As a team, research the current status of this agreement. Which countries are participating? Which are not? What primary concerns surrounding this agreement have resulted in a number of countries choosing not to participate? Do you believe this agreement will be successful in the long run? For those countries not participating, what will it take to enable them to participate in this agreement? Prepare a presentation on this subject and be prepared to present your findings to your fellow classmates.

Case for Discussion

Canada has a problem. So, too, do a number of other countries globally. The problem is what to do with nuclear waste. Although nuclear power facilities have been around for decades, and research on radioactive waste has been assessing the situation for more than 30 years, no one has yet figured out what to do with it. In fact, no country in the world as of this writing has a permanent radioactive waste storage facility (although Sweden and Finland are in the process of creating permanent underground storage repositories). In Canada, for example, radioactive waste up to this point is being stored temporarily at plants and research facilities. The Nuclear Waste Management Organization (NWMO), created by the federal government in 2002, has been tasked to solve this problem. Their solution is to bury what will be an estimated 3.6 to 5.5 million used fuel bundles (depends on number of reactors operating), created by our nuclear reactors, a half-kilometre below the ground in a deep geological repository.[24] The waste will be secured in corrosion-resistant containers, shielded by man-made barriers of clay, and isolated from the environment and groundwater. This solution is what is believed to be required, as nuclear waste will continue to emit radiation at hazardous levels long after it is

buried (estimates peg this at more than one million years). So, who wants this in their backyard? Well, to date, six communities in Canada have thrown their hats into the ring. These communities have been identified as Ignace, Ear Falls, and Schreiber, Ontario, and English River, Pinehouse, and Creighton, Saskatchewan. A couple of other communities are still in the discussion stage with NWMO as well. Why this level of interest? Many of these communities are located in isolated areas, and are currently economically depressed and struggling to survive. The lure—jobs and economic revitalization! The facility, once built, could provide hundreds of jobs. In addition to the waste management facility, NWMO also intends to build a "Centre of Expertise" on the site for research purposes, and expects to attract experts in the field from all over the world. Leading up to the opening of the facility and the centre is the estimated $24 billion in construction projects needed to support it. Once started (still a few years away), the construction alone is expected to take until 2035. For Ignace, Ontario, the potential economic spinoff was such that the town council at the time (2009) was the first community to communicate its interest to NWMO. That does not mean that everyone in Ignace is on board. People there agree that something needs to be done to save their town, but not everyone is sure this is the right solution.[25]

QUESTIONS

What do you think? How do you feel about NWMO's solution regarding radioactive waste storage? Is this the right approach to this problem? Anti-nuclear groups believe we should cease considering nuclear energy as a solution to our future energy needs until we have a solution for the waste it generates. What is your position? What about the transportation risk? NWMO estimates that transporting 3.6 million bundles to a permanent underground repository location would require 53 shipments per month, by road, for 30 years. If you were a resident of Ignace, Ontario (or one of the other towns that has indicated interest), how would you feel?

Practise and learn online with Connect. Connect resources include additional and interactive study exercises, videos, and practice quizzing, as well as additional material you won't find in the printed text.

5 Ethics and Corporate Social Responsibility

Learning Objectives

This chapter is designed to provide students with:

Lo1 An understanding of the key challenges managers and members of an organization's board of directors face when wrestling with the concept of ethics

Lo2 An overview of techniques managers can use when making decisions involving ethical issues

Lo3 An understanding of the role of the board of directors in developing the culture of the organization with respect to ethical codes of conduct and behaviour

Lo4 An introduction to the growing importance of corporate social responsibility (CSR) in the marketplace and the various levels of CSR involvement

Lo5 An understanding of the complexity and challenges associated with integrating CSR and corporate strategy

Snapshot—What to Expect in This Chapter

This chapter focuses on the role of ethics and social responsibility within the managerial decision-making process. The content emphasized in this chapter includes the following:

- Ethics in Management

- What Is Ethics?
  - Ethics and the Individual
  - Ethics and Culture
  - Regulating Ethics

- What Is CSR (Corporate Social Responsibility)?
  - Why Is CSR Becoming So Important?
  - The Interdependency of CSR and Corporate Strategy
  - The Challenge Behind CSR Implementation

- A Note Pertaining to Not-for-Profits

- Management Reflection—It Is All About Trust

From the Student's Perspective

In the past, managers have followed one rule in making business decisions: make the most money possible. Companies that did things the fastest and the cheapest were the industry leaders. Everyone wanted to be on top, taking nothing into account except for the bottom line. Profit was king.

However, what happens when profit comes at the expense of the environment, social well-being, or even somebody's life? Transparency in the media has shown us the consequence of business without ethics: global warming, impoverished communities, and, just two years ago, the biggest financial crisis in history. When companies like Walmart have sales equal to the GDP of hundreds of countries, they have the responsibility to further the well-being and sustainability of all their stakeholders—not just their shareholders. They have the responsibility to instigate change for the better. In the end, we have to acknowledge the virtuous cycle in which all of us operate: in order to survive, what we take, we must give back.

Further, instead of being a hindrance to profitability, ethical business has actually become *good business*. Consumers today demand socially responsible initiatives from most, if not all, companies—whether it be through fair trade practices or the preservation of human rights. Companies centred on corporate social responsibility are actually thriving in today's business environment. And what has happened to companies like Nortel, Enron, and Lehman Brothers? Society has doled out its justice.

Nevertheless, as with any moral issue, all decisions are based on free will and choice. As future managers, the choice is up to you. What will you do?

Joanna Pleta is a Queen's University BComm'10 who is currently working as an Assistant Marketing Manager for American Express. She is originally from the Philippines but has also lived in Switzerland, the United Arab Emirates, and the United Kingdom. At Queen's, she was a recipient of the Certificate of Corporate Social Responsibility and the D.I. McLeod's Dean's List Scholarship for four consecutive years. She has also been involved in organizations such as the Queen's Finance Association Conference, the Principal's Innovation Fund, and Unilever. In the future, she aspires to excel in the marketing field, become fluent in French and Spanish, and work in Europe or Latin America.

BUSINESS *in Action*

Enron

How can a company increase its share price without actually increasing its profitability? The answer, according to Enron Corporation's management, was to manipulate its balance sheet and accounting policies. As their massive fraud came to light over a six-month period in 2001, Enron—formerly a Fortune 50 Company—tumbled quickly into bankruptcy in December of that year. Ever since, the name Enron has been synonymous with corporate corruption and greed.

1400 Smith Street

Enron was formed in 1985 with the merger of InterNorth and HNG, two natural gas companies. Kenneth Lay, the head of the smaller HNG, became CEO of the merged company within a year of its formation and quickly set about diversifying Enron's lines of business. Capitalizing on the deregulation of energy markets in the late 1980s, Enron began buying and selling "futures" contracts in electricity and natural gas. During the 1990s, Enron traded all kinds of complex derivatives (including weather-based ones) and entered into many seemingly unrelated lines of business including water and broadband Internet. It also built power plants around the world. Unfortunately for Enron, all this expansion came with two main problems: (1) Enron needed to take on huge amounts of debt to pay for it, and (2) most of these businesses turned out to be unprofitable.

Perhaps in part due to a pay structure that was heavily weighted toward option-based compensation, Enron management appeared to have felt an extraordinary pressure to increase the company's share price. The only way to do this, in their minds, was by meeting Wall Street analysts' profit expectations every quarter. When Enron's actual performance failed to live up to these expectations, management, led by president (and, briefly, CEO) Jeffrey Skilling, and CFO Andrew Fastow, began to manipulate Enron's accounting to inflate its earnings. They accomplished this by booking non-existent revenues and by creating special-purpose entities (limited companies or partnerships created by a firm in order to fulfill some specific objective, usually with the goal of isolating risk) to remove debt from Enron's balance sheet (to make it appear healthier to investors). Fastow was the primary architect of these SPEs and, along with employing them to hide Enron's debt, used them to defraud his employer out of more than $60 million.

While these practices persisted from 1997 until Fastow's termination in 2001, Enron was not the only company at fault. Arthur Andersen LLP, Enron's auditor and consultant, allowed its dependence on its biggest client (in terms of revenue) to get the better of it as it frequently looked the other way when Enron insisted on engaging in questionable accounting practices. Enron's management and accountants were able to successfully exploit loopholes in U.S. generally accepted accounting principles (GAAP); in many cases, they were technically adhering to the rules, but the professional judgment of a diligent auditor would have found them to be very obviously violating their intent. Enron's banks also contributed to the fraud by investing in Enron's special-purpose entities despite having reservations, in order to secure future business from Enron.

When the market caught on to Enron's unethical practices in 2001 its stock price and bond rating plummeted, both of which contributed to its rapid descent into bankruptcy. In the scandal's aftermath, Kenneth Lay, Jeffrey Skilling, and Andrew Fastow were all charged with a

variety of corporate crimes. While Lay and Skilling maintained they had done nothing wrong and knew nothing of Fastow's schemes, Fastow fully confessed to his crimes and turned informant on his fellow executives. He eventually earned a reduced sentence (six years and a $23.8-million fine) for two counts of wire and securities fraud. Skilling was sentenced to 24 years and 4 months in jail (and a $45-million fine) for conspiracy, insider trading, making false statements to auditors, and securities fraud. Lay was charged with 11 counts of securities fraud, wire fraud, and making false and misleading statements, but died of a heart attack before he could be sentenced. As their roles in the fraud came to light (and after it was found that they had shredded countless Enron-related documents), Arthur Andersen LLP surrendered their licence to practise accounting in the United States; their auditing practice quickly dissolved. Undoubtedly, the harshest consequence of Enron's bankruptcy was that its 21 000 employees all lost their jobs, and their pension savings were obliterated due to the actions of the management team.[1]

Ethics in Management

LO1

In March 2009, Bernie Madoff pleaded guilty to 11 federal felonies including securities fraud, investment adviser fraud, money laundering, theft from an employee benefit plan, falsifying SEC filings, and perjury associated with the **Ponzi scheme** he created while overseeing his investment company, Bernie L. Madoff Investment Securities LLC. Madoff, one of the most active traders in the marketplace, achieved what many described as legendary fame for the double-digit returns his company was able to return to investors. What was hidden for so long was that Madoff was using money from new investors to reward older investors, while at the same time siphoning off significant amounts of money for himself. Equally concerning was the fact that reputable financial institutions, credible hedge funds, and prominent investors were included among the ranks of those swindled by Madoff. Fairfield Greenwich Advisors, an investment management fund, was reported to have had more than 50 percent of its investment portfolio (an estimated $7.5 billion) with Madoff. Australian bank Bank Medici, and Spanish bank Banco Santander both had exposure with Madoff in excess of $2 billion. The Dutch bank Fortis, the Swiss bank Union Bancaire Privée, the British bank HSBC, and the French bank Natixis SA, to name a few, were all investors with Madoff. In total, the reach of Madoff's Ponzi scheme is estimated to include thousands of investors, including not-for-profit organizations and charities, universities, pension plans, prominent Hollywood personalities, and professional sports stars. Some individual investor losses were in the tens to hundreds of millions of dollars. In all, prosecutors estimated that Madoff's fraudulent activities resulted in him scamming investors out of an estimated US$13 billion, making it one of the largest Ponzi schemes ever. On June 29, 2009, Madoff was sentenced to 150 years in prison, the maximum allowed under the law.[2]

> **Ponzi Scheme** is a type of investment fraud that involves the payment of purported returns to existing investors from funds contributed by new investors.

In November 2004, Nortel Networks Corporation announced it would again postpone the release of financial restatements that the company was working on and that would impact previous company filings as far back as 1999. The restatements were the result of an accounting scandal that led to the firing of 10 executives and the commencement of two criminal investigations (by the Ontario Securities Exchange Commission and the RCMP). At the heart of the matter was an admission by Nortel that it may have overstated revenue, in 1999 and 2000, by more than $3 billion. This overstatement involved some revenue recognized in those years that should have been deferred to future years, as well as an estimated $250 million in revenue in 2000 that was to be permanently reversed (removed). This $250 million of fictitious revenue represented 10 percent of revenue for that year, and pointed to a concern that internal controls were being overridden by individuals working within the company. The results of the investigations at Nortel concluded that most of the alleged fraudulent acts occurred between 2002 and 2003. It was during this period when members of the senior management team are alleged to have intentionally inflated Nortel's earnings in order to achieve management bonuses. As revenue was not sufficient to deliver the required income, those accused allegedly engaged in the practice of changing revenue recognition policies and of accruing or deferring variable costs and operating expenses in order to improve the bottom line. In reporting the inflated earnings, bonuses were subsequently paid. It is alleged that those involved then attempted to cover up their actions by stating the misrepresentation was due to internal errors. In June 2008, three members of Nortel's management team were arrested by the RCMP for a variety of fraud charges. If convicted, each could face from 5 to 14 years in prison. For Nortel investors, the scandal became the telling end of a once great company. In 2000, Nortel Networks Corporation had a share price of $124, possessed capital of $394 billion, and employed more than 94 000 people. Two years later (2002), its capitalization had fallen to $5 billion and its share value to $0.47. Faced with debt in excess of $4.5 billion, and billions of dollars more in supplier and pension plan claims, in January 2009 the company filed for protection under the Companies' Creditors Arrangement Act (CCAA). In August 2009, the formal liquidation of the company commenced.[3]

What Is Ethics?

LO2, LO3

What causes people to behave like Bernie Madoff did? What drives a major component of an organization's senior management team to become involved in records falsification and the misrepresentation of results? After all, the two cases mentioned above are hardly the only ones we have become witness to over the past few years. In 2009, Canadians in Quebec learned how investment money manager Earl Jones misused an estimated $12 million of the funds entrusted to him to pay for his life of luxury that included the purchase of cars, condos, and private schooling for his children. Those impacted included Jones's own brother and sister-in-law.[4] Canadian Conrad Black, who once headed Hollinger International Inc., was convicted of obstruction of justice in 2007 and, along with three former executives of Hollinger, was convicted of siphoning more than $6 million out of the company. Think of the company names Enron, WorldCom, and Tyco, and some of North America's greatest corporate fraud cases come to mind. These types of situations are not limited to the private sector; both government and the not-for-profit sector have had their challenges. Canada's federal government (i.e., the 2004 sponsorship scandal) and a number of provincial governments (i.e., Quebec's construction industry/labour unions/politics, Nova Scotia's legislature expenses scandal, Ontario's Ontario Lottery Corporation expenses scandal, British Columbia's BC rail sale controversy) recently have faced questions surrounding their ethical behaviour. The Orion Foundation (closed in May 2010), a charity supposedly in support of fighting AIDS in Africa, is alleged to actually have been operated for the private gain of its founder, who is alleged to have benefited from hundreds of thousands in management fees, trips to Las Vegas and Cuba, and home renovations, with auditors finding little money actually flowing to the intended cause. So, why are we seeing and hearing about such brash dismissals of what we, in general, define as unethical behaviour?[5]

To answer this question we need to assess ethics within an organization at two levels. The first level has to do with the individuals themselves. The second level is the culture of the organization within which individuals work.

Ethics and the Individual

Ethics is a reflection of the moral principles or beliefs about what an individual views as being right or wrong.

In its purest sense, the term **ethics** reflects the moral principles or beliefs about what an individual views as being right or wrong. These beliefs are built in part around the norms or standards of conduct society views as acceptable behavioural practices. In many ways, ethics can be thought of as an invisible hand that guides each of us as we make decisions.[6] Because ethics is so personal, herein lies the problem, or challenge, with respect to assessing the ethical boundaries within which an individual will operate. Individual motivations, cultural and environmental upbringing, personal pressures, and lack of information or ignorance will all influence—positively or negatively—an individual's ethical behaviour. For some, ethics is based solely on legality: if it is legal, it is therefore ethical. For others, it is about fairness: if the situation I find myself in is perceived to be unfair, then I am entitled to any course of action to right the wrong. Misinterpretation of what society values also plays into questions relating to ethics. If society has demonstrated both reward and a blind eye to particular actions, then such actions will become, in the minds of some individuals, acceptable practices. If self-worth is communicated on the basis of what you have, the size of your house, and the type of car you drive, then individuals will become driven to achieve this level of societal acceptance to the point that it changes the type of person we should aspire to be. Rather than being viewed as a values-based decision model, the desired outcome is viewed as an economics-based decision model.

> In many ways, ethics can be thought of as an invisible hand that guides us as we make decisions.

As managers, we are challenged daily with a multitude of decisions, many of which may carry ethical overtones to some degree. Although decisions associated with financial integrity seem to dominate the spotlight, ethical decision challenges can occur across a wide operational spectrum. Is the discovery of mould or exposed asbestos in the workplace followed by the choice to cover it up rather than remove it unethical behaviour? What about biases associated with employees because of gender or ethnic background? How about not hiring a candidate for a position that requires extensive training because she mentioned she is pregnant, thereby resulting in your belief that she will take a full year of maternity leave when her child is born?

The same holds true for our employees. They, too, are challenged daily with decisions relating to ethics. Is an employee who routinely comes in late, takes extended lunch breaks, and then leaves early from work guilty of unethical behaviour? Is calling in sick when you are not ill in order to have an extended weekend unethical behaviour, even though the company provides you with 12 sick days per year? What about asking the gym where you work out to give you a letter that states you have attended at least three times per week for the past year, as this is what is required for your employer to reimburse you for your membership, when in actuality you have been going to the gym this often for only the past month? How about a bartender who gives a "friend" a couple of free drinks one night because he/she wants to impress him/her, even though the company policy forbids employees to give away drinks?

Taking a poll of your fellow students regarding their responses to the questions asked above might yield some surprising results. Some individuals may view all of the examples provided as unethical behaviour. Others may see unethical actions in only some of the examples. Again, this points to the dilemma of ethics. Each of us has a different interpretation of what is acceptable or non-acceptable behaviour. This interpretation is influenced by our own personal upbringing as well as societal and other external influences. With respect to business decision making in general, the formation of our ethical interpretation—and, therefore, the invisible hand that guides us—comes from four fundamental sources (see Figure 5.1).

FIGURE 5.1 Ethics Wheel

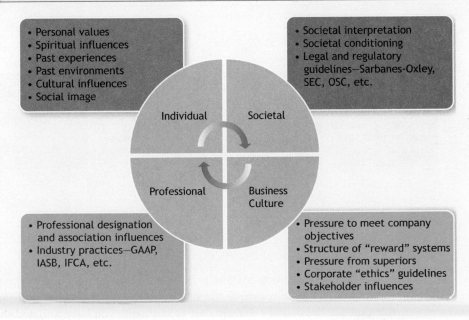

FIGURE 5.2   The "Triple-Yes" Rule

- Yes #1—Does the decision that I am making fall within the accepted values or standards that typically apply to all organizational environments?
- Yes #2—Would I be willing to have this decision communicated to all of my organization's stakeholders, and have it reported on the front page of the newspaper or serve as the lead story on a news channel?
- Yes #3—Would the people in my life with whom I have a significant personal relationship (family, spouse, etc.), as well as managers of other organizations, approve of and support my decision?

These sources are individual, societal, professional, and business culture influences. In making decisions, we need to think in terms not of what is in our personal best interests, but of what is in the best interests of the stakeholders and the public at large. A key aspect of this process is to recognize where the boundaries lie, which should aid us in framing our decisions. As a CEO, I, like many other managers, was challenged a number of times by decisions that carried with them ethical issues. In weighing the ethical considerations associated with these decisions, I utilized what I term the "triple-yes" rule (see Figure 5.2) to determine whether the ethical issues from the decision were effectively dealt with. The triple-yes rule is as follows:

> In making decisions, we need to think in terms not of what is in our personal best interests, but what is in the best interests of the stakeholders and the public at large.

A key aspect of decision-making is being able to live with your decisions. I have found that using the triple-yes approach causes one to fully assess the ethical ramifications of the decisions made and the preservation of personal integrity, which is so fundamental to the role of a manager, employer, and individual in today's society. A second methodology that I have found of value, and use in conjunction with the triple-yes rule, is what I refer to as the ethical decision-making process (see Figure 5.3).

FIGURE 5.3   The Ethical Decision-Making Process

Identify whether an ethical dilemma exists.	In recognizing the dilemma, gather as many facts about the situation as possible.	Evaluate the alternatives available from the perspective of the various ethical positions.	Choose what you believe to be the best alternative, and then "test" it, with a valued adviser, to ensure your correct interpretation.	Initiate your decision and closely monitor the results.

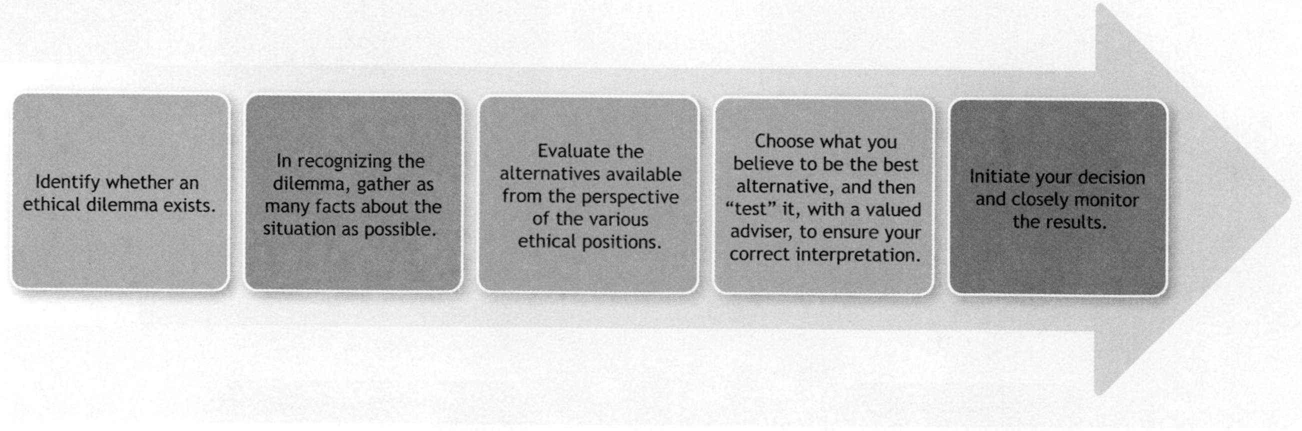

This ethical decision-making process is designed to get a manager to slow down and think through all the consequences of a decision he/she is about to make. With respect to this process, the two key elements are (1) ensuring you have initiated the proper depth of assessment to fully understand the ethical dilemmas and/or consequences that may permeate the decision or exist below its surface, and (2) testing your interpretation of your intended decision with a mentor or key adviser to ensure you are correctly interpreting the situation and that your decision-making frame of reference is complete. This check with a sounding board can—and, in many situations, will—bring forward potential issues you may not have thought of.

The most important skill you can bring to the workplace is your **integrity**. You can be the brightest individual, possessing the best skills, and backed by the best training, but if people cannot trust you, they will not want to work with you. Business is about team work and being able to execute strategy and make decisions in a team-based environment. This means you have to be reliable, trustworthy, and honest. It also means being willing to take responsibility for mistakes you have made. Ethical behaviour, and the decisions associated with it, means being able to look in the mirror each day and know that you are defined by your actions and have the courage to do what is right for the people who work with you and support you.

> **Integrity** is honesty, reliability, ethics, moral judgment.

> The most important skill you can bring to the workplace is your integrity.

Ethics and Culture

Much of this textbook has focused on the need for businesses to build efficient structures and processes in order to succeed. Chapter 7 comments on the need to create a positive work culture where employees are motivated and create high-performance teams to define and execute strategy and tactics in a way that results in a sustainable competitive advantage over their competitors. The responsibility for cultural development does not end, however, with motivation and employee performance. An additional critical component of an organization's culture is the defining of the boundaries of acceptable behaviour for its management team and employees. Just as companies are vulnerable to shifts in market conditions, changes in the intensity of competitive rivalry, disruptive technologies, and changing customer behaviour, so too are they vulnerable to the serious consequences and brand equity erosion that accompanies unethical behaviour within their management and employee ranks. For many organizations, the responsibility for developing policies relating to values, ethics, and financial integrity lies with the organization's **board of directors**. Yes, management needs to execute the policy, but first the board of directors needs to define the parameters of what is meant by ethics and integrity and develop the necessary structure and processes that will enable it to gauge the conscience of the organization. Where a board of directors does not formally exist, advisory boards, equity partners, and individual owners need to ensure the parameters that define ethical behaviour and business integrity are in place and are fully communicated to all employees.

> **Board of Directors** is the term for the governing body of a corporation, comprising individuals chosen or elected to oversee the management of the organization.

> Just as companies are vulnerable to shifts in market conditions, changes in the intensity of competitive rivalry, disruptive technologies, and changing customers, so, too, are they vulnerable to the serious consequences and brand equity erosion that accompanies unethical behaviour within their management and employee ranks.

In forming a culture of ethical behaviour and financial integrity, boards of directors are, in essence, trying to establish the accepted zone of business actions and activities for an organization. The establishment of this structure within the culture keeps an organization's decision-making process and its activities within what is considered to be the "green zone" of accepted business principles around which a company is to operate. The green zone acts as a barrier to keep managers and individuals from straying into the zone of ethical and decision-making uncertainty (the grey zone), or the zone of clearly defined unethical behaviour (the red zone) (see Figure 5.4).

FIGURE 5.4 Zones of Decision Making

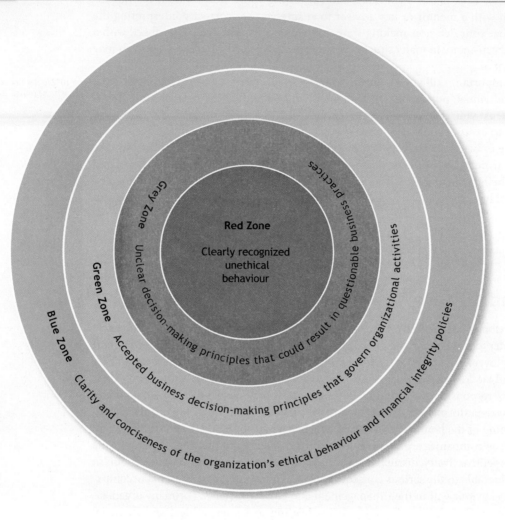

Building this behaviour-containment process begins with the establishment of the mission and core values of the organization and flows through its goals and objectives and right into its business decision-making framework design process. The process, however, does not end here. To truly create a culture of ethical behaviour and financial decision integrity, the board of directors (or owner-representative body) must be active in the ongoing monitoring of the organization and take a leadership role in the tightening of such processes when and where it is required. For example, if a board of directors is expecting its CEO regularly to justify his/her actions and the organization's performance, then this periodic assessment needs to include not only financial and business result benchmarking but also financial integrity and ethical behaviour benchmarking. For boards to effectively create a culture of ethical behaviour and financial integrity, they must commit to the following specific actions:

1. The board must clearly define and establish boundaries of acceptable behaviour and financial integrity, and create performance standards to evaluate adherence to these parameters.
2. These boundaries must be clearly understood and communicated to all employees in the form of a policy or code of conduct. This code of conduct is not limited to financial integrity, but should clearly identify boundaries associated with ethical behaviour, both internal and external, and the consequences for failure to adhere to such a policy or code

of conduct. A key requirement at this level is that senior management fully buy into the development process and the integration of the code of conduct into the organization's policies, protocols, and overall culture.

3. The board of directors must appoint a representative (individual or committee), at the board level, whose responsibility is to audit managerial and employee performance and action in critical areas of this policy or code of conduct. This representative or committee would also be a key participant in reviewing compensation packages and other personnel-related policies to ensure these are not designed in a way which would encourage unethical behaviour.

4. The board of directors must create and support a mechanism for the reporting of ethical concerns within the organization (called **whistleblowing**), with such a process designed in a way that ensures employees who utilize such a process are not penalized or ostracized.

> **Whistleblowing** is the process through which an individual informs someone in authority of a dishonest act or the dishonest behaviour of another person.

5. The board of directors or its representative must interact with senior management and external agencies monitoring the organization's activities in order to discuss issues that could arise with respect to management or employees, and represent the best interests of the organization and its shareholders with respect to questions of ethical behaviour or financial integrity.[7]

> To truly create a culture of ethical behaviour and financial decision integrity, the board of directors (or owner-representative body) must be active in the ongoing monitoring of the organization and take a leadership role in the tightening of such processes when and where it is required.

The key takeaway from the list above is that the board of directors, as representatives of the stakeholders of an organization, must see itself as the creator and sentinel of the organization's conscience. To ensure this occurs, boards must take a lead role in the development of management compensation policies, the shaping of an organization's personnel policy, the review of senior management's performance, and the communication of organizational activities to stakeholders. Board members should never be caught blindsided by events such as what occurred at Nortel. By actively developing an ethical behaviour and financial integrity policy and process, the board of directors and its members can define what is acceptable behaviour for the organization's employees and develop the necessary parameters needed to keep behaviour clearly in the green zone. Should such behaviour move beyond the green zone, the board, via its auditing process, should be able to react to such unethical practices quickly and in accordance to established consequences as defined by its organizational **code of conduct**. The board of directors and the organization's senior management team should also set the expectation and look for full compliance to the organization's code of conduct by supply chain and channel distribution partners. The shared risk and liability exposure that supply chain and distribution partners (as well as all related or interdependent business organizations) have with an organization cannot be overemphasized given the vast global reach of outsourcing and offshoring, which are now embedded into many organizations and their operations.

> **Code of Conduct** is the name for a statement that describes the required responsibilities, actions, and rules of behaviour of an organization's employees.

> The board of directors, as representatives of the stakeholders of an organization, must see itself as the creator and sentinel of the organization's conscience.

The Bombardier "Code of Ethics and Business Conduct," a comprehensive guide to addressing ethical behaviour and financial integrity requirements at Bombardier, is an excellent example. It explains employee obligations with respect to the working environment, business practices and relationships, and interaction with external stakeholders. Bombardier provides this Code of Ethics and Business Conduct in 14 different languages. Information on how to access the code is provided at the end of this chapter.

Regulating Ethics

Recognizing the concerns associated with defining ethics and the challenges organizations face in regulating the behaviour of their employees and management teams, governments and agencies worldwide have created regulations that define how organizations should comply with financial integrity obligations and ethical decision making and behaviour. The criminal acts associated with organizations such as Enron, Tyco, and WorldCom in the United States, led to the passing of the Sarbanes-Oxley Act of 2002 (SOX). In Canada, the equivalent to SOX grew, initially, out of a provincial government of Ontario budget measures act titled Bill 198 (in Canada, securities regulation is handled at the provincial level versus the national level, as is the case in the United States). This was further supplemented by multilateral instruments (regulations) titled 52-108, 52-109, and 52-100, all of which now form the basis of our various provincial securities commission responses to questions of financial integrity and ethical behaviour. These acts, and the accompanying multilateral instruments, focus on protecting the interests of investors and all stakeholders by heightening the financial operational requirements of organizations around such areas as auditor independence, audit committee responsibilities, CEO and CFO accountability for financial reporting and internal controls, faster public disclosure, and stiffer penalties for illegal activities. Similar acts, many that are referred to as Sarbanes-Oxley equivalents, have been adopted in countries globally. Japan's Sarbanes-Oxley Act equivalent is referred to as J-SOX; in Australia, the Sarbanes-Oxley equivalent is referred to as CLERP-9 (Corporate Law Economic Reform Program Act).[8]

The financial crisis of 2008 carried with it a whole new need for financial integrity reform. Whereas the response by governments to business misrepresentation and fraud rests fundamentally in Sarbanes-Oxley (and equivalents), the financial crisis demonstrated heightened concern about the relationship between ethics and risk management. Concerns over the degree of financial leverage that had permeated the marketplace, along with an absence of necessary levels of liquid asset management required to protect against such exposure, is one of many of the market challenges this crisis brought, and around which governments are now seeking to place boundaries. Both international and national organizations—such as the International Accounting Standards Board and the Financial Accounting Standards Board— have called for heightened reporting standardization and regulation to ensure such a situation does not repeat itself. The G20 has agreed, in principle, to the development of high-quality global accounting standards, and initiatives are now underway to make this a reality. A key outcome of all these initiatives will be the development of a single set of global reporting standards that utilize consistent reporting methodologies, provide accurate, unbiased information, and offer full risk disclosure, regardless of the location of the business, organization, or financial institution.[9]

FORENSIC ACCOUNTING

In addition to the heightened regulatory responses to issues pertaining to ethical behaviour and financial integrity, the field of **forensic accounting** has grown significantly over the last decade. Forensic accounting is the integration of accounting, auditing, and investigative skills. Forensic accountants are specialists in looking beyond the numbers in order to interpret what exactly is transpiring within an organization. Forensic accounting audits and investigations are critical to determining the potential extent of damage an organization may have incurred due to unethical employee behaviour or financial integrity issues. They are also key to providing assistance at trial, and during pre-trial discovery periods, in order to provide a professional and credible opinion on the cause and effect of actions taken by individuals, or to settle disputes relating to valuation, economic damage, breach of contract, fraud, and personal injury, to name a few.

Forensic Accounting is the integration of accounting, auditing, and investigative skills.

BUSINESS *in Action*

Walmart

Think that what constitutes ethical business is always cut and dried? Consider the case of Walmart's labour practices, which, from a business ethics standpoint, are anything but. Walmart, the largest company in the world based on sales ($405 billion in 2010), employs more than 2 million people around the globe. Although Walmart has created an impressive number of jobs, the manner in which it treats these employees has come under tremendous scrutiny in recent years. Plaintiffs in *Dukes versus Walmart Stores*, a class-action lawsuit initiated in 2000 but still ongoing in 2010, allege that Walmart systematically discriminates against its female employees with regard to promotion and training opportunities. The suit claims that only 14 percent of Walmart's top managers are female and that, while women make up two-thirds of its hourly employees, they make up only one-third of its salaried managers. In addition, the suit alleges that male employees earn between 5 percent and 15 percent more than their female counterparts, even after taking into consideration seniority, store location, and other factors. On the surface, these look like damning claims that severely undermine Walmart's goal to "honor (founder) Sam Walton's legacy by making the world a better place."

Sometimes, however, statistics can be misleading. Men and women may have different job preferences for hourly positions and could potentially seek promotions at different rates. Indeed, Walmart has countered the suit by claiming that women apply for promotions far less frequently than men do; those who do apply are actually promoted at a higher rate than men are. Perhaps it is Walmart's promotional criteria themselves that are discriminatory. Walmart tends to promote its employees based on their "teamwork, ethics, integrity, and the ability to get along with others." While these criteria appear reasonable on their own, their subjective nature could enable individual managers to act upon their prejudices.

Another somewhat-ambiguous labour issue for which Walmart has been criticized is its policy of locking employees of certain stores in overnight. While this policy is rooted in keeping its employees safe in dangerous neighbourhoods and preventing thefts of its products, some employees have found themselves in emergencies with no way out. Walmart executives maintain that such employees are able to exit the stores through the fire exits, but many employees attest to managerial-level pressure to not use these doors unless there is an actual fire.

Walmart also faces heavy criticism for not allowing its employees to be represented by unions. Critics argue that, as a result, Walmart employees receive substandard pay and benefits. Recent studies have found, however, that wages are competitive with those of other big-box retailers and that,

on top of competitive wages, employees are offered access to retirement plans, profit-sharing, comprehensive insurance coverage, and free confidential professional counselling and assistance, along with child-care discounts and scholarship bonuses.

While Walmart is clearly making an effort to run its business ethically, these examples just go to show how hard it is for any organization to appease all of its critics.[10]

WEB INTEGRATION

For more on Walmart and its operations in Canada, see www.walmart.ca.

What Is CSR (Corporate Social Responsibility)?

LO4, LO5

So, just what is the moral purpose of business? Is it simply to earn profits? Is it limited to providing jobs, buying and selling products and services, and making capital investments that will return a positive ROI (return on investment) to its investors and shareholders? One would like to believe that the responsibilities of business extend beyond this limited moral purpose and strive to create a broader and healthier relationship with society. One reason why corporate social responsibility, as a buzzword, generates such debate in companies, boardrooms, and across society is that, like the definition of ethics, its meaning, and the interpretation of that meaning, is different for almost everyone. For some, it is about not doing anything illegal or dishonourable, or simply supporting a personal or "pet" public project with which a business owner or management team has some connection. For others, it is interpreted as being "philanthropic," in the form of donations to causes that are viewed to be of value to society. A third interpretation might simply be the restoration of environmental degradation that is determined be a consequence of the operations and actions of an organization, thereby protecting the brand and the image of the organization. One thing is certain, however. The old belief that if an action is profitable then it automatically serves the public's best interest no longer applies. To understand the concept of corporate social responsibility, businesses and organizations must first recognize that business and society are interconnected and interdependent. The relationship between the two is not "win or lose," but rather needs to be based upon the fundamental realization that decisions being made within the business organization need to result in profitability, but also need to be in the best interests of society. This is, in essence, what **corporate social responsibility (CSR)** is all about. It is the understanding that the purpose of an organization is to create shared value (business and society) by strategically integrating into its actions a partnership mentality with society where the objectives of both parties are met. It means treating the public interest as a key stakeholder in an organization's operational success, thereby resulting in an attitude shift from "winning for me," or "looking out only for me," to one of participating in activities that enable the organization to win while serving the public good. Making decisions in this broader context is the key to moving the organization beyond the development of a strong corporate reputation and image, which may or may not add value to society, to that of an organization whose core premise is built on creating shareholder value by actively partnering in environmental, social, and public policy programs and initiatives that contribute to the long-term health of society.

> **Corporate Social Responsibility (CSR)** is the understanding that the purpose of an organization is to create shared value (business and society) by strategically integrating into its actions a partnership mentality with society where the objectives of both parties are met.

Why Is CSR Becoming So Important?

Recognizing this underlying uncertainty by many with respect to what CSR is all about, why, then, is it becoming so fundamentally important in the minds of so many executives and members of their boards of directors? The answer lies in what can be thought of as a slow but definitive evolutionary trend on the part of consumers worldwide. A 2010 survey by Penn, Schoen & Berland Associates, in conjunction with Burson-Marsteller and Landor,[11] identified three trends that are assisting in driving the CSR agenda:

1. Despite the financial crisis of 2008, and the recession/recovery of 2009 and 2010, social responsibility has remained an important issue in the minds of more than 75 percent of the consumers surveyed.
2. The ability to leverage CSR initiatives as a key differentiator between two businesses is an important part of an organization's overall value proposition, especially when the organizations against which one is being compared are offering what are otherwise similar products/services.
3. A growing percentage of consumers are willing to spend the same, or more, on products or services from organizations that demonstrate the effective execution of CSR initiatives.

   Although uncertainty remains as to what CSR is or should be, consumers have formed some fairly definitive opinions as to what they believe CSR should represent. For a significant percentage of consumers surveyed, at a minimum, CSR is interpreted to mean that:

1. Companies should be giving back to local communities.
2. Companies need to self-regulate their actions and be willing to be held accountable for their decisions.

Giving back to society; helping others; operating ethically, honestly, and lawfully; being environmentally responsible; offering quality products and services at fair prices; and caring about the impact of their products both globally and the way they are used by their customers were also identified as being fundamental to the CSR definition. Being environmentally responsible and treating employees fairly were identified as key performance measures in terms of what companies need to do to be viewed as more socially responsible. Creating energy-efficient and environmentally sensitive products, providing appropriate levels of pay and benefits for employees, demonstrating equality and equity in hiring practices, caring about the public's well-being, and helping people in need ranked high on the consumer importance list. The results depicted in the Penn, Schoen & Berland Associates survey appear to reinforce similar research conducted by Bonini, McKillop, and Mendonca and published in *The McKinsey Quarterly* in 2007.[12] In a research brief titled "What Consumers Expect from Companies," Bonini, McKillop, and Mendonca identified a number of important areas where consumers felt that companies were doing an unsatisfactory job. The identified areas included transparency about business practices, transparency relating to product and service risks, the development of socially and environmentally responsible products and services, and fair pricing and appropriate accessibility levels of products and services. Consumers also felt that companies performed inadequately with respect to issues associated with political influence, acceptable profit levels, and compensation plans relating to senior management. It should be noted that not all industries or market sectors studied exhibited the same level of concern relating to the perceptions associated with areas of performance identified above. Some market sectors, such as the petroleum industry, exhibited heightened concern in the areas of pricing and environmental impact, while other areas, such as retail, focused their concerns more toward energy consumption, packaging, employee pay and benefits, and the impact of large retailers on local competitors within their communities. For pharmaceutical companies, consumers identified the need for greater equality of health care between fully developed and developing countries as a key concern.

Although the field of CSR is still evolving, the implications of the work done to date are leading managers and boards of directors to three key conclusions relating to the development and execution of business strategy:

1. Consumers are paying attention to companies and their positioning with respect to CSR. Companies perceived as being CSR conscious are finding true opportunities for differentiation, while companies that are lagging in the development and execution of CSR initiatives are being increasingly challenged by individual consumers and activist groups.
2. A true key to creating a positive CSR bond with consumers is by demonstrating, through the products and services being offered, the social benefit of the organization's offerings. This can and, increasingly, will make the difference in the minds of consumers at the time of the purchase decision.
3. Communication strategies are the critical link between consumers and organizations. To be effective in leveraging the CSR initiatives undertaken, organizations need to communicate to their stakeholders how they respect and give back to the communities within which they operate, and how they holistically manage the environment and resource base that they use in the design, development, and delivery of products and services.[13]

The result of the two works identified above, as well as others in this field, point toward the same conclusion: companies that do a better job of understanding consumer perceptions and expectations relating to CSR, and that utilize this knowledge in the delivery and support of their product/service value propositions, ultimately will be more successful in winning the public's trust.

The Interdependency of CSR and Corporate Strategy

With a broad-level understanding of CSR in place, let's now take a closer look at how we can achieve the establishment of a CSR culture into our business organization and systems. Prior to commencing with this discussion, however, it is important to recognize that businesses alone cannot solve all of the world's problems, nor do they have the resources to do so. What businesses can do, however, is identify where they can have a positive effect on society (people, communities, environment) and actively incorporate these initiatives into their overall strategy.

As mentioned in the opening discussion on corporate social responsibility, interpretation as to what this responsibility constitutes does vary by individual and organization. One way to visualize the current variety of approaches associated with corporate social responsibility is to view it via the CSR pyramid (see Figure 5.5).

FIGURE 5.5 CSR Pyramid

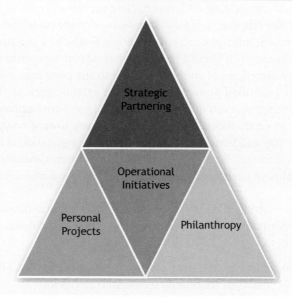

The CSR pyramid illustrates the four primary views associated with the integration of CSR into an organization. At the bottom of the pyramid are the two methodologies that represent arm's-length organizational CSR involvement. At this lower level of the pyramid, participation in CSR initiatives is predominantly focused on personal projects by a business leader(s) or by philanthropic involvement through cash or in-kind donations. Although both of these methodologies do provide a positive contribution to society, in many cases they are the result of decisions that do not significantly influence forward-looking corporate strategy but rather seek to enhance or reinforce the company's image or brand in the marketplace. Their role, in terms of organizational benefits, is largely focused on generic social issues (in many cases, personally driven) external to the organization's operations and long-term competitiveness. An example of "philanthropy," from the base level of the CSR pyramid, is Walmart's decision to provide (through *The Oprah Winfrey Show*) the McGhee sextuplets of Columbus, Ohio, with a generous gift of $250 000 in products and services to help the family transition the six children from infancy to adulthood.[14] An example from the "personal projects" area of the pyramid is the M&M Meat Shops' annual BBQ day in support of the Crohn's and Colitis Foundation of Canada (CCFC). Again, the initiative is noteworthy in that it is in support of a social issue. Mac Voisin, founder and chair of M&M Meat Shops, and M&M franchisees have raised more than $18 million for CCFC.[15] Although these examples are monetary-based, it should be noted that many companies are actively involved, at these levels, within their communities not only in terms of money, but also in terms of time and talent, referred to as "in-kind services." When the YMCA of Kingston, Ontario, made the decision to build a new aquatics centre, the Kingston organization Homestead Landholdings Inc. donated land adjacent to the YMCA and provided engineering design and development support and project management expertise toward the new centre. Without the expertise provided by this commercial development organization, the Kingston YMCA would not have been able to undertake the project without considerable additional expense.

The true integration of CSR initiatives into corporate strategy does, however, require movement beyond the base level. A key transition component to this evolution is for a company to start to view operational systems and tactics with social responsibility outcomes in mind; this forms the middle area of the pyramid, called "operational initiatives." This area is separated from the two base-level areas by the transition from arm's-length social issues to that of social issues impacted as a result of the organization's day-to-day operations. The emphasis here is an awakening, within the organization, of a desire to mitigate social harm as a result of its business system activities (see Figure 5.6). The decision-making focus lies in seeking to enhance efficiencies while, for example, minimizing environmental harm.

FIGURE 5.6 Integration of CSR into Strategy I

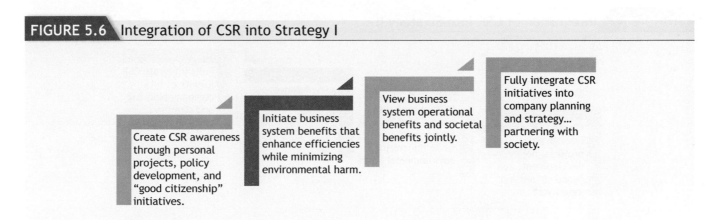

An example is the use of water in the extraction of bitumen by energy-based companies associated with the Alberta oil sands project. Over the past few years, the industry has developed water recycling technology that enables an industry average recycling of 80 percent of the water used (with a number of more efficient companies, the steam injected into the extraction process has reached 90 percent to almost 100 percent recyclable levels). In addition, the current steam to oil bitumen ratio is approximately 3 to 1. With an industry average recycle recovery rate of 80 percent, this results in an estimated 0.6 barrel of (brackish) water per barrel (bbl) of oil produced. Again, new technologies being employed anticipate the ratio of water to bitumen to be reduced to 2 to 1, and industry recycling averages to move up to 90 percent. This will result in a reduction in water use to 0.2 bbl of (brackish) water per bbl of oil.[16] As this is non-potable water taken from deep-well sources, the efficiency gains via recycling and use reduction will reduce the cost base associated with the deep-well water source tapping process and the bitumen extraction process, as well as generate the secondary benefit of enhanced water conservation.

Again, as with the discussion associated with personal projects and philanthropy, this movement toward efficiency enhancements yields positive, although in many cases secondary, benefits to the social agenda. It does not, however, result in the true integration of social responsibility into the strategy development and execution process of an organization. Achieving this level of corporate social responsibility requires a cultural shift within the organization to the top of the pyramid, which is an area titled "strategic partnering." This transition to true corporate social responsibility is identified by two fundamental shifts in the integration of strategy and the social agenda. These two shifts are:

1. The organization's decision-making process evolves from one that responds to social issues identified (in many cases, from external sources) as being pertinent to the organization, to a process that treats corporate social responsibility as a core root of the organization's strategic planning process.
2. The organization recognizes that certain social issues impact the key drivers of its competitiveness and, therefore, seeks to actively develop the necessary social partnerships in order to leverage such competitiveness in a way that positively impacts the people, communities, and environment around which it conducts its business.

Although not always the case, for many companies this is a two-step process (see Figure 5.7). The first phase is shifting the analysis of its business system beyond simply enhancing efficiencies and effectiveness, with secondary benefits derived to society, to that of fully viewing the benefits to society and the organization's operations jointly. This means providing full transparency of its business practices and the risks associated with the products/services it offers, as well as creating socially and environmentally responsible products.

FIGURE 5.7   Integration of CSR into Strategy II

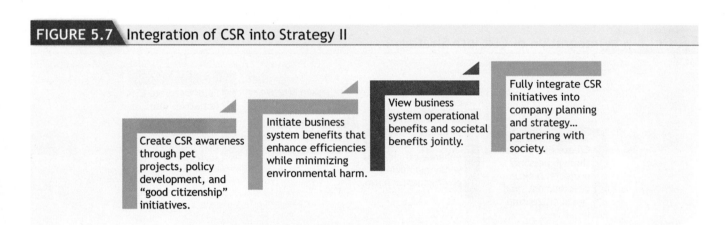

Create CSR awareness through pet projects, policy development, and "good citizenship" initiatives.

Initiate business system benefits that enhance efficiencies while minimizing environmental harm.

View business system operational benefits and societal benefits jointly.

Fully integrate CSR initiatives into company planning and strategy... partnering with society.

The difference between this stage of CSR evolutionary development and the prior one is based on the organization's acknowledgment of its interdependence with society and that the benefits derived from the desire to maximize social benefits across its operations and overall value chain will also assist in maximizing business gains. This means auditing each area within the business system, identifying the positive and negative social benefits that result from the organization's activities within each one, and then seeking to change the organization's activities within each business system area in a way that provides the greatest operational value while achieving the greatest social benefit. This business system evaluation process should enable the organization to identify the negative contributors to the social partnership, thereby providing an opportunity to remedy such practices and transition this work into competitive advantages and new strategic value.

This type of decision making and cultural transition requires leadership from the top. It means conducting a complete risk/reward audit of the full business system and strategic approach to the social partnership. For managers, this approach needs to be conducted on two levels. The first is to identify key social interactions that will occur on a day-to-day basis throughout the organization's business system. By assessing each of these areas of responsibility, managers can then move to step #2, which is to identify those social impacts that are critical to the organization's success and then create definitive and sustainable solutions to such issues. Figure 5.8 provides an example of some of the key factors that could form part of this business system CSR audit process.

FIGURE 5.8 CSR and the Four Quadrants of Managerial Responsibility

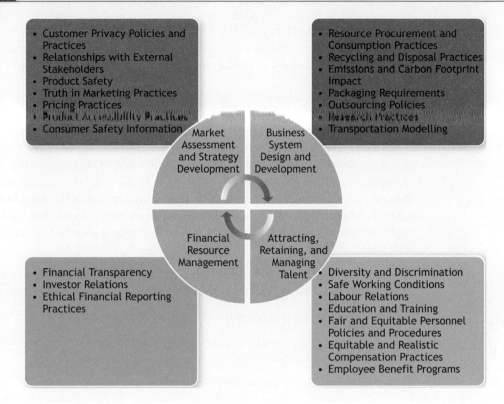

- Customer Privacy Policies and Practices
- Relationships with External Stakeholders
- Product Safety
- Truth in Marketing Practices
- Pricing Practices
- Product Accessibility Practices
- Consumer Safety Information

- Resource Procurement and Consumption Practices
- Recycling and Disposal Practices
- Emissions and Carbon Footprint Impact
- Packaging Requirements
- Outsourcing Policies
- Research Practices
- Transportation Modelling

Market Assessment and Strategy Development

Business System Design and Development

Financial Resource Management

Attracting, Retaining, and Managing Talent

- Financial Transparency
- Investor Relations
- Ethical Financial Reporting Practices

- Diversity and Discrimination
- Safe Working Conditions
- Labour Relations
- Education and Training
- Fair and Equitable Personnel Policies and Procedures
- Equitable and Realistic Compensation Practices
- Employee Benefit Programs

A recent situation in the rental car industry illustrates this interdependency between the organization and social responsibility. In February 2011, the National Highway Traffic Safety Administration (NHTSA) in the United States released the results of a recently completed study of major car rental companies. The study looked at the percentage of vehicles subject to recall that were being rented out to customers prior to the recall defects being repaired. This study was initiated because of growing concerns relating to incidents with rental vehicles and allegations of personal injury and death due to rental car company practices pertaining to recalls. Most notable was an incident involving two California women who were killed in an accident involving an Enterprise Rent-A-Car vehicle. In this particular situation, the car they were driving, a Chrysler PT Cruiser, had an outstanding recall on it. The recall was for a possible leak in the power-steering fluid reservoir, which could result in the engine catching fire. The two women were killed when, while driving, their engine caught fire, resulting in them hitting an oncoming semi-tractor trailer. The investigation that followed showed this same vehicle had been rented out to others prior to the two women, with the recall repairs never made. The follow-up study by the NHTSA continues to raise concerns about the practice of renting out vehicles prior to ensuring that those subject to recalls are repaired. The study confirmed that the big three industry players—Enterprise, Avis/Budget, and Hertz—were continuing to rent vehicles with outstanding recalls on them during the 90 days following the recall notice in more than 50 percent of the recall situations analyzed. In defence of these companies, change is coming. Hertz, for example, has indicated that it now grounds all cars subject to recalls for any type of reason. Hertz cites safety advocates and public attention to the situation as primary reasons for the policy change.[17] "Product safety" is a key CSR impact factor in the "Market Assessment and Strategy Development" zone of the four quadrants of managerial responsibility. For the rental car industry, a true corporate social responsibility approach—which envisions a partnership with society—would, at the forefront of decision making, recognize the need to balance the safety of its customers with its desire to drive volume and profitability from its car rentals. Such an approach would shift away from making decisions on a recall-by-recall basis, interpreting what is a sufficient reason to ground a fleet of vehicles (i.e., making internal judgments as to what may or may not constitute risk to customers), to an operational position where any recall results in the grounding of the vehicles involved until such repairs are made (i.e., what Hertz is now doing).

Steam Whistle Brewing, a micro brewer serving the Ontario, Alberta, and British Columbia markets, is an excellent example of a company whose management team has worked diligently to incorporate green and sustainability-based initiatives across the four quadrants of managerial responsibility and to embed such initiatives into its business practices. Recognized by MediCorp Editors (Globe and Mail) as one of the Top 50 Greenest Companies in 2010, Steam Whistle Brewing reflects, in its operational decision making, the concept of environmental stewardship, resulting in one of the most sustainable breweries in North America.[18] Socially responsible impact factors that illustrate why this organization was awarded this prestigious designation on Earth Day in 2010 include the following:

- Its signature green bottles are made of 30 percent more glass, resulting in a recycling and refill rate that is more than twice the standard brown-bottle-based industry average.

- The brewery is powered using 100-percent green energy from Bullfrog Power.

- Its refrigeration system is chilled using deep water from Lake Ontario (versus conventional refrigeration systems).

- Its delivery trucks are fuelled with biodiesel.

- Its waste diversion program sends leftover food items from brewery events to a local street mission. Organic waste is sent to commercial composting. Cardboard, shrink wrap, broken glass, and sheet metal are all recycled, as well.

- It provides employees with showers and towel service and a secure and sheltered bike storage program, which encourages them to come to work via a "clean air commute."

- Its energy systems and its water savings systems have resulted in significant reductions to water (two-thirds reduction) and energy use (25-percent reduction).

Organizations that are able to climb to the top of the pyramid and develop the necessary social partnerships in a way that positively impacts the people, communities, and environments around which they conduct their business are those that are able to fuse and synthesize their organization's values and financial aspirations into such a partnership (see Figure 5.9). These organizations have learned how to leverage their business competencies and capabilities to utilize their resource base and their expertise to drive maximum benefit for society and, as a consequence, themselves as well.

> Organizations that are able to climb to the top of the pyramid and develop the necessary social partnerships in a way that positively impacts the people, communities, and environment around which they conduct their business are those that are able to fuse and synthesize their organization's values and financial aspirations into such a partnership.

In reaching these levels, organizations and their management teams recognize that the long-term health of society is fundamental to the long-term health of the organization; the two are interconnected versus being separate and distinct. As was indicated earlier, the

FIGURE 5.9 Integration of CSR into Strategy III

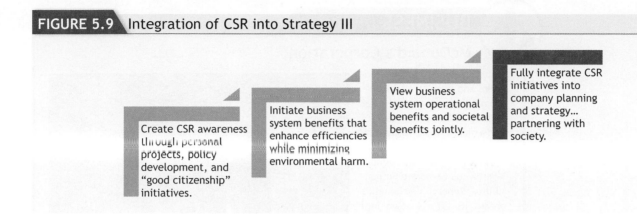

Create CSR awareness through personal projects, policy development, and "good citizenship" initiatives.

Initiate business system benefits that enhance efficiencies while minimizing environmental harm.

View business system operational benefits and societal benefits jointly.

Fully integrate CSR initiatives into company planning and strategy... partnering with society.

achievement of this level of fusion between society and the organization needs to be the result of a focused execution strategy across critical business system components and long-term strategic planning and positioning. An example of the fusing of positive societal impact with corporate strategy and business system needs is Gap Inc. Women make up 70 percent of the Gap's workforce, with many of these employees residing in developing nations. Recognizing that the long-term health of Gap Inc. is based on the ability of these workers to excel in the workplace, in 2007 Gap Inc. initiated the P.A.C.E. program (Personal Advancement and Career Enhancement). This program focuses on training female garment factory workers to have both workplace and social skills, so that they can develop the efficiency skills needed to handle their existing jobs as well as the professional and personal skills needed to advance. The company realizes that by moving these workers beyond their entry-level jobs, they personally advance and thrive and so too do the communities in which they live. According to GAP Inc. and its partners, the International Center for Research and Women and the Swasti Health Resource Center, more than 3500 women have participated in the program, and women who completed the program were promoted 4.7 times faster. Initially implemented in India, the program has now been expanded to Bangladesh, Cambodia, China, and Vietnam.

Chip market leader Intel Corporation also has reformulated its philanthropic approach over the past few years. Again, it is a situation where Intel has redirected its efforts in a way that works with its business strategy—the end result is the creation of a strong society/business partnership. For example, one sector where Intel focuses its monetary and organizational support lies in the area of engineering and math education. Intel has invested in teacher training programs in partnership with ministries of education, with the end result of providing support to more than 8 million teachers in 70 countries. The company also provides resources to support the Intel Science Talent Search, one of the oldest student science competitions in the United States. The Intel International Science and Engineering Competition attracts more than 6 million participants worldwide for awards and scholarships exceeding $4 million.

For companies like Gap Inc. and Intel Corporation, the anticipated benefits of investments in social partnership go beyond simply enhancing the corporate reputation. For these companies, the social strategic partnerships they become engaged in are all integrated with the corporate strategy with the intent of producing long-term value creation and competitive advantage. The investments in social initiatives are complementary to the organization's business goals and objectives. Although the benefits derived may be longer-term, if properly executed the intended outcomes of reduced business risk, increased revenue, or operational cost reductions can be realized as a result of such social integration strategies.[19]

BUSINESS *in Action*

McDonald's Corporation

What does a comprehensive ethics and corporate social responsibility program look like? One would be hard-pressed to find a more comprehensive one than that of the McDonald's Corporation. In its annual "Worldwide Corporate Responsibility Report," McDonald's breaks its efforts down into seven categories: corporate governance and ethics, sustainable supply chain, nutrition and well-being, environmental responsibility, employment experience, and community.

McDonald's ensures strong corporate governance via a variety of means. First, its corporate governance principles require that all of the members of its board (save for its CEO and president) be independent of management. All directors of its board must also abide by a code of conduct, and six standing committees are charged with key roles in contributing to the oversight of management and the decisions management makes. McDonald's regularly updates its Standards of Business Conduct to reflect its ethical ambitions.

McDonald's ensures the sustainability of its supply chain by sourcing fish from fisheries with favourable sustainability ratings and beef from abattoirs with certified animal welfare policies, and has begun to maintain an environmental scorecard for suppliers of its other agricultural products. McDonald's has also conducted a number of initiatives to reduce waste in its packaging; in 2008, 82 percent of its consumer packaging came from renewable materials and 30 percent came from recycled fibre. McDonald's participates in a number of environmental initiatives, such as the LEED Retail Pilot Program, and has created a Global Energy Council to compile best-energy practices from its worldwide operations.

While maintaining a historically unhealthy menu (it is fast food, after all!), McDonald's has made a concerted effort to improve the healthiness of its offerings by eliminating trans fats from its U.S. restaurants and by introducing healthier options, such as salads and wraps, in recent years. McDonald's also provides nutritional information for all of its products.

McDonald's seeks to augment its employee experience by providing them with retirement plans, profit-sharing, and other benefits. McDonald's also operates seven Hamburger Universities, which serve as training centres for restaurant employees and corporate staff. McDonald's strives to create a comfortable environment for people of all cultures and backgrounds to work in, and has received several diversity awards.

McDonald's community involvement includes a long history of Olympic sponsorship and various philanthropic initiatives (on local, regional, national, and international scales). Undoubtedly, however, McDonald's Corporation's best-known charitable initiative is the Ronald McDonald House Charities.

McDonald's Corporation's wide-ranging efforts in CSR and ethics have certainly done well for its business. *Forbes* magazine has named it one of America's most inspiring companies as determined by consumers.[20]

WEB INTEGRATION

Want to learn more about McDonald's Corporation's corporate social responsibility policy? Visit **www.mcdonalds. ca/en/community/social.aspx.**

The Challenge Behind CSR Implementation

Given what we have discussed about CSR up to this point, we legitimately should wonder why all organizations have not raced swiftly to the top of the CSR pyramid. For many companies, transitioning to the top of the CSR pyramid would require a significant change not only in operating procedures and processes, but also in the entire culture of the organization.

In many industries, such a change will require significant investment up front and potentially an additional cost layer to the operating budget. CSR research does indicate that a majority of customers have indicated a willingness to pay more for products/services, but the unanswered question is just how much more. The risk for companies willing to consider a CSR transformation is, of course, "If we do it and our competitors do not, how will that impact our competitiveness?" A second and equally pressing problem lies in quantifying the benefits of CSR initiatives. In other words, how do we assign a financial value to enhanced corporate reputation, improved employee recruitment and retention, or the attractiveness of long term, value-based social initiatives? In addition to the initial potential outcome value of CSR initiatives, considerable uncertainty exists in how to realistically create and measure the metrics needed to evaluate these very subjective areas. Finally, although CSR ideas may appear to be logical, under normal economic conditions what will be the impact toward sustaining these initiatives in periods of global market or company distress? Will shareholders be willing to sacrifice returns during such periods to maintain a longer-term social contract in areas that benefit non–financially committed stakeholders?

The answers to the questions posed above lie in the ability of management and the board of directors to create the necessary data that demonstrate how CSR initiatives are—and why they need to be—fully integrated into an organization's strategy and operations. This means developing the very metrics identified above, which will enable investors to understand their value and to see how a conscious effort toward the "triple bottom line" of people, planet, and profits really does enhance the final P—profits. Such an outcome can be achieved only by a disciplined approach to business planning that identifies CSR as a core pillar within the strategic planning process. Equally challenging for management and the board of directors will be the task of communicating the societal partnership benefits to the external stakeholders and communities while communicating, internally, the win/win nature of the arrangement.

A Note Pertaining to Not-for-Profits

The March 8, 2011, front-page headline on the *Toronto Star* was "Game Over for Shady Charity"; the accompanying subheading indicated that an organ donation association's licence had been yanked after an audit confirmed the charity misspent cash it raised. The article went on to detail how the Organ Donation and Transplant Association of Canada, which made emotional pleas to Canadians to help save lives, had in actuality spent most of the money it raised on fundraising fees and administrative expenses. In fact, it was reported to be one of six health-based charities where more than 70 percent of the amount raised was spent for reimbursing telemarketers and covering other administrative expenses (the CRA, in 2009, communicated a directorate that indicated 35 percent was the maximum safe level for fundraising costs). The audit also found that the charity had initiated practices designed to hide its high costs. This resulted in the charity reporting that only 20 percent of revenues raised went to fundraising and administrative expenses, when the audit concluded that 71 percent of the dollars raised were used to cover such expenses.[21]

For not-for-profits and charities, the goodwill associated with the work they do and the integrity with which they conduct themselves are fundamental to their existence. Unlike for-profit entities, which can use private equity as a basis for acquiring the capital needed to sustain themselves, not-for-profits are heavily dependent upon monetary gifts (donations) from others to keep their operations rolling. For each Organ Donation and Transplant Association, there are hundreds of charities that conduct their business operations in a fully transparent and ethical manner. The challenge for these not-for-profits is how to communicate to potential donors the legitimacy of their work in a donation environment that is becoming increasingly concerned about fraud. Canadians are generous supporters of the not-for-profit sector, but recent survey results reflect a growing uneasiness with the industry as a whole. Canada Helps and Capital One Canada completed their second annual charity fraud awareness quiz in early 2010. The results reported that more than 65 percent of Canadians were worried about fraudulent charities, and more than 50 percent indicated they were less likely to give to charities because of fraud concerns.[22] For managers of charities and not-for-profits, these numbers are nothing but alarming. Not-for-profits and charities must earn and maintain the trust of Canadians in order to be the recipients of their generosity. This means that these same managers must be able to communicate to Canadians the legitimacy of their organizations, be able to provide clear outcomes for the programs and services that they are providing, and be fully able (and credible) to provide prospective donors with an accounting for how their organization spends their money.

Management Reflection—It Is All About Trust

Business courses worldwide continually reinforce the need for organizations to encourage entrepreneurship, innovation, and risk taking. Managers and executives have hundreds of articles and books at their disposal on how to manage and motivate their employees. Organizations continuously look for ways to empower people to develop new processes and operating efficiencies. So, just what is the common thread that allows for all these things to occur within successful organizations? The common thread is trust. Trust is fundamental to all that we do and to everyone that we interact with. As indicated in this chapter, the best asset you can bring to work, on a day-to-day basis, is your integrity. This means being honest, respecting the dignity of others, listening before you speak, being accountable for your mistakes, doing what you say you are going to do, demonstrating transparency in the decisions you make, not presuming you have all the answers, and thanking people for their feedback. Successful managers are open and authentic. They encourage open discussion, communicate their concerns, actively discuss risk, and don't manipulate people or distort facts.

The same holds true for organizations. Trust is a two-way street. To effectively create a societal partnership, organizations need to gain the trust of the external stakeholders who will be impacted by the decisions being made. Corporate social responsibility is just that. It is all about trust. It is making sure that other parties do not perceive the existence of a hidden agenda. It is ensuring that the organization is not distorting or hiding the facts in order to create private gain. It is not trying to spin our public relations in a way that sugarcoats a broken commitment. It is a willingness to address the tough actions quickly and not break the confidence of others when doing so.

As managers, we have an obligation to our employees, our organization, our society, and our planet to make decisions that benefit all, and to do the right thing. Remember, our value and our rewards come from what we do.

Chapter Summary

The purpose of this chapter is to provide students with an understanding of the importance of ethics in the decision-making process, for both individuals and managers. In this regard, the chapter focuses on identifying the critical elements that make up the interpretation of ethical behaviour and financial integrity. It also discusses the challenges that managers, employees, and organizations and their boards of directors face in attempting to build and maintain an ethical environment. The chapter also discusses the concept of corporate social responsibility (CSR) and the development of societal partnerships as a core component of strategic planning. The chapter comments on the growing importance of CSR, the various levels of CSR that exist in today's market environment, and the transition process that occurs as organizations become more connected to the societal partners they influence and, ultimately, can work with for the betterment of all. The chapter also provides a summary overview of the challenges organizations face in implementing CSR into their business strategy. The chapter closes with a discussion of the importance of integrity in the not-for-profit field and the need to demonstrate full operational transparency as a key success factor within this process. The management reflection offers some final comments on the importance of trust as the basis of all decision making and human interaction within the workplace.

Developing Business Knowledge and Skills

KEY TERMS

Ponzi scheme *p. 119*

ethics *p. 120*

integrity *p. 123*

board of directors *p. 123*

whistleblowing *p. 125*

code of conduct *p. 125*

forensic accounting *p. 126*

corporate social responsibility (CSR) *p. 128*

QUESTIONS FOR DISCUSSION

1. What do you feel is the main challenge for managers and boards of directors with respect to ingraining ethics into an organization's culture and decision-making environment?

2. What is the difference between ethics and financial integrity? How are they interconnected?

3. What does a board of directors and an organization's senior management team need to do in order to ensure that decision making stays in the "green zone" of accepted business principles that govern organizational activity?

4. With new initiatives such as Bill 198 and Sarbanes-Oxley (SOX) put into place, and new global reporting standards coming on-stream in this decade, do you feel that government and regulatory bodies on their own can fully define and manage business ethics and ensure financial integrity? Why, or why not?

5. What do you feel is the major barrier preventing organizations from reaching the top of the CSR pyramid?

6. Do you feel that consumer concerns relating to CSR will accelerate in the years to come? Will this be enough to fundamentally change the current view of CSR around the board of directors' table?

QUESTION FOR INDIVIDUAL ACTION

Arrange an interview with an owner of a small or medium-sized business, or the executive director or CEO of a not-for-profit in your community. Ask him/her if they have created a Code of Conduct for employees. Ask him/her, as well, if any formal ethics-based training has been initiated within the organization. Be prepared to share the results of your interview with your class.

TEAM EXERCISE

Using Bombardier Inc.'s Code of Ethics and Business Conduct[23] and your university/college's academic integrity policy as templates, create a Code of Conduct for this business course. Be sure to make your code all-inclusive, commenting on areas beyond simply academic honesty. Look to broaden your policy to include commentary pertaining to work environment, peer and external stakeholder relationships, team-based exercise support, and classroom practices. Present your Code of Conduct to your peers for review and discussion.

Case for Discussion

Larry Pollock, President and Chief Executive Officer of the Canadian Western Bank Group (CWB), paused to consider his company's newest growth opportunity. Larry has held his position with CWB since 1990; over the past 20 years he has led the company to aggressive growth, accomplished primarily through acquisitions. In the past three years alone, CWB's revenues have increased by 47 percent, to $320 million; profits have also increased by 47 percent, to $106 million. CWB currently maintains 37 branches spanning from British Columbia to Manitoba.

Larry is currently considering whether to acquire Cash Mart, a payday loan company with 40 locations of its own and $50 million in annual revenues. This acquisition would, undoubtedly, make good business sense, as it would represent a logical expansion of CWB's lending business that could eventually bring in future customers to its banks. CWB has a strong brand in Western Canada that could be leveraged to increase Cash Mart's business. Larry's concerns about this potential deal, however, lie with the ethical issues associated with it.

Cash Mart operates under the typical model for payday lenders. It offers two-week loans for amounts between $100 and $500 to customers who typically cannot receive credit elsewhere. Cash Mart charges $15 in interest on a $100 loan, which represents an annual percentage rate (APR) of 390 percent and an effective annual rate (EAR) of 3685 percent. Interest rates above 60 percent were once considered criminal in Canada, but Federal Bill C-26 recently amended the criminal code to exempt payday lenders from this restriction.[24]

Cash Mart (and other payday lenders) charges such high rates of interest in part to compensate for the high default rates on payday loans that are typically provided to customers who have such poor credit that they cannot approach banks or other traditional lenders. Payday lenders have long been criticized for exploiting the poor for profit; their exorbitant interest rates are difficult to repay on time and, thus, create a cycle of dependency on expensive credit, doing nothing to encourage borrowers to save. Critics of the industry argue that payday borrowers do not understand how quickly interest rates will compound; they also charge that payday lenders behave negligently by not educating their customers on the value of saving and building a strong credit rating. Payday lenders can, however, provide a valuable service to those who use it responsibly. People who need a one-time emergency source of cash benefit tremendously from Cash Mart's services.[25]

QUESTIONS

CWB's Web site claims that "it's the fact that (they) bank on people that sets (them) apart" (http://www.cwbank.com). Does acquiring a payday lender compromise that mission? Should Larry go ahead with acquiring Cash Mart, or should he stay out of the payday loans business?

Practise and learn online with Connect. Connect resources include additional and interactive study exercises, videos, and practice quizzing, as well as additional material you won't find in the printed text.

6 Developing a Business Strategy

Learning Objectives

This chapter is designed to provide students with:

Lo1 An understanding of the concept of business strategy

Lo2 An appreciation of the importance of developing a strategy within a business operation

Lo3 An overview of the key areas around which business strategy is developed

Lo4 Exposure to the fundamentals of the strategy planning and implementation process

Lo5 An understanding of the unique strategy planning requirements of the not-for-profit sector

Snapshot—What to Expect in This Chapter

This chapter provides students with an introductory overview of business strategy and the strategic planning process that management teams undertake in order to determine the market position they visualize their companies owning, and the actions they intend to pursue, within the market segments in which they choose to compete. The content emphasized in this chapter includes the following:

- The Concept of Business Strategy
  - Strategy Made Simple

- Core Elements for Assessing Business Strategy
  - Purpose
  - Markets
  - Products and Services
  - Resources
  - Business System Configuration
  - Responsibility and Accountability

- The Strategic Planning Process
  - I/E (Internal/External) Analysis
  - Competitive Advantage(s) Identification
  - Strategy Development
  - Strategy Execution

- Strategy Challenges in the SME (Small and Medium-Size Enterprises) Sector

- Strategic Planning in the NFP (Not-for-Profit) Sector (Social Economy)

- Management Reflection—The Need to Plan

From the Student's Perspective

When I think of business strategy, I think of how the organization is achieving its goals. In other words, a strategy is a plan. It is a plan that directs the organization's business operations so that, eventually, it is able to achieve its goals. Strategy is what helps provide greater value to the customer through a different, yet sustainable, product or service offering.

It sounds easy, right? Well, strategy and strategy formulation are actually very challenging. Tireless lists of concepts and principles exist that highlight dominant theories behind strategic positioning. There is no single principle that everyone adheres to, no guiding beacon that says businesses should operate this way in order to be successful. This makes strategy difficult.

Yet, with some help from a few guiding principles, all organizations can be successful at strategy formulation and implementation. It is important that organizations first understand themselves. Accordingly, questions like "What are we good at? What are our core competencies? How far do we want to penetrate our current market or new markets? What products or services do we want to provide? How would a competitive advantage be gained?" must all be answered. Once defined, an organization must identify unique activities for implementation. These unique activities should differentiate the organization from its rivals and should be difficult to imitate. Tradeoffs and tough choices must be willingly made in order to sustain these unique activities as competitors begin to reposition themselves against the organization. Finally, all activities should consistently fit together so that they reinforce each other, thwarting any imitators as the strategy is being implemented.

Simply put, in my perspective the essence of strategy is the identification and linkage of unique activities that differentiate a company from its rivals and provide a sustainable competitive advantage. All in all, Michael Porter summarizes the importance and difficulty of strategy very clearly: "If there were only one ideal position, there would be no need for strategy."

Margaret Walsh graduated in 2008 with a Bachelor of Commerce, Honours degree. In 2009, Margaret received her Master of Industrial Relations degree from Queen's University. She is currently working in the rail industry and is enjoying life to the fullest.

BUSINESS *in Action*

Walmart Canada: Changing the Communication Strategy

Have you watched a Walmart commercial lately? If you have, did you pick up on the shift in the message communicated to consumers? Yes, Walmart still emphasizes price, but the company also recognizes that, as technology improves and competitors become more cost efficient, its price advantage may become less pronounced. Walmart Canada also understands that although "low prices" may be a powerful message to some market segments, it is not necessarily the prime purchase motivator for others. Although some Walmart Canada commercials will continue to reinforce the price message, a number of others will focus on shifting the message to savings. Why? It's all part of Walmart's new strategy to reach more customers and to create more distance between its brand and that of its competitors. For many customers, low prices can also imply low quality. The shift to savings is designed to send the message that spending less by buying products at Walmart will enable its customers to enjoy a better lifestyle. Hence the new Walmart tag line, "Save Money. Live Better." Why change now? As part of its recent strategic planning process for its Canadian operations, Walmart conducted marketing research on who its customers are and what additional potential customers it could tap into. Walmart's core customers remain the price-value shopper, thus the reason why a portion of its communication strategy will focus on reinforcing the low prices message. Walmart, however, also found that two additional market segments are worth pursuing: the "brand aspirationals" and "price-sensitive affluents." Simply stated, "brand aspirationals" are individuals who want specific brands at lower prices. Walmart's size and buying power have enabled it to attract to its stores name brands such as Dell and Sony, and offers them at prices that are lower than those of its leading competitors. "Price-sensitive affluents" are generally older consumers who are looking to save money by being more intelligent shoppers. They take the approach that nobody should pay more than they have to when purchasing a product. Getting a deal makes them feel smarter. Walmart's research had identified that these three market segments make up more than 60 percent of the market. With consumers worrying about the economy, and with saving money becoming a higher priority, Walmart's new strategy is designed to provide the solution. You can save money and live better by buying the products you need at Walmart. For Walmart Canada, the shift in the communication message is but one part (albeit an important one) of its new strategy to increase its market share in Canada. Integrated into its strategy is its shift to 200 000-sq.-ft. supercentres in the suburbs and the development of smaller (100 000-sq.-ft.) yet full-service operations (including groceries) for urban and city centre locations. With groceries being one of the most requested items by customers in its current store locations, Walmart Canada fully intends to continue its aggressive expansion in this area. After all, customers stopping in to pick up groceries become prime candidates for purchasing Walmart's general merchandise products. The current strategy also calls for the addition of an estimated 30 new stores annually, as Walmart strives to make its locations more convenient

to its potential new customers. With over 300 locations nationally, Walmart Canada's focus is to aggressively continue to grow its reach in Canada. Carrying national brand electronics, maintaining its position as the number-one seller of toys, and actively competing in the grocery and fresh food sector are all part of this vision and strategic initiative.[1]

WEB INTEGRATION

Want to learn more about Walmart Canada? Go to **www.walmart.ca.**

The Concept of Business Strategy

LO1, LO2

The development of an organization's business strategy is fundamentally one of the most important responsibilities of a senior management team or, in the case of a small business, the business owner. For an organization to be successful over the long term, managers need to have a game plan as to where and how to compete in the markets in which they intend to serve. As we pointed out in Chapter 1, the long-term success of an organization, and its ability to evolve and grow, is predicated on two fundamental principles (see Figure 6.1):

FIGURE 6.1 Interdependency of Strategy and Tactics

1. the ability to define and create a strategic direction and market position for the organization (strategic plan); and
2. the ability to execute the core tactical initiatives within the plan in a manner that ensures the organization's success.

This chapter deals in detail with the first part of this equation, the development of a business strategy. It also provides an overview of the execution of this strategy to achieve the organization's objectives (covered more extensively in the remaining chapters of this textbook).

> The long-term success of an organization and its ability to evolve and grow is predicated on two fundamental principles: the ability to define and create a strategic direction and market position for the organization (strategic plan), and the ability to execute the core tactical initiatives within the plan in a manner that ensures the organization's success.

Strategy Made Simple

For many students, the concept of business strategy is one of the most difficult to understand and apply. This is largely due to the fact that strategies are generally customized for each business, given the market conditions that they face and the desired business goals they aspire to reach. In its most basic form, business strategy is all about understanding what opportunities exist in the marketplace and which ones should be pursued. Based on these conclusions, managers then have to decide upon their path of action in pursuit of capitalizing on the opportunities chosen (see Figure 6.2). Think of strategy simply as being summarized by the answers to two

FIGURE 6.2 Business Strategy in Simple Terms

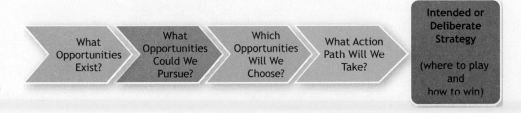

questions: "Where do we want to play," and "How do we plan to win." By answering these two questions, we develop the seeds for what is called our intended or deliberate strategy; that is, the specific direction and actions we plan to take in order to guide our organization's decisions going forward. Whether we can hold our course or are forced to change our direction is based on our abilities to execute our strategy, given competitive actions and external market influences.[2]

Core Elements for Assessing Business Strategy

LO3

For business managers, the development of a business strategy means making decisions and determining direction in six key areas (see Figure 6.3):

1. Purpose
2. Markets
3. Products and services
4. Resources
5. Business system configuration
6. Responsibility and accountability

Purpose

Purpose refers to the mission of the organization and the vision its managers or owner(s) have

> **Mission** defines an organization's purpose or reason for existence.

for the business. **Mission** refers to the fundamental purpose the business has identified as being its predominant reason for existence. Mission statements usually identify the broad goals around which a company was formed. They also can reflect on how an organization will get to where it wants to go. For example, Walmart's mission is currently identified as "helping people save money so they can live better." Canadian Tire Corporation's mission, or statement of purpose, is "We exist to create customers for life and shareholder value." Bombardier Inc.'s mission statement (shown on the next page) seeks to identify the core essence of what Bombardier is all about.

FIGURE 6.3   Core Elements of a Strategy

BUSINESS *in Action*

Bombardier Inc.'s Mission Statement

Our mission is to be the world's leading manufacturer of planes and trains.
We are committed to providing superior value and service to our customers and sustained profitability to our shareholders by investing in our people and products.
We lead through innovation and outstanding product safety, efficiency and performance.
Our standards are high. We define excellence—and we deliver.

Source: www.bombardier.com

Mission statements, when combined with ethics policies and statements of behaviour or values, guide the overall direction and activities of a business. Decisions made by managers within an organization should reinforce the mission the company is aspiring toward.

A **vision** statement is a forward-thinking statement that defines what a company wants to become and where it is going. Walmart's vision is to become the worldwide leader in retailing. Jim Treliving and his partner George Melville's initial vision for Boston Pizza was to have it become Canada's #1 casual dining chain.[3] Canadian Tire Corporation's vision statement (shown below) identifies what the company aspires to become and how it plans to achieve it.

> **Vision** is a forward-thinking statement that defines what a company wants to become and where it is going.

BUSINESS *in Action*

Canadian Tire Corporation

Our vision is to create sustainable growth by being a national champion and Canada's most trusted company. We will grow from our strengths—leveraging our brands, core capabilities, assets and extraordinary people.

Source: http://corp.canadiantire.ca

As part of developing and reviewing a business strategy, managers or business owners will revisit their mission and vision statements to ensure they are still applicable and represent desired outcomes for the firm's direction and decision-making process. Required changes will be made at the front end of the strategic planning process. A review of these two "purpose" fundamentals is a necessary first step in deciding where and how to compete.

Markets

Markets refers to the specific markets or market segments the business sees itself competing in. As part of the strategy development process, managers and owners need to assess their success in existing markets and evaluate the potential of new markets. Markets should be assessed in terms of their current and future profitability and growth potential. Markets that represent opportunities for future growth and enhanced profitability will receive greater managerial attention and resource support. Markets that have become unprofitable or marginally profitable and lack significant future growth will be evaluated in terms of market exit strategies or **harvesting** strategies.

> **Harvesting** is a strategy that reflects a reduced commitment to a particular market given its perceived weak future growth or profitability potential.

Products and Services

Products and Services refers to a review of the current products and services offered by a business, as well as potential new products/services that are to be added to the products portfolio. Over time, products and their related services can become obsolete or no longer desired by the organization's customers. This can be the result of technological innovation, changes in consumer needs and tastes, or new direct substitutes for existing products and services being offered by competitors. A critical part of the strategy development process is to determine which products and related services are to remain part of a business's portfolio, as well as which are to receive additional R&D (research and development) support, and which new ones are to be added. Examples of strategic business decisions regarding services could relate to whether customers should be offered payment terms for buying products, whether financing options should be offered by the company itself or sourced to an external financing supplier, and so on. For example, in 2006 the Hudson's Bay Company (HBC) made a strategic decision to sell its credit card division to GE Money (a division of General Electric Canada) for $370 million. This sale resulted in a shift in responsibility for accepting credit card applications and managing credit risk from HBC to GE Money. For HBC, it meant an immediate influx of money and elimination of the credit risk of providing its customers with credit card purchase options. For GE Money, it represents an opportunity to acquire a customer base of 3.1 million active customers who use credit for purchases (approx. $1.1 billion in value) and—assuming it properly manages this risk, using its expertise and many years of experience—to profit annually from managing this new addition to its product portfolio.[4]

Resources

Resources refers to the allocation of a business's resources in support of its strategic decisions. Businesses, like all of us, have only so many resources. There are capacity limitations as to the amount of products businesses can produce, the amount of money they can commit to projects, and the variety of tasks their workforce can handle at any given time. In recognizing this, as part of the strategy development process businesses must make decisions on where to allocate these limited resources. Similarly, businesses may not have the expertise in-house to effectively execute strategies. In this situation, managers will have to decide if they need to go out and acquire required expertise, or if their plans need to be modified or redirected due to the lack of competencies or technology within a business in order to succeed with a desired strategic direction. The plant closings and dealership terminations by General Motors and Chrysler that dominated the news in 2008 and 2009 illustrate the process of companies making decisions relating to resource allocations as they seek to divest of areas that are not profitable and reallocate such resources to areas that will support profitability and growth within the business.

Business System Configuration

Business System Configuration refers to modifying the organization's infrastructure and the way it does business to ensure the success of the plan. This could mean making changes to the organization's distribution outlets, warehousing or product delivery, plants and facilities, manufacturing or assembly processes, marketing campaign, and so on. (The development and management of business systems is covered in more detail in Chapter 7.) A good example of a business configuration strategy shift could be the addition of an ecommerce-based Web site for the sale of products/services. Another example is Avon Products Inc.'s (fragrance, cosmetics, skin care, hair care) 2007 restructuring of its distribution channel in order to reposition Avon in the global marketplace. This involved a decision to close some smaller distribution centres and replace them with a larger, state-of-the-art regional centre, as well as an earlier decision to expand the availability of Avon products beyond its in-home salesforce to offer products online and through Avon's own mall-based kiosks and retail outlets. In entering the Chinese market, Avon made a further shift in its distribution strategy by selling its products not only through an in-home salesforce but also through alternate cosmetics-focused retail operations, such as its partnership with Masson, a well-known direct seller of beauty products in China.[5]

Responsibility and Accountability

Responsibility and Accountability refers to identifying who within the business will be responsible for each aspect of the strategic plan. A fundamental underlying element to the success of a business strategy is to identify the key objectives to be achieved and who will be responsible for their attainment. To assist managers in meeting such objectives, initiatives within a strategic plan are built around what are termed SMAC principles: specific, measurable, actionable, and controllable. (Another popular acronym in this regard is SMART: specific, measurable, actionable, realistic, and time sensitive.) For example, a manager who is given an objective to "increase sales" has little to base his overall effort on or success against, and accountability measures for evaluation purposes are not really identified or communicated. Modify this directive based on SMAC (or SMART) principles, and it becomes "increase the sales revenue of products A, B, and C by 10 percent over the upcoming three-month period, with 50 percent of the sales growth coming from new customer accounts and 50 percent coming from higher sales to existing customers." The manager in charge of products A, B, and C now has a much clearer idea of the objective he/she has been given, and understands the accountability measures against which he/she will be evaluated. These SMAC (or SMART) principles could be further expanded to define which customer segments will be attacked, how much money will be provided for promotional purposes (budget), and how staff involved will be rewarded for the success of this initiative. Strategic plans must identify who is responsible for each element within the plan and also identify how accountability for the success of the plan will be measured.

As you have probably sensed, considerable crossover and interaction exists among the six areas noted in this section. Developing a business strategy looks at each of these areas individually, but also holistically in determining the road an organization should take. Decisions and adjustments relating to products and markets impact the business configuration. Likewise, a revision to the organization's mission or a shift in its vision can result in its strategy taking a whole new course. Competitor actions and the resources that an organization has at its disposal will influence decisions on where and how to compete. Developing a business strategy is a lot like planning a trip. You need to determine where you are, where you want to go, and what the best route to take is given the amount of money you have to spend, your means of getting there, and what you hope to accomplish on the trip. For businesses, a strategic plan is its road map to success. It defines a specific route the business intends to undertake, provides benchmarks to measure its success along the way, and identifies where and how the organization will interact with its customers as it seeks to meet its overall mission and vision.

> For businesses, a strategic plan is the road map to success. It defines a specific route the business intends to undertake, provides benchmarks to measure its success along the way, and identifies where and how the organization will interact with its customers as it seeks to meet its overall mission and vision.

The Strategic Planning Process   LO4

With a base-level understanding of strategy and the core elements that are assessed as part of its development, let's now turn our attention to how managers and organizations actually take this knowledge and information and turn it into the stated "road map" (organizing framework) for success. The building of this road map is called the strategic planning process. This process is all about observations, analyses, choices, and actions. Again, recognizing that strategy is specific to each company and therefore may require some tailoring of the approach, the

FIGURE 6.4   Strategic Planning Process

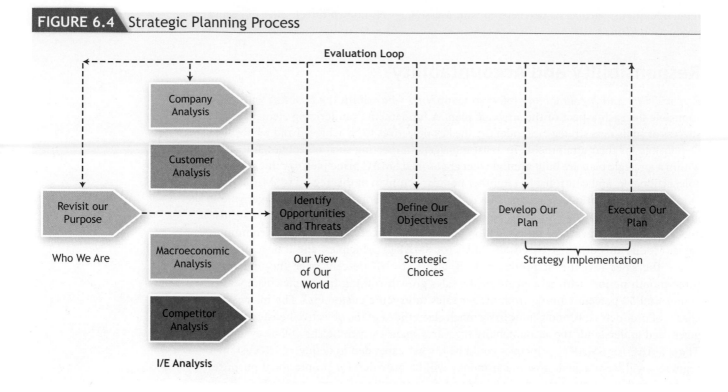

following represents a general overview of the steps associated with the development of a strategic plan (see Figure 6.4):

- **Revisit our purpose:** Who are we and where do we want to go?

- **Undertake an I/E (internal/external) analysis to understand our environment:** What changes or shifts are occurring that threaten us or that provide us with opportunities?

- **Assess our view of our world:** Based on what we know, what are our choices?

- **Choose a direction:** Given our capabilities, competencies, competitive advantages, and resources, which strategic choices should we pursue (where will we play)? What threats must we respond to?

- **Implement our strategy:** How do we develop the strategic thrusts and tactics to achieve our objectives and successfully execute the plan (how we will win)?

The strategic planning process is really an organizing framework around which the company can first assess what is changing in its macroeconomic environment, what strategies its competitors are pursuing, who its customers are and how they are changing, and what its capabilities, competencies, and advantages are. Given this analysis, its focus then shifts toward identifying the opportunities that exist in the marketplace, choosing which opportunities to pursue, and then developing an implementation plan to successfully achieve the identified objectives. With this in mind, let's take a quick look at each of the phases within the strategic planning process in order to better understand a management team's focus (see Figure 6.5). Note that a discussion of the need to revisit an organization's purpose (mission and vision) was discussed earlier and will not be repeated here.[6]

I/E (Internal/External) Analysis

The I/E (internal/external) analysis is all about assessing business risk and change in four key areas. These areas are identified as macroeconomic, industry, competitor, and company (see Figure 6.4). The external portion of the I/E analysis focuses on understanding what is

FIGURE 6.5   Where Is Our Focus?

Stage of Strategic Planning Process	Focus
Revisiting Our Purpose	Assessing the fit of the current mission and vision of the organization
I/E Analysis	Understanding the external and internal environment
	External—PESTEL, Porter's five forces, competitor SWOT
	Internal—company SWOT, 3C analysis—competencies, capabilities, capacity
	Customer—changes in attitudes, behaviour, needs
Our View of Our World	Given what we know about ourselves, our customers, our competitors, and the overall environment, what are our options? What is/are our competitive advantage(s)?
Strategic Choices	Which opportunities make the most sense, given our market position, resources, and environmental dynamics? What threats must we respond to?
Strategy Implementation	Develop the plan. Define the key performance indicators for monitoring it. Execute it.

influencing markets today and what will influence them going forward. In many cases, it is an assessment by management of the magnitude of change that is occurring within a given market arena and what shift in business risk has occurred, or will occur, as a result of such changes. The business models that we discussed in Chapters 1 and 2 (PESTEL, Porter's five forces, competitive markets, 3C analysis) are all critical in assisting us with the development of this analysis, as is the inclusion of a competitor and company-focused **SWOT** (strengths, weaknesses, opportunities, threats) analysis (see Figure 6.6).

SWOT stands for strengths, weaknesses, opportunities, and threats.

FIGURE 6.6   I/E Analysis: What the Models Tell Us

Business Model	Focus of Analysis
PESTEL	Guides us in developing an understanding of the macro-economic environment— political, economic, societal, technological, environmental, legal
Porter's Five Forces	Guides us in understanding the dynamics of the industry within which we compete— Porter's five forces are: • Intensity of rivalry within the industry • Threat of new entrants into the industry • Threat of new product/service substitutes within the industry • Power or control of suppliers within the industry • Power or control of buyers within the industry
Types of Competition	Guides us in understanding the nature of the industry's competitive landscape: • Perfect competition • Monopolistic competition • Oligopoly • Monopoly
SWOT Analysis	Strengths, weaknesses, opportunities, threats Competitive SWOT to size up competition Company SWOT to define company strengths, weaknesses, opportunities, and threats
3C Analysis	An assessment of our competencies, capabilities, and capacity with respect to the resources that we possess.

As was discussed in earlier chapters, conducting a PESTEL analysis enables us to get a sense of the broad market environment and external influences that could impact demand for our products and services, and change the nature of the way in which we do business. This would include assessing the potential impact of factors such as geopolitical events, new regulations, economic growth potential, foreign exchange rate influences, inflation, demographics, societal changes, accessibility to credit, technology disruptions, environmental impact factors, and legal exposures in the areas of product liability and environmental risk management.

At the industry level, our main focus would be on Porter's five forces. The value of Porter's five forces lies in its ability to assist us in identifying fundamental changes or disruptions to the industry within which we compete with respect to five key areas (as previously noted in Chapter 2):

1. Rivalry among existing competitors
2. Threat of new entrants
3. Threat of substitute products or services
4. Bargaining power of suppliers
5. Bargaining power of buyers

The following examples illustrate how, having conducted a Porter's five forces analysis, we are able to recognize changes or disruptions that are occurring in key market areas. The arrival of Lowe's Companies Inc. into Canada creates a new direct competitor for RONA and Home Depot, and will indirectly compete with companies such as Canadian Tire, Walmart, and Zellers for customer expenditures relating to home improvement and home decor. Wireless phones (cell phones) have become a direct substitute for land-line phones for a growing percentage of the population. Companies such as Canada Payphone Corporation are facing increasing market pressures from wireless carriers, as the need and demand for payphones is reduced due to the growing popularity of wireless communication technology. Nokia, a historical market leader in cell phone manufacturing, has seen its market share significantly reduced due to the technological savvy of smartphone manufacturers such as Apple and RIM. Canada Post and the United States Postal Service are facing reduced revenues due to substitute products such as text messaging and email. Walmart, given its economies of scale and buying power, is able to exercise considerable price control over its suppliers and then leverage such cost advantages against its direct and indirect competitors. Competitive rivalry intensity continues to rise within the retail sector in Canada with the arrival of U.S. banners such as Marshalls, Victoria's Secret, J. Crew, Bath & Body Works, Crate & Barrel, and the soon-to-come Target.

Identifying anticipated moves by major and up-and-coming competitors is also a key component of the external analysis. Businesses need to anticipate and react to new initiatives and changes in strategies and market positioning by their competitors. Walmart's decision to expand its Canadian retail operations to the Walmart SuperCentre format has required organizations such as Loblaw Companies and Metro to develop strategies in response to Walmart's full entry into the Canadian grocery business in Ontario. Canadian Tire has modified its store design in an effort to increase its product/service offerings (food, kitchen and bath, house and home) and drive additional dollars from its customer base in response to changes in the competitive landscape. Tim Hortons and Starbucks both will need to respond to McDonald's growing presence in the coffee market. Assessing competitors means looking at their operations, understanding how they intend to attack the marketplace, determining what message they will send to consumers as part of their positioning/differentiation strategies, and identifying what their perceived competitive advantages are (price, brand awareness, product quality). It also means assessing their management team and getting a feel for how managers make decisions, what their vision for the organization is, and how quickly they will react to shifts or changes in your organization's strategy. A popular way to assess a competitor is through the use of a SWOT analysis. A SWOT analysis asks managers to analyze a competitor on the basis of four elements: what are the competitor's strengths, what are its weaknesses, what market opportunities will it seek to attack, and what threats does it pose to your organization if it is successful in its operating initiatives, new market thrusts, and overall strategies to grow the company? Reviewing the annual reports of competitors, reading their quarterly earnings reports and forward-looking assessments of the future, and listening to their C-level management team's comments relating to market conditions and opportunities are also excellent sources of information relating to intended competitor strategies and actions.

> Businesses need to anticipate and react to new initiatives and changes in strategy and market positioning by their competitors.

A customer analysis focuses on trying to identify what shifts have taken place in our customer base in terms of attitudes, behaviours, and needs. The analysis will take into consideration demographic changes to our customer base, shifts in the desires of customers for the types of products and services they are looking to buy, and the impact of the economic climate on both current and future demand for our goods and services. A key outcome of this analysis is the identification of any significant shifts in customer expectations and requirements for our products and services in the markets we serve. The customer analysis will also look to assess our existing customer base for new sales and revenue-generation opportunities. Although controversial, an example of this is the BC Lottery Corporation's decision in August 2009 to increase its online gambling limit (PlayNow Web site) for its customers from $120 to $9999 per week. Citing the rapid growth of online gaming, with revenue expected to reach $20 billion per year by 2010, and the fact that there are more than 2000 online gaming sites without limits, the BC Lottery Corporation's move represents an opportunity to gain a greater share of the expenditures on online gaming by its more than 100 000 PlayNow players (its online Web site).[7]

An organization's customer analysis will attempt, as well, to identify opportunities to reach new customers through new market development (finding new market segments to serve), new product/service offerings, or potentially as a result of acquiring a company and its customer base. Lowe's Companies Inc.'s decision to come to Canada was based on recognizing, as part of its planning process, that new market opportunities for its products and services existed outside of the United States, with Canada being a primary market for such an expansion. Costco Wholesale merged with Canadian-based Price Club (Quebec) in 1993 as a way of gaining access to the Canadian market and further expanding its North American presence and business scale (and doubled its size).

> A customer analysis focuses on trying to identify what shifts have taken place in our customer base in terms of attitudes, behaviours, and needs.

As part of the organizational evaluation process, managers (and business owners) need to assess the competencies of their own organization and the level of resources (financial, operational, etc.) they have access to in order to determine what their capacity and overall capabilities are as a company. This is the internal portion of the I/E analysis. Just as managers are encouraged to assess competitors via a SWOT analysis approach, managers also are encouraged to conduct a SWOT analysis on their own organization. For organizations to properly assess their position in the marketplace and the probability of success of the various business opportunities they are considering, a full internal audit (strengths and weaknesses) of the firm's financial resources, organizational competencies, operational capacities, human resource skills, and overall capacity should be conducted and then measured against key competitors. By conducting such an internal analysis, managers can determine which markets the organization can successfully compete in and which initiatives should be avoided due to the resource, competency, and capacity limitations of the organization. For managers, the internal analysis represents a form of enterprise risk management.

It seeks to identify the financial, operational, technological, and market risks that would need to be assumed if a certain opportunity were pursued, and measures the ability of the organization to be able to respond to—and manage—such risks prior to the implementation of these initiatives.

From this I/E analysis phase, the organization hopes to be in a position to determine where, and how, it wants to compete. A critical part of this I/E analysis process is to identify opportunities that exist for the organization, as well as any threats that may be present and that must be appropriately assessed from a risk perspective. Another key outcome should be the ability of the organization to define any temporary or sustainable competitive advantages it has over its competition.

Competitive Advantage(s) Identification

For managers, a key outcome of the I/E analysis is identifying the competitive advantages an organization believes it possesses when compared to its competitors. As discussed in Chapter 1, a company enjoys a competitive advantage when it can provide customers with a product/service that offers more value than alternate products/services offered by its competitors. The key words in the definition of competitive advantage are *more value*. The ability to enhance the value of a product or service when measured against competitive offerings is what fundamentally entices customers to select your product as the best solution to their needs. Another way of stating this is that the real measure of a competitive advantage is the reason why a customer chooses to purchase your product over those of your competitors. Competitive advantages are either strategic or operational. Strategic competitive advantages can be thought of as "first mover" actions in a marketplace; that is, the ability to see how your organization can change the rules of the game in the markets the company chooses to compete in. Apple Inc.'s innovative approach to the integration of entertainment and technology, and the new customer demands being driven from it, is an example of a strategic competitive advantage. From this strategic sense of market direction and needs, Apple has been able to create innovative products such as the iPod, iPhone, and iPad. Operational competitive advantages are the result of being able to execute the day-to-day activities required of the transformation and marketing support processes within the organization in a manner that is superior to the same execution requirements of competitors. This means being more efficient and effective than competitors in the processes the organization undertakes to deliver products and services to the market, being more responsive to customer needs, offering superior quality, being able to offer new product enhancements faster, and being more flexible toward change as markets evolve. Figure 6.7 provides an overview of the four major areas where companies can seek to establish competitive advantage opportunities.[8]

FIGURE 6.7 Areas for Establishing Competitive Advantage Opportunities

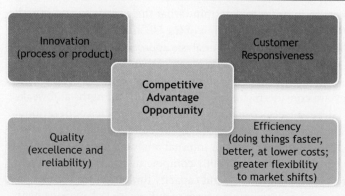

Strategy Development

For managers, the next step after completing the I/E analysis and identifying the organization's competitive advantages is to make decisions as to which opportunities to pursue and how resources will be allocated in support of these market opportunities. These decisions are then formulated into the organization's strategic plan, which can be thought of as possessing three parts: the corporate-level strategy, the business-level strategy, and the operating plan. The **corporate-level strategy** defines *what* the organization intends to accomplish and *where* it plans to compete (the markets to be focused on). It identifies which businesses to compete in, which new businesses to add, which business areas to exit, and where the business emphasis should be placed. In general, it is considered the high-level strategy that guides the organization's overall activities; think of it as outlining the "big picture." Once this direction has been determined, the organization then develops its **business-level strategy**. This defines *how* the organization intends to accomplish the corporate-level strategy. Business-level strategies respond to questions of how to compete in the market sectors where the organization has chosen to do business. This level of planning would be determining specific objectives it hopes to achieve for each of its identified business initiatives or business units. Finally, with these objectives identified and understood, the organization would develop the specific tactics or what is called its **operating plan**, which it will need to execute in order to ensure the business strategy—and, therefore, the corporate strategy—is met. Figure 6.8 provides an overview of what this process and its sequencing looks like.

Corporate-Level Strategy defines what the organization intends to accomplish and where it plans to compete.

Business-Level Strategy outlines specific objectives the organization hopes to achieve for each of its identified business initiatives and/or business units.

Operating Plan is a detailed, immediate-term set of objectives and corresponding tactics designed to achieve a specific business initiative.

FIGURE 6.8   Strategy Alignment

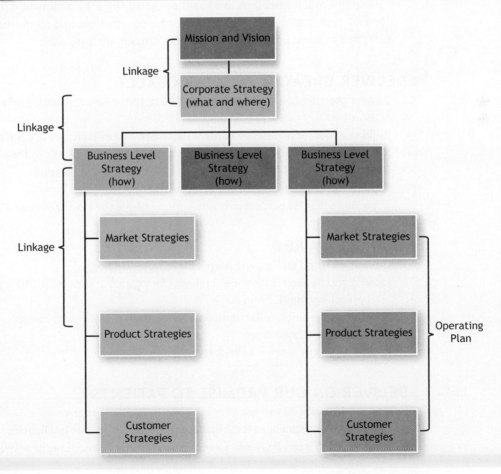

Let's use Merck & Co., a major pharmaceutical player, as an illustration to highlight the relationship between corporate-level and business-level strategies. Heading into 2009, Merck & Co., as part of a recent strategic planning process, identified the following outcomes:

"To achieve our mission of discovering and developing medicines and vaccines that improve the lives of people around the world, we are fundamentally changing this company."

"Our vision is to emerge as the leader in the pharmaceutical industry of the future." Based on this planning process and the desired outcomes identified above, Merck & Co. created its corporate strategy supported by five key corporate-level strategy objectives (the "big picture"):

Drive ongoing performance through their products
Deliver greater value globally
Improve their research productivity and accelerate their discovery process; create a pipeline (products under development) full of potential
Deliver on their promise to patients; improve accessibility to medications globally
Create a leaner, more responsive organization; drive efficiency and productivity

To ensure the achievement of these corporate objectives, Merck & Co. developed its business-level strategy. The business-level strategy was supported by specific objectives, all designed to link to and support the objectives of the corporate-level strategy. These business-level strategy objectives (summarized for brevity) were as follows:[9]

DRIVE ONGOING PERFORMANCE THROUGH PRODUCTS

Pursue the expansion of eligible patents for drugs such as Gardasil & Zostavax
Pursue approval for Isentress as a first-line therapy for HIV treatment
Develop new fixed-dose combinations for Januvia, Instress, and Metformin
Continue to invest in studies for promising drugs in their pipeline

DELIVER GREATER VALUE GLOBALLY

Expand presence in emerging markets: China, India, Korea, Russia, Turkey, Poland, Brazil
Build stronger local presence in identified markets; key launches in China and India
Shift investments, based on opportunity, from developed markets to these markets
Be first to market with new drugs across all major emerging markets
Expand current market presence in Japan and the UK
Drive more than 50 percent of revenue from outside the United States

TRANSFORM R&D

Continue to fund and expand Merck Bioventures (biologics)
Identify and develop "follow-on" biologics for patent expirations in 2017; three new drug applications with FDA in 2009
Seek out acquisitions, collaborations, and strategic alliances that complement existing products and capabilities
Invest 20 percent of revenue back into R&D

DELIVER ON OUR PROMISE TO PATIENTS

Increased accessibility to the Merck Patient Assistance Program
$15-million investment in the Alliance to Reduce Disparities in Diabetes
Support of U.S. Health Care Reform; remain actively involved in the solution process
Improve worldwide access to medicines, vaccines, and healthcare

CREATE A LEANER, MORE RESPONSIVE ORGANIZATION

Merger with Schering-Plough, August 7, 2009: $41.1B in cash and stock
$923-million investment in restructuring the organization

Once corporate-level and business-level strategies and objectives have been identified, operating plans are developed that will ensure their successful execution. Key components of the operating plan development process include:

a) Specifics as to how to compete (for each business initiative or business unit)
b) Identification of the key revenue drivers and an assessment of the total potential revenue forecasts the business can expect from a particular initiative
c) Identification of the upfront and ongoing cost commitments necessary to develop the market opportunity that the business has decided to focus on.
d) Identification of the required market position and marketing communication initiatives required to support the business initiative or unit in question.
e) Identification of staffing, infrastructure, and process realignment required in support of the initiatives undertaken.

Figure 6.9 provides a summary of the key fundamentals that managers need to fully develop when formulating operating plans.

FIGURE 6.9 Fundamentals to Operating Plan Formulation

At the end of the day, the organization's strategic plan should identify where and how it intends to compete in the marketplace; identify which weapons of competitive rivalry it will leverage as its products/services battle for market share; and define the marketing and operational plans required to effectively and efficiently execute the plan. A good way to assess the "fit" of the strategy being recommended is to assess it against the five questions provided in Figure 6.10.

Prior to the implementation (execution) of the strategic plan, managers should review the plan with the intent of confirming the following:

1. The operational activities within the plan are properly aligned to achieve the plan's objectives.
2. The budgets established, and the money to be generated, are realistic when compared to sales forecasts.

FIGURE 6.10 Five Critical Questions to Review When Developing Strategy

1. Does your proposed strategy leverage your organization's resources and capabilities?
2. Does your strategy fit with current and anticipated industry/market conditions?
3. Are the competencies that you plan to leverage considered to be sustainable for the required period?
4. Are the key drivers of your strategy consistent with the organization's strategic objective and position?
5. Do you have the ability and wherewithal to successfully implement the chosen strategy?

Source: Ken Wong, Queen's University

---

3. The resources needed to successfully execute the plan are available or can be acquired.
4. A series of benchmarks or performance indicators have been established that will enable the management team to effectively monitor the plan's progress.

> At the end of the day, the strategy being recommended should define, for the organization, where and how it intends to compete in the marketplace, which weapons of competitive rivalry it will leverage as its products and services battle for market share, and the marketing and operating plans that will be required to effectively and efficiently execute the plan.

Strategy Execution

The final phase of the strategic planning process is the strategy execution phase. It is this portion of the process where management shifts its emphasis from what it wants to do, and hopes to achieve, to actively engaging the business into executing the desired strategic thrusts and tactics. It is in this stage where the organization becomes fully committed to the plan, resulting in a degree of "directional lock-in" taking place. The level of **directional lock-in** directly equates to the level of riskiness of the plan, as the higher the capital amount and resource-base being committed, the greater the impact on the organization should the plan not be executed properly and fail to meet its required objectives.

Directional Lock-in is the level of financial and operational commitment an organization incurs as a result of implementing the organization's strategies.

In the execution phase, organizations commit their capital resources for needs such as building plants, retooling existing plants, building new equipment, funding research and development for new products and services, undertaking marketing and advertising campaigns, funding warehouse and distribution logistics support, and hiring staff. The amount of investment into these items that is required by an organization at the front end of the execution of a strategy results in the degree of directional lock-in that a company experiences. The more money invested up front the greater the risk to the company, as the return of this investment is determined by the success of the strategy in the marketplace. For example, a small-business owner may decide to open up a second store for his/her retail business in a neighbouring town as part of its new business strategy. This decision requires the owner to make a considerable locked-in investment prior to the receipt of any revenue (sales) from this new location. The owner will have to build a building or commit to a lease for retail space. Inventory and equipment will need to be purchased. Staff will need to be hired. Such a decision could result in a capital investment running into the hundreds of thousands of dollars. Going back to our example of Merck & Co., one of its key objectives was the acquisition of Schering-Plough for US$41.1 billion. The decision to acquire Schering-Plough represents a tremendous investment on the part of Merck & Co. Once the acquisition takes place, Merck & Co. would be "locked in" to ensuring the addition of Schering-Plough to its portfolio contributes to its desire to create a leaner, more responsive organization and enables Merck & Co. to meets its vision of becoming the leader in the pharmaceutical industry of the future.

For any business to be successful in recovering its capital investment and covering the operating costs associated with delivering products and services to customers, the execution plans need to be effectively implemented. This means that their operations must be efficient, their marketing plans must be effective, their staff must deliver on meeting customer needs, and their management teams must make good decisions on how to respond to issues and challenges that occur as the strategy is executed. The end result is that the company has to generate enough revenue from the sale of its products and services to cover its operating costs, meet its financial obligations relating to debt it has taken on (if applicable), and return the investment back to the company. Only if this performance level occurs will the organization actually experience true growth.

A key requirement of the strategy execution phase is for managers to continuously monitor the success of the implementation of the strategy and to take corrective action quickly in the event that things are not going well. Managers keep their finger on the pulse of the execution of the strategy by measuring success against predefined benchmarks or objectives. Sales forecasts become sales targets for sales managers. Operations managers monitor and manage processes and materials purchases, as well as labour levels, to ensure that costs stay in line. Finance managers monitor the cash flowing into and out of the business to ensure the company can continue to pay its bills and that the revenue coming in from business operations is sufficient to meet current and future cash requirements. Periodic senior-level management meetings take place in order to fully evaluate the company's progress with the strategy and determine whether adjustments to the plan need to be made. They also focus on assessing the impact of competitor actions and responses to the plan. This ongoing evaluation process is designed to ensure that managers look to see if the organization, at the end of the business cycle period, will meet the objectives being strived for. If they sense that such objectives are not currently on track, then alternate corrective tactics or revised objectives will be developed and put into place to get the organization back on track or to minimize the negative consequences of the weak performance (see Figure 6.11).[10]

> A key requirement of the execution phase is for managers to continuously monitor the success of the implementation of the strategy and to take corrective action quickly in the event that things are not going well.

FIGURE 6.11 Monitoring Plan Success

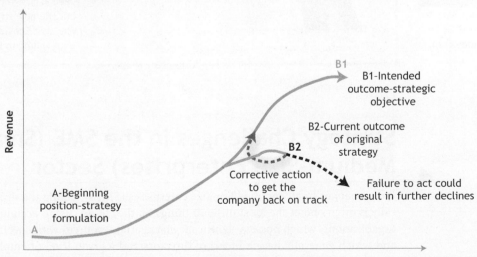

BUSINESS *in Action*

Sony Corporation: Reawakening the Sleeping Giant

Howard Stringer really has his work cut out for him. Stringer, who became Sony's CEO and chairman of its board of directors in 2005, remains optimistic but also senses urgency in seeking to redirect Sony's global marketing and operations efforts. Already challenged by a seemingly endless line of competitors, the recent economic downturn is adding to his woes. Historically a profitable company, Sony's year-end financial statements (March 31, 2009) saw the organization stumble from record profits of just over US$5 billion in 2008, to an operating loss in excess of US$2 billion, its first operating loss in nearly a decade; this, on revenues of approximately US$80 billion, down almost US$13 billion when compared to 2008. For Stringer, the task at hand is a total reworking of Sony's strategy and operational execution. Once dominant in a number of major markets, Sony not only has been slow to bring new products and services to the market, but also its understanding of what consumers want and its ability to develop and deliver products while controlling costs has been a challenge. Yes, the current economic climate is an issue, but it does not explain Sony's loss of its dominant position in the portable music player business (Sony Walkman) to Apple, the lacklustre performance of its video recorders against upstarts such as Pure Digital, or its higher-than-average manufacturing costs for its TVs when compared to direct competitors such as Samsung. Although Sony spends almost $5 billion per year on research and development, Stringer knows that he needs to get better bang for his buck. Sony has produced some innovative, top-notch products recently, but the question is whether the company truly understands what consumers want. The Sony PS3, although state of the art, was expensive to make and generated only marginal returns, while Nintendo's Wii caught the fancy of a new generation of video system buyers. Sony's PS-700 digital reader is struggling against Amazon's (and Oprah-backed) Kindle. A key defect in the Sony product is the lack of wireless download capabilities. For Sony and Stringer, the time to act is now. Within the current planning cycle, Howard Stringer is attacking Sony on all fronts. Stringer and his management team are slicing away over US$3 billion in expenses as they seek to streamline Sony's manufacturing and support operations processes. His team is also reworking supplier contracts and reducing the number of suppliers Sony will work with as part of this initiative. Stringer is also busy restructuring the organization to be more responsive to customer needs and reawakening Sony's culture

through a series of top-level management changes. Research and development is redirecting its efforts not only to bring back Sony's history of innovation and quality, but also to ensure the products Sony makes better meet the needs of the markets it competes in. Will Stringer succeed in his efforts? Time will tell, but the new strategy in place is one that Sony and Stringer are both willing to bet on.[11]

WEB INTEGRATION
Want to track Sony's progress? Go to www.sony.com.

Strategy Challenges in the SME (Small and Medium-Size Enterprises) Sector

For owners of small and medium-size enterprises (SMEs), taking the time to plan strategically is often one of the most difficult things on the "to do" list to accomplish. Unlike large organizations, which possess significant managerial resources with specific specializations, and which generally have a board of directors and a given level of emphasis on assessing strategic direction at defined periods of time, SME managers and owners often find themselves acting as the marketing, human resource, operations, and financial managers, all rolled into one. Their daily, weekly, and monthly efforts seem to be focused on fighting fires or fixing problems. When they do get a chance to plan, it is often focused on short-term planning efforts, generally geared toward current-year initiatives. In addition to having little time to plan, small and medium-size business owners often lack access to the expertise and resources needed to undertake a strategy review. Having said this, the need to plan strategically is just as important for a small business as it is for a major multinational organization. Small and medium-size business owners must assess and anticipate the changes that are occurring within their markets, the need for their products, and new opportunities that could exist. Strategic planning also enables these managers and business owners to make more efficient use of their resources and to minimize impulse spending or copycat initiatives that may result in little to no revenue or profitability gains for the organization. A good example is the temptation to spend large amounts of money on a radio or television advertising campaign. To maximize the return on such an expenditure (or to make such an expenditure at all), business managers and owners should first determine whether this is the correct approach to reaching their primary target market, whether it is the best route to take in delivering such a message, whether it is the right time of the year for the message to be delivered, whether the anticipated return on the advertising investment warrants its costs, and whether this expenditure makes sense given the objectives the business hopes to achieve going forward. Creating a strategy for the business, determining where and how to compete, and laying out a plan for an upcoming specified period will enable SME owners to make better decisions as to how to allocate their monetary, staffing, and operational resources. Taking a planning cycle approach, as discussed in Chapter 1, will provide clarity and direction to the business and enable it to better define benchmarks against which operational performance can be measured.

> The need to plan strategically is just as important for a small business as it is for a major multinational organization.

BUSINESS *in Action*

Planning a Small Business Strategy

For Elwin Derbyshire, risk taking is nothing new. A veteran Canadian Tire Corporation dealer, Elwin has seen the competitive landscape change significantly over his illustrious career. He is a recipient of numerous community and Canadian Tire corporate awards and is the owner of Canada's largest-volume (sales) Canadian Tire store. Elwin credits much of his success to the belief that it is critical to understand market trends, both in terms of the consumers' wants and in-store technology. Understanding trends is only the start—you must then deliver products that meet the customers' needs. A key component of this process is competitive intelligence. Elwin diligently reads trade periodicals and monitors key market indexes to keep abreast of shifts in market dynamics and trends. Visiting both direct and indirect competitor retail operations also provides him with a sense of where the competition is going and what new trends are taking hold in the marketplace. Elwin is also a firm believer in the need to maximize the use of technology to drive operating efficiencies and effectiveness. Entrepreneurship is about risk taking. To quote a baseball analogy (a favourite of Elwin's), if you never take a step off first base, you will never steal (or reach) second base. Risk taking, however, can be managed. With Elwin, it means continuous interaction with suppliers at trade shows and Canadian Tire Corporation buyers, and seeking the involvement of his managerial people and other team members in the long-range planning and the day-to-day buying and service-related decisions in the store. Where is

this decision-making effort focused? Right at the end user—the customer! In Elwin's mind, the emphasis is on the shopper and the delivery of a positive and unique shopping experience. The most important part in the customer's shopping experience in a "needs-driven" store like Canadian Tire is having the product that the customer came looking for. A lot of time is devoted to ensuring the store is stocked and products are on the floor, particularly with the flyer-advertised items—it is critical to deliver on what you promise. A key ingredient in the store's success is recruiting and training skilled staff and then following up and assessing staff competencies and empowering people with responsibility and accountability for getting the job done. Yes, there are some risks to being the first to introduce new products and enter new markets. In today's competitive retail environment, with increasing sales volumes, the inventory risks become larger (over $10 million in inventory in this one store), but the benefits can be huge. Possessing many years of business experience, natural leadership qualities, and an uncanny aptitude for instinctively sensing new opportunities, Elwin knows strategically where he envisions his operation going. As he states, "If you always do what you have always done, you will always get what you have always got." Reaching out to tap new customer needs and desires, involving his team in the community, and not waiting for customers to simply show up at the store are the key drivers in his strategy-planning philosophy.[12]

WEB INTEGRATION

Want to learn more about Canadian Tire and its franchisees? Go to http://corp.canadiantire.ca.

Strategic Planning in the NFP (Not-for-Profit) Sector (Social Economy)

LO5

Strategic planning in the not-for-profit sector poses some unique challenges over and above those mentioned up to this point in our discussion. Like for-profit entities, not-for-profits, in many instances, must develop strategies and tactics that produce positive financial results for the organization. If they don't, then they run the risk of becoming unable to sustain their operations. Where the difference lies, however, is in what drives the overall mission of the organization and whom, collectively, the management team needs to respond to. In the for-profit sector, the overarching objective of a business's strategy is ultimately focused on driving profitability and maximizing gains on behalf of business owners or shareholders. This is accomplished via the sale of goods and services, and funding is provided through operations, debt financing, or equity financing. In the social economy, not-for-profit leaders have a different mandate in that they are challenged to succeed while balancing the effectiveness of their economic activities (if they provide goods or services for a fee) with the social goal or purpose of the organization (see Figure 6.12). Their strategies involve a stronger inclusion of needs delivery based on the collective interest and social goals of a segment of society. Rather than having shareholders or direct business owners, their actions are assessed by some organized collective (membership base, government entity, or community board). Financing is, in many cases, the result of philanthropic donations, government allowances or grants, and private grants, in addition to dollars generated through the sale of goods and services, and/or dollars borrowed (debt financing). In a number of cases, there may actually be no revenue generated by the not-for-profit, making it totally reliant on external funding mechanisms, such as government.

FIGURE 6.12 Social Economy: Strategic Conclusions

Private Sector		Social Economy
Profitability Maximizing Gains	Overarching Objective	Needs Delivery via Collective Interest and Social Goals
Management Shareholders	Influences	Democratic Foundation Organized Collective
Debt/Equity Financing Internal Reserves	Financing	Diversified Base—Members, Government, Community
Sales of Goods and Services	Predominant Revenue Model	Sponsorship—Government, Foundations, etc. Sales of Goods and Services

Source: Adapted from Reseau d'investissement social du Quebec: Guide for Analysis of Social Economy Enterprises.

In formulating and implementing strategy in the social economy, managers must ensure that their actions, in addition to guiding the economic activity of the not-for-profit (NFP), effectively respond to the following (see Figure 6.13)[13]:

1. **Mission balance:** Maintain the balance between the need to create an effective economic base for the NFP while ensuring that the social mission and goals of the NFP are met.
2. **Vitality:** Enhance the **vitality** of the organization through maintenance and growth of its membership or community support base.

> **Vitality** refers to the ability of the NFP to grow and sustain its membership base and donor base.

FIGURE 6.13 Social Economy: Strategy Considerations

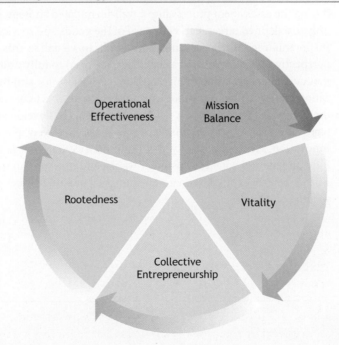

Source: Adapted from Reseau d'investissement social du Quebec: Guide for Analysis of Social Economy Enterprises.

Collective Entrepreneurship ensures that the involvement of the community where an organization is located and the population that it serves are reflected in the formulation and implementation of the strategy.

Rootedness refers to the extent to which the NFP is interwoven into the fabric of the community that it serves and is supported by a broad representation of its organizations, businesses, and citizens.

3. **Collective entrepreneurship:** Maintain an atmosphere of **collective entrepreneurship**, which means ensuring that the involvement of the community where it is located and the population it serves are reflected in the formulation and implementation of the strategy.
4. **Rootedness:** Enhance the **rootedness** of the organization by strengthening partnerships and not-for-profit networks that are supportive of the mission and work of the NFP.
5. **Operational effectiveness:** Operate in a manner that demonstrates the products and services offered by the NFP are priced at levels that ensure their accessibility by the targeted social audience, and provide mechanisms for support for those who are in need yet truly unable to pay.[14]

Management Reflection—The Need to Plan

Sun Tzu, in *The Art of War*, comments that "strategy without tactics is the long road to victory; tactics without strategy is the noise before defeat." For managers, regardless of the size of their business, defining the direction of the company and determining where and how the business is going to compete is essential. Successful businesses have one very common denominator: they take the time to plan how the business will be positioned in the marketplace, and what markets it will serve, and then they execute the critical components of their strategy better than their competitors. A successful business person will be able to tell you why his/her business is different from its competitors and unique to its customers. In essence, they know what their competitive advantages are, and they know how to leverage them to ensure their business is "best of breed."

In summary, then, what constitutes a successful strategy? A successful strategy is one that properly assesses the external environment, defines the changes and opportunities within market segments the organization intends to serve, and effectively allocates resources and maximizes capabilities in a manner that is supportive of the products and services it delivers to the marketplace. A key outcome of the strategy formulation process should be the identification of the key competitive advantages the organization possesses and the successful leveraging of these advantages within its marketing communication and operational delivery processes. To be successful, the organization must be able to transfer the knowledge gained during the assessment process into a well-formulated strategy, which it then executes successfully to a defined target market in need of the goods and services being offered. To be successful in this regard, the organization needs to visualize this process from the customers' perspective. This means that as managers we need to fully understand the key buying criteria that customers are using in making purchase decisions, and then determine how our organization can best align our products and services to meet customer expectations identified via these criteria. This process is what will enable us to develop and sustain competitive advantages, and will help us determine how to most effectively allocate resources in order to drive innovation, efficiency, quality, and customer responsiveness initiatives. Only when we have fully understood what the customer wants, and how we can most effectively respond to this, will we be able to embark on a well-thought-out path toward profitability and organizational wealth creation.

Chapter Summary

This chapter provides students with an introductory overview of the concept of business strategy and of the fundamentals of the strategic planning process. A key emphasis within the chapter is the identification of the key elements that managers need to assess as they develop a strategy for their business or organization. These include the creation of vision and mission statements, defining the products/services to be offered, assessing the resources the organization has or has the capacity to acquire, configuring the business system to ensure the execution of the intended set of actions, and defining managerial responsibility and accountability to ensure its success. Also discussed, in detail, is the strategic planning process itself and the key stages within it (revisiting the organization's purpose, I/E analysis, the identification of strategic choices, strategy formulation, and strategy implementation). Included within this discussion is an understanding of the difference between corporate-level strategies, business-level strategies, and operating plans, and the linkages among the three. The chapter closes with some thoughts relating to the challenges that strategy development poses for small and medium-size businesses, as well as the unique influences that not-for-profits need to consider when assessing and developing their organizational strategies. For not-for-profits, strategic plan development is uniquely challenged by the balancing requirements between financial stability and meeting the needs of a collective interest, defined by its social mandate and, in many cases, the altruistic goals of an organized collective.

Developing Business Knowledge and Skills

KEY TERMS

mission *p. 146*

vision *p. 147*

harvesting *p. 147*

SWOT *p. 151*

corporate-level strategy *p. 155*

business-level strategy *p. 155*

operating plan *p. 155*

directional lock-in *p. 158*

vitality *p. 163*

collective entrepreneurship *p. 164*

rootedness *p. 164*

QUESTIONS FOR DISCUSSION

1. What are the six key areas that managers need to assess when developing a business strategy? How does managerial responsibility and accountability factor into this process?

2. What are the major stages of the strategic planning process? Why is revisiting an organization's mission and vision such a critical beginning point of the strategic planning process?

3. Why do managers need to assess the internal and external environment as part of the strategy development process? What key takeaways do you believe should be the result of this analysis?

4. What is the difference among corporate-level strategies, business-level strategies, and operating plans? How are they interconnected?

5. How is strategy formulation different in the not-for-profit sector when compared to the for-profit sector? In your mind, does this make the development of strategy in the NFP sector more challenging? Why, or why not?

QUESTION FOR INDIVIDUAL ACTION

Assume that *Canadian Business* magazine has asked you to write a short reflective commentary on the role of strategy and/or the strategic planning process as it relates to organizational growth and market position. You are to craft a creative essay that will communicate to readers your unique perspective on the role of strategy and the importance of strategic planning in the life cycle of an organization. The approach you take in responding to this question is open to you. You may choose to focus on a specific aspect of strategy or strategic planning, or tackle it at a more "macro" level. The intent is not simply to re-state information from the chapter, or to re-word basic definitions, but rather to develop a truly reflective discussion on the subject matter you choose to explore. You may quote other sources in your commentary, but remember that it is meant to be your personal interpretation. It should not be thought of as a research paper, but as a learning tool written from the position of a knowledgeable student within this field.

TEAM EXERCISE

Conduct interviews with two or three small-business owners in your local area. Ask them to describe their strategy development or business planning process. Discuss with them the strategy development approach presented in this chapter, and ask them to comment on some of the barriers they envision in utilizing this methodology as part of their business planning approach. Prepare a presentation that summarizes your discussions and provides recommendations for best practices for small businesses looking to assess their current market position and future strategy.

Case for Discussion

So, just how would you take on the likes of Rogers Communications, Bell, and Telus? Well, a bunch of wireless cell phone providers are going to have to figure this out. One in particular, Globalive, has aspirations of becoming Canada's newest national wireless carrier. The Canadian government auctioned off additional licences for wireless operations in 2008. Globalive spent over $400 million at this auction acquiring operator licences for every province except Quebec. Backed by both domestic and foreign venture capital, Globalive plans on spending an additional $1.4 billion over the upcoming decade to build a network that will enable it to compete on the national level. Their vision: to grab 15 percent of the Canadian market over the next 10 years. Analysts estimate that 30 percent of Canadians still are not cell phone users. For Globalive, this represents an opportunity to acquire first-time buyers versus having to steal customers away from the Big 3. Having said this, Rogers, Bell, and Telus also see opportunities with this untapped market. All three have increased their marketing efforts, recognizing the increasing intensity of competition that is about to hit the market. In addition to simply creating a higher profile, these major players have introduced new brands focused on price-sensitive buyers, and are busy locking up customers with long-term user contracts. Globalive also has to consider the other upstarts that will be looking for market opportunities as a result of their participation in the government auction.

For Globalive to survive, it has to determine strategically where and how to compete, what market segments represent its greatest opportunities, how its network development should roll out, which manufacturers' products to highlight, and what differentiated communication message to use in order to create profile, awareness, and uniqueness for its product against the Big 3. Then there is the matter of distribution, in terms of finding the best way to reach Globalive's target audience and determining what areas of the country should be pursued first.[15]

QUESTIONS

What are your thoughts? Strategically, what recommendations would you make to Globalive? Which customer segment(s) and geographic regions do you think represent their best opportunity? If you were the head of Globalive, how would you position your service offering against Rogers, Bell, and Telus?

Practise and learn online with Connect. Connect resources include additional and interactive study exercises, videos, and practice quizzing, as well as additional material you won't find in the printed text.

7 Developing Your Business Structure and Culture

Snapshot—What to Expect in This Chapter

This chapter provides students with insight into the core characteristics associated with business system design, the outcome of which provides the formal framework for successful execution of the tactics required to meet the organization's overall objectives. The content emphasized in this chapter includes the following:

- Business System Design

- Developing the Organizational Framework
  - Structure
  - Culture and Environment
  - Management Approach

- The Concept of Restructuring

- Management Reflection—The Importance of Business System Design

From the Student's Perspective

Every organization is a unique entity characterized by its people, purpose, and operations. At the core of every organization is a blend of personalities, work ethics, values, and drives—otherwise known as its culture. As current business students and, potentially, future managers, our success is reliant on the degree of understanding we develop for the "blend" of our organizations.

Of course, the job description of a "manager" may entail a multitude of responsibilities; however, a key success factor for managers is to be able to positively influence the people they work with. To do so, managers need to develop a profound understanding of how the organization functions by asking questions like: Who are the people I am working with? What motivates them? How are they tied to the success of the organization? What differentiates us from the others? By devoting the time to asking questions and deciphering what makes the organization work, managers will be better equipped to lead.

Organizational structure and culture are never static. Look at any organization and you will notice that changes of all sorts have been implemented over time to improve its competitiveness and its ability to keep up with the ever-changing world we live in. In order for us to excel in our future roles as managers, we must first learn the tools that will help us to better decipher the code to our organization's specific structure and culture so that we can ask the right questions and implement the right changes.

Prior to taking the Commerce route at Queen's University, I knew that I was interested in understanding more about how the world works. Obtaining an education across various aspects of business has helped me to achieve that goal. Particularly, I have decided to begin my career in the financial industry due to my enjoyment of combining numerical analysis with logical reasoning to make sense of current events. After completing a semester at the Singapore Management University, I have developed an appreciation for learning about business from different cultural perspectives. I hope to one day be able to gain some professional experience abroad. Aside from business, I am incredibly passionate about music—particularly playing the piano, as I have been doing so for more than 15 years. If there is anything I have learned thus far, it is to always remember to keep doing the things you love!

BUSINESS *in Action*

Lessons from Jack Welch

Jack Welch is considered by many to be one of the greatest business leaders and managers of all time. During his more than 20 years as the CEO of General Electric, Welch increased the market capitalization value of the company from approximately US$13 billion to more than US$400 billion. An award-winning, best-selling author, Jack's lessons and philosophies relating to a variety of management topics are read and practised by managers across the globe and in almost all industry settings. In a discussion relating to organizational hierarchy in *BusinessWeek* magazine (June 2007), Welch offered some insight as to his views regarding the pitfalls associated with building too much bureaucracy and having too many layers of management within an organization. For Jack, adding layers of management into an organization's structure must be fully thought out before it is implemented to avoid four fundamental pitfalls. First, today's marketplace is changing at a faster rate than ever before; a risk of too many layers of management is that it slows down the decision-making process. Too many people have to approve a decision before it can actually be implemented. Second, having increased layers of management can impede communication if information and decisions need to be communicated through too many individuals. This has the potential for information distortion because every time the information changes hands the intent and the facts within it risk the potential for change. Third, too many layers of management can stifle creativity and innovation within the organization. Bureaucratic red tape, and the need to gain too many approvals, can sap the energy out of new and promising ideas. Fourth, too many layers of management can promote meddling; with small spans of control, managers often find the need to overmanage. In Jack's mind, managers should spend their time leading and energizing others to get the work done. Organizational conflict and productivity issues arise when managers meddle in areas where their attention is not required, or when higher-level managers get themselves directly involved in areas where middle and front-line managers have been assigned such supervisory tasks. For an organization, the effective use of layers and managerial hierarchy lies in its ability to reinforce cultural behaviours within the organization that will foster innovation, creativity, the sharing of ideas, the elimination of bureaucracy, and the instilling of confidence and an attitude of accountability within its workforce. The organization's structure should encourage the free flow of ideas, quick and effective responses to changes in market dynamics, and the elimination of barriers impeding success. As Jack has so often stated, managers should lead more and manage less. They need to articulate the vision and then energize others to accomplish the goals of the organization. And, by the way, everyone should have fun while they are doing it. Jack retired as CEO of General Electric in 2001, and is currently the head of Jack Welch LLC, where he serves as a special partner with the private equity firm Clayton Dubilier & Rice. A regular guest on CNBC, Jack also speaks regularly to business audiences and students around the world. Jack was named "Manager of the Century" by *Fortune* magazine in 2000.[1]

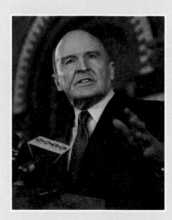

WEB INTEGRATION

To learn more about Jack Welch's managerial ideas, visit www.**welchway.com** or read one of Jack's bestsellers, *Winning*, or *Jack: Straight from the Gut*.

LO1   Business System Design

When we think of a business system, four key components should come to mind for the seasoned manager. You can think of these as the cornerstone to the structural foundation of a business, how it operates, and how its tactical execution is tied to its strategic plan. These components, when properly designed, aligned, and developed, ensure the successful execution of a business strategy.[2] These components are as follows, and are illustrated in Figure 7.1:

- Organizational structure, culture, and management approach

- Control systems to manage strategic intent

- Mechanisms for effective talent management

- Operational processes and market support and alignment

FIGURE 7.1 Business System Design

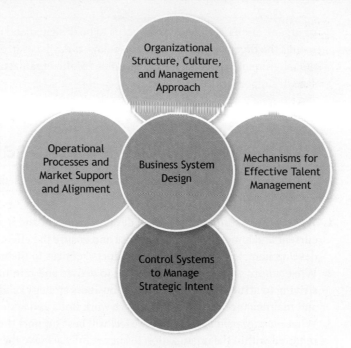

Organizational Structure, Culture, and Management Approach relates to the formal framework around which the business system is designed and how such a structure directs and influences collaboration, the exchange of knowledge, the communication and sharing of ideas, and the work environment surrounding the accomplishment of tasks and the meeting of responsibilities (the focus of this chapter).

Control Systems to Manage Strategic Intent defines the managerial evaluation and control processes utilized to determine the success of the organization in meeting its strategic and operational goals and objectives. This would include financial management systems, along with the establishment of key success metrics relating to productivity, market share growth, and asset performance, to name a few. It also refers to the formalized communication tools used to disseminate critical information up, down, and across the organization. These control systems are designed to guide managers and employees during the integration of business-level strategies in support of the overall corporate-level vision and mission. (These systems are introduced in this chapter and discussed more thoroughly in Chapter 14.)

Mechanisms for Effective Talent Management refers to the decision-making hierarchy, the delegated span of control within an organization, and the allocation of position power within it (discussed in this chapter and further supported by Chapter 8).

Operational Processes and Market Support and Alignment focuses on the processes and initiatives needed to support and direct product/service transformation within the organization, the creation of the value proposition applicable to such products/services, and the distribution, marketing, sales, and service in support of these products/services. These operational and market support processes are commonly referred to as the **value chain**. The various components that make up the value chain are discussed in detail in Chapters 9 through 11.

> **Value Chain** is the term for the processes and initiatives needed to support and direct the product/service transformation within the organization, the creation of the value proposition applicable to such products/services, and the distribution, marketing, sales, and service in support of these products/services.

An organization's business system needs to be designed and developed in a way that ensures the organization functions on a day-to-day basis in a manner that maintains solid alignment between the strategic intent of the organization and the activities taking place in support of this intent. As briefly illustrated above, this need to maintain alignment between the organization's strategy and structure is fundamental to the successful achievement of its goals and long-term vision. With this in mind, the balance of this chapter focuses on demonstrating how managers design an organization's structure, influence its culture, and define its decision-making approach in order to provide the framework for accomplishing this task.[3]

> An organization's business system needs to be designed and developed in a way that ensures the organization functions on a day-to-day basis in a manner that maintains solid alignment between the strategic intent of the organization and the activities taking place in support of this intent.

Developing the Organizational Framework

LO2, LO3, LO4, LO5

When developing the organization's framework, managers should take into consideration three key questions:

1. What is the best *structure* that will develop, connect, and maintain relationships with our current and anticipated customer base and ensure the effective and efficient design, development, and delivery of our products/services to the marketplace?
2. What *culture or environment* is needed to deliver and reinforce the market position we are striving to achieve (as outlined in our business strategy) and facilitate the development and maintenance of high-performance work units and systems within our organization?
3. What *management approach* do we feel will best support the activities and interactions required within the organization to successfully achieve the goals and objectives defined in our strategic plan?

These questions can be visualized as three spheres around which the development of an organization's framework, which will ultimately guide its business system, will be created (see Figure 7.2).

As Figure 7.2 illustrates, the spheres representing each of these areas overlap. This is intentional in that each area influences the others with respect to the development of an organization's framework and the consequences realized. The end result is the creation of a framework that provides the backbone as to how the organization will facilitate the delivery of its operational plan and, ultimately, its vision and mission.

Structure

Structure is the formal framework around which tasks are organized and responsibilities allocated within an organization.

As noted above, **structure** relates to the formal framework around which tasks are organized and responsibilities are allocated within an organization. As managers, we need to view the requirements of our business in meeting the expectations of our customers and determine the

FIGURE 7.2   Developing an Organization's Framework

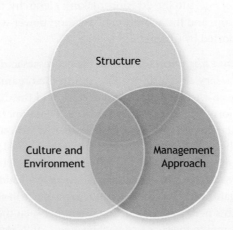

best structural approach to take in order to support and accomplish this. Behind this decision is the concept of customer "touch points." In designing structure, we need to think about how we interact with customers, and design the organization's framework in a way that best facilitates these interactions and ensures the highest level of responsiveness to meeting the needs of the individuals or businesses who buy and use our products. We must also realize that the design and development of a structure should not be thought of as being static (i.e., a one-time event), but rather requires ongoing monitoring to ensure it continues to meet the needs of the organization as it evolves and grows (or contracts). What is recognized as an acceptable structure for a new or emerging single-product-focused company may no longer apply as the organization grows to two, three, or more product/service offerings, adds additional divisions focused toward unrelated markets, expands geographically, or utilizes an acquisitions approach toward growing its business. Structures also need to be assessed against changes occurring in the marketplace to ensure they remain pertinent to maintaining our connection with defined target markets, respond to competitive pressures, support stakeholder and/or shareholder expectations, and, where applicable, meet compliance or legal requirements. Structure is also about driving efficiency and effectiveness. Regardless of the focus of our strategic intent (premium price, low cost, niche market player), our structure must ensure we deliver our products/services to the marketplace in a manner that is superior to the competition. Our structure is a core component of the framework behind how this is accomplished.

> Managers need to realize that the design and development of a structure should not be thought of as being static (i.e., a one-time event) but rather requires ongoing monitoring to ensure it continues to meet the needs of the organization as it evolves and grows (or contracts).

TYPES OF STRUCTURE

As indicated above, the structure of an organization most likely will change over time as the organization evolves and its strategic goals and objectives change. Efficient structures will reflect the best framework for a company at a given point in time. Structures are fluid in that as needs and conditions change, so too must structures. Having said this, many organizations have a tendency to follow a generalized structure development path as they flow through their life cycle. In their infancy stage, organizational structures tend to be fairly flat and simple. If you think of an entrepreneur launching a new business, in many cases the number of employees and the managerial decision-making structure will be fairly straightforward (owner and a few employees; no formal hierarchal structure). As the organization grows, there may be a need for better controls to maintain efficiency and effectiveness. In this situation, the organization may shift to a functional structure, where it is departmentalized around specific tasks such as marketing, sales, manufacturing, service, engineering, finances, and HR. As the organization grows further, there may be a perception that the company can be better managed if it reorganizes around specific customer categories, with each category acting as a separate value cell or operational unit. The rationalization might be that this will enable the teams assigned to a specific type of customer to more fully concentrate and specialize on the products or services applicable to this defined customer base, with the end result being improved connections and interactions with the specific customer category assigned to them. Within each customer category, marketing, sales, manufacturing, and service may be dedicated to a single purpose (the product(s) they are involved in), whereas other areas of the organization, such as finance and HR, may remain centralized depending on the size and desired outcomes of the organization. As the organization continues to evolve similar product lines may materialize, resulting in a desire to restructure around product lines or divisions. Also, organizations may possess multiple business interests through acquisitions or new market development. This may result in organizations structuring their operations almost as separate businesses, often referred to as strategic business units (SBU). Transitioning from a regional player to a national or international player may also result

FIGURE 7.3   Sample: Structural Evolution

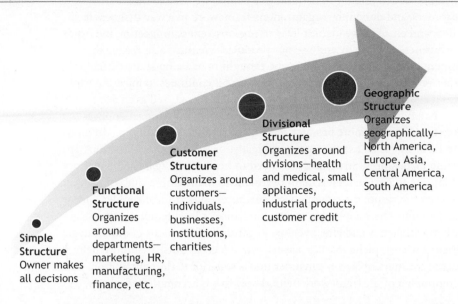

Simple Structure
Owner makes all decisions

Functional Structure
Organizes around departments—marketing, HR, manufacturing, finance, etc.

Customer Structure
Organizes around customers—individuals, businesses, institutions, charities

Divisional Structure
Organizes around divisions—health and medical, small appliances, industrial products, customer credit

Geographic Structure
Organizes geographically—North America, Europe, Asia, Central America, South America

in organizations structuring their businesses geographically. Figure 7.3 provides a sample of one possible evolutionary path an organization's business structure framework could follow. It should be noted that this is simply an illustration, as organizations often will combine components from each type to develop the customized business system approach that they feel best meets the needs of the organization, is most responsive to their customer and stakeholder requirements, and maintains a culture of innovation and opportunity development. Figure 7.4 provides a simplified example of each different type of structure noted above.

FIGURE 7.4   Types of Organizational Structures, Simplified

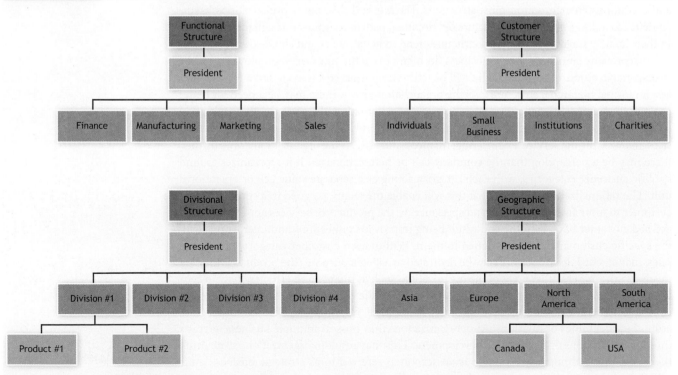

The structures discussed thus far have been largely traditional in their nature and have emphasized some form of departmentalization as a core component of their framework for development. It should be recognized that such structures may not be viewed as the best approach or natural evolution for all companies. Departmentalized approaches to structure seem to fit best for traditional organizations where some aspect of task specialization is present. In this situation, the grouping of jobs into departments seems to make logical sense from the perspective of efficiency and effectiveness as well as ease of managerial control. In some companies or industry sectors, however, task specialization and the need for departmentalization may not be the best organizational structural approach. A good example is companies or industries where project management makes up a predominant component of the organization's operations. In these situations, employees from various departments need to work jointly, in a cross-functional environment, on a project or specific initiative for a defined period of time. An example of an organizational response to such a situation would be a matrix-style structure. A matrix organizational structure takes into consideration that individuals will have specific expertise related to defined departmental areas. The difference, however, is that this expertise can be considered fluid in that different types of expertise may be needed for each project the organization currently has on the go. In this situation, the organization defines project managers who then draw on the resources and expertise of various departments to successfully complete the projects designed. Engineering firms, construction companies, and large project-driven organizations are the types of companies that are more likely to consider a matrix-style approach to organizational structure. Figure 7.5 provides an example of a matrix-style organizational setup.

The best organizational structure for a particular company is related to a number of factors. The organization's size, geographic dispersion, range of business undertakings, task specialization requirements, general nature of the work, and perceived best way to connect with customers all will influence how an organization structures its work responsibilities and its management decision-making process. It also has been emphasized that structures are not static, and that organizations will revisit and modify their structures throughout their evolution. Periods of growth—whether the result of acquisition, current product growth, or new market opportunity development—as well as periods of organizational contraction due to economic or financial challenges, or simply a need or a desire to be more efficient and effective, can all result in substantial changes in the appearance and framework of an organization. Organizational structures can, and should, be thought of as almost a customization of the manner in which an organization perceives it is best able to manage its business system and

FIGURE 7.5 Matrix-Style Organizational Structure, Simplified

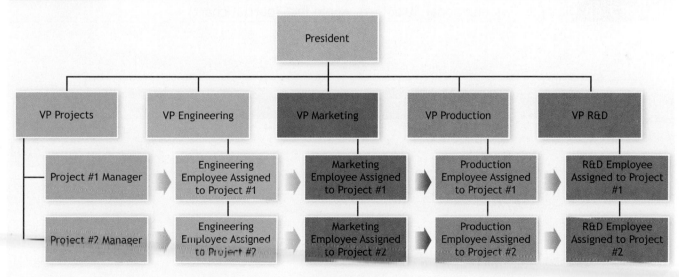

deliver its products/services to the marketplace. The ability to create a more efficient and effective structure, and to create stronger customer relationships, can result in a competitive advantage in the marketplace. The creation of these structures often results in a hybrid use of components of the various structural options highlighted above. Figures 7.6A, 7.6B, and 7.6C provide examples of some aspects of the current organizational structures in place with a sample of companies. Again, keep in mind that these structures are fluid and that changes to what is shown in Figures 7.6A, 7.6B, and 7.6C could already have occurred or be in the process of occurring. One of the unique charts shown is the top-level management structure of Research In Motion, which utilizes a co-CEO approach to managing the company.

> Organizational structures can, and should, be thought of as almost a customization of the way an organization perceives it is best able to manage its business system and deliver its products/services to the marketplace.

BUILDING BLOCKS OF STRUCTURE

Just what do management teams look at when determining where and how to initiate or modify their organizational structures in order to best meet the needs of their companies? Recognizing that the need to revisit the current structure can be influenced by external and internal factors, the reorganization of a business's structure generally focuses on some or all of the

FIGURE 7.6A Sample Organizational Structure, Research In Motion (partial chart)

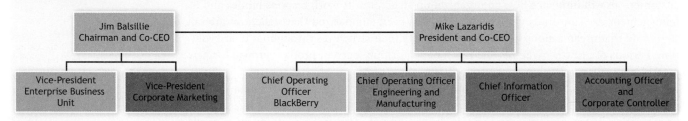

Source: Cogmap, Organizational Charts by Cogmap, www.cogmap.com, May 26, 2010.

FIGURE 7.6B Sample Organizational Structure, Apple Inc. (partial chart)

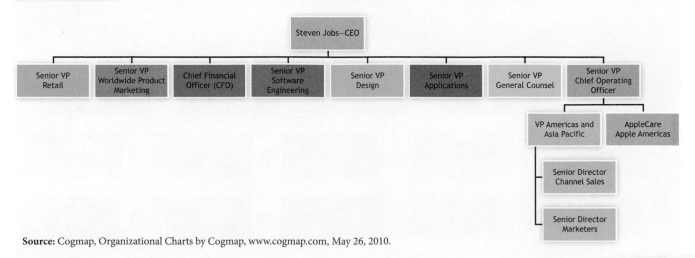

Source: Cogmap, Organizational Charts by Cogmap, www.cogmap.com, May 26, 2010.

FIGURE 7.6C Sample Organizational Structure, eBay Inc. (partial chart)

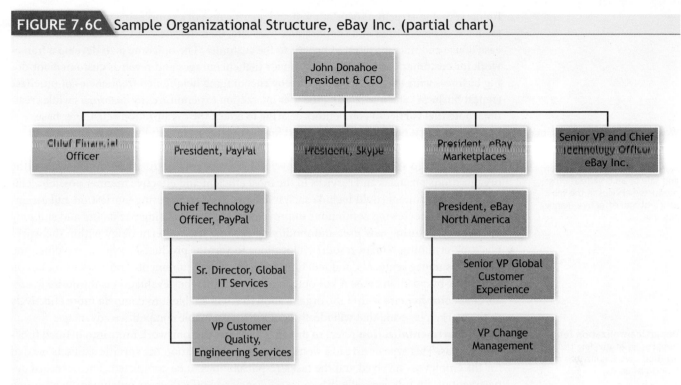

Source: Cogmap, Organizational Charts by Cogmap, www.cogmap.com, May 26, 2010.

building blocks illustrated in Figure 7.7: customer intimacy, work efficiencies, and degree of departmentalization.

Customer intimacy refers to ensuring the structure an organization designs and puts into place is built on interactions and connectivity to customers in order to meet their expectations for contact, service, and support. As organizations grow, the tendency can be to build structure more around internal efficiencies and practices versus ensuring that such structures are designed to support the value proposition around which products and services are sold. Managers must ensure that customer "touch points" (i.e., mechanisms for interaction) are

> **Customer Intimacy** is the term for the interactions and connectivity that organizations seek to foster with their customers in order to meet their expectations for contact, service, and support.

FIGURE 7.7 Building Blocks of Organizational Structure

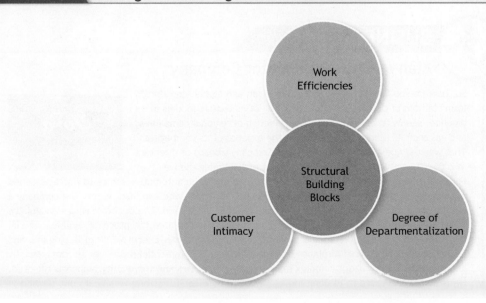

fundamental to structural development and alignment. For example, if a decision is made to facilitate customer sales and support via a Web site, then the site must be designed to ensure ease of use and maximization of benefit to the customer. The outcome is to develop a framework for customer connection and intimacy that encourages and rewards customers for doing business with the organization, thereby encouraging heightened frequencies of purchase (repeat business) and maximizing the "per interaction expenditure" by customers while creating a potential barrier to competitors desiring to attack the organization's customer base.

Work Efficiencies refers to the alignment of the tasks required to support the design, development, marketing, distribution, and sale of an organization's products/services in the most efficient and effective manner possible.

Work efficiencies refers to the need for the organization to fully analyze the type, number, and responsibilities of the various positions within the organization and align these to the tasks required to support the design, development, marketing, distribution, and sale of the organization's products and services in the most efficient and effective manner possible. This analytical assessment could include such initiatives as re-engineering fabrication and assembly processes, reviewing continuous improvement tactics, assessing packaging and shipping procedures, defining new uses and modifying existing uses of technology within the workplace, determining human resource allocations to various products/services, implementing quality assurance protocols, and redefining specific task requirements and responsibilities on a position-by-position basis. A key outcome of work efficiency evaluation is the desire to create core competencies within the organization that will enable it to compete more effectively in the marketplace and that will ideally result in a sustainable competitive advantage.

Departmentalization refers to the process of dividing the organization's work units into defined functional areas.

Departmentalization refers to dividing the organization's work units into defined functional areas. This type of division would take into consideration the specific skill sets needed for the employees involved and the tasks/responsibilities to be completed. The degree of departmentalization is generally driven by efficiency and effectiveness outcomes. By grouping employees into defined functional areas the organization is striving to centralize the tasks involved, thereby creating synergies within the department with the end result ideally being the maximization of efficiency and effectiveness. A common example of departmentalization is found within functional structures where organizations create defined departments, such as finance, engineering, manufacturing, and marketing. Often-listed advantages of departmentalization include the sharing of tasks, economies of scale resulting from the centralization of tasks, ease of managing due to the narrowly defined skill focus, and greater control over the quality of work being produced. Disadvantages that need to be recognized are that departmentalization can lead to a "silo mentality" where decisions are made in isolation of other organizational needs, reduced cross-organizational communication, loss of the organizational "big picture" or vision by employees, and a tendency to focus on internal priorities versus external customer, market, and stakeholder needs.[4]

BUSINESS *in Action*

Alan Mulally, Ford Motor Company

So, how do you turn around a North American and global icon that is losing billions of dollars, suffers from a lack of innovative models in its pipeline, seems to be operating as a collection of regional companies, and has seen its market share erode at the expense of its competitors? That was the question facing Ford Motor Company's board of directors in 2006. *The answer*: Recruit a CEO capable of redefining the way that Ford Motor Company operates. *The solution*: Go outside the automotive sector to find a seasoned manager and leader who understands business systems and who can instil within the company a culture focused on operational discipline and creative innovation. *The decision*: Hire Alan Mulally. Hired in September 2006, Mulally devised a plan and then created the processes and managerial system necessary to ensure its successful execution. The former Executive VP of Boeing Inc. and CEO of Boeing Commercial Airplanes (the manufacturer of commercial passenger aircraft), Mulally knows a thing or two about complex manufacturing processes and the quality emphasis required. He is also well-versed in understanding the need to establish strong financial controls and in

Feel the difference

meeting time-to-market deadlines to ensure the company stays competitive in today's intense global marketplace. In taking over Ford in 2006, Mulally knew the task at hand would not be an easy one. You don't turn around a company with Ford's track record overnight—2006 saw Ford lose US$12.6 billion, with an additional US$2.7 billion loss in 2007. Add to this the financial meltdown of 2008 (in which Ford lost US$14.7 billion) and the recession that followed, and one can see just how challenging Mulally's task is. However, progress is being made, the results are turning positive, and Mulally has Ford on track to finally becoming the global player it has aspired to be for so many years. Ford saw a net income of US$2.7 billion in 2009, and the first quarter of 2010 recorded an impressive US$2 billion in profit. Along with this profit turnaround, Ford Motor Company has seen a definitive improvement in its stock price as well. Ford's stock price has risen from a low of $1.80 in November 2008 to $14.21 at the end of April 2010. Equally important, Ford Motor Company was the only North American "Big 3" automobile manufacturer that did not need a government bailout (both General Motors and Chrysler Corporation required government financial assistance to weather the financial crisis of 2008–09). Mulally's approach is a straightforward one. It combines a commitment and focus to the brand; a desire to compete in the targeted market areas with carefully defined products; a plan to simplify the processes associated with design, development, and manufacturing; and a commitment to being "best of class" in the key areas that are most meaningful to customers (quality, fuel efficiency, safety, and overall value). To succeed, Mulally has created a business system at Ford that places a strong focus on understanding the mission, communicating requirements and results, and maintaining a clear visibility on what needs to be done. This means placing a strong emphasis on cross-functional team work. Mulally ensures that senior managers from every functional discipline are included on his decision-making team, as everyone in the organization needs to know what is going on if Ford is to succeed. For Ford, in 2006, it was all about regaining confidence, discipline, and the desire to win. The board of directors' decision to bring Alan Mulally on as CEO was exactly what Ford needed. Mulally's approach of analyzing the situation, accepting the facts, and then creating the solution is fundamental to redesigning this organization's systems and culture. As members of his management team have commented, Alan is the type of person people want to follow. Combine this with a business acumen that fully understands the need for a well-directed and well-aligned business system, and a vision and mission, and you can see why Ford's future looks bright. Ford's market share is up, its products are leading-edge, its relations with its unions are better than ever, and its operations are finally under control.[5]

WEB INTEGRATION

Want to learn more about Ford Motor Company's turnaround strategy? Visit **www.ford.com**.

Culture and Environment

While organizational structure can be thought of as the skeleton and muscles of the organization, where a framework is developed for supporting the day-to-day processes and activities, the culture of the organization can be thought of as its conscience and its heart. **Culture** defines how the individuals within the organization behave and how the organization as a whole will react to both internal and external challenges and stimuli. Culture can be thought of as the manner in which all the layers of the organization interact with each other (see Figure 7.8). It reflects the behavioural aspect of the internal processes and procedures the organization uses to facilitate the completion of tasks and the management of outcomes. It is the underlying values, attitudes, and interactive relationships that govern how work is to be accomplished. When developing the framework for an organization, managers need to take into consideration the environment within which they want employees to work, the norms or behaviours they desire to reinforce, and the interactive and interconnectivity opportunities they desire to incorporate into the decision-making and task completion process.

Culture defines how the individuals within the organization behave and how the organization as a whole will react to both internal and external challenges and stimuli.

FIGURE 7.8 Cultural Interconnectivity

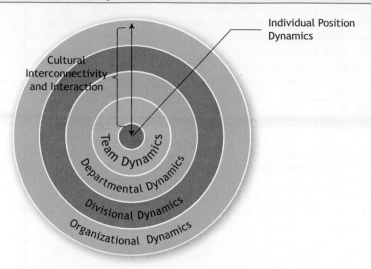

Individual Position
Dynamics

Cultural
Interconnectivity
and Interaction

Team Dynamics
Departmental Dynamics
Divisional Dynamics
Organizational Dynamics

> While organizational structure can be thought of as the skeleton and muscles of the organization, where a framework is developed for supporting the day-to-day processes and activities, the culture of the organization can be thought of as its conscience and its heart.

Managers also need to recognize that immigration and the interconnectivity of the global marketplace will bring individuals from a variety of cultural backgrounds into contact with each other, both within and outside of the workplace. This cultural diversity impacts not only how individuals interact, but also how individuals perceive authority, how they negotiate solutions to problems or challenges, how they view decisions (long-term versus short-term), how gender influences perceptions of authority, and their overall view of structure and hierarchical constraints and parameters. One of the leading authorities in assessing the influence of culture on structural efficiency and strategy execution is Professor Geert Hofstede of Maastricht University. His cultural dimensions model (see Figure 7.9) outlines five key dimensions that managers need to assess as they evaluate the impact of cultural interaction both within and outside of their organizations. Hofstede's widely used model provides managers with a good starting point to assess changes to their organizational culture as the organization evolves and as the interconnectivity with different global cultures grows.[6]

WEB INTEGRATION

Want to learn about the cultural dimensions model and Geert Hofstede's work? Visit **www.geert-hofstede.com**, or Google "Hofstede cultural dimensions model."

FIGURE 7.9 Hofstede Cultural Dimensions Model

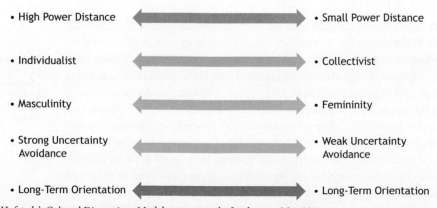

- High Power Distance ⟷ • Small Power Distance
- Individualist ⟷ • Collectivist
- Masculinity ⟷ • Femininity
- Strong Uncertainty Avoidance ⟷ • Weak Uncertainty Avoidance
- Long-Term Orientation ⟷ • Long-Term Orientation

Source: Geert Hofstede, Hofstede's Cultural Dimensions Model, www.geert-hofstede.com, May 2011.

FIGURE 7.10 Zones of Cultural Influence

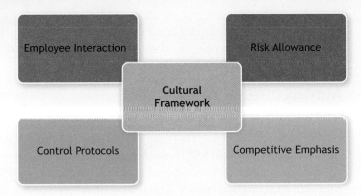

With a focus on the internal culture, managers can, in a sense, set the tone and seek to develop a measure of control over the environment within which the organization operates daily. They do this by defining the type of culture desired in advance of implementing organizational framework modifications. This is accomplished by defining behavioural norms and boundaries around four fundamental zones (see Figure 7.10).

Employee interaction refers to the level and style of interaction that occurs among employees and between work units and their management teams. It defines the participatory nature of the work environment, the sense of teamwork that is fostered within the organization, and the commitment of the management team toward supporting and developing each employee's skills and capabilities.

Risk allowance refers to the degree of entrepreneurship that is embedded into the organization. It is the extent to which the environment allows and encourages risk taking and flexibility in making decisions, supports innovation and innovative ideas, and rewards creativity in the workplace.

Control protocols refers to the rigidity or flexibility associated with the application of, and adherence to, rules, policies, and procedures within the organization. It is the degree of rigidity, order, and uniformity that is embedded within the organization, and the overarching emphasis on work conduct defined by efficiency and effectiveness protocols. Financial systems, quality control systems, and reward systems are examples of control protocols developed by an organization to oversee and direct operational performance.

Competitive emphasis refers to the extent to which the organization rewards and reinforces goal achievement, emphasizes competitiveness (internal and external), and defines its success on the basis of market superiority. This can also be thought of as the degree of passion that the organization communicates to its employees (and the frequency of such communications) relating to organizational successes and achievement of performance benchmarks. This also includes the effective use of logos and other visual representations by the organization in order to create a profile and define its market uniqueness.

The key with respect to this cultural framework is to develop a culture that passionately pursues the attainment of the vision and the mission of the organization.[7] This cultural framework becomes the underlying fabric of the organization and governs the connectivity of each individual employee to the organization and its "raison d'être." Organizations that will benefit from a positive work culture are those that enable the flow of information horizontally as well as vertically, and that resist the development of silos by creating protocols that involve team dynamics and cross-functional decision making, information transparency, the sharing of vision and mission, and the belief in employees as assets versus an expense. The same can be said of setting and communicating expectations. Employees who understand the expectations placed on them and who perceive such expectations, although challenging, as doable and realistic will challenge themselves to achieve these heightened levels of performance. This

Employee Interaction refers to the level and style of interaction that occurs among employees and between work units and their management teams.

Risk Allowance refers to the degree of entrepreneurship that is embedded into the organization.

Control Protocols refers to the rigidity or flexibility associated with the application of, and adherence to, rules, policies, and procedures within the organization.

Competitive Emphasis refers to the extent to which the organization rewards and reinforces goal achievement, emphasizes competitiveness (internal and external), and defines its success on the basis of market superiority.

assumes, of course, that these expectations are provided in an environment and culture that celebrates such successes and ensures employees have the resources needed to succeed.[8]

> The key with respect to this cultural framework is to develop a culture that passionately pursues the attainment of the vision and the mission of the organization.

Management Approach

As part of our discussion on developing an organizational framework, we also need to direct our focus toward defining (in broad terms) how the organization will be managed and the hierarchal structure that will be used to communicate the managerial process to employees. As you will see, the managerial approach really is reflective of the conclusions reached with regard to structure and culture. This includes decisions on the centralization or decentralization of managerial decision-making authority and responsibility, the extent of responsibility that various managerial positions will oversee (referred to as span of control), the coordination of the work effort that is considered most efficient to effectively direct the operational and market support processes within the organization, and the nature of the specific tasks that individuals within the organization accomplish on a day-to-day basis. Figure 7.11 illustrates the core criteria that ultimately will influence an organization's managerial approach.

FIGURE 7.11 Key Management Approach Criteria

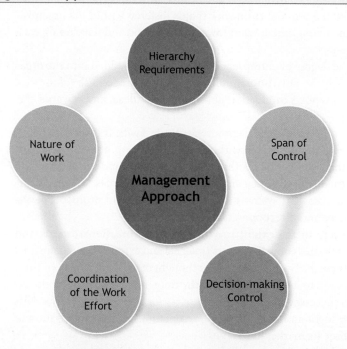

Managerial Hierarchy refers to the number of levels of management deemed necessary to effectively manage the organization, and the sequential ranking of the managerial positions in relationship to one another.

Managerial hierarchy refers to the number of levels of management deemed necessary to effectively manage the organization, and the sequential ranking of the managerial positions in relationship to one another; this hierarchy is often referred to as the "chain of command." It will be driven by the structural design of the organization (functional, geographic, customer, product focus). The number of layers of management will ultimately determine how tall or flat the organization is (see Figure 7.12). In general, the larger and more complex the organization, the more layers of management are required to effectively manage it. The key to hierarchy development, however, is where to position decision-making control so that the organization can effectively respond to the needs of the marketplace it serves in a manner that

FIGURE 7.12 Tall versus Flat Organizations

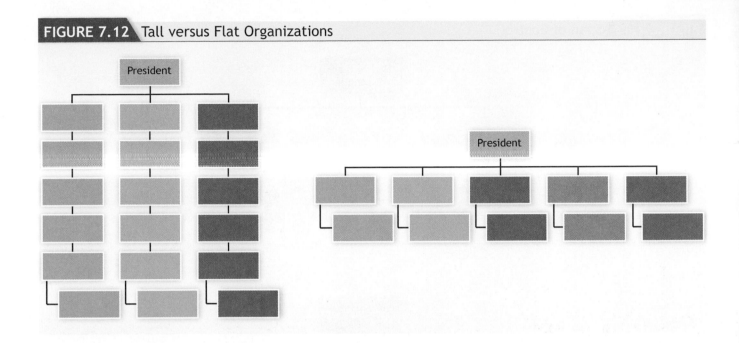

enables "management acumen" to be viewed as a competitive advantage. It is for this reason that organizational structures are continually being assessed and reassessed, as ineffective design can lead to poor or uninformed decision making.

Decision-making control refers to the level of responsibility and decision-making authority that is transferred to each specific managerial position. Again, structure will influence this, but so will the confidence that top-level management has in its lower-level managers to effectively make decisions that will benefit the organization. Decision-making control, in essence, reflects the location of organizational authority. Will it be centralized or decentralized? Centralized authority generally retains managerial control and decision making at the top of the organization. Supporters of centralized approaches believe that this results in the greatest efficiency and ensures that decisions are made in a consistent manner across the organization. They also argue that a centralized approach better ensures that the organization's operating plan remains aligned with its strategic objectives and vision. Opponents to a centralized managerial approach argue that this results in lower-level managers feeling less empowered and therefore reluctant to make decisions. This can result in a slower response to customer needs, lower morale among such managers, and heightened organizational conflict due to the inability to respond to day-to-day planning, organizing, and directing requirements. Many also believe that this approach inhibits the development of lower-level managers, resulting in long-term negative impact to the organization's overall health. A decentralized managerial approach is believed by its proponents to provide the organization with a quicker response mechanism to internal and external issues, stronger developmental outcomes, higher morale levels for lower-level managers, and less overall organizational conflict as decisions are made on the spot. As with any situation there are opponents who express concerns about such a managerial approach, pointing to the potential for inconsistency across the organization as various managers will interpret policies and procedures differently. They also point toward the increased risk of poor decisions due to some managers lacking experience or the information needed to make a fully informed decision, as well as loss of control over business operations as decisions may not be made in alignment with the overall corporate strategy and operating plan.

Span of control refers to the number of subordinates a manager will have reporting to him/her (see Figure 7.13). The span of control is generally determined by an analysis of the position's breadth and complexity of responsibilities, the degree of day to day interaction with subordinates, and the experience, expertise, and capabilities of both the individual in the

Decision-making Control refers to the level of responsibility and decision-making authority that is actually transferred to each specific managerial position.

Span of Control refers to the number of subordinates a manager has reporting to him or her.

FIGURE 7.13 Span of Control

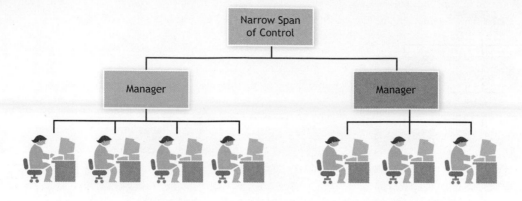

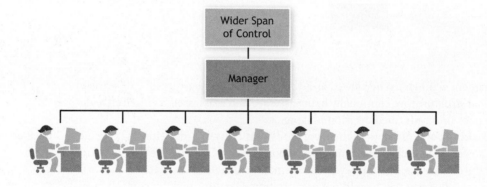

Coordination of the Work Effort is the organization and allocation of the HR complement, and the development of the structure surrounding it, in a manner that produces the most effective and efficient business system.

position and those who report to him/her. In general, the more the manager has to be involved in the day-to-day interactions of an area of responsibility, and the more complex the tasks associated with the responsibility assigned, the narrower the span of control will be.

Coordination of the work effort refers to the grouping of tasks and the facilitation of collaborative efforts among departments that must occur within the organization to ensure its products/services are designed, developed, produced, packaged, and distributed in a manner that successfully reaches the desired markets, and that customer connectivity and intimacy are achieved and their benefits maximized. This coordination of work effort will have a significant impact on the managerial hierarchy (or chain of command) that an organization puts into place, as well as the span of control associated with each managerial or supervisory position created. Work effort coordination also assesses the nature of the work that needs to be accomplished, and seeks to identify the most efficient processes for accomplishing such work. Decisions relating to process standardization or customization, production protocols, cross-functional project team formation, job rotation, training initiatives, and new technology deployment are but a few of the decisions that would fall under work coordination analysis. The determination of whether to consider outsourcing versus in-house manufacturing or support processes is another possible decision area relating to the coordination of work effort. In the Business in Action feature relating to Ford Motor Company, a key emphasis for Alan Mulally was to reassess how Ford conducted business on a global basis. Prior to Mulally's hiring, Ford Motor Company was largely product- and decision-focused on the basis of geographic units, with the North American unit making decisions relating to North America, the European unit being focused solely on Europe, and so on. This regional geographic focus resulted in a duplication of engineering and design teams, similar models being produced for different markets, and an overall failure to maximize the competitive leverage and economies of scale that a globally focused organization could bring. Under Mulally's tenure, Ford has reassessed how work is accomplished within the organization. Mulally's vision is that of "One Ford," as he calls it. It is the ability of the company to integrate its work processes to create vehicles for the global market. This means looking to reconfigure the way in which the company operates to increase the number of distinctive models it offers from fewer production platforms. For example, in 2008 the Ford Focus was produced for both the European market and the North American market. The Focus was designed and manufactured on two separate platforms that shared few similar components. Ford visualizes an international Ford Focus in 2013, with as many as five different variations of the vehicle being manufactured from a common platform. Mulally's vision does not stop here. A critical component of his work also includes the con solidation and alignment of the Ford Motor Company, its suppliers, and its dealers in order to improve these relationships and enhance the operational efficiencies of the organization.

Nature of the work refers to the specific tasks that need to be accomplished at the individual job level within the organization. Are we manufacturing a product? Are we a retail operation that purchases finished products and then resells them to customers? Are we a service industry, such as an investment bank, a real estate brokerage firm, or a charitable entity focused on serving the homeless? Assessing the nature of the work means defining what tasks are required in order for us to meet the needs of our customer base, whether such customers are other businesses, consumers, or a combination of both. It then means determining the best way to develop our response to the need identified. Ford Motor Company is, again, an example. Alan Mulally and his management team must assess what exactly needs to be done at each level of the organization, and within each position, to ensure that Ford reaches "best of class" status with respect to quality, fuel efficiency, safety, and overall vehicle value. The team is also assessing how and where Ford will interact with customers, dealers, employees, suppliers, unions, investors, and bankers, to name a few.

> **Nature of the Work** refers to the specific tasks that need to be accomplished at the individual job level within the organization.

IMPLEMENTING THE MANAGERIAL APPROACH

Mulally's "One Ford" plan is designed around the concepts of one team, one plan, and one goal. The objective is to foster within the organization a culture of functional and technical excellence, create a collaborate environment of teams and people working together, improve the quality and sustainability of products, and create a decision-making process that delivers the operating results expected by its shareholders as well as stakeholders. Mulally is accomplishing this by defining the needed managerial approach and building the framework for achieving the stated strategy utilizing the core components noted above. We need to do exactly the same thing in our day-to-day management of the organizations we oversee. General managers and C-level managers need to think beyond today's fires and seek to define how the business system is going to be developed and adjusted to continually meet the needs of the organization's customers and stakeholders. A core fundamental aspect of this is a regular review of the organization's structure and its management decision-making approach. As strategies change, so must the business system framework required to ensure the successful execution of the revised strategic direction (see Figure 7.14). Take Eastman Kodak as an example. In the 1990s, a large percentage of Eastman Kodak's revenue and profitability was driven by its film-based products and services. With the arrival of digital processing into the mainstream market at the turn of the millennium, Kodak has had to completely change its organizational strategy and modify its business system and supporting structure in response. Technologies that it previously did not have were developed or acquired; markets that it did not have products in were entered; and divisions were eliminated or sold and new ones added. The end result is that the Eastman Kodak of today is far different from the Eastman Kodak of 20 years ago.

> General managers and C-level managers need to think beyond today's fires and seek to define how the business system is going to be developed and adjusted to continually meet the needs of the organization's customers and stakeholders.

Management Approach Process

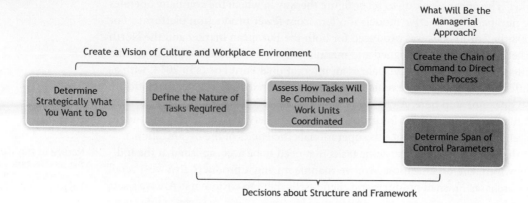

Create a Vision of Culture and Workplace Environment

What Will Be the Managerial Approach?

Determine Strategically What You Want to Do

Define the Nature of Tasks Required

Assess How Tasks Will Be Combined and Work Units Coordinated

Create the Chain of Command to Direct the Process

Determine Span of Control Parameters

Decisions about Structure and Framework

Decisions relating to structure and framework are derived from an assessment of the nature of the tasks required and the most efficient and effective grouping of these tasks to maximize the efficiency and effectiveness of the organization and meet its strategic objectives. As such an assessment takes place, it is important for managers to also visualize the culture and work environment they feel will best enable the talent within the organization to respond to the challenges such strategic objectives bring. With these two areas defined, managers can then determine the managerial approach that best fits the alignment of the structure to the organization's objectives and creates the culture and work environment envisioned as being fundamental to the achievement of the current objectives and the organization's long-term vision and mission.

BUSINESS *in Action*

Eastman Kodak

Eastman Kodak has been a company in transition for over a decade. As far back as 1991, analysts were sensing that Eastman Kodak's business model—and the company itself—was at risk. Driving significant revenue and profitability from its film-based product lines, Eastman Kodak was slow to react to the emerging digital trends in the marketplace. With a share value peaking at just over $90 in 1997, Eastman Kodak seemed to be content in floating along, seemingly oblivious to the market forces that were  quickly surrounding it. Fast forward to 2004, and what was once the world's biggest film manufacturer had eliminated more than 27 000 jobs in recent years, closed a number of factories, sold off major portions of its operations, and was spending billions of dollars in an attempt to catch up to what were now formidable competitors in the digital photography and imaging business (Canon, HP, Ricoh, Fuji, Xerox, Lexmark, Sony, and Emerson, to name a few). Once employing more than 145 000 employees (1988), Kodak, in its revised form, now employs approximately 30 000, and has a share value of $4.46 (June 2010). So, are Kodak's days numbered, and has it spiralled into the "whirlpool of death"? It depends on whom you talk to. However, one thing is for certain: its management team has focused, over the past 10 years, on transforming Eastman Kodak, from a film-based product-line organization into an emerging competitor in the digital realm. The question is whether or not it can effectively restore its revenue and profitability in the face of an onslaught of competitors, all better financed and currently better positioned as specialists in the markets they serve. So, just what is Eastman Kodak doing to get itself into the digital game? A major effort is centred on digital printing and related peripheral services, which some are calling Kodak's best bet for the future. Kodak views the global printing industry as a real opportunity for its future growth. Considerable time, money, and effort have been placed on positioning Kodak as a major player in the continuous inkjet market. This means taking on HP and Lexmark in the consumer market, and Xerox (among others) in the commercial sector. Kodak has also positioned itself in the digital still and video camera market and the document scanning market, where it hopes it can leverage its brand name and profile. The company also has created Kodak's online gallery and imaging services division, with the hope of supplementing the deterioration of its film-based product lines with digital development services. To say the change at Kodak has been "paradigm" has been an understatement. A US$13-billion company in 2000, with US$10 billion of this revenue coming from consumer film-based and health-imaging sales, Kodak's revenue in 2009 had fallen to US$7.6 billion with an operating loss of US$117 million. Film-based and traditional photography products and services, which made up more than 60 percent of Kodak's sales in 2000, now represent less than 10 percent of the organization's revenue. The health imaging division was sold in 2007. In a complete transformation, Kodak has gone from being focused on the photographic film business to being a digital imaging company. Its three current divisions are the consumer digital imaging group; the film, photo-

finishing, and entertainment group; and the graphic communications group. The jury remains out on Eastman Kodak. The company has seen ongoing additions and departures at the senior management level. Risks challenging the organization range from the sluggishness of the economy to the swiftness of technology in the markets they are competing in, the global competitive pressures that are impacting prices and overall profitability, and ongoing questions as to whether Kodak has indeed invested in the right markets for the future. A key short-term issue is profitability. Although it has initiated ongoing cost-cutting measures, taken advantage of outsourcing opportunities, and sold off underproducing assets, all to improve the bottom line, the company currently continues to operate barely above breakeven, and the organization's total liabilities exceed the value of its asset base. Kodak's management team will continue to focus on transforming the company going forward. For CEO Antonio Perez and his team, the situation remains fluid, with change being the only constant.[9]

WEB INTEGRATION

To follow Kodak's organization redesign process, use Google Finance, or visit Eastman Kodak's Web site at **www.kodak.com**.

The Concept of Restructuring

LO6

Often, when browsing the business section of a newspaper or a Web site, we come across an article about a company that has announced a **restructuring** initiative. For many, the questions that come to mind ask what restructuring is, and what the rationale is for an organization to initiate such an exercise. Restructuring generally occurs when companies recognize a disconnection to their intended strategy as a result of disruptions that have occurred either internally or from the external marketplace. Recognizing that a change to their business system or their desired position in the marketplace is required, organizations decide to make fundamental changes to the way in which they do business. Restructuring an organization can be in response to such activities as an immediate need to reduce costs, a longer-term need to redirect the organization's business efforts due to a fundamental shift in the demand for the products/services they offer, competitive pressures, a change in customer behaviour, technology obsolescence, or bankruptcy. The Business in Action vignette on Eastman Kodak is designed to provide an example of when and why a business restructuring might occur. Restructuring does not have to be a reactive business decision, nor is it solely focused on downsizing, or retrenchment, due to liquidity or solvency issues challenging an organization (although we tend to hear more of such situations via the media). Although these are valid reasons for initiating a restructuring strategy, restructuring can be due to positive circumstances,

Restructuring addresses the need to change an organization's business system or desired position in the marketplace, or to make fundamental changes to the way an organization does business.

such as significant growth, the launch of new products or services, the acquisition of a company, or a future anticipated move in the marketplace by the organization. Ultimately, the goal of any restructuring initiative should be to increase the value and the long-term health of the organization. When thinking about restructuring, managers should focus on three common elements to the plan: structural design, execution, and communication.

> Restructuring generally occurs when companies recognize a disconnection to their intended strategy as a result of disruptions that have occurred either internally or from the external marketplace.

- **Structural design:** The first element is the structural design of the restructuring plan. What changes or adjustments to the organizational structure will be required to successfully achieve the desired objectives of the restructuring plan? What impacts to our culture are anticipated? Are significant changes being implemented that will fundamentally change our chain of command and managerial decision-making process?

- **Execution:** What will the restructuring process look like? What are the various phases to the plan that will need to be implemented? Is this simply a subtle change as a result of challenging the status quo in order to maintain or enhance the organization's competitive position, or is this a significant and drastic move as a result of very real and significant market disruptions? Will the restructuring process severely disrupt the organization's business operations? If so, what is the intended strategy to help keep business flowing?

- **Communication:** What is the communication plan? How are we going to communicate the restructuring to the various stakeholder groups impacted? Have we definitively tied the restructuring plan to the revised organizational strategy to ensure a full understanding of the rationale for the action? How can we minimize negative impact to morale and preserve our employee culture if such an impact is perceived to exist?

A key determination in the success of a restructuring initiative lies in the extent of the change the organization is undertaking. In general, restructuring single, isolated business processes or initiatives is easier to implement, with a higher probability of success. For example, the desire to restructure the fabrication process of a single product via enhanced technology application is easy for a managerial team to focus on and guide to its completion. The risk of implementation gets considerably greater, and the probability of success lower, as the degree of change required, the broadness of the change focus, and the length of time to completion all increase. As Eastman Kodak is finding, a total fundamental change to the direction of the business, the markets in which it plans to compete, and the change in the integrated business processes that it needs to successfully execute its strategies is a monumental task, to say the least. It is, in fact, a challenge that has spanned several years, and one that analysts remain unsure of as to the level of success Eastman Kodak will actually achieve. Figure 7.15 provides an illustration of the risk and complexity impact on the probability of success for a restructuring effort.

Keep in mind that to be successful at any restructuring effort an organization's management team must remain focused on the objectives desired, get actively involved in the transformation process, and commit with the staying power required to see the project to its successful completion. Prioritization and sequencing of what needs to be accomplished, the amount of change needed to ensure that the desired results are achieved, a full understanding of the learning curves for staff involved, and an accurate sense of the time and investment requirements needed are all fundamental success metrics to achieving the desired organizational goals.[10]

> To be successful at any restructuring effort an organization's management team must remain focused on the objectives desired, get actively involved in the transformation process, and commit with the staying power required to see the project to its successful completion.

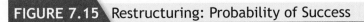

FIGURE 7.15 Restructuring: Probability of Success

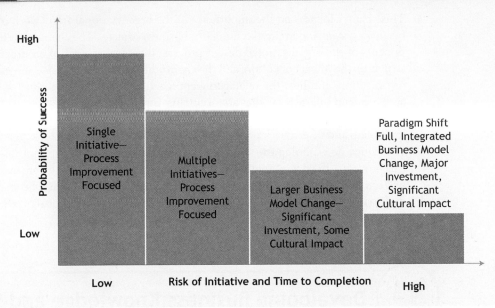

Management Reflection—The Importance of Business System Design

Managers need to recognize the important role that an organization's business system structure and its culture and work environment play in the accomplishment of its business strategy. The structure, culture, and managerial approach fundamentally influence the flow of communication, the level of collaboration, and the efficiency and effectiveness of the work being performed. Structure and culture are what forms the backbone of the organization. It is the formalized process through which tasks within the organization are aligned with the strategic objectives of the company, and are executed in support of this stated strategy. The development of the "chain of command" or managerial hierarchy directly influences the speed with which decisions are made, the approval processes required to make things happen, and the responsibility and accountability levels within the organization. As managers, we need to take the time to plan this hierarchy in a manner that drives efficiency and effectiveness, but that also creates a culture and work environment that energizes our workforce, encourages the sharing of ideas, fosters innovation and creativity, eliminates bureaucracy, and articulates the organization's vision and mission.

> The development of the chain of command or managerial hierarchy directly influences the speed with which decisions are made, the approval processes required to make things happen, and the responsibility and accountability levels within the organization.

Chapter Summary

This chapter focuses on the importance of the organizational framework in the design of a business system and in the execution of a business strategy. The chapter outlines the key components of the organizational design process: the development of an organization's formal structure, the impact of culture and the environment on the efficiency and effectiveness of an organization, and how the managerial approach will, ultimately, influence and support the activities and interactions that are occurring within the business. The chapter also seeks to familiarize students with the different types of organizational structures companies can utilize to develop and direct work processes and tasks, and the building blocks managers should review when determining the structural approach to be utilized. An important component of this process is the determination of the managerial approach that the organization as a whole will implement and the key factors that will influence this decision. The chapter ends with a discussion of the concept of restructuring and the relationship of the extensiveness of the change and the amount of time required for the redesign process.

Developing Business Knowledge and Skills

KEY TERMS

value chain *p. 171*

structure *p. 172*

customer intimacy *p. 177*

work efficiencies *p. 178*

departmentalization *p. 178*

culture *p. 179*

employee interaction *p. 181*

risk allowance *p. 181*

control protocols *p. 181*

competitive emphasis *p. 181*

managerial hierarchy *p. 182*

decision-making control *p. 183*

span of control *p. 183*

coordination of the work effort *p. 184*

nature of the work *p. 185*

restructuring *p. 187*

QUESTIONS FOR DISCUSSION

1. What are the four key components that are used to formulate the design of a business system?

2. In developing an organization's framework, what three questions should be utilized to drive the development process? How are they interrelated?

3. In your opinion, what are the key criteria for determining the type of organizational structure a business should evolve toward?

4. Why is developing the right culture so important for a business system? What are the key zones of impact that should be assessed when seeking to influence the cultural framework of an organization?

5. Discuss the five key criteria that are used to determine the managerial approach an organization develops to guide the organization's decision-making process. How are these combined to form a process for finalizing the intended managerial approach?

6. What is restructuring? When thinking about restructuring, what three common elements should managers focus on to ensure that a successful restructuring takes place?

QUESTIONS FOR INDIVIDUAL ACTION

Using annual reports and an Internet search, analyze three or four leading publicly traded Canadian companies and draw conclusions as to the focus of their organizational structure. What does their organizational setup (i.e., their org charts) tell you? How are they currently focused (functional, product-focused, customer-focused, matrix, etc.)? How do their structures enable them to better serve their customers and maintain their advantage in the marketplace?

TEAM EXERCISE

Using the Business in Action vignette as a guide, develop a detailed analysis, for presentation to the class, of the organizational changes that have occurred within Eastman Kodak over the past two decades. What significant changes have occurred in the way this company does business? How have its markets and overall strategic focus changed? How has this impacted the organizational structure and culture of Eastman Kodak? How much change has occurred within the management team?

Case for Discussion

Tony J. Condie, president (and owner) of Club Athletica, is in a bit of a dilemma. His organization has grown considerably over the last three years, and a real opportunity exists to significantly expand the business operation and become a major player in the delivery of fitness services within the community of New Bedford. The dilemma, however, is how he should restructure his organization to continue to meet the needs of his current customer base and effectively manage his business while taking advantage of these new opportunities.

New Bedford is a municipality of 200 000 residents just outside of Toronto. The municipality is predominantly made up of white-collar occupations, with heavy emphasis on government and university-related services. There is a newly evolving biotech industry within the municipality as well. The community is considered to have slightly above-average incomes and is projected to grow at a rate of 9 percent per year for the next five years.

As part of his five-year plan, Tony is focused on growing his business through the establishment of additional Club Athletica locations. This will enable Club Athletica to provide programs and services that are convenient and in close proximity to the various geographic sectors within the city. With its current facility centrally located, the plan is to open two additional locations in the southeast and northwest sections of New Bedford. Both areas are expected to realize significant population growth over the near term.

Success, however, does not come without its share of challenges. Tony's current Club Athletica location has doubled its membership over the past couple of years, causing considerable strain on the facility and his management team. Tony, as the owner, continually finds himself directing day-to-day facility issues and operations. It seems that he is constantly putting out operational fires, acting as the IT "go to" person, and responding to customer concerns personally. This already leaves him with little time for strategic planning and new site development. With his previously publicly announced commitment to open his two additional facilities over the next 12 months, locations leased, and marketing beginning to ramp up, a sense of the loss of control is beginning to creep into his mind. Clearly, the current organizational structure is not set up to handle a multi-site operation.

The focus to date has been on a single-site operation, with responsibility accountability as shown below:

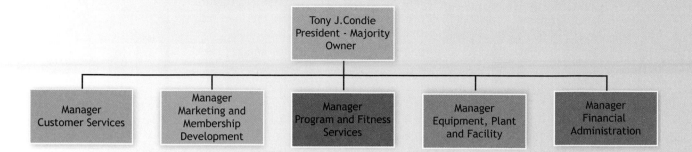

Tony has reached the following conclusions regarding the anticipated expansion of Club Athletica:

- Although smaller in size than the current facility, the two new locations will essentially offer the same services currently offered at his existing Club Athletica location (fitness centre, group fitness classes, personal training, water massage therapy, tanning, and temporary child care services for children of members using the facility).

- Facility cleaning, membership services, program requirements, and maintenance issues will exist at all three locations and must be accounted for.

- Membership access must be transparent at all locations. Club Athletica members should be able to access any of the three facilities seamlessly, and see consistency in the delivery of services and programs regardless of which facility they are in.

- Current server and software systems will need to be reassessed and upgraded. A key requirement will be the implementation of a new member management software system that can track member usage and provide other key membership data and statistics for all three locations.

- Administration services and marketing will be housed at the central location for all three facilities, as will IT and other core support services.

In addition to the new locations and the operational issues associated with them, Tony also recognizes that he needs to spend more time out in the community, networking and increasing the profile of Club Athletica. After all, generating new business, soliciting new organizations for corporate memberships, and creating better prospecting links requires face-to-face interaction on the part of the business—and Tony knows and understands that this is what he does best. In addition, it is rumoured that new competitors may be popping up in the area given its population growth and attractive demographics. So much to think about—so little time!

With all this in his mind, Tony knows that a redesign of the way he conducts business and of his current organizational structure is required. The current functional structure (as shown above) just doesn't seem to make sense given all the changes that will take place in the upcoming 12 months and the need to create a stronger image and profile for Club Athletica. The private investors backing Tony, all true supporters of the Club Athletica concept, are reminding him, however, of the need to maintain control over unnecessary expenditures during this expansion. They do, however, recognize the need for additional employees if the growth is to be properly managed. Unsure where to begin, Tony has asked you and your team to review his current situation and provide him with some initial thoughts, and assist him by outlining a process that he can follow in redesigning his organization.

QUESTIONS

What recommendations would you make to Tony and Club Athletica? Specifically:

1. Identify what you believe are the three to five key decision criteria Tony needs to consider in redesigning Club Athletica's current operating model and organizational structure.

2. Develop a simplified process that you would recommend to enable Tony to fully assess the core requirements for a successful transition to a multi-site location.

3. Assuming you could hire two additional managerial positions, what would they be? How would you redesign the organizational chart to reflect these new additions?

Practise and learn online with Connect. Connect resources include additional and interactive study exercises, videos, and practice quizzing, as well as additional material you won't find in the printed text.

8 Managing and Leading the Organization's Talent

Learning Objectives

This chapter is designed to provide students with:

Lo1 An appreciation for considering employees assets rather than expenses

Lo2 An appreciation for the fundamentals needed to create a positive work environment

Lo3 An overview of the motivational tools that are key for managers

Lo4 An understanding of the competencies a manager must possess to be successful in managing talent

Lo5 An understanding of the internal and external challenges managers face in managing talent

Snapshot—What to Expect in This Chapter

This chapter focuses on managing and leading an organization's talent. The content emphasized in this chapter includes the following:

- The Importance of Talent

- The Employee Transformation Process
  - What Constitutes a Great Company?
  - What Makes for a Great Job?
  - Compensation and Lifestyle Influences

- The Motivational Tool Kit

- Managing Your Workforce

- The Danger of Short-Term Pressures

- Putting It All Together

- HR Management in the Small Business Setting

- Management Reflection—Finding the Right Balance

From the Student's Perspective

Although "leadership" is a term that is difficult to define, we tend to know when we are in the presence of good or bad leadership. Based on my personal experiences in university and in the workforce, I can say that there are at least three abilities that great leaders need to possess in order to motivate and inspire others toward a common goal.

First, leaders *establish direction*. They tend to have a clear vision, self-confidence, and supreme organizational skills. To you, this may mean writing out an agenda for a group meeting—or, better yet, sending it out 24 hours prior. Second, leaders *mobilize action*. It is crucial to provide your teammates with the tools they need, ensure that everyone is on task, and, above all, maintain an enthusiastic and positive attitude. Third, leaders understand the importance of the *development* of their team. This requires understanding, empathy, and a willingness to change. It is extremely important to let others on your team take ownership of different responsibilities and to give them proper recognition when it is due. After all, leaders would not be leaders if they had to do everything themselves!

At university, you will have many opportunities to practise and advance your leadership skills. I encourage (and challenge!) you to get involved in activities about which you are passionate or even curious. It is in those areas that your energy will engage others and enable you to, ultimately, reach success.

And, once success is achieved, remember that celebrations are in order.

Cheers!

Katharine Berger (B.Comm '09) is one of the first grads hired for the grad@Loblaw program in the Marketing and Loblaw Brands stream. She has received both theoretic and hands-on training in the core departments of the grocery industry, and currently works on some of Canada's top brands at the Loblaw office in Brampton, Ontario. Katharine was involved in several committees while in the Queen's Commerce program. She was the co-chair of the Alma Mater Society charity ball, the yearly events coordinator for the Queen's Marketing Association Conference (QMAC), the retail manager of Oil Thigh Designs (OTD), and obtained her certificate in Corporate Social Responsibility. In the near future, she plans to pursue an MBA, travel to China, and explore photography.

BUSINESS *in Action*

The War for Talent

For many of the world's global business players, the war for executive talent is just heating up. Over the upcoming decade, one of the most defining issues that will challenge organizations across all business areas is the acquisition and retention of managerial staff. Whereas companies in the past have benefited from a large management pool of baby boomers in their 30s and 40s, this age group has now moved into their 50s and 60s, with retirement shortly to follow. Organizations are already feeling the pinch, as companies are finding in their search for executive talent that the marketplace is becoming increasingly crowded. Recent statistical research shows that the number of 35- to 44-year-olds in North America will decline by 15 percent between now and 2015. Add to this the fact that the surge of women—who historically have provided employment expansion opportunities for the marketplace—has peaked, thereby further tightening the available labour pool. Attitudes of executives have also changed, as more university graduates, MBAs, and young business professionals are looking for opportunities with smaller upstart companies where the risk/reward opportunity (excitement, flexibility, ability to impact, financial and equity-based rewards) is believed to be sufficiently more attractive from a career perspective. Today's younger managerial professionals are also much more "job mobile," viewing their careers as bridging several organizations and opportunities versus staying with a single business organization for their career duration. For organizations in need of top-level management talent to guide and grow their business, this declining supply of talent is further compounded by the need for even more sophisticated skill sets in the managers they do manage to recruit and retain. Today's global marketplace is demanding managers with significantly greater global exposure and acumen, strong leading-edge technology competencies, multicultural management experience, and entrepreneurial skill sets needed to keep organizations innovative and at the forefront of the industries within which they compete. As Elizabeth G. Chambers, Mark Foulon, Helen Handfield-Jones, Steven M. Hankin, and Edward G. Michaels III stated in their article "The War for Talent," organizations will be increasingly chal-

lenged to define and redefine their employee value propositions in order to communicate to prospective employees why they should come work for them rather than the company next door. The challenge then becomes how to develop these employees once recruited, and how to continue to challenge them in a way that results in success for them and for the organization, thereby retaining their talents for the benefit of the organization for the long term.[1]

The Importance of Talent

LO1

In very broad terms, the opening chapters of this textbook have attempted to create a sense as to the overarching role of C-level managers, general managers, and small business owners with regard to managing their respective organizations. This overarching role can be thought of as encompassing four broad areas of responsibility: market assessment and strategy development and execution; business system design, development, and implementation; financial resource management (discussed in detail in Chapters 12, 13, and 14); and the fourth, discussed in this chapter, attracting, retaining, and managing talent. Recognizing that all four areas are important and, in many ways, interconnected, the objective of this chapter is to discuss the pivotal role that the organization's talent plays in directing its strategy, capital, and financial resources and business system components in order to achieve excellence in operational performance.

To provide some additional insight, let's assume you are getting ready to embark on a trip. Initially, you must define where you need to go—just as a business, in its strategic development process, needs to define the company's overall business direction. The *market assessment and strategy development* responsibility involves determining a destination, choosing a route, and providing a GPS to ensure you stay on track. The *business system design and development* responsibility involves determining the type of vehicle to be used, deciding whether to use your own vehicle or rent a vehicle, arranging pre-trip maintenance, booking hotels, and purchasing maps and trip tickers. The *financial resource management* responsibility involves establishing a budget, allocating the required financial resources to ensure the monetary needs of the trip are met, and ensuring financial obligations incurred during the trip are covered. Finally, the *talent* responsibility involves driving the vehicle, interpreting the route and GPS directions, ensuring the schedule is maintained, and arriving at the destination as planned. As you can recognize from this simple illustration, although the strategy direction is defined, the financial resources are provided, and the system is developed to meet the trip's requirements, it still comes down to the "talent" to ensure the trip is completed successfully. Herein lies the importance of an organization's human resource complement, or what is called its talent. An organization's success is only as good as the management team that leads it and the talent that executes the strategy and is responsible for delivering on the key success metrics. Knowing this, then, why does it appear that so many organizations still view their managerial staff and employees as an expense line on the income statement rather than as an asset similar to the capital and financial assets that appear on their balance sheets? The answer appears to be that too many organizations think of their talent as a tactical versus strategic resource—and, therefore, manage it on the basis of short-term needs—versus as a core strategic component and integral part of the organization's long-term strategy. As managers, we need to recognize our employees are a core area from which we can develop and leverage a sustainable competitive advantage, and design and implement human resource recruitment and development strategies in a way that makes them an integral part of the strategic planning and execution process.

Demographics, globalization, and the need for higher-knowledge skill-based employees are requiring us to take a longer, more "asset versus expense" approach to our human resource team. This means defining human resource objectives that are in line with business objectives, and targeting talent at all levels within the organization for skill, knowledge, and capability improvement as an opportunity to raise operational productivity, sales, and profits. A key component of this asset-base approach to human resource management is recognizing that managers need to spend more time on talent development; managers need to focus their efforts on coaching and providing feedback to employees, ensuring that a culture of collaboration and communication exists within the organization, effectively addressing underperformance, providing rewards that reflect the level of performance given, and investing in the resources needed in order for all to be successful in their work endeavours. It is hoped that, once you have read this chapter, you will gain some insight into how managers can successfully respond to the challenges of managing their human resources team.

> Managers need to spend more time coaching and providing feedback to employees, ensuring that a culture of collaboration and communication exists within the organization, effectively addressing underperformance, providing rewards that reflect the level of performance given, and investing in the resources needed in order for all to be successful in their work endeavours.

The Employee Transformation Process

Organizations spend a tremendous amount of time and money on attracting, developing, motivating, and retaining their employees. In keeping with our aim to view each employee as an asset versus an expense, as managers we should seek a return on our investment in each employee just as we look to achieve a return on the investments we make in technology, equipment, buildings, and so on. To receive this anticipated return means that we need to view and treat our human assets in the same way we would treat our other capital and financial assets. Assume, for example, we are looking to purchase a new piece of equipment for our organization. In making the purchase decision we will determine the type of equipment needed, develop the specifications the decision should be based on, assess the different purchase options, choose the equipment to be purchased, determine the level of support needed to maintain this equipment, and ensure it is being properly used. We will also need to make periodic investments in the equipment to maintain its efficiency, consider other uses that make sense for the equipment, and plan to retain the equipment for as long as it continues to contribute to the organization's operating productivity, sales revenue generation, and overall profitability.

The same approach should be fundamental to decisions involving our human assets. We should first determine the need within the organization that we are trying to solve and develop a set of specifications that identify the specific skill set required to fill the position. Then, we should determine the type of individual best suited to filling the need, recruiting and selecting a preferred candidate from a list of applicants. Once this person has been hired, we must provide orientation, training, and skill support development to the new employee, seek to maximize the individual's potential through periodic or ongoing investment in new or existing skill development, look to enrich the employee's experience through additional opportunities for contribution to the organization, and evaluate and provide feedback on the employee's overall productivity and contribution to the sales and profitability of the organization. Just as capital assets have a life cycle, so, too, do employees. The key as managers is to maximize the length of this life cycle for as long as the benefits to the organization continue to accrue in terms of productivity, sales revenue generation, and profitability. Success in this regard means that employees feel valued and are given the opportunity to grow and excel in the areas of responsibility and accountability applicable to them, and are rewarded in a manner that they feel is commensurate with their commitment.

As with investment decisions relating to equipment or a building, the recruitment and development of human resource assets requires a significant upfront investment on the part of an organization. It also recognizes that there will be a period during which the investment in the employee will exceed the productivity value of that employee. Figure 8.1 provides a simplified overview of the transformation process that an organization incurs in moving an employee into the organization and then to a fully productive level.

With few exceptions, employees do not simply walk in the door on their first day of work and instantly contribute to the organization at 100 percent of their productive potential. A significant amount of time and money is invested by the organization in attracting the preferred candidate, hiring this individual, and then transitioning the new hire into the organization and into the specific position. This investment takes the form of costs associated with:

- preparing the job specification or job description

- identifying the type of candidate required and advertising and recruitment (agency fees, etc.)

- interviews and aptitude or behavioural testing (if required)

- travel, relocation, and job acclimatization, such as orientation and training

- hiring bonuses and other job-related expenses

Keep in mind that once the prospective employee is hired, wage and benefit costs are incurred as well. Recruiting top-level managers can take months and can require an

FIGURE 8.1   Employee Transformation Process

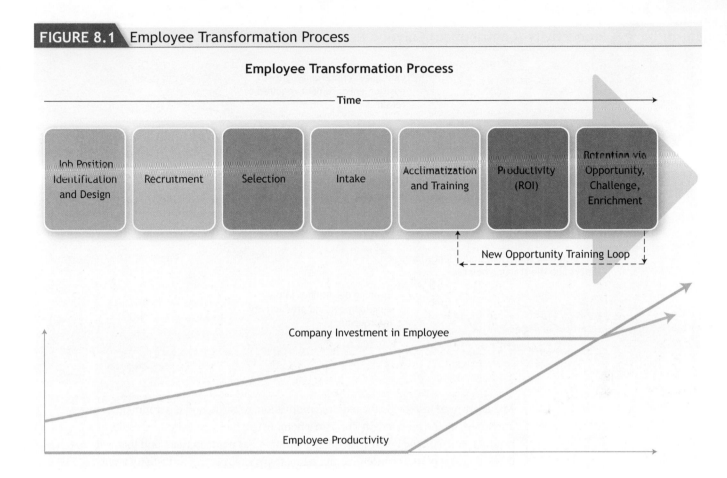

investment of several thousand dollars on the part of the organization. Once the employee is in the position, time also has to be allowed for the individual to understand the organization's culture, its decision-making structure and process, its customer base, and the operational processes driving its products and services. It is not unusual for this acclimatization and training period to extend from six months to the first full year that an employee is with an organization.

This discussion demonstrates that each employee hired represents a considerable investment on the part of the hiring organization. As managers, it is essential that we think through the process and plan for hiring an employee in the same way that we look to purchase equipment and other valuable organizational assets. In addition to this investment attitude, we also need to consciously think in terms of what will be required to ensure the new hire becomes productive and remains of value by making a contribution toward meeting the organization's vision and mission. As managers, a major part of ensuring our organization reaps the benefits of its employees' productivity lies in our ability to effectively manage our workforce and invest in them the time, energy, and financial resources that will enable them to effectively perform their jobs. This means that, as managers, we need to provide the motivation, rewards, and environment to move our employees up the productivity curve to a point where their contribution results in a positive return on the investment we have made in them, and that will provide, on an ongoing basis, the incentive and desire to maintain such productivity levels (see Figure 8.2). We must also recognize that a failure to provide the right work *environment*, *rewards*, and *recognition*-based incentives (ERR) will heighten the probability of employee defection (turnover), thereby forfeiting any potential return on our investment and requiring us to spend new dollars to attract new employees to take their place.

FIGURE 8.2   Productivity (Contribution) Curve

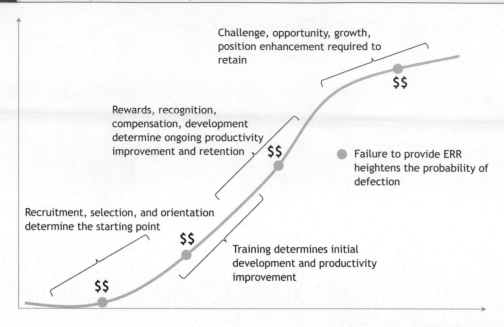

Managers need to provide the required motivation, rewards, and environment to move employees up the productivity curve to a point where their contribution results in a positive return on the investment the organization has made in them and that will provide, on an ongoing basis, the incentive and desire to maintain such productivity levels.

So, just what does it take to create a work environment that encourages employees to reach and maintain high levels of productivity? The remaining parts of this chapter try to provide some guidance for managers with respect to this question. The answer lies in our ability, as managers, to deliver a work environment that leads each of our employees to conclude that they work for a great company, they have a great job, and the reward system offered meets their compensation and lifestyle expectations (see Figure 8.3).[2]

FIGURE 8.3   Creating a Positive Work Environment

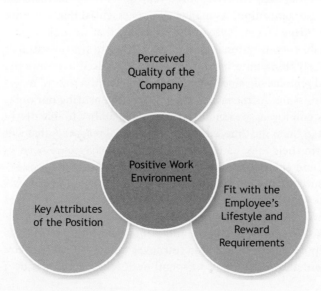

BUSINESS *in Action*

Steven Jobs on Finding Talent

In 2008, in an exclusive interview, *Fortune* magazine senior editor Betsy Morris had the privilege of talking with Apple CEO Steve Jobs. The interview covered a variety of topics relating to Apple's success and future prospects. One of the questions that Morris posed to Jobs had to do with finding talent. In his response, Jobs indicated that when he hires somebody for Apple, the core determinant for him is whether the person will fall in love with Apple. Yes, the person has to be smart, but, more importantly, they have to be passionate about what Apple does and believe in the essence of the company itself. For Jobs, if a person falls in love with Apple it means they will do what is best for Apple, not what is best for them or anyone else. Jobs went on to indicate that recruiting is difficult. As he put it, it is like finding needles in a haystack. Recognizing that you cannot possibly find out everything about a person in one or two interview sessions, Jobs indicated that much of it is about "gut" feelings. How do you feel about this person? What are they like when they are challenged? Why are they here? Like Steve Jobs, managers involved

in hiring are constantly challenged to attract and acquire the best talent for their organizations. For managers, a key component of the hiring and promotion process should be in measuring an individual's passion. People with passion have the ability to fight back in the face of obstacles and difficulties. They also seem to have an innate ability to get things done and to make things happen. A second key characteristic is focus. Does the individual have the ability to stay focused on the most important issues? Being focused means recognizing the core essence of what needs to be done, and being able to weed out those options or alternatives that will result in the organization straying from its intended path. It is also finding those individuals with leadership potential. It is recognizing the ability for an individual to develop his/her capacities and abilities, as well as the capacity and the ability of others. With the heightening global competitiveness across markets, it is critical that companies make the investment to recruit emerging leaders and to encourage leadership development among existing staff.[3]

What Constitutes a Great Company?

As the saying goes, everyone loves a winner. The same holds true regarding our choice of where to work. Employees like to be part of a winning team. This does not necessarily mean the company has to be the biggest competitor within its industry. It really refers to the fact that employees need to believe the organization is perceived as an industry leader or a challenger and innovator within the market segments that it serves. This could be at the international, national, regional, or local level. For many employees, their work environment is a major aspect of their overall life. Employees like to feel that the organization they work for offers exciting challenges for the future, possesses values that are in line with their own thinking, and is composed of talented people all working toward a well-defined goal or vision, recognized within the industry and the community as an innovator and strong performer, led by a high-quality management team, and provides an acceptable level of job security for its workforce. As managers, it is important that we recognize this fundamental underlying requirement and seek to communicate to our employees the victories and the positive attributes of our company in a way that instils pride in being part of that organization.

What Makes for a Great Job?

Although attracting and retaining individuals who want to work for a great company is essential, ensuring that the job we are asking them to do challenges them and fits into their career aspirations is a second key component of keeping individuals at optimal performance levels. For managers, this means that we need to meet the expectations of employees on three levels. First, it is important that we communicate to employees how their job fits into the big picture of the organization overall and contributes to the mission and vision of the organization. Employees need to understand how they fit in if they are to view their job as being meaningful—each employee, no matter whether they are the CEO of the organization or a front-line server dealing with customers on a day-to-day basis, must have a sense as to the purpose of their work in delivering the organization's mission. Second, employees need to feel that their current position provides challenges commensurate with their background and skill set. Great jobs offer employees opportunities for advancement, the ability to grow through job enrichment or job enhancement, and the ability to take on a sense of ownership and accountability for the work being performed. Third, employees need to perceive a good fit with their immediate supervisor or boss. Employees value feedback and interaction with their managers. They are looking for approval, praise, and recognition of a job well done, as well as positive, constructive criticism delivered in a professional manner when corrections to their performance need to be communicated. They are also looking for their managers to respect them, trust them, set expectations that will realistically challenge them, provide the appropriate level of resources, and remove barriers that stand in the way of their ability to perform their work. Two-way communication via establishing objectives and sharing performance expectations is essential to a culture and an environment where employees can excel.

Compensation and Lifestyle Influences

The final component of creating an environment for optimal productivity within a workforce, and for attracting and retaining employees, is the establishment and communication of a reward system that meets their compensation and lifestyle needs. Recognizing that compensation levels are limited by the financial capabilities of an organization, employees fundamentally need to perceive that the organization's compensation system is equitable in its underlying performance/reward framework. In other words, organizations need to ensure that inequity within their reward system, driven by internal and external comparisons, does not result in employees feeling undervalued or unappreciated. Recognizing the difference between high and low performers and ensuring that poor performers are not unfairly rewarded at the same levels as high performers is an important component of the internal equity assessment process. Keep in mind that, although we think of compensation largely in terms of salaries or wages, compensation also encompasses bonuses, such as signing bonuses, longevity bonuses, and performance bonuses; long-term incentives, such as stock options; employee benefits, such as life and health insurance; and pensions or retirement plans. An additional component to establishing a high-performance work environment is the requirement for employees to recognize that their organization understands and respects their need for a balanced lifestyle. The ability to provide flextime options, meaningful and valued fringe benefit options, performance-based financial incentives, acceptable levels of stress, a manageable work pace, opportunities for advancement, developmental programs for personal and job-related growth, and recognition reward systems all work to create an underlying framework for positive performance.[4]

> High levels of employee performance are directly related to employees' belief that they work for a great company, have a great job, and enjoy a reward system that meets their compensation and lifestyle expectations.

BUSINESS *in Action*

Creative Ways to Reward Employees

Companies worldwide are learning more and more that building a highly productive workforce staffed by happy and highly motivated people can be accomplished in many ways. Although stock options, performance bonuses, and regular wage increases are still important, business leaders and their boards of directors are finding that supporting lifestyle balance and providing day-to-day reinforcement that employees are valued can result in far greater returns in terms of work performance, employee retention, and active company loyalty. Although these "new-style" benefits come with a price tag, for many companies the return they receive from their workforce far exceeds the cost. So, just what are some of the more creative ways that organizations are using to attract, retain, motivate, and meet the needs of their workforce? Well, here are just a few of the many creative benefits currently being offered. SAS provides employees with an onsite health-care centre staffed by 4 physicians and 10 nurse practitioners. It also has a 66 000-sq.-ft. fitness centre, a natatorium, and a lending library at its Cary, North Carolina, head office. SAS also provides onsite day care, and has an unlimited sick-day policy. Google engineers are given 20 percent of their time to devote to projects of their own choosing. Colgate-Palmolive employees can participate in a vacation exchange program where they can buy additional vacation days or sell unused days. The company also provides employees access to a mortgage assistance program.

Research In Motion gives new employees a free BlackBerry smartphone on their first day of work, and provides onsite massage services, flu shot clinics, and discounted gym memberships to help employees stay healthy. Qualcomm employees participate in baseball games, are offered surfing lessons, can sign up for kayaking tours, go bowling, and have company-sponsored bonfires. Cisco, one of private industries' largest providers of company-provided child care, has a system that enables parents to track their kids via computer while in their child care centres. Southern Ohio Medical Centre, located in Portsmouth, Ohio, provides employees with $3500 in adoption aid. Canadian companies, such as Johnson Inc., Goldcorp Inc., and Amec Americas Limited, offer maternity/paternity leave compensation "top-up benefits" to new mothers, fathers, and adoptive parents.

Arnold and Porter, a law firm, provides employees with bonuses for referring customers to the firm. Mattel Inc. has milk and cookie socials, while General Mills offers subsidized infant care at its company headquarters. Intuit, the financial software innovator, provides its employees with a $65 daily subsidy for in-home care when a child is sick or a school is closed. Mountain Equipment Co-op of Vancouver supports its staff with onsite yoga classes, shower facilities for bicycle commuters, and a private nap room for breaks during the day. The company also has an employee lending program for computers, bicycles, and boats. Companies such as Adobe Systems and Intel offer employees the opportunity for paid sabbaticals. Intel, for example, gives employees eight paid weeks of sabbatical for every seven years of service. And, more and more, employers are recognizing the value of longer-term employees. Retention bonuses and profit-sharing opportunities are becoming popular ways of reinforcing the value of longer-service staff.

Companies also are seeing increased value in assisting employees with personal development goals. Loblaw Companies Limited provides both online and in-house training programs, and offers tuition subsidies (up to $1200 per year), subsidies for professional designations, and career planning advice. Other Canadian companies, including Research In Motion, Cameco, and Digital Extremes, offer similar types of programs.

Not all perks or benefits are financially related. Many creative ideas are designed to enable workers from all levels to participate in company decision making and to ensure that the organization's mission and vision are effectively communicated to employees. McCormick & Co. of Sparks, Maryland, has 14 "junior boards of directors" that give employees from all levels within the organization the opportunity to voice their ideas to the company. Marriott International CEO Bill Marriott's annual letter to his workforce is translated into 28 languages, reflecting the diversity of Marriott's workforce. Mercedes-Benz USA has an MB community blog where employees can share ideas on company changes. Empire Financial Group, located in Kingston, Ontario, regularly assembles all of its employees at the local Cineplex for an "all company" briefing, outlining the direction, goals, and objectives the organization is aspiring toward or has accomplished.

Given the turbulent economic times we have recently experienced, companies are also seeking to provide their employees with reassurance that they are valued and that concerns relating to job security and downsizing will be handled in a manner that communicates to employees the importance of their contributions to the company's success. A number of companies, such as NuStar Energy, have initiated "no-layoff" policies. Others, where layoffs are necessary, are offering heightened severance packages and enhanced out-placement support services.

For smaller companies, and those with less financial capacity, some of the perks described above may not be possible. This does not mean, however, that employees cannot be recognized for a job well done. Creative ideas used by companies to reward their employees include "employee car washes," morning fruit baskets, subsidized gym memberships, wellness fairs, community volunteer days, and subsidized lunch days. The CEO of Canadian company Digital Extreme donated one month of his salary so that one of his employees could afford home renovations to ensure accessibility for a loved one who lives with disabilities.

As you can see, the diversity of programs and services being used to reward employees reaches far beyond simple salary or wage-based compensation. As managers, it is important to take the time to observe and interact with our employees to learn how we can better support both their work environment and their individual development. Creativity is at the core of developing potential reward and recognition instruments, with the ultimate goal being the desire to develop and maintain an environment that values its employees within the organization in which we manage.[5]

The Motivational Tool Kit

On a day-to-day basis, a manager's main task within an organization is to develop a productive workplace. This means making decisions associated with both the strategic objectives and tactical plans within his/her area of responsibility. With regard to human resource decisions, managers need to individually motivate each worker, as well as collectively motivate the team that he/she oversees. Gone are the days of using punishment and coercion as methodologies for driving productivity from a workforce. Today's managers need to recognize that high-performance teams and productive employees are the result of an environment of collaboration, cooperation, positive reinforcement, competent leadership, and effective communication. Creating a positive and productive work environment is not always easy, but there are some fundamental things that managers can, and should, keep in mind when looking to work with, enhance the productivity of, and motivate their employees. These can be thought of as your motivational tool kit and are easily remembered by the acronym TALENT (see Figure 8.4).

T = TRUST AND RESPECT

One of the key attributes of great work environments is that they are developed on the underlying principle of trust and respect. Employees value managers and companies that trust them and respect their views and opinions. A recent survey by the McKinsey Group revealed that trust between a company and its employees is a key attribute of a dedicated workforce.

FIGURE 8.4 Motivational Toolkit: TALENT

- **T** • Trust and Respect
- **A** • Approval, Praise, Recognition
- **L** • Lead By Example
- **E** • Enrichment
- **N** • Negotiation Skills
- **T** • Treasure

A = APPROVAL, PRAISE, AND RECOGNITION

Often cited as one of the most important motivators, employees respond positively to praise and recognition for a job well done. Managers should not underestimate the role that regular, positive feedback plays in maintaining a high-performance work unit. Recognition of a job well done heightens levels of employee satisfaction in the workplace and is a key driver of employee retention. It should be noted that recognition does not always have to be monetarily focused. Research has demonstrated that praise and commendation, attention, and opportunities for new challenges are as strong a motivator as money. In fact, a recent McKinsey survey concluded that three non-cash motivators—praise from immediate managers, attention from leaders, and a chance to direct projects—were as effective a motivator as three leading money-based motivators (performance cash bonuses, increase in base pay, and stock options).

L = LEAD BY EXAMPLE

Employees expect their managers to lead by example. The willingness of managers to work side by side with employees, as part of the team, to get the job done results in employees building stronger bonds with these managers and having greater respect for them.

E = ENRICHMENT

Employees often value the opportunity for new work experiences and additional challenges. Enriching the opportunities for individual growth on the job will result in a more productive and higher-skilled workforce. When such enrichment opportunities can be offered, this also reinforces the respect that the organization has for an employee, recognizes the skills that the employee possesses, and reinforces the value that the employee provides in assisting the organization with meeting its mission and vision.

N = NEGOTIATION SKILLS

Negotiation skills refers to a manager's ability to deliver two key areas of support to his/her employee base. The first has to do with a manager's ability to orchestrate, on behalf of his/her team, the removal of barriers, the acquisition of resources, and the enhancement of processes that will enable the team to achieve the level of performance needed to accomplish the stated goals and/or objectives. This means creating an environment that supports success. The second support area is the ability of managers to effectively communicate to their employees the desired level of expectations for each individual, as well as the team overall, in a manner that reinforces an environment of collaboration, accountability, and interdependence.

T = TREASURE

Employees are motivated by financial incentives that are directly related to work performance and levels of productivity. Performance-based cash bonuses and other creative financial incentives are valued by employees as long as they are felt to be equitable, realistic, and achievable. It should be understood, however, that financial incentives by themselves are not as strong a motivator as the other tools within TALENT. For individuals who are satisfied with their compensation levels, additional short-term bursts of financial rewards may result in only short-term bursts of additional productivity. Another key concern with financial incentives lies in their "sustainability." Once given, removal of such rewards due to market pressures, economic downturn, or company solvency and liquidity issues may actually act as a demotivator rather than a motivator. It should, however, also be noted that, in general, insufficient monetary rewards cannot be fully compensated for by good human relations activities on the part of managers.

BUSINESS *in Action*

Evolution of Motivational Theory

Today's views on how to motivate employees and develop productive work environments are the result of significant research and contributions by many over the past 100+ years. Modern practices have evolved from a number of published works by some of the foremost business thinkers. Frederick Taylor, often referred to as the "father of scientific management," published a leading study of productivity analysis in 1911 titled "The Principles of Scientific Management." For Taylor, it was all about studying workers to find the most efficient ways of doing things, and then teaching other employees these same techniques.

Abraham Maslow conducted a series of studies on human behaviour between 1939 and 1943 which resulted in what is now known as "Maslow's hierarchy of needs." Maslow's work found that employees, based on their individual situations, are motivated by varying types of needs, beginning with the most basic (physiological and safety) and evolving toward more intrinsic needs, such as love or belonging, self-esteem (recognition and appreciation), and self-actualization (self-development, creativity, and job satisfaction).

In the 1960s, two additional important studies were released regarding motivation and workplace performance. Frederick Herzberg provided valuable insight into what managers can do in the workplace to motivate employees. Herzberg's work sought to divide factors influencing work performance into two categories, hygiene factors and motivational factors. Hygiene factors focused on the work environment and were found to be factors that did not necessarily motivate, but when they were absent or not adequately provided would result in worker dissatisfaction and, therefore, lower levels of performance. Hygiene factors were found to be general working conditions, policies and administrative procedures, salary, job security, organizational structure, and type of supervision. For Herzberg, true motivational factors were directly related to what makes people happy and what will result in higher levels of work performance. Herzberg found that true motivational factors were related to achievement, recognition, interest in the task being performed, responsibility given, and potential for advancement. A second study during this same time period, by Douglas McGregor, examined theories relating to individual behaviour in the workplace. In his "Theory X and Theory Y" McGregor concluded that managerial attitudes toward their workforce directly influenced performance and productivity. Theory X managers believe that workers have an inherent dislike for work, dislike responsibility, are motivated solely by financial rewards, and need to be threatened or coerced in order to be productive. At the opposite end of the continuum are managers who have a completely different set of assumptions. Theory Y managers believe that people like work, will commit themselves without coercion or punitive outcomes toward objectives that they are challenged by, will accept and seek responsibility and accountability for their work, and are motivated by a variety of rewards beyond monetary compensation. McGregor concluded that, where possible, implementation of Theory Y attitudes by managers led to higher levels of productivity, because workers will contribute more to an organization if they are treated as responsible and valued employees. Conversely, an unsupportive atmosphere at work generally leads to lower levels of productivity and higher levels of employee turnover.

In his 1967 publication titled "The Human Organization," Rensis Likert examined the different types of leadership styles within organizations. Likert concluded that in order for an organization to achieve maximum profitability and to have good labour relations and high levels of productivity, organizations need to make optimal use of their human resources. Recognizing that organizations have different structures and are guided by different managerial styles, Likert identified that organizations that have confidence in their employees, provide them with the opportunity for input and participation in the goal-setting process, give them true responsibility for the attainment of those goals, offer them a cooperative environment, and communicate with them regularly receive, in return, the highest levels of employee performance. Victor Vroom offered managers the "expectancy theory," which theorized that the amount of effort an employee exerts on a given task is directly related to the outcome desired and the reward to be received. Employees will be much more motivated to initiate and successfully complete a task if the expectations are such that the employee sees a meaningful outcome for the effort.

As can be expected, ongoing research continues into what it takes to motivate people in the workplace. Additional theories continue to be offered, all designed to enable organizations to improve the overall productivity and performance of their workforce. Today's marketplace and work environment is significantly different than the world that Frederick Taylor and Abraham Maslow experienced. Global competition, and changes in attitudes toward work and life, all have resulted in shifts as to what it takes to manage in today's complex, fast-paced society. Although our workforce needs and desires have changed, one thing has fundamentally remained constant. As managers, we need to continually view our human resources talent as a core asset to the organization and to encourage their active participation in the decisions relating to the goals and direction the organization is striving toward. If you would like more information on motivational theory, do a Google search for "employee motivation."[6]

Managing Your Workforce

LO5

Managing a workforce in today's complex business setting requires a diverse skill set. Managers need to be able to engage employees, build consensus, develop and execute strategy, anticipate and remove productivity barriers, enhance operational efficiencies, and manoeuvre their way through increasingly complex regulatory, environmental, and legal environments. On a daily basis, managers need to figure out what to do despite increasing uncertainty in an ever-changing global economy, and the ever-growing enormous amounts of relevant information that today's technological and data-mining tools place in front of them. To be able to successfully organize, develop, direct, and lead their team, managers themselves need to fully understand the direction the organization is pursuing and the key competitive advantages it hopes to bring to the table as it seeks to acquire and retain customers. They then need to be able to take this information and develop a road map for success, as well as a framework for ensuring that objectives are met, and communicate this effectively to their employees. Once the direction is set and the road map established, managers then need to be able to monitor the progress being made via the benchmarks they have developed and make the appropriate corrections to keep the effort on

FIGURE 8.5   Workforce Management Focus

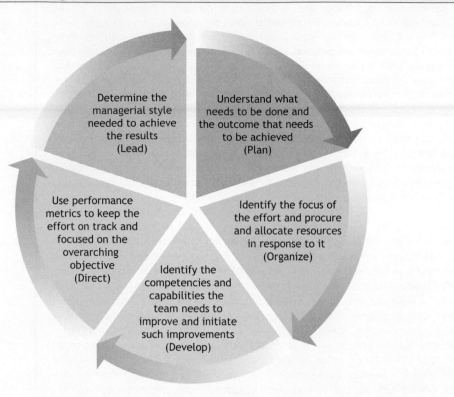

track, thereby ensuring that objectives are met. Knowing what needs to be done and how to do it is one thing. To succeed in carrying out these tasks, managers need to be able to transcend this analytical assessment of what needs to be done and "lead" employees in ensuring the goals and objectives are accomplished in a manner that exceeds customer expectations and outperforms competitive rivals. Managers must also be realistic in the current competencies and capabilities of their team and take the time to identify employee skill gaps that may prevent the team from accomplishing both current and anticipated future initiatives. With the identification of skill gaps, managers must then embark upon the appropriate skill-development strategies to ensure these gaps are closed, thereby providing their team with the best possible chance of success. Figure 8.5 outlines these key areas of workforce management focus.[7]

> To be able to successfully organize, develop, direct, and lead their team, managers need to fully understand the direction the organization is pursuing and the key competitive advantages it hopes to bring to the table as it seeks to acquire and retain customers.

To be successful in their planning, organizing, developing, directing, and leading endeavours, managers must recognize that their skill set needs to encompass four key competencies. These critical skills are what separate high-performing managers from lower-performing individuals (see Figure 8.6). It should be noted that of the four key skill sets identified, three have to do with communication and employee interaction.

- **Conceptual skills:** As noted above, managers need to be able to visualize, understand, and communicate the big picture. This means that managers need to be able to describe to their employees how their work and their efforts contribute to the overall success of the organization. The ability to continually reinforce this positioning message to their team is critical to the ongoing maintenance of high levels of productivity.

- **Leadership skills:** Strong leadership skills are fundamental to successful managers. Leading means being able to build continuous momentum within your workforce, and building

FIGURE 8.6   Managerial Skill Set

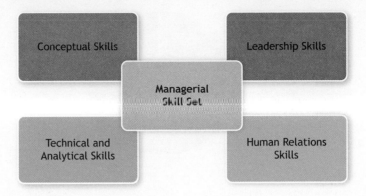

a system that encourages innovation, creativity, and can survive beyond a single individual (succession management). Leadership is all about inspiring others to achieve identified levels of expectations. Successful leaders—via maturity, energy, charisma, intuitiveness, empathy, and controlled emotion—will frame the culture of their organization or work unit. Leadership is all about accepting responsibility when things do not go well, and sharing credit when success is realized. A fundamental characteristic of great leadership is the willingness to place the organization's needs above those of the individual. Great leaders trust their team and are not afraid to have their ideas challenged. Strong leaders also demonstrate a true passion for their team and their company, and communicate an underlying desire to be the best at whatever they undertake.[8]

- **Technical and analytical skills:** Simply put, to be successful managers must have a solid understanding of the work that needs to be accomplished. This is essential to be able to identify the relevant issues that need to be addressed, barriers that need to be removed, and performance metrics that need to be achieved if the organization's goals and objectives are to be met. Managers may not be required to understand every facet of an employee's work responsibilities, but they need to have a technical understanding of the core fundamentals of the positions that they are overseeing if they are to be successful in coaching, mentoring, and supporting an employee's work effort. The ability to recognize operational inefficiencies and ineffectiveness is directly related to the technical knowledge one has of the processes being undertaken and the analytical ability to assess the individual steps within such processes. Managers need to take the time to learn the core fundamentals of the positions they supervise. An often overlooked source of organizational conflict is the lack of managerial competency to develop and guide the process a work unit is expected to follow, and to appreciate the complexity of tasks that employees are challenged by on a day-to-day basis.

- **Human relations skills:** The ability to communicate expectations in an engaging, motivating, and collaborative manner is key to successful management. Successful managers understand that their role is to develop and motivate their HR asset. Daily interaction means responding to the needs of their employees in a manner that reinforces the fundamentals laid out in the acronym TALENT. A second fundamental to strong human relations is the recognition, by managers, of which power base to use when interacting with their employee team (see Figure 8.7).

> The ability to communicate expectations in an engaging, motivating, and collaborative manner is the key to successful management.

Managers have at their disposal two bases of power. The trick is to know when to use each of them in order to ensure that interactions with employees build a culture and environment of collaboration and professionalism, yet enable the manager to meet the needs of the organization in terms of organizing and directing the task(s) at hand. The two key power bases of a

FIGURE 8.7   Manager's Power Base

Personal Power is the power that a manager possesses as a result of his/her leadership competencies. It is the ability to motivate, facilitate, demonstrate empathy, and collaborate with staff in order to meet organizational expectations.

Position Power is the power that a manager legitimately holds due to the title he/she has within an organization. This power is derived on the basis of expertise, legitimacy of rank, the ability to control rewards and resources, and the obligation to assess performance.

manager are personal power and position power. **Personal power** is the power that a manager possesses as a result of his/her leadership competencies. It is the ability to motivate, facilitate, demonstrate empathy, and collaborate with staff in order to meet organizational expectations. **Position power** is the power that a manager legitimately holds due to the title he/she has within the organization. This power is derived on the basis of expertise, legitimacy of rank, the ability to control rewards and resources, and the requirement to assess performance. Let's take an example to illustrate the effective use of each. Suppose a manager has been informed, by his supervisor, that sales of the product line he manages have really taken off. Although delighted with the success, the manager realizes that this unanticipated growth will result in the existing complement of staff having to work additional hours (overtime), including weekends, for the next two to four months, until HR can recruit, select, and intake additional employees to meet current and anticipated future demand. Recognizing that this will affect upcoming vacation schedules and lifestyle activities for his team, the manager will need to ask his staff to work with him in resolving this issue in a manner that meets organizational expectations and recognizes the imposition the situation will cause to their personal lives. To approach this on the basis of position power, mandating (without employee input) how the situation will be handled could result in a significant negative impact. The manager would be better suited to approach this on the basis of personal power, and collaborate with his staff to find a solution that best meets their needs and ensures the organizational objectives are met. In a second situation, assume that an employee's performance is below expectations and that prior efforts to coach the employee have resulted in little to no performance improvement. The manager is now faced with placing the employee on formal notice that his/her performance is in need of improvement, otherwise additional consequences will occur. In this situation, the manager is best suited to approach the meeting and discussion on the basis of position power, and provide the employee with a straightforward discussion of the issues and potential outcomes of the performance deficiency. The position power enables the manager to communicate that his/her responsibility for the performance of the entire team and each individual team member necessitates the formality of the discussion. It should be noted here that the manager, in utilizing this power base, should focus on the behaviour correction required, dealing only with the issues that have manifested themselves. The discussion should be handled in a professional, courteous manner, absent of any unrelated personal references toward the employee as an individual/person.

Leadership styles and effective management strategies are, ultimately, driven by the power base that a manager perceives he/she needs to use in overseeing his/her responsibility within an organization. The style can also be influenced by the nature of the tasks being performed, the organizational culture, the centralization or decentralization of decision making that occurs, and the capabilities and experience of the workforce itself. In general, managers who exhibit participative, managerial decision-making approaches, and who understand the decision factors influencing the power base from which to determine where, and how, to approach a situation, are believed to produce more effective results from a motivational, collaborative, and performance perspective.

Leadership styles and effective management strategies are, ultimately, driven by the power base that a manager perceives he/she needs to use in overseeing his/her responsibility within an organization.

The Danger of Short-Term Pressures

As discussed earlier, managers are continuously being challenged by market uncertainty and what appears to be an endless and diverse supply of potentially relevant information that can influence the direction and implementation of business goals and objectives. In today's corporate environment, the challenge to drive toward higher levels of productivity and continually increase performance efficiency and effectiveness targets seems to never end. For managers, it is all about time management and responding to the latest internal and external pressures. This constant pressure to meet shareholder expectations and monthly, quarterly, and current-year operating targets has a tendency to shift managers into a short-term focus mode. The danger of this pressure is that it causes managers to shift away from their five fundamental zones of effort (planning, organizing, developing, directing, and leading), and concentrate on the three that are designed to most efficiently respond to such short-term pressure (planning, organizing, and directing). When this shift to short-term pressure occurs, the areas of leadership and development—two fundamentals of long-term strategic and operational health—often get relegated to a lower priority, while a third area, planning, focuses more on immediate operational plans, which may lose their synergy with the organization's overall strategic plan and long-term vision. The potential near-term impact of this short-term management approach, referred to as "short-termism," is the following:

- Organizations tend to decrease their emphasis on talent management strategies.

- Organizations and their decision-making processes have a tendency to become "siloed," with a reduced emphasis on collaboration and information sharing.

- Company investment decisions tend to be dominated by immediate short-term financial results and shareholder return expectations.

- Talent development costs are viewed more as an operational expense than a capital investment.

- HR actions tend to be more "knee-jerk" driven, hiring only at the last minute and where absolutely necessary, as such hiring is viewed as a potentially profit-reducing expense.

- Absence of career and competency development is viewed as a near-term requirement; that is, as a tactical issue versus a strategic issue.

Although economic pressures may legitimately require an organization to think in terms of the immediate future (due to solvency or liquidity problems), a number of firms fall into this trap, again, due to the perceived need on the part of the management team or its board of directors to continually exceed shareholder/investor expectations in the immediate term. The long-term consequences, however, given this movement away from protecting the investment in the talent component of an organization, can result in failure over the longer period to develop the competencies in their staff and their management team to meet the strategic requirements of the company going forward. For many, the end result of this short-term focus is that managers do not spend enough time on talent management strategies, and that these strategies become no longer aligned with the organization's long-term business strategy. This "short-termism" loop and the consequences of this type of decision-making attitude are illustrated in Figure 8.8.[9]

The constant pressure to meet shareholder expectations and monthly, quarterly, and current-year operating targets has a tendency to shift managers into a short-term focus mode.

FIGURE 8.8 Short-Termism Loop: Impact to Talent Development

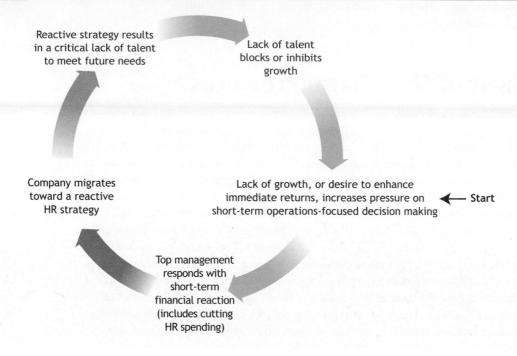

The de-emphasis of long-term goal setting and talent development initiatives can, and often does, result in heightened organizational conflict. If short-termism permeates an organization for an extended period, the end result can be myriad disruptors, all of which can cause an organization to drift away from its intended goals and objectives. Incompatible goals due to **silo mentality** can arise among what are meant to be cross-functional units. The staffing resources needed to get the job done and meet the increasing complexity of the tasks required can become insufficient, and the managerial competencies needed to guide the organization forward can become lacking. In responding to this challenge, managers must resist the temptation to become predominantly focused on meeting and exceeding short-term expectations, and recognize that, while important, these results need to be balanced in consideration of the long-term health of the organization. Shareholders, for example, are but one component of our stakeholder base. Customers, suppliers, employees, and other parties connected to our organization all need to have their expectations met as well. Successful firms do just that—they balance the needs of all stakeholders, and manage the organization in a manner that not only ensures its survival today, but also protects its long-term competitiveness and sustainability going forward.

> **Silo Mentality** refers to managerial decisions that do not take into consideration the cross-organizational impact that such decisions will have.

> Successful firms balance the needs of all stakeholders and manage the organization in a manner that not only ensures its survival today, but also protects its long-term competitiveness and sustainability going forward.

Putting It All Together

Managers must interact with their workforce in a manner that builds continuous momentum, inspires high levels of performance, ensures an understanding of the work to be accomplished, and creates "buy-in" on the part of employees to the vision and goals of the organization. To accomplish this, managers have to operate on a number of different planes—leading by example; organizing or creating an environment that fosters collaboration and guides the process; and empowering their staff, enriching their experiences, and creating mechanisms that assure accountability and responsibility for the work or tasks assigned to each staff member. They also need to provide support mechanisms and provide feedback to ensure employees understand what is expected of them. Creating and maintaining a positive work environment requires a consistent, methodical approach on the part of managers. It begins and continues to develop with each interaction a manager has with his/her staff. Getting off on the right foot is fundamental, but so is genuinely striving to ensure that employees feel valued and are recognized for their accomplishments regularly. Although not meant to be all-inclusive, Figure 8.9 provides a checklist for effective talent management that managers can refer to in order to ensure the environment within which they manage is a positive one for the individuals who work under them.[10]

| FIGURE 8.9 | Checklist for Effective Talent Management |

✔ Do my employees know and understand the organization's vision and mission?

✔ Do my employees know and understand what is expected of them?

✔ Do my employees have the tools to do the job right?

✔ Am I providing each of my employees the opportunity to do his/her best every day?

✔ Have I provided each of my employees with the opportunity to learn and grow?

✔ Do I provide each of my employees with regular feedback as to how they are doing?

✔ Do I provide my employees with coaching and mentoring, when needed, to ensure that they meet the expectations asked of them?

✔ Do I ask my employees for their opinions prior to implementing changes that will impact their work productivity and performance?

✔ Have I provided my employees with opportunities to make friends at work?

✔ Have I sat down with each employee recently and provided them with a formal performance appraisal on how well they are doing their job?

✔ Do my employees believe that I truly care about them?

HR Management in the Small Business Setting

The HR issues for entrepreneurs and small business managers are the same as those that face much larger organizations. Entrepreneurs and small business managers must still determine how to motivate their workforce, inspire them to commit to the organization and seek to excel, and create recognition and compensation systems that encourage high levels of productivity, retain employees, and ensure equity and fairness to all. Having said this, the challenge for small business owners and entrepreneurs is that all of this often has to be done without the support of a fully established HR department—in reality, many entrepreneurs and small business managers *are* the HR department. Constantly challenged by day-to-day market and financial risk pressures, entrepreneurs and small business managers often relegate the establishment of formal HR policies and procedures to the back burner, always intending to deal with them but rarely finding the time. It is important for these individuals to understand two important fundamentals in this regard. First, given their size and lack of manpower in the HR area, a mistake that entrepreneurs and small business managers often make is trying to apply large-business structures to their small operations. The key is to keep it simple. Entrepreneurs and small business owners should seek to use mechanisms that are sustainable and that can be applied consistently with little bureaucratic infrastructure. Second, in establishing their approach, entrepreneurs and small business managers should look to develop strategies toward those performance factors that represent the best win/win outcomes for them and their employees: compensation, benefits, training, flexibility and work balance, and a feeling of inclusion. Note that promotion and advancement does not appear in this list—this is not because they are not valued, but because, in many small business settings, the opportunity to reward in this fashion may be limited. If they are available, then they certainly should be added to the list. The idea, just as with large businesses, is to create a positive work environment. Small business employees want to understand the owner's vision, and often are a great resource of ideas for greater cost efficiencies and growth opportunities. Entrepreneurs and small business owners should seek to tap in to their employees in this way. Employees in many small business settings often look for greater responsibility. In fact, one recommended strategy for delegating is for the small business owner to identify five things that routinely consume his/her time and assign those tasks to a dependable and competent employee. Entrepreneurs and small business owners who can succeed in delegating can find their day-to-day operational load lightened, thus allowing greater time for planning and developing growth and profitability initiatives. Compensation can be an issue when trying to retain employees, but many small-business owners and entrepreneurs have found that retention bonuses (say, at three, six, and nine years) have been an effective mechanism for developing staying power with employees and providing positive reinforcement for a job well done. Others have found that profit sharing also yields positive benefits. Operating a small business is all about getting personal with your employees, and communicating both the good and the bad in a collaborative manner. Employees who understand the business as a whole are more likely to demonstrate increased accountability and responsibility, take initiative, and seek to protect the business owner's investment. In small business, culture is everything. If nothing else, entrepreneurs and small business owners need to create a fun, team-based place to work. In today's market, young professionals are looking to entrepreneurship and small companies more and more as an exciting career choice. For owners of small businesses, this represents an opportune time to receive maximum benefit from the knowledge and skill set that these highly qualified employees can offer. The trick is for entrepreneurs and small-business owners to fully leverage these critical skills in a way that encourages these individuals to excel, and create a sense of ownership in them via a reward system that places value on their contribution.[11]

> Employees who understand the business as a whole are more likely to demonstrate increased accountability and responsibility, take initiative, and seek to protect the business owner's investment.

Management Reflection—Finding the Right Balance

Managers are constantly being challenged with finding the right balance in setting strategy, operating the business, and designing and developing the organization's asset and resource base. A critical component of this process is determining where, and how, to make the best use of the organization's talent assets in a manner that provides an advantage in the marketplace and meets or exceeds customer and stakeholder expectations. To create a truly productive and efficient workforce, managers need to recognize that employees are as important an asset as the equipment and infrastructure used within the business. A key component to talent asset management is the creation of a work culture that encourages collaboration and cooperation among employees and the management team. Cross-functional communication, open dialogue on problem solving, recognition of work well done, and the willingness to accept responsibility and accountability for individual actions form the foundation of such a high-performance culture. As a manager, it is your ability to lead by example, as well as to develop your team's competencies, that will mark your success. Planning, organizing, and directing your team is fundamental to your success as well. The key is to communicate what you want your team to focus on and achieve, and then provide the culture and environment to ensure that each member of the team has the tools and the opportunity to succeed.

> As a manager, it is your ability to lead by example, as well as to develop your team's competencies, that will mark your success.

Chapter Summary

This chapter was designed to provide you with an overview of the managerial requirements associated with managing and leading an organization's talent. Fundamental to this was a focus on defining the skills and competencies that managers must possess in this regard. To be successful, managers must be able to plan, organize, develop, direct, and lead their employee talent. To truly motivate their workforce, organizations and their management teams must develop a relationship of trust and respect, recognize efforts on the part of their staff and offer praise, enrich their work experience through new opportunities and challenges, lead by example, exhibit strong negotiation skills both with employees and on their behalf, and provide them with acceptable levels of compensation and rewards. Managers also must be able to conceptualize how an employee's work fits in with the overall vision and mission of the company. They must be able to exhibit strong leadership skills to motivate their work units to higher levels of performance and productivity, provide support via strong technical and analytical skills, and possess strong human relations skills in interacting with employees on a day-to-day basis.

The chapter also provides an overview of the ongoing challenges and pressures managers will face in leading their staff and in managing their areas of responsibility. Critical to this is to recognize the dangers associated with short-termism and the potential loss of strategic direction and long-term organizational health that can result from such a mentality. In closing, as described in the opening "From a Student's Perspective," managers need to recognize three fundamental requirements to their work. They must establish direction, mobilize action, and develop their teams to successfully meet the expectations of the organization, its customers, and its stakeholders.

Developing Business Knowledge and Skills

KEY TERMS

personal power *p. 210*

position power *p. 210*

silo mentality *p. 212*

QUESTIONS FOR DISCUSSION

1. So, you're the boss. Now what? Assume you have just been promoted to a managerial position. What key thoughts and actions would you reflect on in order to develop and maintain a highly productive workforce?

2. Compensation by itself not believed to be a strong, long-term motivator of employees. Why is this? Conversely, why can't the other motivational tools found in the acronym TALENT fully compensate for insufficient compensation levels in the workplace?

3. What are the four critical skills that separate high-performing managers from low-performing individuals? In your mind, which of these skills is most important? Why?

4. Why should organizations and managers be wary of the short-termism loop? What is its potential long-term impact on talent development?

QUESTION FOR INDIVIDUAL ACTION

Arrange to meet with a couple of entrepreneurs or business owners in your area. Ask them what they believe are the most pressing human resource issues within their organizations. How do they try to motivate and retain their employees? Which approaches have they found most successful in their desire to develop a dependable, high-performance work team?

TEAM EXERCISE

As a team, meet and discuss what you believe young professionals such as yourselves are looking for from an employer as you leave your post-secondary education and venture into the workforce. Look beyond salary and wages and seek to describe what you feel will be the true motivators for you to excel within an organization. What about retention? What will keep you with an employer? Do you see yourself wanting to work for multiple employers over your career? If so, then why? Prepare a presentation summarizing your views and opinions and share this with your class.

Case for Discussion

Matt Wilson, co-owner and president of CFP Inc., a growing technology sensor component company, realizes that CFP is at a crossroads. The business, which opened in 2002, has grown from operating out of a small garage in Surrey, British Columbia, with Matt, his wife, Sarah, and his brother Robert as its sole employees, to a $12-million operation with 45 full-time and 25 part-time employees. The business plan up to this point has been well executed, developing a strong customer base made up of a number of loyal (if finicky) customers across North America who need a variety of sophisticated sensor applications. With Robert's engineering and design expertise, Sarah's office management skills, and Matt's strong business acumen (MBA class of 1999), managerial responsibilities for critical aspects of the business have been effectively distributed among these three principal owners.

The strong business growth, intensifying global competition, and ever-increasing customer demands for smaller, more complex, and higher-performing sensors are causing Matt, Sarah, and Robert to feel increasingly stretched. Almost 100 percent of Robert's time is consumed with design, prototype development, and related R&D projects. The design team, which he also oversees, has grown to 10 employees. Sarah is consumed, on a daily basis, with human resource issues, payroll and administration requirements, customer and supplier interactions, and ever-increasing government regulations (tax compliance, health and safety, etc.). As more and more of CFP Inc.'s customer base lies outside of Canada, international shipping considerations, NAFTA compliance, and paddling through the newly implemented "Buy America" legislation and its Canadian-exception rules eat into her valuable time as well. Like Robert's R&D department, the administration area has also grown, taking on four full-time and two part-time employees to assist with the continually growing workload. Add to this the learning curve associated with the newly installed financial management computer system and, well—you get the picture.

Matt, too, is feeling the pressure. Although technically the company president, Matt, up to this point in time, has largely played the role of a general or operations manager. Matt and his team of managers (five in total) oversee the operations, marketing and sales, customer service, and plant and facility aspects of CFP Inc.'s business system. Growth of the operation has resulted in the manufacturing area moving to a two-shift operation, covering 16 hours per day. Customization of plant equipment seems to be occurring almost every quarter, as Robert and his team seek to keep CFP Inc.'s customers happy with leading-edge sensor solutions. Add to this the required technology applications that need to be continually introduced in

order to improve efficiencies and effectiveness and remain competitive with Asian manufacturers, and the constant search for suppliers that can meet CFP Inc.'s sharp tolerance and performance expectations. Beyond manufacturing, Matt is also dealing with sales force and dealer development, and the increasing customer support requirements that growing businesses like CFP Inc. face as a result of their success.

All of this has been fairly manageable but things are set to change again, which is resulting in the need to reassess how the business will be managed going forward. As part of the recently completed planning-cycle process, which CFP Inc. initiated in 2008, the company decided to take advantage of what was viewed as a great growth opportunity in Brazil. CFP Inc., supported by Export Development Canada, recognized a real demand for a complex sensor application in Brazil's emerging ethanol-manufacturing sector. Following six months of negotiations, the deal has now been finalized, and the potential to double the size of CFP Inc. over the next two to four years has gone from an idea to a reality. With such a major initiative under way, Matt knows that his time will be totally consumed with getting the Brazilian operation up and running. Robert will also need to be heavily involved, as his unique, patented, sensor design is core to the entire business arrangement. Both Matt and Robert will be spending a large chunk of their time in Brazil interacting with, and supporting, their newly acquired Brazilian customers. Matt and Robert both know that, as good as Robert's initial leading-edge design is, modifications will need to be made once prototypes and actual product implementation takes place. This time requirement means two things: Matt can no longer oversee the existing operation on a day-to-day basis, and Robert will need to transfer the day-to-day supervision of his R&D team to someone else. Sarah, in addition to overseeing the administration area, is transitioning into the role of CFO (chief financial officer) for CFP Inc., overseeing all financial management responsibilities. In addition, a significant number of employees will need to be hired, beginning in as little as three to six months, to meet not only the growing North American demand but also the volume requirements anticipated from Brazil.

At a meeting of the three principals (Matt, Sarah, and Robert) and their advisory board, it was concluded that the time had come to hire a COO (chief operating officer) who could manage the operation, thereby allowing Matt and Robert the time and focus necessary to ensure the Brazilian deal is a success. The only remaining question coming out of this meeting was just what type of person they should be looking for, and who should this person be.

QUESTIONS

CFP Inc. has turned to you for an answer to the question of what type of person they should be looking for. Develop an overview of the characteristics of the type of individual CFP Inc. should find to fill the position of COO. What types of skills does he/she need to possess? Based on this list of skills, where would you place your emphasis? What are your top two prioritized competencies that this individual must possess? Why did you choose these?

9 Operations and Supply Chain Management

Learning Objectives

This chapter is designed to provide students with:

Lo1 An understanding of how operations management fits into an organization's overall business system

Lo2 Recognition of the key areas of responsibilities of operations managers

Lo3 A description of the primary and support activities that make up an organization's value chain

Lo4 Exposure to the core managerial decision-making areas that reside within an organization's operations cycle

Lo5 An understanding of the importance of establishing quality standards and embedding these within the culture of the organization

Lo6 An overview of operations management for small businesses

Snapshot—What to Expect in This Chapter

As identified by the learning objectives, this chapter focuses on managing an organization's operations and supply chain. The content emphasized in this chapter includes the following:

- Operations Management: Fitting Into the Big Picture

- Responsibilities of Operations Managers

- The Organization's Value Chain
  - Value Chain Analysis: Primary Activities
  - Value Chain Analysis: Support Activities

- The Operations Cycle
  - Process Management
  - Supply Chain Management
  - Product/Service Management

- Establishing Quality Standards

- Operations Management in Small Businesses

- Management Reflection—Operational Success

From the Student's Perspective

Does "operations and supply chain management" remind you of an automotive plant manager standing in front of an assembly line? Are you wondering why you have to study this engineering-like topic as part of your business curriculum?

Actually, studying operations is about understanding the backbone of every company plan and their ability to control or improve their business processes. Every business competes on operations-based principles; it is fundamental to an organization's ability to build and sustain a competitive advantage. After studying this chapter, you will begin to understand the fundamentals of operations strategies and how they are used by successful companies such as Amazon.com or Walmart—which dominates its industry based upon its mastery of these concepts. Even for an industry such as investment banking, every trade that is agreed upon, every new product that is launched, or every market that is entered into—ultimately, every transaction that is completed—has operations processes embedded within its business flow.

In addition to learning how to forecast demand, reduce inefficiencies, or eliminate bottlenecks, operations management principles will help you to develop your problem-solving skills relating to complex and uncertain situations. After all, all you need to do is put yourself in the shoes of a manager of a particular company and understand the conflicting demands of people, technology, and economics. In doing so, you will get a sense of the importance of operations management.

Hyuk Tae Kwon received his Bachelor of Commerce in May 2010. He fluently speaks Korean, English, and Chinese. During his third year of university, he went on a one-year exchange to Peking University in China. In his fourth year, he founded his university's Asian Central Banks Shadow Committee, which studied East Asian economies. In July 2010, he will be working at Goldman Sachs in its Tokyo office. After acquiring additional business experience, he hopes to start his own business and also plans to contribute his knowledge and experience in helping the underdeveloped nations through international organizations such as the IMF or the World Bank.

Managing the Value Chain

BUSINESS *in Action*

Toyota Production System (TPS)

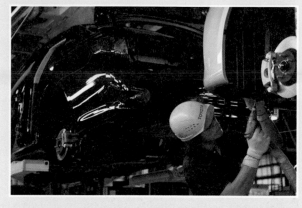

It is hard to talk about excellence in operational processes without a mention of Toyota's famed TPS (Toyota Production System). Steeped in a philosophy of continuous improvement and operational efficiency, TPS is core to Toyota's competitive advantage in today's global automobile marketplace. This lean manufacturing system, based on the concepts of JIT (just-in-time) and jidoka (highlighting and visualizing problems), has resulted in Toyota developing and executing operating processes that are among the most efficient in the world. So efficient, in fact, that a number of its competitors (and other companies at large) are adopting some, if not all, of the tactics associated with TPS. Toyota seeks to drive two specific outcomes as it manufactures its products and services. The first is the complete elimination of waste. Toyota continuously studies exactly what it needs within its production processes and strives to eliminate duplication and unnecessary inefficiencies associated with the wasteful use of resources. Waste refers not only to unused parts or defects, but also to inefficient use of equipment and assets and carrying unnecessary inventory. Idle equipment and assets are non-productive, and therefore wasteful. Eliminating unnecessary inventory means to make only what is needed, when it is needed, and in the amount needed. The system is designed to produce Toyota vehicles as they are ordered, but to do so in the quickest and most efficient manner possible for delivery to customers. The second outcome is quality. Quality is ingrained within the TPS manufacturing process. At Toyota, if defects are discovered they are dealt with efficiently and effectively. It also means that production stops until such defects are properly dealt with. Toyota prides itself on quality, and the brand has become synonymous with dependability and reliability.

In the first quarter of 2010, when Toyota faced a massive recall on a number of models due to concerns relating to "sticky" gas pedals, the company did exactly what the concept of jidoka demands: it ceased production until it believed it had effectively solved the problem. During the recall assessment period, Toyota also instructed its dealers not to sell any vehicles from their lots and showrooms until the problem had been completely analyzed and a solution developed. At Toyota, dealing with such recalls is almost unheard of. Its management team, in responding to global concerns relating to Toyota products, ordered a full review of the design, engineering development, and production processes to ensure that recalls of such magnitude do not reoccur. Key outcomes of this review, as announced by President Akio Toyoda in March 2011, included a new global vision as well as significant changes to the decision-making process at Toyota. These changes, designed to streamline decision making within the organization, included reducing the number of members on the board of directors, reducing the three-tier decision-making structure within Toyota, and—most importantly—implementing a more decentralized decision-making approach for its overseas regional operations. The core outcome of these changes was to provide regional operations with a bigger say in policy formulation and greater authority in responding to issues arising in their operational spheres (a key criticism of Toyota and its handling of the 2010 recall). Also announced in the new vision was the establishment of a regional advisory structure to provide additional external insight into ways to further improve its operations and decision-making protocols.

As President Toyoda announced, the global vision of Toyota outlines the values that the company, and its execution of TPS, is committed to honouring. The revised global vision reads, "Toyota will lead the way to the future of mobility, enriching lives around the world with the safest and most responsible ways of moving people. Through our commitment to quality, constant innovation, and respect for the planet, we aim to exceed expectations and be rewarded with a smile. We will meet challenging goals by engaging the talent and passion of people who believe there is always a better way."

As the complexity of manufacturing continues to grow, with more significant use of technology becoming embedded into such processes than ever before, all manufacturers will be challenged to ensure that their manufacturing processes remain focused on defect-free execution. For Toyota, its historical advantage has been the culture and the structure it has ingrained within its organization and within TPS, which has enabled Toyota to efficiently produce vehicles with different specifications on common platforms while ensuring the highest quality. Their JIT supply system orders, stores, and retrieves parts only as needed, and reorders only when parts have been used. Connectivity to its dealers results in customer orders being promptly received and incorporated into the production process. Toyota's culture of jidoka seeks to make daily improvements in the way that products are produced to ensure that quality remains a top priority. At Toyota, it is all about using leading-edge technology that enables them to produce vehicles in the most efficient and effective manner possible. A key lesson of the 2010 recall, however, is that the use of this technology must be balanced with the "human touch" to ensure that Toyota's most important resource—its talent—remains active in the process, responsive when issues arise, and constantly visualizing where and how improvements can be made. The lessons learned, as identified and ingrained into the new global vision, reinforce the need for an active and participative decision-making process as part of the productivity cycle to ensure that when issues occur they are handled effectively, efficiently, and compassionately.[1]

WEB INTEGRATION

Want to learn more about Toyota, TPS, and the company's new global vision? Visit **www.toyota.com/about/ our_values/**, or Google Toyota Production System (TPS).

Operations Management: Fitting Into the Big Picture

LO1

As Hyuk-Tae Kwon indicated in "From the Student's Perspective," operations management is all about the ability of a company to control and/or improve its business processes. In fact, operations management goes beyond the ability to control or improve, and fundamentally focuses on the design and development of such processes as well. Based on your readings of prior chapters, you should be getting a sense as to the importance of developing a business system within the organization and ensuring that this system is aligned properly to the business's strategy, vision, and mission. Chapter 6 focused on the framework for developing this strategy, and chapters 7 and 8 emphasized the importance of developing the formal business structure, culture, employee productivity initiatives, and decision-making hierarchy—or, in summing up all of these items, the framework to direct and control it. For a business to truly be successful, a third fundamental component to its business system must be present: the organization must develop and maintain efficient and effective operational processes that deliver to the marketplace the products or services the organization offers. Successful organizations understand the interconnectivity of strategy, business structure, and operations, and seek to ensure that all three are integrated into the decision-making process and that structure and operations are aligned and in support of the organization's strategic goals (see Figure 9.1).

FIGURE 9.1 Business System Components

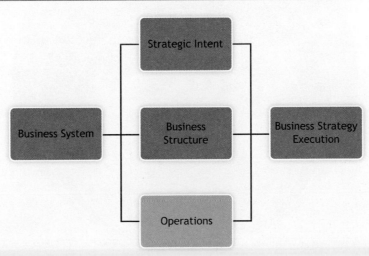

> Successful organizations understand the interconnectivity of strategy, business structure, and operations, and seek to ensure that all three are integrated into the decision-making process and that structure and operations are aligned and in support of the organization's strategic intent.

When we visualize the interconnectivity of these three business system components, we should conclude the following:

- Strategy is what we want to accomplish.

- The business structure should provide the controls and the formal communication and responsibility framework that will guide the organization as it seeks to realize its strategy.

- Operations are understood to be the actual processes employed, which, when combined with the utilization of the organization's capital assets, enable strategic outcomes to be actualized.

These three components and the corresponding actions that take place within the operations area result in getting the right product or service to the right customer at the right place at the right time for the right price. Keep in mind that the decisions we as managers make are focused on developing customer interactions and selling our products and services (see Figure 9.2).

As stated in earlier chapters, successful businesses look to establish within their business systems competitive advantages that enable them to deliver their products and/or services to their targeted market segments in a manner superior to that of the competition. These advantages could be the result of more effective market positioning and brand strength, more effective use of technology and process advantages, or pure cost advantages due to economies of scale, lower labour or production costs, and so on. What will ultimately create these advantages for an organization within its competitive market environment is the ability of the

FIGURE 9.2   The Big Picture

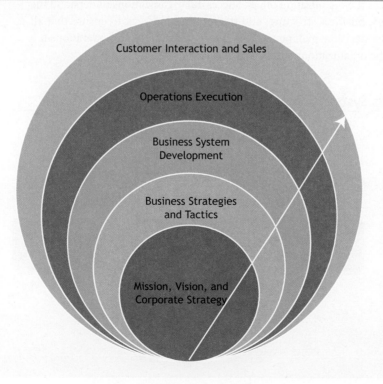

management team to transfer such strategic intent through the decision-making structure and into the effective execution of operational processes.

> Successful businesses look to establish within their business systems competitive advantages that enable them to deliver their products and/or services to their targeted market segments in a manner superior to that of the competition.

Responsibilities of Operations Managers   LO2

Operations management is all about the effective design, development, and management of the processes, procedures, and practices embedded within an organization's business system for the purpose of achieving its strategic intent. In broad terms, the mandate of the operations management team can be thought of as encompassing three broad categories of responsibility (see Figure 9.3). The intent of the operations management team is to design and develop such processes, procedures, and practices in a way that takes into consideration time requirements associated with getting products/services to the market. In addition, decisions need to be made relating to the quality/cost trade-offs that are designed to support the value proposition being communicated to the target market by the marketing team via the organization's marketing mix strategy. It is important to recognize that the areas of responsibility identified in Figure 9.3 overlap, as there is a definitive interconnectivity between decisions made within each of the areas noted.

- Process management
- Supply chain management
- Product/service management

  Process management is the design and development of the work flow and connectivity of the operational requirements (processes) needed to ensure that an organization's products and services are efficiently produced and effectively delivered to the marketplace. Process management looks at the specific tasks that need to be accomplished by the organization and orders or sequences them to result in the most effective and efficient work flow. It is similar to the development of blueprints or schematics associated with building a structure or outlining a work flow. As indicated above, this process development and task sequencing is assessed with respect to time, quality, and cost requirements and constraints. A key outcome of process

> **Operations Management** is the effective design, development, and management of the processes, procedures, and practices embedded within an organization's business system for the purpose of achieving its strategic intent.

> **Process Management** is the design and development of the work flow and connectivity of the transformation requirements (processes) needed to ensure that an organization's products and services are efficiently produced and effectively delivered to the marketplace.

FIGURE 9.3 Operations Management: Areas of Responsibility

management decision making is the determination of how the transformation process for products and services will be designed. It also looks at what equipment and structures will be used to ensure that the transformation maximizes efficiency and effectiveness objectives and is aligned with the organization's market position and the related communication message. This may result in an assembly-line approach, a fully automated technology-manufacturing process making extensive use of robotics, or a handcrafted, customized approach to the fabrication or finishing of products and services. A further discussion of process management factors occurs in the next section of this chapter, which relates to the value chain.

Supply Chain Management is the management of the interdependencies among suppliers, manufacturers, and distributors; it seeks to develop the terms and conditions that will enable all parties to efficiently and effectively meet their obligations to one another due to their business relationships.

Supply chain management refers to the management of the flow of materials and/or products, information, and costs through the front end of an organization's value chain. It includes interactions such as the purchase of materials from suppliers and the coordination of just-in-time (JIT) inventory practices. It also considers the warehousing and distribution logistics required to move finished product from the organization's manufacturing or distribution facility to its channel partners, who ultimately sell the product to its final users (customers). Supply chain management is all about relationship management. It is the management of the interdependencies among suppliers, manufacturers, and distributors. It also seeks to develop the terms and conditions that will enable all parties to efficiently and effectively meet their obligations to one another due to their business relationships. Supply chain management is discussed in more detail in the next section of this chapter.

Product/Service Management refers to the variety of activities that commence with the design and development of potential new products in R&D and extend to the post-purchase support of products/services now in the hands of customers.

Product/service management refers to the variety of activities that commence with the design and development of potential new products in R&D and extend to the post-purchase support of products and services now in the hands of customers. Product/service management includes supporting product modifications, enhancements, and other changes made throughout the product's life cycle. It also involves the decision trade-offs associated with quality and cost. Decisions relating to functionality, durability, and performance are just some of the factors that need to be assessed within this area of responsibility. Product/service management decisions are made in close cooperation with the organization's R&D, marketing, and engineering departments. Consumer wants and preferences must be identified, and decisions jointly made prior to the product/service management team incorporating them into the design or redesign of a new or current product. Product/service management decisions also consider competitor product/service adjustments that are known to be "in development" or that have been presented to the marketplace, as well as emerging technologies that potentially could disrupt a marketplace. Product/service management decisions also focus on assessing the cost base of a product by analyzing its various components and determining which features need to remain, to be added, and to be removed or modified.

As demonstrated by this initial discussion of the responsibilities associated with operations management teams, the decision-making focus is quite broad and highly connective not only across the three areas identified above, but also in the sense that it requires considerable collaboration and communication across the entire organization. Let's now drill deeper into the realm of the operations management team by analyzing the process flow that will occur, to some degree, within all organizations, and how the supporting capital asset base and business structure are integrated to form a cohesive business system.[2]

LO3 The Organization's Value Chain

Keeping the discussion relating to operations management simple is, in itself, a difficult task. The evolution of technology, when combined with the emergence of heightened competition in global and domestic markets and the increasing efficiencies driven from specialization, is resulting in increasingly sophisticated ways in which we produce and deliver products/services to the marketplace. Techno-savvy production processes, warehouse and distribution logistical software, sophisticated material procurement analytical methodologies, and enhanced outsourcing and offshoring strategies all make for increasingly complex operations management arenas. To try to maintain some order to our discussion, and to gain a full appreciation of the complexity of the interconnectivity across the organization, our focus will be on tying this discussion to a business concept called *value chain analysis*.

The value chain is a business concept that was first proposed by Michael Porter of the Harvard Business School in 1985, in his book *Competitive Advantage: Creating and Sustaining Competitive Performance*. At the centre of Porter's value chain model is the underlying principle that managers should seek to make decisions across the chain's activity areas in a manner that contributes positively to the overall value of the products or services being produced or offered. By "value," it is implied that the benefit a decision would deliver to the product or service would outweigh the cost associated with it, thereby enhancing its value. The idea behind using this model is to get managers to think about how to plan their work, schedule the required activities, determine the most efficient allocation of resources, and execute those activities in a way that maximizes the value of the process. This maximization of value can be in the form of cost efficiencies, or it can be in the form of high quality standards, customization or product uniqueness, or high performance standards (to name a few). Again, the key is to think in terms of adding value that cannot be easily duplicated or mimicked by the competition in order to create a sustainable competitive advantage inherent within the activities the organization undertakes. To illustrate this concept, think of the release of Apple's iPad. The iPad, in actuality, is a collection of glass, metal, and electronic parts and components that on their own represent little value to the iPad customer. The market research firm iSuppli estimated the cost of the iPad (parts and manufacturing, as of April 2010) at approximately US$260. Of this $260, just over $250 was for components, with the touch screen making up the largest expense, and the manufacturing costs being just under $10 per unit.[3] Apple's initial retail price for the iPad was $499 (base model). This means that, for the finished product, Apple is generating a 48 percent gross profit margin from the sale of each unit (1 − 260/499). Keep in mind that Apple still has other expenses that must be recovered from this $499 selling price (marketing, development costs, general sales and administration, and so on). The point is that as part of its overall value chain process, from which the value proposition materializes, Apple is able to command a significant price increase over the core costs of the components it is using in the manufacturing of the iPad because of the value that the iPad represents to the final consumer. This is the root concept of value chain analysis (value maximization), and one that often can be best assessed by asking the question, "What is it that we must do to deliver maximum value to our customers?" In defining the key success metrics associated with this response, we should then tailor our value chain initiatives to execute the required tactics, processes, and methodologies essential to achieving **value maximization** in the eyes of our customers.

> **Value Maximization** refers to maximizing the benefits (price/quality comparison) that an individual or set of customers will realize as a result of using a product or service.

> At the centre of the value chain model is the underlying principle that managers should seek to make decisions across the chain's activity areas in a manner that contributes positively to the overall value of the products or services being produced or offered.

Value Chain Analysis: Primary Activities

In managing our value chain, we as managers must look at the connectivity between two key areas of business system activity. These two areas are called primary and supporting activities. **Primary activities** relate to the specific activities through which the development and transformation of a product or service occurs as it is produced and delivered to the marketplace. These areas (which may or may not occur in all organizations) are as follows, and are shown in Figure 9.4:

> **Primary Activities** relate to the specific activities through which the development and transformation of a product or service occurs as it is produced and delivered to the marketplace.

- Inbound logistics
- Operations
- Outbound logistics
- Marketing and sales
- Customer service

FIGURE 9.4   Value Chain: Primary Activities

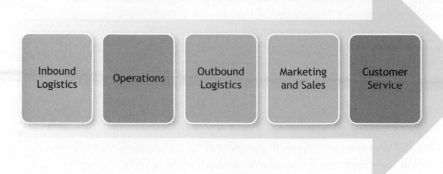

Source: Adapted from Michael Porter—Value Chain Analysis. See Michael Porter Value Chain Model framework, Value Based Management.net, www.valuebasedmanagement.net, May 25, 2010; and The Value Chain, Michael Porter, QuickMBA Strategic Management, www.quickmba.com/strategy/value-chain/, May 25, 2010.

Inbound Logistics refers to the management of supplier relationships relating to those parts and/or components, or finished products, that are brought into the organization in order to produce finished products for delivery to the marketplace.

Inbound logistics refers to the management of supplier relationships relating to those parts and/or components, or finished products, that are brought into the organization in order to manufacture finished products for delivery to the marketplace. Again, using our iPad example to illustrate a manufacturing setting, this would relate to the scheduling, shipping, and temporary warehousing of the glass, metal, and electronic parts and components. For a retailer purchasing finished goods—for example, a shirt from Thailand—this would relate to the coordination of the shipping and delivery of these shirts to the retailer's warehouse, and their temporary storage until they were shipped out to retail sites around the country.

Operations refers to the manufacturing and/or product change processes set up to ensure that the final product the organization is manufacturing or handling is ready for the marketplace.

Operations refers to the manufacturing and/or product change processes set up to ensure that the final product the organization is manufacturing or handling is ready for the marketplace. In our iPad example, this would be the manufacturing process used to combine the various parts and components into an actual iPad. For a retailer purchasing a finished product—again, for example, a shirt from Thailand—this may mean packaging the product and attaching the required labels to ensure that it meets information regulations specific to Canada, and/or branding the shirt under their company's name. Operations decisions would include process application, labour, and production management activities.

Outbound Logistics refers to getting the finished product to the customer via a distribution channel that is accessible, convenient, and able to minimize stockouts and other sales impediment factors.

Outbound logistics refers to the distribution activities required to get the right product to the right place at the right time. This means getting the finished product to the customer via a distribution channel that is accessible, convenient (in terms of the customer's ability to purchase), and able to minimize stockouts and other sales impediment factors that could result in customers shifting to an alternate provider. Outbound logistics decisions focus on warehouse needs, distribution, and inventory management activities, as well as on transportation and routing activities. In the case of the iPad, outbound logistics refers to decisions and activities relating to shipping the iPad to Apple's own stores, determining other retailers that will be authorized to sell the product (when a decision is made to broaden the distribution), and delivering the product to them. The same holds true for the sale of finished products through retailers. Outbound logistics also manages the warehousing, inventory, and transportation logistics for these organizations. The Business in Action vignette relating to Walmart on page 227 is a good example of this.

Marketing and Sales refers to those activities that create profile and awareness for the organization's products, services, or brand(s), and the benefits derived from the acquisition and use of such products or services.

Marketing and sales refers to those activities that create profile and awareness for the organization's products, services, or brand(s), and the benefits derived from the acquisition and use of such products or services. Referring back to Chapter 1 and our discussion relating to the creation of a value proposition, it is the role of marketing to effectively communicate the benefits of the products and services being offered in a manner that creates preference for, and commitment to, the organization's products and services on the part of its customer base.

Advertising, sales promotion, packaging, and point of sales communication, as well as contributing to decisions relating to distribution channel selection and setup, all form a part of marketing and sales activities. One of Apple Inc.'s core strengths is its brand strength and the ability of its marketing and sales departments to leverage this strength, and the emotional tie that individuals have to the brand. Apple Inc.'s ability to communicate the uniqueness of its products and the high levels of satisfaction derived by users of its products are fundamental to its success.

Customer service refers to the support provided to customers before, during, and fol-lowing the purchase process. Customer service can be thought of as technical support, repair support, warranty service work, installation, replacement parts management, upgrading options, and customer training, to name a few. A key desired outcome relating to customer service is to maintain and, where possible, enhance the value of the product/service purchased by the customer. Achieving this can result in high levels of customer satisfaction, which translates into customer loyalty and commitment. When effectively implemented, these activities can result in active customers who recommend others to your company, as well as strong customer loyalty that minimizes the potential of customer desertion to competitors.

Viewing the primary activities (inbound logistics, operations, outbound logistics, marketing and sales, and customer service) together as a chain should allow you to visualize the interconnectivity between process management, supply chain management, and products/services management. Operations management teams need to look at the types of processes to initiate in order to smoothly manage the inflow of materials and the transformation of such materials into finished goods, followed by the outflow of such products and services from the organization. The ability to design, develop, and effectively implement these processes in a way that is superior to those of its competitors can enable the organization to achieve a significant and sustainable competitive advantage in the marketplace. Management must then seek to optimize the relationships with its supply chain (inbound logistics, operations, and outbound logistics) partners. The development of strong supplier and distributor relationships is invaluable to the organization. Suppliers and distributors assist the organization in understanding market trends and shifts, maintaining a watchful eye on competitive innovation, and ensuring that cost control management practices are put into place throughout the supply chain in order to maintain competitive pricing strategies. Finally, while these two areas are being actively managed, the operations team must also look toward the future, designing, developing, enhancing, and maintaining the various products and services being offered to the marketplace.[4]

> **Customer Service** refers to the support provided to customers before, during, and following the purchase process.

> The development of strong supplier and distributor relationships is invaluable to the organization with regard to understanding market trends and shifts, maintaining a watchful eye on competitive innovation, and ensuring that cost control management practices are put into place throughout the supply chain in order to maintain competitive pricing strategies.

BUSINESS *in Action*

Walmart: A Lean, Keen Operating Machine

Walmart is #1 again, according to *Fortune* magazine. For an unprecedented seventh time in 10 years, Walmart (WAL MART STORES INC.) sits on top of the *Fortune* 500 ranking of U.S. businesses (based on sales volume). With sales exceeding US$408 billion, Walmart has been either #1 or #2 in revenue each year for the past decade. With 8416 stores worldwide and a workforce exceeding 2 million employees, Walmart serves more than 140 million customers per week. What makes Walmart so great? The company is founded on three basic principles: respect for the individual, service to its customers, and striving for excellence. It is this third principle that has resulted in Walmart becoming the lean, keen operating machine it is today. At its roots, founder Sam Walton created a culture that was never satisfied that prices were as low as they could be,

or that quality was as good as the customer expected. This culture continues to drive Walmart today, as it relentlessly pursues continuous improvements to its operations in the search for more efficient and cost-effective ways to bring to the marketplace the goods and services that its customers desire. A key component of this strategy has been to develop a sustainable, competitive advantage within its supply chain. Few, if any, companies in the world are more effective at moving goods and services through the front end of the value chain (supply chain) than Walmart. Walmart has effectively combined technological sophistication and innovation, transportation modelling, inventory management efficiencies, and global buying power given its economies of scale to evolve its operations into the largest retail organization in the world. For Walmart, the operation's focus is straightforward. The company continuously develops and applies a wide range of innovative merchandising approaches. Its regional hub-based distribution model, utilizing cutting-edge inventory management processes, efficiently handles hundreds of thousands of cases of merchandise each day. Its sophisticated computer system automatically transmits order replenishment information to many of its suppliers, saving time and money. This same system, via its inventory tracking model, also keeps Walmart on top of the changing buying patterns of its customers, thereby enabling it to quickly modify its product offerings. Walmart's buyers, backed by its tremendous buying power, work closely with its supplier network to develop and support partnerships that enable this retail giant to meet its (and its customers') expectations of quality.[5]

WEB INTEGRATION

Want to learn more details about Walmart's supply chain efficiencies? Google Walmart supply chain management, or visit **www.walmart.com**.

Value Chain Analysis: Support Activities

Support Activities are those areas within the organization that are not directly associated with the actual processes the organization uses to produce products and/or deliver services but that are an integral part of the support structure the primary activities rely on to successfully execute strategy.

Although one might get the impression that the primary activities noted above form the basis of the responsibilities of operations managers, it is equally important that these managers recognize and effectively manage—collaboratively, with the rest of the organization—the support activities needed to ensure the strategy execution is a success. **Support activities** are those areas within the organization that are not directly associated with the actual processes the organization uses to produce products and/or deliver services; these activities, however, are integral parts of the support structure the primary activities rely on to successfully execute strategy (see Figure 9.5). Some examples of support activities include:

FIGURE 9.5   Value Chain: Support Activities

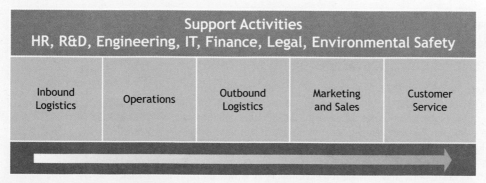

Source: Adapted from Michael Porter—Value Chain Analysis

- The IT department, which will collaborate with the operations department on the development and application of new technologies in support of the value chain process.

- The research and development and engineering departments, which primarily focus on new product development, existing product enhancement, and process design and development.

- Human resource management, which assists in recruitment, employee development, and support services for employees.

- Other supporting departments such as finance, accounting, legal, and environmental safety.

> The successful execution of the primary activities of the organization is facilitated by the organization's support activities.

The Operations Cycle

LO4

The initial part of this chapter dealt with identifying where, and how, operations management teams fit into the overall business system that an organization has developed to successfully deliver its products and/or services to the marketplace. The broad concept of the flow of activities within this business system has also been illustrated utilizing the value chain as a basis for this discussion. With this in mind, we turn our attention toward how operational tactics are integrated into the organization's overall strategy. We will also more fully define where operations managers spend their time and effort on a day-to-day basis.

Going back to Chapter 6 and the development of a business strategy, an organization will need to determine and confirm its mission and vision. This information, combined with a resource and capability assessment and market assessment, is then formulated into a business strategy. The strategy is then executed with the intention that strong market performance and profitability will follow, thereby meeting the company's current strategic expectations and maintaining the course toward the fulfillment of its vision and mission. As discussed in chapters 1 and 6, this process is outlined in what has been defined as the business planning cycle (see Figure 9.6).

FIGURE 9.6 Business Planning Cycle

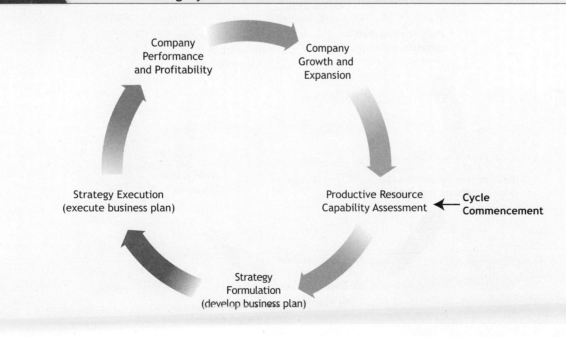

Why mention this again? Because a key area of responsibility with regard to the strategy execution phase of the planning cycle lies with the operations management team. Operations managers need to understand the strategic intent of the organization and, using this information, translate it into the action plans that will drive the execution of the organization's strategy. A key component of this process is to take the information derived from this strategy review and implement it through what is called the **operations cycle**. The operations cycle is the alignment of the operational tasks within an organization by its management team in order to meet the strategic outcomes defined in the organization's business strategy (see Figure 9.7).

For example, if the organization's intent is to focus on differentiated markets via the development of feature-rich products and services and communication of uniqueness and value-added benefits to customers, then the operations cycle within the organization needs to reflect this. This would imply an operations cycle that possesses flexibility and customization, and high-quality processes and operations. It also includes an emphasis on product research and development to stimulate innovation and creativity, and strong relationships with suppliers and distributors to ensure that this market position can be supported. Conversely, if the organization's desired strategic position is to focus on low price and acceptable quality, then the operations cycle will more likely place an emphasis on **process standardization** and **process simplification**. This requires a focus on process research and innovation versus product research and innovation, highly centralized material procurement to maximize economies of scale, and a focus on capital investment that drives ease of manufacturing design and execution.[6] Figure 9.8 provides an outline of the alignment between strategy and operational execution.

> Operations managers need to understand the strategic intent of the organization and, using this information, translate it into the action plans that will drive the execution of the organization's strategy.

With the operating cycle as a framework, operations managers must now delve into how best to respond to the specific objectives that have been formulated with the organization's strategic plan. This means that they need to determine how best to execute the operating cycle, taking into consideration their three spheres of responsibility (refer back to Figure 9.1): process management, supply chain management, and product/service management.

Operations Cycle is the alignment of the operational tasks within an organization by its management team in order to meet the strategic outcomes defined in the organization's business strategy.

Process Standardization is the design and utilization of common platforms and common task sequencing to produce/develop a variety of products or services.

Process Simplification is the design and utilization of a minimum number of tasks when developing products and/or services.

FIGURE 9.7 Operations Cycle

- Make the required operational changes and investments
- Manage the process to realize desired performance
- What Is the Strategy? ← Start
- Does this translate into an emphasis on lower prices or better quality?
- Determine what needs to be done to execute the strategy

Source: Notes and Slides, 2007 AMBA Mission Critical Marketing, Ken Wong, Queen's School of Business.

FIGURE 9.8   Strategy and Operational Alignment

Strategic Intent	Operations Management Focus	Operations Application Focus
Low Cost/Low Prices	Tight cost control Structured organization Tight process supervision Meeting volume-based targets	Process standardization Process simplification Economies of scale Technology intensive Low-cost distribution R&D process improvement focus
Differentiated Strategy/ Higher Prices	Focus on quality vs. quantity Emphasis on culture of collaboration and communication Greater allowance for creativity and self-achievement Emphasis on defining and adding value to products	Higher labour skills Stronger emphasis on creativity skills Strong tie-in with marketing Strong R&D product development focus Strong partnership approach with distributors

Source: Notes and Slides, 2007 AMBA Mission Critical Marketing, Ken Wong, Queen's School of Business. Used with permission of Kenneth Wong

Process Management

In terms of process management, operations managers have four core decision areas that need to be examined (see Figure 9.9). These are as follows:

1. Process design, layout, and execution
2. Materials management
3. Facility design and layout
4. Capital asset evaluation and acquisition

FIGURE 9.9   Process Management: Key Decision Areas

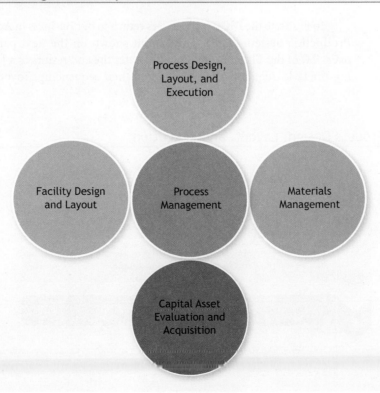

Process Design, Layout, and Execution refers to the assessment and implementation of the tasks necessary to get the required work accomplished, and how such tasks will be grouped and sequenced to ensure that the most efficient and effective processes are utilized in the production of products and/or services.

Process design, layout, and execution refers to the assessment and implementation of the type of tasks needed to get required work accomplished, and how such tasks will be grouped and sequenced to ensure that the most efficient and effective processes are utilized in the production or delivery of products and/or services. Depending on the nature of the industry and the work required, this could include fabrication processes, assembly processes, quality assurance processes, clerical and administrative support processes, internal and external transportation processes, environmental initiatives, and hazardous waste handling processes. Decisions will need to be made, as well, as to how the flow of work will be sequenced and what steps must be initiated into the process to ensure that quality, timing, performance, and service expectations are met. Other decisions could be related to the flexibility required, the technology to be used, and the level of human interaction at various points throughout the process. As an example, one decision could be determining if the greatest output efficiency would be one based on a fixed process approach, where the process being developed is focused on one product line only, versus a flexible production approach capable of handling more than one product but recognizing that retooling time and other factors may add additional costs to the work flow process. In general, a good way to think of process design and layout is to view it as a flowchart, or as the analysis of a road map. Visualizing the work flow needed, and using process management software, tools, and models, managers will define not only a starting point for the various tasks required, but also an ending point, which results in the product/service getting to the right place at the right time and to the right customer in a manner that meets the organization's strategic positioning and financial performance objectives. This means defining the work that needs to be done, identifying the task sequencing that will result in the most efficient and effective work flow necessary to accomplish the required transformation, creating this work flow, and then executing and continuously evaluating the performance results. An easy way to remember the key fundamentals associated with process design, layout, and execution is by the acronym DICE—*define, identify, create,* and *execute* (see Figure 9.10).

> Process management decisions will need to be made as to how the flow of work will be sequenced and what steps must be initiated into the process to ensure that quality, timing, performance, and service expectations are met.

To illustrate the DICE process, let's return to our Business in Action example of the Toyota Production System (TPS). The exhibit shown on the next page provides a broad-level overview of the TPS concept[7] and illustrates the end results of a DICE analysis. After defining the tasks required and determining their sequencing, Toyota created its TPS process.

FIGURE 9.10   DICE: Process Design, Layout, and Execution

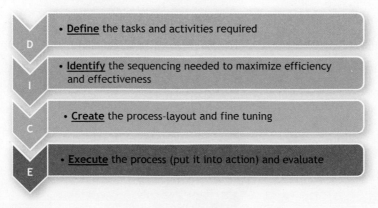

- **D** — **Define** the tasks and activities required
- **I** — **Identify** the sequencing needed to maximize efficiency and effectiveness
- **C** — **Create** the process-layout and fine tuning
- **E** — **Execute** the process (put it into action) and evaluate

Now fully implemented, Toyota's operations management team monitors and manages the system, assessing its overall efficiency and making ongoing decisions relating to continuous improvements in order to maximize its effectiveness and contribute to the achievement of the organization's overall business strategy.

Although we have focused our discussion of process design largely on the development of continuous-process work flows, short-term or outcome-specific project management analysis can also form a critical component of operations management responsibility in many business sectors. These would include areas such as engineering and commercial real estate

TPS Concept

Jidoka
—Highlighting/visualization of problems—

-Quality must be built in during the manufacturing process!-

If equipment malfunction or a defective part is discovered, the affected machine automatically stops, and operators cease production and correct the problem. For the Just-in-Time system to function, all of the parts that are made and supplied must meet predetermined quality standards. This is achieved through jidoka.

1. Jidoka means that a machine safely stops when the normal processing is completed. It also means that, should a quality / equipment problem arise, the machine detects the problem on its own and stops, preventing defective products from being produced. As a result, only products satisfying quality standards will be passed on to the following processes on the production line.

2. Since a machine automatically stops when processing is completed or when a problem arises and is communicated via the "andon" (problem display board), operators can confidently continue performing work at another machine, as well as easily identify the problem's cause to prevent its recurrence. This means that each operator can be in charge of many machines, resulting in higher productivity, while continuous improvements lead to greater processing capacity.

Just-in-Time
—Productivity improvement—

-Making only "what is needed, when it is needed, and in the amount needed!"

Producing quality products efficiently through the complete elimination of waste, inconsistencies, and unreasonable requirements on the production line. In order to deliver a vehicle ordered by a customer as quickly as possible, the vehicle is efficiently built within the shortest possible period of time by adhering to the following:

1. When a vehicle order is received, a production instruction must be issued to the beginning of the vehicle production line as soon as possible.

2. The assembly line must be stocked with required number of all needed parts so that any type of ordered vehicle can be assembled.

3. The assembly line must replace the parts used by retrieving the same number of parts from the parts-producing process (the preceding process).

4. The preceding process must be stocked with small numbers of all types of parts and produce only the numbers of parts that were retrieved by an operator from the next process.

Source: "Toyota Production System," http://www.toyota-global.com/company/vision_philosophy/toyota_production_system/.

development and construction. Project management can also relate directly to new product development and the launch of a new product or service. As with continuous process layout methodologies, business design technology software tools and models exist to assist managers with these critical project management tasks. Two commonly used project management tools are the **PERT chart** and the **Gantt chart** (see Figures 9.11 and 9.12). Both PERT charts and Gantt charts are project management tools that offer a decision-making framework to assist managers in estimating the time, money, and people required to develop and execute a business project. PERT (Program Evaluation and Review Technique) charts focus on the identification and dependency relationships of the tasks required and the recognition of the critical components of the project that must be completed at given points in a project's life, otherwise project delays will occur (critical path analysis). Gantt charts, which provide similar information to that provided by PERT charts, focus more on the communication of the task timeline and the time duration anticipated within each task. PERT and Gantt charts are used to detail the design and development of the work flow for a project, and can also be customized or modified to assist in managing continuous process situations.

Materials management refers to the management of the inputs required in order to develop the products or services that the organization is intent on delivering to the marketplace. Materials management could be associated with inputs/items such as:

- components for assembly purposes

- parts for repair and maintenance of products sold

- raw materials, such as molten aluminum for the fabrication of transmission casings or pistons for automobiles

- hazardous waste disposal

- sanitary practices for the safe handling of food at restaurants

- regulation compliance for the handling of goods such as prescription drugs

- the handling of fully finished goods that the organization has purchased with the intent of reselling such items through its retail outlets

PERT Chart is a scheduling methodology that focuses on task sequencing and the identification of the critical path of steps that will most greatly impact the ability to complete a project, and the length of time needed for completion.

Gantt Chart is a methodology used to schedule the steps associated with a project and the time required to complete each step.

Materials Management refers to the management of the inputs required in order to develop the products or services that the organization is intent on delivering to the marketplace.

FIGURE 9.11   Example PERT Chart

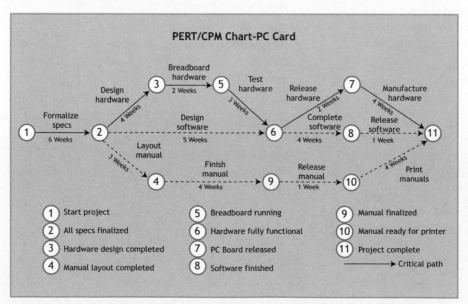

Source: PERT Chart Example, RFF Electronics, RFF Flow5 Professional Flowcharting, www.rff.com/sample_pert.htm, May 2010.

FIGURE 9.12   Example GANTT Chart

[Project Name]
[Company Name]

Project Lead: John Doe
Today's Date: 2/24/2009   (Tue)(vertical red line)
Start Date: 1/5/2009   (Mon)

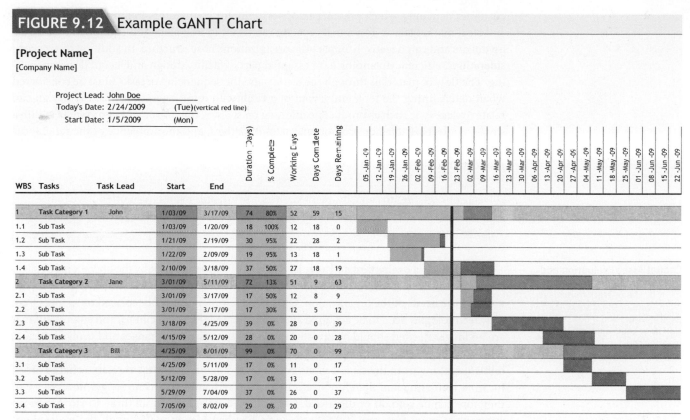

WBS	Tasks	Task Lead	Start	End	Duration (Days)	% Complete	Working Days	Days Complete	Days Remaining
1	Task Category 1	John	1/03/09	3/17/09	74	80%	52	59	15
1.1	Sub Task		1/03/09	1/20/09	18	100%	12	18	0
1.2	Sub Task		1/21/09	2/19/09	30	95%	22	28	2
1.3	Sub Task		1/22/09	2/09/09	19	95%	13	18	1
1.4	Sub Task		2/10/09	3/18/09	37	50%	27	18	19
2	Task Category 2	Jane	3/01/09	5/11/09	72	13%	51	9	63
2.1	Sub Task		3/01/09	3/17/09	17	50%	12	8	9
2.2	Sub Task		3/01/09	3/17/09	17	30%	12	5	12
2.3	Sub Task		3/18/09	4/25/09	39	0%	28	0	39
2.4	Sub Task		4/15/09	5/12/09	28	0%	20	0	28
3	Task Category 3	Bill	4/25/09	8/01/09	99	0%	70	0	99
3.1	Sub Task		4/25/09	5/11/09	17	0%	11	0	17
3.2	Sub Task		5/12/09	5/28/09	17	0%	13	0	17
3.3	Sub Task		5/29/09	7/04/09	37	0%	26	0	37
3.4	Sub Task		7/05/09	8/02/09	29	0%	20	0	29

Source: Gantt Chart Template, Microsoft Excel, www.vertex42.com/Files/gantt-chart-template-MF.xls, May 2010.

As you can sense, materials management and process management are quite interconnected. Materials management refers to the specific tasks associated with the handling of materials, while process design, layout, and execution detail how this handling of materials is to be orchestrated within the full work flow of the organization.

Facility design and layout refers to infrastructure layout and related facility components that will be required to house and support the processes noted above. Key decisions in this area of operations management responsibility include decisions relating to production **capacity**, plant, facility, and/or retail locations, warehousing, storage, and other similar decisions. Walmart, as an example, uses a regional hub approach to supporting its various store locations. As Walmart builds and opens new stores, it also has to consider how it is going to support the stocking and restocking of these stores through its distribution system. This means that further expansion plans associated with Walmart go beyond individual store selection and require a larger, regional expansion approach.[8] Similarly, Shoppers Drug Mart, in launching its newly designed stores, had to make a significant number of decisions relating to the square footage allocation of its newly expanded departments (cosmetics, convenience foods) and what each of these store areas was going to look like as part of its process of attracting customers. Toyota Motor Company, in building its new Canadian manufacturing facility in Woodstock, Ontario, had to make decisions relating to the size of the facility and the types of vehicles to be built there. The plant, announced in 2005, took approximately three years to build, with the first vehicle rolling off the assembly line in December 2008. Designed to build Toyota's RAV 4 sports utility vehicle, the plant was built with an annual production capacity of 270 000 vehicles. Economic conditions in 2008 resulted in production initially being limited to approximately 75 000 vehicles annually, and has since been bumped up to approximately 150 000 vehicles annually.[9] Decisions relating to capacity, plant size (footprint), and plant layout often have to be made years in advance, based on estimated sales forecasts given anticipated market conditions. Building too little capacity can result in not being able to meet

Facility Design and Layout refers to infrastructure layout and related facility components that will be required to house and support the processes and materials used by the organization.

Capacity refers to the maximum amount of product that can be produced, or services delivered, given facility, equipment, and process constraints.

customer demands, which presents an opportunity for competitors to move in to the market and steal market share. Too much capacity can result in idle plant and equipment, which tie up dollars and can negatively impact the organization's cost structure. In addition to size considerations, efficiency planning is an essential part of facility design and layout decision making. The flow of materials through the facility and the sequencing of tasks must be considered when determining the look and layout of a facility. In retail operations, facility design can relate to decisions such as product positioning on shelves, the movement of products within a store to reflect seasonal or promotional sales initiatives, and the ambiance of the retail location to reflect a theme or contribute to the uniqueness and appeal of a particular brand or product line.

> Decisions relating to capacity, plant size (footprint), and plant layout often have to be made years in advance, based on estimated sales forecasts given anticipated market conditions.

Capital Asset Evaluation and Acquisition refers to an assessment by the operations management team of the state of current capital assets and a determination as to their applicability to meeting the needs of the organization.

Capital asset evaluation and acquisition refers to an assessment by the operations management team of the state of current capital assets and a determination as to their applicability to meeting the needs of the organization. Obsolete equipment must be replaced or modernized. New technologies need to be acquired and implemented. Plants, facilities, and equipment that are no longer needed should be divested of. As the organization changes and evolves, so, too, do its capital asset requirements. Managers must continuously assess the operational capabilities resulting from the capital assets available, and determine what to retain, what to invest in, what is missing and therefore needs to be acquired, and what is no longer necessary and therefore can be sold off or discarded. Over the past several years, all three North American automobile manufacturers (GM, Ford, and Chrysler) had to make tough decisions about which brands to keep, which vehicles to keep producing, and which plants will continue as central to the production process. GM, for example, has eliminated the Oldsmobile, Saturn, and Pontiac brands. Ford is considering closing its Mercury division. These types of decisions have resulted in the closing of many plants, the elimination of hundreds of dealers, and the early retirement or termination of thousands of employees. The decisions relating to which plants to close and which brands to eliminate were the result of assessing the organization's strategic intent, conducting a resource and market assessment, and then evaluating the efficiency, effectiveness, and competitiveness of the capital asset infrastructure at various plant locations. These factors determined which assets to keep and which assets to sell or discard.

BUSINESS in Action

Harvey's: Redesigning Its Restaurants

For Canadians, the Harvey's brand name represents a "David versus Goliath" saga, as this Canadian company has been challenged to compete with mega-brands such as McDonald's, Burger King, and Wendy's. In its fight to maintain and grow its market share, Harvey's has followed the industry leaders' forays into menu expansion, such as breakfast items and non-burger-related sandwiches. The end result has been little revenue growth and a constant pressure on profitability. So, what's next in Harvey's quest to improve its overall market position in Canada? Rick McNabb, Harvey's CEO, thinks that he has the answer. McNabb, a former successful franchise owner from Parry Sound, Ontario, plans to take Harvey's back to its roots. In McNabb's mind, the addition of breakfast items and non-burger sandwich items caused Harvey's to lose sight of what makes it unique: the customization of hamburgers. (After all, Harvey's does make a hamburger a beautiful thing.) With this in mind, McNabb has a strategic plan that is designed to grow Harvey's restaurant base by an additional 150 stores, bringing its total market penetration to more than 400 locations nationwide. In addition to revamping its hamburger's fat content and being a first mover in shifting to trans-fat-free cooking oil, a key part of this strategy is the redesign of its store format. Harvey's new stores will be smaller (2200 sq. ft. versus 3200 sq. ft.),

have less seating (65 seats versus 100), and be much more eco-friendly. Why the change? The new stores will cost less money to build and operate. This means that initial franchise costs will be reduced to around $550 000. Lower operating costs mean franchisees will need to drive less revenue to cover their expenses and provide a greater allowance for profit for both the franchisee and the parent corporation (Cara Operations Limited). This lower initial start-up cost and stronger operating margins are what McNabb hopes will attract its next generation of franchise owners and enable Harvey's to build significantly more corporate-owned stores than could be realized under the old model. Hamburgers are a multi-billion-dollar business in Canada, and McNabb and Harvey's believe that a smaller, leaner, and more efficient capital asset base means less overhead, which can be translated into lower costs, which will enable it to expand its footprint (add additional stores) and improve its value proposition in the eyes of customers.[10]

WEB INTEGRATION

Want to learn more about the success of Harvey's expansion plans? Visit **www.harveys.ca**.

Supply Chain Management

As indicated earlier in the chapter, supply chain management refers to the management of the flow of materials and/or products, information, and costs through the front end of an organization's value chain. This means planning, sourcing, and delivering the required components, parts, or products purchased for resell to the organization, and then delivering the finished products to the marketplace either through business-to-business relationships (B2B) or business-to-customer (B2C) sales locations. An additional function of supply chain management—and one that is often overlooked—includes the development of a responsive network for dealing with defective merchandise and/or unsold items (excess inventory), if these are to form part of the organization's customer service strategy. For an organization, a key aspect of supply chain management is an understanding of the various partners the organization will need to interact with to ensure that it successfully develops the network needed for the efficient flow of goods and services into and out of the organization. Figure 9.13 provides an overview of some of the key partners that need to be included in an organization's supply chain network.

When we think about supply chain management in general, three areas of ongoing responsibility come to mind. These are as follows (see Figure 9.14):

1. Supply chain planning
2. Supply chain operating execution
3. Supply chain performance evaluation

Supply chain management refers to the development of the supply chain structure and the accumulation of the necessary information needed to make effective supply chain decisions. Examples of activities that form a core part of the planning mode are:

- Making decisions relating to outsourcing of various supply chain functions versus keeping such activities in-house.

- Assessing the various software and ebusiness services that will be required to effectively manage supply chain tasks.

Supply Chain Management refers to the development of the supply chain structure and the accumulation of the necessary information to make effective supply chain decisions.

FIGURE 9.13　Supply Chain Partners

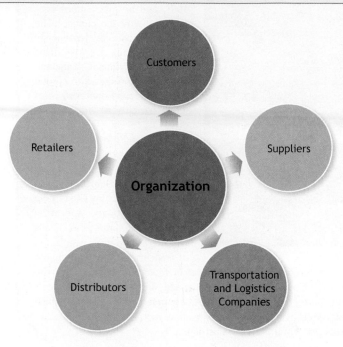

FIGURE 9.14　Supply Chain Management Responsibilities

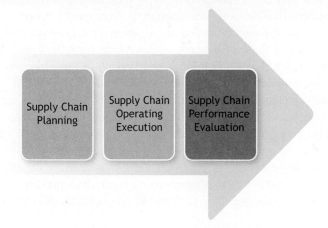

- Analyzing sales forecasts to determine appropriate product quantities to purchase.

- Designing the transportation and warehouse networks to effectively manage the flow of products through the organization's value chain.

Supply Chain Operating Execution refers to the execution of the specific tasks necessary to ensure that key performance results are achieved.

Supply chain operating execution refers to the execution of the specific tasks necessary to ensure that key performance results are achieved. This would include activities such as the management of inventory levels, efficient utilization of the organization's transportation fleet, effective use of technology systems in place, accurate and timely invoicing and collection, ensuring that products reach the market in a timely fashion, and the achievement of the required manufacturing quantities to meet the expectations of retailers and other product distributors.

Supply chain performance evaluation refers to the critical outcomes that the supply chain must achieve in support of the organization's overall operating performance. Two critical outcomes in this regard are (1) maximum utilization of the capital asset base, and (2) minimization of the time involved within the cash operating cycle. Maximization of the capital asset base has been alluded to earlier in this chapter. This represents the focused desire, on the part of the supply chain management team, to minimize unnecessary and wasteful expenses due to inefficient transportation flows, poor inventory management and warehouse inefficiencies, and poor capacity management due to inaccurate sales forecasting and demand interpretation. Inefficiencies in capital asset and infrastructure management often result in an upward pressure on expense lines and profitability erosion. The **cash operating cycle (COC)**, also known as the cash-to-cash cycle, refers to the amount of time it takes for an organization to recover the cash (product is sold and money is received) it has paid out for the development, production, and distribution of products. It represents the amount of time it takes for money you are spending to finance the transformation of inputs into products and/or services (process flow across the stages of the value chain) to be returned to you in the form of cash once sales have been made and accounts receivable collected. Figure 9.15 illustrates a simplified cash operating cycle. In general, the shorter the cash operating cycle, the more quickly the organization is getting back the cash it has expended on producing its goods and services and, therefore, the less the organization needs to rely on cash reserves or short-term debt financing to cover the expenditures. An additional generalization associated with cash operating cycles is that the longer it takes for a company to produce its products, move them into the market, have them sold, and receive the revenue from them, the more expensive the cost of producing these products will be. In business, time is money. The concept of the COC and its financial impact on the organization will be discussed in more detail in Chapter 14.

Supply Chain Performance Evaluation refers to the critical outcomes that the supply chain must achieve in support of the organization's overall operating performance.

Cash Operating Cycle (COC) refers to the amount of time it takes for an organization to recover the cash (product is sold and money is received) it has paid out for the development, production and distribution of products.

> In general, the shorter the cash operating cycle, the more quickly the organization is getting back the cash it has expended on producing its goods and services and, therefore, the less the organization needs to rely on cash reserves or short-term debt financing to cover the costs of the expenditures incurred.

FIGURE 9.15 Cash Operating Cycle

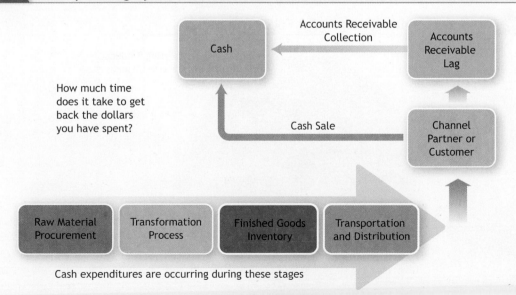

The idea behind supply chain management is to assist the organization in reducing its cost base, thereby offsetting market pressures toward lower prices. It does this by trying to make the most effective use possible of the dollars it must invest, and by striving to maximize the financial performance of the organization through superior management of inventories, warehouses, transportation fleets, distribution networks, and sales forecasting methodologies. This means ongoing assessment and analysis of sourcing and procurement practices, labour allocation, distribution processes, inbound and outbound warehouse practices, inventory management practices, and supplier payment options, to name a few. The core idea is to provide the right products and/or services to the market at the right time, at the lowest supply chain costs possible.[11]

Product/Service Management

As identified earlier in this chapter, one of the spheres of responsibility of operations managers is their collaborative involvement (with R&D, marketing, and engineering) in the design and delivery of existing product enhancements, as well as new products/services. As markets evolve and customers' needs, expectations, and attitudes change, organizations will continually review their existing product portfolio to determine where to enhance existing products, launch new products, or invest in emerging opportunities and/or technologies that will spur future product/market opportunities. In assessing the organization's current business planning cycle and its overall longer-term strategy, operations managers play a key role in determining the ability of the organization to execute changes to the existing product line and/or develop future products and services. Discussions relating to product/service management opportunities are generally focused around three specific areas: existing product/service changes, new product opportunities, and long-reach opportunities (see Figure 9.16).[12]

These three areas are as follows:

- Existing product/service changes

- New product opportunities

- Long-reach opportunities

Existing product/service changes relates to the existing products and/or the existing level of services offered to the marketplace within which the organization currently competes.

FIGURE 9.16   Product/Service Management Focus

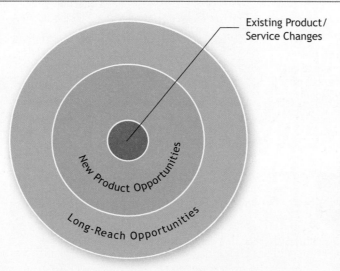

Decisions associated with this area of operations management relate directly to the product modifications or enhancements that are deemed necessary from a competitive perspective (such as component input changes, feature/benefit modifications, level of service support, and stocking of replacement parts). It represents an assessment of the current value of an existing product within the market it currently serves, and the additions, adjustments, or deletions required to enhance or maintain its current position (or to successfully reposition it). The laundry product Tide, for example, has gone through a number of evolutions since its debut in 1943, all with a focus on defending and growing its market leader position in the laundry detergent market. The years since 1943 have seen Tide evolve, through powder, crystal, and liquid product offerings, to its current availability of product choices, such as compact powder (puck), quick stick (Tide to Go), and target market options such as Tide with Febreeze, Tide Stain Release, and Tide Washing Machine Cleaner.[13] Apple's iPod, the industry leader in the MP3 player market, has been the recipient of continuous innovation and upgrades as Apple sought to drive ongoing revenue and profitability from this particular product offering. Again, existing product/service adjustments can be thought of as core enhancements or changes that are deemed necessary because they are fundamental to maintaining the product/service's competitive position, meeting its revenue and profitability objectives, or improving its overall appeal in the marketplace.

New product opportunities refers to the development of new products for market opportunities that exist today and for which research has concluded there is near-term revenue potential. Apple Inc.'s development of the iPad, which provides a new product option applicable to both the electronic reader market and the netbook market, is an example of this immediate-term type of opportunity. New product opportunity development is critical in that existing products and services have defined lives. As these products mature and decline, they must be replaced by new products and services if the organization is going to continue to grow. Using Apple again as an example, its main cash cow (cash provider) for much of 2000 through 2009 was its iPod product. Through the use of core enhancements, combined with a strong market position, Apple Inc. realized tremendous profits from its iPod portfolio. The first quarter of 2010, however, saw this change as the iPhone, which represented a solid 40 percent of Apple's revenue during that quarter, actually contributed greater profitability to the company than the iPod. Although the iPod is still profitable, Apple Inc. is looking for new products to replace the significant cash provided to the organization from the iPod, as iPod sales have begun to flatten (down 1 percent in first quarter 2010) and the product will become a lower priority in Apple's future growth plans. Apple's product pipeline, consisting of newer iPhone, Mac, and iPad product versions, is poised to take up this slack and reflects this company's ability to launch new products for existing markets.[14]

Long-reach opportunities refers to the investment in, and development of, new product research for potentially emerging markets of the future. The intent of these types of R&D decisions is to develop leading-edge technologies and/or products and services that will enable the organization to obtain "first mover advantage" when, and if, these markets emerge. Examples include prescription drug research and development, electric car battery development, and hydrogen fuel cell technology development. For example, at Apple Inc. R&D dollars are being spent today on emerging technologies that will, hopefully, supply Apple with its products of tomorrow. The marketplace remains uncertain, so investments may not materialize into actual product opportunities. The need exists, however, to focus on such emerging markets if Apple is going to maintain its market leader position in the target segments it serves.

Establishing Quality Standards   LO5, LO6

As one can see, the role of the operations management team is complex and challenging. With the rapid change in technology, the ongoing maturing of the global market, and the influx of new competitors from all parts of the world, operations managers must seek to design, develop, implement, and manage processes vital to the successful execution of an organization's strategy. A key part of this challenge is to continually protect and, in many cases, enhance the quality of the products and services being offered in the face of constant downward pressure on price. This means that operations managers and their teams must work to continually improve the efficiency and effectiveness of the organization's operations cycle, while at the same time striving to reduce the costs incurred in doing so (see Figure 9.17). A key weapon in this ongoing challenge to preserve quality and maintain the product standards expected by customers in the face of pressure to reduce costs lies with the organization's culture and the development of performance standards. Operations managers know that the ability to establish within the organization a culture focused on preserving quality and maintaining product consistency is fundamental to maintaining a competitive advantage in the face of intensifying competition. Managers also recognize that their ability to supply their products to customers in B2B settings is predicated on their capability to meet consistent and measurable quality standards. With an increasing focus on specialization and automation, finished goods producers rely on their suppliers to deliver consistent (quality) parts and components for integration into their production/transformation processes. Operations and supply chains are becoming truly global, with manufacturing partners and suppliers performing more and more of the transformation work on the products and services sold by many companies. Legal, environmental, ethical, and social responsibility issues are impacting the operations of organizations more extensively than ever before.

> A key weapon in this ongoing challenge to preserve quality and maintain the product standards expected by customers in the face of pressure to reduce costs lies with the organization's culture and the development of performance standards.

FIGURE 9.17   Quality Impact Factors

In response to this, organizations and their operations management teams are implementing behaviour-directed methodologies designed to assist in the control of consistency and quality standards within the organization. For many, **ISO (International Organization for Standardization)** certification is an essential first step in ensuring that they meet the expectations of their customers. The ISO has developed more than 18 000 standards relating to the manufacturing and supplying of products and services. Its focus is to make the manufacturing of products and services safer, more efficient, and more socially responsible. Its work results in customers benefiting from knowing that manufacturers have conformed to international standards relating to reliability and quality. By achieving ISO certification, manufacturers agree to adhere to the product and process specification requirements and criteria in the manufacturing of products and services within their industry classification, and to use a common technological language in their communication with suppliers and customers. ISO standards cover a wide range of industry sectors, such as agriculture, construction, engineering, manufacturing, distribution, and information and communication technologies, to name a few. The ISO's best-known categories of standards cover general management practices and quality standards (ISO 9000 series) and environmental management standards (ISO 14000 series).[15]

> **ISO (International Organization for Standardization)** is the world's largest developer and publisher of international standards.

Although ISO certification is a good first step for many organizations, particularly in the manufacturing and distribution sectors, organizations often look to develop a culture of quality (beyond ISO compliance) in order to achieve a sustainable competitive advantage over their competitors. Toyota's development of TPS is a good example of an organization developing standards to guide its operations-based processes and to embed within its culture a sense of discipline toward uncompromising quality. Alan Mulally's Ford One program (highlighted in Chapter 7) is another example of attempting to shift the cultural attitude within an organization toward quality. Other companies have turned to developed methodologies such as Six Sigma and TQM to assist in redefining cultural attitudes toward quality and to significantly upgrade their quality performance results. **Six Sigma** is a methodology that focuses on a philosophy of total improvement. It seeks to integrate within an organization's culture an organized approach for the analysis of processes, with the intent of minimizing (and eliminating) the occurrence of defects—which, ultimately, impact the quality of the products/services being delivered to the marketplace and the costs incurred in their creation. Based on a methodology of DMAIC (define, measure, analyze, improve, control) for existing operations, or DMADV (define, measure, analyze, design, verify) for new operations, Six Sigma analyses guide managers to map the processes being used within the organization, align these with customer needs, and then seek to improve or develop such processes and implement the necessary controls for maintaining the heightened (required) quality levels. Although historically best suited for situations where quantitative data are available and defect rates can be measured, the Six Sigma approach has been extended to non-quantitative situations as well. Developed by Motorola Inc. in the 1980s and made famous by General Electric (under CEO Jack Welch), Six Sigma has resulted in significant savings for many companies across a wide variety of manufacturing sectors. Six Sigma gets its name from its statistical orientation of deviation from the mean. Attainment of Six Sigma represents a situation where the manufacturing processes being employed are virtually free of defects (3.4 defects per 1 000 000 chances). An easy way to think of Six Sigma is that better processes, with lower defect rates, mean lower costs, which results in improved profit margins.[16]

> **Six Sigma** is a methodology that focuses on a philosophy of total improvement.

WEB INTEGRATION
Want to learn more about ISO certification? Visit www.iso.org.

WEB INTEGRATION
Want to learn more about Six Sigma and its use in today's marketplace? Google Six Sigma methodologies.

While Six Sigma focuses more on the specific processes within an organization, **TQM (total quality management)** can be viewed as more of a broad-based approach to managing quality within the organization. TQM can be thought of as a management system that seeks to assimilate the concept of quality improvement across the entire organization. TQM challenges the organization to be customer focused and to strive for total employee involvement to ensure that quality (in the delivery of products or services) is fully integrated as a core component into the organization's strategy, processes, and communication messages. Similar to

> **TQM (Total Quality Management)** is a broad-based approach to managing quality within the organization.

FIGURE 9.18   Successful Quality Initiative Implementation

WEB INTEGRATION
Want to learn more about TQM
and how to incorporate it into
the workplace? Google TQM or
total quality management.

Six Sigma, TQM looks for managers to implement quality improvement initiatives on the basis of facts and on the utilization of analytical thinking in determining ways to become more efficient and effective. TQM also directs its emphasis on the processes used within the organization to interact with customers. The focus of quality improvement needs to be in those areas of the organization that influence the quality perception at known critical customer touch points.[17]

Six Sigma and TQM are but two of the many approaches organizations and their operations management teams can initiate to improve and maintain heightened quality levels. For example, BPR, or business processing engineering, focuses on how organizations transform production and manufacturing processes to improve the way that people work. In reality, companies often take components of the various models offered and use them to formulate their own customized approaches to managing quality through their manufacturing and/or service-based delivery processes. Toyota's TPS approach is, again, an excellent example. Regardless of the path chosen or the methodology selected, managers need to recognize that certain core fundamentals will determine their overall degree of success. These fundamentals can be summarized as follows (see Figure 9.18):

- Quality initiatives, such as those described above, are successful only if they are accompanied by strong management support and commitment.

- To be successful, quality initiatives must be supported by a well-structured approach and deployment process. This needs to include clear identification of the roles and responsibilities of those involved. Specific, measurable, actionable, and controllable objectives must be identified.

- Quality initiatives must be viewed as requiring a team-based approach. Involvement, input, rewards, and recognition must be shared with all involved.

- The progress and results of the initiatives must be effectively communicated to all involved. The sharing of knowledge and successes is fundamental to developing a quality-focused culture.

Operations Management in Small Businesses

Operational efficiency and effectiveness is one of the predominant challenges facing the small business owner. Possessing, in many cases, limited resources and expertise, small business owners often do not have the abilities or the financial capabilities required to take full advantage of the technologies and practices available to maximize the cost-effectiveness of their businesses. Also, lacking the depth and functional expertise of full-time operations management professionals, small business owners must generally seek to tackle the intricacies of operations management while attending to the broader business issues (sales, finance, HR, and so on). A small, generally more transient employee base also limits their ability and desire to commit significant financial resources into the training and education of what are perceived to be non-critical business positions. With all of these challenges noted, just how does a small business owner seek to tackle the need to create as efficient an operation as is possible? The answer to this question lies in the fact that, although limitations do exist, the small business owner can incorporate many of the key characteristics of successful operations management. Small business owners should look to understand customer expectations and translate this into processes designed to support customers at the key interaction touch points where the business and customers connect. Small business owners should also think in terms of product consistency, striving to deliver consistent experience with each customer interaction. A key component of this process is to determine what skills are fundamentally required at the point of customer contact and seek to ensure that employees are recruited, trained, and educated to support this interaction. Small business owners should also take the time to plan their business layout. A good way to do this is to walk through every step associated with the process of delivering products and/or services to the customer and then design the layout and process in support of this. Taking the position of the customer and working backwards through this process is an eye-opener for many small business owners and professionals. Finally, small business owners need to be careful not to make operational decisions "on the fly," but rather based on facts and via a systematic, analytical process that ensures the changes or adjustments being made enhance service and do not negatively impact the delivery of service in other areas. For many small business owners, a key to success is communication of the business strategy and effective communication of how operational areas are linked to this plan. Often feeling alone, small business owners should seek to involve their employee team in discussions relating to facility layout, process planning, and service delivery changes. Employees "in the trenches" of the day-to-day operations can often provide positive and constructive ideas on how to improve services and/or make better use of technology. The additional benefit is the sense of involvement they will get from such discussions and the motivational impact the process will have on their future work effort.

Management Reflection—Operational Success

More and more organizations understand that the battle to develop sustainable competitive advantages lies at the front end of the value chain. The need for efficient and effective transformation processes and supply chains can, and will, dramatically influence the ability of an organization to compete in today's global marketplace. The ability of marketing to build brand differentiation is dependent upon the consistent and effective delivery of quality products and services at price points that customers are willing to pay for the value received. To be successful in meeting customer expectations and in contributing to the organization's overall value proposition, operations managers must develop the deep functional expertise and the general business skills needed to develop and manage the processes and methodologies required for competitive purposes. They must also understand and seek to eliminate those costs within their operations that do not add value to the products or services being offered. Decisions relating to this cannot be made in isolation of others. Operations managers need to integrate a cross-functional approach to their decision making that includes internal stakeholders, such as sales, marketing, customer service, and finance, to name a few, as well as external stakeholders, particularly supply chain partners and distribution channel representatives. This collaborative and cooperative approach is vital to ensuring that decisions made within one area of the transformation and distribution process do not negatively impact other areas. Finally, organizations must tailor their operations to the needs of their customers, ensuring that the expectations of these customers are met, and that the right product is delivered to the right place at the right time for the right price.

To be successful in meeting customer expectations and in contributing to the organization's overall value proposition, operations managers must develop the deep functional expertise and the general business skills needed to develop and manage the processes and methodologies required for competitive purposes.

Chapter Summary

The focus of this chapter is on acclimatizing students to the responsibilities of operations managers. The chapter begins with a discussion of the important role operations management plays within the organization's business system and in the execution of the organization's business strategy. The role of the operations manager is discussed, as are the three areas of responsibility associated with this position: process management, supply chain management, and product/service management. This is followed by an analysis of the value chain, including the identification of the primary activities and support activities associated with it. With this broadened understanding of the role of the operations management team provided, the chapter then focuses on an overview of the key decision-making areas that operations managers will face on an ongoing basis. These include decisions relating to process, materials, facility layout, asset management, and supply chain planning, execution, and performance monitoring. In addition to this, a commentary is offered with respect to the importance of establishing quality standards for an organization and embedding these into its culture. This discussion includes references to ISO certification, the use of Six Sigma and TQM methodologies, the identification of quality impact factors, and the managerial competencies required for the successful implementation of quality initiatives. The chapter closes with a brief discussion of the challenges facing small business owners and their use of operations management tools and techniques, as well as a final reflection on what managers need to understand in order to initiate successful operations management strategies and tactics.

Developing Business Knowledge and Skills

KEY TERMS

operations management *p. 223*

process management *p. 223*

supply chain management *p. 224*

product/service management *p. 224*

value maximization *p. 225*

primary activities *p. 225*

inbound logistics *p. 226*

operations *p. 226*

outbound logistics *p. 226*

marketing and sales *p. 226*

customer service *p. 227*

support activities *p. 228*

operations cycle *p. 230*

process standardization *p. 230*

process simplification *p. 230*

process design, layout, and execution *p. 232*

PERT chart *p. 234*

Gantt chart *p. 234*

materials management *p. 234*

facility design and layout *p. 235*

capacity *p. 235*

capital asset evaluation and acquisition *p. 236*

supply chain management *p. 237*

supply chain operating execution *p. 238*

supply chain performance evaluation *p. 239*

cash operating cycle (COC) *p. 239*

ISO (International Organization for Standardization) *p. 243*

Six Sigma *p. 243*

TQM (total quality management) *p. 243*

QUESTIONS FOR DISCUSSION

1. What is meant by the term operations management? What are the three areas of responsibility that decisions relating to operations management revolve around?

2. What is the underlying principle behind the value chain business model? Describe the primary activities that make up the value chain and how they are integrated with support activities in order to allow organizations to effectively manage the design, development, and distribution of products and services.

3. What is meant by the "operations cycle"? How does it integrate with an organization's business planning cycle?

4. What are the four key decision areas associated with process management? How are they all interconnected?

5. What is the major focus of supply chain management? What are the primary areas of responsibility of supply chain managers?

6. What are the key factors that impact quality within an organization? How do managers successfully manage quality implementation initiatives?

QUESTIONS FOR INDIVIDUAL ACTION

Interview a small retail business owner in your town about how he/she manages his/her operation. Who makes decisions regarding facility layout? How are these decisions made? What about inventory management? How are decisions made regarding what products to buy and how far in advance the products must be ordered? What factors influence the types of products they carry? What about warehousing? How much of their facility square footage is allocated to inventory storage?

TEAM EXERCISE

In the 1980s, Motorola Inc. developed what is known today as the Six Sigma methodology. Recognizing its value in managing quality and in reshaping a culture focused on quality, General Electric adopted Six Sigma as a major component of its operational strategy. Since then, a large number of major corporations across the globe have adopted Six Sigma. As a team, prepare a presentation that traces the origin of Six Sigma and provide an overview as to how this methodology works. Be sure to discuss how Six Sigma is implemented within an organization. Also develop two or three success stories from organizations that have implemented Six Sigma and that demonstrate the cost savings realized. Think about this in terms of a cost/benefit trade-off.

Case for Discussion

Sasha Wong and her partner, William Lee, have always had a desire to get into business for themselves. Sasha's parents, entrepreneurs in their own right, have owned a successful specialty food market in their Greater Vancouver neighbourhood for several years since immigrating to Canada. Having worked in her parents' business for a number of those years (where she also met William), Sasha has developed a good understanding of the business management complexities associated with even this small an operation. Sasha and William's plan is to open a wholesaling company, called Sasha Foods, which will specialize in importing high-quality Japanese sauces and foods. Sasha and William have both spent considerable hours researching the local marketplace and have determined that the growing Asian market in the Greater Vancouver area represents a tremendous opportunity. Unlike the current North American brands of soya and teriyaki sauces, and rice noodles and cakes (as examples), Sasha and William intend to offer their customers authentic sauces and related food products

imported directly from Asia. Their plan is to offer these products through their own store-front location, as well as through specialty and gourmet retail locations (such as Sasha's parents' store) in British Columbia. William also visualizes an opportunity to provide these products to the growing Asian restaurant industry, which now makes up a significant portion of the dining landscape in Vancouver. For Sasha and William, the question is where to begin. The market research has been done. The decision to proceed makes sense given the data collected and analyzed—but, where to start? What types of operations decisions need to be made to move Sasha Foods from a concept to a reality?

QUESTIONS

1. Using the primary activities within the value chain as guide, develop an operations plan for Sasha and William. What types of broad-level decisions must Sasha and William think about? Develop a list of questions you would ask Sasha and William in regard to getting the right products to the right place at the right time.

2. Using the information generated from question #1 above, and your knowledge of operations process design and development, prepare a flowchart of the operational process and its requirements for Sasha Foods. Identify the critical capital asset investments that will need to be made in order to support this flow.

3. Returning to the value chain, identify the requirements associated with support activities that also will have to be developed in order to support an efficient and effective operation.

Practise and learn online with Connect. Connect resources include additional and interactive study exercises, videos, and practice quizzing, as well as additional material you won't find in the printed text.

10 The Marketing Challenge

Learning Objectives

This chapter is designed to provide students with:

Lo1 An understanding of the purpose of marketing

Lo2 Recognition of how marketing is linked to strategy

Lo3 Knowledge of the importance of positioning in the formulation of marketing strategy

Lo4 An appreciation of the importance of marketing research, segmentation, and targeting in the marketing process

Lo5 A base-level exposure to where, and how, marketers seek opportunities for new product/service ideas, development, and growth

Lo6 An awareness of how an organization's marketing team seeks to influence customers and create loyalty for the products these customers buy

Snapshot—What to Expect in This Chapter

As identified by the learning objectives, this chapter focuses on exposing students to key concepts associated with the role of marketing within an organization. The content emphasized in this chapter includes the following:

- Marketing's Purpose

- Marketing: Its Link to Strategy

- The Concept of Positioning

- Segmentation and Target Marketing
  - Marketing Research: A First Step in the Segmentation Process
  - Transitioning Segmentation Analysis to Target Marketing

- Marketing's Challenge
  - Need Identification
  - Understanding the Consumer Decision-Making Process
  - Responding to Needs: Value Proposition Development and Communication

- A Note Pertaining to Not-for-Profits

- Management Reflection—Back to Strategy

From the Student's Perspective

If you like thinking creatively about strategy, you are about to read *the* ultimate section of this textbook. Marketing is pure strategy. As a manager, you must analyze the competitive landscape to determine how to best compete in the marketplace. As your competitors make their moves, you must respond accordingly. The art of marketing is designing a strategy that will be both proactive in the industry (being a first mover, in some cases) and reactive to your competitors and consumer trends.

But, what exactly is marketing? Is it sexy billboards? Is it hilarious commercials? Is it punchy slogans? All of those things are often a product of a marketing strategy; however, marketing is far more than quirky ad campaigns. Marketing is the integral business function that designs and executes strategies, effectively positioning a product or service in the market. The ultimate goal of a marketer is to create value in the eye of the consumer, and to justify the highest possible price. In other words, you must optimize the ratio of relative price to relative quality.

The focus of this section is marketing and positioning. To effectively position a product, service, or experience in the market, immense amounts of research must be conducted. Marketing managers are constantly challenged to filter massive amounts of industry and consumer data to make winning business decisions. Marketing is the best, and most important, business function. To learn why, read on.

A true marketer at heart, Rachel Zimmer is pursuing a career in brand management and sales. In the long run, she hopes to dabble in the world of marketing consulting; eventually, she would love to start her own business. Rachel enjoyed putting her skills to the test in a variety of competitions in her final year of school. She won the Queen's University Emerging Markets Competition, the Queen's University Marketing Association Challenge, the Queen's University Commerce Society Business Plan Competition, and Canada's Next Top Ad Executive Competition.

BUSINESS *in Action*

Social Networks

Globally, Facebook now possesses more than 500 million users. Twitter, whose users currently number more than 170 million, has aspirations of seeing its user base climb to 1 billion. Social Web sites such as LinkedIn, Bebo, MySpace, Orkut, Vkontakte, and the up-and-coming LikeALittle continue to emerge almost daily across the globe. Yuri Milner, a major partner in Russia's Web-based social network company Digital Sky Technologies (DST), which also owns a 10 percent stake in Facebook, has proposed what he calls the "Zuckerberg theory." According to Milner, every 12 to 18 months the amount of information being shared among people on the Web doubles. This sharing of information, over time, could result in people bypassing more general search-based Web sites—such as Google—in favour of sites built atop social networks, where they can rely on friends' opinions to figure out where to get the best handbag, how to change batteries in a smoke detector, or whether to vacation in Istanbul or Rome. According to Milner, people will pick their network and the network will become their main filter for everything. If we assume that Milner's interpretation of the trend evolving over the Web is accurate, this acceleration to social Web sites as a main source of information and impression formation could have tremendous influence on marketing strategy, the development of value propositions, the formation of brand impressions, and the way in which we communicate to potential target markets. Already important, digital marketing could become an even more powerful determinant of where and how to reach our customers and to obtain feedback from those customers. Already, a growing number of companies are leveraging Facebook and Twitter as core components to their marketing strategies. Not-for-profits are using Facebook as well, to generate support for the causes they represent—all in an effort to more effectively reach individuals who share an inter-

est in the work of the not-for-profit, and to interact with those who are willing to support the NFP monetarily. As you read through this chapter and the one that follows, think about the variety of uses and benefits social networks could support within an overall marketing strategy. Given what you know about social networking, how might it influence how you would communicate the products and services of a company that you manage or work for to the marketplace at large?[1]

LO1 Marketing's Purpose

When you think of the word "marketing," what comes to mind? For most people, it refers to the development and delivery of an advertising or media campaign. While this is indeed a part of the marketing process, the development and delivery of an advertising and/or media campaign is often the last step in the development and delivery of a marketing strategy. The marketing process (discussed in more detail later in this chapter) begins long before the advertising strategy is developed and delivered to the targeted customers. It is really a much broader process that encompasses assessing market dynamics, identifying needs and solutions, and determining what price to charge. It also encompasses ensuring that customers have access to the product through the development of distribution channels and options, and delivering the communication message in order to create awareness and preference for the products and/or services that an organization is offering to its existing, and potentially new, customers. Having said this, what is the purpose behind the development of a marketing strategy? In its simplest context, the purpose of **marketing** is to design, develop, and communicate value. Value in this context refers to the ability of an organization to communicate, to existing and potential customers, why its product/service offering meets the needs of these individuals and businesses, and why it should be judged superior to those of competitive alternatives.

Marketing is the process through which organizations design, develop, and communicate the value of their products and/or services.

> In its simplest context, the purpose of marketing is to design, develop, and communicate value.

Let's look at two fundamental principles associated with customer behaviour that will, hopefully, highlight the importance of this value-based approach to understanding the purpose of marketing.

Principle #1 Customers don't buy products or services—they buy solutions to problems or needs.

Principle #2 Customers will not pay more for a product if they can get a similar product for less.

Assuming agreement with these two fundamental principles underlies the challenge and, therefore, the purpose of marketing. The greater the ability of an organization to deliver to its existing and new customers solutions to their problems or needs that are interpreted to be of higher quality, uniqueness, importance, or convenience, the greater the product/service's value becomes to these customers. This perceived difference in value is what truly differentiates a company's products/services from those of its competitors. This differentiation can then be used to create a preference for the organization's products/services over those of its competitors, thereby resulting in loyalty and commitment for its products, its brands, and the organization in the marketplace. This value does not always have to be tangible; for example, based on functionality. Value, real or perceived, can equally be based on intangible attributes such as peer acceptance, status, emotional benefits, pride of ownership, brand commitment or loyalty, and so on. In fact, as discussed in Chapter 1, value propositions identify the value attributed to a product/service offering through the following development equation:

Value Proposition = Service Benefits + Product Benefits + Brand Benefits + Cost Benefits + Emotional Benefits

A customer's value relationship with an organization can, in many ways, be summed up as the overall experience that the customer has when interacting with an organization. Keeping this "value" purpose in mind, let's now take a look at the role of marketing within an organization and how the development and execution of a successful marketing strategy will assist the organization in meeting its business objectives, its long-term vision, and the organization's intended mission.[2]

Marketing: Its Link to Strategy

LO2

As Rachel Zimmer pointed out in her opening commentary, found under "From the Student's Perspective," marketing is a critical component associated with the successful execution of an organization's strategy. Largely perceived as the communications link between an organization and its marketplace, marketing is fundamentally responsible for connecting customers to the products and services offered by an organization, and reinforcing the needs and desires that are being satisfied. This means understanding the six R's of marketing: the *right need* to pursue, the *right solution* to offer, the *right value proposition* to position the organization's products and services around, the *right methodology for delivery*, the *right price to charge*, and the *right communication message* to use.

In developing an organization's marketing strategy and ensuring its alignment to meeting the objectives of the overall corporate and business-level strategies that it supports, marketers need to be able to demonstrate an effective response to six core challenges (see Figure 10.1). These six core challenges can be framed into a series of six questions that marketers must be

FIGURE 10.1 Core Challenges of Marketing

able to answer in order to assess the viability or success of the potential of a product and/or service offering. The six questions are as follows:

1. Do we understand our targeted customers' needs and desires?
2. Do we believe that our current or anticipated product and/or service represents a viable solution to the targeted customers' needs and/or desires?
3. Can we create a value proposition that positions our product and/or service as the best solution to our targeted customers?
4. Is there an existing or potential viable distribution model for delivery of our product and/or service to the marketplace in a manner that effectively reaches our targeted customers?
5. Can we support the product and/or service and its delivery to the marketplace at a price point that is attractive to the targeted customer and that allows us to be profitable?
6. Can we develop and deliver to the targeted customers a communication message that will attract these buyers to our product and/or service?

You will notice that the term "targeted customers" has been used within each of these questions. This is because within a given marketplace not everyone will be interested in our product and/or service offering, or, if interested, will be able to afford it (or desire to purchase it) at the price point we have established as being necessary to ensure that our business model is profitable. The concept of targeting customers and its relationship to the mechanics of segmentation are discussed later in this chapter.

To be successful in the execution of its overall strategy, an organization must be successful at both the product strategy level and the business strategy level. Marketing is integral to this success. Properly positioned products, combined with a superior (in terms of effectiveness) marketing effort, lead to organizational profitability and growth (see Figure 10.2). This, in turn, leads to the achievement of product and/or service objectives that support the achievement of business objectives and, ultimately, organizational objectives and the company's overall vision and mission (see Figure 10.3). Properly positioning a product and/or service is the focus of this chapter, while the execution of a superior marketing effort via the

FIGURE 10.2 The Marketing Formula

FIGURE 10.3 Marketing's Impact on Strategy

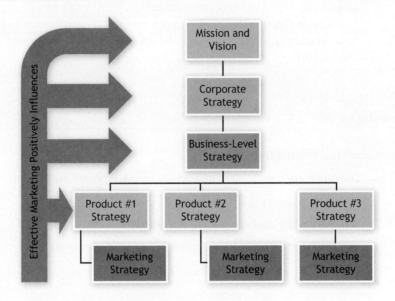

development of the elements that make up a product and/or service's marketing mix is the focus of Chapter 11.

> To be successful in the execution of its overall corporate strategy, an organization must be successful at both the product strategy level and the business strategy level.

The Concept of Positioning

LO3

As alluded to throughout this textbook, a key fundamental associated with the development of an organization's business strategy is how it will position its brand, products, and/or services in the marketplace. Figure 10.2 (the marketing formula) goes one step further and definitely states that in order to execute a successful marketing strategy a management team must establish an effective and well-defined market position. So, what are we referring to when we talk about positioning? The easiest way to think about the concept of **positioning**, according to social marketer Francois Legarde,[3] is to think about it as being the place in the consumer's mind that you want your organization's brand, products, and/or services to own. When potential purchasers think about solving a particular need, we want them to think about the brand, products, and/or services that we offer and the benefits that will accrue to them by selecting our offerings over those of our competitors. Positioning is all about developing a

Positioning is the ability of an organization to develop a unique, credible, sustainable, and valued place in the minds of our customers for its brand, products, and/or services.

unique, credible, sustainable, and valued place in the minds of our customers. It is how we distinguish ourselves from our competitors in the marketplace. Market position can be built around product and/or service features and attributes, functional and/or emotional benefits, or cultural values. Brands, products, and/or services that are well positioned automatically come to the consumer's mind when making repeat purchases, or seemingly float to the top of the purchase potential list when customers are thinking about making a first-time purchase. For example, if you were considering purchasing a 46-inch flat-screen television, what would be your three first choices of retail locations to visit in order to purchase this TV? For many Canadians, the response would include two prominent retail businesses, Best Buy and Future Shop. This is because both are well positioned in the minds of a majority of consumers as possessing the brands and products, supported by the necessary services, to result in a positive purchase experience. Similarly, Tim Hortons has firmly established itself as the market leader in Canada in the "to-go" coffee beverage category, in part due to its positioning strategy of aligning its brand to being "truly Canadian."

In order to effectively position our brand, and the products and/or services that we attach to it, marketing managers need to be successful in the attainment of four key objectives (see Figure 10.4).

FIGURE 10.4   Positioning to Win

Successful Positioning Objectives

- Communicate the solution effectively to the targeted customers
- Understand the market to be served
- Understand the customers to be targeted
- Deliver the solution in a way that is superior to competitors

> Positioning is all about developing a unique, credible, sustainable, and valued place in the minds of our customers for our brand, products, and/or services.

A key requirement associated with effective positioning is the development and validation of marketing research relating to both market dynamics and customer needs. As will be discussed later in this chapter, this involves conducting analyses relating to competitors, customers, potential market segments, and internal competencies in order to determine where, and how, the organization will position its brand, products, and/or services. In closing, positioning is built around a value proposition that clearly differentiates an organization's brands, products, and/or services from those of its competitors and, based on a solid understanding of market fundamentals, effectively delivers on the identified target customer's needs. Critical to this process is the ability to establish in the minds of our targeted customers that the price/quality relationship of our offering is superior to that of our competitors, and results in customers concluding that our solution best meets their needs.

LO4   Segmentation and Target Marketing

Successful companies recognize that they cannot be all things to all people. Attempting to provide a standardized product to the entire marketplace often results in failing to meet the needs and expectations of customers seeking a specific value or benefit from a product or service. To avoid taking this average approach to the market, successful marketers focus on trying to identify particular segments within the market and then delivering products/ services specifically aligned with meeting the needs of customers within these segments. Research In Motion (RIM), for example, focused on meeting the needs of government and business customers during the initial development of its BlackBerry device. Recognizing the unique needs of these segments (security, text messaging), RIM focused its software and logistics development on meeting the needs of this core customer group in a way that provided services judged to be superior to its competitors. This specialization enabled RIM to become the initial leader in smartphone technology and build a market leader position within these segments.

Marketing Research: A First Step in the Segmentation Process

As noted above, a core ingredient for success in business is to understand the needs of our current and potential customers and then to deliver on these needs in a manner that is superior to our competitors. Critical to this is the development and utilization of marketing research in determining how best to respond to the needs of a targeted market segment. The concept of market segmentation recognizes that "one size does not fit all." This means that we need to define the best way to segment the market, and determine how this **segmentation** will result in an improved probability that we can be successful in targeting a given segment and marketing our products and/or services to these potential customers.

Segmentation refers to determining the best way to divide the market in a manner that will result in a better understanding of potential customer needs, interests, preferences, attitudes, and behaviours.

> The concept of market segmentation recognizes that "one size does not fit all."

The development of marketing research information that we can use in determining which segments to target can be thought of as coming from two sources:

1. Primary sources; and
2. Secondary sources.

Primary sources of information are those that an organization develops and/or utilizes to generate information specific to the organization and the products and services it offers. Examples of primary sources of information are customer surveys; customer input via social media sites such as Facebook, tweets from Twitter users, and company Web sites; focus groups that we establish to test and/or obtain comments on existing products and services or new product concepts; formal test marketing initiatives; and behavioural observations. As an example, a manufacturer of ice cream may use a focus group to taste and rate new flavours prior to launching these flavours into the marketplace. McDonald's may choose to test new menu items in a limited geographic area to determine overall customer acceptance and to receive feedback with respect to taste and quality. Organizations, more and more, are using Facebook and other social media Web sites to gather customer information relating to the market segments they are pursuing. Whereas focus groups may provide organizations with a better understanding of the value of their product or service, the sample size is quite small. Social media networks enable marketers to monitor comments, opinions, and results from a much larger sample. These sites also enable marketers to get a much earlier and stronger sense of trends occurring in the marketplace. Reviewer blogs provide information on the strengths and weaknesses of product releases. Behavioural and attitudinal trends can also be monitored and better understood as a result of assessing the commentary and "chat" occurring among specific demographic groups.

Primary Sources of Information are those that an organization develops or utilizes to generate information specific to the organization and the products and services it offers.

Secondary sources of information are those that already exist and are available at no cost or on a fee basis; managers use these information sources to conduct research and draw conclusions. Examples of secondary information would be researching the Statistics Canada Web site to gather demographic information (age, gender, family, income, households) about a particular geographic area; reviewing various media options to better understand current and forward-occurring social and cultural trends; accessing Conference Board of Canada

Secondary Sources of Information are those that already exist and are available at no cost or on a fee basis; managers use these information sources to conduct research and draw conclusions.

information relating to national economic trends; conducting generic information searches via Google or Bing; undertaking information searches of competitors via company Web sites, annual reports, or third-party commentary; and evaluating product test results from third-party testing organizations (Consumer Reports, CNET, etc.) and blogs of identified experts in a particular field.

In tying marketing research to segmentation, marketers and managers will strive to create a profile of the customers within the various segments identified within a market. This profile is often developed around a combination of four core characteristics:

1. Demographics—age, gender, income
2. Geographic clustering—location, reach
3. Psychographics—lifestyle, status, ego, emotion, tastes, trends
4. Behavioural—use, buying patterns

This information is then used to help determine which segments to target and in the facilitation of the response to three fundamental questions that will, ultimately, drive the marketing effort (see Figure 10.5):

1. What are the key decision criteria that potential and/or existing customers use in determining which product(s)/service(s) they will buy?
2. What is the priority or ranking of these criteria? Is there any one criterion that will predominantly influence the purchase decision?
3. How can we best position our product/service offering to align most closely to meeting these key decision criteria used by our sought-after customer base when measured against our competitors?

FIGURE 10.5 Segmentation

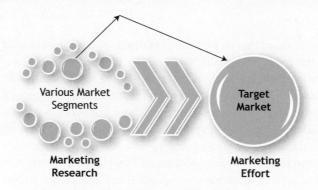

Transitioning Segmentation Analysis to Target Marketing

Utilizing marketing research to assist in better understanding the marketplace and how it is segmented enables marketers and managers to determine which segments are the most attractive recipients to the marketing message that the organization intends to convey and, ultimately, those prospective customers that represent the highest probability of buyers for the products and/or services being offered. This evolution from market assessment to target marketing forms the front end of what is called the marketing process (see Figure 10.6).

> Utilizing marketing research to assist in better understanding the marketplace and how it is segmented enables marketers and managers to determine which segments are the most attractive recipients to the marketing message that the organization intends to convey.

FIGURE 10.6   The Marketing Process

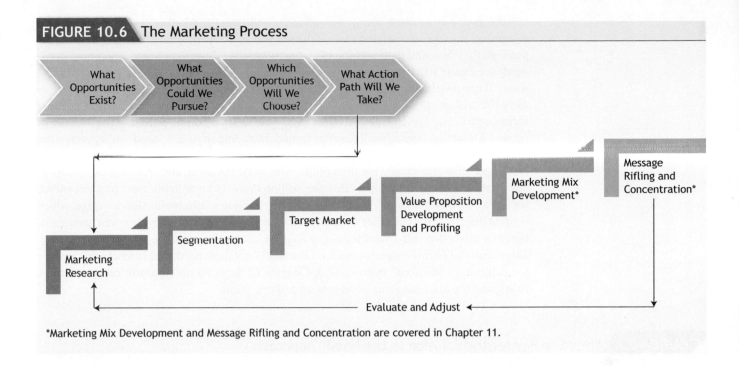

*Marketing Mix Development and Message Rifling and Concentration are covered in Chapter 11.

Target marketing is leveraging the information acquired during the research and segmentation process and determining which market segment(s) the organization feels is/are its primary or best opportunity for penetration and sales success. By defining target market segments, the organization can develop its value proposition around those decision criteria that the customer values the most, thereby tailoring the product and/or service offering to best meet the needs of the target market identified and the customer profile created. Target marketing also recognizes that although a large portion of the market may be aware of our product and/or service offering, the ability, desire, or willingness to purchase it may lie with a much smaller percentage of the market. Target marketing enables organizations to focus on those potential customers who are most likely to purchase the product and who have the capacity to do so. This enables these organizations to concentrate their marketing resources on reaching these customers and tailoring their marketing message in a manner that presents their product and/or service offerings as the best solution to the potential customers' needs (see Figure 10.7).

> **Target Marketing** is the process whereby organizations determine which market segments represent the strongest clustering of potential customers who are most likely to purchase the product and who have the capacity to do so.

FIGURE 10.7   Segmentation Analysis to Target Market

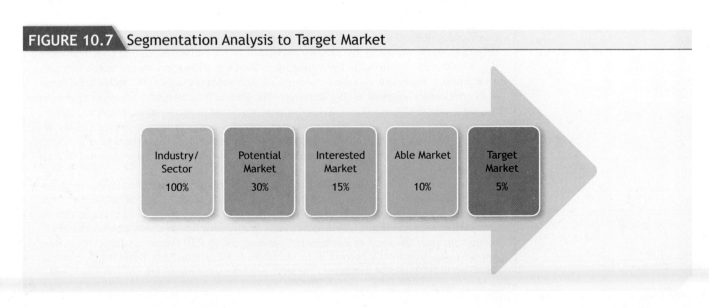

An easy way to think about segmentation and target marketing is that segmentation determines the level of need that various clusters within the marketplace have with respect to a problem they face, and their viewing of an organization's product/service as a solution to this need (see Figure 10.8). By "need," we mean the overall desire to solve a problem and satisfy a want. Target marketing then looks at the segments exhibiting the greatest need (desire to solve the problem or satisfy the need), and looks to identify those segments with the greatest willingness to pay for the solution to the need—or, in other words, purchase the product or service. Marketing research will assist us in understanding what the "need" is. Segmentation defines the level of need, and target marketing defines those who will pay for the need. As marketers, understanding what the need is, who has it the most, and who is most willing to pay for it enables us to develop a value proposition that is tailored to offer our product and/or service as the best solution. This then enables us to create a communication message, which is rifled directly at the customer's reason for the need, along with the development and execution of a marketing mix strategy, thereby aligning our product/service as the ideal solution. The remainder of this chapter focuses on the additional tools needed to leverage the "pay for the solution to the need" process, with Chapter 11 focusing on communication message rifling and the marketing mix development and execution.

FIGURE 10.8   "Need to Pay for the Solution to the Need" Approach

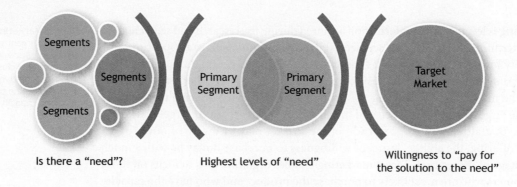

Is there a "need"?   Highest levels of "need"   Willingness to "pay for the solution to the need"

BUSINESS *in Action*

3M Company

Ever wonder where the Post-it Note came from? It is just one of the many innovative products developed and marketed by 3M Company (Minnesota Mining and Manufacturing Co.). With more than 55 000 products offered to the marketplace, 3M seems to be everywhere. Scotch Tape—it's a 3M product. Thinsulate insulation—made by 3M. Ace bandages—again, 3M. Your iPhone—some of its components are made by 3M. Sandpaper—you guessed it: a 3M innovation. In fact, you can find 3M products embedded in a number of products found in automobiles, hospitals, offices, and your home. In 2009 alone, 3M released over 1000 new products. With revenue of US$23 billion in 2009, 3M is #106 on the *Fortune* 500 list of the largest companies in the United States. Its sales growth is up an astonishing 21 percent in the first half of 2010, and net income is up 43 percent.

Established in 1902, 3M has evolved around a business model focused on innovation and new product development. For 3M, a key fundamental performance metric is to have at least 30 percent of its revenue produced by new products launched within the last five years. To achieve such performance benchmarks, 3M needs to have a continuous flow of new products in its development pipeline. This requires a culture of innovation and an R&D budget to support it. 3M does just that. Approximately 9 percent of its workforce is focused on R&D. Despite the economic downturn in 2008–09, 3M continued to spend more than US$1 billion per year on new product

development. 3M allows its R&D scientists to use 15 percent of their time to pursue ideas on their own. The results are new and innovative ideas spread across such business areas as infection prevention, abrasives, adhesives, and imaging. 3M technology is behind what enables us to have brighter traffic signs, better-gripping golf gloves, and micro-needles that could soon replace hypodermics, thereby lessening the pain associated with the delivery of medicines. At 3M, it is not so much about creating the "next big thing," but about creating hundreds and hundreds of solutions per year to the little things that its customers need and value. A key aspect of this development is the need to effectively market these products through its sales and distribution channels. This requires a significant and well-executed marketing effort. Backed by its strong brand recognition, 3M works closely with its customers to identify new product opportunities in its existing core businesses. It also means exploring new business opportunities in areas such as renewable energy, water infrastructure, and mobile digital media, to name a few.[4]

WEB INTEGRATION

Want to learn more about 3M Company and its strategy and marketing focus for the future? Visit **www.3m.com**.

BUSINESS *in Action*

Starbucks: Changing Its Market Focus

A significant change has been brewing at Starbucks. Known globally for its coffee bistros, Starbucks wants to position its brand and its company beyond its core operation. Yes, coffee will continue to be a core focus of the organization, and they will continue to strive to be the leading purveyor of quality coffee worldwide, but the long-term strategy is to move beyond a coffee-centric product line. This means communicating to customers that the Starbucks brand is more than just coffee. An initial first step in this repositioning process is a major change to its logo. The Starbucks siren is still there, but gone are the words "Starbucks" and "coffee." The removal of "coffee" is focused on communicating to customers, going forward, to think of Starbucks in terms of a much broader line of goods and services. Although plans are to continue to grow the Starbucks coffee line and retail store unit, mainly via international expansion, even greater growth aspirations lie in growing a variety of products through licensing, franchising, acquisitions, and branding opportunities. Partnerships with companies such as Pepsi-Co and Unilever have resulted in a broadening of the Starbucks product line to include bottled Frappuccino, Starbucks DoubleShot espresso drinks, Starbucks Discoveries chilled beverages, Tazo Tea ready-to-drink beverages, and Starbucks super-premium ice cream products. Its recent acquisition (November 2011) of upscale juice maker Evolution Fresh Inc. will push Starbucks into juice-related product categories, which it can sell in outlets beyond its coffee-based retail locations. Add to this an intent

to franchise its Seattle's Best Coffee brand, expand its VIA single-serve coffees, and develop additional food service account relationships and licensing opportunities, and one can quickly see that the company intends to grow in a number of directions beyond its core retail operation model. Even the company-operated retail store operation is not going to stand still. Finishing a period of consolidation that saw Starbucks close hundreds of retail stores and reduce its new-unit growth expectations, the company continues to experiment and test various concept configurations, all with the idea of driving additional revenue and profitability through this side of the operation. New store designs, drive-through business operations, and new product offerings through these retail locations are all designed to improve sales at existing and newly opened locations. In October 2010, a Seattle store became the first Starbucks to offer alcohol: craft beer and wines are available for purchase after 4 p.m. The idea is to provide customers with additional reasons to visit a Starbucks beyond the traditional early morning "java fix." Whether beer and wine will become a mainstay at Starbucks is yet to be determined. The point of all of this, however, is that Starbucks envisions its brand and its future market position to be built beyond the purchase of coffee. With this in mind—and in much the same way that Apple Computer Inc., with its original focus on computers, is now known as Apple Inc., a compu-entertainment organization—Starbucks wants you to think of it beyond coffee. Will it succeed? The answer lies in the future.[5]

WEB INTEGRATION

To learn more about the transformation taking place at Starbucks, visit **www.starbucks.com**.

LO5, LO6   Marketing's Challenge

As indicated in Figure 10.1, marketers within an organization must respond to six core challenges. Within each of these challenges is a multitude of tasks that, if executed properly, will lead to the effective positioning of the product in those market segments the organization intends to serve. With a base-level understanding of positioning, segmentation, and target marketing in place, let's now begin the process of assessing these challenges in more detail.

Need Identification

Need identification focuses on assessing opportunities that exist within the marketplace for our current and potential (soon-to-be-launched) products and/or services. It means attempting to identify untapped or unmet needs within the marketplace and leveraging our R&D capabilities to develop products and/or services that will meet such needs. It also means looking at our current portfolio of products and/or services and deciding where opportunities exist that will enable us to maximize their revenue and profitability potential (via the product/opportunity matrix). Finally, need identification considers whether our emphasis should be on new customer acquisition, further leveraging relationships with existing customers, or a combination of the two (see Figure 10.9).

When we think about need identification, we need to assess the marketplace we are reviewing in two fundamental ways:

1. Where do opportunities exist?
2. What market dynamics present themselves in the segments we are considering?

FIGURE 10.9 Marketing Challenge: Need Identification

Seeking out opportunities that enhance the success of the products/services we offer or that identify untapped needs in various market segments furthers the achievement of the organization's overall strategy and is a fundamental role of marketing. As managers, we need to recognize that such opportunities can come from a variety of sources. To assist managers in analyzing the various potential options for further revenue and profitability growth, Igor Ansoff developed a growth strategy opportunity identification model called the Ansoff matrix. This matrix is more widely known today as the product/opportunity matrix (see Figure 10.10). Within this matrix, Ansoff suggests that managers should focus their analytical review in four areas when assessing market opportunity[6]:

1. Market penetration opportunities
2. Product/service development opportunities
3. Market development opportunities
4. Diversification opportunities

Market penetration opportunities focus a manager's attention on growing the sales revenue of the organization's existing products through its existing customer base. This means seeking ways to (a) get its existing customers to purchase the organization's products/services more frequently, or (b) increase the average transaction revenue per purchase at the time when these customers are buying. For example, according to Canadian Tire, more than 50 percent of Canadians shop at Canadian Tire at least once per month, while 40 percent shop there once per week. Statistics Canada's estimated population of Canada in 2009 was 33 739 900. Based on Canadian Tire's estimates,[7] this means that 16 869 950 Canadians shop at Canadian Tire once per month, and that 13 495 960 Canadians shop at Canadian Tire once per week.[8] Assuming that when they visit Canadian Tire Canadians spend an average $20 per visit, Canadian Tire can potentially increase its annual retail sales by an estimated $2.7 billion if it can get the additional 10 percent (50% – 40%) of these Canadians who shop at Canadian Tire once per month (3 373 990) to shop there once per week. Likewise, if Canadian Tire can improve its average transaction revenue per customer (basket size) from $20 to $25 across the 40 percent of Canadians who shop there weekly (13 495 960), then Canadian Tire could increase its revenue by an estimated $3.5 billion. Market penetration opportunities are all about trying to increase one's market share from an existing market and/or driving a greater "share of wallet" of existing customers each time they spend. To be successful with such strategies, an organization's marketing team must develop ways that will stimulate the additional frequency of purchase (and/or repurchase) or provide incentives for customers to increase the share of wallet they are willing to spend with the organization. Incentives to encourage customers to purchase larger quantities of a product, trade discounts to acquire premium shelf space in order to make products more visible, advertising initiatives focused on stimulating renewed

FIGURE 10.10 Ansoff Matrix (Product/Opportunity Matrix)

Source: Ansoff Matrix, QuickMBA Strategic Management, www.quickmba.com/strategy/matrix/ansoff, July 2010; www.ansoffmatrix.com; www.vectorstrategy.com.

product/service interest, rebates, coupons, and other sales stimulation initiatives are just some of the many weapons that organizations will use to create additional demand for their products and services.

New product and/or service opportunities focus a management team on identifying and developing new products and/or services for the existing markets within which it competes, and/or the existing customer base that it serves. For example, a retail operation that sells gas fireplaces makes a decision to develop an annual preventive maintenance program for the fireplaces it has sold, and looks to sell this additional service to its existing customer base. Businesses such as Best Buy and Future Shop develop and sell to their customers extended warranty programs designed to cover the various electronic products these customers purchase. Walmart, recognizing an opportunity to better serve its existing market and customer base, shifts to a Supercentre format that results in Walmart adding a fully integrated grocery store operation into its retail concept. A potato chip manufacturer decides to market a bean dip under its own brand name and market this in conjunction with its chips. Apple Inc. created its iTunes Web site to support the purchase of music by users of its iPod. For many companies, a critical part of the ongoing marketing and organizational strategy process is their investments into R&D for the purpose of creating new products and services for their existing and potential customer base. This chapter's Business in Action vignette about 3M Company (page 260) underscores the value of new product and service development to an organization's long-term success.

Market development opportunities focus a management team on identifying and cultivating new customers for the existing products an organization currently offers. Market development opportunities can be the result of product line extensions of existing products designed to capture new customers via **segmentation stretch**, or simply finding new uses for existing products that attract previously uninterested customers to purchase an organization's existing product. General Mills saw the potential for additional sales of its Cheerios cereal to additional similar but different market segments by adding variations of the original Cheerios product offering. Confident in its brand name and in its ability to retain existing Cheerios customers, General Mills has repositioned Cheerios toward that of a more health-focused cereal (whole-grain oats, lowers cholesterol), and introduced additional brand extensions such as Multi-Grain Cheerios, Banana-Nut Cheerios, Yogurt Burst Cheerios, and Berry Burst Cheerios. In initiating brand and/or product extension strategies to stretch a product/service offering across wider market segments, managers need to consider two key points. The first has to do with **cannibalism**. Managers need to determine whether any sales volume erosion has occurred to the existing product/service offering, and, if so, whether this volume decrease is offset by the newly launched extended brand's sales gains. The marketing team also has to be careful about sending mixed messages when marketing a similar product toward similar but distinct segments (kids, families, adults). Second, when accompanied by a repositioning shift, marketing managers need to ensure that **customer desertion** to a competitive offering does not occur due to the change in brand or product communication message focus. In addition to stretching a product's reach through brand extension strategies, marketing managers can also seek to uncover new uses for existing products and services. The ability to successfully transition a product toward multiple uses can open new significant sales opportunities for products/services. Arm & Hammer Baking Soda, a product produced by Church & Dwight Co. Inc., has recognized considerable revenue growth due to the many additional uses for this product beyond simply baking. As far back as 1927, Church & Dwight began communicating the personal healthcare potential of Arm & Hammer Baking Soda for bath, body, and teeth. As a result of the tremendous success of its "baking soda in the refrigerator and the freezer" campaign, 1972 marked a significant shift in the way that baking soda was perceived by both customers and the company. This new view of the various solutions that baking soda offered to cleaning and maintenance problems within the household produced a variety of market opportunity spin-offs. Utilizing a brand extension strategy, Church & Dwight has broadened Arm & Hammer Baking Soda's positioning around that of an economical, gentle, and environmentally safe cleaning, deodorizing, and medicinal product.

Segmentation Stretch refers to expanding the focus of a product/service to similar and related market segments that share a positive affinity for the product/service offering.

Cannibalism is the reduction in sales of an existing product/service due to the launch of a new, similarly targeted product/service offering.

Customer Desertion occurs when customers move to a competitive offering due to a change in brand or product communication message focus.

WEB INTEGRATION
To view a historical timeline of the evolution of this popular product's market development strategy, visit **www.armhammer.com/timeline.aspx.**

Diversification opportunities focus managers on assessing opportunities that lie outside the organization's current products and/or services, and represent the creation or development of new markets served by new products and/or services. In many cases, diversification opportunities represent new business initiatives by an organization. Diversification could be the result of natural organic growth by the organization, or could be due to an acquisition. Diversification opportunities could be in related or unrelated areas of current market and business expertise. Apple's original business premise was focused on manufacturing and marketing computers. Apple has since diversified, organically, into the music distribution industry and into the smartphone industry as a catalyst for further growing the organization. Google has embarked on a significant acquisition strategy in order to gain access to a variety of technologies relating to social networking, cloud computing, and phone applications—all markets that the organization sees as critical to its long-term growth strategy. Aardvark, reMail, and Picnik are examples of recent acquisitions designed to provide Google with access to the technological expertise and products/services needed to continue to expand its reach in these emerging and rapidly growing markets.[9] The Tata Group of Companies (India) is one of the most widely diversified organizations in the world. Tata has business operations spanning seven different market sectors: information technology and communications, engineering products and services, materials (steel and composites), services (hospitality, real estate, financial, insurance), energy (oil and gas), consumer products (watches, jewellery, automobiles), and chemicals (pharmaceuticals, fertilizers).[10]

Utilizing Ansoff's matrix is just one of a number of interrelated steps in determining what and where opportunities exist in the marketplace and which ones are best to explore and pursue. Additional key steps involve conducting marketing research to identify the fit between potential market needs and the products and/or services that we intend to offer, determining whether this identified opportunity is substantial enough to meet financial and market share performance expectations and current and anticipated competitive activity in the targeted segment, and assessing the resource and capability requirements needed to effectively deliver on the identified opportunity.

Understanding the Consumer Decision-Making Process

As stated above, a critical aspect of marketing is the identification of needs that exist in the marketplace to which an organization can respond. Equally important, however, is ensuring that we understand why potential customers purchase a particular product and/or service, and how they determine, out of a number of competitive offerings, which product/service to buy. Significant marketing effort is allocated to understanding this critical question of why and how people buy.

> A critical aspect of marketing is the identification of needs that exist in the marketplace to which an organization can respond.

THE BUYING PROCESS[11]

In making a decision to buy, potential customers will fundamentally go through a four-phase process (see Figure 10.11). The length of time spent within each stage of this decision-making process will be dependent upon the potential customers' familiarity with the product/service, the various alternatives offered in the marketplace, whether it is a first-time purchase or a repeat purchase, and the level of financial commitment associated with the transaction.

For marketers, a key fundamental requirement in developing the marketing strategy for an organization's products/services is to devise the positioning strategy and marketing mix tactics (discussed in detail in Chapter 11) that will enable its products/services to occupy the dominant position in the minds of potential customers as they enter into, and transition

FIGURE 10.11   Consumer Decision-Making Process

through, this decision-making process. As marketers, our goals with respect to this decision-making process are the following:

- Be at the top of the potential customer's purchase list as he/she enters into the decision-making process, and reinforce and support the purchase of our product as the potential customer transitions to the point of purchase.

- If we are not at the top of the potential customer's purchase list during the initial consideration of purchase alternatives, then our goal is to disrupt the potential customer's predetermined list of viable purchase alternatives in a way that creates awareness and preference for our products and/or services.

- Assuming that we have won the battle for the initial purchase, reinforce and support the customer in a way that encourages him/her to develop a loyalty and commitment to our product, thereby making future purchases almost automatic with little consideration of alternative products and/or services being offered by our competitors.

Figure 10.12 provides an illustration of the influence and impact associated with this decision-making process with respect to the three goals identified above.

Figure 10.12 illustrates a situation where the potential customer is looking to make an initial purchase of a product and/or service, or is making a repurchase where no loyalty has been generated to a previously purchased product and/or service. As such, the potential customer is open to considering, or can be influenced to consider, alternatives available in the marketplace. As marketers, this non-loyal situation means that we (as well as our competitors) have the opportunity to disrupt the potential customer's predetermined purchase choice at several key points in the decision-making process (noted by the starbursts). We can disrupt this process and, ideally, influence the potential customer to purchase our product and/or service through the use of a number of different marketing tools. Examples of these tools, which can be referred to as the marketer's tool box, are as follows (see Figure 10.13):

- Company-driven marketing techniques

- Consumer-driven marketing techniques

- Channel support and interaction techniques

FIGURE 10.12 Consumer Decision-Making Process: The Marketer's Goals

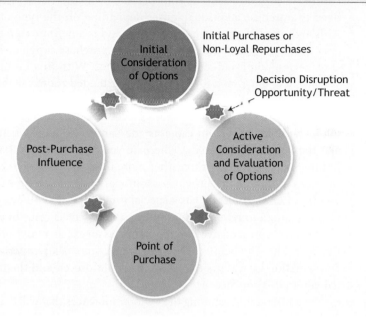

FIGURE 10.13 Marketer's Tool Box

Category	Tools of the Trade
Company-Driven Marketing Techniques	Advertising Sales Promotion Publicity Point of Purchase Displays Dedicated Sales Force
Consumer-Driven Marketing Techniques	Internet Searches Product Reviews Peer Recommendations Analysts' Blogs Social Media Websites and Commentary
Channel Support and Interaction Techniques	Dealer Incentives Point-of-Purchase Discounts Channel Member Training Exclusivity Arrangements Salesperson Recommendations

Let's use an example to illustrate the way that marketing works to influence the customer decision-making process. Assume you are in the market to purchase a new digital camera; the question you face involves which brand to purchase. Your initial thought is to consider a Canon camera, because your current, although somewhat dated, camera is a Canon. Recent advertisements, however, have led you to consider stepping up to a dSLR camera versus a simple "point-and-shoot" digital camera. The Canon Rebel immediately comes to mind. However, you have also taken note of recent advertisements for Olympus and Sony cameras, brands you also have heard good things about. Jumping onto various Web sites and reading a number of product reviews and "best buy" lists expands your options to include cameras by Fuji, Panasonic, Nikon, and Casio (a brand you initially did not consider). A good friend of your parents owns the Canon Rebel and reminds you of the need to purchase additional lenses depending on the type of pictures you want to take. Although the Rebel takes great pictures and is a definite step up over regular digital cameras, the initial price point and the need to purchase supplemental lenses leads you back to considering point-and-shoot digital cameras. With this in mind, this same friend makes you aware of the Canon SX30, which has extended zoom capabilities and is highly regarded by industry experts. Armed with this information, and desiring the extended zoom option, you revisit the Internet, seek ideas and comments through Facebook, and reduce your potential purchase list to four cameras: the Canon SX30, the Panasonic FZ35, the Nikon P100, and the Fugifilm HS10. Now, where do you buy the camera? You decide to visit Best Buy, Future Shop, and Henry's to gather more information and to compare prices. At Best Buy, the sales representative provides additional information on each camera and also informs you that Canon currently has a special promotion that allows you to trade in your current Canon camera to receive a discount on the purchase price of the Canon SX30. Reinforced by the sales representative that the camera is an excellent option, you decide to purchase the Canon SX30. The familiarity of the brand, your prior experience with a Canon product, confirmation by reviews that it is a solid performer, and the trade-in discount promotion led you to this conclusion.*

In addition to illustrating the various influences that will occur throughout this decision-making process, there is another key point associated with marketing: the need to effectively manage and positively reinforce the post-purchase phase of the decision-making process. Effective marketing does not end at the point of purchase. Considerable emphasis is placed on the post-purchase period, which is where true customer loyalty and commitment is developed. This is important for three reasons:

1. Customers need immediate and ongoing reinforcement that the purchase they made was the right one. Reinforcing the purchase decision, particularly decisions that require a significant financial commitment, is fundamental to developing customer loyalty and commitment.
2. For many purchases, particularly business-based purchases, ongoing servicing and training may be core aspects of the buying decision. The quality of such support services is, in many cases, as important as the initial purchase.
3. Satisfied customers tell others about the quality of the products and services that they purchase and use. Active referrals from current customers assist us in broadening our customer base.

> Marketing does not end at the point of purchase. Considerable emphasis needs to be placed on the post-purchase period, which is where true customer loyalty and commitment is developed.

As marketers, we need to realize that having current customers repurchase our products/services is fundamental to building the scale we need in order to sustain our organization. It is critical to develop within our customer base a level of loyalty and commitment to our products/services that moves our customers to skip the initial stages of the customer decision-making process at the time of repurchase and go directly to the "purchase" phase, repurchasing our product/service without considering other competitive alternatives. Figure 10.14 illustrates this ideal position of maximum customer loyalty.

For marketers, the challenge is a continuous need to reinforce and reward our existing customers, thereby minimizing customer desertion (customers leaving us) while attempting

---

*The choice of the Canon SX30 as the product to be purchased is for illustration purposes only. The author is not stating that this brand and model is superior to any of the other brands and models mentioned.

FIGURE 10.14 Consumer Decision-Making Process: Maximum Customer Loyalty

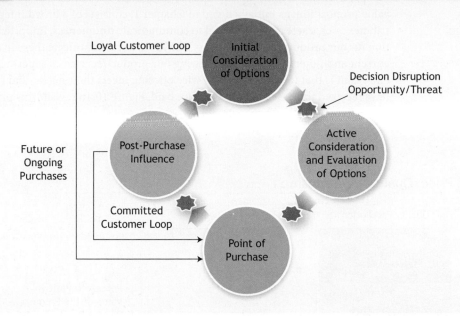

FIGURE 10.15 Growing the Customer Base

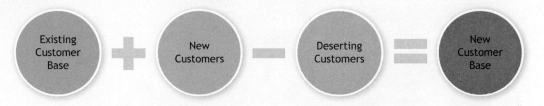

to continually attract new customers in order to further grow our customer base (see Figure 10.15). Growing the company is all about reinforcing to our current customers that we offer the best value proposition in the marketplace, while attempting to disrupt the purchase patterns of potential customers by getting them to actively consider our products and/or services as viable options and, ultimately, purchase them to meet their needs or solve their problems. To effectively accomplish this, we need to understand which market segments are closely aligned to having their needs solved by our products/services, and target those with the ability to transition their "need" into "paying for the solution to the need." Then, in understanding their decision-making process, we must best position our value proposition in a way that results in the purchase of our products/services instead of competitive offerings.

Responding to Needs: Value Proposition Development and Communication

The role of marketing, as reinforced throughout this chapter, is to communicate the value proposition for an organization's products/services as the "best" solution to the needs of a targeted market of prospective customers. This value proposition demonstrates, beyond the functionality of the product and/or service, why our organization's product/service offerings should be considered superior to those of our competitors when assessed from a price/quality perspective. Understanding that quality and, therefore, value can be real or perceived, our value proposition, as initially noted in Chapter 1, consists of a broad integration of valued attributes or characteristics designed to communicate uniqueness, importance, and differentiation for our product/service offering. The key is to communicate these in a way that results in current and potential customers viewing our product/service as superior. For customers, the end result is that (a) the product/service offering meets their needs, and (b) they believe they have received the best value for the price paid. Figure 10.16 revisits this price/quality relationship as illustrated in Chapter 1.

FIGURE 10.16   Price/Quality Relationship

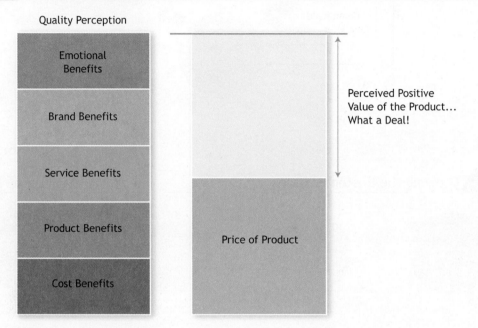

Recognizing that the entire organization needs to deliver on the value proposition, marketing's role is to communicate this message to targeted customers and to continuously reinforce the product and/or service offering's ability to deliver on this message. This means that marketers must have a full understanding of who their customers are, why they buy, and how they buy. They also must recognize what aspects of the buying process require the use of which marketing techniques in order to ensure that the value proposition is effectively delivered and that the value message is reinforced. Recent work by McKinsey and Company[12] on the impact of the various tools within the marketer's tool box (Figure 10.13) has shown that the need for effective marketing strategy goes beyond simply a strong company-offered media campaign. The need to respond to consumer-driven marketing techniques and channel support point-of-sale techniques grows in importance the farther the potential customer moves through the decision-making process (see Figure 10.17).

> The need to respond to consumer-driven marketing techniques and channel support point-of-sale techniques grows in importance the farther the potential customer moves through the decision-making process.

FIGURE 10.17 Impact of Influencers

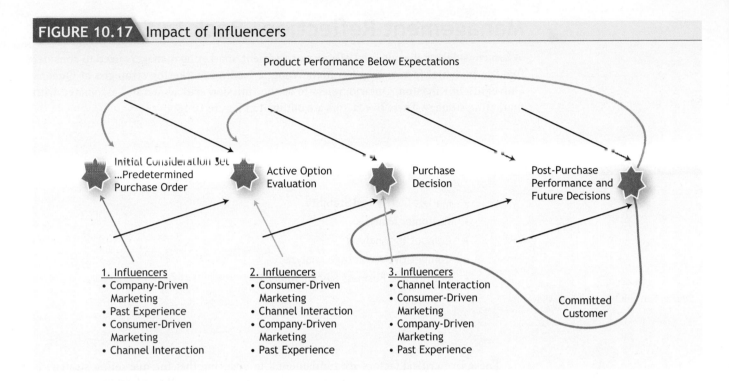

Product Performance Below Expectations

Initial Consideration Set ...Predetermined Purchase Order

Active Option Evaluation

Purchase Decision

Post-Purchase Performance and Future Decisions

1. Influencers
- Company-Driven Marketing
- Past Experience
- Consumer-Driven Marketing
- Channel Interaction

2. Influencers
- Consumer-Driven Marketing
- Channel Interaction
- Company-Driven Marketing
- Past Experience

3. Influencers
- Channel Interaction
- Consumer-Driven Marketing
- Company-Driven Marketing
- Past Experience

Committed Customer

A Note Pertaining to Not-for-Profits

Just like for-profit entities, not-for-profit organizations need to create and sustain demand for the products and services they offer. Equally important, they must be able to communicate, as core to their marketing process, the value that the mission and vision of the organization has to the community and a broader set of stakeholders. For not-for-profits, this concept of social marketing needs to ensure that the organization becomes fully rooted as a valuable resource to the community it serves, and is seen as a valued benefit in a way that encourages individuals, businesses, and government(s) to support the delivery of such products and services through philanthropy, membership or program fees, or budgetary commitment. The vitality of the not-for-profit organization is predicated on positioning itself as the preferred provider of products and/or services, and in meeting the needs of its user base in a way that generates loyalty, empathy, and commitment to the cause the not-for-profit aspires to respond to. As an example, the Humane Society of Canada works to protect dogs, cats, horses, birds, rabbits and small animals, livestock, lab animals, wildlife, and the environment.[13] Its local community-based affiliates offer services relating to caring for injured, abused, and homeless animals, finding homes for such animals, promoting responsible pet ownership, organizing spay and neuter programs, undertaking emergency animal rescues, and providing education services relating to animal care.[14] To be effective in this work, the Humane Society needs to create a position in the community as the preferred delivery agency for such services, and to create the necessary profile and awareness to generate the dollars needed in the form of fees for services rendered, donations, government support, contractual arrangements, and so on. Not-for-profits, like for-profit entities, need to recognize, as well, that not all individuals, businesses, and organizations will need, appreciate, or respond to their mission and/or vision. The concepts of marketing research, segmentation, and target marketing are equally important to the not-for-profit in determining which services to offer, where and how to deliver such services, and how best to tap into the various private philanthropic, public and private grant, and government funding opportunities vital to their success.

Management Reflection—Back to Strategy

When considering the potential of a market segment, marketing managers need to consider five fundamental factors that Kenneth Wong, a leading marketing strategist at Queen's University in Kingston, Ontario, refers to as the "mission critical factors" associated with marketing strategy. These five factors are outlined in Figure 10.18.

FIGURE 10.18	Market Dynamics: Critical Factors

- Market Clarity and Stability
- Customer Analysis
- Competitor Analysis
- Competitive Advantage Analysis
- Culture and Business System Analysis

Source: Kenneth Wong, Queen's University

These five critical factors are fundamental to ensuring that the marketing strategy is linked with an organization's overall strategy, vision, and mission. By understanding marketing's role as a key component in our ability to execute strategy, in conducting such an analysis managers can validate that the marketing effort will be aligned with the organization's strategy and that the structure of the organization will be appropriately directed to ensure its successful execution. The alignment of marketing's effort to an organization's strategy can be fully assessed through the response to the following questions:

- **Market clarity and stability:** Will things stay right within this market long enough for us to fully implement our intended marketing strategy and achieve our targeted financial goals? Are there external pressures, political influences, industry innovations, or competitive responses that will close the perceived window of opportunity prior to the successful execution of our strategy? Is there clarity and stability in the market segment(s) we intend to pursue?

- **Customer analysis:** Are we marketing our products/services to the right set of customers? In other words, have we identified the primary market segments that have the greatest need and will be receptive to our product/service offerings?

- **Competitor analysis:** Have we analyzed our competitors and their respective positioning strategies? Do we understand and can we anticipate their competitive actions and responses?

- **Competitive advantage analysis:** Have we identified the right competitive advantage around which to position our product? Has this perceived advantage been validated via marketing research and/or some other objective basis?

- **Culture and business system analysis:** Do we have the right culture, capital capacity, and business system to support our intended positioning strategy and marketing effort? Can we deliver on what marketing intends to communicate to the targeted market segment(s) in terms of needs solution, benefits, services, and features?[15]

Chapter Summary

This chapter is designed to familiarize students with the fundamentals needed to develop a marketing strategy for an organization. Critical to this process is recognizing the purpose of marketing and understanding the role it plays in influencing the execution of an organization's corporate and business-level strategy. A major emphasis within this chapter is recognizing the importance of segmentation and target marketing as central to the marketing process. Knowing which segments of the market will be most receptive to the products and services being offered is key to the success of any business. The chapter also attempts to provide students with guidance on where organizations can look for new growth opportunities, and on understanding the customer decision-making process and how this will influence the development of an organization's communication and positioning strategy. A central focus of this discussion is on understanding the components that make up the marketer's tool box, as well as recognizing the importance of how these various marketing elements impact value proposition development. The chapter closes with a discussion relating to positioning not-for-profit organizations, as well as with a "management reflection" that synthesizes the critical factors driving marketing strategy execution. Understanding the five big questions that marketers need to ask when formulating marketing strategy is the key outcome of this closing discussion.

Developing Business Knowledge and Skills

KEY TERMS

marketing *p. 252*

positioning *p. 255*

segmentation *p. 257*

primary sources of information *p. 257*

secondary sources of information *p. 257*

target marketing *p. 259*

segmentation stretch *p. 264*

cannibalism *p. 264*

customer desertion *p. 264*

QUESTIONS FOR DISCUSSION

1. What are the six core challenges that marketers must be able to respond to when assessing the viability or success of a product or service offering?

2. What is the importance of positioning with respect to marketing and the development of a marketing strategy?

3. What is the difference between segmentation and target marketing? How does marketing research influence this process?

4. What are the predominant tools that make up the marketer's tool box? How are these tools used within the consumer decision-making process?

5. What constitutes a value proposition? How is this different from simply communicating the core functionality of a product and/or service?

6. How is marketing a not-for-profit organization different from marketing a for-profit entity's products and services? How are they similar?

QUESTIONS FOR INDIVIDUAL ACTION

Both Apple and Nike have been successful in creating logos absent of names or other words. Do you believe Starbucks will be successful with this same approach? What do you believe Starbucks needs to do to achieve a logo that is recognized worldwide on the same level as those of Apple and Nike? What do you believe are the biggest challenges for Starbucks in attempting this logo approach?

TEAM EXERCISE

Choose a not-for-profit organization in your community. Based on your research and resulting understanding of the mission and vision of this not-for-profit, create a social networking positioning campaign for the organization. Where and how do you believe it should concentrate its social networking effort? What market segments should it target? How should it judge the success of this initiative? What other key positioning initiatives would you recommend in addition to the social marketing effort?

Case for Discussion

Isaac Larian, founder and CEO of MGA Entertainment, looked out the window of MGA's headquarters onto Roscoe Boulevard, located in the San Fernando Valley area of Los Angeles, California. MGA was preparing a major re-release of the Bratz line of dolls, and Isaac was pondering how MGA should position its flagship brand. Since 1997, when the children's toy company was founded, MGA has established a number of product lines including Moxie Girlz, 4Ever Kidz, and Rescue Pets. It has even acquired the rights to iconic children's toy brand Little Tikes. Since MGA's inception, however, no product has been more important to its success than Bratz, a line of dolls that, while competitors to Barbie, are much edgier and feature skimpier outfits and greater use of makeup. The Bratz line, which was released in 2001, has been controversial from the start, both for its dolls themselves and for the fact that they, unlike Barbie, never pretended to care about anything other than shopping and fashion.

Bratz were a huge hit with girls, despite their parents' concerns. Their success has been partly attributed to their multi-ethnic nature; they come in four different skin tones. Since 2008, however, MGA has not been able to profit from this success. In 2004, Mattel launched a suit against MGA that alleged that Carter Bryant, the dolls' creator, was an employee of Mattel at the time of their development, and that, as a result, Bratz were Mattel's intellectual property. A judge initially found in favour of Mattel, ordering, in 2008, that MGA pay its rival $100 million and turn over the production rights to Bratz. That ruling was overturned in July 2010, but the two years in between saw the production of Bratz dolls slow to a virtual standstill.

In the years since the Bratz release in 2001, the children's toy and doll markets have evolved tremendously. The continued evolution of pop culture has desensitized both children and parents, making dolls that were once shocking in 2001 seem much tamer today. Children's relationships with toys have also changed over time. Mattel's 2009 annual report identifies the shorter life cycles that now exist for toys, as well as the increasing propensity for children to outgrow toys at younger ages and to show preference for increasingly sophisticated technology applications in their toys. In the past, Bratz had been at the forefront of the use of media to promote toy products; MGA had featured Bratz in television shows, online games, and movies.[16]

QUESTIONS

Isaac wondered how MGA should position Bratz today. What segments of the doll and toy market should it target? Is there some way in which MGA should incorporate modern media to rebuild the Bratz brand? Does the same need exist today for an edgy, fashion-conscious doll as existed 10 years ago?

Practise and learn online with Connect. Connect resources include additional and interactive study exercises, videos, and practice quizzing, as well as additional material you won't find in the printed text.

11 Understanding the Marketing Effort

Learning Objectives

This chapter is designed to provide students with:

Lo1 Familiarity with the key marketing mix elements that make up the four pillars of the marketing effort

Lo2 An understanding of the importance of intrinsic value proposition attributes in the formulation of an organization's product and/or service differentiation strategy

Lo3 Exposure to the four key fundamental factors that will impact the setting of price for an organization's products and/or services

Lo4 An awareness of the key decision-making factors that will influence the type of distribution and delivery system an organization develops for its products and/or services

Lo5 An appreciation for the marketing process associated with the development of the communication message applicable to an organization's product and/or service offerings

Lo6 A base-level exposure to the intricacies of product life cycle

Lo7 An introduction to portfolio management

Snapshot—What to Expect in This Chapter

As identified by the learning objectives, this chapter focuses on exposing students to key concepts associated with the execution of marketing strategy. The content emphasized in this chapter includes the following:

- Four Pillars of the Marketing Effort
  - Product Strategy: Value Proposition Attributes versus Product Attributes
  - Pricing Strategy: Return on Sales Maximization
  - Distribution Strategy: Connecting with Customers
  - Communication Strategy: Communicating the "Fit"

- Managing a Product's Life Cycle
  - Managing across the Life Cycle

- Managing a Product Portfolio

- A Note Pertaining to Not-for-Profits

- Management Reflection—Managing the Marketing Effort

From the Student's Perspective

The marketing mix is often referred to as the "four P's" (product, price, place, and promotion). Like any recipe, the ingredients within your marketing mix need to be chosen carefully. They must work together to create a competitive position. Get just one element of the mix wrong and your brand will not deliver on its promise. After all, how good is a sandwich without bread, or a pizza without cheese? It is, therefore, a strategic imperative for managers to understand and develop a marketing mix for their organization. So, how do you promote the right product in the right place for the right price? You need to talk to your target market. Savvy marketers rely on consumer insights, market research, and strong analytics to make these critical decisions. In fact, one major marketing myth is that marketers are averse to crunching numbers and, instead, rely on creativity alone to excel. The reality is that marketing is much more strategic. In a game where a single percentage point of market share can easily represent six figures of revenue, today's companies are demanding that marketers demonstrate an ROI (return on investment). Managers who can execute an optimized marketing mix will best transition their consumers from awareness to loyalty. However, just like in the culinary arts, a healthy dose of intuition and artistry, grounded in years of professional experience, also has its place. This balance of creativity and pragmatism is what differentiates the marketing stream from all the other business disciplines. Embrace the four P's—the marketing mix is your friend!

Bram Warshafsky graduated with a degree in Commerce in 2010. Bram enjoys playing squash, listening to jazz, and discovering new features on his beloved MacBook Pro. After graduation, Bram will be working in brand management at a consumer packaged goods company and dreams of eventually starting his own creative agency.

BUSINESS *in Action*

Online Grocers

How important is distribution to business? In the case of online grocery stores, it *is* the business. During the dot-com boom of the late 1990s, online grocers were seen as the next big thing. It was expected that consumers would rapidly adopt this new shopping model that allowed them to save both gas and time going to, coming from, and at the grocery store. New companies such as Webvan and HomeGrocer expanded rapidly and raised tremendous amounts of money, but quickly failed due to their inability to make their businesses profitable. There are still more than 250 online grocers operating in North America today, but most are smaller outfits; many are designed to take advantage of the organic and locally grown food movements and to provide hard-to-find items. Many traditional bricks-and-mortar retailers have attempted to establish online stores in North America only to pull back after some early struggles.

Why has it been so difficult to make online grocers profitable? The answer lies in the complexity of their distribution requirements. Whereas a company that distributes digital media online needs only to add additional servers as sales increase, online grocery stores are forced to rapidly expand their warehouse systems to keep up with increasing demand. Huge online retailers, like eBay and Amazon, are able to cope with stress in their distribution systems because they employ the postal service or other couriers for their deliveries. When they are swamped for orders, they can hold on to their wares and send them a day or two later. Grocery stores, however, do not have that luxury. Not only do groceries tend to include perishable items that must be kept cool or frozen, but they also are expected to arrive at a specific time. Consumers do not like to put off eating. Delivering groceries is made even more difficult by the fact that they are almost always ordered at the end and at the beginning of the week, which means that vehicle and warehouse space added to be able to meet the "Friday" demand sit unused for most of the week.

In Great Britain, where higher population density makes delivering groceries more efficient, there are several big players in the online groceries industry, a segment whose sales make up more than 5 percent of the national grocery market. Online grocers in that country tend to employ one of two distribution methods: pure-pay online merchants, such as Ocado, distribute food directly out of their warehouses, while traditional retail grocers, such as Tesco, send packers to their own physical stores. In response to some retail customer complaints that the online store packers interfere with their shopping, Tesco has even opened some "ghost" stores whose sole purpose is to serve the online market.

Big market participants have not given up yet in the United States, however, and (relatively) new entrant FreshDirect has been quietly expanding its market outward from Manhattan, New York—where, as of 2010, it served more than 600 000 customers and earned over $250 million in sales. Expanding to the suburbs increases the cost of gas but decreases the cost of labour, as only one person is needed to drive, park, and deliver groceries. In the city, two people are often needed for this process due to security and parking concerns.

It is difficult to predict whether online grocery shopping will ever truly be embraced in North America. If it is, and if dedicated online grocers are to be successful, they will require a superior mastery of their distribution requirements.[1]

Four Pillars of the Marketing Effort

In Chapter 10, our analysis relating to marketing opened with a discussion pertaining to the six R's of marketing: understanding the *right need* to pursue, creating the *right solution* to that need, getting the right product backed by the *right value proposition* and the *right methodology for delivery*, along with the *right communication* messaging strategy and the *right pricing strategy*. Chapter 10 then focused on concepts, models, and tools relating to need identification and solution positioning, including a preliminary discussion on value proposition development. This chapter directs its attention toward the remaining four R's, and the marketing effort focus needed to ensure our organization's success in an increasingly competitive market environment. This marketing effort is most easily understood as the creation and execution of an organization's **"marketing mix,"** comprising strategic and tactical decisions relating to its product/service offerings, pricing, distribution, and marketing communication efforts and approaches. Historically referred to as the four P's of marketing (product, price, place, and promotion), the ability to create and integrate these four decision areas into a unified marketing approach can be more effectively thought of as the "four pillars to the marketing effort." It should be noted that the term "promotion" has since been replaced with the word "communication," and the term "place" has been replaced with the word "distribution," meaning the channels used to ensure that the product is accessible to purchasers. These changes have been made to more accurately reflect today's marketing approach, which goes far beyond simply promoting products and/or services at bricks-and-mortar locations (see Figure 11.1).

> **Marketing Mix** refers to an organization's strategic and tactical decisions relating to its product/service offerings, pricing, distribution, and marketing communication efforts and approaches.

In creating our marketing mix via these four pillar components, our effort is on developing, demonstrating, and communicating to our current and potential customers why our product is the best solution to their need, and then ensuring that it is available for customer acquisition through a convenient delivery option (bricks-and-mortar location, online, etc.) and at a price point that represents the best price/quality trade-off. Assuming that our marketing research, segmentation, and target marketing analysis is accurate, an effective marketing mix effort should result in achieving a definitive "fit" between our product/service offering and the needs of our potential customers. Traditionally, marketing textbooks and marketers have been trained to think of the marketing mix around four concepts: product strategy, pricing strategy, distribution strategy, and company-managed communication strategies. Although valid in terms of a company-centric approach, an alternate view is to think of a successful marketing effort as including these areas, but to design it and build it with a more

---

| FIGURE 11.1 | Four Pillars of the Marketing Effort (Marketing Mix) |

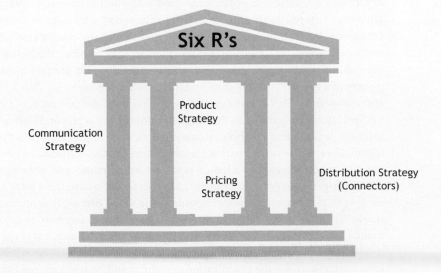

FIGURE 11.2 A Different Way to Think about the Marketing Mix

Traditional	Revised
Product Strategy	Value Proposition Attributes
Pricing Strategy	Maximize Return on Sales
Distribution Strategy	Connect with Customers
Communication Strategy	Communicate "Fit"

customer-centric slant (see Figure 11.2). Let's take a look at each of these areas in order to explain the value of this different approach to creating a marketing mix.

> Assuming that our marketing research, segmentation, and target marketing analysis is accurate, an effective marketing mix effort should result in achieving a definitive "fit" between our product/service offering and the needs of our potential customers.

Product Strategy: Value Proposition Attributes versus Product Attributes

When one thinks of product strategy, one has a tendency to focus his/her concentration and efforts on the tangible attributes of the product and/or service that an organization is offering. Although valid in that such attributes (functionality, packaging, component make up, etc.) are important and necessary decision-making areas relating to product and/or service offering design, this potentially hard or somewhat tunnelled vision of what the product and/or service strategy is all about may result in marketers failing to develop and leverage other essential and core-differentiating attributes. As was noted in Chapter 10 (as well as Chapter 1), viewing the product strategy as that of value proposition attributes brings into play a considerably broader range of attributes that can be used to more fully align the organization's offerings to the needs of the target market and create greater opportunity for differentiation. Creating a value proposition strategy broadens the focus to include such additional items as branding, emotional bonding, peer acceptance, and post-purchase service support. The product strategy essentially becomes the overall "experience" that the customer has with the product and the organization offering it. When combined with the functional, packaging, and component attributes, this results in a much stronger differentiated message to communicate to potential customers. When thinking about product positioning and product strategy, the key is to think about how the product and/or service offers to the customer the best solution in the face of competitive alternatives. As an example, companies that are positioned as premium-price players in a market segment may find their customer base being attacked by a low-price, low-cost competitor. This can be especially troublesome if the competitor offering's tangible product quality is comparable to that of the premium-price player. However, by offering a total solution package that combines financing options, a higher level of service support, stronger technical expertise on the part of its sales representatives, specialized or customized product options, longer warranty periods, a reputable brand name, and strong product reliability, the premium-price player can, in many cases, retain its competitive edge. The important takeaway is that in viewing product strategies via value proposition attributes, the focus of the marketing team shifts from simply "building a better mouse trap" to creating positive performance gaps between the company and its competitors in such a way that even if the tangible mouse traps become of equal quality, other differentiators have been created that continue to create preference for the organization's products and/or services (see Figure 11.3).

FIGURE 11.3 Value Proposition Strategies

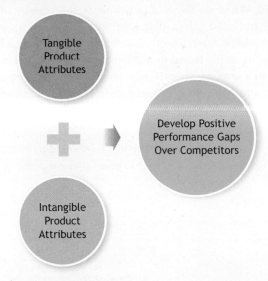

Viewing product strategies as the development of value proposition attributes shifts the marketing team's focus from simply "building a better mouse trap" to creating positive performance gaps between the company and its competitors.

Viewing product strategies through value proposition attributes can often result in the discovery of new market space as well. The ascension of Netflix and the demise of Blockbuster can be largely attributed to Netflix's recognition of the core value proposition–based solution to the customer's need, that being the attribute of convenience. Rather than focusing on building a strategy whose predominant focus is around titles of movies, Netflix chose to build a product/service strategy around the concept of the convenience of acquiring the product. Thinking in terms of value proposition attributes gets marketers to look at the product across a number of different potential advantage points (see Figure 11.4).

THE POWER OF BRANDS

Name recognition is one thing, but a brand name that communicates and epitomizes positive performance attributes that are judged to be superior to those of competitors is huge in today's competitive market environment. Companies spend millions of dollars on creating brand image, and rightly so. A brand that carries emotional ties and strong intrinsic value into

FIGURE 11.4 Value Proposition Attributes

a value proposition greatly improves the chances for its success. Strong brand names communicate quality, reliability, product consistency, and peer acceptance in many market sectors. When we think of snowboards, the brand name Burton comes to mind. Images of coffee, in Canada, immediately bring up Tim Hortons and Starbucks. Think of fast food, and McDonald's is often top of mind. So, just what makes a brand so powerful? The answer lies in the ability of the brand to move its customer market beyond simply awareness of the brand itself to a level of commitment that is unmatched by competitors. Truly successful brands, which add power to a company and/or its products and services, are those that have evolved to the top end of the brand ladder (see Figure 11.5).

> Truly successful brands, which add power to a company and/or its products and services, are those that have evolved to the top end of the brand ladder.

FIGURE 11.5 Brand Ladder

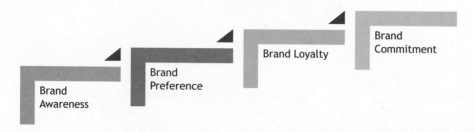

Predetermined Purchase List refers to the ranking of products/services that purchasers develop for all the options available when making a purchase decision.

Brands that have reached the "brand commitment" level on the ladder have an active and loyal customer base that continually places the brand at the top of their **predetermined purchase list**, resulting in their immediate migration to the purchase decision without further consideration of alternate competitive options. One way to visualize this would be to think of a person so committed to Starbucks coffee that he/she is willing to drive past several Tim Hortons and Second Cup outlets in order to find the nearest Starbucks location. Brands seldom command this type of allegiance overnight. It is a level that is obtained over time and is the result of the organization continually meeting and exceeding its customers' expectations across all value proposition components. In many cases, to achieve such a relationship level with their customers, organizations must successfully connect with them on three levels: product attributes, benefits, and emotional ties (see Figure 11.6).

> Brands that have reached the "brand commitment" level have an active and loyal customer base that continually places the brand at the top of their predetermined purchase list.

Brand awareness is often gained as organizations communicate, and the market accepts, that the brand offers distinctive features that set it apart from its competitors. The movement up the ladder toward brand preference and brand loyalty results in customers using this brand and, recognizing the benefits from it, choosing to repurchase the brand and concluding that its benefits (versus those of competitors) are such that a relationship to the brand is formed. Brand commitment evolves as ongoing use results in the brand becoming an automatic response when the need for this product or service presents itself. The decision to purchase is automatic, and the belief toward substitute brands is that they simply will not result in the same level of satisfaction. In essence, the brand has created an emotional or psychological link

FIGURE 11.6 Brand Success

Distinctive Emotional or
Psychological Commitment

Distinctive Product
Benefits

Distinctive Product
Attributes

with the customer in such a way that the intrinsic value of the brand is transferred to the customer as a result of using the brand. As an example, the General Motors brand "Cadillac" historically has focused its marketing efforts toward creating an emotional tie or bond with customers with the implication that ownership of a Cadillac is directly correlated with business success. (Yes, you are constantly the last one to leave the office. Yes, you are the "go to" person when decisions need to be made—and, yes, you shoulder the major responsibilities within the organization. As you look out your office window, however, at the last car remaining that evening in the employee parking lot, it is yours, and it is a Cadillac. You have truly made it.) Keep in mind that perception is reality when it comes to brands. Think of Toyota and how many people perceive the brand to represent quality. Think of Apple; the brand communicates innovation. The retail company Target in the United States (and now coming to Canada) also has been successful in developing its brand in this way. Target's success did not happen overnight—the development of its customer brand commitment took many years to build. Its success, however, is that it was able to communicate to its customers not just the variety of products it offered, but, more importantly, that its middle-class audience could purchase designer-style clothing at discount prices. Target customers were able to dress and feel like they were wearing high-end fashions, at price points they could afford. The ability to transition a brand from awareness to commitment is all about delivering the value proposition in a way that demonstrates distinctiveness and creates emotional and psychological ownership with customers as the proven solution to solving their needs. Again, this means going beyond the core tangible attributes of a product and tapping into the emotional "psyche" of the customer in terms of attributes such as style, ego, status, peer pressure, and lifestyle affiliation, to name a few. Tim Hortons' "truly Canadian" theme-based brand affiliation is at the heart of its marketing success and is an excellent example of how to create an emotional bond with an organization's customer base.

> The ability to transition a brand from awareness to commitment is all about delivering the value proposition in a way that demonstrates distinctiveness and creates emotional and psychological ownership with customers as the proven solution to solving their needs.

BUSINESS *in Action*

Great Canadian Brands

Just which brands are Canada's most loved? For the past two years, *Canadian Business* magazine, in partnership with Reputation Institute, has endeavoured to answer this question. Its annual survey of Canada's most loved brands looks at depth and integrity of an organization's reputation as a key barometer for determining just who is #1. As stated in its report in June 2011, what makes a great company is not just the success of its products and services, but also a reflection of how its customers perceive the organization itself. The study, which assessed 50 of Canada's biggest consumer-focused companies (based on revenue), judges the organizations in seven areas: governance, innovation, workplace, corporate citizenship, leadership, performance, and product/service offerings. Also assessed were the trust, esteem, and goodwill the brand was perceived to possess. The #1 ranked company was the Jean Coutu Group, the pharmaceutical retailer located in the province of Quebec. Tim Hortons finished a close second, followed by Shoppers Drug Mart, WestJet, and Research In Motion. Although relatively unknown outside of Quebec, Jean Coutu possesses a beloved family-values core brand appeal within the province. By no means a small player, with annual sales in excess of $2.5 billion (CAD), this drugstore chain scored high on public image and excellence in service. Its founder, Jean Coutu,

is a cultural icon in Quebec on the same level as Dave Thomas of Wendy's and Colonel Sanders of KFC. The Jean Coutu stores, with the slogan "You can find everything here, even a friend," fill one-third of all prescriptions in Quebec, and possess strong appeal for Quebec's working-class and rural shoppers. The appeal lies with the working-class roots of Jean Coutu and the heart and sweat that he put into building what is still a family-based business. The company is, in many ways, a reflection of Coutu himself, a reflection that many Quebecers can identify with and love to support. Although the Jean Coutu brand is regional to Quebec, the Jean Coutu Group is not a regional player. The company does operate in Ontario, under the name Maxi Drugs, and is also considering acquisitions, should they present themselves, in Western Canada.

Like Jean Coutu, WestJet also benefits from a strong perception of trust among its customers. WestJet customers have a strong allegiance to the company, which they consider to be well managed and customer focused, in addition to loyalty to the products and services it offers. The same can be said of Tim Hortons, last year's #1 ranked company. For many, this is an attribute from which RIM could benefit. Noted for its strong line of products and services, the RIM company brand itself lacks the emotional allegiance and passion (by Canadians) that is felt for the higher ranked organizations in this survey.

The end result is that although it scored well on innovation, leadership, and products and services, its scores were lower on trust, esteem, and admiration. Given its current global and North American market share slide in the face of aggressive marketing by Apple and Android-based phone competitors, RIM may benefit from seeking to re-launch its image in a manner that enables it to better compete (brand-wise) against companies such as Apple and Samsung not just on the basis of products and services, but in terms of company image as well. This is not lost on RIM investors, who feel that part of RIM's challenge, looking forward, is to further improve its market appeal and brand in a manner similar to the value that the Apple name brings to its products and services.

Finally, which companies saw their rankings drop over the last year? Scores fell for a number of banking, energy, and telecommunications companies. The conclusion is that many of these brands are met with at least some level of consumer skepticism in the evaluation areas identified above. Which industry sector scored the best? This accolade was claimed by "food retail."[2]

WEB INTEGRATION

Want to learn more about Canada's best loved brands, and see which companies did not score so well? Go to **www.canadianbusiness.com** and search "Canada's most loved brands."

Pricing Strategy: Return on Sales Maximization

Is business all about obtaining the largest market share? Should a company's pricing strategy be solely based on undercutting our competitors in order to get the sale? Does our pricing strategy truly reflect the value of the products and services we offer? Does the strategy support our brand and the positioning behind our value proposition? These are just some of the several questions that will challenge marketers and managers when it comes to pricing the products and services their organizations offer. In the face of a growing global marketplace, companies are being challenged across many sectors with a relentless downward pressure on price. Increasing competitive intensity and product substitutability, coupled with the rapidity of technological innovation and change, continues to contribute to this downward pressure. This, coupled with the constant challenge of "expense creep," places additional pressure on organizations to maintain and protect their operating margins. Upward pressure on capital costs, HR costs, R&D requirements, market development costs, and process development costs, to name a few, all contribute to this upward pressure on an organization's cost base. As managers, we can respond to this ongoing pressure in one of two ways (see Figure 11.7).

Our ability to respond to this globalization trend fundamentally comes down to how well we can differentiate our products and services from our competitors' products and services in the markets we are serving. The ability of our marketing mix to demonstrate and communicate this to our target markets is, and will be, a core component of our success. In situations where we are unable to truly differentiate our products and services, price will become a major point of comparison and, therefore, a core decision-making criterion as to which product and/or service is chosen by potential customers. The ability to effectively differentiate

FIGURE 11.7 Responding to Price Pressures

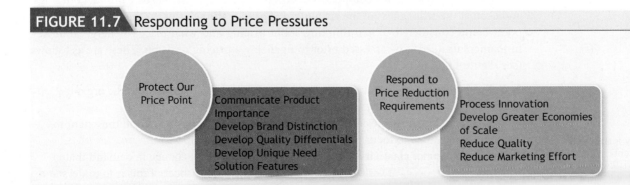

Protect Our Price Point
- Communicate Product Importance
- Develop Brand Distinction
- Develop Quality Differentials
- Develop Unique Need Solution Features

Respond to Price Reduction Requirements
- Process Innovation
- Develop Greater Economies of Scale
- Reduce Quality
- Reduce Marketing Effort

FIGURE 11.8   Influence of Price–Purchaser Decision Criteria

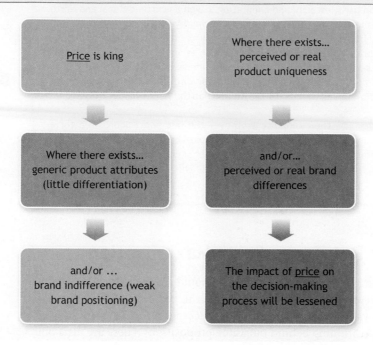

ourselves will enable us to minimize price as a major point of comparison, thereby reducing its influence on the decision-making process (see Figure 11.8).

> The ability to effectively differentiate ourselves will enable us to minimize price as a major point of comparison, thereby reducing its influence on the decision-making process.

MANAGING THE PRICING PROCESS

Determining what price to charge is critical to the execution of the marketing strategy and to the overall success of the marketing effort. Pricing involves considering a number of factors and requires solid knowledge of both internal and external influences. Internally, managers and marketers must fully understand the cost base of the organization and the margins that are needed in order to ensure that the price being charged is sufficient to cover the operating expenses and to support the investment needs of the organization. Chapter 12 provides a detailed analysis of how managers assess their cost base and how the concepts of breakeven analysis and margin management influence the pricing process. Externally, managers and marketers need to assess the competitiveness of their price against alternate product offerings, and against the willingness of the customer to "pay for the solution to the pain" at the price point being considered. When thinking about pricing and what price to charge, four key fundamentals need to be assessed prior to finalizing a pricing decision. These are as follows (see Figure 11.9):

1. Fully identify the cost structure components of the product/service that the organization intends to offer to the targeted market.
2. Research and identify the cost structures of your major competitors, and the extent to which they intend to focus on price as a major point of comparison.
3. Analyze the **price elasticity** of the target market; that is, the change in demand that is anticipated to occur at various price points. An additional aspect of this is to understand the price range that consumers will conclude is acceptable for the product/service you

Price Elasticity is the change in demand that is anticipated to occur at the various price points the organization is considering for its product and/or service.

FIGURE 11.9 Key Fundamentals to Setting Price

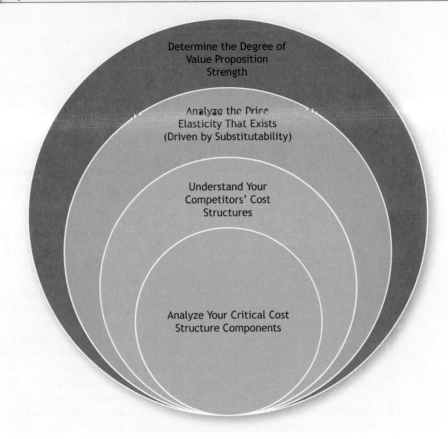

Determine the Degree of Value Proposition Strength

Analyze the Price Elasticity That Exists (Driven by Substitutability)

Understand Your Competitors' Cost Structures

Analyze Your Critical Cost Structure Components

intend to offer. A core fundamental is the ability to define the **consumer price threshold**: the maximum price point that the customer is willing to pay for your product or service.

4. Determine the degree of value proposition positioning strength that the product/service commands in the marketplace. This will enable marketers and managers to identify the premiums that can be allocated to the base pricing model given core differentiators such as brand strength, emotional ties, psychological attribute uniqueness, publicity initiatives, and other positioning-based communication message tactics.

Consumer Price Threshold refers to the maximum price point that the customer is willing to pay for a product or service.

With information generated from analyses within the four areas noted above, managers will also need to consider the required margin that must be incorporated into the pricing structure in order to ensure that additional organizational-based expenditure obligations—such as debt repayment, equipment and capital asset replacement, inflationary cost pressures, product-line growth initiatives, and allowances for unforeseen contingencies—are factored into the pricing formula. Profit expectations, which should include acceptable returns on the investment made in the product within a defined **payback period**, also need to be taken into consideration. As noted above, the details of the pricing process are more formally discussed in Chapter 12, on cost-base analysis and pricing.

Payback Period represents the length of time required to recover, or earn back, the cost of an investment.

As one can conclude, pricing is not an easy thing to do. For an organization, however, the setting of price is one of the most important components of the marketing process. Price reflects the cost that the customer must endure in order to acquire the desired product or service. It fundamentally impacts the perceived value of the product, as it is one-half of the measurement (the other being the value proposition being purchased) that the customer will use when determining if, and when, to buy, and which product or service to buy. For managers, the focus of setting price should be on the following questions: how can we maximize our return on sales on the product/service we offer in a way that ensures competitiveness, lies within our customers' acceptable price range, results in a recognized value advantage between our product/service and those of our competitors, and contributes to the long-term wealth of the organization? Again, Chapter 12 seeks to provide the process essential to implementing a successful pricing strategy.

> Successful pricing strategies seek to maximize the return on sales on the product/service we offer in a way that ensures competitiveness, lies within our customers' acceptable price range, results in a recognized value advantage between our product/service and those of our competitors, and contributes to the long-term wealth of the organization.

BUSINESS *in Action*

The YMCA of Kingston: How Understanding Price Impacts Business Decisions

As indicated in the opening chapter of this textbook, the author served as the Chief Executive Officer of the YMCA of Kingston, Ontario, for 14 years. During this tenure, the YMCA of Kingston faced a crossroads with respect to its main facility (called Wright Crescent), which dated back to 1955. The focus was to decide whether the organization should build a new YMCA facility in Kingston or renovate the existing facility. At the time, construction costs for a new YMCA facility were estimated at approximately $12 million. Alternatively, the investment needed to modernize and expand the existing facility was placed at approximately $6 million ($2 million for required upgrades to HVAC and other infrastructure needs, and $4 million for a significant addition to its aquatics centre). The renovation approach, however, while enhancing the capabilities of the YMCA, would still leave it with a relatively old structure, one that would require further financial expenditures down the road. In deciding which direction to take, the board of directors hired a consulting firm to undertake a significant marketing research study relating to both the potential for membership growth as a result of building a new facility and the overall price elasticity (including consumer price threshold identification) for YMCA membership fees. Analyzing and drawing conclusions relating to the fee structure range was fundamental to ensuring that the YMCA could pay the cost of debt associated with building the new facility. Financial calculations conducted by the management team at the time concluded that a monthly membership fee in the $60+ per month per adult member range would be required to support the cost of debt that would be needed to build a new facility and appropriately support its revised operating expense projections. The facility would need to attract a larger membership base in order to support this initiative as well. The conclusions reached by the consulting firm, based on its market analysis, was that the upper end of the price range for YMCA memberships in Kingston hit a price threshold at a price point significantly below the needed $60+ per month per adult member range. The price threshold was estimated to be $45 per month per adult member. At the time, the YMCA was charging approximately $35 per month per adult member. The research further concluded that there was little impact on demand elasticity between $35 and $45 per month per adult member, but at the $45 per month threshold demand dropped significantly. This information played a significant role in the decision of management and the board of directors that, based on the fundraising abilities of the organization, the cost of debt that would be incurred, and concerns over pricing at a point needed to ensure the future solvency of the organization, building a new facility was not feasible without significant risk. The board and the management team, in their wisdom, opted for an expansion of the existing

facility, recognizing that the price point of $45 per month per adult member would be sufficient to enable this registered charity to undertake such an initiative without exposing the organization to significant financial risk. The enhanced facility, including a major addition to its aquatics centre, was opened to the public in the fall of 2008.

WEB INTEGRATION
For more information regarding the YMCA of Kingston and its services and facilities, visit **www.kingston.ymca.ca.**

Distribution Strategy: Connecting with Customers

The development of a distribution strategy is all about connecting with customers. Channels of distribution and the development of channel intermediary relationships fundamentally revolve around ensuring that customers have convenient and accessible ways of purchasing our products and/or services. What was once predominantly thought of as a "bricks-and-mortar" development process has been dramatically changed by the development of Web-based technology services. In establishing a distribution strategy, it is important for marketers and managers to think in terms of how and where customers will purchase our products/services, and then to create the linkage that allows them to do so. In establishing these connection links, a number of key decision areas will come to mind. These decisions are not made in isolation of each other, but are best thought of as an integrated decision process, with decisions across all three jointly determining where, and how, we believe customers will have the best access to our product coupled with the optimal level of sales support. These key decision areas are as follows (see Figure 11.10):

1. Direct, indirect, or mixed systems
2. Product/service delivery options
3. Degree of sales support

DIRECT, INDIRECT, OR MIXED SYSTEMS

Direct, indirect, or mixed channel configurations (systems) refers to the amount of involvement and control an organization desires to maintain over the final sale of its products and/or services. **Direct distribution** implies that the organization intends to connect directly with its customers to handle the final sale of its products and/or the delivery of its services without the assistance of a **channel intermediary** (see Figure 11.11). Organizations tend to use direct

Direct Distribution refers to connecting directly with customers and handling the final sale of products and/or the delivery of services without the assistance of a channel intermediary.

Channel Intermediary refers to an organization that assists a company in the distribution and delivery of goods or services to its customers.

FIGURE 11.10 Channel Decision-Making Process

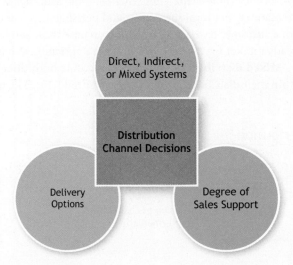

FIGURE 11.11 Direct Distribution

| Company | - - - - - - - - - - - - → | Customer |

Absence of channel intermediaries

distribution channels as a result of a belief that their product is better supported by dedicated, company-employed sales personnel, and/or that they can gain greater customer loyalty and greater "share of wallet" by dealing directly with the customer. Amazon.com's business model has been predominantly built around a direct distribution, Web-based model. In the cosmetics industry, Avon Products Inc. and Mary Kay Inc. both use direct sales personnel to sell their products and services to families across North America. Direct distribution approaches can also be the result of organizations believing that they can more effectively control the transportation and distribution costs associated with their products. In addition, organizations spearheading the creation of new market space and/or product areas may feel that a direct approach is necessary to effectively educate customers on the benefits of their products/services or new technologies. Direct distribution tactics can take into consideration single-customer contact points, or utilize multiple purchase option arrangements to facilitate the delivery of goods and services to customers.

Indirect distribution implies the use of a channel intermediary, such as a broker, wholesaler, or retailer, to facilitate the sales of an organization's products and/or services to the customer (see Figure 11.12). Organizations tend to use indirect distribution tactics as a result of the belief that significantly greater market reach and support can be provided by leveraging the expertise, locations, facilities, and experience of channel intermediaries. An example of an indirect distribution approach is an individual who desires to sell his/her home. In most cases, the homeowner will hire a real estate agent/broker to facilitate the sale and handle the transaction on their behalf. The ability to reach buyers and interact with them, along with the expertise and knowledge that a real estate agent/broker can provide regarding property valuation and the legal transactions associated with it, are predominant reasons why this approach is viewed by many as the preferred route to take. Indirect distribution is also used when an organization feels that customer familiarity with the use of the product is sufficient that a personal- or company-dedicated selling approach is not essential to the overall value proposition strategy, and/or when the cost of reaching customers is significantly higher than that incurred by using a channel intermediary. For many agricultural-based operations, the necessity of getting a product quickly from the fields where fruits and vegetables are grown to the supermarket aisles in urban areas requires the expertise of transportation and handling brokers and wholesalers. These channel intermediaries are experts in moving these products in a manner that minimizes costs and perishability. They also have the established contacts with a customer base that is ready to purchase these products and services, thereby providing a ready market for the products that these agricultural-based operations produce.

Mixed distribution systems incorporate both direct and indirect distribution options within their distribution strategy (see Figure 11.13). The ongoing development of Web-based

Indirect Distribution implies the use of a channel intermediary, such as a broker, wholesaler, or retailer, to facilitate the sales of a company's products and/or services to its customers.

Mixed Distribution Systems are distribution systems that incorporate both direct and indirect distribution options within their distribution strategy.

FIGURE 11.12 Indirect Distribution

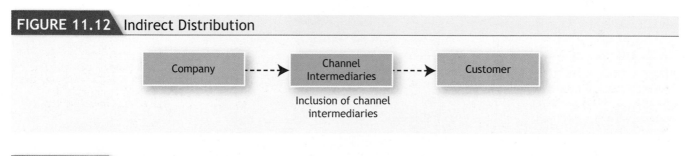

FIGURE 11.13 Mixed Distribution

models has resulted in more and more organizations viewing this distribution tactic as a preferred business model. The use of mixed distribution systems is not limited simply to the addition of Web sites. Coach (Leatherware) Inc., maker of the famous Coach purses, sells its products in Canada both direct to customers via company-owned and operated stores, and via its Web site (www.coach.com). In the United States, however, in addition to company-owned stores and its Web site, Coach Inc. sells these same products through select (authorized) indirect channel intermediaries (in this case, retail operations such as Macy's Inc., Bloomingdale's, and Lord & Taylor[3]). Dell Inc. originally sold its computers direct to customers through its online Web site and customer service centres. Dell has expanded its distribution strategy to a mixed distribution approach by making its computers available for purchase at Walmart.[4]

PRODUCT/SERVICE DELIVERY OPTIONS

As stated earlier, the best way to think of the development of an organization's distribution strategy and its accompanying tactics is in terms of creating a methodology for "connecting" with customers. This means that the organization needs to think in terms of accessibility and convenience in addition to cost and distribution efficiencies. More and more organizations are adopting a distribution approach that seeks to maximize the options customers can use when purchasing a product or service. With Web-based strategies becoming more fully developed, technology advances pushing costs down, and customer buying trends exhibiting non-traditional behaviours, the addition of a variety of purchase opportunity options is becoming more and more necessary to maintaining customer interest and loyalty. Sears Canada, as an example, uses a variety of purchase opportunity options in order to attract and retain customers and to build convenience and flexibility into its customer "connection" (distribution) strategy. The Sears bricks-and-mortar distribution network includes corporate stores, dealer stores, and Home showrooms. Sears also has been experimenting with what it calls "pop-up" stores. These are temporary storefronts, stocked with selected merchandise, designed to appeal to the university-age demographic. These temporary stores have appeared at selected universities in Canada such as McMaster University, University of Western Ontario, Brock University, and Queen's University. Pop-up stores are generally open on campus during the month of September and are designed to take advantage of the back-to-school needs of the students at the universities where they are located. In addition to this bricks-and-mortar approach, Sears also provides customers with access to its products via its catalogue division. This division consists of a telephone and a store-based sales centre approach backed by more than 1850 catalogue merchandise pickup locations across Canada. Sears has over 106 travel offices to support its travel division, and offers a network of home maintenance, repair, and installation services across Canada to support its appliance and home-improvement product lines. Sears also provides access to online shopping, for a large percentage of its products, at www.sears.ca. A recent test initiative underway in the United States through its parent company, Sears Holdings Corporation, is the idea of selling the Sears **private label brands** through other retailers. A number of the company's private brands, such as Kenmore, Craftsman, and Diehard, are well known across North America and command significant customer loyalty. Sears management hopes that, by offering these brands beyond Sears alone, additional revenue and brand recognition can be achieved. If successful, this could provide Sears with a new, currently untapped revenue stream and business opportunity. In addition, it ideally could also translate into more customers visiting Sears stores as these customers seek additional products offered under these brands, but not available through the external channel partners.[5] Organizations that incorporate a number of different channel connections through which customers can purchase a product and/or service are undertaking a **multi-channel distribution** strategy. Like Sears, Coach Inc., as noted above, also follows a multi-channel distribution approach.

DEGREE OF SALES SUPPORT WITHIN THE CHANNEL

In addition to considering the broad-level distribution approach to connecting with customers (direct, indirect, mixed) and the channel configuration to be used (product delivery options),

Private Label Brands are products that are created by one company for sale by another company under this latter company's own brand name.

Multi-Channel Distribution refers to the incorporation of a number of different channel connections through which customers can purchase a product and/or service.

managers must also think about the type of channel they believe will best support the customer during the buying process. A key decision associated with determining the type of channel system lies in determining the level of sales support that is needed for your product and/or service. Although customers care about the quality of the product and its price, a positive buying experience is what really drives value. A key part of this experience is ensuring that customers are supported in the selling process by channel intermediaries and at the point of purchase. The buying process, as discussed in Chapter 10, consists of four stages: need identification, information search, alternative selection, and the purchase decision. The distribution channel's maximum value lies in the stages of alternative selection and supporting the purchase decision (although it also supports the two initial stages, relating to need identification and information search). Determining how extensive a distribution channel to develop is, in many ways, directly related to the sales support required in educating customers on why the purchase of an organization's product and/or service represents the best solution to their needs. In general, the greater the complexity of the product, the greater the lack of familiarity with the product category by the customer, and the greater the price, the more important the sales support becomes at the time of the purchase. When assessing the types of channel relationships to pursue, managers tend to assess the best fit around the following channel relationship categories:

1. Intensive distribution arrangements
2. Selective distribution arrangements
3. Exclusive distribution arrangements

> Although customers care about the quality of the product and its price, it's a positive buying experience that really drives value.

Intensive Distribution is a decision by an organization to distribute the product and/or service through as many locations or channel outlets as is possible.

Convenience Goods are goods purchased by customers on a regular basis, with minimum effort and little emotional connection.

Intensive distribution arrangements seek to maximize product availability in the marketplace. Intensive distribution implies a desire by an organization to distribute the product and/or service through as many locations or channel outlets as is possible. The idea is to have customers see your product and/or service wherever they go. A good example of this lies with **convenience goods**, which are products and services that we use every day. Often, decisions to buy are based on convenience and availability in addition to brand loyalty and commitment. The desire to purchase a soda is a good example of this. Sodas can be found in restaurants, vending machines, grocery outlets, arenas, convenience stores, office building kiosks,

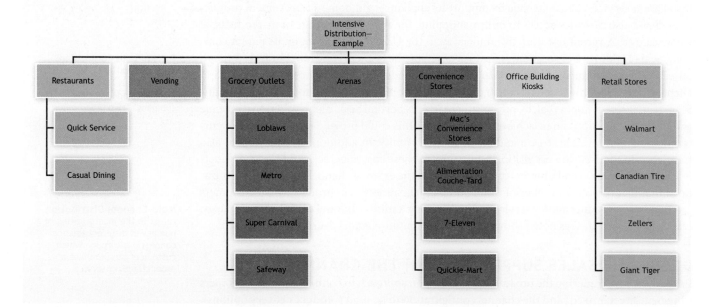

and retail stores. As indicated, the advantage of this distribution approach is that it maximizes market penetration and offers tremendous potential for achieving significant scale. The risk for the organization is that it requires a significant financial commitment in inventory to achieve this broad-based availability. It also results in having the product handled by a larger number of distributors, many of whom are carrying a wide variety of products, a number of which are most likely in direct competition with the products/services the organization is trying to sell. This means that the ability and the willingness of the distributor to focus his/her selling efforts on our product are limited, as there is no focused commitment on our product/ service offering.

Selective distribution arrangements narrow the breadth of access that products and/or services have in the marketplace. The decision to limit the extent of the reach could be based on the need for heightened sales support at the time of purchase. As an example, Sofame Technologies Inc. of Montreal limits the sales of its technologically advanced, energy-efficient heat recovery systems to a selected list of authorized dealers. These dealers are considered by Sofame Technologies to possess the necessary expertise and marketplace contacts to assist Sofame in the sale and support of its products. This decision could also be based on a desire to reinforce a brand name or a particular image for a product or service.[6] Going back to our Coach Inc. example, this organization uses a selective distribution channel for the sale of its products. The purchase of a Coach handbag must take place at either a Coach Inc. retail location or at one of its authorized distributors (Macy's, Bloomingdale's, Lord & Taylor). You will

Selective Distribution refers to a decision by an organization to sell its products and/or services through a limited number of channel intermediaries.

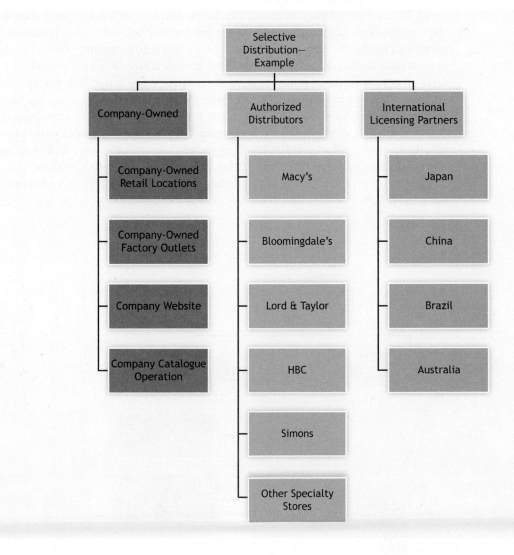

not find Coach purses at Walmart or Zellers. These retailers are simply not in line with the customer profile and image that Coach Inc. seeks to communicate to the marketplace. Selective distribution may also be based on geographic clusters, differentiation initiatives, joint ventures, and strategic alliances. Organizations using selective distribution arrangements do so because they believe their products or services will be better supported at the point of sale by these channel intermediaries. They also feel that they can retain a greater degree of control over how the product is priced, marketed, and sold. Finally, these same organizations, by offering an authorized dealer status, can contractually limit the number of competitive offerings that the channel member agrees to carry, thereby minimizing direct competition at the point of purchase for the product or service the organization is seeking to sell.

Exclusive Distribution refers to a decision by an organization to offer its products and/or services through a single market representative.

Exclusive distribution arrangements reflect a further focusing on the distribution of products through a single, authorized channel intermediary. For manufacturers of products, this means offering these products through only one market representative. As an example, new Ford Motor Company vehicles can be purchased only at Ford dealerships. Organizations often use exclusive distribution arrangements when the selling process associated with their products requires the highest levels of support, or when the organization is attempting to break into new markets. Distribution exclusivity is also a key to franchise-based operations, where the franchisor agrees to provide to the franchisee a full business operating model governed by an exclusivity contract. As an example, M&M Meats Inc. provides access to its operating model, and its products and services, only to contractually licensed franchisees. The benefit for organizations is that it is anticipated that awarding an exclusive distribution contract to a channel intermediary will result in a total commitment, or a higher level of commitment, by that intermediary. In general, exclusive distribution arrangements should also give the organization maximum say in how the product/service will be marketed and sold, and generally prohibit the channel intermediary from carrying competitive lines. The risk for the organization is that, should the exclusive distribution arrangement not result in the required level of sales success, then the organization may have few immediate alternate options to stimulate demand for the product, as contractual provisions may prevent the organization from terminating the relationship in the short term. For the channel intermediary, the benefit is that it can add to its portfolio a product/service that cannot be purchased elsewhere. Assuming that the product is well received by its target market, this can result in enhanced loyalty not only to the organization's brand, but to the channel intermediary as well. Initial forays into international markets are often undertaken via exclusive distribution arrangements with dealers, brokers, or other channel intermediaries.

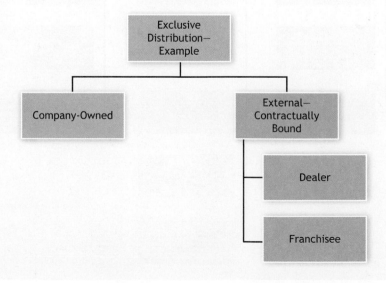

IMPORTANCE OF CHANNEL INTERMEDIARIES

Although recent trends have seen many businesses shift their distribution strategies to Web-based, direct-reach sales options, managers and marketers should not underestimate the power and importance of channel intermediaries. Successful companies recognize that channel intermediaries are not simply an outlet for the sales of an organization's products and services, but rather are viewed as a key stakeholder and partner in the overall demand-generation and selling process. Channel intermediaries, when properly cultivated and incentivized, can become instrumental in building market share, shaping the product mix through key information gathering and feedback, forecasting demand, participating in and sharing the costs of sales and marketing efforts, educating customers, and acting as critical contacts at the front end of the organization's customer relationship model. In many situations, channel intermediaries bring to the market experience and expertise that the manufacturing and/or service company does not possess in-house. Significant risk mitigation can also take place through channel intermediaries, who commit to purchasing products and/or services in advance, and absorb the cost of unsold inventory once these products are purchased. Used effectively, channel intermediaries help make the connections with customers more effective, assist in driving down costs, and help to identify **profit leaks**, thereby improving the overall performance of product and service-supplying organizations.

Profit Leaks are inefficiencies within an organization's marketing mix that result in margin erosion and loss of profit.

> Successful companies recognize that channel intermediaries are not simply an outlet for the sales of an organization's products and services, but rather are viewed as a key stakeholder and partner in the overall demand generation and selling process.

BUSINESS *in Action*

Business-to-Business (B2B) Sales

The global financial crisis and subsequent recession have caused both sellers and buyers to reflect on their current business relationships. The trimming of human resources and the renewed emphasis on productivity maximization have challenged employers, on both the buying and the selling ends, to do more with less. Add to this the upward cost pressure currently being felt across sales and distribution channels due to ever-climbing transportation expenses, and the pressures to improve efficiency and effectiveness initiatives have never been greater. Competitive intensity, coupled with the need to grow or at least maintain profitability in the face of declining or stagnating sales volume, has resulted in a significant shift in business models across the globe. The end result is that the way in which businesses interact with each other in the B2B (business-to-business) setting is fundamentally changing. For the selling organizations in this value chain relationship, it means trying to provide heightened levels of customer service in the face of tighter and scarcer resources. For the buying organizations, it means seeking out solutions that will enable them to create and sustain competitive advantages in the face of waves of competitive turbulence.

The above commentary is meant to reflect on the fundamental question that is occurring in sales-based organizations today: How do we continue to grow our sales revenues when the business customers we work with have seen theirs flatten? Do we simply try to take sales away from our competitors who are also serving this same client base, or can we develop a more productive and solution-based relationship with this client base, thereby advancing the needs of both our and their organizations? The answer to this lies in responding to both of the challenges noted by these questions. To accomplish this, we need to understand better than ever before what our customers want and need. Then, we need to make sure that our salesforce delivers this better than any of our competitors. Recent research by McKinsey & Company has identified the following trends in the relationships between buyers and sellers. First, buyers are becoming increasingly demanding and are, more and more, looking for customized solutions to the challenges they are facing. Second, these buyers are asking sellers to accept more risk and provide greater monetary allowance and benefits, particularly with respect to significant purchase commitments. They are also requiring that these sellers maintain an ongoing relationship presence with these contracts, providing ongoing support, expertise, and value. Finally, customers are looking for solutions, not simply products and/or services. They expect sellers to provide higher levels of expertise at the front end of the sale to ensure that the benefits the buyers hope to achieve are realistic and realizable.

For sellers, these increasing requirements on the part of buyers result in the need to re-structure the sales approach to meet these needs and keep profitability objectives obtainable. To do this, sellers must consider three key responses to the heightened demands of customers. First, selling organizations need to commit to long-term training initiatives for their staff to ensure that sales representatives are capable of meeting the expertise requirements of custom-ers. If this is not feasible, then organizations need to develop "pools of expertise" that sales representatives can draw on when needed. Second, selling organizations need to do a better job of assessing the forward profitability potential of each client, and adjust their selling efforts accordingly. Buying organizations, whose potential for future sales is greatest, should be allo-cated higher levels of salesforce commitment. Finally, as buyers are becoming more accustomed to enhanced technologies, sales organizations should make better use of technology-based sales techniques such as Web conferencing tools, video conferencing, online order platforms, and telephone-based technical support (versus the continuous and costly pressures of meeting face to face). More than ever, customers are willing to accept simple, fast, and inexpensive transaction vehicles, as long as the level of support is there and they see savings derived from these mecha-nisms reflected in an organization's pricing going forward. Sales representatives must also pay closer attention to the forward-thinking strategies of their customers in order to anticipate and position the organization toward upcoming sales opportunities.

In closing, selling organizations must align themselves with what customers perceive to be important in maximizing the selling experience, while managing the process in a way that en-ables the achievement of profitability objectives. This needs to be accomplished without sacri-ficing the perceived level of commitment the organization has to its customer base. Stronger assessment of customer value, technology options, and required levels of in-house expertise are core to this process.[7]

Communication Strategy: Communicating the "Fit"

The fourth pillar of the marketing effort is an organization's communication strategy. Often thought of as advertising and promotion, this marketing mix element involves significantly more than just the development of a media-based message. The key fundamental of this pillar is that the communication strategy needs to demonstrate the "fit" of the value proposition developed as the best solution to the needs of the target market being focused on. Communi-cation strategy development takes the information discussed in Chapter 10 (segmentation, target market selection, customer profiling and positioning) and embodies this within a focused message, driven by a well-defined and well-developed value proposition and targeted specifically at a defined audience (see Figure 11.14). This is referred to as **message rifling**.

Message Rifling is a focused message, driven by a well-defined and developed value proposition, that is targeted specifically at a defined audience.

Message rifling is all about making sure that you are communicating the right product/service value proposition components, to the right audience, at the right time, via the right message mechanism. As managers, we have a variety of communication options. Message communication can be via company-based media programs, direct marketing efforts, chan-nel incentives to stimulate sales support via our channel partners, third-party initiatives such as product reviews, blogs, and publicity-based initiatives designed to draw positive attention to our offerings. These options were discussed in Chapter 10, and form what has been identi-fied as the marketer's tool box (shown again in Figure 11.15). These communication options are best thought of as tactical tools designed to deliver on the overall marketing effort being implemented for a particular product/service value proposition.

> Message rifling refers to making sure you are communicating the right product/service value proposition components, to the right audience, at the right time, via the right message mechanism.

FIGURE 11.14   Communicating the "Fit"

FIGURE 11.15   Marketer's Tool Box

Category	Tools of the Trade
Company-Driven Marketing Techniques	Advertising Sales Promotion Publicity Point-of-Purchase Displays Dedicated Sales Force
Consumer-Driven Marketing Techniques	Internet Searches Product Reviews Peer Recommendations Analysts' Blogs Social Media Websites and Commentary
Channel Support and Interaction Techniques	Dealer Incentives Point-of-Purchase Discounts Channel Member Training Exclusivity Arrangements Salesperson Recommendations

The development of the marketing communication strategy is really the commencement of the selling process. As was mentioned above, the key is to determine how to link the strategy for the products and services being offered to the marketplace in a manner that enables us to get targeted potential customers to listen to our message and to build a relationship with them, which results in their adoption of our products and/or services. This means we need to think about the best approach to personalizing the relationship, while showing them how our products/services will solve their needs. In developing a communication strategy, managers must think about four key questions:

1. Do we understand why these customers need our products and/or services?
2. Do we understand the level of knowledge that our customers possess concerning the products and/or services we are asking them to purchase?
3. Do we understand who the actual decision maker is when making such a purchase?
4. Are we able to clearly define, in simple terms, what makes our products/services different?

By answering these four questions, we can then use this information to determine where and how best to apply our marketing budget to create awareness for our products and/or services, build interest in them, explain what customers will receive for the purchase, and reinforce the conclusion that our offering is the best fit for solving their need. Armed with this information, and based on our understanding of the buying process, we can finalize decisions on whether we should pursue targeted potential customers through traditional media channels (TV, radio, print media), direct marketing (online, telemarketing, and other offline options), event sponsorship, publicity and public relations tactics, trade shows, merchandising and point-of-sale options, Web-based channels, packaging, or a combination of the above.

GROWING IMPORTANCE OF SOCIAL MEDIA AS PART OF THE COMMUNICATION STRATEGY

As discussed in Chapter 10, consumers move through a multi-stage process when determining which products and/or services to purchase. Historically, this process has led marketers to believe that their efforts should be in two specific areas: creating brand awareness, and swaying purchasers to buy. This meant emphasizing traditional advertising approaches and selling incentives at the point of purchase, in what many interpreted as a "hard sell" environment. Today's customers, armed with access to almost unlimited information via digital and Web-based resources, are looking for marketers to engage them in the buying process, not dictate to them what they should buy. Developing the communication strategy in support of products and/or services today, given the power of the digital environment, means shifting the emphasis to a much broader marketing mandate. This would include:

1. Coordinating communication activities in a way that engages the customer through an increasingly Web-based information and social-network-driven purchase decision.
2. Creating interest in the brand in a way that enables the customer to personalize a relationship with the brand and, hence, act as an ambassador for it.
3. Recognizing the need to create and manage access to an increasing demand for content relating to the products and/or services being offered, the distribution channels being used, and the promotions being offered.
4. Increasing the emphasis on selective utilization of social media and third-party Web-based options in a way that ensures targeted potential customers are reached.[8]

To illustrate the impact that social media is playing in the execution of marketing communication strategies, we take a brief look at some significant findings relating to both the well-known social media engines (Twitter, Facebook, YouTube) and the power of blogs. In a recently published case study, "Social Media Opportunities for Public Companies, Case Study: Players Network, Inc.," NewMediaPlus—an organization that provides real-time solutions for social media, Web development, graphic design, and online advertising—provided the following insights into the dramatic impact that social media is having on the way customers search for, stay informed about, and buy products and services:

- Studies have shown that people who follow companies and their brands on Facebook and Twitter are more likely to purchase products or services from those companies. They also are more likely to recommend those companies to their friends. More than half of those surveyed indicated a greater willingness to buy a product they follow, and over 60 percent indicated a willingness to recommend brands that they follow to others.

- The primary reasons why users follow a brand on Facebook are (a) to receive discounts and promotional information for the brand, (b) to identify themselves as customers of a particular brand or company, (c) to draw others to the brand, and (d) because doing so is fun and entertaining.

- Individuals in fully developed countries in Europe, North America, and Asia spend, on average, more than four hours per month watching YouTube videos. Canadians, for example, watch an average of 4.4 hours of YouTube videos per month.

- Companies that blog are found to have more visitors to their Web sites and create more inbound links to their Web sites. Blogging also results in more indexed pages in support of company products, services, and brands.

To place these findings in perspective, let's look at the current level of activity relating to the Internet and social media. Recent estimates of global internet users are as follows[9]:

North America	252 908 000
Europe	418 029 796
Asia	738 257 230
Latin and Central America	20 970 490
Africa	67 371 700

There are currently more than 500 million participants on Facebook. It is estimated that there are more than 126 million blogs. More than 2 billion YouTube videos are streamed daily, and there have been more than 10 billion "tweets" since 2006.[10] A recently illustrated example points to the power of the reach of social media networks. A university student, on break at his parents' home, had a disagreement with his mother over cleaning his room. The disagreement centred on whether he should clean his room before the family's cleaning service arrived to clean the house. The mother felt that the room should be tidied up. The student disagreed, indicating that if he were to clean the room, then what would be the value of having a cleaning service. The student, in frustration, decided to post the question on Facebook, asking for comments as to whether it made sense to clean his room prior to the arrival of the cleaning service. The student received hundreds of thousands of responses to this query from all over the world, some in support of the student and some in support of his mother's position. The point is simply that other communication vehicles could not generate such activity, on a global scale, in such a short period of time.

The conclusion to be drawn is that social media marketing, if managed properly, can create reach for an organization and can build loyalty for its products and services in a way never before seen. The most prominent newspapers in the world cannot claim anywhere near the reach of Facebook and Twitter in terms of numbers of subscribers. The key to remember, however, is that despite its tremendous reach, social media marketing requires a strategy, just as any other business decisions need to be made with strategy in mind. Effective social media marketing requires identification of established objectives and evaluation measurements against quantifiable performance metrics. Even before the development of such objectives, companies need to realize that venturing into social media marketing requires a significant commitment. Content has to be frequently updated to ensure that it stays relevant; failure to do so will lead to customer desertion and dissatisfaction. Commitments also have to be made around site and blog monitoring to ensure that relevant data generated by the social media sites used are collected and incorporated into current and future business decision making. When used correctly, social media marketing can provide significant benefits to the organization across a variety of fronts. Companies today are using social media marketing to improve customer relations, inform customers of product promotions and sales, provide coverage for events the organization is participating in, reinforce advocacy of issues understood to be of importance to its followers, monitor customer perceptions of new product releases, assess competitive actions, notify investors of upcoming information releases, and protect and reinforce the organization's reputation. Undertaking social media marketing, like anything else, does not mean automatic success. Managers must recognize its value and its limitations. For social media marketing to be successful, it needs to accomplish four critical things (see Figure 11.16):

1. Capture interest among general Internet traffic
2. Increase customer engagement with the organization
3. Turn interest and engagement into sales
4. Build active customer loyalty

Take Tim Hortons as an example. Tim Hortons launched its Facebook page in 2009; today, it is one of Facebook's most popular Canadian-based sites, with more than 1.5 million fans.[11] This means that approximately one in every 12 Canadians using Facebook is linked to Tim Hortons. The site encourages Tim Hortons customers to post comments on what they love about Tim Hortons. For Tim Hortons, it is a new relationship-building approach to marketing, one that gives the company a unique way to engage with customers. Instead of talking at its customers, it is talking with them. Social media is a venue to gain information and learn about customer likes and dislikes, as well as get responses on key purchase-based decisions. For instance, did you know that 67 percent of Tim Hortons' Facebook followers order a large or extra-large coffee, and that 25 percent of these customers visit Tim Hortons more than twice per day? Forty-nine percent of these same customers visit Tim Hortons at the start of the day, and 31 percent order a double-double when they stop in. Why Tim Hortons? More than 55 percent of the respondents to the Facebook survey on the Tim Hortons site indicated that it is the special taste of the coffee that keeps them coming back. Information like this, from an organizational perspective, is valuable for inventory, staffing, and general operational purposes. Tim Hortons is now expanding its Facebook presence by purchasing ads on Facebook, or what Facebook likes to refer to as "engagement units." Tim Hortons hopes that this combination of a site presence supported by an advertising campaign will assist in growing sales and further building customer loyalty.[12]

Lululemon Athletica's Facebook site, with more than 300 000 fans, provides customers with an opportunity to comment on upcoming designs, stay up to date on Lululemon events, offer inspiring stories to others, and get the latest news on yoga and fitness tips and trends. Like the Tim Hortons site, Lululemon's site is all about creating the special bond with customers that will enable the organization to create strong brand commitment and active loyalty—all of which results in customers becoming ambassadors for the organization and the products and services it offers.[13]

FIGURE 11.16   Social Media Success Factors

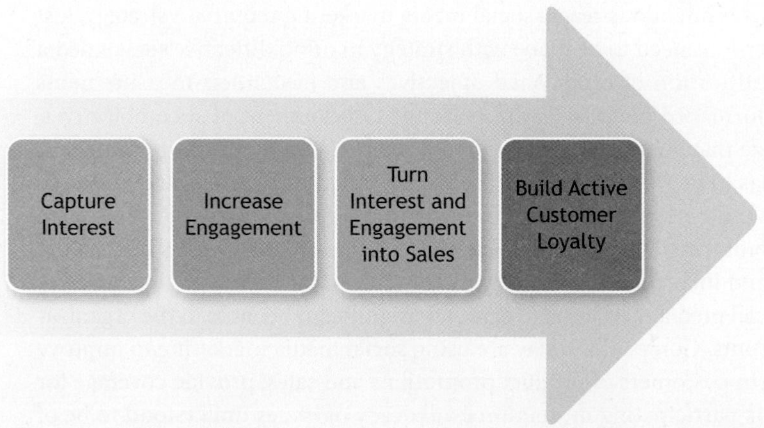

Capture Interest → Increase Engagement → Turn Interest and Engagement into Sales → Build Active Customer Loyalty

Returning to our general discussion concerning communication, marketing communication strategies are designed to support the specific objectives an organization has established for a defined business period. These objectives could be focused on building market share, improving the profitability of the current volume, educating customers on product/service benefits, creating profile and awareness, reinforcing brand preference and commitment, supporting point-of-sale initiatives, enhancing the organization's reputation, and delivering post-purchase reinforcement of purchase decisions. Communication tactics form a vital part of this strategy, as their fundamental goal is to effectively deliver the message to the marketplace, thereby defining and reinforcing the purpose of such objectives. A critical aspect of the communication effort lies in its support of the execution strategies in place as a product and/or service, positioned by its value proposition, moves through its life cycle.

Managing a Product's Life Cycle   LO6

The lives of products and services, like companies, are defined by what is called a life cycle. The length of this life cycle and the success that a product or service has within it is determined by both the success of the positioning strategy designed for the product/service and the successful execution of its marketing effort (marketing mix). Traditionally, products that have achieved some initial level of success will transition through five specific stages of life during their life cycle: development, introduction, growth, maturity, and decline (see Figure 11.17). Although most textbooks on this subject start the product life cycle at the introduction stage and, therefore, define the cycle as having four stages, the initial stage of development is included here because it does reflect a significant risk to the organization in terms of both resource consumption and financial commitment. The development stage refers to the steps associated with the creation of a new product/service. This includes the development of an idea or concept; the assessment of its feasibility to be commercialized; the development of a physical prototype (if a product); an analysis of its market potential via focus groups (customer and channel partner), surveys, or third-party testing; resource allocation approval; test marketing; and pre-launch communication initiatives.

FIGURE 11.17   Traditional Product Life Cycle

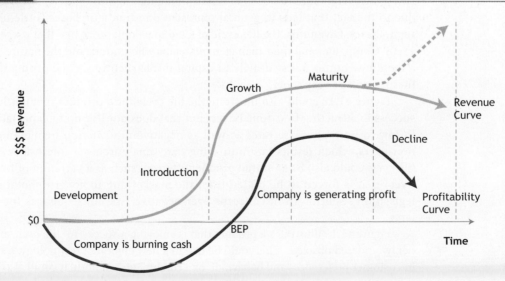

Figure 11.17 illustrates a traditional product life cycle. It is traditional in that all five stages are defined and that the revenue and profitability curves reflect a standard growth model where the product, once developed, is introduced to market and, after a period of time, gains market acceptance with its targeted customers. This is then followed by a period of growth where more and more customers become aware of the product and become more familiar with the product and its benefits. Assuming that the marketing strategy is effective, demand for the product begins to accelerate significantly. This increased demand and accelerated product adoption rate enables the product to generate sales sufficient to cover its operating expenses (identified as the BEP—breakeven point), followed by initial profitability (BEP is discussed in more detail in Chapter 12). As first-time customers continue to purchase the product, coupled with repeat purchases of the product by existing customers, revenue continues to climb, resulting in the product line becoming able to generate profits. Again, assuming success in this manner, sales volumes will continue on an upward trend with improved profitability occurring as the product moves through this growth phase. Moving forward in time, at some point the first-time buyers of the product will begin to decline in number (because most people who desire the product have now purchased it), thereby resulting in the sales growth of the product to slow and potentially flatten. Demand for the product, at this point, can be thought of as being largely driven by repurchase rates. The length of the maturity stage will be determined by our ability to stimulate repeat purchases and find additional pockets of new customers via segmentation and target marketing techniques. Product innovation and enhancement, product-line extension strategies, market penetration tactics, and market consolidation strategies are all examples of initiatives that can be employed in a mature market to continue to lengthen this stage and maintain or enhance sales and profitability strategies (see the dashed line in Figure 11.17). At some point, the product will begin to experience a decline in sales. This could be due to product obsolescence, a shift in customer needs and demand, or a combination of the two. As the product progresses through this decline stage, a decision will need to be made as to how long to support the product and when it would be appropriate for the organization to divest itself of it.

The discussion above is for illustration purposes only. Not every product follows the same path. Product life cycles, and the reason for their length and overall success, are influenced by a number of both controllable and non-controllable factors. For managers, however, it is important to assess what a potential life cycle would look like, and be prepared to make adjustments to the marketing effort and the overall product strategy once the life cycle is underway. In some cases, life cycles can be very short. In other cases, life cycles can extend over many years. As an example, consider the life cycle of a fad. In many cases, the overall duration of a fad can be thought of in months versus years. This is largely due to the fact that fads in general represent one-time purchases (little opportunity for repurchase). Given this, the life cycle of a fad may look more like that presented in Figure 11.18. Companies and their management teams who understand the nature of a product as a fad know not to invest heavily in capital infrastructure for the product, given that its lifespan will be very short.

Figure 11.18 could also illustrate the life cycle for a product that has had some early success in attracting first-time buyers but that does not live up to expectations, resulting in low to no repurchase rates as well as negative information being communicated to non-users, which results in diminishing first-time purchaser interest. A similar type of life cycle could also be an initial product offering (such as a variation of financial derivatives) that is forced to be pulled from the market due to governmental regulations or legislation resulting from concerns over negative risk consequences for the market at large.

Figure 11.19 illustrates a product that is enjoying a successful life cycle and then is suddenly rendered obsolete. This could be due to a new emergent technology, a significant shift in customer preferences and behaviour, or a combination of both. It could also be the result of an unanticipated and uncontrollable risk trigger impacting the company and its industry. A

FIGURE 11.18 Fad versus Traditional Product Life Cycle

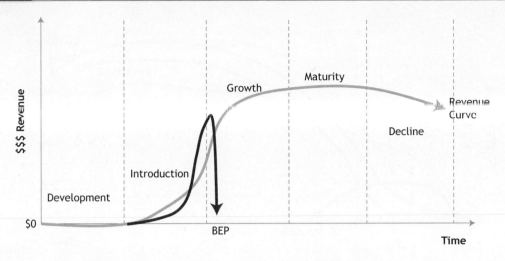

FIGURE 11.19 Obsolescence versus Traditional Product Life Cycle

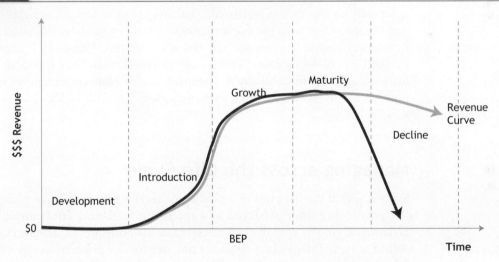

good example of this would be the dramatic decline in the sale of music CDs as a result of the advent of disruptive innovators, such as Napster and Kazaa, and the downloading of music via similarly focused Web sites.

The ability to effectively position a product and execute a successful marketing effort will also significantly influence the length and success of its life cycle. Let's take the example of an emerging market, such as the market for smartphones. This industry represents a significant opportunity for a number of mobile phone manufacturers globally. Although many of these manufacturers may enter the market at early stages of market development, not all will be successful. Figure 11.20 provides some potential outcomes for companies involved in this market.

In Figure 11.20, five companies have entered our hypothetical smartphone industry. The orange line represents the industry growth curve for this period from the time of the initial emergence of this industry to the current date. As you can see, companies A, C, and D all entered the industry at its inception. Companies B and E entered a bit later. Company A has ended up being the industry leader, with its growth rate exceeding that of

FIGURE 11.20   Life Cycle Outcomes

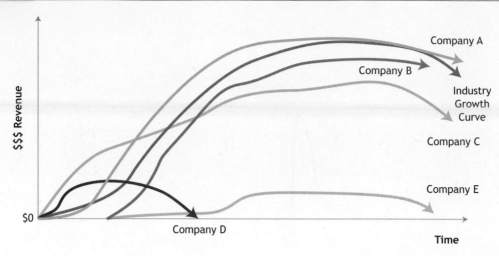

FIGURE 11.20   Life Cycle Outcomes

the industry. Company C initially looked to be the market leader, with a quick growth spurt early on, but then experienced a flattening of sales coinciding roughly with the time that Company B entered the market. Company D had some brief success early on, but then simply was unable to compete, and exited the market. Company B continued to show strength despite being a later entrant into the market, and has ended up #2 and a main market challenger to Company A. Company E, also a late entrant, never really did find a position in the marketplace that customers identified with and, as such, ends up being a marginal player.

Managing across the Life Cycle

Success within the life cycle of a product or service comes down to possessing an effective positioning strategy backed by a successful marketing effort formulated around a meaningful (in the eyes of customers) value proposition. As managers, we need to be able to sense the stage of development not only for our product/service offering, but also for the industry itself. We also need to anticipate competitive actions, coupled with their potential for disruptive innovation, and shifts that can, and most likely will, occur in consumer preferences and/or behaviour. Life cycle management is all about knowing what the key success factors are within each stage (see Figure 11.21), and the potential triggers that will cue managers to the transition in focus that is necessary as the product/service offering shifts from one stage to the next. Having said this, managers also must take care that their actions do not result in a self-fulfilling prophecy. An example of this would be assuming that the marketplace for a particular product or service will soon decline due to the belief that because we are in a mature market, decline is inevitable. Given this belief, the managers then make decisions to pull back on supporting the product, thereby reducing the marketing effort and, ultimately, leading the product or service offering into decline.

> Success within the life cycle of a product or service comes down to possessing an effective positioning strategy backed by a successful marketing effort formulated around a meaningful (in the eyes of customers) value proposition.

FIGURE 11.21 Managing across the Product Life Cycle

	Development	Introduction	Growth	Maturity	Decline
Marketing Objective	Viable product idea. Can be commercialized.	Customer acquisition. Grow market share and required scale. Properly position with primary target audience.	Customer acquisition and customer retention. Grow market share and required scale.	Customer retention and segmentation stretch. Defend market share, and/or seek to create new market space.	Harvest or milk the product. Treat it as a cash cow. Assess possibility to revitalize the product.
Marketing Effort	Test marketing. Pre-launch advertising and publicity. Establish initial channel partners.	Create awareness and profile. Meet expectations. Successful product launch. Define market position and key differentiators.	Create product and brand preference and loyalty. Reinforce early adopters' decisions to buy. Stress differentiation.	Reinforce brand and product differentiation. Increase market penetration and market development activities. Assess potential for product line extensions.	Data mine to determine most profitable customers. Maximize efficiency and effectiveness of expenditures.
Financial	Manage burn rate. Sufficient enough capital.	Manage burn rate. Get to breakeven point. Sufficient capital to cover operating expenses and launch needs.	Achieve breakeven point. Sufficient capital to continue to support product and business system needs.	Maximize return on sales. Maximize the returns on additional incremental investment.	Maintain margins in the face of diminishing volumes. Assess attractive divestiture options.
Profits	Non-existent—no revenue stream	Generally, no profits early on.	Achieve profitability objectives.	Seek profit and ROI maximization.	Maintain profitability for as long as possible
Competitors	First to market concerns. Protecting intellectual property.	Starting to emerge or are already in the market. Who has first mover advantage?	New entrants entering the market. Enhanced product offerings from competitors.	Watch for market consolidation. Assess risk of disruptive innovations.	Look for additional revenue opportunities as competitors exit the market.
Common Stage Transition Triggers	Concept can be shifted to working prototype. Focus groups (customers and suppliers) respond positively to idea. Test marketing meets or exceeds expectations. Pre-launch publicity and promotion generates interest.	Product launch occurs, signalling commercialization. Initial customer acquisition takes place.	Demand for the product accelerates, placing pressure on infrastructure capacity and operating margins. Competitive segmentation activities emerge.	Demand in core markets slows. Repurchase dependency heightens. Competitors further segment the market. Consolidation activity increases. Niche market activities increase.	Repurchase rates slow. Segmentation opportunities diminish. Some competitors exit the market. Consumer trends shift is readily apparent. Innovation opportunities become minimal.

BUSINESS *in Action*

Transportation: Cost Implications (Global Reach)

One only has to look back over the last 10+ years to see the significant impact that globalization has had on the competitive landscape of many commercial sectors. With the rise of the emerging economies (as discussed in Chapter 3), many organizations have sought to take advantage of the market and production-based opportunities that these economies have offered. The end result has been the ability to offer the global consumer more products than ever before at very attractive price points. Taking advantage of outsourcing and the comparative advantages that various countries across the globe offer, businesses have become experts in managing global supply chains. The efficiency and effectiveness of this model has resulted in the development of

complex and highly sophisticated transportation systems predicated on cost efficiencies that enable products to be assembled across the globe and transported to customers at a lower cost than if the products were produced at home. This model, however, has been largely developed around the theory that the additional cost of transportation is more than offset by the savings achieved in labour and other direct product costs that result from producing abroad. The challenge going forward lies in whether this model will hold true in the face of rising standards of living in emerging economies, and the increasing cost of transportation in light of demand and supply issues. As an example, Air Canada estimates that for every dollar increase in oil prices, its fuel costs increase by $25 million on an annualized basis. Transportation costs impact the margins and profitability of companies at all levels of business activity. Emerging economies and their growth have already placed an upward pressure on the cost of commodities. Add to this increased transportation costs to deliver such raw materials to their markets, and the end result is an already higher cost base at the front end of the manufacturing and/or assembly process. These costs then make their way through the distribution channel when transportation costs continue to impact an organization's overall cost base and, therefore, the price that needs to be charged to the final user. As the cost of oil rises, as an example, so, too, does the cost of gasoline, jet fuel, and other product categories that are petroleum based. The upward trend in fuel prices is impacting and will continue to impact trucking companies and their cost of doing business. Although there may be a willingness, perhaps, to absorb short-term increases to remain competitive, these trucking companies will ultimately be required to pass on these costs to buyers. Manufacturers and suppliers will continue to use technology and enhanced transportation modelling in an effort to offset this upward cost creep.

Rising transportation costs also impact the buying capabilities of customers. The global marketplace is driven by the demand for goods and services, with the consumer accounting for a significant portion of this overall demand. Consumer-based goods companies, which are facing upward price pressure given transportation costs, also must recognize that these same cost pressures are being felt by consumers themselves, thereby impacting their propensity and their ability to purchase goods and services. With the price of oil, on a per barrel basis, expected to continue to move upward as the global demand and supply relationship tightens, transportation costs will continue to be front and centre in the minds of managers and marketers, as well as consumers.[14]

Managing a Product Portfolio

LO7

Up to this point, our focus has been on managing a single product. In many organizations, managers are responsible for the growth and financial solvency of an entire product portfolio. This could be with respect to a family of products marketed under a primary brand (Cheerios, Honey-Nut Cheerios, Multi-grain Cheerios), or a series of complementary products such as Frito-Lay snacks (Lay's, Fritos, Doritos, Tostitos, Cheetos, Sun Chips, Rold Gold Pretzels,

Smartfood Popcorn, Cracker Jack, Miss Vickie's).[15] Each product needs to be evaluated and value propositions adjusted and repositioned through continuously focused and refocused marketing communication efforts. As managers, we need to make decisions on where to expand the investment in support of a particular product and/or product line, where to maintain a given level of investment, when to reduce investment (harvest), and, finally, when to divest ourselves of it. This means constantly assessing the market potential of the product or service that we are evaluating, making adjustments to its positioning in the market, and revisiting the marketing communication efforts in a way that reinforces or revitalizes the product and its brand, its awareness, preference, loyalty, and commitment. Portfolio management is all about making decisions on where to invest in order to improve the organization's market position going forward. As managers, one fundamental we can almost always count on is that the resource needs of the organization will exceed our ability to supply such resources. This means that, given the finite nature of our financial and physical resources, and the fact that our needs will exceed our supply, we will continually be pressed to define priorities on where to invest and grow the organization. Decisions relating to this will impact the various products and/or services within our portfolio. As managers, however, our responsibility lies in doing what is best to improve the overall performance of the organization versus any one individual product line. Trade-offs will, ultimately, have to be made. One approach to making decisions relating to where to invest, maintain, harvest, and divest is called the growth/share matrix, made popular by the Boston Consulting Group. This business model suggested that, as a frame of reference in making portfolio management decisions, managers focus on the growth potential of a product relative to the product strength that it currently possesses in the marketplace. A variation of this model is presented in Figure 11.22.[16]

> Portfolio management is all about making decisions on where to invest in order to improve the organization's market position going forward.

Taking the core components of the growth/share matrix, the model presented in Figure 11.22 is designed to focus managers on the core cost/benefit trade-offs that need to be considered given the relationship between market potential and the current market position that a product's value proposition has within the marketplace. This revised model also recognizes that market potential may not always be categorized as high or low, but that a given, acceptable level of market potential may offer managers opportunities to further grow a product line

FIGURE 11.22 Assessing Future Product Potential

		Strong	Weak
Future Market Potential	High	What should be done to further expand our scale and our returns, given our strong market position?	What can we do to change things? Will rebranding or repositioning get us back on track?
	Medium	Is there an opportunity to stretch or tap further into secondary markets to improve returns?	Can we improve "harvesting" or "niche" marketing results by increasing the efficiency and effectiveness of our marketing effort? If not, should we divest?
	Low	Should we simply seek to maximize the "cash cow" effect? Can the dollars being generated be better used elsewhere versus reinvested in this product?	Why are we here? Does divestiture mean that freed resources can be better used elsewhere?

Current Value Proposition Strength

and/or service opportunity via selective strategies. As managers, we need to recognize that growing markets require investment. The key question, however, lies in the return that such an investment can generate over the anticipated life of the product's life cycle. Similarly, products that have failed to achieve acceptable returns should be questioned, with the focus being on either correcting the situation via positioning and renewed marketing effort, or divesting of the product in order to reallocate the resources toward more profitable ventures.

A Note Pertaining to Not-for-Profits

As with for-profit entities, not-for-profit organizations (NFPs) must also be skillful in the execution of their marketing efforts. For not-for-profits, these efforts focus on both communicating the mission of the organization and stimulating and reinforcing the demand for the NFP's products and services. Of significant challenge for the NFP is to be successful in doing this without creating the perception that the NFP has abandoned its altruistic motives for financial purposes. Not-for-profits must also seek to make use of the same tools that for-profit entities use in the creation of their marketing mix. Social networks, focus groups, media-based advertising, and channel partner development are of equal importance in the NFP arena. Utilization of Facebook and other social media sites enables stakeholders to provide a real "voice" in support of the not-for-profit's efforts. Social media sites, organized by the NFP, provide a viable, low-cost opportunity for communicating the organization's community activities, and solicit requests for assistance on meaningful objectives organized by the not-for-profit. For the NFP, the key components for survival lie in the ability of the organization to achieve rootedness within the community and vitality through membership, philanthropic gifts, and the meaningful delivery of its services in support of its mission. To successfully accomplish this, the NFP needs to achieve the same outcomes as for-profit organizations with respect to brand recognition and a value proposition that is judged by its customers and users to be superior to those of other for-profits and NFPs competing for the same dollars. Sustainable business models, even in the not-for-profit sector, are built around the four pillars of marketing. The life cycle of an NFP is subject to the same market pressures as those of companies and products in the for-profit sector. Failure to communicate and deliver a meaningful solution to a need can result in the desertion of support from both monetary and altruistic stakeholders.

> Sustainable business models, even in the not-for-profit sector, are built around the four pillars of marketing.

Management Reflection—Managing the Marketing Effort

The effective execution of an organization's marketing mix is one of the critical success factors that managers must focus on in their bid to ensure the immediate and long-term health of their organization. Profits and profitability come from satisfied customers who have received value as a result of their purchase experience. In planning an organization's overall strategy, and in executing the tactics associated with it, committed expenses often precede operating performance. Recognizing this, managers must be sure of the direction that the organization is taking in positioning its products and services and of the effective execution of its marketing effort. In many sectors in today's marketplace, the choices that customers have have never been greater. This explosion of choice has required organizations to further customize their product and/or service offerings in order to create uniqueness and improve the overall perception of the importance of their product in solving a customer's problem. Doing so, however, results in an even finer segmentation and target market slicing and dicing approach.

Driven by this need to specialize in order to create enhanced differentiation, marketers and managers also increase the probability of error that the alignment executed will not yield the required success results. In many product and/or service categories, customer expectations are such that many believe the perfect solution to their needs and/or problems must exist. For managers and marketers, this results in a growing complexity of how to position and market. It also means that the ability to create brand profile, preference, and commitment are becoming more fundamental to the success in many product and service categories. Faced with an almost endless number of choices, customer decision making has become so overwhelming, in some cases, that those customers are often forced to default to the most familiar brand and/or the one that is most easily accessible. As managers, we need to recognize the demands that all of these interrelated pressures are placing on our ability to be successful in the delivery of products and services in the segments in which we are marketing. Being at the top of the predetermined purchase list at the time of the purchase decision is paramount to our success. For the customer, in some ways it may not matter whom they choose—as long as they choose. For us as managers, whom they choose is core to our sustainability and success. Our marketing mix needs to communicate why that choice should be us.

Chapter Summary

This chapter focuses on understanding the marketing effort that we, as managers, will need to direct in order to ensure a successful execution of our marketing strategy. A core emphasis in this chapter is on understanding the key fundamental elements associated with developing our value proposition, price position, distribution approach, and communication tactics, which are critical to the success of products and services associated with our organization. The recognition of the importance of brand power, as well as the influence of price on the purchase decision-making process, is a key component of this discussion. The distribution tactical discussion is supported by commentary associated with channel selection requirements and the integration of sales support and channel intermediary decision-making involvement in the product/service delivery process. The chapter also revisits the concept of the "marketer's tool box" from Chapter 10, adding to this discussion the integration of these tools with the concepts of segmentation, target marketing, customer profiling, and value proposition development into a rifled communication message, which results in the product and/or service being offered as the best "fit" for responding to a customer's needs. The chapter then transitions into a discussion of the key stages of a product and/or service's life cycle, and how we, as managers, can and should manage this process, defining the key objectives to be achieved within each stage and cueing us to the required tactical marketing shifts that will influence our success. An extension of this discussion is a broadening of our responsibilities to actively assess, on an ongoing basis, the overall market potential of our entire portfolio of products, drawing conclusions as to where to invest, expand, maintain, retrench, and divest, depending on overall current product strength and future market potential. The chapter closes with a note relating to the importance of not-for-profits to recognize that the four pillars of marketing (marketing mix) are fundamental to their success as well, along with the importance of maintaining their balance between altruistic mission requirements and the economic realities of financial stability and sustainability.

 Developing Business Knowledge and Skills

KEY TERMS

marketing mix   *p. 279*

predetermined purchase list   *p. 282*

price elasticity   *p. 286*

consumer price threshold   *p. 287*

payback period   *p. 287*

direct distribution   *p. 289*

channel intermediary   *p. 289*

indirect distribution   *p. 290*

mixed distribution systems   *p. 290*

private label brands   *p. 291*

multi-channel distribution   *p. 291*

intensive distribution   *p. 292*

convenience goods   *p. 292*

selective distribution   *p. 293*

exclusive distribution   *p. 294*

profit leaks   *p. 295*

message rifling   *p. 296*

QUESTIONS FOR DISCUSSION

1. What are the four pillars of marketing? How do these pillars (marketing mix elements) combine to create an organization's marketing effort?

2. The average supermarket can offer 40 000+ items to its customers. A quick look at the market can identify as many as 90 different types of shampoos and almost 100 different varieties of toothpaste. One manufacturer of orange juice has over 20 different varieties itself. What does this say about the importance of branding in today's marketplace?

3. What are the two primary ways in which managers can seek to respond to the globally driven downward pressure on price? Of the two, which do you feel is the more effective? Why? If your answer is "it depends on the situation," then what key positioning indicators would determine which route you would take?

4. What are the four key fundamental factors that managers need to assess when determining what price to charge for an organization's products and/or services?

5. The distribution of products and/or services can impose upon an organization some of its largest transaction costs. How do channel intermediaries assist in reducing these costs for manufacturers and suppliers?

6. What do you believe are the key marketing objectives that managers need to focus on within each stage of a product and/or service's life cycle? Given your response, where would you focus your marketing effort in order to ensure that these identified objectives are met?

QUESTIONS FOR INDIVIDUAL ACTION

Choose a product or service that was recently introduced into the marketplace, but was then pulled from the market by the company. Why did the company cease offering this product and/or service? Based on your knowledge of marketing, what, in your mind, was the fundamental reason for this product and/or service failure? Was it due to poor positioning, an ineffective execution of the marketing mix, or a combination of the two? Be prepared to present your analytical findings to your fellow classmates.

TEAM EXERCISE

As a team, identify a not-for-profit organization in your city or town that you have some familiarity with. Research its current use of social marketing media in communicating its mission and message to its community stakeholders. How effective do you believe its social media approach is? What recommendations would you make to this NFP to improve its use of this communication tool? Create a fundraising idea for this NFP and provide an outline as to how you would implement a social media marketing campaign in support of it. Prepare a presentation outlining your fundraising idea and the social media campaign that you have developed in support of it.

Case for Discussion

At 6 feet 5 inches, Peter Simons is an imposing figure. Peter, who heads up the Quebec-based retail chain known by his family's name (Simons), is getting ready for a major shift in the company's strategy. Up to this point a regional player in the retail clothing sector, Peter and his management team are looking west and south. With sales exceeding $300 million, this privately held company is poised to move beyond Quebec, with ideas of becoming a major player in the Canadian retail sector; a sector that is becoming increasingly crowded, with a number of U.S.-based players looking north in an effort to realize their own growth objectives.

Founded in 1840, Simons currently has seven stores operating in Quebec. Their plan is to add 12 additional stores to their banner across Canada, and then, assuming things go well, look south to the United States. A geographic-niche player that has had success with a strategy of cheap-chic styles alongside more expensive designer lines, Simons sees a real opportunity to duplicate its regional success into English Canada. Although small in size (compared to its major competitors such as The Bay), Simons is an experienced and efficient operator. The organization, in fact, is one of the most productive retailers in Canada. Simons generates more than $600 of sales on a per-square-foot basis, as much as three times the volume of its main competitors.[17] This is an astounding feat considering that Simons stores, on average, exceed 100 000 square feet, thereby placing them in the megastore category. Set to open its first English Canada store in 2013 in Edmonton (West Edmonton Mall), Simons also is currently assessing location opportunities in Toronto, Ottawa, and Calgary. Why the decision to move forward now with expansion plans? Peter knows that the waves of competition in Canada are only going to become more turbulent. Minneapolis, Minnesota–based Target has announced it is coming to Canada, with initial store openings slated for 2013. Kohl's, one of the fastest growing U.S. retailers, has also indicated a desire to come north. Add to this the already entrenched Walmart and a host of other recently arrived and soon-to-come competitors (Marshalls, Victoria's Secret, J. Crew, J.C. Penney, etc.), and one can see that the market is going to get very busy very quickly. It is not just U.S.-based retailers that Simons needs to think about. Canadian-based Loblaw Companies Ltd., as an example, has announced plans to open 20 stand-alone Joe Fresh stores across Canada, beginning with three in Ontario and one in Alberta in 2011.[18] Despite all of this new retail activity, Simons still sees an opportunity to expand and grow. Their advantage lies in their ability to couple value-based pricing with distinctive and unique fashions created by talented, yet relatively unknown, designers. Each store also has a different design, to eliminate the cookie-cutter store layout approach used by most of the major retail players. For Simons, it is all about creating a unique shopping atmosphere. Industry analysts recognize that Simons is very good at what it does, and the company has demonstrated solid success up to this point. The question is whether it can successfully grow the chain, as Peter envisions, in a market that is becoming increasingly infiltrated by major U.S.-based retail players.

QUESTIONS

Using the four pillars of a successful marketing effort, outline what you believe are the key success factors at which Simons, as an organization, will need to excel if it is to be successful in its venture outside of Quebec. Create a value-proposition statement for Simons that you believe will be attractive to English Canadians. Identify the critical challenges that Simons will face as it seeks to expand outside of Quebec.

For more information on Simons, visit www.simons.com.

Practise and learn online with Connect. Connect resources include additional and interactive study exercises, videos, and practice quizzing, as well as additional material you won't find in the printed text.

12 Cost-Base Analysis and Pricing

Learning Objectives

This chapter is designed to provide students with:

Lo1 An exposure to the composition of an organization's cost base

Lo2 A familiarity with the two fundamental categories of an organization's operating costs (variable and fixed)

Lo3 An understanding of the importance of the relationship between variable and fixed costs within an organization's total cost structure

Lo4 Recognition of the importance of the ability to understand an organization's breakeven point and the process associated with its identification

Lo5 An understanding of the value of recognizing a product or service's optimal price point

Lo6 An overview of the key impact factors associated with setting prices for the products and services an organization offers

Snapshot—What to Expect in This Chapter

As identified by the learning objectives, this chapter focuses on understanding business concepts and practices associated with cost-base analysis and pricing. The content emphasized in this chapter includes the following:

- Understanding the Organization's Cost Base
  - The Composition of an Organization's Cost Base

- The Concept of Breakeven Point Analysis (BEP)
  - Using BEP to Understand Profit Objectives
  - Using BEP to Ensure That Full Cash Flow Needs Are Realized
  - Using BEP to Assist in the Setting of Price

- Mark-up Pricing and Other Pricing Considerations
  - Additional Comments Relating to Pricing

- Management Reflection—The Importance of Cost-Base Analysis

From the Student's Perspective

When entering the boardroom or seating yourself behind the CEO desk for the first time, you might have a vision of how to increase sales or how to steal market share from your main competitor. Maybe you dream of introducing a sensational and pioneering product to the market. It is indeed great to have visions, but maximizing revenues or having the best product is, unfortunately, not enough to become a successful manager. The cost side of the income statement may not always be as exciting as the revenue side; however, it is worth more than just a brief look.

Unsurprisingly, every company wants to make its products as profitable as possible by squeezing costs while keeping the prices high; however, there is more to understanding the cost base than minimizing the costs. Is the company able to adjust production without cutting margins when facing an economic recession? How many units must be sold in order to cover the costs and make the new product profitable? To what extent do the costs and profit depend upon your company's decisions rather than external events that it cannot control? These are just a few of the essential questions you will be able to answer if you understand your organization's cost base and its composition. Finally, it is worth mentioning that it is generally easier to reduce your own costs by a dollar than increasing sales by a dollar. In other words, the ability to manage your costs can be one possible shortcut to success when managing your organization.

Niklas Flofsam graduated from Uppsala University (Sweden) in 2010 with a Master of Law degree and a Bachelor of Business degree. Niklas was an international student at Queen's School of Business in 2009, and he is currently working as an associate at a major business law firm in Sweden.

BUSINESS *in Action*

Air Canada's Cost Transformation Program (CTP)

As with many players in the North American airline industry, Air Canada continues in its quest to return to profitability. The recession of 2008-09 significantly impacted air travel revenue, just as it impacted many other major business sectors. Although still "in the red," reporting 2009 fourth-quarter losses of $83 million, Air Canada is headed in the right direction, as this 2009 reported loss is a much improved position over its 2008 fourth-quarter operating performance where the company lost $146 million. Although 2009 fourth-quarter revenue per average seat mile flown (RASM) was down 7 percent, when compared to the same period in 2008, Air Canada has been able to offset this revenue reduction through improvements in cost management and the resulting reductions in its cost base. Recognizing the challenges that the company (and the industry) was anticipated to face throughout the period of 2009 to 2011 (due to the financial crisis and the recession), Air Canada, in mid-2009, launched its Cost Transformation Program, or CTP. The key objective of this program was to deliver company-wide cost savings through the implementation of effective cost controls throughout the organization, thereby protecting its operating margin in the face of decreasing revenues. The program targeted cost savings of $50 million in 2009, $250 million in 2010, and $500 million in 2011. For many airline carriers, their largest expense lines are fuel, wages and benefits expense, and aircraft maintenance. With fuel prices largely uncontrollable due to the volatility of oil prices, Air Canada's CTP program sought to initiate cost savings from contract improvements with suppliers and other operating partners, salary and benefit reductions, and operational process and productivity improvements. Now one year into its Cost Transformation Program, Air Canada is seeing solid signs of improvement. Its costs per average seat mile (CASM) decreased by 3.2 percent versus those in fourth-quarter 2008, without taking fuel savings (due to the lower price of oil) into consideration. When adding fuel savings to the equation, CASM decreased by 9.8 percent. Targeting CTP annual savings, in 2009, of $50 million, actual results were $20 million better, providing Air Canada with $70 million in savings. The company has indicated that it is also on track in meeting its 2010 objective of $250 million, and remains optimistic that it will also achieve its 2011 objective of $500 million in cost savings. Air Canada's management team credits CTP with assisting in stabilizing the company's financial situation during what has been a very difficult economic period. The improvements in cost performance and productivity are key drivers in improving Air Canada's operational performance. When reviewing full-year results for 2009, Air Canada reported a net loss of $24 million, a significant turnaround over the net loss of $1.03 billion recorded in 2008. Air Canada anticipates that it will continue to reduce its CASM (excluding fuel expenses) by 3 percent to 5 percent per year for 2010 and 2011. These actions, combined with initiatives taken to better manage fuel price volatility (hedging techniques) and

a stronger Canadian dollar, should enable Air Canada to get back to operational breakeven. Air Canada remains cautiously optimistic on the revenue side. The company visualizes a slow, but steady, recovery in passenger demand, with average seat mile (ASM) capacity growing by 1.5 percent to 2.5 percent in 2010. A key concern, however, in this regard remains the ability of the industry to move beyond fare discounting as a core mechanism for stimulating traffic.[1]

WEB INTEGRATION

To learn more about Air Canada's progress in moving the company toward profitability, visit **www. googlefinance.com** and type in Air Canada, or go to Air Canada's Web site at **www.aircanada.com**.

Understanding the Organization's Cost Base

LO1, LO2, LO3

One of the fundamental requirements for managers is to understand the configuration of the cost base of the organization for which they are developing strategies, making operations decisions, and, ultimately, determining where and how the organization is to compete in today's marketplace. A key element of this process is to identify the various costs that the organization will face, the percentage impact that key cost areas have on the total cost base of the organization, and the degree of controllability that managers have, in the near term, on costs being incurred. Having a good understanding of such cost base information will enable managers to better assess their financial options in the event of unexpected changes in market dynamics, unanticipated reductions in revenue, and strategic positioning shifts that the organization is planning.

In order to develop a good understanding of an organization's cost base, managers need to focus on the following:

1. The make-up of their cost base.
2. The percentage of the cost base that lies within their control in the near term.
3. The market pressures that will impact the cost base going forward.
4. The volume and dollar requirements necessary to achieve breakeven.
5. Evaluating their cost structure with respect to "good" costs versus "bad" costs.
6. Evaluating their costs in comparison to the cost base of their competitors.

> Having a good understanding of cost base information will enable managers to better assess their financial options in the event of unexpected changes in market dynamics, unanticipated reductions in revenue, and strategic positioning shifts that the organization is planning.

The Composition of an Organization's Cost Base

In simple terms, an organization's cost base is made up of the total costs associated with delivering the organization's products or services to the marketplace. A good way to think about the composition of this cost base is in terms of all the costs (across all value chain components) an organization incurs as it manufactures, distributes, markets, and sells products to other businesses or to consumers such as you and me. Assume that your company (XYZ Corporation) manufactures electronic sensors, which, following fabrication, are sold to other businesses that then place these sensors into finished products that are sold to the marketplace at large. In this example, the cost base of the XYZ Corporation would be made up of the various costs identified in Figure 12.1 below.

As managers, we need to understand the cost structure within each of these areas. This enables us to fully understand the costs incurred in producing and supporting each sensor, a critical requirement in determining, ultimately, what price to charge for the sensors we are manufacturing. In addition to recognizing the costs incurred within each of these areas, we also need to determine whether these costs are directly involved in the manufacturing process (called direct or variable costs) or whether they are operational support costs (indirect, fixed, or semi-fixed costs) that exist because we are in business, but that are not directly tied to the creation of the product (in this case, our sensor). Figure 12.2 provides an easy formula for analyzing an organization's cost base.

In analyzing the composition of an organization's cost base, there are two fundamental conclusions that we, as managers, hope to identify:

1. The percentage of our costs that are considered to be direct or variable costs versus the percentage that are considered to be indirect (fixed or semi-fixed).
2. The cost areas (if any) that make up a significant percentage of our overall cost base.

FIGURE 12.1   Cost Base: XYZ Sensor Organization

Procurement of Parts → Manufacturing Costs → Distribution Costs → Marketing and Sales Costs → Administration Costs → Post-Purchase Service and Support Costs

FIGURE 12.2   Computing the Total Cost Base

VARIABLE VERSUS FIXED COSTS

Variable Costs (also referred to as direct costs) are those costs that are directly tied to the manufacturing of a product or the delivery of a service depending on the type of business being assessed.

As noted above, **variable costs** (also referred to as direct costs) are those costs that are directly tied to the manufacturing of a product or the delivery of a service depending on the type of business being assessed. Common examples of variable or direct costs are the cost of materials that are used in the manufacturing of a product, the direct labour costs associated with this transformation process, and distribution costs associated with getting the product to the right customer at the right place at the right time. As an example, let's assume that we manufacture and distribute laptop computers (think of Dell Inc.). The variable or direct costs associated with the manufacturing and distribution of laptops would include the following:

- The cost of the components that are used in the laptop (memory chips, processors, video cards, etc.)

- The cost of the labour needed to assemble each laptop

- The cost of the packaging the laptop is shipped in

- The shipping costs associated with delivering the laptop to the customer (retailer, or direct customer)

A good way to think about variable costs is that, in terms of our laptop example, in the event that we stopped manufacturing laptops these costs would disappear. If we no longer manufactured laptops, we would have no need to purchase the components, hire people to assemble them, or incur shipping costs, because we would no longer be selling them.

Fixed Costs (also referred to as indirect costs) are those costs that, although not directly tied to the manufacturing of a specific product or the delivery of a specified service, nonetheless exist as a result of conducting our business and operating our company.

Fixed costs (also referred to as indirect costs) are those costs that, although not directly tied to the manufacturing of a specific product or the delivery of a specified service, nonetheless exist as a result of conducting our business and operating our company. Examples of fixed or indirect costs—which a business must account for in its cost base and must, therefore, ensure are incorporated into its pricing strategy—are insurance, utilities, interest expense on debt, and administration costs. An additional uniqueness of fixed costs is that these costs represent an expense that is, for the most part, uncontrollable in the near term. This means that managers have little ability to change the amount of the expense. As an example, if you sign a five-year lease for a building that obligates you to lease payments of $5000 per month, then you have little ability to modify this monthly payment during the lease period regardless of the success of your business. The amount owed during the lease period ($5000/month) is, in essence, fixed. Another type of indirect cost that should be assessed is called *committed costs*. These are costs that the organization commits itself to within an operating year, and that often are spent in advance or at the front end of a manufacturing/sales cycle. Examples of a committed cost would be the marketing costs associated with launching a new product or service, advertising expenditures designed to further promote a product or service, software technology upgrades within a given year, and research and development costs that the organization has committed to spending. When analyzing an organization's fixed or indirect cost base, think in terms of the equation shown in Figure 12.3.

With an understanding of the types of costs we are looking for, organizations will now seek to build an understanding of their cost base. This is accomplished by working through

FIGURE 12.3 Computing the Indirect Cost Base of an Organization

Fixed Costs **+** Committed Current Period Costs **=** An Organization's Indirect Cost Base

the various zones within an organization's value chain and determining the cost composition of each. A good way to think of this is in terms of a ladder, with each rung of the ladder representing a cost zone. By working through these areas and identifying the cost structure within each, we can identify the total costs that an organization will incur in delivering its products and/or services to the marketplace (see Figure 12.4).

Going back to our original equation, which states that Variable Costs + Fixed Costs = Total Costs, we can also get a pictorial feel for what our total cost base looks like at various production and sales levels (see Figure 12.5). As the following section ("Degree of Managerial Control") will illustrate, it is important to understand this relationship, as it does impact the degree of control that a management team has over its cost base. Understanding an organization's cost base is essential in determining the required pricing strategy that will be utilized in the marketing of a product and its corresponding impact on profit.

> Understanding an organization's cost base is essential to determining the required pricing strategy that will be utilized in marketing the product and its corresponding impact on profit.

DEGREE OF MANAGERIAL CONTROL

In addition to identifying the various types of costs associated with an organization's cost base, managers must also understand how the composition of this cost base (relationship between variable and fixed costs to the total cost base) will influence their ability to manage

FIGURE 12.4 Cost Ladder

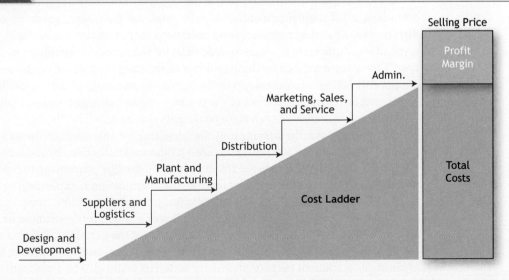

Source: Based on *The Definitive Business Plan*, Richard Stutely, 2nd Edition, Prentice Hall, 2007.

FIGURE 12.5 Total Cost-Base Composition

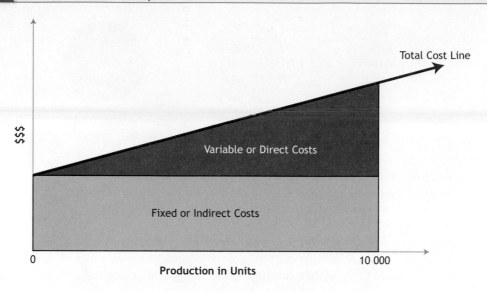

their company. In general, the more the cost base is composed of variable or direct costs, the more control managers have over the actual management of this cost base on a day-to-day basis. Conversely, the more the cost base is composed of fixed or indirect costs, the more difficult it is for managers to use cost-reduction strategies to protect the organization's profitability in response to decreases in demand for products and services and their corresponding reductions in revenue. To illustrate this, let's look at a couple of examples of organizations with differing cost structures.

> The more the cost base is composed of fixed or indirect costs, the more difficult it is for managers to use cost-reduction strategies to protect the organization's profitability in response to decreases in demand for products and services and their corresponding reductions in revenue.

Let's first return to our discussion of the laptop manufacturer. Manufacturing operations often have a substantial percentage of their total cost base being made up of variable (or direct) costs. By nature, manufacturing operations are production focused and, therefore, can respond fairly quickly to downturns in demand for their products simply by reducing production. This is accomplished by shutting down or reducing the volume on the production line, temporarily laying off workers, and reducing future purchases of the materials and components used in the manufacturing of the product sold by the organization. Figure 12.6 shows the initial configuration of such an organization's cost base.

Let's now make the assumption that demand for the product drops by 25 percent (from 10 000 units to 7500 units). Figure 12.7 demonstrates that, by reducing production, the total cost line will be reduced (from A1 to A2), thereby attempting to balance the costs of the organization with the loss of revenue the organization is experiencing (as a result of moving from 10 000 units to 7500 units). Yes, profitability will be impacted, as the fixed costs that were being paid for through the sales of 10 000 units must now be redistributed across 7500 units, but the organization is able to save the variable (direct) costs of producing 2500 fewer units. Given that a significant level of the costs are variable, the utilization of cheaper component parts or packaging materials could also be a mechanism for further reducing the total cost base of the organization, in the near term, in order to maintain an acceptable level of profitability.[2]

FIGURE 12.6   Manufacturing Operation with Significant Variable Cost Zone

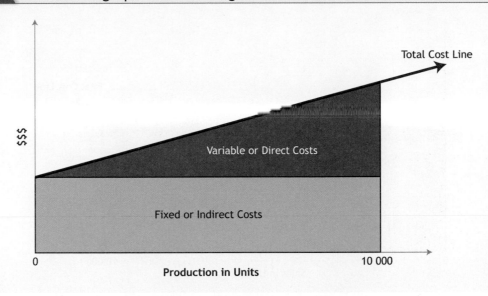

FIGURE 12.7   Manufacturing Operation with Significant Variable Cost Zone: Reduced Production

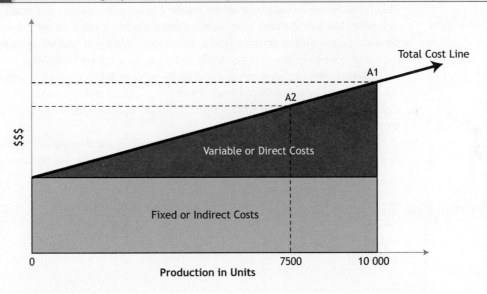

For our second example, let's shift our focus to that of a retail operation. In retail (as well as in many service-focused operations), the ability to reduce costs in the face of reduced demand is more difficult in the short term. This is because retail operations, by the nature of their business model and cost configuration, have a higher percentage of their cost base made up of fixed or indirect costs. As they are not manufacturing products but rather reselling finished goods and/or services, their expenses are largely made up of costs such as lease expenses, utilities, and core staffing levels, which are based more on the hours the business is open than on the number of units being sold. Given this, their cost configuration looks more like that shown in Figure 12.8.

Unlike our laptop manufacturer in our first example, again, the retail operation does not have the same flexibility to reduce costs in the short term in the event of a reduction in

FIGURE 12.8   Retail Operation with Significant Fixed Cost Zone

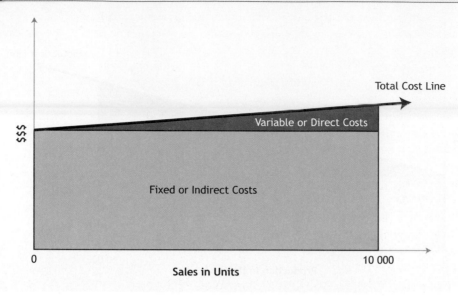

demand, as most of their cost base is made up of fixed or indirect costs. The reduction in sales, from 10 000 units to 7500 units, has little impact on the total cost line (see Figure 12.9). This is because the cost of the actual product being sold makes up a small percentage of the cost base. Most of the cost base, as mentioned above, is made up of expenses, such as store lease costs, minimum staffing levels, and so on. Also, for retailers leasing space in malls, reducing operating hours is generally not an option (given their lease contracts). The end result is that, although revenue is down by 25 percent, total cost reductions cannot be used to offset the reduction in sales volumes. For retailers, small reductions in sales volumes can have significant impact on the profitability of the organization. This is due to its largely fixed near-term cost structure.

At this stage, we have attempted to keep our discussion very general and quite simplistic. The impact of the configuration of an organization's cost base will be made clearer later on in

FIGURE 12.9   Retail Operation with Significant Fixed Cost Zone: Reduced Sales

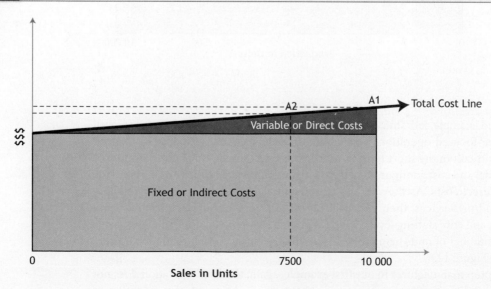

this chapter when we discuss the concept of breakeven. Prior to this discussion, however, it should be noted that our commentary up to this point has been with a singular focus (that of cost-base mechanics). It is important to understand, as well, that market dynamics will influence the composition and overall competitiveness of an organization's cost base. The global marketplace brings to the customer increasing options in terms of both the depth and width of product choices available to meet their specific needs. With increasing choice comes greater price awareness and sensitivity on the part of consumers. Quality, uniqueness, importance, and overall value are continually being assessed by customers against the prices that companies are charging. The ability to manage one's cost base more efficiently and effectively than competitors can lead to competitive advantage, resulting in greater market share and/or profitability. Specialization is also impacting the marketplace, with many manufacturers relying on key suppliers to produce the needed components and/or services to support their manufacturing operations and the products/services that they sell in the marketplace. Dependency on suppliers for critical components can also impact and/or restrict a management team's ability to control costs. The end result is that the ability to manage an organization's cost base is not limited to the relationship between variable costs (VC) and fixed costs (FC). It is also dependent on the ability of management to have flexibility and choice in adjusting these costs in order to effectively support and execute an organization's corporate and business-level strategies. This has to be further assessed against competitor product offerings and cost-base advantages in order to, ultimately, determine where and how to compete.

> The ability to manage an organization's cost base is not limited to the relationship between variable costs and fixed costs, but also is dependent on the ability of management to have flexibility and choice in adjusting these costs in order to effectively support and execute an organization's corporate and business-level strategies.

BUSINESS *in Action*

What Is the Best Way to Cut Costs?

As one would anticipate, a large percentage of companies have had to cut costs in the face of the financial crisis of 2008, the recession of 2009, and the slow economic recovery occurring in 2010. With a number of industry sectors facing percentage revenue reductions in the double-digit range, the need to assess cost allocations in order to maintain organizational liquidity and solvency has become almost a quarterly standard operating procedure for many senior-level executives. With this in mind, and recognizing that almost all companies will need or desire to cut costs at some time during their life cycle, the question becomes what is the most effective way to do so. The answer is to enter into cost-cutting discussions with a mindset that ensures cost-cutting decisions and tendencies remain aligned with the organization's overall strategy. Although it may be easier, in the perceived interest of fairness and equity, to indicate that cost reductions should be made across the entire organization at an agreed-upon rate (say, for example, 10 percent), such an approach and action generally does not result in the most effective support of the organization's strategic intent. The key to cost cutting is to ensure that actions focused on reducing the cost base of the organization do not impact the sources of value (called value cells) that the organization relies on to compete in the marketplace. In the McKinsey & Company article "A Better Way to Cut Costs," authors Dennis Layton and Risto Penttinen suggest that there is a best-practice process organizations can follow when considering cost-reduction tactics. This approach advises managers, when restructuring, to be sure to restructure with the future of the company in mind. This means thinking about the current business model and its applicability to the future, as defined by the organization's strategy. This will result in the decision-making process focusing on the applicability of the structure to support the critical value chain processes in those areas of the organization that are core to its revenue generation future, and to ensure that resources are not depleted from these areas. It also means, when considering cuts to what is perceived to be the "fat" of the organization, to, again, ensure that the cuts

made do not erode productivity standards or accountability, or eliminate vital processes, functions, or activities, especially within value cell zones. Managers need to think in terms of eliminating redundancies, low-value activities, and management layers in a way that does not impede the ability of the organization to remain competitive. Finally, cost-cutting should be built around the concept of building capabilities, not destroying them. Decisions need to focus on redirecting resources to reinforce and enhance the organization's strengths and, where weaknesses do exist, to reduce resource allocation initiatives in a way that makes sense and does not jeopardize the organization's overall competitive ability. This process means that managers need to determine where they foresee future potential gain and marketplace strength, and build the organization around these value centres (cells). It goes without saying that cutting costs is never easy. For managers, however, developing such decisions around the organization's strategy and clearly articulating the link between cost cuts and resource reallocation, and communicating this to the organization's employee base, will enable such cuts to be better understood and accepted. The results of such an approach should also better position the company for the future than would be the case with an across-the-board "cuts" approach designed to have everyone share the same level of pain.[3]

The Concept of Breakeven Point Analysis (BEP)

LO4, LO5

Breakeven Point (BEP) is the level of sales revenue or volume that is required for the organization to cover all of its costs.

A critical outcome of analyzing an organization's cost base is taking this information and utilizing it to determine the level of revenue required for the organization to break even. The **breakeven point (BEP)** is the level of sales revenue or volume required for the organization to cover all of its costs. It is most easily thought of as that point where the total revenue of the organization equals its total costs, resulting in a profit of $0 (see Figure 12.10).

For managers, the breakeven point is considered to be the minimum acceptable position for the business in the short term. Operating below the breakeven point means that the organization is operating in a loss position and, therefore, would need to draw upon its cash reserves and/or access to external cash resources (debt financing or equity financing) in order to assist in covering its expenses. If the organization did not possess sufficient cash reserves, and did not have access to additional cash from external sources, the end result could be insolvency and business closure. Operating at breakeven point does mean that total costs are being covered. It also means, however, that the organization is not making a profit. This lack

FIGURE 12.10 Breakeven Point

Minimum Acceptable Position for the Short Term

of profit could result in the organization not generating future cash reserves and resources to cover such things as equipment replacement, new product development, and other strategic initiatives deemed essential to the long-term sustainability of the organization. Businesses, of course, need to earn current-period profits and sustain ongoing profitability in order to ensure their long-term success. The ability for managers to understand the sales volume(s) it takes to reach breakeven is an important part of the process of setting profitability objectives. Computing an organization's BEP is a two-step process:

- Step #1 is to estimate (within a degree of decision-making credibility) an organization's costs, and determine the nature of these costs (variable or fixed costs).

- Step #2 is to take this cost analysis and incorporate it into the breakeven point formula in order to effectively calculate the BEP for the organization. Keep in mind, again, that BEP is that point where total sales revenue equals total costs.

Looking back to earlier in this chapter, and with reference to our initial discussion of cost-base analysis, we attempted to define what the cost base for a given organization would look like. This was initially shown in Figure 12.5, and is repeated below as Figure 12.11.

> Breakeven point (BEP) is considered to be the minimum acceptable position for the business in the short term.

Breakeven point analysis takes this information and adds to it the anticipated revenue of the organization, based on its intended selling price, for the volume of units to be manufactured and sold. The point where the revenue from the sales of the products (units) offered to the marketplace equals the total costs (variable costs + fixed costs) associated with producing these products (units) is the breakeven point, as illustrated in Figure 12.12.

On the graph shown in Figure 12.12, the BEP is illustrated for this fictional company and production situation. At BEP, the volume being produced and sold by the organization, at its current selling price, is sufficient to cover its costs. Volumes of production above this point would yield a profit (assuming that they were sold), while volumes and sales below BEP would mean that the organization is not generating enough revenue to produce a profit for the firm. This is due to the fact that the revenue flowing into the firm (represented by the sales revenue line) is insufficient to cover all the costs (variable and fixed) that the firm is incurring as a result of being in business.

FIGURE 12.11   Total Cost-Base Composition

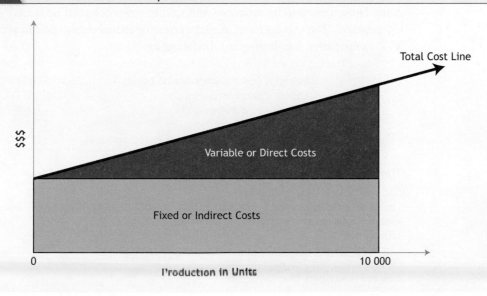

FIGURE 12.12   Breakeven Point (BEP)

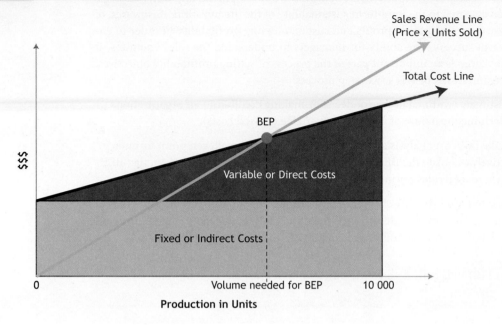

CALCULATING BEP IN UNITS

Computing BEP is relatively easy once the costs of the organization have been determined and the allocation between variable costs (direct costs) and fixed costs (indirect costs) is understood. Whether the BEP calculation seeks to develop the breakeven point based on the number of units that need to be produced and sold or based on the total amount of revenue that needs to be generated is often determined by how the costs are best understood by the organization's management team. If costs are generally looked at on a per unit basis, as one would generally find in manufacturing operations, then calculating BEP in units may be the easiest approach. If costs are best understood as a percentage of sales revenue, then calculating BEP in dollars makes the best sense. Our intent is to illustrate both approaches. We will, however, start with the formula calculation that provides BEP in units.

For illustration purposes, let's again go back to our laptop manufacturer. Assume that the XYZ Corporation is a manufacturer of laptops. Its management team wants to know how many laptops need to be produced and sold to cover the total operating costs of the XYZ Corporation. The management team, in assessing the total costs of this product line for the XYZ Corporation, has determined the following:

Material costs (components) per unit	$ 80.00
Labour costs per unit	$ 20.00
Packaging costs per unit	$ 6.00
Shipping costs per unit	$ 9.00
Total Variable Costs (direct costs) per unit	$115.00

The fixed or indirect costs have been calculated and determined to be:

Plant overhead (utilities, insurance, service contracts, maintenance, etc.)	$1 500 000
Administration costs (payroll, accounting, IT, etc.)	$2 000 000
R&D costs	$ 500 000
Marketing costs (promotions, advertising, branding, etc.)	$1 500 000
Interest expense on debt	$ 500 000
Total Fixed Costs (indirect costs)	$6 000 000

XYZ Corporation sells its laptops to retailers, such as Best Buy, Future Shop, and Staples, which then resell the computers to individual customers. XYZ Corporation's average selling price (ASP) for its laptops is $240 per unit. The question is how many units XYZ Corporation must produce and sell in order to break even (keep in mind that BEP is where profit equals $0).

The BEP formula is as follows:

$$BEP \text{ (units)} = \frac{\text{Total Fixed Costs}}{\text{(Selling Price per Unit} - \text{Variable Costs per Unit)}}$$

$$BEP \text{ (units)} = \frac{\$6\,000\,000}{\$240 - \$115} = 48\,000 \text{ units}$$

In order for the XYZ Corporation to break even, it must produce and sell 48 000 units at an average selling price of $240 (see Figure 12.13).

Once the BEP (in units) is determined, the BEP (in $$$) can easily be calculated by multiplying the BEP (in units) by the selling price. In this situation, the required sales volume needed to break even would be 48 000 × $240 = $11 520 000.

If XYZ Corporation fails to sell at least 48 000 units at an average selling price of $240 per unit, it will suffer an operating loss. If it can produce and sell more than 48 000 units at an average selling price of $240 per unit, then it will enjoy an operating profit.

Keep in mind that selling prices and costs do not remain static, but change over time. This means that managers need to continually reassess their breakeven position in order to understand how changes to their cost structure or to their selling price will impact BEP. As an example, assume that, due to price increases in the cost of components and agreed-upon wage increases to employees, the variable cost (direct cost) of producing a laptop increases to $125 per unit. How does this impact BEP?

$$BEP \text{ (units)} = \frac{\text{Total Fixed Costs}}{\text{(Selling Price per Unit} - \text{Variable Costs per Unit)}}$$

$$BEP \text{ (units)} = \frac{\$6\,000\,000}{\$240 - \$125} = 52\,174 \text{ units}$$

FIGURE 12.13 XYZ Corporation: BEP (Units)

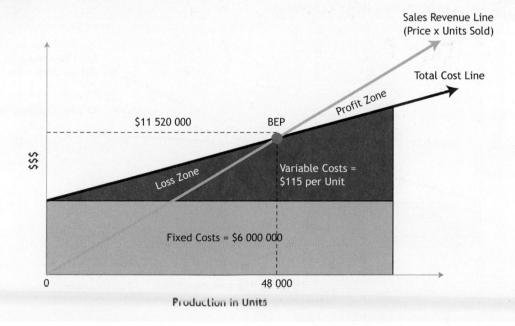

In order for the XYZ Corporation to break even, it must produce and sell 52 174 units at an average selling price of $240. Given this change, the required sales volume needed to break even would be 52 174 × $240 = $12 521 760, or an additional $1 001 760 in sales revenue.

> Managers need to continually reassess their breakeven position in order to understand how changes to their cost structure or to their selling price will impact BEP.

What if competitive price pressures force XYZ Corporation to reduce its selling price, resulting in an average selling price (ASP) of $210? Going back to our original example of variable costs of $115 per unit, the revised BEP in this situation would be:

$$BEP \text{ (units)} = \frac{\text{Total Fixed Costs}}{(\text{Selling Price per Unit} - \text{Variable Costs per Unit})}$$

$$BEP \text{ (units)} = \frac{\$6\ 000\ 000}{\$210 - \$115} = 63\ 158 \text{ units}$$

In order for the XYZ Corporation to break even, it must produce and sell 63 158 units at an average selling price of $210.

Once the BEP (in units) is determined, the BEP (in $$$) can easily be calculated by multiplying the BEP (in units) by the selling price. In this situation, the required sales volume needed to break even would be 63 158 units × $210 = $13 263 158.

Figure 12.14 shows the movement in BEP based on the two changes we just discussed (an increase in variable costs and a change in the average selling price).

CALCULATING BEP IN DOLLARS ($$$)

In some situations, in servicing their customers companies provide such a wide variety of products and services that it makes it unrealistic to compute BEP on a per unit basis. In this situation, these organizations, based on their cost analysis process and their business model, may be in a better position to compute BEP, initially, on the basis of total sales revenue ($$$). A good example of an industry that would likely assess BEP on this basis is the restaurant industry. Let's assume you are the manager of a coffee shop called the Coffee Mug. As the

FIGURE 12.14 XYZ Corporation: BEP Comparison

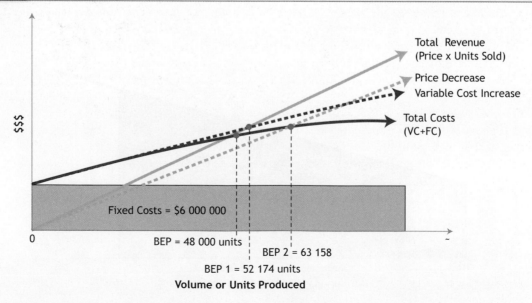

manager, you and your team have just recently completed a cost analysis of Coffee Mug's cost base. The results are as follows:

Variable (Direct) Costs as a % of Revenue	
Food costs	32%
Labour costs	33%
Paper and supply costs	7%
Franchise royalty	6%
Advertising fund contribution	2%
Total Variable Costs	80%

Fixed (Indirect) Costs	
Lease	$40 000
Insurance	$ 2 500
Utilities	$20 000
Professional fees	$ 1 500
Building overhead	$10 000
Interest on debt	$14 000
Total Fixed Costs	$88 000

To compute the BEP (in $$$) for Coffee Mug, the formula used is slightly different. The BEP formula in this situation is:

$$\text{BEP } \$\$\$ = \frac{\text{Total Fixed Costs}}{1 - \text{Variable Cost \%}}$$

$$\text{BEP } \$\$\$ = \frac{\$88\ 000}{1 - .80} = \$440\ 000$$

In this situation, we are indicating that 80 percent of each $1 of revenue received is consumed in the variable costs of delivering the product and services to the customer. This leaves only $0.20 of each dollar left over to pay for the fixed costs, which total $88 000. The organization (Coffee Mug) would need to generate $440 000 in sales in order to cover all of its costs. If it generates less than $440 000, it will suffer an operating loss. If its sales exceed $440 000, it will enjoy a profit.

As a manager, you will most likely be interested in understanding what this means in terms of the number of customers you would need to serve annually, weekly, daily, or hourly in order to achieve this required sales volume of $440 000. An analysis of your operation determines that customers, on average, spend $4 per visit to your Coffee Mug. Given this, you would need 110 000 customers annually to break even. This could be further broken down to 2115 per week (assuming 52 weeks), or 302 per day. If you were open 10 hours per day, you would need, on average, 30 customers per hour, or approximately 7.5 customers every 15 minutes.

As with the XYZ Corporation, noted above, if Coffee Mug incurs higher than anticipated costs, it will result in its BEP being moved upward. As an example, assume that Coffee Mug's material costs increase to 35 percent, instead of 32 percent. This will increase the variable cost percentage to 83 percent. This movement will result in BEP being revised to:

$$\text{BEP } \$\$\$ = \frac{\text{Total Fixed Costs}}{1 - \text{Variable Cost \%}}$$

$$\text{BEP } \$\$\$ = \frac{\$88\ 000}{1 - .83} = \$517\ 647$$

A 3 percent erosion (increase) in the variable cost base of the organization results in the organization needing an additional $77 647 in revenue to break even (cover its costs).

> BEP is used to identify the level that sales revenue has to reach in order to cover the total operating costs of an organization.

Using BEP to Understand Profit Objectives

As was indicated earlier, BEP is used to identify the level of sales revenue required in order to cover the total operating costs of an organization. It also has been noted that BEP should be considered the minimum acceptable position for an organization in the short run. The failure to achieve BEP will result in the organization requiring additional cash from other sources. Ongoing operating levels below BEP will eventually result in the organization becoming insolvent and possibly ceasing to exist.

Having said this, investors, shareholders, and management teams are not in business to break even. Expectations are that organizations will strive to achieve a defined level of profit in a given year, as well as ongoing profitability. For managers, understanding the level of sales activity (volume or revenue $$$) is fundamental to determining the feasibility of various profit objective levels and the determination of what profit objective the organization should strive for. The BEP formula can be modified in a manner that will enable the organization to see the sales volume requirements of such objectives.

> Investors, shareholders, and management teams are not in business to break even. Expectations are that organizations will strive to achieve a defined level of profit, in a given year, as well as ongoing profitability.

Going back to the XYZ Corporation, a manufacturer of laptops, let's revisit the original cost premise upon which the BEP calculation was based:

Material costs (components) per unit	$ 80.00
Labour costs per unit	$ 20.00
Packaging costs per unit	$ 6.00
Shipping costs per unit	$ 9.00
Total Variable Costs (direct costs) per unit	$115.00

The fixed costs were calculated and determined to be:

Plant overhead (utilities, insurance, service contracts, maintenance, etc.)	$1 500 000
Administration costs (payroll, accounting, IT, etc.)	$2 000 000
R&D costs	$ 500 000
Marketing costs (promotions, advertising, branding, etc.)	$1 500 000
Interest expense on debt	$ 500 000
Total Fixed Costs (indirect costs)	$6 000 000

Average selling price (ASP) per unit is $240.

Now, let's assume that, in addition to the costs noted above, the board of directors of the XYZ Corporation has challenged the management team to realize a profit of $800 000 in the upcoming year. For management, the question becomes what sales volume is required in order to cover all of our costs and achieve a profit of $800 000. A simple modification to the BEP formula can calculate this for us:

$$\text{BEP} + P = \frac{\text{Total Fixed Costs} + \text{Profit Objective}}{(\text{Selling Price per Unit} - \text{Variable Costs per Unit})}$$

$$\text{BEP} + P = \frac{\$6\ 000\ 000 + \$800\ 000}{(\$240 - \$115)} = 54\ 400\ \text{Units}$$

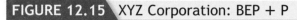

FIGURE 12.15 XYZ Corporation: BEP + P

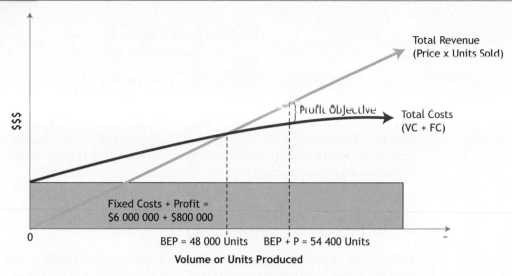

The original BEP was 48 000 units. In order to achieve a profit objective of $800 000, XYZ Corporation needs to produce and sell an additional 6400 laptops at an average selling price of $240 per unit (see Figure 12.15). Keep in mind that in the event that costs change, or the selling price is reduced, the number of units required to achieve this profit objective will change. As an example, if the selling price is forced down, due to competitive pressures, to $210 per unit, the number of units that must be produced and sold to realize the $800 000 profit objective will increase to 71 579 units (assuming that all costs remain unchanged).

As with the BEP (in units) formula, we can also modify the BEP (in $$$) formula in order to recognize the total sales revenue needed to ensure we reach our profit objective. Going back to the Coffee Mug example, let's review the initial cost base assumptions, and then add a profit objective.

Variable (Direct) Costs as a % of Revenue	
Food costs	32%
Labour costs	33%
Paper and supply costs	7%
Franchise royalty	6%
Advertising fund contribution	2%
Total Variable Costs	80%

Fixed (Indirect) Costs	
Lease	$40 000
Insurance	$ 2 500
Utilities	$20 000
Professional fees	$ 1 500
Building overhead	$10 000
Interest on debt	$14 000
Total Fixed Costs	$88 000

Let's assume that the owner of Coffee Mug invested $400 000 to set up his franchise. Let's also assume that his objective was a 12 percent return on this investment annually. This would mean that the owner desires an annual net profit of $48 000 ($400 000 × .12). Modifying the BEP (in $$$) formula in the same manner as we did the BEP (in units) formula, the revised sales revenue required to break even and meet the desired profit objective would be as follows:

$$\text{BEP \$\$\$} + P = \frac{\text{Total Fixed Costs} + \text{Profit Objective}}{(1 - \text{Variable Cost \%})} = 54\ 400 \text{ units}$$

$$\text{BEP \$\$\$} + P = \frac{\$88\ 000 + \$48\ 000}{(1 - .80)} = \$680\ 000$$

The required sales volume needed to break even and achieve the profit objective would be $680 000. The original BEP (in $$$) was $440 000, so the Coffee Mug operation needs to generate an additional $240 000 in revenue if the owner is to achieve his desired 12 percent annual return on his investment.

Using BEP to Ensure That Full Cash Flow Needs Are Realized

Another way in which the BEP formula can be helpful is in determining what the sales revenue level requirement would be in order to cover the organization's full operating costs, meet its profit objective, and meet any principal repayment debt obligations that the organization is required to pay in the current year. As an example, let's go back to the Coffee Mug. Let's assume that the cost structure remains unchanged, as is, again, shown below. Let's also assume that the profit objective remains at 12 percent annually, based on the $400 000 investment by the owner.

Variable (Direct) Costs as a % of Revenue	
Food costs	32%
Labour costs	33%
Paper and supply costs	7%
Franchise royalty	6%
Advertising fund contribution	2%
Total Variable Costs	80%

Fixed (Indirect) Costs	
Lease	$40 000
Insurance	$ 2 500
Utilities	$20 000
Professional fees	$ 1 500
Building overhead	$10 000
Interest on debt	$14 000
Total Fixed Costs	$88 000

In addition, let's further assume that the owner borrowed $196 000, at 7.5 percent for 10 years, as a way to assist in financing his coffee shop start-up. This debt obligation would require an annual principal repayment in addition to the annual interest payment on the debt. Let's make this annual principal repayment obligation $15 000. Assuming that the owner wants all of these expenses to be paid for by the operation, and he still wants his $48 000 net profit (12 percent of $400 000), what is the required sales volume needed to support this?

$$\text{BEP \$\$\$} + P + DRP = \frac{\text{Total Fixed Costs} + \text{Profit Objective} + \text{Debt Repayment}}{(1 - \text{Variable Cost \%})}$$

$$\text{BEP \$\$\$} + P = \frac{\$88\ 000 + \$48\ 000 + \$15\ 000}{(1 - .80)} = \$755\ 000$$

For the owner, we can conclude the following based on our calculations:

- Operational BEP is achieved at a sales revenue volume of $440 000 (all operating costs are covered).

- Operational BEP and the profit objective are achieved at a sales revenue volume of $680 000.

- Operational BEP, the profit objective, and the loan repayment requirement are achieved at a sales revenue volume of $755 000.

In breaking this down, the owner can now track his annual, monthly, weekly, and daily sales volume to determine if his Coffee Mug is on track to deliver on the desired financial outcome. Assuming that he is open every day (365 days per year), he now knows that his daily sales need to be:

- $1205 to break even (BEP/365)

- $1418 to break even and realize his profit objective

- $2068 to break even, realize his profit objective, and fully pay the principal owed on the loan

At an average sale per customer of $4, he also knows that he needs:

- 302 customers per day to break even

- 355 customers per day to break even and realize his profit objective

- 517 customers per day to break even, realize his profit objective, and fully pay the principal owed on the loan

Using BEP to Assist in the Setting of Price

Another benefit of breakeven analysis is its value in assisting managers with understanding the optimal price to charge for products and services offered to the marketplace. Let's use an example with the AAPL Corporation, a manufacturer of smartphones, to illustrate how a derivative of the BEP formula can be used to determine where an organization, assuming total control of market factors, should price its product to ensure that all costs are covered and that its desired profit objective is met.

Let's assume that AAPL Corporation plans to launch a new smartphone, called the SASS, into the Canadian marketplace. The SASS, which features touch-screen technology, single-key access to Facebook and Twitter, and access to current applications available through the AAPL App store, is targeted toward the university student marketplace. In analyzing manufacturing and operating costs, AAPL's management team has concluded the following:

1. The direct costs associated with manufacturing the SASS have been estimated at $75 per unit.
2. The indirect costs associated with the SASS smartphone (plant overhead; selling, general, and administrative expenses; R&D expenses; interest on debt), for the first year of the product launch are estimated at $20 000 000.
3. The profit objective set for the SASS smartphone for the first year is $4 000 000.
4. The manufacturing capacity of the facility that will produce the SASS is 400 000 units in year one. Discussions with distributors (Rogers, Telus, Bell, Phones R Us) indicate that, assuming it is a hit, the SASS will be able to sell all 400 000 units.

Management's key initial question is what is the required selling price that AAPL will need to receive for the SASS smartphone in order for it to cover all of its costs and meet its targeted profit objective? This optimal price point can be calculated via the formula illustrated in Figure 12.16.

FIGURE 12.16 Optimal Price Point

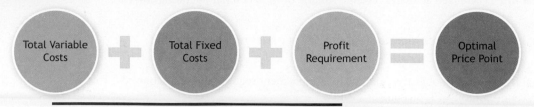

Quantity Produced and Estimated to Be Sold

In the case of AAPL, the optimal price point for the SASS smartphone would be calculated as follows:

> Optimal Price Point (also referred to as Cost Plus Pricing)
>
> $$OPP = \frac{\text{Total Variable Costs} + \text{Total Fixed Costs} + \text{Profit Objective}}{\text{Quantity Produced and Expected to Be Sold}}$$
>
> $$OPP = \frac{(\$75 \times 400\ 000 \text{ units}) + \$20\ 000\ 000 + \$4\ 000\ 000}{400\ 000 \text{ Units}}$$
>
> $$OPP = \$135$$

The $135 price represents the (optimal) price that AAPL will need to charge to ensure that it covers all of its costs and meets its desired first-year profit objective. For AAPL, this ideal or optimal price point needs to be assessed against a number of different factors. These would include, but not be limited to, the following:

- Is this price competitive with other similar competitive units and anticipated new competitive units in the marketplace?

- Is this price acceptable to our distributors, who, when adding their mark-up, will anticipate a strong and profitable addition to their product portfolio?

- Is this price point, and the corresponding mark-up that will be added to our product by our distributors, in keeping with our company and brand position in the marketplace?

Mark-up refers to the addition to the manufacturer's price that distributors add to the price of a product to ensure that their own direct and indirect costs are covered and that their profit margin is achieved.

Mark-up pricing is the addition to our price (which becomes our distributors' cost base) that our distributors will add to ensure that their own direct and indirect costs are covered and that their profit margins are achieved. As an example, assume that Phones R Us is one of our leading distributors. Phones R Us purchases our SASS smartphone at a price of $135. In order to cover their retail bricks-and-mortar operations' direct and indirect costs, Phones R Us adds a mark-up of 120 percent to the cost of the phone. This means that Phones R Us will retail the SASS smartphone for $297 ($135 + ($135 × 1.20)). Both AAPL and Phones R Us need to assess this price point's ability to compete in the marketplace, and determine whether this optimal price point and corresponding mark-up can be achieved. If it is believed the price point is too high, then adjustments to the mark-up of Phones R Us, to the profit objective of AAPL, and/or to the cost base of the phone (reduced features, less expensive products, etc.) will need to be made to ensure that the SASS smartphone enters the marketplace properly priced.

Managers should not assume that the optimal price point is the only price point that can be used for a product as it enters the market. Often times, the optimal price point may simply be too rich for the market to accept, and/or may not be in keeping with the overall brand and pricing strategy of the company. It is meant to simply be one element of a full pricing discussion and plan. Trade-offs will have to be made. In some cases, the introductory price will need to be set low to stimulate interest and demand. In other cases, it will need to be set high in order to recapture the significant development costs associated with the product.[4]

Managers should not assume that the optimal price point is the only price point that can be used for a product as it enters the market.

BUSINESS *in Action*

The Forzani Group Ltd.: Consolidating Business Efficiencies

The Forzani Group Ltd. (FGL), one of Canada's leading retail organizations, is now a member of the Canadian Tire (CTC) family. The friendly takeover, valued at $770 million, brings into Canadian Tire Canada's largest sporting goods and sports apparel operation. For Canadian Tire, it offers an opportunity to gain access to some of the sports industry's highest-profile brands and gain considerable additional customer reach. Viewing FGL as a complementary business, Canadian Tire believes that the move will make Canadian Tire a dominant player in the sporting goods industry, provide a strong defence against potential U.S.-based entrants coming to Canada (e.g., Dick's Sporting Goods), and create supply chain and operational synergies between the two companies with estimated savings of $25+ million annually.

A key aspect of the deal is that Forzani will continue to operate as a separate entity within the Canadian Tire portfolio. Known historically as one of the best operationally managed businesses, FGL, owners of banners such as SportChek, Sport Mart, Nevada Bob's Golf, Sports Experts, and Fitness Source, will continue to simplify the way it does business and, in the process, improve its overall productivity. Over the past several years, FGL itself has grown as a result of acquisitions and new store openings. Its purchases of Athletes World and Fitness Source are two of its most recent additions to its growing banners across the North American landscape. Yes, if opportunities arise, Canadian Tire and FGL may still look to add to its banners, but, for the most part, their focus will be on continuing to consolidate FGL's operational processes and to integrate best practices between CTC and FGL in order to drive greater business efficiencies and improve operating margins and returns on invested capital. Growing revenue will still be a major objective, and FGL's goal to increase revenue by 10 percent per year over the next five years should remain a core priority.

A key focus of this business efficiency initiative is the harmonizing and unifying of business processes and technologies. Whereas each FGL banner has operated somewhat autonomously, banners are now being consolidated around product categories in order to minimize duplication of effort; streamline and centralize purchasing; share and take advantage of best practices in operations, marketing, and product assortment; and enhance the use of technology. These initiatives are designed to make Forzani a more efficient and effective organization, and one that generates superior cash flows. As an example, based on sales per square foot and gross margin realization, Forzani's Sports Experts banner is one of the most profitable sporting goods chains in North America. While also profitable, SportChek simply does not deliver the same per-square-foot return. By importing the best practices found in Sports Experts into SportChek, as well as consolidating what are currently separate operational areas, FGL hopes to see SportChek's returns move to the same level. In addition to these types of internal process consolidations, FGL also plans to consolidate its products and take greater advantage of its product winners across all of its banners. Products from its Nevada Bob's Golf stores have been integrated into a number of its SportChek operations, and several product assortment integration decisions have been made across its Sport Mart, SportChek, and Coast Mountain operations. Look for Nevada Bob's Boutiques in SportChek stores as an example of this intended product assortment integration initiative. Product assortment integration also allows FGL to get a better sense of potential product winners earlier. The new integration strategy enabled FGL to realize the market opportunity in sports bikes, a $780 million business in Canada. Smart and quick repositioning of FGL's banners to service this market has resulted in a doubling of market share from 5 percent to 10 percent in this category. The goal is, rather than having separate buying teams and a separate managing of the marketing approach for each banner, FGL will unify its market approach and have category-buying teams so that more opportunities, such as sports bikes, can be picked up early, communicated across the organization, and be fully leveraged in terms of financial results. FGL's transformation does not stop here. FGL is also shifting its focus away from new store openings and seeking to grow by expanding its current stores and by redesigning its market approach. SportChek stores, where possible, will see their square footage expanded in order to house the new product categories to be offered and leverage the economies of scale that can be driven off the slightly larger footprints. FGL believes that by adding approximately 5000 sq. ft. to existing stores, versus building new stores, greater operating efficiencies will be gained and less business risk will be incurred. FGL has also contracted the management of its ecommerce operations to GSI, an ecommerce specialist, with the intent of driving more revenue and greater operating efficiencies from this part of the organization.

Forzani Group Ltd. knows that some areas of the business will always be uncontrollable. Unseasonably warm winter weather in a given year, as an example, historically has resulted in an overall decline in fourth-quarter sales. It is also aware that it will always be challenged by upward cost pressures relating to marketing (due to the competitive intensity of the marketplace), and wages (scheduled minimum wage increases, etc.). Recognizing this, FGL is focusing its efforts on what it can control. It is striving to maximize the efficiencies of its inventory management and buying, minimize unnecessary discounting of inventories throughout its banners, consolidate its operations to yield lower costs, and drive more revenue dollars from its existing retail square footage. So far, the results are promising. Revenue into 2011 continues to grow, gross profit margins are improving, and earnings before taxes were up a full percentage point when compared to the prior year. Adding Canadian Tire's own expertise, the new scale realized by the combination of these two organizations, and access to its 485 retail outlets across Canada should enable Forzani to continue to grow its revenue opportunities. Given its operational expertise, this should speak well to adding value to Canadian Tire as a company, and to its shareholders.[5]

WEB INTEGRATION

Want to learn more about Canadian Tire's acquisition of Forzani? Google Canadian Tire acquires the Forzani Group.

Mark-up Pricing and Other Pricing Considerations

LO6

Much of our discussion within this chapter has focused on manufacturing operations and the use of cost-base and breakeven analysis to ensure that the organization's pricing strategies are derived from a full understanding of their cost structures. Retail organizations that purchase finished goods with the intent of reselling these products also need to fully understand the costs incurred in the purchase and delivery of these finished products to the marketplace. As an example, assume that your organization purchases dress shirts from a manufacturer in Thailand for resale through your company stores. Although not technically manufacturing the shirt, costs are still incurred in importing the shirt to Canada, transporting it to the various retail outlets that the company owns, and maintaining and supporting its outlets. Going back to Figure 12.9, we are reminded that a very high percentage of our cost base is not directly related to the cost of the shirts, but to fixed or indirect costs associated with our operation's intent to resell the shirts in the Canadian market. When faced with a situation such as this, our focus is all about making sure that we price the shirt high enough to cover the total costs incurred by the organization and meet its profit objective. This means that we have to mark up the cost of the shirt to a level that ensures that full cost recovery and profit objectives are realized. An easy way to initiate such a pricing approach is to utilize what is called mark-up pricing (also referred to as step-up pricing). To illustrate this process, let's assume the following cost structure:

Costs identified below are on a per-shirt basis	
Cost per shirt (purchase price from Thailand manufacturer)	$ 6.00
Transportation costs to Canada	$ 2.00
Import and customs fees for entry into Canada	$ 0.50
Port docking and unloading fees (Canadian port)	$ 0.50
Transportation charges to our regional warehouse	$ 1.00
Labelling and packaging costs under our brand	$ 1.00
Delivery and freight charges to retail outlets	$ 1.00
Total variable or direct cost per shirt	$12.00

As noted, the variable, or direct, cost of the shirt is $12. In addition to this cost, however, we must also cover the fixed, or indirect, costs of our organization. This would include marketing costs, general selling and administrative wages and expenses, warehouse plant and facility costs, leases and other business expense obligations (utilities, insurance, supplies, etc.) associated with our retail outlet operations, and the wages and benefits associated with our retail and distribution support staff. Let's make the assumption that this has been calculated by our finance department and requires a standard mark-up of 150 percent over the direct cost of the products that we sell. Our company's board of directors has also indicated that they are looking for management to deliver a 15 percent profit margin for the upcoming year. Both the additional indirect costs and the profit margin need to be incorporated into the pricing model in order to calculate a price that is sufficient to cover all of our company's expenses and yield the desired profit. An easy way to understand this retail pricing example is by viewing this pricing decision via a "step-up" process (see Figure 12.17).

As is shown in Figure 12.17, the mark-up pricing process results in the need for us to charge $34.50 for this shirt if it is to cover the 150 percent standard mark-up recommended by our finance department, as well as the 15 percent profit margin being sought by our board of directors, as part of our organization's financial requirements for profitability and long-term solvency.

Keeping in mind the price consideration comments made with respect to optimal price point pricing, managers similarly need to assess the ability of the marketplace to accept the full results of a mark-up pricing calculation. Pricing decisions cannot be made in isolation of competitive price points and the willingness of the market to pay the price being offered. As an example, assume that you are interested in purchasing a refrigerator for your apartment or

FIGURE 12.17 Mark-up (or Step-up) Pricing Illustration

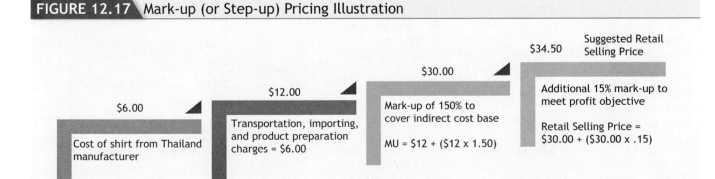

house. In assessing your options, you make a decision to check the prices of three retailers that offer the style and model of refrigerator you are interested in. During this search of these three retailers, you notice a price differential among the three. Why does this occur? This price differential could be the result of different cost structures of the three organizations. The cost structure differential could be the result of one retailer selling significantly greater volume than the others, resulting in its ability to purchase the product from the manufacturer at a lower price. It could also be the result of a more efficient business operation, which requires a lower mark-up to cover the organization's cost versus that of its competitors. It could further be the result of additional services that one competitor offers to differentiate itself from others. If not cost-related, the price differential could be the desire of one of the organizations to take a **price discounting** approach to drive market share or increase volume, or a **price skimming** approach, where the emphasis is on maximizing the profit margin on each of the units sold. This would be reflected in the profit margin objective attached to a particular product or service (see Figure 12.18). To further complicate the pricing process, some retailers may choose to incorporate **psychological pricing** (i.e., pricing at $33.99 versus $34.00) into their final price position, adjust prices for seasonality, provide **rebates**, coupons, or price reductions via temporary sales promotions, or offer customers quantity discounts should they buy certain amounts of the product.

> Pricing decisions cannot be made in isolation of competitive price points and the willingness of the market to pay the price being offered.

Additional Comments Relating to Pricing

With the emergence of the global marketplace and the ongoing explosion of online selling and buying, the challenges associated with pricing are greater than ever before. Whereas the marketplace at one time could depend on a relatively fixed price approach, where an initial price could be set and held for an extended period of time, pricing decisions today are more fluid and dynamic. Competitors are continually utilizing price as a weapon of competitive rivalry in order to gain awareness and drive demand for their products and/or services. Conversely, retailers are also looking to use price as a key component of a differentiation strategy that, as an example, could seek to establish a luxury-focused brand identity in the

Price Discounting is a reduction in the price of the product with the intent to stimulate the sale of the product over a defined period of time.

Price Skimming refers to the utilization of a premium price strategy in order to maximize the margin return on the sale of each individual unit of a particular product.

Psychological Pricing is the utilization of pricing tactics that are designed to respond to the psychological tendencies of purchasers.

Rebate refers to a temporary price reduction offered on a product or service in order to stimulate sales. Rebates can be offered at the point of sale or on a deferred basis (example: mail-in).

FIGURE 12.18 Mark-up Pricing Comparison

Retailer	Cost of Refrigerator from Manufacturer	Retailer's Standard Mark-up	Profit Objective	Rebate or Sales Promotion Discount	Final Price to Customer
Retailer #1 High-End Retailer — fine furniture and appliances	$300.00	200%: includes free delivery, financing options, etc.	20%	$100.00 in-store rebate	$980.00
Retailer #2 Big Box Store — re-labels under own brand	$270.00 volume discount	160%: no frills - cash and carry only	10%	None	$772.20
Retailer #3 Specialty Appliance Store	$300.00	180%: trained staff, full installation, follow-up service, extended warranty	15%	10% discount	$869.40

marketplace, thereby enabling organizations to drive greater margins from the sale of individual products/services. Volatility in transportation costs due to rapid changes in the price of fuel have resulted in industries, such as the airline industry, adopting variable pricing strategies that add surcharges to base prices in order to compensate for uncontrollable fluctuations in costs. With more companies doing business globally, currency exchange rates, combined with market size (in international regions) and different environmental and other regulatory requirements, add further complexity to the pricing decision-making process.

With all this in mind, one can readily see that the art of pricing a product or service has become an almost customized process, for which one needs to consider four fundamental impact factors (see Figure 12.19):

- The total cost base of the product or service to the organization

- The product or service's value (actual and perceived) to the customer

- The degree of price sensitivity within the product or service sector

- The effectiveness of marketing efforts to communicate uniqueness, quality, and importance

As has been discussed earlier in this chapter, managers need to fully understand both the variable and fixed costs associated with their organization's operations. In addition to understanding these fundamental operational requirements, managers also need to anticipate the required additional financial contingencies associated with the organization, as well as its future needs, to ensure that price points being considered adequately cover both the current and future organizational financial requirements (see Figure 12.20). In terms of the required additional financial contingencies, managers need to think about the establishment of reserves sufficient to fund the replacement of equipment, plant, and facility, and other capital assets, due to wear and tear and obsolescence. Debt repayment requirements, and **expense creep** due to inflationary pressures, are additional factors that should be assessed and incorporated into a product or service's pricing formula. In addition to these known needs, future needs also must be analyzed. This could be focused on such items as product development through R&D investment, technology-based initiatives to enhance organizational processes, service systems or process support systems, market studies focused on new market opportunities, or

Expense Creep refers to the tendency for expenses associated with the organization's various cost lines to rise due to inflationary pressures, union negotiated contracts, and so on.

FIGURE 12.19 Price Impact Factors

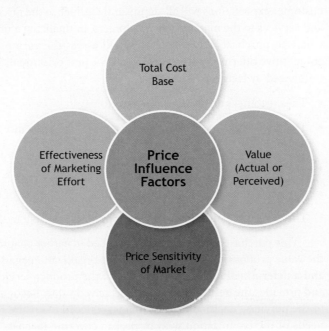

FIGURE 12.20   Total Cost-Base Analysis

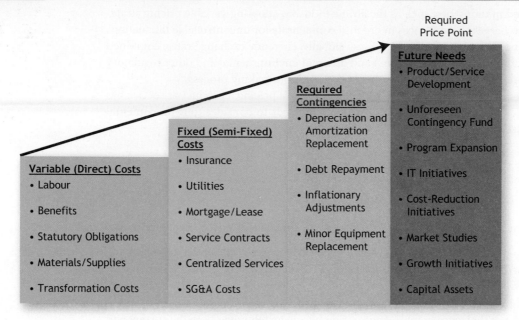

other potential growth initiatives. It is important to understand that revenue is the result of price times quantity sold, and as such is the core source of the dollars that an organization has at its disposal. What it does not generate internally through the sale of its products and/or services will need to be secured externally (this is discussed more in Chapter 13). Although it is recognized that the total financial needs of the organization generally cannot be generated internally, the operations of the organization are what will, ultimately, need to be used to repay the costs incurred, and the debt taken on, in support of organizational activities. This needs to be considered and assessed when determining price points for the various products and services offered by the organization.

As managers, we must also understand that pricing decisions cannot be made in a vacuum, focused solely on costs, but that external influences, competitive offerings, and customer expectations will all significantly influence the price at which we offer our products and services to the marketplace. Customers, in finalizing a product selection or a decision on where to purchase needed services, will assess the various options and determine which competitive offering they feel represents the best price/quality trade-off. This decision will be influenced by factors such as:

- The customer's ability or willingness to pay

- The preferences of the customer in terms of functionality and intangible "psychographic" benefits

- The importance of quality and performance

- Behavioural issues, such as the regularity and intensity of use

- The number of direct alternatives or options available in the marketplace

This purchase process (as was discussed in earlier chapters) is based on a comparison of the value proposition being offered by the organization against that of its direct competitors, and a determination, by the customer, of the product/service that best meets his/her needs and provides the best functional and perceived value. Recognizing this as a core fundamental to the purchase decision process, managers need to ensure that the price they set meets the needs of the organization with respect to covering its costs and driving the required profit

FIGURE 12.21 Pricing Incentive

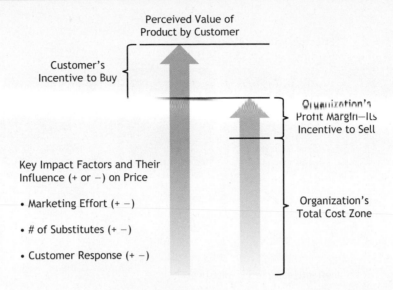

Perceived Value of
Product by Customer

Customer's
Incentive to Buy

Organization's
Profit Margin—Its
Incentive to Sell

Key Impact Factors and Their
Influence (+ or −) on Price

Organization's
Total Cost Zone

• Marketing Effort (+ −)

• # of Substitutes (+ −)

• Customer Response (+ −)

margin (organization's incentive to sell). They must also, however, match this with the price that provides customers with an acceptable incentive to buy (see Figure 12.21).

> Pricing decisions cannot be made in a vacuum. External influences, competitive offerings, and customer expectations will all significantly influence the price at which we offer our products and services to the marketplace.

As was noted in Chapters 10 and 11, which focus on market positioning and marketing mix execution, the ability of an organization to effectively differentiate itself from its competitors, via uniqueness, quality, or importance, can mitigate the use of price as a weapon of competitive rivalry by its competitors. Marketing effectiveness, focused on brand, product, or use differentiation, can be fundamental to enabling an organization to achieve stronger margins through premium pricing strategies that buyers accept as valid "value" reinforcement. The absence of such effective marketing messages can, and often does, result in price becoming a more critical decision criterion on the part of purchasers (see Figure 12.22).

As has been previously noted, the pricing process, on an ongoing basis, remains a challenging aspect of management's responsibility. It is, after all, the root from which revenue is generated. By clearly identifying the profit objectives of the organization, and more fully understanding its cost base and the external impact factors that will influence price, managers can more effectively price products and services in a way that reinforces the firm's overall strategic positioning in the marketplace and maximizes the value proposition the organization offers to its customers. Once price is set, the process does not end. Ongoing assessment of profitability, costs, and competitive conditions is required to continually ensure that market reaction to the pricing strategy in place maintains the necessary balance between the needs of the organization and meeting the expectations of its customer base (see Figure 12.23).[6]

> By more fully understanding the cost base of an organization and the external impact factors that will influence price, managers can more effectively price products and services in a way that reinforces the firm's overall strategic positioning in the marketplace and maximizes the value proposition the organization offers to its customers.

FIGURE 12.22 Pricing: Marketing Effectiveness

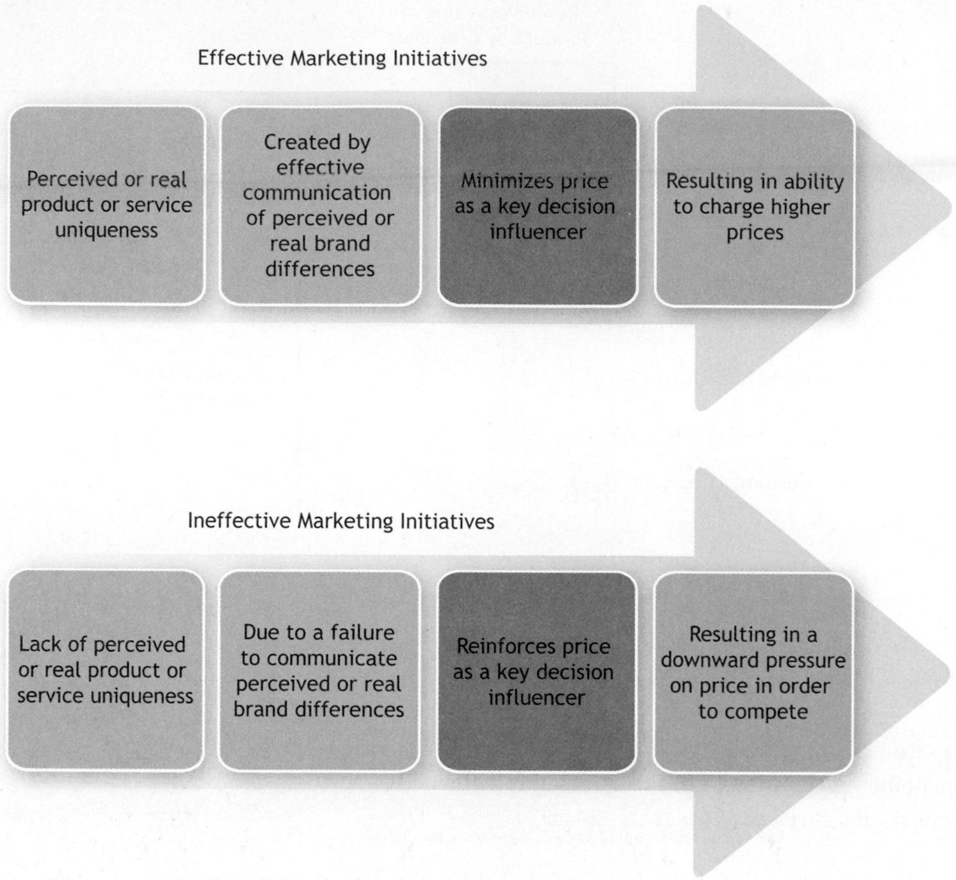

Effective Marketing Initiatives

| Perceived or real product or service uniqueness | Created by effective communication of perceived or real brand differences | Minimizes price as a key decision influencer | Resulting in ability to charge higher prices |

Ineffective Marketing Initiatives

| Lack of perceived or real product or service uniqueness | Due to a failure to communicate perceived or real brand differences | Reinforces price as a key decision influencer | Resulting in a downward pressure on price in order to compete |

FIGURE 12.23 Pricing Process

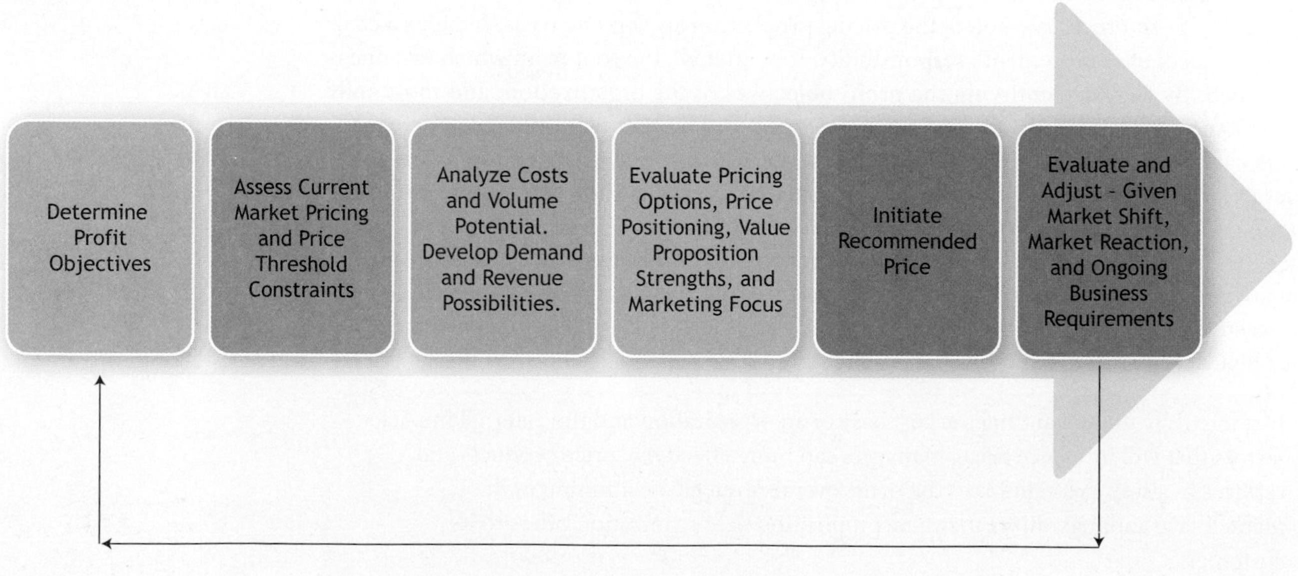

| Determine Profit Objectives | Assess Current Market Pricing and Price Threshold Constraints | Analyze Costs and Volume Potential. Develop Demand and Revenue Possibilities. | Evaluate Pricing Options, Price Positioning, Value Proposition Strengths, and Marketing Focus | Initiate Recommended Price | Evaluate and Adjust - Given Market Shift, Market Reaction, and Ongoing Business Requirements |

Management Reflection—The Importance of Cost-Base Analysis

Managers need to make intelligent decisions regarding price based on fully understanding their cost base and the profit objectives that the company desires from products within its portfolio. To continue to grow, organizations need adequate returns on their investments and require products and services to meet profit expectations throughout the duration of their life cycles. Understanding the cost base of the organization is essential in ensuring that pricing decisions are determined in such a way that the organization recognizes their implications to its cost lines and profitability position. Whether it is a defensive response to competitor pressures, the leveraging of competitive advantage due to a cost base that is lower than that of its competitors, or the desire to utilize a premium price approach to reinforce a luxury brand image, managers need to effectively incorporate their knowledge of their cost base into their pricing strategy.

> Understanding the cost base of the organization is essential in ensuring that pricing decisions are determined in such a way that the organization understands the implications to its cost lines and profitability position.

The ability to manage an organization's cost base is not limited to understanding the differences between direct and indirect costs. It is also dependent on the ability of managers to recognize the flexibility and choice (or lack thereof) they have in adjusting such costs in order to effectively support and execute an organization's strategies. It means looking across all elements of the cost ladder, as well as understanding the future cost environment the company will face. Understanding an organization's breakeven point and potential changes to this point are also core requirements to effective cost management, as is the recognition of the required research and development costs, equipment replacement costs, and allowances for unforeseen contingencies that a company needs to plan for.

Pricing decisions cannot be made in a vacuum. Understanding the customer's ability and willingness to pay, the quality expectations of the target market, the number of direct alternatives or options available in the marketplace, and the intangible attributes that provide customers an incentive to buy, must be integrated with the organization's cost-base position. Remember, revenue growth and profits are the result of satisfied customers. Understanding the relationship between price and costs is a critical step in determining which markets to pursue, our ability to emphasize volume, and the level of quality that can be incorporated into the products and services we offer. Customers purchase products whose perceived value exceeds the price being asked. As managers, we need to ensure that the price point offered is sufficient to cover our total cost base and our profit margin (incentive to sell).

Chapter Summary

The focus of this chapter is on ensuring that students understand the importance of the need to understand the cost base of an organization. Understanding the cost base and how such costs are structured is fundamental to ensuring that an organization maintains control of its ongoing financial requirements. Managers need to understand the relationship between variable and fixed costs that make up their cost structure, and how changes to these costs, and/or changes to revenue flowing into the organization, given these costs, will affect its overall profitability. A core fundamental to this process is the ability to identify and monitor an organization's breakeven point (BEP). The ability to calculate the BEP, in volume (units) or in dollars, enables managers to determine whether the organization is going to face liquidity and, potentially, solvency issues in the near term. It is considered by many to be the benchmark for the minimum acceptable position at which an organization can operate in the short term. The utilization of breakeven calculations, when combined with profit objectives and other cash flow requirements, ensures that managers get a true picture of the levels of activity and revenue actualization needed to sustain the operation and to protect the financial health of the organization. In addition to understanding the cost base, managers must also have a solid understanding of the external factors that will influence the price points that can be charged for the various goods and services the organization offers. The ability to assess competitor actions, market trends, demand and revenue potential, and value proposition strength are all central to the development and finalization of pricing decisions. The utilization of optimal price point calculations, which are designed to identify to managers the ideal price point at which an organization's profit objectives can be realized, is a key addition to this process as well. In determining this optimal price point, the question becomes, however, whether the organization can realistically charge this ideal price in the marketplace. Will this price be competitive? Will the market view the price point as being appropriate, given the value proposition of the product or service against which the price is being compared, and the effectiveness of the marketing initiatives developed to communicate it? The chapter closes off with a general discussion associated with an overview of the pricing process managers should refer to when setting prices in today's competitive environment.

 ## Developing Business Knowledge and Skills

KEY TERMS

variable costs *p. 318*

fixed costs *p. 318*

breakeven point (BEP) *p. 324*

mark-up *p. 334*

price discounting *p. 338*

price skimming *p. 338*

psychological pricing *p. 338*

rebate *p. 338*

expense creep *p. 339*

QUESTIONS FOR DISCUSSION

1. What is an organization's cost base? What are three things that managers might look for in analyzing it? Why is it so important that managers be able to understand their organization's cost base?

2. What is the difference between variable (direct) and fixed (indirect) costs? Which of these do you think is easier for an organization to control, and why?

3. How would a restaurant's direct and indirect costs differ from those of a manufacturer? For which type of organization are direct costs more important, and for which type are indirect costs more important?

4. All companies strive to make a profit. Breaking even every year is not considered an acceptable return on an organization's investment. Explain why, in spite of these statements, it is still crucial that a company understands its breakeven point.

5. What is mark-up pricing? Why is it important to understand how mark-up pricing works when pricing a product and conducting a breakeven analysis?

6. What are the four impact factors that will influence the setting of a price for a product or service?

QUESTIONS FOR INDIVIDUAL ACTION

Approach a local business and ask its managers if they conduct a breakeven analysis. Do they use it to determine their pricing? Do they use it to ensure that their full cash flow needs are realized? What other business decisions do they use it for? Prepare a report of your findings.

TEAM EXERCISE

As a team, prepare a cost analysis for opening a new restaurant. Your analysis should consider the impact of direct and indirect costs, as well as a detailed units and sales-based breakeven analysis. You will likely have to conduct some research to determine the costs and potential prices for the type of restaurant that you would like to establish. Prepare a presentation of your analysis.

Case for Discussion

The presentation having just ended, Linda Martino, CEO of Palmero Jeans Inc., has a decision to make. Does she break with a long-standing vision that Palmero Jeans will be 100 percent made in the USA, and recommend to her board of directors that the company shift production of its jeans to Costa Rica? The decision, not to be taken lightly, is one that will fundamentally change not only the way the organization operates, but also how it positions the brand in an increasingly competitive marketplace.

PALMERO JEANS INC.

Established in 1976, Palmero Jeans Inc. is a manufacturer and distributor of high-end jeans wear, competing directly with the likes of Rock Star, Chip and Pepper, Dylan & George, Paper Denim, and Sass & Bide, to name a few. Focused on a California style, Palmero Jeans Inc. distinguishes itself with a vintage feel that is all about comfort. As their ad campaigns state, Palmero Jeans fit like a glove. Recently featured on Oprah, Palmero Jeans Inc.'s "Superfine" collection has received rave reviews by jeans critics. Comments such as "they are so rad" and "these jeans are super cool" populate blogs and discussion boards serving this select and finicky niche market. A second line, called "Skinny Pockets," is focused toward a younger crowd, and emphasizes the perfect fit with fabrics that feel super soft. The tag line associated with the Skinny Pockets campaign is "Skinny Pockets are the jeans that you buy, wear, love, buy more, wear more, love more."

MARKET DYNAMICS

Although well distinguished in the designer jeans market, the situation at Palmero Jeans Inc. is not as bright and cheerful as the product line and its advertising suggests. For one thing, the market for designer jeans has taken a beating over the last two years, as the recession has negatively impacted demand and sales have declined. Considered by many to be a luxury good, the more mature shoppers are becoming much more discriminating in their brand selection and more reluctant to part with their hard-earned dollars. Simply put, the consumer psychology is not so upbeat these days, with many buyers in this category playing more the part of "lookers" versus "buyers." In addition to the woes an economic downturn brings, the market continues to see new entrants, both domestically and globally. New emerging brands, such as Acne, Red Monkey, J Brand, and G-Star, further slice up what is already a niche specialty market. Add to this new entrants from Asia, such as Fugian, Xian, and Nikesell, and the end result is a very crowded market where consumers have greater choice and prices are being forced down. Sure, an initial response, particularly with respect to the Asian brands, is that they are imitators versus true designer originals. Having said this, one has to admire the quality these brands possess and the unbeatable price points they are using to lure customers, particularly first-time buyers, to this product category. In particular, a Chinese manufacturer, Key2Fashion, has made significant inroads into the market in a very short period of time. Their success formula: cutting-edge design at a fraction of the cost. The recent signing of Jessica Alba, Lindsay Lohan, and Fergie to endorsement contracts sets the stage for a major North American launch.

AT A CROSSROADS

For Linda, the stakes are high. Palmero Jeans Inc., a smaller industry player, is at a turning point. Historically a differentiator on the basis of product quality, technology has now enabled all manufacturers to produce their product lines at excellent quality levels. Yes, designs speak for themselves, but what customers are saying is that more and more companies are producing excellent fashion designs focused on competing segments of the market; the end result is that price, which was not considered to be a key purchase decision criterion, is becoming much more meaningful. In the short term, Palmero Jeans Inc. has responded with price decreases to ensure that fashion buyers remain committed to the brand, thereby protecting Palmero's relationships with its distribution channel members. These exclusive shop retailers have indicated, however, that other manufacturers, with lower price points, enable these retailers to expand their margins by buying low and selling high. Key2Fashion, in particular, has used this strategy as a way to ensure that their jeans receive significant shelf space in an increasingly crowded market. Recent announcements also point to both Levi Strauss and Lee entering the designer market in pursuit of the younger demographic. This would place their products in direct competition with Palmero's Skinny Pockets line. Both of these companies moved jean production out of the United States a while back, with Levi Strauss now producing its products in Mexico, and Lee in India. Lee, in particular, is a potential threat, having just signed a deal with the Olsen twins to design and brand their new product offering.

INITIAL ANALYSIS

Although Palmero Jeans Inc. has been committed to remaining a made-in-USA brand, Linda knows that an analysis needs to be conducted to determine whether the company should shift some, or all, of its manufacturing operations outside of the United States. Costa Rica's growing garment industry, its government's commitment to assist with the cost of building the manufacturing facility, and its close proximity to the United States all make it a viable option for consideration. Not wanting to change too much too soon, Linda's initial thought is to focus on a financial assessment for the Skinny Pockets product line (initially scheduled to be launched this year). As it has yet to be released, a shift in the manufacturing of this product is

possible, as an initial short-run manufacturing process could be established at Palmero's Venice, California, plant until the manufacturing facility could be completed in San José, Costa Rica. This strategic shift might result in a reduction in projected profits in the initial year, but this should be more than offset with savings once the Costa Rican plant is up and running. Also mentioned is the possibility of delaying the introduction of Skinny Pockets into the marketplace until next year, giving the necessary time needed to build the Costa Rican plant and thereby maximizing the perceived cost advantage. Still, others on the board of directors seem adamant about keeping production in the United States given the short time that designer jean labels remain popular (the average is three years to peak, followed by one year of harvesting). The company is, after all, contemplating the commitment of $10 million to the development of a full-scale manufacturing operation in Costa Rica (the Costa Rican government is matching this investment at no cost to Palmero Jeans Inc.), with the intent of producing not only jeans, but also other fashion-related products at this new facility.

Before making a decision, however, Linda needs to at least get a feel for the financial numbers associated with this product line and the potential costs and benefits that could be realized if the manufacturing shift takes place.

ANALYTICAL FINDINGS TO DATE

Linda has assigned you the task of analyzing the changes in the cost base that could be realized if a decision were made to relocate the manufacturing operation for the Skinny Pockets jeans line to Costa Rica. Associated with this, please note the following:

1. The annual costs associated with manufacturing Skinny Pockets at the Venice, California, plant are as follows:
   a. Plant overhead, interest expense, and administration costs: $1 200 000 annually (years 1, 2, and 3)
   b. Current (year 1) labour cost per unit (pair of jeans): $15.00
   c. Current (year 1) material cost per unit (pair of jeans): $10.00
   d. Current (year 1) shipping cost per unit (pair of jeans): $3.00
   e. Union contract—cost of wage adjustment for upcoming two years: 3% per year (years 2 and 3)
   f. Anticipated material cost increases for the upcoming two years: 2% per year (years 2 and 3)
   g. Anticipated increase in shipping costs for the upcoming two years: 10% per year (years 2 and 3)

Total production capacity of Skinny Pockets jeans at the Venice, California, plant: 200 000 pairs per year

2. The projected annual costs for the initial year (year 2) associated with manufacturing Skinny Pockets at the San José, Costa Rica, plant are anticipated to be:
   a. Plant overhead, interest expense, and administration costs: $2 500 000 annually
   b. Current labour cost per unit (pair of jeans): $4.00
   c. Current material cost per unit (pair of jeans): $7.00
   d. Current shipping cost per unit (pair of jeans): $6.00
   e. Costa Rica—cost of wage adjustment for upcoming two years (years 3 and 4): no change
   f. Anticipated material cost increases for the upcoming two years: 2% per year (years 3 and 4)
   g. Anticipated increase in shipping costs for the upcoming two years: 10% per year (years 3 and 4)

Total production capacity of Skinny Pockets at the San José, Costa Rica, plant: 360 000 pairs per year

3. If production is moved from the Venice, California, plant, it is assumed that this section of this plant will be closed and its employees will no longer be needed.

4. The initial pricing strategy for Palmero Jeans Inc.'s Skinny Pockets line is set for entry into the market at $48 per unit (pair of jeans). Feedback from distributors/retailers is already pointing toward the need for a more aggressive pricing strategy in order to be competitive with this demographic. It is entirely feasible that a price point of $38 per unit (pair of jeans), or even $35 per unit (pair of jeans), may need to be considered. This potential to move toward these lower price points will have to be considered as part of the decision-making process. Based on prior styles and designs, marketing anticipates the pricing curve to look like the following:

Skinny Pockets	Price per Unit (pair of jeans)
Launch Year (both locations)	$48.00
1 Year later	$38.00
2 Years later	$35.00
3 Years later	$35.00

5. The board of directors has set a minimum annual return on the capital investment in a product line at 10 percent. With a $1.5 million investment in Skinny Pockets, this means that the annual profit to be driven from this line must be at least $150 000. This, too, needs to be part of the financial evaluation.

6. The marketing department, in conferring with key distributors and retailers, has estimated that first-year sales of the Skinny Pockets jeans line would be in the 125 000 to 165 000 units (pairs of jeans) range. Assuming that targeted sales projections are met, this could climb to between 200 000 and 300 000 units by its anticipated peak demand in year three. In fact, the following probability scale has been established by the marketing department in this regard:

Skinny Pockets	90% Probability	75% Probability	60% Probability
Year 1	125 000 units	150 000 units	165 000 unit
Year 2	150 000 units	175 000 units	200 000 units
Year 3	200 000 units	250 000 units	300 000 units
Year 4	180 000 units	160 000 units	125 000 units

QUESTIONS

1. Conduct a breakeven analysis (BEP) for the first three years of production for the Venice, California, plant and the San José, Costa Rica, plant.

2. Revise this BEP analysis to include the $150 000 annual profit from the Skinny Pockets product line as desired by the board of directors.

3. Based on the information provided in the case, your BEP analysis, and on business concepts learned to date, identify what you feel are the five most important decision criteria that must be taken into consideration in making this decision. These criteria can be qualitative or quantitative.

4. In terms of a recommended strategic direction for the company, how would you rank the following options (1 = best to pursue, 3 = least attractive to pursue).
   a. Launch Skinny Pockets this year, with all three to four years of manufacturing taking place at the Venice, California, plant.
   b. Launch Skinny Pockets this year, with year 1 production at the Venice, California, plant, and years 2, 3, and 4 at the San José, Costa Rica, plant.
   c. Delay the launch of Skinny Pockets one year, and then produce all units at the San José, Costa Rica plant.

5. Explain why you chose the strategic action you identified as #1 above. Explain further why you thought that the action identified as #3 above was the least attractive to pursue.

Practise and learn online with Connect. Connect resources include additional and interactive study exercises, videos, and practice quizzing, as well as additional material you won't find in the printed text.

13 Introduction to Capital and Financial Markets

From the Student's Perspective

I remember thinking that stocks and bonds were just those random numbers wasting the last pages of the business section of the newspaper. I thought that no one actually followed or cared about them and that acronyms like TSX and S&P were simply mysterious and intangible systems that generated artificial gains or losses by chance. Was I ever wrong! Those hundreds of numbers are what actually drive business financing, allowing for the most efficient use of capital by the market and massively expanding the possibilities for investment and growth.

To me, the most interesting and important aspects of capital markets are their role in financing a company's start-up and/or growth initiatives. Capital markets carry out the desirable economic function of directing capital to productive uses. The savers (governments, businesses, and people who save some portion of their income) invest their money in capital market instruments like stocks and bonds. The borrowers (governments, businesses, and people who spend more than their income) borrow the savers' investments that have been entrusted to the capital markets. Capital markets create the opportunity for companies to issue equity or debt in order to obtain immediate capital to pursue investments with higher returns than the cost of such financing. This opportunity is what allows effective companies to thrive and continue to grow. Ineffective companies will not be able to obtain a high enough rate of return on investments to make such financing beneficial, hence capital markets allocate capital most efficiently.

Understanding this fact is the key to appreciating the importance of capital markets, even if their intricacies seem overwhelming at first. Don't give up, business students, because one day capital markets will inevitably become a part of your lives!

Heather Hawks was born in the small town of Port Perry, Ontario, and decided to specialize in accounting, entering her chosen Commerce program in 2006. She received the Dean's List with Distinction scholarship in 2008 and graduated on the Honour Roll in 2010. She is employed at PricewaterhouseCoopers in Toronto and is currently pursuing her CA designation. She plans on becoming an expert in the conversion of Canadian GAAP to IFRS standards and hopes, one day, to make partner at an accounting firm.

BUSINESS *in Action*

Facebook: Is an IPO Coming?

You have to hand it to Mark Zuckerberg. In just six short years, he has transformed Facebook from a social networking concept based out of his Harvard University dorm room to one of the Internet's most popular destinations. Analysts believe it is only a matter of time before Facebook, currently privately held, goes public via an IPO (initial public offering—the initial sale of stock by a corporation through a public exchange). Because it is a privately held corporation, full financial information relating to Facebook is currently not available. What we do know is that, with more than three-quarters of a billion users, Facebook has successfully transitioned from a social information sharing network to a sustainable business model, built on an advertising-revenue-driven formula similar to the one that catapulted Google Inc. to business fame. Facebook's user explosion is an advertiser's dream; their numbers, according to company news releases, grew from approximately 150 million at the beginning of 2009 to an estimated 350 million by year-end. It is estimated that the number of users will be in the range of 650 million to 750 million by the end of 2011. In June 2011, the number of Facebook users in Canada topped 16 million. With user growth comes revenue growth as the ability to reach this user base via target marketing is an attraction that marketers and advertisers simply cannot afford to not be a part of. Facebook's 2009 revenues were estimated to have been between US$600 million and US$800 million, with the *Wall Street Journal* reporting revenue estimates of US$750 million. Estimates for year-end 2011 revenue top $1 billion, according to analysts who closely track Facebook's business activities.

Up to this point in time, Facebook has relied on private-equity funding to transition the social networking organization into a business-savvy operation. Key financial backers include Digital Sky Technologies, Microsoft Corporation, Accel Partners, Greylock Partners, and Meritech Capital Partners. Hong Kong venture capitalist Li Ka-shing is also a key investor. Additional investors were added to the mix when the investment house Goldman Sachs and a private Russian investor committed more than $500 million to the company in the first quarter of 2011. Goldman Sachs, on behalf of Facebook, also is overseeing the raising of an additional $1.5 billion in private-equity investments through the international investment community (underway as of this writing). Those following this private-equity offering have indicated that more than $7 billion in customer inquiries were received for the potentially $1.5 billion in equity being offered.

Although Facebook has indicated that an IPO is not imminent in the near future (the company has indicated it is not a near-term priority), investors know that this type of operating performance will encourage Facebook's private-equity partners to seek to realize their return on their investments. The current Goldman Sachs estimates of Facebook's market value exceed US$50 billion. Facebook, already challenging the likes of Yahoo Inc. and even Google Inc. for leadership in attracting advertising revenue, is thought by many to be poised to become the largest Internet player in the very near future. Because of the type of information its users share, Facebook's strength is that it can provide advertisers with information relating to exactly what people are interested in—information that results in advertisers and marketers being able to rifle messages directly to the target audience that needs or desires a given product or service the most. Other Internet players to date simply cannot provide this same level of user information. For Facebook, the future appears bright. If and when it decides to go public (some speculate that this will now happen in the second or third quarter of 2012), a marketplace for its shares is certain to exist. Assuming that it can balance privacy concerns and the social networking needs of its users with the needs of advertisers and marketers, which is necessary to support the business model, Facebook could launch one of the most successful IPOs ever.[1]

Opening Comments

The title of this chapter—Introduction to Capital and Financial Markets—may cause you to wonder what its content will be all about. This chapter is designed to expose you to two important fundamentals associated with managing a business. The first has to do with business formation and the advantages and concerns of the three prominent ways to legally structure a business entity. The second is to provide you with a base-level understanding of the different ways in which a business generates or procures financial resources in order to fund its business opportunities, and the management decisions applicable to these options. This relates to its ability to generate money internally, as well as the key considerations applicable to external financing options, generally referred to as credit (debt) or equity financing. Although not immediately recognized as being interrelated, these two elements of business management (legal structure and financing) do go together. As a business organization commences and grows, the need for additional cash resources often acts as a catalyst for the way that its legal structure evolves, and sets the stage for decisions relating to the source, as well as the acquisition of the financial resources required to support its growth. With this in mind, let's now proceed to more fully understand the key characteristics of each of these two business decision areas, and the interrelationship that occurs as a business organization moves through its life cycle.

Business Ownership Options

LO1

Starting a business is often one of the most exciting decisions an individual, or group of individuals, can make. A key initial decision associated with the formation of a business is the type of legal structure to be utilized in order to enable the individual, or individuals, to commence business operations. In making this decision, five main factors will influence its final outcome. Although not meant to be all-inclusive, these factors are felt to be predominant influences in determining the type of legal structure to utilize in commencing business operations (see Figure 13.1):

FIGURE 13.1 Factor Analysis: The Legal Formation of a Business

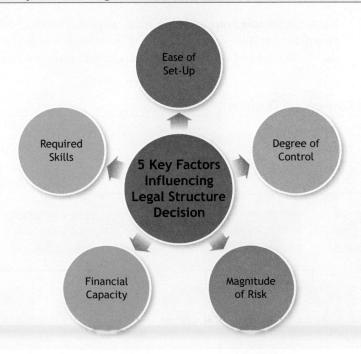

1. Ease of business set-up and operation
2. The degree of control that an owner desires
3. The magnitude of risk that individuals are willing to take on
4. The capacity of individuals to provide the financial needs required
5. The anticipated skills required for success

Ease of set-up relates to how easy it is to get a business up and running, and the various government regulations and required "filings" associated with a particular legal structure. The degree of control refers to the degree of ownership and level of decision-making authority that an individual (or individuals) desires within the business operation. The magnitude of risk refers to the level of financial, operational, and legal liability that individuals are willing to accept in owning and operating a business. Financial capacity refers to the financial resources that individuals have access to in order to invest in commencing business operations and supporting its ongoing cash requirements. A required skills analysis evaluates the degree of expertise that is needed to successfully manage the business against the skill set of the individual or individuals. Although these five factors are discussed in the context of commencing a business operation, it is important to note that a review of these factors will occur at several points during an organization's life cycle, as the business owners assess the needs within each of these areas and draw conclusions as to the capacity of the existing structure and ownership base to accept the risk and deliver the required resources and skills essential to sustaining the business operation. As the needs of the organization change, or the level of risk magnifies, the need to adjust the business organization's legal structure may be in the best interests of all those involved.

Using these four factors as a base for decision-making purposes, individuals can seek to form their business under one of three legal structures: a sole proprietorship, a partnership, or a corporation (see Figure 13.2). It should, again, be noted that commencing with one legal structure does not inhibit the ability of an individual, or individuals, to change the business structure in the future should it be in the best interests of the business organization.

> As the needs of the organization change, or the level of risk magnifies, the need to adjust the business organization's legal structure may be in the best interests of all those involved.

Sole Proprietorships

Sole Proprietorship refers to a business that is owned by one person and that is initiated without a requirement to create a separate legal entity.

For many, the **sole proprietorship** is the easiest way in which to commence a business. A sole proprietorship is the commencement of business by a single individual. In a sole proprietorship there is no real creation of a separate legal business entity. In essence, the individual and

FIGURE 13.2   Business Ownership Options

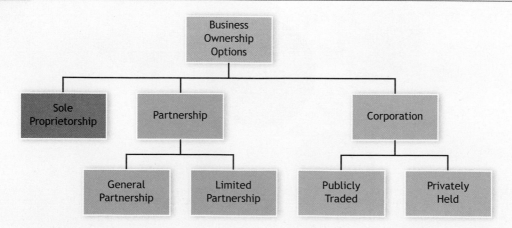

the business are one and the same. Business commencement generally takes place (it varies slightly by province) by registering your business, if in a name other than your own, and paying the required registration fee. In many cases, the name of the business is simply the name of the individual. If this is the case, most provinces do not require any formal registration at all. The debts of the business are also deemed to be the debts of the owner. Any income earned by the business is treated as the personal income of the owner. The key advantage of the sole proprietorship beyond the simplicity of the commencement of the operation is that the sole proprietor has 100 percent control of the business with regard to ownership and in making decisions relating to the business. A key risk issue is that the sole proprietor is 100 percent personally exposed to the liabilities incurred by the business. In the event that the business is unable to pay its debts (i.e., monies that it owes), the sole proprietor becomes personally obligated for such debts. A second concern with sole proprietorships is that the skill set of the business is limited to the skills possessed by the sole proprietor. For example, an individual who is skilled at building houses may not have the business acumen to successfully own and operate a residential or commercial real estate development business. Finally, sole proprietors are limited to their own personal capacity to invest and/or borrow money in support of the business organization. Those sole proprietors with limited financial capacity may find that they are unable to invest the necessary resources in the business organization in order to sustain it on an ongoing basis. Using our factor analysis approach (identified in Figure 13.1) in considering the legal formation of a business, the sole proprietorship can be summarized as shown in Figure 13.3.

> The key advantage of the sole proprietorship, beyond the simplicity of the commencement of the operation, is that the sole proprietor has 100 percent control of the business with regard to ownership and in making decisions relating to the business.

Partnerships

Recognizing some of the limitations of sole proprietorships, individuals desiring to undertake the formation of a business often opt to take the route of a **partnership**. A partnership is a business organization that is formed by two or more individuals. Although we often think of partnerships as being two partners, it is important to note that many partnerships have more than two partners. Legal and accounting firms are a good example of this, with a number of these firms possessing many partners. Although you don't technically have to have a **partnership agreement**

Partnership is a business organization that is formed by two or more individuals.

Partnership Agreement is a written agreement among the partners that outlines the expectations of each partner and details how the partnership is going to work.

FIGURE 13.3	Factor Analysis: Sole Proprietorship

Factor	Summary Conclusions	Advantage	Potential Concern
Ease of Set-up	Generally requires little more than registering the business name	√	
Degree of Control	100% ownership and full decision-making control	√	
Magnitude of Risk	Unlimited personal liability for risks associated with the business		√
Financial Capacity	Limited to the financial resources of the sole proprietor		√
Skills Required	Limited to the skill set and business competencies of the sole proprietor		√

to commence a business partnership in Canada (the partnership act of the province where the business is located may rule that a business is a partnership on the basis of its structure), it is highly recommended that such an agreement be developed and put into force at the time of inception of the business. Creating a partnership agreement ensures that the expectations of each partner, and the details of how the partnership is going to work, are fully understood by all partners involved. The partnership agreement also outlines the percentage of ownership that is attributed to each partner. As with a sole proprietorship, partnerships are not separate legal entities when it comes to liability and taxation. Income earned and liabilities incurred by the partnership are treated as personal income and personal liabilities to each of the partners. Business income or losses pass through the partnership and are reported on each partner's personal income tax return. In the event that the partnership itself is unable to pay its liabilities, these then become the personal obligations of the partners. Partnerships also carry the obligation of what is called **joint and several liability**. This means that each partner could be liable for the total debts of the partnership if other partners are unable to pay their portion of a partnership's obligations. As can be inferred from the name "partnership," individuals often choose to initiate this form of business formation as it enables the partners to jointly share the risk, jointly contribute the dollars needed to fund the business (thereby enabling a greater level of financial capacity than partners could provide on a stand-alone basis), and take advantage of the combined skills and competencies of all partners involved. An additional concern relating to partnerships is the sharing of ownership and decision-making control. This can be especially disconcerting in small partnerships with two or three partners. Differences of opinion on strategic direction, commitment to the business, or competencies in operating the business can, and often do, occur. To protect from this type of discord impacting the business, many partnership agreements include a **buy-sell agreement**. Using our factor analysis approach to considering the legal formation of a business, a partnership can be summarized as shown in Figure 13.4.

Joint and Several Liability refers to the liability obligation of partners as the result of a legal contract. Partners can be held individually liable for their share of the obligation (several), or fully liable for the full obligation (joint) in the event that the other parties to the agreement are unable to pay their obligations.

Buy-Sell Agreement is a written agreement among the partners that details the sale by one partner and the purchase by another of the business interest of the selling partner.

> Creating a partnership agreement ensures that the expectations of each partner, and the details of how the partnership is going to work, are fully understood by all partners involved.

FIGURE 13.4 Factor Analysis: Partnership

Factor	Summary Conclusions	Advantage	Potential Concern
Ease of Set-up	Easy to set up; however, the development of a partnership agreement is highly recommended. A time delay may result, and legal fees will most likely be incurred.	√	
Degree of Control	Ownership and decision-making control is divided among partners, in accordance with the partnership agreement.		√
Magnitude of Risk	Unlimited personal liability (joint and several) exists for risks associated with the business.		√
Financial Capacity	Financial resource capacity is expanded to include the capabilities of all partners.	√	
Skills Required	Skill set and business competencies are expanded to include the capabilities of all partners.	√	

Our discussion above has been largely focused on what are termed "general" partnerships, where all partners are active in the business and share the full business risk associated with the organization. It is important to mention that another type of partnership arrangement does exist; this is called a **limited liability partnership (LLP)**. A limited liability partnership is a partnership that is made up of both general partners (at least one) and limited (passive) partners. Limited partners are individuals who contribute equity capital (money in exchange for a percentage of ownership) to the organization, but are not actively involved in the management of the business operation and have minimal control over daily business decisions. Given this minimal business involvement, the partnership agreements associated with LLPs clearly stipulate the limitations of the liability exposure of these limited (passive) partners to the value of their investment. The general partner(s) assume(s) the full liability exposure on behalf of the partnership. Limited liability partnerships are commonly found in the real estate sector, where large sums of capital are required for development purposes but the day-to-day management responsibilities can be delegated to a small management team.

> **Limited Liability Partnership (LLP)** is a partnership that is made up of both general partners (at least one) and limited (passive) partners.

Corporations

The formation of a **corporation** results in a marked change in the legal status of a business organization. Unlike sole proprietorships and partnerships, which are not viewed as separate legal entities, a corporation is just that. By virtue of its business definition, a corporation creates a distinct legal entity separate from its owners. This distinct, separate legal entity is established by the process of **incorporation**. In Canada, this can be done at the provincial level, which enables the business to legally operate in a given province, or federally, which enables the business to operate throughout Canada. A key advantage in incorporating federally is that you are able to use the same business name in all provinces. It should be noted, however, that federal incorporation is more expensive to set up, and requires additional paperwork over and above that found at the provincial level. In addition, incorporation brings with it requirements associated with corporate governance. A **board of directors** will need to be established, officers of the corporation elected, minutes of meetings kept, and resolutions associated with business decisions approved and documented.

> **Corporation** is a business entity that, legally, is separate and distinct from its owners.

> **Incorporation** is the legal process of setting up a corporation.

> **Board of Directors** is an appointed or elected body of a for-profit or not-for-profit corporation that oversees and advises management on issues challenging the organization on behalf of its stakeholders and shareholders.

Given the commentary above, it can be rightfully assumed that the incorporation process will result in a longer time frame to get a business up and running, as well as a higher cost to do this. Although the cost of incorporation varies by province, and between provincial incorporation and federal incorporation, it can be assumed that the cost of the incorporation process will be in the hundreds, if not thousands, of dollars. So, why incorporate if it is so much easier to just open up a sole proprietorship or to form a partnership? First, forming a corporation protects the organization's owners (shareholders) by limiting their liability. As a separate legal entity, the liabilities of the corporation do not automatically transfer to the owners in the event that the corporation is unable to pay its bills. This, in itself, is a very attractive feature of a corporation. Second, ownership rights are clearly defined and are based on the percentage of stock owned by its owners. Third, the ability to issue shares of stock as a means of raising additional cash (capital) for the business organization is unique to the corporation. In addition, business organizations need to be incorporated in order to be eligible for many federal government programs, and to take advantage of tax incentives relating to capital gains exemptions and small business deductions. The corporate tax rate, for those business organizations that are earning profits, may also result in a lower total tax obligation than if the business were left as a sole proprietorship or partnership. Having said this, incorporation does require the filing of a tax return on the part of the corporation, and then including income received from the corporation (dividends), by its owners, on their personal income tax returns, where it could be subject to additional taxation. Again, using our factor analysis approach to considering the legal formation of a business, a corporation can be summarized as shown in Figure 13.5.

> Because it is a separate legal entity, the liabilities of the corporation do not automatically transfer to the owners in the event that the corporation is unable to pay its bills.

FIGURE 13.5 Factor Analysis: Corporation

Factor	Summary Conclusions	Advantage	Potential Concern
Ease of Set-up	More cumbersome to set up. A search needs to be conducted of the corporate name (to verify its availability). Articles of Incorporation need to be created, and incorporation documents need to be filed. It is, initially, the most expensive form of business set-up. As a separate entity, incorporation requires the filing of a separate tax return for the corporation, as well as other annual reporting requirements. Governance set-up and procedural requirements also exist.		√
Degree of Control	Ownership is based on the percentage of shares in the corporation owned by an individual.		√
Magnitude of Risk	As the corporation is a separate, legal entity, the liabilities of the corporation are limited to the corporation itself.	√	
Financial Capacity	Financial resource capacity is expanded, as the corporation has the ability to issue shares of stock to raise capital. The corporation can also borrow money in its own name.	√	
Skills Required	Skill set and business competencies are expanded to include the capabilities of all shareholders, and/or a professional management team.	√	

Private Corporations are corporations whose ownership is private. The shares of stock of the corporation are not publicly traded.

Public Corporations are corporations whose shares of stock are traded on at least one stock exchange or are publicly available in the over-the-counter market.

Initial Public Offering (IPO) refers to the initial sale of stock, by a corporation, through a public exchange.

Exchange is an organization that facilitates the trading of securities, stocks, commodities, and other financial instruments. Exchanges provide a platform for selling these financial instruments to the public at large.

Over-the-Counter (OTC) refers to stocks being publicly traded through a dealer network versus an exchange.

As noted in Figure 13.2, there are two main types of corporations that students need to familiarize themselves with—private corporations and public corporations. **Private corporations** are business organizations whose ownership is privately held. This means that the shares of the corporation are not publicly traded and are not available to the general public for purchase. As an example, assume that a business located in Montreal, Quebec, is incorporated in that province as a private corporation. The Province of Quebec would assign this business a provincial corporate registration number; let's assume that it is Quebec 9647-0500. The articles of incorporation would identify that shares have been issued to the owners involved in this private corporation, reflective of the percentage of ownership attributed to each. These shares, however, are not available for sale to just anyone. As a private corporation, the selling of the shares would be a private transaction between the current owner of the shares and a potential purchaser. The articles of incorporation may restrict just how shares may be purchased and offered for sale. For example, there may be an obligation to offer existing shareholders what is called "first right of refusal" on the shares to be sold before a shareholder can seek an outside buyer. In a private corporation, the shares do not trade on one of the public exchanges as publicly traded companies do. This results in greater difficulty in establishing a price for these shares, and, potentially, the selling of these shares, than that experienced with the selling of shares relating to a public corporation.

Public corporations are corporations whose shares of stock are initially issued via an **initial public offering (IPO)**, and whose shares are then traded on at least one stock **exchange**, or are publicly available in the **over-the-counter (OTC)** market. Public corporation shares, once issued, are then considered to be publicly held. Unlike the private corporation, whose share price is difficult to value due to the fact that the shares are not publicly traded, the share value of publicly traded corporations is set as the result of daily trading activity on these shares by the marketplace (public) at large. Publicly traded corporations also have significantly more regulatory and periodic information filing requirements that they need to abide by. These requirements are set out by the securities commission that oversees the exchange the company is trading its shares on. In Canada, securities exchange governance has been established at the provincial level. In Ontario, for example, this commission is referred to as the OSC, or Ontario Securities Commission, which administers and enforces the security legislation of the province of Ontario. In Alberta, it is the Alberta Securities Commission. In Quebec, it is the Autorité des marchés financiers (AMF). Within the United States of America, a single federal regulatory agency has been established for this purpose: the U.S. Securities and Exchange Commission, or SEC.[2]

Business Evolution

LO2

As stated at the beginning of this chapter, the decision on which type of legal approach to take when forming a business will depend on a number of factors, five of which have been presented in our factor analysis summary of each of the three legal options discussed (sole proprietorship, partnership, and corporation). For many individuals, commencing business operations is easiest via the establishment of a sole proprietorship. As the business moves from its initial embryonic phase and begins to grow and mature, its cash requirements, as well as the potential liability exposure, may necessitate a revisiting of the initial legal formation. As an example, the need for additional cash necessary for investment into the business in order to support growth may result in the need for a sole proprietor to take on a partner, or to incorporate in order to sell shares of stock to venture capitalists or venture capital companies. Let's use the example of Lululemon Athletica Inc. to illustrate this evolutionary process. Keep in mind that although Lululemon Athletica's growth led to a particular path in terms of legal formation and transition, other companies have taken different paths with equal success. Lululemon Athletica Inc.'s path of business formation and evolution is illustrated in Figure 13.6.

Most Canadians are aware of Lululemon Athletica Inc. and its yoga-inspired apparel line built around a value proposition of healthy living. Lululemon, with annual sales now exceeding US$450 million, is already one of Canada's great business success stories and is poised to be one of Canada's next great global brands. Things were not always this way at Lululemon Athletica. As discussed in a Business in Action vignette in Chapter 3, Lululemon founder Dennis (Chip) Wilson commenced business operations, on his own, in 1998. Wilson, as owner, was successful in growing the business through a combination of business credit, cash he personally invested into the business, and profits generated by the business. This business approach served Wilson well initially, as he stretched his brand recognition and opened additional store locations. He recognized, however, that in order to gain access to the level of investment required to significantly grow Lululemon Athletica, financial resources beyond

FIGURE 13.6 Lululemon Athletica: Evolutionary Path

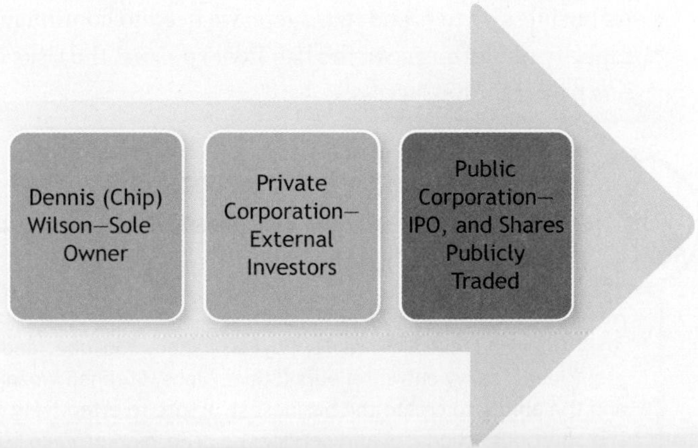

his personal capacity would be necessary. With this in mind, Wilson restructured Lululemon Athletica Inc. as a private corporation in 2005, and successfully sold shares of stock in his business to private investors. Two of the most noteworthy private investors were the Boston-based venture capital firms Advent International Corp. and Highland Capital Partners. These two companies invested approximately US$195 million in Lululemon Athletica Inc., for a significant minority (estimated at 48 percent) ownership stake in the company. In addition to the capital investment, the two firms also brought to Lululemon Athletica Inc. a wealth of new business competencies to complement the skills that Chip Wilson possessed. Yes, Wilson had to give up some decision-making control of Lululemon Athletica Inc. and saw his ownership stake decrease, but the additional financial capacity and skills, along with better management of the expansion risk being undertaken, made the shift in business structure worthwhile. As Wilson indicated publicly, when commenting on the equity infusion being provided by Advent International Corp. and Highland Capital Partners, "We like the Advent/Highland group because of whom they have brought to the table. The expertise of the board and management will ensure that we are successful in the U.S. and worldwide." With this new influx of cash, Lululemon Athletica Inc. continued its successful growth path. In 2007, seeing additional opportunity to further expand and grow, Lululemon Athletica Inc. made a decision to further restructure from a private corporation to a public corporation. This transition was high-lighted by the launch of its IPO (initial public offering) and the listing of Lululemon Athletica Inc. shares on both the Toronto Stock Exchange (TSX, listed as LLL) and the NASDAQ (listed as LULU). The issuance of these additional shares of ownership in Lululemon Athletica Inc. enabled the company to raise approximately US$320 million, thereby providing the additional capital needed to finance the company's future growth aspirations. The 2007 IPO was ranked the third best IPO offering in the United States that year (out of 177).[3]

Again, the example of Lululemon Athletica Inc. was intended to provide an illustration of how the evolution of the business, and the changing needs of the organization, can result in shifts in the legal structure behind the business operation. As business owners and managers, we need to continually be aware of the financial capacity of our business, the liability exposure, the risks being incurred, and the skill sets necessary for success. Using these factors as a basis for a business review, we can then make forward-thinking adjustments as to how we operate our business in order to ensure its ongoing success. The need to raise capital to fund future needs can, and often does, play a key role in this decision-making process. The remainder of this chapter focuses on providing some insight into where, and how, managers utilize internal and external financial resources in order to fund their growth strategies and maintain their financial stability. Most of our discussion will pertain to corporations, as the flexibility of the capital structure within these organizations provides us with the best framework for discussion. A macro-based discussion relating to not-for-profits is also provided, as there are some unique differences between the sources of cash between for-profit organizations and not-for-profits (NFPs).

> As business owners and managers, we need to continually be aware of the financial capacity of our business, the liability exposure, the risks being incurred, and the skill sets necessary for success.

BUSINESS *in Action*

Sequoia Capital

Have you ever wondered how businesses such as AdMob, Apple, Cisco, eHarmony, Electronic Arts, Google, LinkedIn, Oracle, PayPal, Yahoo, YouTube, and Zappos got started? Yes, it takes great ideas, savvy entrepreneurs (Steven Jobs, Stephen Wozniak, Larry Page, Sergey Brin, etc.), and the ability to create the business structure to effectively design, develop, and communicate the solutions (products and services) to the marketplace to meet the needs of the targeted

customers. It also takes money. The amount of money that a business will burn through in its initial start up phase, and in moving the organization to breakeven point, can be staggering. It can take years and cost millions of dollars. So, where do entrepreneurs get the cash to sustain a business until its revenue is sufficient to cover its costs? Well, one option is to get venture capital companies, such as Sequoia Capital, to invest in them. In exchange for an equity stake in the business (percentage of ownership), firms such as Sequoia Capital invest the required thousands, or millions, of dollars necessary to get these young but potentially lucrative upstarts off the ground. We say lucrative because, in return for this investment, the venture capital company will expect the market value of the business it invests in to grow, thereby enabling it to get a solid return on its investment when, and if, it chooses to sell its share of the business. Sequoia Capital specializes in venture capital funding in business sectors such as energy, financial services, health care services, Internet, mobile, outsourcing services, and technology markets. The organization seeks to collaborate with the founders in a way that enables these entrepreneurs to successfully launch and sustain their businesses. By collaboration, Sequoia Capital provides more than just money. They also provide access to seasoned professionals and managers who provide much-needed guidance and expertise to the development of the business idea and the launch of the business into the marketplace. Sequoia Capital has three rounds of business financing that entrepreneurs can apply for. The first is "seed" funding, which is designed to assist in getting the business off of the ground. Sequoia typically invests $100 000 to $1 million in such start-ups. The second round of funding is what is called "early stage" funding. This funding seeks to assist business ideas that have gained traction in the marketplace and now need the necessary financing and support to build and sustain the business model and its supporting structure. Sequoia Capital typically invests between $1 million and $10 million in this stage into the selected companies that it chooses to support. The third stage of funding is "growth stage" funding. Typically, with investments in the $10 million to $100 million range, this stage of funding is focused on assisting these companies with the necessary capital to expand their markets, make necessary acquisitions, grow the depth of competencies and expertise, and prepare for the launch of the organization's IPO. Companies funded by Sequoia Capital (founded, in 1972, by Don Valentine) now account for more than 14 percent of the value of the NASDAQ. Recent funding announcements (May 2010) by Sequoia Capital include investments in Klarna, a Swedish-based company that specializes in payment solutions for the ecommerce sector, Taykey, an Israel-based company that offers interest-based advertising platforms, and Sipera Systems, a Texas-based leader in solutions in "unified communications" technologies, to name a few. With more than US$1.5 billion in funds, and worldwide exposure with offices in China, Israel, and the United States, Sequoia Capital thinks of itself as the entrepreneur behind the entrepreneurs. Oh, and by the way—all of the companies listed in the opening sentence of this "Business in Action" received start-up funding from Sequoia Capital.[4]

WEB INTEGRATION

For more information regarding Sequoia Capital, visit **sequoiacap.com**. On Twitter, Sequoia Capital is available @sequoia_capital, or Google Sequoia Capital.

Funding the Organization

LO3

One of the core responsibilities of a manager is to assess the financial resource requirements of an organization and determine how those needs are going to be met. This means that managers need to review the **capital structure** of their organization and make decisions as to how the organization is going to finance its operations and what will be the mixture of use of the different sources of funds it will have at its disposal. A key component of this analysis will be to manage the debt/equity ratio (discussed in more detail in Chapter 14), which provides managers with an understanding as to how much debt the organization has incurred, or is willing to incur, in financing its operations, and whether this has added significant negative risk to the organization's financial stability.[5]

Capital Structure refers to an organization's mixture (use) of debt, internal cash reserves, and external equity-based investments in financial support of operational activities.

Sources of Funds

In general, for-profit organizations have three sources of funds available to them (see Figure 13.7). These sources of funds are as follows:

- Funds derived from operations
- Funds obtained via credit facilities (debt)
- Funds obtained via equity financing

FIGURE 13.7 Sources of Funds

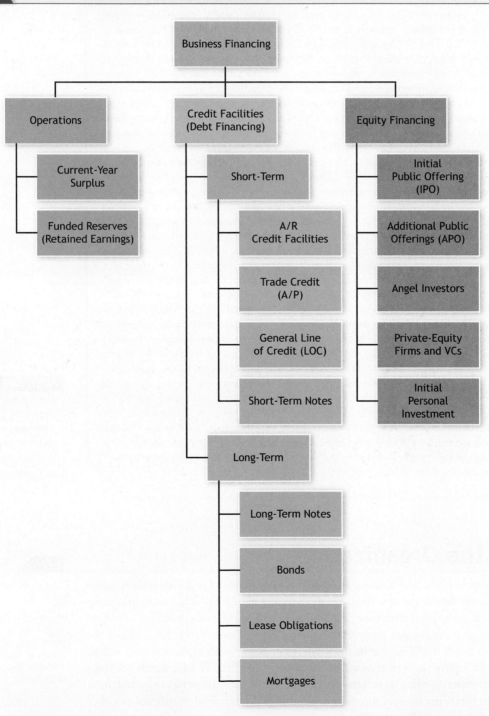

Funds Derived from Operations

Funds derived from operations refers to two internal sources of funds that managers can look to in order to fund current and future activities within an organization. These two internal sources of funds are:

- Current-year operating profits

- Retained earnings

Current-year **operating profits** (or operating surplus, in the case of not-for-profits) are the excess dollars that organizations have generated, and have at their disposal, during the current operating period as a result of their business activities after their current expense obligations have been paid. It can be best understood as total revenue minus total operating expenses during a defined period of time (i.e., month, quarter, or year). The organization's income statement (discussed in Chapter 14), which reflects operating results for this defined period of time, identifies the profit that the organization has realized from its operations. This profit, unless paid out to investors/shareholders, becomes an immediate source of new capital for an organization, which it can then choose to reinvest in support of future growth opportunities, enhanced R&D exploration, or the acquisition and/or replacement of equipment in support of the organization's activities.

Operating Profits equal total revenue minus total operating expenses.

Retained earnings represents the dollar amount of net earnings that an organization has accumulated over the history of its operations, and that it has chosen to hold within the organization (not pay out to investors/shareholders). Identified under the owners' equity section of the balance sheet (discussed in Chapter 14), retained earnings becomes a source of funds for the organization to draw upon in the event of operating losses during a given period, or in the event that additional investment needs to be made into the organization (growth, R&D, equipment replacement, acquisitions, and so on). Retained earnings will also be used to compensate for operating losses occurring in a given year. An important caution to identify, at this point, is that although retained earnings is considered a source of capital, managers need to also view the cash position of the company (found on the balance sheet) to be sure that the dollar amount identified in retained earnings is still available to the organization in a liquid form (cash, near cash). The ability to draw from prior earnings, which is what retained earnings represents, is based on the belief that the prior earnings remain within the organization and have not been used for other purposes, thereby diminishing the cash position of the company. The cash position of the company, as reflected on the balance sheet, is the most accurate recognition of the capacity of the organization to draw on its cash reserves to fund its current and future needs.

Retained Earnings refers to the dollar amount of net earnings accumulated over the history of an organization that it has chosen to hold within the organization.

The concepts of current-year operating profits and retained earnings are fully explained in Chapter 14. At this point, it is important to understand that the operation itself represents a viable source of cash as long as it is, and has been, profitable.

Credit Facilities (Debt Financing)

Credit facilities refers to debt that an organization has taken on in support of its business activities. It represents the organization borrowing money or receiving products or services on a credit basis from another organization or individual(s). Credit facility arrangements provide the borrowing organization with access to money that it normally would not have access to, under the stipulation that it will be paid back over a defined period of time, or on a definitive date. The repayment terms may include an obligation to pay interest on the money borrowed as well. Credit facilities are generally viewed as falling into one of two debt categories: short-term credit facilities and long-term credit facilities (see Figure 13.8).

Credit Facilities refers to debt that an organization has taken on in support of its business activities.

Credit facilities are a type of debt financing. With debt financing comes a legal obligation to pay both the interest on the debt, if applicable, and the debt principal, when due, regardless of the organization's financial position.

FIGURE 13.8   Credit Facilities

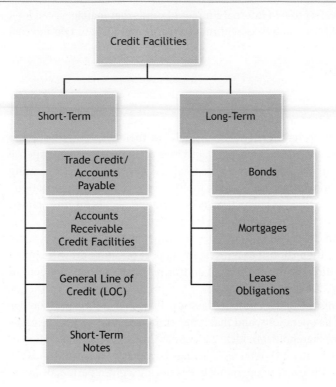

SHORT-TERM CREDIT FACILITIES

Short-Term Credit Facilities refers to debt obligations that an organization takes on for a short period of time, generally less than one year.

Accounts Payable refers to money owed by an organization to its suppliers and other short-term service providers.

Accounts Receivable refers to money owed by customers of the organization for products or services that the organization has delivered to such customers, but has not yet received payment for.

Line of Credit refers to an arrangement with a lending institution that provides an organization with a pre-arranged borrowing ceiling (maximum) that the organization can draw on at any time, and in any amount, up to the agreed-upon limit.

Collateral refers to capital assets or monetary assets used to secure a credit facility. The collateral would be used to pay off the lender in the event that the organization cannot meet the credit facility repayment obligations.

Short-term credit facilities refers to debt obligations that an organization takes on for a short period of time, generally one year or less. Typical categories of short-term credit include trade credit, borrowing against the organization's future flow of accounts receivable, borrowing against a general line of credit the organization has established, or borrowing on a short-term-note basis (i.e., borrowing a specific sum of money for a specified period of time—three months, six months, one year). Trade credit, for example, is used when the organization orders products or receives services from another organization but payment for these products or services is deferred until a later date (e.g., "30 days to pay"). These are commonly referred to as the **accounts payable** of the organization, and are found under the current liabilities section of the balance sheet (discussed in Chapter 14). Credit facilities relating to borrowing against the future inflow of **accounts receivable**, or against a **line of credit**, relate directly to the cash operating cycle (discussed in Chapters 9 and 12) and the managing of the cash flow needs of the organization. A line of credit (LOC) is a credit facility that gives the organization immediate access to a predetermined sum of money at a specified interest rate. Pre-approved through a lending facility, the line of credit provides the organization with the ability to draw on this account to meet frequent, short-term capital needs. As an example, if the cash flow of the organization is such that its accounts receivable collections may not be sufficient in time to meet a payroll obligation, then the organization could borrow the money to meet its payroll obligation through its line of credit and then pay off this short-term borrowing when the accounts receivable are collected. Borrowing against a future flow of accounts receivable works in a manner similar to a general line of credit. It is just that the accounts receivable of the organization are used as **collateral** against this loan or credit facility. An example of an industry that makes significant use of such arrangements is the furniture retail and distribution industry. Deferred payment purchase options for customers (think of Leon's Furniture and its "don't pay a cent event") result in very elongated cash operating cycles for these companies. In order to continue to finance the purchase of new products from manufacturers given the long repayment time allowances to its customers, these retailers and distributors rely on lenders to provide capital to them, with their future accounts receivable repayment streams acting as collateral. Short-term notes are obligations that an organization agrees to as a result of borrowing a defined sum of money for a fixed period of time (one year or less). Short-term notes are commonly written for periods such as one month, three months, six months, or one year. Organizations with short-term borrowing requirements make use of this type of credit facility in order to cover the cost of short-term projects, quarterly seasonal fluctuations in their business, bridge financing for longer-term projects, or other definitive short-term borrowing needs. These notes may be secured with collateral, or, assuming a strong credit rating on the part of the company, could be lent without a formal collateral requirement (i.e., secured versus unsecured notes).

Overall, short-term financing, and its integral support of the cash operating cycle, is a common activity with most organizations. The particular type of short-term financing undertaken will vary by organization and business sector. An understanding of the amount of short-term credit (debt) that an organization has taken on can be achieved by analyzing the current liability section of the organization's balance sheet (discussed in Chapter 14). Credit facilities, defined as short-term, are expected to be repaid by the organization during the current operating year and are a key factor in assessing the liquidity of a company.

> Credit facilities defined as short-term are expected to be repaid by the organization during the current operating year and are a key factor in assessing the liquidity of a company.

LONG-TERM CREDIT FACILITIES

Long-term credit facilities represent debt that an organization obligates itself to repay over a time frame that exceeds one year in duration. As with short-term credit facilities, these debt obligations may, or may not, include an interest expense obligation; although, with long-term credit facilities, it is likely that such a **cost of borrowing** will apply. Examples of some of the more common long-term credit facilities that organizations tend to utilize in procuring borrowed capital for infusion into their operations are bonds, mortgages, long-term notes, and lease obligations. The amount of cash required to build the capital asset infrastructure needed to compete would be beyond the scope of many organizations if long-term financing capabilities, through the use of credit facilities, were not part of their funding mix. The costs, as an example, of the plant and facility investments required to build manufacturing facilities in the automotive, aerospace, and technology sectors can run into the millions of dollars. Long-term credit arrangements enable organizations to construct such facilities by providing the needed dollars up front and then allowing the organizations to repay these debt obligations over the useful life span of the capital assets that the debt has funded. For plant and facility capital assets, this could be periods of 15, 20, or 25 years or more. Given the importance of this source of funding, let's take a bit of time to discuss, in more detail, some of the more common long-term credit facility options used by organizations.

Long-Term Credit Facilities represent debt that an organization obligates itself to repay over a time frame that exceeds one year.

Cost of Borrowing refers to the total sum of money over and above the principal borrowed paid by an organization as a result of incurring and repaying a debt obligation. This would include interest paid as well as costs incurred in setting up the credit facility.

Bonds   A **bond** (also referred to as a fixed-income security) is a credit facility by which an organization (corporations, governments) borrows money for a stipulated period of time. In return for the use of these funds, the organization promises to pay the holder of the bond an agreed-upon amount of interest at regular intervals (generally, semi-annually) during the period of time for which the funds are borrowed. At the end of the stipulated period of time, the organization borrowing the money agrees to repay the full amount borrowed (bond principal or face value). A number of different types of bonds are available in the marketplace (treasury, convertible, step-up, put bonds); for the purposes of our discussion, we will focus on what is termed a straight bond. Figure 13.9 provides an illustration of how a 10-year straight bond would work.

Bond refers to a credit facility with which an organization borrows money for a stipulated period of time. In return for the use of these funds, the organization promises to pay the holder of the bond an agreed-upon amount of interest at regular intervals (generally, semi-annually) during the period of time for which the funds are borrowed.

FIGURE 13.9   How a 10-Year Bond Works

Year 1	Money, in the amount of the bond's face value, flows into the company when the bond is issued. Interest payments begin, to the bondholder, generally, on a semi-annual basis.
Years 2–9	Interest is paid to the bondholder.
Year 10	Principal and remaining interest is paid to the bondholder.

Example: 10-year bond, $1 000 000 principal at 11% interest

Year 1	$1 000 000 flows into company. The company will need to make pro-rata interest payments on the amount borrowed.
Years 2–9	Annual interest payment of $1 000 000 × .11 = $110 000 (paid semi-annually) to the current bondholder. This means two payments of $55 000 at six-month intervals.
Year 10	Payment of $1 000 000 face value and any applicable interest, for partial year up to maturity date, to current bondholder.

Although bonds are considered a credit facility (debt instrument), the purpose of a bond for many organizations is to raise capital for the firm. The dollars raised from the issuance of a bond are often used to provide an organization with the capital necessary to build infrastructure, fund acquisitions, or provide new working capital to the organization for the purpose of developing and growing the business. The issuance of a bond is generally handled through an investment firm or bank that facilitates the bond offering in the marketplace (see Figure 13.10).

> Bonds represent a legal obligation to pay the face value of the bond on a given date in the future. This requires the organization to establish reserves for these bonds prior to this date so that when the maturity date is reached the bond repayment can be made.

As identified in Figure 13.10, once a bond has been issued and sold to a potential investor, that investor may resell the bond in the marketplace to new potential investors. In re-selling the bond, the initial investor transfers the rights to future interest paid on the bond by the bond issuer, as well as the receipt of the face value of the bond at its maturity date, to the new bondholder. Because the length of time to maturity on a bond can span 10, 20, or 30 years or more, the market value of the bond (in the marketplace), prior to its maturity, may change. This is due to movements in interest rates that make holding the bond more or less attractive,

FIGURE 13.10   Bond Issuance Process

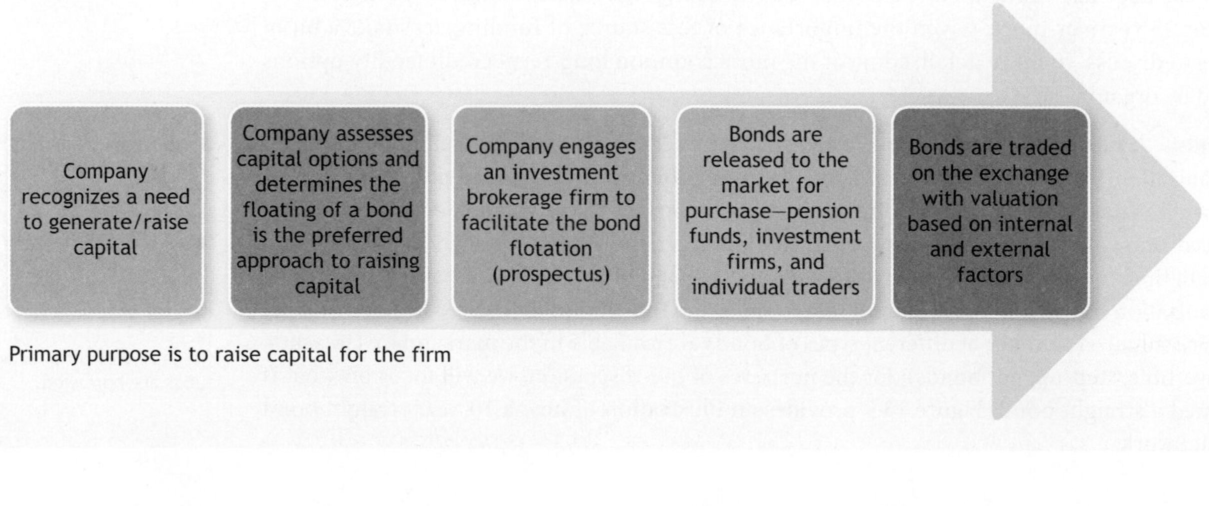

Company recognizes a need to generate/raise capital	Company assesses capital options and determines the floating of a bond is the preferred approach to raising capital	Company engages an investment brokerage firm to facilitate the bond flotation (prospectus)	Bonds are released to the market for purchase—pension funds, investment firms, and individual traders	Bonds are traded on the exchange with valuation based on internal and external factors

Primary purpose is to raise capital for the firm

FIGURE 13.11 Bond Life Cycle

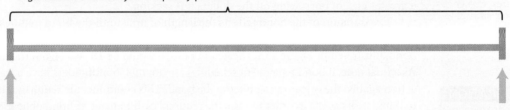

During the life of the bond (period between issuance and maturity date), the bond may be resold, by bondholders, to new investors. The interest on the bond is paid to the holder of the bond on the date that interest payments are due. The market value of the bond may change during this period, depending on market factors and changes in the bond's rating and/or changes in the issuing organization's solvency and liquidity position.

Bond Issuance
- Company issues bond through investment firm or bank
- Proceeds from the sale of the bond go to company, less investment firm's or bank's fees
- Company begins to pay interest to bondholders

Bond Maturity
- Bond is retired
- Company pays any remaining interest obligation to bondholders
- Company pays the face value (par value) of the bond to bondholders on maturity date

or changes in the liquidity and/or solvency position of the issuing organization that may change the risk associated with owning the bond. Figure 13.11 provides an overview of the key characteristics associated with a bond's life cycle.

The issuance of bonds is not limited to corporations. In Canada, municipalities (with some issuing restrictions and unique debt repayment requirements), provincial governments, and the federal government are all common issuers of bonds for the purpose of financing a variety of other activities essential in supporting their citizens. When discussing bonds, potential buyers focus their attention toward three key areas: the coupon rate, face value, and maturity date. The *coupon rate* is the interest rate that the bond promises to pay on the *face value* of the bond. Again, interest is generally paid on a semi-annual basis. The face value (also known as the par value or the principal borrowed) is the value that the issuing organization (the organization borrowing the money) agrees to pay to the bondholder on the *maturity date* of the bond, which is the day that the principal payment is due.

The following two factors determine the coupon rate (interest rate) at which a bond is issued:

1. The risk-quality rating of the organization issuing the bond
2. The duration of the bond

The risk-quality rating refers to the probability that the organization issuing the bond will be able to repay to the bondholder the face value of the bond on its maturity date, as well as meet the required interest payments on the bond during the period when the bond is outstanding. **Rating agencies**, such as Dominion Bond Rating Service Limited (DBRS), based in Toronto, Moody's Investors Service Inc., Standard & Poor's Inc., Fitch Inc., and A.M. Best Company Inc., to name a few, will assign a bond rating to organizations issuing bonds, or that currently have bonds outstanding. The purpose of these agencies is to provide current and prospective bondholders (investors) with an objective and independent creditworthiness assessment of an organization's solvency, liquidity, and overall long-term organizational health. In drawing these conclusions, analysts from these agencies will review an organization's current and historical performance, have meetings and discussions with an organization's management team, review publicly released financial documents and statements, and may conduct site visits in order to accurately assess an organization's financial capacity and effectiveness.[8] This

Rating Agencies refers to organizations that offer an objective and independent creditworthiness assessment of an organization's solvency, liquidity, and overall long-term organizational health.

information is then translated into a rating classification for the bond (debt) being issued, or which has previously been issued, by the particular organization in question. Ratings can range from a high of AAA, which is the highest ranking and indicates virtually no chance of default, to lower rankings, such as BB or lower, which reflect **junk bond** status. In general, the lower the bond rating an organization receives, the higher the required interest rate will need to be in order to attract investors to buy the bond. This will result in an organization incurring a greater cost of borrowing on the dollars it is seeking.

> **Junk Bonds** refers to a high probability of default; commonly referred to as speculative bonds due to their potential for default on either their interest rate or principal payment obligations.

The duration of the bond reflects the length of time until the bond matures. This refers to the time period between the bond issue date and its maturity date. In our example of the 10-year bond, illustrated in Figure 13.9, the length of time would be 10 years from the date of issuance. As a final note, if bond repayment schedules are not met, bondholders have a legal right to take action against the organization issuing the bond. This could include requiring the organization to liquidate its assets in order to raise the required cash to meet its bond obligations.

> If bond repayment schedules are not met, bondholders have a legal right to take action against the organization issuing the bond. This could include requiring the organization to liquidate its assets in order to raise the required cash to meet its bond obligations.

> **Mortgage** refers to a credit facility that is backed by real estate collateral (generally, the real estate the mortgage underwrites), and that sets forth a defined schedule of periodic payments for the full repayment of the debt owed, plus interest, over a defined period of time.

Mortgage   A **mortgage** is a credit facility that is backed by real estate collateral (generally, the real estate that the mortgage underwrites) and that sets forth a defined schedule of periodic payments for the full repayment of the debt owed, plus interest, over a defined period of time. Mortgage credit facilities are generally built around four characteristics. These are as follows (see Figure 13.12):

- Mortgage value
- Amortization period
- Interest rate
- Interest rate term

FIGURE 13.12   Mortgage Characteristics

FIGURE 13.13   Mortgage: Savik Industries

- Mortgage Value $4 000 000
- Amortization Period   20 years
- Interest Rate   6%
- Interest Period   5 years

Based on these terms, the required monthly payment for the first five years of the mortgage is $28 487.54

Source: Vorton Financial Power Tools, Loan Calculations, June 2010.

The mortgage value refers to the amount of money that is being borrowed, or what is called the **principal**. This will generally be based on an appraised value of the real estate or property, its actual purchase price, and any applicable down payment being made by the purchaser. The **amortization period** refers to the length of time for which the mortgage will be underwritten. The interest rate identifies the cost of borrowing or the rate at which the money is being lent to the borrower. The interest period refers to the length of time that the interest rate, on which the repayment schedule is currently based, will be applicable. At the end of this period, this rate will then be reassessed against the current cost of borrowing, and a revised principal plus interest repayment schedule will be set up based on the original amortization rate. As an example, assume that Savik Industries has decided to purchase an industrial building to house its manufacturing operation. The purchase price is $5 million. Savik Industries will make a down payment of $1 million and take out a 20-year mortgage for the remaining $4 million. The initial interest rate is set at 6 percent for the first five years of the mortgage. Savik Industries' mortgage would be structured as shown in Figure 13.13.

Principal refers to the amount borrowed or the amount remaining on a loan separate from the cost of borrowing, as represented by the interest expense charges applicable to the credit facility (loan).

Amortization Period refers to the length of time over which a credit facility (loan) will be paid off.

The monthly payment of $28 487.54 comprises two parts: a repayment of a portion of the principal, and the interest expense allocation (i.e., cost of borrowing). A sample of what this repayment schedule would look like (for the initial five months) is shown in Table 13.1:

TABLE 13.1

Monthly Payment of $28 487.54	Interest Paid	Principal Paid	Mortgage Balance
Month #1	$19 755.49	$8 733.05	$3 991 266.95
Month #2	$19 711.36	$8 776.18	$3 982 490.77
Month #3	$19 668.02	$8 819.52	$3 973 671.25
Month #4	$19 624.46	$8 863.08	$3 964 808.18
Month #5	$19 580.69	$8 906.85	$3 955 901.33

Source: Vorton Financial Power Tools, Loan Calculations, June 2010.

If the interest rate and the amortization period remained unchanged for the entire mortgage duration, the total amount that Savik Industries would pay for this mortgage would be $6 837 009.70. This would be represented by the repayment of the principal borrowed ($4 000 000.00) and the cost of borrowing over the 20-year period (at 6%) of $2 837 009.70. At this stage, the development of the actual payment schedule is not important. What is important to understand is that the repayment obligation includes both a principal and a cost-of-borrowing amount. It should also be noted that the cost of borrowing is considered to be a business expense (interest expense) and will appear as an expense on the organization's income statement (discussed in Chapter 14).[7]

Long-Term Note refers to a credit facility under which an organization borrows a stipulated amount of money for a defined period of time (which exceeds one year), and with a defined interest rate schedule (fixed or variable).

Long-Term Note   A **long-term note** refers to a credit facility under which an organization borrows a stipulated amount of money, for a defined period of time (which exceeds one year), and with a defined interest rate schedule (fixed or variable). Long-term notes are similar in their set-up to that of a mortgage (defined repayment terms), except that they are generally written for a shorter time duration. Long-term notes can be underwritten either with or without a collateral requirement (secured or unsecured). As an example, assume that YMR Industries needs to purchase new equipment and related technologies in support of the manufacturing of its products and services. The total cost of the new equipment and related technologies is $350 000. Let's assume that YMR Industries decides to borrow this amount from RBC, repayable over five years, with a financing cost of 7.5 percent. The execution of this credit facility takes place on June 1, 2010, and results in YMR Industries adding $350 000 of long-term debt (liability) to its balance sheet as of this date. Its monthly payment obligation would be $7013.28. As with the mortgage example discussed above, this $7013.28 includes both the interest expense (based on the remaining balance on the note for the given month that the payment is for), plus an allocation toward paying off the principal ($350 000) so that, at the end of 60 months, this five-year note would be fully paid. Table 13.2 provides an illustration of the initial 12-month breakdown of the interest and principal payments made, as well as the remaining balance on the note. Borrowing $350 000 for five years at 7.5 percent will result in YMR Industries paying RBC a total of $420 796.92. The cost of borrowing the $350 000 over the five-year period equals $70 796.92 ($420 796.92 – $350 000.00). Borrowing the $350 000 enables YMR Industries to purchase the equipment now and utilize this equipment to generate additional sales revenue and/or reduce costs in other areas. YMR Industries, without the use of debt financing, may not have had the cash to make a purchase of this magnitude—or, with limited cash reserves, may believe that better uses of its cash exist.

> Interest expense paid by the organization on its credit facilities is considered to be a business expense.

It should be noted that although Table 13.2 demonstrates a long-term note with a monthly repayment schedule, these notes can be written with a variety of periodic repayment options (quarterly, semi-annually, annually) and may also include customized features such as

TABLE 13.2

Monthly Payment of $7013.28	Interest Paid	Principal Paid	Five-Year Note Balance	Total Amount Paid
Month #1	$2 187.50	$4 825.78	$345 174.22	$7 013.28
Month #2	$2 157.34	$4 855.94	$340 318.27	$14 026.56
Month #3	$2 126.99	$4 886.29	$335 431.98	$21 039.85
Month #4	$2 096.45	$4 916.83	$330 515.15	$28 053.13
Month #5	$2 065.72	$4 947.56	$325 567.59	$35 066.41
Month #6	$2 034.80	$4 978.48	$320 589.10	$42 079.69
Month #7	$2 003.68	$5 009.60	$315 579.50	$49 092.97
Month #8	$1 972.37	$5 040.91	$310 538.59	$56 106.26
Month #9	$1 940.87	$5 072.42	$305 466.18	$63 119.54
Month #10	$1 909.16	$5 104.12	$300 362.06	$70 132.82
Month #11	$1 877.26	$5 136.02	$295 226.04	$77 146.10
Month #12	$1 845.16	$5 168.12	$290 057.92	$84 159.38
Month #60	$43.56	$6 969.72	$0.00	$420 796.92

Source: Vorton Financial Power Tools, Loan Calculations, June 2010.

balloon payments or other "return of principal" options. A balloon payment occurs when a major portion of the principal owed on a loan is not included in the periodic payments made on the loan, but is deferred to a later date. In many cases, a balloon payment will come due at the end of the amortization period. It should also be noted that although we have illustrated the use of a fixed interest rate within a credit facility's structure, interest rates can be of the variable rate (adjustable rate) structure. An example of a variable rate loan would be one that is tied to the **prime lending rate**, such as prime + 1 percent. This means that the interest rate on the loan will be adjusted whenever there is an adjustment to the prime lending rate. Assume that the prime lending rate is 2.50 percent. In this example, the interest rate on the loan would be 3.50 percent (2.50% + 1.00%). If the prime rate is moved upward to, say, 2.75 percent, this would result in an increased cost of borrowing, to 3.75 percent.

> **Prime Lending Rate** refers to the base lending rate used by banks. It is also often interpreted to be the rate at which banks lend money to their most preferred customers.

Lease Obligations Lease obligations that cover periods in excess of one year are considered long-term debt obligations of an organization. Lease obligations represent a legal obligation to pay a service provider with an agreed-upon amount of money, via a defined periodic payment schedule over an identified period, in return for the use of property, equipment, or some other service. At the end of this period, provisions may, or may not, be included in the lease to provide the organization with an opportunity to purchase the asset that has been leased. If such a provision does exist, lease buy-back provisions, along with a residual value formula computation to be used in determining the purchase value of the leased asset, generally at the end of the lease term, will be fully defined within the lease agreement. For many organizations, leasing represents a preferred option over the outright purchase of an asset. Leasing enables the organization to minimize the upfront cash outlay for equipment and other assets, and ensures that the organization stays current with the latest technology. As an example, assume that ABC Industries is in need of a high-capacity, high-speed, multi-functional photocopy, printing, and scanning unit to support its marketing and administration departments. After reviewing the potential options with distributors of a variety of brands and models, ABC Industries settles on its preferred choice. The cost of this photocopy, printing, scanning, and document-sorting machine is $63 000. ABC Industries can either choose to purchase the unit outright, or enter into a five-year lease agreement offered by the manufacturer. The lease agreement enables ABC Industries to pay $3000 down, and then make monthly lease payments based on the $60 000 remaining balance on the machine, plus a financing/leasing cost of 9 percent. These payments would be made for 60 months (five years). Based on the $60 000 remaining balance, with a financing/leasing cost of 9 percent for a period of 60 months, the monthly payments would be $1245. The total cost of the machine at the end of the five-year period would be $77 700 ($3000 + ($1245 × 60)). At the end of the lease period, assuming that there is no desire or opportunity to purchase the unit, the machine is returned to the manufacturer. In leasing, the person or organization that owns the land, equipment, or property is called the lessor. The person or organization that rents the land, equipment, or property from the lessor is called the lessee. Again, it is the recognition of the legal obligation to pay, under the lease agreement, that results in the requirement to recognize it as a liability of the organization.

Impact of Credit Facilities The ability to utilize credit facilities to assist with financing the cash operating cycle, and with enabling organizations to develop and grow their capital asset base, is a major reason for the creation of the incredible global business marketplace that we have today. This ability to secure access to significant amounts of capital, at reasonable costs of borrowing, is what enables companies to utilize the capital assets acquired to generate revenues and investment returns that exceed the cost of borrowing. The risk to organizations that take on debt is that, by utilizing credit facilities, these organizations are adding to the size of their fixed-cost base. Both the principal and interest payments associated with the various credit facilities tapped will need to be made, regardless of whether an organization's sales increase, remain unchanged, or decrease. The addition of this debt will also modify this same organization's breakeven point, as additional sales will need to be realized in order to pay for the costs associated with servicing and retiring this debt. As managers, in making decisions to utilize debt financing (credit facilities) as a source of funds for our business, we must ensure that the repayment obligations associated with the credit facilities undertaken do not jeopardize the liquidity and solvency of our organization. Debt, in the absence of revenue enhancement or cost reduction, results in nothing other than an increase to the cost base of the organization. Knowing this means that we need to be careful on how, and when, we use debt as a mechanism to fund the growth and/or expansion of our organization. This discussion of debt, and the concern associated with the amount of debt an organization should undertake, is meant to be an introduction to this topic. Chapter 14, Understanding Financial Statements, expands upon this topic to ensure that students have a good base-level understanding of the role of credit facilities and the advantages and risks associated with the concept of **debt leverage**.

> As managers, in making decisions to utilize debt financing (credit facilities) as a source of funds for our business we must ensure that the repayment obligations associated with the credit facilities undertaken do not jeopardize the liquidity and solvency of our organization.

Equity Options

Up to this point, we have discussed two ways in which an organization can meet its capital requirements. The organization can obtain capital for reinvestment purposes from profitable current and/or past business operations. The organization also can utilize credit facilities as a way to assist in financing its cash operating cycle and in raising the needed capital to meet its development and growth requirements. The third way in which an organization can raise capital is through the procurement of equity financing. Depending on its legal structure (sole proprietorship, partnership, corporation), an organization will have access to private equity and/or public equity funding options (see Figure 13.14).

Private equity is equity capital (money) that is obtained by an organization from private sources (not through one of the public exchanges). Examples of private equity include the equity contribution to the business by the owner(s), family, friends, or some other initial backer (commonly referred to as an angel investor), private-equity firms, or venture capitalists. Private-equity investment opportunities are available to sole proprietorships, partnerships, and corporations. Private-equity investments can be either a direct monetary investment into the company (for sole proprietorships and partnerships) or monetary investments as a result of the issuance (sale) of **stock** (for corporations). Regardless of the situation, equity-based investments into an organization represent the acceptance of an ownership stake in the business in exchange for the capital invested. Going back to the example of Lululemon Athletica Inc. used earlier in this chapter, private-equity investments into Lululemon Athletica Inc. would include the personal investments made by Chip Wilson, potential early start-up capital from family and/or friends, and the private-equity firms Advent International and Highland Capital Partners. Sequoia Capital, highlighted in the Business in Action vignette, is also an example of an organization that provides private equity to businesses.

Public equity refers to equity investments in an organization, by investors, as a result of the purchase of publicly traded shares (stock) due to an initial public offering (IPO), or an additional public offering (APO), also referred to as a **secondary offering**. Public-equity investment opportunities are limited to corporations. Again using Lululemon Athletica Inc. (TSX: LLL) as an example, the IPO executed in 2007 resulted in Lululemon Athletica Inc. selling 18 200 000 shares at an average selling price of $18 per share, raising just over US$327 million.[8] Toys R Us, currently a privately held corporation, announced on Friday, May 28, 2010 that it would launch an IPO with the intent of raising as much as US$800 million. The company plans to use the capital it raises from its IPO to pay off some of its debt (estimated at US$5.2 billion) and for other general purposes. When launched, Toys R Us will be listed on the NYSE under the company symbol TOYS.[9] One of the largest IPOs in Canada, during the

Debt Leverage refers to the use of debt to finance an organization's capital asset base.

Private Equity refers to equity capital that is obtained by an organization from private sources (not through one of the public exchanges).

Stock is a security that represents a percentage of ownership in a corporation's assets, and entitlement to a pro-rata claim on earnings when released.

Public Equity refers to equity investments in an organization, by investors, as a result of the purchase of publicly traded shares (stock) due to an initial public offering (IPO) or an additional public offering (APO), also referred to as a secondary offering.

Secondary Offering refers to an additional public offering of an organization's stock for the purpose of raising new capital.

FIGURE 13.14 Equity Options

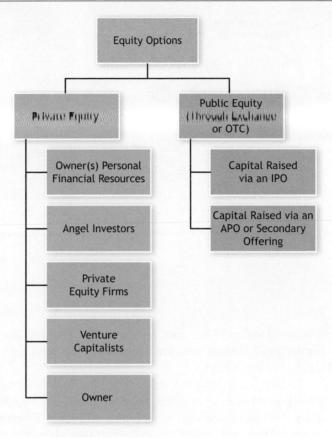

first quarter of 2010, was a $190 million stock issue by Leisureworld Senior Care Corporation (TSX: LW). Monies raised from this IPO will be used to acquire shares, which currently reside with the parent company (Leisureworld Senior Care GP Inc.), and repay approximately $60 million in debt. A recent example of an APO is that of General Maritime Corporation (NYSE: GMR), which announced, on June 17, 2010, that it was offering for sale 30 600 000 additional shares of stock at $6.75 per share. The intent of this secondary offering is to raise approximately US$195.6 million (net of underwriting and share-offering expenses). The company is intending to use the proceeds from this APO to fund the acquisition of seven additional tankers for its maritime fleet.[10]

In discussing public-equity options, there are a couple of important points that managers need to understand. First, a company receives the proceeds from the sale of stock only at the time of its initial issue and sale. After that, the trading (selling) of shares that occurs in the marketplace is between the owners of the stock (sellers) and the new purchasers (see Figure 13.15).

Understanding this means that managers and members of the board of directors, in consultation with the investment banking firm handling the initial sale, must determine whether the conditions are right for the launch of an IPO or a secondary offering, and if the asking price will be received from public investors. As an example, upstart Porter Airlines (Porter Aviation Holdings Inc.), based in Toronto, made a decision to drop plans for an IPO in May 2010 due to the volatility and turmoil in the equity markets at that time. Robert Deluce, CEO of Porter Aviation Holdings Inc., indicated that it was prudent to defer the IPO until better market conditions existed that would enable Porter Aviation Holdings Inc. to get a better price for its shares. For Mr. Deluce and Porter Aviation Holdings Inc. the utilization of private-equity options may be a better route to take in the interim. Porter's IPO was initially priced

FIGURE 13.15   Public-Equity Offering: Cash Flow

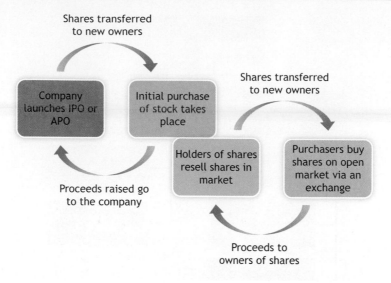

Second, managers, in considering an APO or secondary share offering, must consider the impact on the current share value of the organization's stock in the marketplace. Issuing additional shares of stock can result in **price dilution**, which means that the price of existing shares of stock will decline due to the fact that a larger number of shares (which represent ownership in the company) now exist. As an example, assume that the MTR Corporation currently has 10 million shares of common stock outstanding, and the price of these shares is $20 per share. This means that MTR Corporation has a **market capitalization value** (market cap) of $200 million ($20 × 10 million shares). If MTR Corporation makes a decision to offer an additional 5 million shares to the marketplace, this will have a downward impact on the price of the stock. This is because the number of shares outstanding (circulating in the marketplace) will increase to 15 million. In order for the market cap to remain at $20 million (assuming this is still a valid value for MTR), then the price per share will need to decrease to $13.34. Discounting potential upward movements due to improvements in MTR's cash position resulting from the share offering, the price of the stock will move (be diluted), from $20 toward a per-share value of $13.34. It should also be noted, with respect to secondary share offerings, that the additional money raised is typically applied to organization-based needs that are anticipated to improve the liquidity and/or performance of the company issuing these shares. These actions are intended to improve the organization's value in the eyes of current and potential investors, and its overall position in the industry sector within which it competes. If successful, this action should enable the company issuing the shares to protect its share value against the price dilution to its shares due to the larger number of shares outstanding. The improved performance or financial position of the company would have an upward influence on share value, thereby offsetting some, or all, of the price dilution.

As you can recognize, the issuance of an IPO and/or APO (secondary offering) requires a great deal of thought on the part of the organization. As the organization only receives the proceeds from the initial sale of its shares, the business organization's managers, directors of its board, and the investment firm handling the issuance of the IPO or APO must all be confident that the timing and price point at which the shares are being introduced will result in the maximum benefit that the organization can expect to receive from the share issuance. Figure 13.16 provides an overview of this issuance process.

at between $6 and $7 per share, and then revised to $5.50 per share, before it was pulled from the market. Investors were unwilling to pay this price for shares of Porter Aviation Holdings Inc. at that time.[11]

Price Dilution means that the price of existing shares of stock will decline due to the fact that a larger number of shares (which represent ownership in the company) now exist.

Market Capitalization Value refers to the current market value of an organization. It is calculated by taking the number of shares outstanding multiplied by the current value of its shares.

FIGURE 13.16 Public-Equity (Stock) Issuance Process

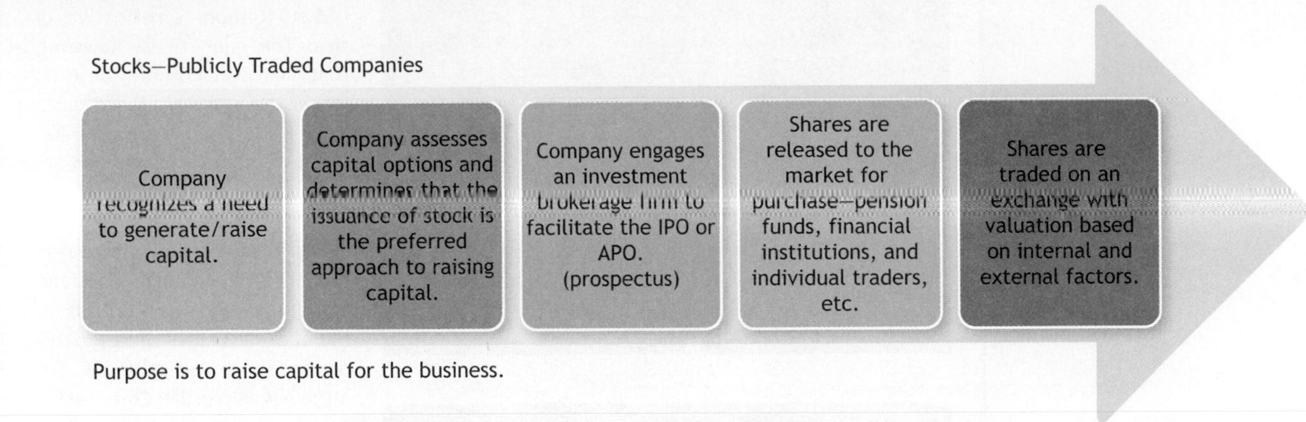

Stocks—Publicly Traded Companies

Company recognizes a need to generate/raise capital.	Company assesses capital options and determines that the issuance of stock is the preferred approach to raising capital.	Company engages an investment brokerage firm to facilitate the IPO or APO. (prospectus)	Shares are released to the market for purchase—pension funds, financial institutions, and individual traders, etc.	Shares are traded on an exchange with valuation based on internal and external factors.

Purpose is to raise capital for the business.

As shown in Figure 13.16, the stock share issuance process is one that takes time and money. Once the company determines that it wants to issue shares of stock via an IPO or a secondary offering, the organization will generally retain and work with an investment firm to determine the asking price for the shares to be offered, the number of shares to be sold, and the timing of the launch of the IPO or secondary offering. The investment firm will prepare, on behalf of the business organization, a **prospectus**. The prospectus is the required legal document to be filed with the securities commission that has jurisdiction for the share issuance; it provides information relating to the current financial stability of the company and the intent of the share issuance, thereby enabling investors to make an informed decision on the risk associated with the purchase of the shares being offered. The investment firm will also facilitate the sale of the shares of stock to institutional buyers (pension plans, financial institutions, etc.) and/or public investors at large. In return for its involvement, the investment firm receives a fee for its services. Once issued, the stock of the issuing company then openly trades on the exchange it was sold through (TSX, NYSE, NASDAQ, etc.), with future trades occurring through this public marketplace vehicle between institutional and individual traders.

> **Prospectus** refers to a legal document to be filed with the securities commission that has jurisdiction for the share issuance; it provides information relating to the current financial stability of the company and the intent of the share issuance, thereby enabling investors to make an informed decision on the risk associated with the purchase of the shares being offered.

BUSINESS in Action

Apple Crowned "King of Technology"

A funny thing happened in May 2010. Funny, if you are Apple Inc.—but not so funny if you are, say, Microsoft Corporation. Historically, Microsoft Corporation has been recognized as the world's most valued technology company; value in this context is defined on the basis of market capitalization, which is calculated by taking the number of shares outstanding (traded publicly) multiplied by its share value. In layman's terms, market capitalization represents what the marketplace believes a company is worth. Think of it as the cost associated with buying all of a company's stock and, hence, obtaining 100 percent ownership of the business.

With Microsoft pursuing the business marketplace, which was embracing a technology revolution over the past 20 years, and Apple Inc. trying to figure out just what to do and how to fit in during the 1990s, Microsoft's dominance as the most valued technology firm seemed unassailable. In fact, a quick look at market capitalization values during this period of time clearly illustrates the significant spread between these two organizations. Microsoft Corporation remains a great business, providing consistent results, year after year, to its investors. With net margins in the 25 percent to 30 percent range, and earnings per share (EPS) consistent at around $1.50 to $2.00 annually, Microsoft continues to reward investors with dividends, as well as a sense of

safety and security. Its current market capitalization value of US$219 billion is reflective of this. The concern is, however, that Microsoft Corporation is no longer the innovator that it once was. It has, more or less, become stagnant, relying on its Windows operating system and its Office suite of products to continue to provide its core revenue and earnings streams. Some analysts refer to this as the click and clack of keyboard-dependent driven solutions. So, although Microsoft Corporation remains a force to be reckoned with, it is more from the position of an industry follower versus an industry leader. One only has to look at its recent product releases, such as Zune, Bing, and even Xbox, to recognize the dependency on others to develop markets first. Meanwhile, Apple Inc. has orchestrated a complete business turnaround. An aggressive innovator in handheld devices, Apple has focused on replacing the click and clack approach toward software integration with the touch-screen approach, and has utilized its innovative advantages in the consumer market, particularly with respect to handheld devices, to strike gold on behalf of its shareholders. The end result is that Apple's share value has skyrocketed, from $7.45 in January 2003 to $270 in June 2010. Earnings per share have also consistently improved, from $0.10 in 2003 to $6.24 in 2009. Its revenue per share has grown from $8 in 2002 to $40.61 in 2009. For Apple Inc., the future looks bright, as its products appear clearly positioned toward digital content (songs, movies, books, photos, etc.). With its market capitalization value at US$246 billion on June 22, 2010, and some analysts predicting its stock to surpass $300 per share or more, Apple Inc. appears to be in a great position to continue to grow the company's overall value. As of May 2010, only Exxon Mobil had a market capitalization value greater than Apple's. If its current trend continues, we might find Apple Inc. is not only the most valued technology company, but also the most valued company in the world.[12]

WEB INTEGRATION

To follow the movement in Microsoft Corporation and Apple Inc.'s share values and market capitalization values, go to **www.googlefinance.com** or **www.yahoofinance.com** and search using Microsoft Corporation (MSFT) and Apple Inc.'s (AAPL) stock symbols.

Putting It All Together

As managers, we will, most likely, end up using a combination of all three funding sources in order to meet the needs of our cash operating cycle and capital asset development requirements. Decisions relating to funds generated from internal operations will focus on how much of the current profit being generated should be used today and how much should be reserved for the future (transferred to retained earnings). It will also be influenced by the need, or desire, to return a portion of the profits to owners as a reward for their investment in our organization. Depending on the type of operation we are managing, we will, most likely, make use of a number of short-term credit options (trade credit being a primary example), as well as consider using longer-term options to support capital asset acquisition and development. With credit comes the risk of leverage. The biggest impact of leverage is that, when we are in a loss situation, the impact on liquidity and solvency magnifies, as we still have to meet our interest and principal repayment options. Although lenders may work with us in the short term, they will not tolerate repayment postponement indefinitely and, in a worst-case scenario, could initiate legal action against us, thereby further crippling the organization's ability to survive. Equity financing represents a viable way to generate capital externally for the organization. It does, however, require consideration of the long-term impact to the organization, particularly for its current owners, in terms of ownership dilution, loss of control, and the potential for decisions becoming more and more influenced by the need to meet investor ROI requirements. Equity financing is also predicated on the fact that the organization has the potential to be profitable, and that the future growth potential results in the best use of an investor's capital. The end result is that, as managers, we need to consciously think about where and how to use and obtain capital. It is an essential part of our strategic plan. Each source of funds (capital) has its own advantages and disadvantages. Taking on too much debt, or becoming overextended on the credit side, can impact our future ability to meet financial obligations or obtain new capital when it is most needed. Although equity financing may appear attractive, we need to be conscious as to how this is going to impact the future direction of the company and decisions supporting the intended strategy. New owners, by virtue of their investment, will, most likely, have a say in how we do business going forward. Figure 13.17 provides a summary of the advantages and disadvantages of each of the sources of funds

FIGURE 13.17 Summary: Sources of Funds

Source of Funds	Advantage	Disadvantage
Funds from Operations	• No external funding source is required • No dilution of ownership occurs • No fixed repayment schedule • No interest payments	• Monies available may not meet the full needs of the organization • Uncertainty may exist as to the amount of money available now and in the future • Monies needed internally cannot be distributed to owners as a return on their investment
Credit Facilities	• No dilution of ownership occurs • Can provide large inflows of capital now, with payments spread out over long periods of time • Enables the organization to use someone else's money to fund organizational needs • Interest expense is considered to be an operational expense	• Requires full repayment, either on a periodic or lump sum basis • Obligations must be met, regardless of the financial condition of the organization • A cost of borrowing is incurred • Collateral is usually required—may restrict future asset use
Equity Financing	• Enables the organization to raise cash without the leverage concerns associated with debt financing • No repayment obligations • External funding source—does not place pressure on operations to fund organization's needs	• Dilutes ownership • If publicly traded—control lies with the owner of a majority of shares (51%) • Short-termism—management decisions may be impacted by shareholder investment needs

discussed in this chapter. Keeping these advantages and disadvantages in mind as we seek to provide the organization with the funds necessary for its success will assist us in maintaining a balanced approach to where and how funds will be procured and used.

For most organizations, managers will have a tendency to look first toward internal funds to compensate owners and to finance new investments. When such funds are not sufficient to provide the necessary capital to finance the required investments deemed critical for the organization's success, the tendency will then be to look toward debt financing, in combination with internal funds or on its own. As noted above, a key issue here will be the ability or capacity of the organization to handle the additional debt load being contemplated. Owners, managers, and boards of directors of for-profit organizations will, in most cases, resort to external equity financing only when it has been concluded that the other sources of funds (internal and debt financing) cannot be used to adequately fund the needs of the business.

LO4   A Note Pertaining to Not-for-Profits

Although similar to for-profit organizations in many ways, one of the key fundamental differences between not-for-profit (NFP) organizations and for-profit organizations lies in their capital structure. For-profit business organizations, as has been illustrated within this chapter, have essentially three sources of capital funding: (1) cash available from internal operations (current profit and retained earnings), (2) the use of debt financing via a variety of credit facility options, and (3) equity investments (private or public) that are acquired in exchange for an ownership stake in the for-profit business. Not-for-profit organizations can utilize cash available from internal operations, as well as debt financing via credit facility options. This does assume, however, that the NFP delivers its products and services for a fee and, therefore, has revenue-generation capabilities. It also assumes that the NFP has established credit and has sufficient capital assets that can serve as collateral on a loan. Both of these situations may not exist. Many NFPs do not generate revenue, but rely on funding totally from outside sources, such as various levels of government. They are, in essence, expense-driven organizations, whose budgets consist solely of transfer payments to them for the purpose of delivering services to the community. Many others do not have a sufficient capital asset base to serve as a basis for collateral, or operate in a manner that enables them to utilize the same breadth of credit facility options available to for-profit entities. Assuming, however, that access to these first two sources of capital exists, where for-profit and not-for-profit organizations fundamentally differ lies in the ability to utilize equity investments as a way to fund an organization's sustenance and growth. As NFPs are not owned by individuals, but rather exist for the collective good of society, and are not permitted to accept equity investments in the business in exchange for an ownership stake, private- and public-equity options simply do not exist for these organizations. Recognizing this absence of a third source of capital, not-for-profit organizations are allowed to fundraise in support of their organization's activities and services (some restrictions may apply, depending on legal formation, location, and articles of incorporation). These fundraising initiatives may take the form of activities such as the direct solicitation for donations, the implementation of fundraising events (runs, walks, auctions, etc.), and the implementation of annual giving campaigns and capital campaigns for the purpose of raising funds in support of programs, activities, and/or capital asset acquisition, refurbishment, and maintenance. The concept of **philanthropy** and the ability to accept donations—and, if registered charities, issue donation tax receipts to their donors—represents a core fundamental source of capital for many NFPs. The end result is that, although different, NFPs also have three sources of capital funding available (see Figure 13.18). Unlike their for-profit counterparts, NFPs in general will prefer to undertake philanthropic initiatives as a viable source of funds prior to exhausting current internal reserves or undertaking new debt financing.

Managing the NFP requires the same type of decision-making skills and risk/reward trade-off analysis as is found in the for-profit sector. Managers need to assess the potential capital available from each of the three sources of funds that the NFP has at its disposal, and

Philanthropy refers to the receipt of funds from another person or organization for the purpose of using them to enhance the well-being of others.

FIGURE 13.18 NFP Sources of Capital

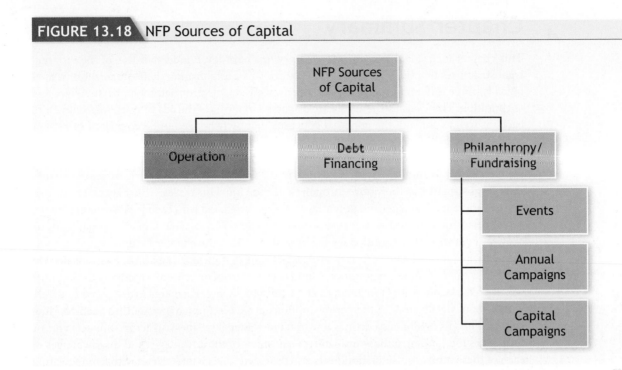

determine where and how to allocate these resources in order to achieve the NFP's mission and vision. In addition, managers of NFPs must recognize that although profit may be the *raison d'être* for for-profit entities, it is the achievement of the social mission and the delivery of its programs that represent an NFP's *raison d'être*. This implies that, in many cases, it is the distribution of wealth and benefits through the NFP's activities, even in the absence of generating a surplus, that must drive its management team's decision-making focus.

Management Reflection—The Need for Capital

With few exceptions, organizations have an ongoing thirst for capital. The need to fund new marketing initiatives, new products and services, new technologies, new equipment, new business locations, and the acquisition of the general capital assets required to make us more efficient and effective appears to be never-ending. With this insatiable appetite for capital comes the realization that decisions will need to be made on the best places or priorities to allocate this precious resource. The ability to acquire capital, either internally or externally, and effectively use it to generate new revenue sources—or higher levels of revenue from existing sources—can be developed into a definitive and sustainable competitive advantage. Access to capital means the ability to fund new initiatives and future growth. As managers, we need to recognize that capital access can come from one of the three sources discussed in this chapter. The trick, so to speak, is to make smart decisions on which source to tap for a particular initiative at a given time in order to maximize the benefit of the use of the chosen source of capital in a way that builds the long-term health of the organization. With this decision-making process comes an analysis of the various needs and desires of its internal stakeholders, as well as how to best position the organization to current external, and future, stakeholders. This process also requires a full analysis of the organization's cash operating cycle and an assessment of its future long-term financial needs. From this analysis comes a financial strategy that, in essence, defines for the organization where its capital is anticipated to come from, thereby enabling it to determine which initiatives will be funded from which source of funds. Without a full analysis in this regard, managers may find that they have exhausted a key source of funds, thereby restricting the ability to generate the capital needed to support the implementation of near-term and long-term opportunities.

Chapter Summary

This chapter focused on providing students with a base-level understanding of the different legal structures that business owners can utilize when establishing their organizations. Specifically, three different legal structures were reviewed: sole proprietorship, partnership, and corporation. These legal structures were discussed in terms of the advantages inherent within each, as well as some of the potential concerns that owners need to be cognizant of as they choose an initial legal structure for their new business. Included within this discussion was the recognition that choosing one legal structure type does not preclude the business owner from changing to another structural option in the future. In fact, many organizations modify their legal structure as they move through their individual life cycles. This may be predicated on the inherent advantages and potential concerns associated with each legal structure, or the direct result of the need to tap new sources of capital to further fund the organization's growth. Following this evolutionary business discussion, the chapter focused on communicating to students the three primary sources of funds that owners can utilize to access needed capital for their business organizations: funds derived from operations, financing through the use of credit facilities (debt financing), and equity financing. Each area is discussed in detail, with a focus on illustrating the various options available to managers within each funding source. This discussion also defines how the type of legal business structure impacts and/or influences the funding options available. A summary of the advantages and disadvantages of each of these fund acquisition options is also provided. The chapter closes with a note relating to the differences between for-profit corporations and not-for-profit organizations (NFP) with regard to the sources of funds available to an NFP's management team.

Developing Business Knowledge and Skills

KEY TERMS

sole proprietorship p. 354

partnership p. 355

partnership agreement p. 355

joint and several liability p. 356

buy-sell agreement p. 356

limited liability partnership (LLP) p. 357

corporation p. 357

incorporation p. 357

board of directors p. 357

private corporations p. 358

public corporations p. 358

initial public offering (IPO) p. 358

exchange p. 358

over-the-counter (OTC) p. 358

capital structure p. 361

operating profits p. 363

retained earnings p. 363

credit facilities p. 363

short-term credit facilities p. 364

accounts payable p. 364

accounts receivable p. 364

line of credit p. 364

collateral p. 364

long-term credit facilities p. 365

cost of borrowing p. 365

bond p. 365

rating agencies p. 367

junk bond p. 368

mortgage p. 368

principal p. 369

amortization period p. 369

long-term note p. 370

prime lending rate p. 371

debt leverage p. 372

private equity *p. 372*

stock *p. 372*

public equity *p. 372*

secondary offering *p. 372*

price dilution *p. 374*

market capitalization value *p. 374*

prospectus *p. 375*

philanthropy *p. 378*

QUESTIONS FOR DISCUSSION

1. What are the three primary forms of business ownership? What are the advantages and disadvantages of each?

2. Given the ease of set-up of a sole proprietorship or partnership, why is it that a number of entrepreneurs choose to incorporate their businesses at the time of inception? What is the driving force behind such a decision?

3. What is the fundamental difference between a privately held corporation and a public corporation?

4. What are the three primary sources of cash (capital) for a for-profit organization? Is one more important than the others? As a manager, what approach would you take to determining how you would finance a new business investment?

5. What are the two key determinants of the coupon rate (interest rate) at which a bond is issued?

6. What is an IPO? How is it different from an APO (secondary offering)?

7. What is the primary difference between for-profit organizations and not-for-profit organizations with respect to the sources of funds available to them?

QUESTIONS FOR INDIVIDUAL ACTION

Arrange an interview with the executive director or the chief executive officer (CEO) of a not-for-profit organization. Discuss with this individual the challenges they face in acquiring external funds to assist in the development and growth of their organization. What is their primary source of external funding? Do they have sufficient assets to enable them to utilize debt financing as a primary funding source? If so, what is their board of directors' position with respect to the use of debt financing? Prepare a brief presentation for your class highlighting the conclusions you have reached and the challenges you have uncovered as a result of your meeting.

TEAM EXERCISE

As a team, review four or five recently initiated IPOs. This may mean researching the prospectus for each IPO chosen in addition to analyzing the actual results realized. What were the fundamental reasons these companies gave for making the decision to become public corporations? What was the objective of each company in terms of the dollars forecast to be raised in the IPO? What was the money primarily going to be used for? Were these IPOs successful? Did the share value realized exceed the initial IPO expectations? Was the IPO withdrawn? If so, why? Prepare a presentation for the class that identifies the information developed on each of the IPOs assessed and the key conclusions reached.

◢ Case for Discussion

On May 3, 2010, Shaw Communications officially announced that it had purchased major portions of the recently restructured Canadian media giant Canwest Global Communications Corporation. The deal, with a value estimated at $2 billion, is a major part of the closing chapter on one of Canada's iconic business entities. For Shaw Communications, the purchase provides it with some of Canwest's most-coveted assets, its over-the-air and specialty television businesses, which include Canada's second largest television network, Global Television, and significant interests in a number of specialty television channels including the home and garden channel (HGTV). The deal, according to the official Shaw Communications announcement, was funded by the assumption of approximately $815 million of net debt that currently resides within Canwest, with the remainder of the purchase price provided in cash via Shaw's cash reserves and established credit facilities, and includes an approximately $65 million cash injection to enable its newly acquired interests in Canwest to emerge from bankruptcy. For Canwest Global Communications Corporation, it is the end of what has been a tumultuous decade. Determined to be an international player, Canwest Global Communications Corporation embarked on an ambitious acquisition strategy, which began in 2000 with its $3.5 billion acquisition of the *National Post* newspaper and other media-related interests from Hollinger Inc. This acquisition, combined with additional acquisitions and newly developed operations in places such as the United Kingdom, Australia, New Zealand, and Turkey, resulted in Canwest incurring debt in excess of $3 billion. This was then followed by the purchase of Alliance Atlantis, in partnership with GS Capital Partners, for $2.3 billion in 2007. The acquisition activity of the first seven years of the decade left Canwest Global Communications Corporation with just under $4 billion of debt and very little breathing room should its operations fail to generate the required revenue to support such a capital structure. For the Asper family (majority shareholders), and Canwest's CEO Leonard Asper, what then materialized was the "perfect storm." In an industry already threatened by changing consumer habits and a shift away from printed media for online information options, the financial crisis of 2008 and the recession of 2009 further accelerated the negative impact Canwest's debt position had on the organization's cash position, as advertising revenues in key divisions fell dramatically. The end result was that Canwest Global Communications Corporation was forced to seek bankruptcy protection under the Companies' Creditors Arrangement Act in October 2009. Following several months of negotiations that resulted in convincing a number of creditors to exchange their debt positions for equity positions, Canwest was still unable to demonstrate to remaining key creditors that a viable business model could be developed that would ensure that outstanding payments, as well as future payments, could be made. Senior creditors, led by Scotiabank and representing most of the major Canadian banks, which were owed approximately $950 million and whose debt was secured by the assets of the corporation, pushed to have Canwest broken up and sold in order to meet its debt obligations. In the early months of 2010, the bankruptcy court sided with these senior creditors, thereby resulting in a bidding process for Canwest's assets and the eventual sale of non-print media assets to Shaw Communications Inc. As indicated, Canwest's newspaper operations, including the *National Post*, are not part of the deal. The sale of print media assets remains subject to bankruptcy proceedings as of this writing, but this part of Canwest appears to be poised to emerge from bankruptcy as a separate legal entity supported by new ownership. This portion of what was once Canwest Global Communications Corporation is anticipated to operate under the name Postmedia Network Inc. (Shaw Communications owns the rights to the Canwest name). For Canwest Global Communications Corporation, the situation that caused its demise was not that its operations were not profitable, but that they were unable to generate the required cash to meet the enormous debt obligations Canwest had committed itself to. At the time of the decision to commence with the selling of Canwest assets, it was estimated that Canwest owed more than $100 million in payments on the various lines of credit and loans that were still outstanding. It was also estimated that it owed more than $600 million to unsecured creditors.[13]

QUESTIONS

1. What lessons can be learned from the demise of Canwest Global Communications Corporation?

2. What does this case say about the risk associated with debt financing and the concept of debt leverage?

3. In seeking to expand through acquisitions, what risks are incurred when purchasing a business largely through debt financing?

4. If Canwest Global Communications Corporation's operations were profitable, then why was it forced into bankruptcy?

Practise and learn online with Connect. Connect resources include additional and interactive study exercises, videos, and practice quizzing, as well as additional material you won't find in the printed text.

14 Understanding Financial Statements

Learning Objectives

This chapter is designed to provide students with:

Lo1 An understanding of the role financial statements play in assisting managers in managing their businesses

Lo2 Exposure to the two types of financial transactions (operational and capital assets) that managers track as part of their financial analysis

Lo3 An understanding of the fundamentals of liquidity, solvency, efficiency, and capacity as they pertain to the financial assessment of a business

Lo4 Exposure to the three primary financial statements (income statement, balance sheet, and statement of cash flows) that managers use in assessing the financial stability of an organization

Lo5 An introduction to the use of trend, comparative, and absolute analytical tools as methodologies for interpreting the financial performance of an organization

Lo6 A base-level insight into the role of forecasting and budgeting in the financial assessment process

Snapshot—What to Expect in This Chapter

As identified by the learning objectives, this chapter focuses on exposing students to the basics associated with financial statement analysis. The content emphasized in this chapter includes the following:

- The Role of Financial Statements
  - Two Fundamental Types of Business Transactions
- Liquidity, Solvency, Efficiency, and Financial Capacity
- Three Primary Financial Statements
  - Income Statement
  - Balance Sheet
  - Statement of Cash Flows
- Analyzing and Interpreting Financial Information
  - Ratio Analysis
  - Leverage Analysis
  - Trend or Comparative Analysis
  - Absolute Analysis
  - Forecasting and Budgeting
- A Note Pertaining to Not-for-Profits
- Management Reflection—Keeping Your Finger on the Pulse of the Organization

From the Student's Perspective

Financial statements should serve as the basis for every managerial decision. Whether one is evaluating the attractiveness of a buyout offer or contemplating the merits of a new product launch, financial statements provide the means with which to understand the potential impact of a business decision.

Together, the income statement, balance sheet, and statement of cash flows detail the financial performance and position of a company. More specifically, they explain how liquid, solvent, efficient, and viable a business is.

Some people may think that only accountants care about financial statements. That could not be further from the truth. Externally, financial statements are reviewed by investors, creditors, and regulators. Internally, they are analyzed by managers and employees. A small business owner might use financial statements to prepare tax returns and operating budgets. A financial officer may use them to model a potential business combination and forecast cost synergies. A division head can use these statements to set goals and assess performance. An entrepreneur might use them to validate a business plan and raise start-up financing. A *Fortune* 500 CEO may use financial statements to benchmark against industry peers and internal targets, while a board of directors might use them to measure growth trends and set manager remuneration.

All this is just a long-winded way to say that every manager needs to be comfortable with preparing, reading, and interpreting financial statements. They tell the story of a company's past and hold the key to charting its future.

Will Fang graduated with a Bachelor of Commerce in 2010. In his spare time, Will enjoys photography, playing the piano, and cheering for the Ottawa Senators. Following graduation, Will began his career in investment banking in New York City.

BUSINESS *in Action*

The Role of the CFO

As part of the C-level management team, CFOs (chief financial officers) hold one of the most important positions in today's corporate environment. With increasing pressure to deliver superior financial results, heightened regulatory requirements, and a rapidly changing global marketplace requiring greater financial investment to fund results, CFOs are challenged more than ever before. Where historically CFOs often focused their attention on budget development and analysis and financial controls, they are now being challenged more and more to actively participate in designing and assisting in the strategic planning and implementation of the organization. Expectations are that CFOs will understand how their companies create value in the marketplace. This means knowing which products are contributing positively to the bottom line, and developing performance measures and metrics that focus not only on financial results, but also on long-term market sustainability. CFOs are also being asked to be more active in integrating financial performance measures and operating competitiveness to ensure that decisions do not focus too much on achieving short-term results while destroying long-term market position

and competitive advantage. This integration is what is important in understanding the non-financial performance requirements that drive financial results. Yes, CFOs remain the guardians of the financial solvency of organizations. They also must now provide leadership in protecting the forward-looking operational and market-based health of the organization in a marketplace that continues to pressure organizations for stronger short-term results.[1]

The Role of Financial Statements

LO1, LO2

As has been discussed throughout this book, the role of the senior management team is to determine an organization's overall direction and then direct and manage the execution of the tactics and strategic thrusts that have been developed to ensure the organization achieves its vision and objectives. This requires the effective utilization of its assets, employees, capital, and management acumen so that its business system delivers a superior value proposition to its customers. Decisions are made across a number of key business areas—such as marketing, operations, business system configuration, and HR, to name a few—with the intent of meeting the organization's customer needs and expectations. So, how does a management team track the effectiveness of its decisions and product/service offerings with respect to growth, profitability, and asset productivity? This is accomplished through the analysis of its financial statements.

Analyzing and interpreting financial statements is what enables a management team to "keep its fingers on the pulse" of the organization. Financial statements keep managers up-to-date on the success of the organization's sales and marketing initiatives, and on the ability of the organization to control its costs and maintain its **gross profit margin** and overall **profitability margin** as it delivers its products and/or services to its target market.

Gross Profit Margin is the portion of an organization's revenue that is left over after the organization has paid the direct costs (wages, components, materials, etc.) associated with its products or services.

Profitability Margin is the portion of an organization's revenue that is left after all operating expenses associated with its products or services have been paid.

Analyzing and interpreting financial statements is what enables a management team to "keep its fingers on the pulse" of the organization.

FIGURE 14.1   Three Fundamental Statements

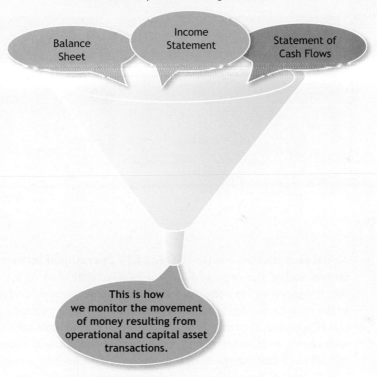

In analyzing the current financial situation of a company, managers generally rely on three primary financial statements: the income statement, the balance sheet, and the statement of cash flows (see Figure 14.1). These statements provide vital information to managers regarding an organization's current liquidity and solvency position, as well as its overall financial capacity to respond to opportunities and challenges that the organization may face in the near term. When assessed over a period of time, these financial statements also provide managers with information relating to the organization's overall growth and profitability trends, as well as its overall operating efficiency. It should be noted that while each statement is of value on its own, managers generate the clearest picture of what is happening within an organization by reviewing all three statements together and drawing conclusions based on the interconnectivity of the information generated from such a combined analysis. We will come back to discussing each of these statements in more detail, and also more thoroughly analyze the concepts of liquidity, solvency, efficiency, and capacity. Prior to doing this, however, it is important to understand the two fundamental types of business transactions that organizations will experience as they seek to grow their business and its overall profitability.

> In analyzing the current financial situation of a company, managers generally rely on three primary financial statements: the income statement, the balance sheet, and the statement of cash flows.

Two Fundamental Types of Business Transactions

Managers are constantly making decisions—and reviewing the results of these decisions—regarding two fundamental types of business transactions: operational transactions and

FIGURE 14.2   Two Fundamental Types of Business Transactions

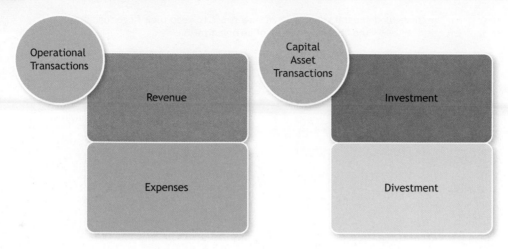

Operational Transactions represent the flow of money within the organization that is directly related to day-to-day business dealings.

Capital Asset Transactions are the decisions managers make with respect to investment and divestment of capital assets (buildings, equipment, business subsidiaries) that may be needed, or are no longer needed, as part of the organization's business system.

capital asset transactions (see Figure 14.2). **Operational transactions** represent the flow of money within the organization that is directly related to day-to-day business dealings. Revenue (generated as a result of selling goods and/or services) and reoccurring expenses relating to the manufacturing, distribution, and selling of such goods or services are primary examples of operational transactions. **Capital asset transactions** are decisions that managers make with respect to investment and divestment of capital assets (buildings, equipment, business subsidiaries) that may be needed, or are no longer needed, as part of the organization's business system. Although these are not directly related to the current year's profit for an organization, they do have an impact on its cash flow over the period being analyzed. The discussion of the three financial statements identified above (income statement, balance sheet, and statement of cash flows) will provide further clarity on how operational and capital asset transactions impact an organization and its ability to earn a profit and ensure long-term sustainability.

Liquidity, Solvency, Efficiency, and Financial Capacity

LO3

An important responsibility of managers, when conducting a financial analysis of their organization, is to draw conclusions about the current and future liquidity and solvency of the organization (see Figure 14.3). As has been noted in prior chapters, *liquidity* refers to the ability of the company, on the basis of the cash it has on hand and the cash it is generating within its operations, to meet its ongoing financial obligations. As an example, an organization will, on a monthly basis, have a variety of expenses that must be paid. Employees are expecting paycheques, suppliers are expecting payment for products/services provided to the business, and financial institutions are expecting that organizations will meet the repayment schedules associated with their credit facilities. In order to meet such obligations, businesses need to generate sufficient revenue from the sale of their products/services, or have sufficient cash on hand to cover such requirements until revenues can reach levels high enough to support these cash requirements. A liquidity assessment by a management team looks at these issues. Can the organization meet its current obligations both today and in the near term?

> An important responsibility of managers, when conducting a financial analysis of their organization, is to draw conclusions about the current and future liquidity and solvency of the organization.

FIGURE 14.3 Current and Future Liquidity and Solvency

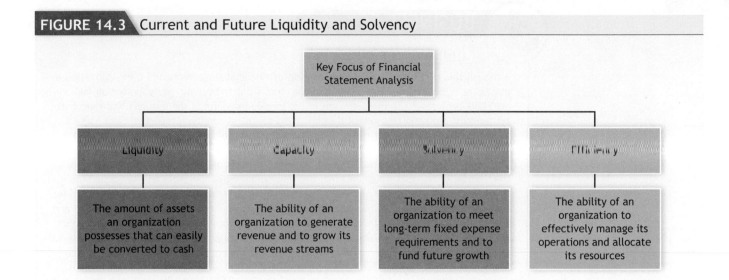

Solvency refers to a longer-term assessment of the financial stability of the organization. Solvency focuses on the forward anticipated profitability of the firm, and whether the firm has or can acquire sufficient capital in order to remain in business. In addition to looking at liquidity issues noted above, solvency also takes into consideration future revenues, products/services under development, market position, and the ability of the company to acquire additional capital resources if necessary. Solvency, in summary, refers to the ability of an organization to meet its long-term expense obligations and to profitably grow the company. An organization that becomes insolvent is unable to operate due to the lack of the necessary financial resources. For insolvent companies that are unable to find new sources of funding, the next step is generally closure and/or bankruptcy.

Efficiency refers to how effective the organization is in deploying its resources and managing its operational processes in the delivery of goods and/or services to the marketplace. Examples of efficiency measures would be how quickly we are collecting money owed to us from customers, how long it takes us to convert our inventory into sales, how productive our employees are, and how effective we are in utilizing our asset base and technology in generating sales for the organization.

Financial *capacity* is a general term that relates to an organization's cash reserves and borrowing power. Companies that have large cash reserves have the capacity to weather a downturn in the markets that results in a decrease in revenue. They also have the capacity (ability) to invest in research and development, launch new products, and initiate strong marketing plans. Companies that have valuable assets, and that have not taken on significant debt financing, also possess the capacity to borrow money in the event that they need to do so. As part of their strategic planning, managers look to assess the financial capacity of an organization in order to determine the amount of financial resources the organization has to work with. This will determine where and at what level the organization feels it can financially support its competitive position in the marketplace.

So, how do we get a read on the liquidity, solvency, efficiency, and capacity of an organization? We analyze and interpret its financial statements. The information provided within the income statement, balance sheet, and statement of cash flows provides us with valuable insight into drawing conclusions relating to these four assessment metrics.

> As part of their strategic planning, managers look to assess the financial capacity of an organization in order to determine the amount of financial resources the organization has to work with.

BUSINESS *in Action*

Financial Myopia

Although this chapter focuses on the analysis of financial statements and their utilization in managing an organization, managers must be careful not to become overly fixated on immediate short-term results to the detriment of the long-term health of the business. Positive short-term results are important in that they can build confidence in the management team's tactics and strategic thrusts. Positive short-term results also ensure that the organization maintains and/or improves its liquidity position and, at the same time, reinforces or delivers on the organization's longer-term direction. The risk, however, is that companies will become so fixated on the next set of financial statements that decision making may focus more on immediate bottom-line results than what is truly needed to nurture and grow the company's competitive edge for the future. The willingness to trade growth opportunities, customer service advantages, and employee-based intellectual capital in order to achieve stronger near-term results can compromise the underlying health of an organization. As an example, Circuit City Inc., once the #2 consumer electronics retailer in the United States, announced in March 2007 that it was going to lay off about 3400 store workers and replace them with lower-paid employees. This action,

along with several other cost-cutting initiatives, was designed to place Circuit City Inc. in a better position to generate stronger financial returns. Although short-term immediate benefits were noticed, there was considerable longer-term concern that this move would hurt employee morale, reduce productivity, drive away customers, and result in a significant loss of intellectual capital. In essence, the concern was that the company traded a significant competitive advantage (knowledgeable and experienced employees) and significantly compromised the long-term operating health of the company. For Circuit City Inc., the drastic actions taken in 2007 did not work, and the company was forced into bankruptcy and liquidation in January 2009. As managers, we need to learn how to balance the need to generate immediate returns with the need to protect and develop market-based competitive advantages that will ensure the long-term viability of the company, its products/services, customers, and other stakeholders.[2]

LO4

Three Primary Financial Statements

Income Statement

Income Statement is the financial statement that responds to the question of whether our business is earning a profit as a result of the sales we have made versus the expenses we have incurred in developing our goods and services and delivering them to the marketplace.

An **income statement** (Figure 14.4) is the financial statement that responds to the question of whether our business is earning a profit as a result of the sales we have made versus the expenses we have incurred in developing our goods and services and delivering them to the marketplace. It should be noted that under new IFRS rules the name income statement will change to the Statement of Comprehensive Income. The income statement, which reflects a specific period of time (year, quarter, month), identifies the revenue we have received and then subtracts the

FIGURE 14.4 The Income Statement

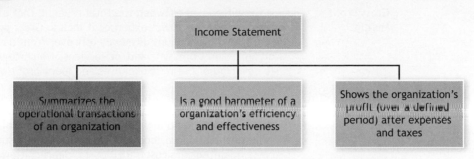

FIGURE 14.5 Simplified Operating (Income) Statement

	Sales Revenue	$$$$
Less:	Product Costs (COGS)	$$$$
Equals:	Gross Profit Margin	$$$$
Less:	General Operating Expenses	$$$$
Equals:	Earnings Before Interest and Taxes	$$$$
Less:	Interest Expense	$$$$
Equals:	Earnings Before Income Taxes	$$$$
Less:	Income Taxes	$$$$
Equals:	Net Profit or Loss	$$$$

expenses the business has incurred in generating such revenue. The residual amount remaining, after all operating expenses have been deducted from an organization's revenues, is profit. If expenses incurred exceed the revenue received, then the business would incur an operating loss for the period of time specified. Figure 14.5 outlines a typical (simplified) income statement format.

The income statement reflects a specific period of time (year, quarter, month), identifies the revenue we have received, and then subtracts the expenses the business has incurred in generating such revenue.

In order to better understand what an income statement is telling us, we can break it down into its individual components as shown in Table 14.1.

TABLE 14.1

| Sales Revenue | Reflects the dollar ($$$) amount that the organization has received as a result of selling its products and/or services. Revenue can be typically thought of as the sales that a company has made (less product or merchandise returns), and can be further broken down into the number of units an organization has sold multiplied by its selling price. |
| Cost of Goods Sold | Are the expenses that are directly incurred in the manufacturing of a product or the delivery of a service. As an example, if an organization were in the business of manufacturing and selling laptop computers, the cost of goods sold (product costs) involved would be the cost of the components used to build the laptop, the labour associated with assembling the laptop, and the packaging and delivery charges incurred to ship the laptop to the customer. |

Continued

TABLE 14.1 *Continued*

Gross Profit Margin	Is the difference between the total revenue that an organization receives and the direct expenses it incurs. Gross profit margin represents the amount of money left over from the sale of the organization's products and/or services, which can then be used to cover other business expenses and meet profit objectives.
General Operating Expenses	Are indirect expenses that an organization incurs and that must be paid from an organization's gross profit margin. General operating expenses include administrative expenses, general marketing expenses, and operational overhead (utilities, insurance, lease costs, maintenance costs, R&D costs, depreciation, etc.).
EBIT (Earnings Before Interest and Taxes)	Is determined by subtracting general operating expenses from gross profit margin.
Interest Expense	Is the interest payments that the organization is obligated to pay during a specified period on the debt that the organization has undertaken in order to finance its operations.
EBT (Earnings Before Taxes)	Is the amount of earnings the operation has produced prior to recognizing its federal and provincial income tax obligations.
Net Profit or Loss	Represents the firm's profit or loss from the sale of its products and/or services to its customers. This dollar amount is typically referred to as net income or net loss.

INCOME STATEMENT EXAMPLE: CAA TRONICS INC.

Let's use the following example to provide an illustration of how an income statement is generated, and how the results can be interpreted.

CAA Tronics Inc. manufactures leading-edge electronic sensors that it sells through an established line of dealers. In reviewing its recent 12 months' results, CAA Tronics Inc.'s management team has established the following revenue and cost information:

Sales	
Quantity Sold	2 000 000 units
Selling Price	$32.00 per unit
Product Costs	
Material Costs	$12.75 per unit
Labour Costs	$ 9.00 per unit
Distribution and Packaging Costs	$ 3.00 per unit
General Operating Expenses	
Depreciation	$ 500 000
R&D Expenses	$4 000 000
General Marketing Expenses	$1 750 000
General Selling Expenses	$1 500 000
Administration Expenses	$1 050 000
Interest on Debt	
Annual Interest Expense	$1 800 000
Corporate Tax Rate	25%

Utilizing the information noted above, the income statement for CAA Tronics Inc. for the year being assessed could be calculated as shown in Exhibit 14.1:

EXHIBIT 14.1

			% Sales
	CAA Tronics Inc. **Income Statement — 20XX**		
Sales Revenue	(Selling Price × Quantity Sold) ($32.00 × 2 000 000 units)		$ 64 000 000 100%
Less:	Product Costs (also called Cost of Goods Sold)		
	Material Costs ($12.75 × 2 000 000 units)	$25 500 000	
	Labour Costs ($9.00 × 2 000 000 units)	$18 000 000	
	Distribution & Packaging Costs ($3.00 × 2 000 000)	$ 6 000 000	$ 49 500 000 77%
Gross Profit Margin			**$14 500 000 23%**
Less:	General Operating Expenses		
	Depreciation	$ 500 000	
	R&D Expenses	$ 4 000 000	
	General Marketing Expenses	$ 1 750 000	
	General Selling Expenses	$ 1 500 000	
	Administration Expenses	$ 1 050 000	$ 8 800 000 14%
EBIT (Earnings Before Interest and Taxes)			**$ 5 700 000 9%**
Less: Interest on Debt			$ 1 800 000 2.5%
Earnings Before Taxes (EBT)			**$ 3 900 000 6%**
Less: Income Tax Expense @ 25% (.25 × $3 900 000)			$ 975 000 1.5%
Net Income or Profit			**$ 2 925 000 4.5%**

As we can see from the above example, CAA Tronics Inc.'s business operations generated $64 000 000 in sales in 20XX. This was the result of selling 2 000 000 electronic sensors at a selling price of $32 per unit. CAA Tronics Inc. spent $58 300 000 on expenses in order to develop, produce, and distribute these units to its customers. Of this $58 300 000 in expenses, $49 500 000 was for product costs associated with manufacturing and distributing the product, while $8 800 000 was for general operating expenses (depreciation, R&D, marketing, selling, and administration). In addition, CAA Tronics Inc. was required to make interest payments on debt to its creditors in the amount of $1 800 000. This left CAA Tronics Inc. with Earnings Before Taxes (EBT) of $3 900 000. Federal and provincial corporate income taxes amounted to $975 000, leaving CAA Tronics Inc. with a net profit of $2 925 000, or a 4.5 percent ROS (return on sales).

Another way to think about this is shown in Figure 14.6.

Revenue represents 100 percent of the dollars flowing into the operation. In order to generate each $1 of sales, CAA Tronics Inc. incurs $0.91 in business expenses (variable costs of $0.77 and general operating expenses of $0.14). This leaves $0.09 to pay for interest expenses and taxes. Interest expense payments cost $0.025 (2.5 cents) per $1 of revenue, and taxes cost another $0.015 (1.5 cents) per $1 of revenue. The end result is that for each $1 of revenue received, CAA Tronics Inc. makes only $0.045 (4.5 cents) in net profit that it can then use to further improve the organization's financial and market position.

FIGURE 14.6   CAA Tronics Inc.: Income Statement

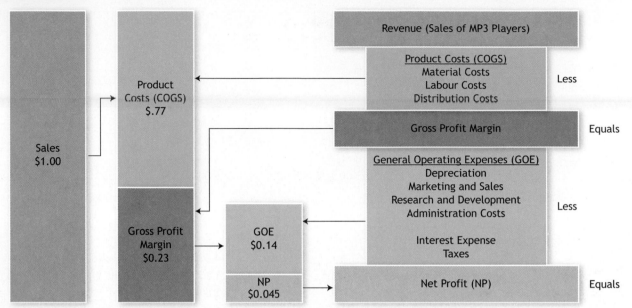

Source: *The Definitive Business Plan*, Richard Stutely, 2nd Edition, Prentice Hall, 2007.

Balance Sheet

Balance Sheet refers to a financial statement that provides managers with an understanding of the resources the organization has at its disposal at a given point in time, and the financial obligations the business has incurred as a result of purchasing these resources.

The **balance sheet** (Figure 14.7) is a financial statement that provides managers with an understanding of the resources the organization has at its disposal at a given point in time, and the financial obligations the business has incurred as a result of purchasing these resources. As with the income statement, new IFRS rules will transition the name of this statement to that of the Statement of Changes in Financial Position. The title "balance sheet" is reflective of the fact that the information being identified in this financial statement must adhere to the following accounting equation:

$$\text{Assets} = \text{Liabilities} + \text{Owners' Equity}$$

As in the equation above, the balance sheet is arranged into three areas: assets, liabilities, and owners' equity. The information contained within each of these sections of the balance sheet is outlined below.

ASSETS

Assets refers to the resources that the organization has at its disposal and that it can utilize in the generation of business activity and, ultimately, profit.

Assets represent the resources that the organization has at its disposal and that it can utilize in the generation of business activity and, ultimately, profit. Assets can be classified as either "current" or "non-current." Current assets are resources that organizations can convert to cash

FIGURE 14.7   The Balance Sheet

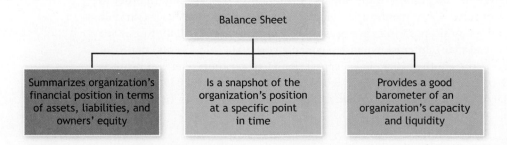

FIGURE 14.8 Assets

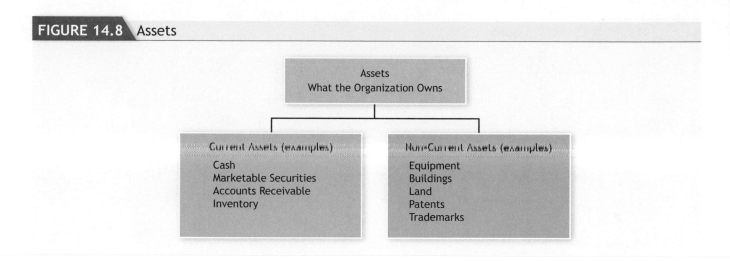

and/or consume, usually within a short period of time (i.e., one year or less). Examples of current assets are cash, marketable securities, accounts receivable, and inventory. Non-current assets are resources that are generally more fixed in nature, and typically represent the capital assets of the organization. Examples of non-current assets are plant and equipment, land, and the value of intangible assets such as patents or trademarks (see Figure 14.8).

LIABILITIES

Liabilities are the debts or financial obligations that an organization has incurred as a result of conducting its business. As with the asset section of the balance sheet, the liability section typically separates such debts or financial obligations into those that are coming due in the short term (current liabilities) and those that extend into the future (long-term liabilities). A standard rule for current liabilities is that they are obligations the organization will need to pay within the current business year. Examples of current liabilities are accounts payable, trades payable, and short-term debt (such as a 90-day loan). Long-term liabilities are obligations that extend out beyond a one-year period. Examples of long-term liabilities are a 5- or 10-year loan, a mortgage on a building, or an obligation such as a 10-year bond (see Figure 14.9).

OWNERS' EQUITY (OR SHAREHOLDERS' EQUITY)

Owners' equity (Figure 14.10) represents the value of capital received from the owners of the business that is used to fund the start-up or ongoing operations of the business, plus the value of the organization's retained earnings. Generally, companies will retain a portion or all of their current-year profits in order to fund future growth opportunities, buy new equipment,

> **Liabilities** are the debts or financial obligations that an organization has incurred as a result of conducting its business.

> **Owners' Equity** represents the value of capital received from the owners of the business that is used to fund the start-up or ongoing operations of the business, as well as reflecting the value of the organization's retained earnings.

FIGURE 14.9 Liabilities

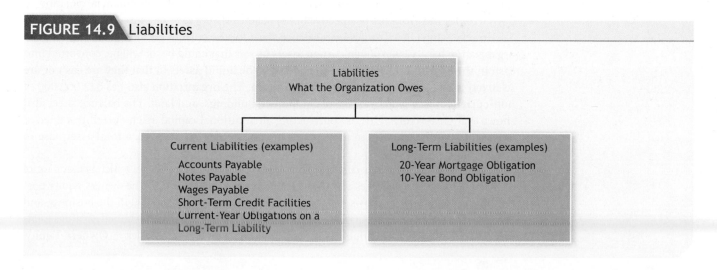

FIGURE 14.10   Owners' Equity

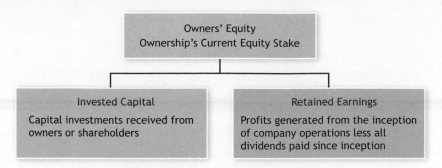

Going back to our balance sheet accounting equation, Assets = Liabilities + Owners' Equity, we can see that, given the composition of the balance sheet, the following additional conclusions can be reached:

Retained Earnings represent the value of prior earnings that an organization has retained for future investment in the business.

purchase new buildings, or develop new products, or to hold in reserve to cover unforeseen contingencies. **Retained earnings** equals the profits generated since the inception of the company's operations, less all dividends paid since inception. An easy equation to help us remember the composition of owners' equity (also called shareholders' equity) is the following:

> **Owners' Equity** = Owners' Capital Invested + Retained Earnings

The term "shareholders' equity" pertains to organizations that have issued stock as a basis of business ownership, with the capital invested reflecting the initial amount for which shareholders purchased their shares from the company.

Going back to our balance sheet accounting equation, Assets = Liabilities + Owners' Equity, we can see that, given the composition of the balance sheet, the following additional conclusions can be reached:

> **Liabilities** = Assets − Owners' Equity
> Owners' Equity = Assets − Liabilities

Knowing the relationships among each of these sections of the balance sheet is important for managers, because this understanding will assist in analyzing the liquidity, solvency, and financial capacity of the organization.

BALANCE SHEET: CAA TRONICS INC.

As with the income statement example shown earlier, let's review the financial position of CAA Tronics Inc. from the perspective of the balance sheet (Exhibit 14.2).

In reviewing CAA Tronics Inc.'s balance sheet for the current period, we can see that the organization has $12 900 000 in current assets (assets that could be, or will be, converted into cash in the near future). These are considered to be liquid assets in that they are cash or are relatively easy to convert to cash in the near term. The organization also has $42 000 000 of non-current assets, which consist of equipment, buildings, and land. The balance sheet also shows that CAA Tronics Inc. is constructing an additional capital asset, currently valued at $10 000 000 (construction in progress). This gives CAA Tronics Inc. a total asset base of $54 900 000.

CAA Tronics Inc. also is currently showing $36 800 000 in liabilities, which is made up of $5 800 000 in current liabilities and $31 000 000 in long-term liabilities. The owners' equity portion of the balance sheet shows that the owners have invested $9 000 000 in the business, and that, given its prior year's profitability, the organization has accumulated retained earnings totalling $9 100 000. Reviewing our accounting equation, Assets = Liabilities + Owners' Equity,

EXHIBIT 14.2

ASSETS		LIABILITIES + OWNERS' EQUITY	
CAA Tronics Inc. Balance Sheet—20XX			
Current Assets		Current Liabilities	
Cash	$ 1 500 000	Accounts Payable	$ 2 500 000
Marketable Securities	$ 2 000 000	Wages Payable	$ 1 800 000
Accounts Receivable	$ 5 400 000	Taxes Payable	$ 975 000
Inventory	$ 4 000 000	Short-Term Debt	$ 525 000
Total Current Assets	**$12 900 000**	**Total Current Liabilities**	**$ 5 800 000**
Non-Current Assets		Long-Term Liabilities	
Equipment	$ 8 000 000	5-Year Note	$ 5 000 000
Buildings	$ 20 000 000	Mortgage	$ 16 000 000
Land	$ 4 000 000	10-Year Bond	$ 10 000 000
Construction in Progress	$ 10 000 000	**Total Long-Term Liabilities**	**$31 000 000**
Total Non-Current Assets	**$42 000 000**		
		Total Liabilities	**$36 800 000**
		Owners' Equity	
		Invested Capital	$ 9 000 000
		Retained Earnings	$ 9 100 000
		Total Owners' Equity	**$18 100 000**
Total Assets	**$54 900 000**	**Total Liabilities & Owners' Equity**	**$54 900 000**

we find that CAA Tronics Inc.'s statement of financial position for the period being reviewed does balance:

$$\textbf{Assets} = \text{Liabilities} + \text{Owners' Equity}$$
$$\$54\ 900\ 000 = \$36\ 800\ 000 + \$18\ 100\ 000$$

Statement of Cash Flows

Going back to our initial discussion relating to financial transactions within an organization, we concluded that businesses will have two types of financial transactions: operational transactions and capital asset transactions. The income statement, as noted previously, provides us with a good understanding of the operational transactions that an organization incurs in its drive to create profitable growth. It must be understood, however, that organizations generate cash inflows and cash outflows beyond operational transactions. The purchase or construction of a building, the selling of additional shares of stock, and repayments of principal on loans are all examples of transactions that deal with the organization's capital assets. These transactions, which require monetary support in the same manner as those expenses being incurred on an income statement, also must be recognized within the managerial decision-making process. This is, in essence, the role of the **statement of cash flows** (Figure 14.11).
While the income statement provides insight into the operational transactions that are occurring within an organization, the statement of cash flows provides managers with a full understanding of the total movement of cash (from all sources) into and out of the business. Given this,

Statement of Cash Flows provides managers with a full understanding of the total movement of cash (from all sources) into and out of the business.

FIGURE 14.11   Statement of Cash Flows

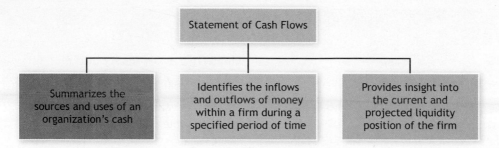

many managers and analysts consider the statement of cash flows to be the best source of information relating to an organization's liquidity situation.

> Many managers and analysts consider the statement of cash flows to be the best source of information relating to an organization's liquidity situation.

As an example, assume that Fit for Life Inc., a large health and fitness operation located in Toronto, decides to add an aquatics centre to its current facility. The anticipated cost of the aquatics centre is estimated at $5.0 million. As a result of unanticipated increases in construction costs, changes to the architectural drawings, and an enhancement of the services to be offered (versus those originally planned), the final cost of the aquatics centre totals $5.8 million. This additional $800 000 of capital represents an additional outflow of cash to the organization beyond the $5.0 million it originally planned to spend and had budgeted for. This $800 000 additional expenditure would not be picked up on the income statement, as it is not an operational transaction. It also may not be recognizable on the balance sheet, as the balance sheet shows only aggregate amounts of the value of assets, not dollars being spent on assets as they are being built or acquired. You would have to check for differences in retained earnings levels or cash balances to pick up on this additional expenditure. Where this additional expenditure becomes immediately noticeable is in the statement of cash flows. It is this statement that shows the full impact of all cash-related decisions within an organization and, therefore, truly enables us to understand and sense what the cash position/situation of the organization is (see Figure 14.12).

To further illustrate how a statement of cash flows is produced, let's go back to our example of CAA Tronics Inc. In addition to the operating results shown on the income statement (Exhibit 14.1) and the balance sheet (Exhibit 14.2), assume that the following additional non-operational transactions took place in 20XX:

1. The $10 000 000, 10-year bond now showing under the liabilities section of CAA Tronics Inc.'s balance sheet was issued in the current year.
2. The $10 000 000 in "construction in progress" showing under the asset section of CAA Tronics Inc.'s balance sheet was spent in the current year.
3. The taxes shown as being owed on the income statement of CAA Tronics Inc. are deferred until the next period, and therefore do not actually have to be paid at this time.
4. Other non-cash items (such as changes to the levels of accounts payable and accounts receivable) netted out to be $100 000.
5. CAA Tronics Inc. repurchased 100 000 shares of company stock at $20 per share.
6. Principal repayment on the five-year note and 20-year mortgage was $1 300 000.

On the basis of this information, and using the information provided in Exhibits 14.1 and 14.2, we can create a statement of cash flows for CAA Tronics Inc. (shown in Exhibit 14.3).

FIGURE 14.12 Simplified Statement of Cash Flows

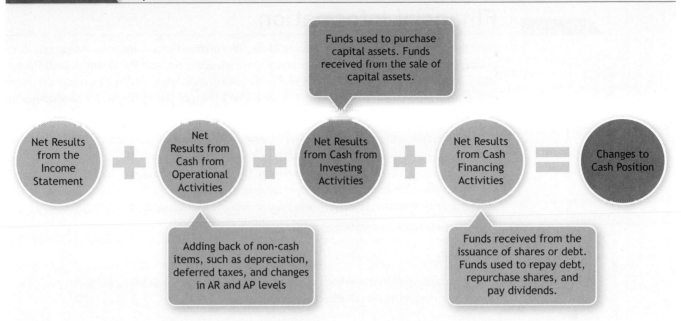

When the net change in cash position is added to the beginning cash position of CAA Tronics Inc. from the prior year's balance sheet, this will equal the amount of cash shown on the balance sheet for the current period. Assume that last year's cash balance on the balance sheet was $300 000. When this year's net change in cash position is added to this, the new cash balance on the balance sheet (Exhibit 14.2) equals $1 500 000.

EXHIBIT 14.3

CAA Tronics Inc.
Statement of Cash Flows—Year 20XX

Cash from Operational Activities

Net Income (Deficit)	$ 2 925 000	(taken from Exhibit 14.1)
Depreciation	$ 500 000	(taken from Exhibit 14.1)
Deferred Income Taxes	$ 975 000	(taken from Exhibit 14.1)
Other Non-Cash Items	$ 100 000	
Net Cash from Operations	$ 4 500 000	

Cash from Financing Activities

Repurchase of Stock	($ 2 000 000)	
Principal Payment on Debt	($ 1 300 000)	
Issuance of 10-Year Bond	$10 000 000	
Net Cash from Financing Activities	$ 6 700 000	

Cash from Investing Activities

Construction in Progress	($10 000 000)	
Net Cash from Investing Activities	($10 000 000)	

Net Change in Cash Position $ 1 200 000

Cash, Beginning of the Period	$ 300 000	
Cash, End of the Period	$ 1 500 000	(reflected on Balance Sheet)

Cash from Operational Activities refers to adjustments to net income to reflect the actual cash provided by operating activities

Cash from Financing Activities refers to sources of cash flowing into the organization from non-operating activities.

Cash from Investing Activities refers to uses of cash flowing out of the organization from non-operating activities.

Net Change in Cash Position refers to the net movement in the cash position of the organization based on operating, financing, and investing activities.

Analyzing and Interpreting Financial Information

Now that we have a better understanding of the information that is contained within our three primary financial statements (income statement, balance sheet, and statement of cash flows), let's take a look at how to further interpret this information when making business decisions and drawing conclusions relating to the financial health of the business. In conducting an analysis of an organization's financial health, our focus is generally in four specific areas:

1. *Ratio analysis*—the process by which we assess and interpret the relationships among the financial results shown on an organization's financial statements.
2. *Leverage analysis*—the process of assessing the impact of the amount of debt an organization has incurred in order to finance its asset base.
3. *Trend or comparative analysis*—whereby we look at trends occurring over time by analyzing financial statements across multiple time periods.
4. *Absolute analysis*—where we look at the specific dollar amount of financial resources available.

Only by utilizing all four methods are we able to get a true sense as to the financial position of the company and the overall direction of its financial health.

Ratio Analysis[3]

Ratios seek to define the relationship between critical components of information found on the financial statements.

Ratio analysis is a primary tool that managers use to assess the financial health of an organization. **Ratios** seek to define the relationship between critical components of information found on the financial statements. Ratio analysis is really a driver for the development of questions to which the management team will seek additional information in order to effectively manage the organization. Managers are cautioned to realize that, although helpful, ratios by themselves are not always indicative of the financial health of the organization. This is why managers need to go beyond simply conducting such an analysis and generate key questions (relating to what is happening within the operation) that will drive a more sound understanding of what is happening financially within the organization.

> Managers are cautioned to realize that, although helpful, ratios by themselves are not always indicative of the financial health of the organization.

Recognizing that ratio analysis can extend into a variety of analytical areas, managers fundamentally utilize ratio analysis to get a feel for the operational efficiency of the organization in four fundamental areas:

1. Profitability
2. Solvency and liquidity
3. Debt
4. Activity

Profitability Ratios focus on assessing the amount of income the organization has earned in comparison to the operating activity that has taken place and the assets that have been used to support its generation.

Profitability Ratios   **Profitability ratios** focus on assessing the amount of income the organization has earned in comparison to the operating activity that has taken place and the assets that have been used to support its income generation. Ideally, an organization will want to be as efficient as possible given the resources expended and the activities that have taken place. In general, the more efficient the organization is in its activities and its deployment of its assets the more profitable it should be (assuming revenues are sufficient to cover costs). Managers often will set target ratios for the organization as part of its planning process, and then compare the actual results against the targets to determine whether the organization is operating as efficiently as anticipated. Examples of profitability ratios often used by managers are as follows:

- Return on sales

- Return on assets

- Return on equity

- Earnings per share

Return on Sales (ROS)   The return on sales ratio identifies to managers the percentage of sales the company has generated that actually represent profit (net income) for the business. Utilizing information from the Income statement, the return on sales ratio is calculated as follows:

$$\text{Return on Sales} = \frac{\text{Net Income}}{\text{Net Sales}}$$

If we use CAA Tronics Inc.'s income statement (see Exhibit 14.1), we can calculate its return on sales as follows:

$$\text{CAA Tronics Inc.'s Return on Sales} = \frac{\$2\,925\,000}{\$64\,000\,000} = 4.5\%$$

Another way of looking at this is that for every $1 in sales that CAA Tronics Inc. makes, it puts $0.045 (4.5 cents) in its pocket. The other $0.955 (95.5 cents) is consumed in covering its expenses and tax obligations. If the target for the year were an ROS of 6 percent, then CAA Tronics Inc. would have fallen short of its objective. Conversely, if the target were an ROS of 3 percent, then CAA Tronics Inc. would have exceeded its expectations.

Return on Assets (ROA)   The return on assets ratio identifies the relationship of net income to the total asset base of the organization. This ratio reflects how productive the deployment of these assets was in producing income for the organization. ROA is calculated as follows:

$$\text{Return on Assets} = \frac{\text{Net Income}}{\text{Total Assets}}$$

Although not shown in the example that follows, return on assets is generally computed using the average total assets of an organization ((beginning assets + ending assets)/2). Sometimes managers and/or investors will add interest expense back into the net income figure in order to get a sense as to the return on assets prior to the cost of borrowing.

Again using CAA Tronics Inc. as an example, the ROA calculation would take the net income figure from the income statement (Exhibit 14.1) and divide it by the value of total assets found on the balance sheet (Exhibit 14.2):

$$\text{CAA Tronics Inc.'s Return on Assets} = \frac{\$2\,925\,000}{\$54\,900\,000} = 5.3\%$$

This ratio means that for each $1 of assets deployed by this organization, it generated $0.053 (5.3 cents) of net profit for the business. Organizations will then compare this ratio against previously defined targets and against industry standards to determine how effective their utilization of assets is.

The next two ratios, return on equity (ROE) and earnings per share (EPS), relate to the return investors will realize on their investment in the business.

Return on Equity (ROE)   The return on equity ratio (ROE) computes the amount of net income that was earned on each dollar of invested capital provided by the business's owners (shareholders). This ratio is computed as follows:

$$\text{Return on Equity} = \frac{\text{Net Income}}{\text{Total Equity}}$$

Referring to CAA Tronics Inc.'s income statement (Exhibit 14.1) and balance sheet (Exhibit 14.2), the ROE for the current year would be computed as follows:

$$\text{CAA Tronics Inc.'s Return on Equity} = \frac{\$2\ 925\ 000}{\$18\ 100\ 000} = 16\%$$

As with the ratios noted above, this means that for each dollar of invested capital provided by owners (shareholders), the company generated $0.16 (16 cents) in net income. This would then be compared against forecast or targeted returns, as well as against the ROEs of competitors, to determine the use of invested capital and the attractiveness of the return when compared to other investment opportunities. Again, although not shown in this example, balance sheet items (such as total equity), within ratio computations, are often averaged over the period of time for which the calculation is being made.

Earnings per Share (EPS) This ratio is calculated for corporations where shares have been issued and investors are looking to see what the return on their investment is for each share purchased. The earnings per share ratio reflects the return that individual investors would recognize for each share of stock that they owned. It should be noted that this does not mean that shareholders would actually receive this money, as the organization may not pay these dollars out but will most likely keep them in order to fund future capital needs.

$$\text{Earnings per Share} = \frac{\text{Net Income}}{\text{\# of Shares Outstanding}}$$

Let's assume that CAA Tronics Inc. currently has 8 000 000 shares of stock outstanding. This means that the organization has issued, and investors have purchased, these 8 000 000 shares. Again, using the net income from the income statement (Exhibit 14.1), we can compute the EPS for shareholders of CAA Tronics Inc:

$$\text{CAA Tronics Inc.'s Earnings per Share} = \frac{\$2\ 925\ 000}{8\ 000\ 000\ \text{shares}} = \$0.365$$

In calculating the EPS for CAA Tronics Inc., we see that shareholders earned $0.365 (36.5 cents) per share. Because shareholders will own different numbers of shares, this is a useful way for an investor to determine the return on his/her individual investment.

Solvency and Liquidity Ratios As noted earlier in this chapter, when an organization is unable to meet its cash obligations in the short term, or becomes insolvent due to its inability to meet its cash obligations for the long term going forward, the end result can be bankruptcy and liquidation. Managers need to understand the amount of cash that will be required to meet their operating needs and financial obligations. **Solvency and liquidity ratios** assist in doing just this. By comparing financial obligations with the financial resources that an organization has, managers can determine whether the organization possesses sufficient capital resources to meet its upcoming needs. In this way, managers can anticipate cash shortages and/or excess cash positions versus being surprised by such events. Common solvency and liquidity ratios used by managers include:

Solvency and Liquidity Ratios analyze the financial obligations that an organization has against its financial resources in order to determine whether the organization possesses sufficient capital to meet its upcoming needs.

- Current ratio
- Quick ratio
- Solvency ratio

Current Ratio One of the most popular ratios used in measuring the solvency and liquidity position of an organization is the current ratio. This ratio shows the relationship between an organization's current assets and its current liabilities. Remember that current assets are those assets that represent cash, near cash, or items that can be converted to cash in the short term (usually within the current operating period). Current liabilities are the financial obligations the organization must meet in the short term.

$$\text{Current Ratio} = \frac{\text{Current Assets}}{\text{Current Liabilities}}$$

Using CAA Tronics Inc.'s balance sheet (Exhibit 14.2), we can compute the current ratio for this business:

$$\text{CAA Tronics Inc.'s Current Ratio} = \frac{\$12\ 900\ 000}{\$5\ 800\ 000} = 2.22$$

What this means to CAA Tronics Inc.'s management team is that the organization has $2.22 in current assets for each $1.00 it has in current liabilities. For the management team, there is comfort in knowing that the organization has sufficient cash and near-cash resources to meet its current financial obligations. It should be noted, however, that what is an acceptable current ratio will vary by industry and by the length of an organization's business cycle (the length of time it takes to develop, manufacture, distribute, and sell its products/services). In some industries, a current ratio of 1:1 may be acceptable, while in others a much higher current ratio may be required. Maintaining a strong current ratio is a best practice for keeping an organization solvent and for meeting its liquidity needs.

Quick Ratio   The quick ratio (also known as the acid test ratio) is a valuable ratio to use when an organization is really concerned about its current liquidity position. The quick ratio looks to remove from the current ratio calculation those assets that are not so easily converted into cash immediately and therefore would take time to generate cash from in the event of a need for immediate cash resources. These remaining assets, referred to as quick assets, are often limited to cash, marketable securities, and accounts receivable. These quick assets are then divided by the total value of current liabilities in order to determine an organization's ability to meet its current obligations strictly from its immediate cash position.

CAA Tronics Inc.'s quick ratio (again, using Exhibit 14.2) would be computed as follows:

$$\text{Quick Ratio} = \frac{\text{Cash + Marketable Securities + Accounts Receivable}}{\text{Current Liabilities}}$$

$$\text{CAA Tronics Inc.'s Quick Ratio} = \frac{\$1\ 500\ 000 + \$2\ 000\ 000 + \$5\ 400\ 000}{\$5\ 800\ 000} = 1.53$$

CAA Tronics Inc.'s quick ratio is 1.53, which means that it has $1.53 of quick assets for each $1.00 of current liabilities. This means that CAA Tronics Inc. is able to cover its short-term obligations from its existing cash and near-cash resources and still have some of these resources left over to meet other financial needs.

Solvency Ratio   The solvency ratio is designed to assess the ability of an organization to meet its long-term financial obligations. This ratio takes an organization's net income, adds back depreciation (which is a non-cash transaction, and is found on the income statement; see Exhibit 14.1), and then assesses it against the total value of an organization's liabilities (see Exhibit 14.2).

$$\text{Solvency Ratio} = \frac{\text{Net Income + Depreciation}}{\text{Total Liabilities}}$$

CAA Tronics Inc.'s solvency ratio would be calculated as follows:

$$\text{CAA Tronics Inc.'s Solvency Ratio} = \frac{\$2\ 925\ 000 + \$500\ 000}{\$36\ 800\ 000} = .093$$

An acceptable solvency ratio does vary by industry, but a general rule is that the ratio should be equal to or greater than .20. In this case, CAA Tronics Inc.'s solvency ratio is .093, which may indicate to management that the amount of debt that CAA Tronics Inc. has assumed is becoming significant and that additional use of debt may not be the most appropriate form of financing, as these obligations could lead to solvency and/or liquidity issues down the road.

Debt Ratios focus on the amount of debt an organization has taken on, the relationship of this debt value against its total asset base, and the ability of the organization to meet its debt servicing (payments) obligations.

Debt Ratios

Debt ratios focus on the amount of debt an organization has taken on, the relationship of this debt value to its total asset base, and the ability of the organization to meet its debt servicing (payments) obligations. Three common debt ratios used by managers are:

- Debt to asset ratio

- Debt to equity ratio

- Times interest earned ratio

Debt to Asset Ratio   The debt to asset ratio assesses the relationship between the value of the debt that has been taken on by an organization and the value of its total assets. This lets managers and analysts know how much of the asset base of the organization has been created via debt financing. This identifies the amount of financial leverage the organization has assumed in order to build the company.

$$\text{Debt to Asset Ratio} = \frac{\text{Total Liabilities}}{\text{Total Assets}}$$

In CAA Tronics Inc.'s case, the debt to asset ratio would be calculated as follows (see Exhibit 14.2):

$$\text{CAA Tronics Inc.'s Debt to Asset Ratio} = \frac{\$36\ 800\ 000}{\$54\ 900\ 000} = .67$$

Based on the ratio as calculated above, CAA Tronics Inc.'s debt to asset ratio is .67. This means that for each $1.00 of assets purchased by CAA Tronics Inc., $0.67 (67 cents) was financed via debt. Acceptable debt ratios will vary by industry, but generally speaking, although some debt is acceptable, high debt to asset ratios worry managers and lenders alike. The higher the ratio, the more creditors own the business versus investors, and the more exposure the organization will have to solvency issues given the high costs of servicing such debt. The value of this debt ratio can also be an indicator of the risk attitude of the management team in that higher debt levels can imply a willingness to be more aggressive with respect to risk and a willingness to borrow money to fund business ventures.

Debt to Equity Ratio   The debt to equity ratio assesses the relationship between the amount of debt that has been taken on by an organization and the value of the equity position of its investors (shareholders). Keeping in mind the accounting equation, Assets = Liabilities + Owners' Equity, the debt to equity ratio calculates the amount of money an organization has borrowed in order to fund the creation of its asset base, against the amount of money that investors have provided.

$$\text{Debt to Equity Ratio} = \frac{\text{Total Liabilities}}{\text{Total Equity}}$$

In CAA Tronics Inc.'s case, the debt to equity ratio (also referred to as a leverage ratio) would be calculated as follows (see Exhibit 14.2):

$$\text{CAA Tronics Inc.'s Debt to Equity Ratio} = \frac{\$36\ 800\ 000}{\$18\ 100\ 000} = 2.03$$

Based on the ratio as calculated above, CAA Tronics Inc.'s debt to equity ratio is 2.03. This means that in building its asset base, CAA Tronics Inc. utilized $2.03 of debt financing for each $1.00 of capital provided by investors. In essence, CAA Tronics Inc. was leveraged a bit more than 2 to 1.

Times Interest Earned Ratio   When an organization takes on debt financing, it is promising to the lender that it will repay the lender both the principal borrowed and the interest charge incurred in borrowing the money. If an organization finds itself in unanticipated trouble, the lender's minimum expectation would be that the organization would at least meet its interest obligation on the debt it has taken on. The times interest earned ratio assesses the ability of the business to do just that. Organizations make such interest payments out of their cash flow, and this obligation is typically budgeted to be taken out of revenues and the profit that is derived from the organization's business operations. The ratio, in essence, lets managers and analysts know if the organization is generating sufficient profit to meet its interest expense obligations. The times interest earned ratio is computed as follows:

$$\text{Times Interest Earned Ratio} = \frac{\text{EBIT (Earnings Before Interest and Taxes)}}{\text{Interest Expense}}$$

In computing the times interest earned ratio for CAA Tronics Inc., we would return to the income statement (Exhibit 14.1) to pick up the required information.

$$\text{CAA Tronics Inc.'s Times Interest Earned Ratio} = \frac{\$5\ 700\ 000}{\$1\ 800\ 000} = 3.16$$

The times interest earned ratio indicates that CAA Tronics Inc. can meet its current interest expense payments on its debt 3.16 times from the income that it is generating from its operations. The higher the number associated with this ratio, the more comfortable lenders are that at least the interest obligation associated with the debt will be paid. A low or negative number in this ratio could raise concerns about the organization's solvency position and its ability to service its debt.

Activity Ratios   **Activity ratios** assist managers in assessing the efficiency and effectiveness of key components of an organization's operations. By computing these ratios, managers can get a sense as to how effectively the organization is utilizing its asset base, whether changes in cash flow into and out of the organization could be negatively impacting its cash operating cycle, and how well capital is being utilized in support of the organization's strategic and tactical decisions. Recognizing that there are a variety of activity ratios at the disposal of management, some of the more common ratios are illustrated below. It should be noted that acceptable ratio levels do vary by industry, so it is important to assess the results of ratio analyses in comparison to the specific market environment within which the organization is competing.

> **Activity Ratios** assist managers in assessing the efficiency and effectiveness of key components of an organization's operations.

Two common activity ratios that managers utilize are as follows:

- Days receivable

- Inventory turnover

Days Receivable   The number of days it takes to convert accounts receivable to cash is an important piece of information for managers to understand. The ability to convert dollars owed to an organization into cash has a definite impact on the company's cash flow and cash operating cycle. Computing this ratio involves a two-step process. The first step is to calculate the average daily sales by an organization. This is accomplished as follows:

$$\text{Average Day's Sales} = \frac{\text{Net Annual Sales}}{365\ \text{Days}}$$

Once the average day's sales is computed, this number is then divided into the current amount of accounts receivable to determine an average collection period, which is called the days receivable:

$$\text{Days Receivable} = \frac{\text{Accounts Receivable}}{\text{Average Day's Sales}}$$

Using CAA Tronics Inc. as an example (see Exhibits 14.1 and 14.2), we can compute this as follows:

$$\text{CAA Tronics Inc.'s Average Day's Sales} = \frac{\$64\,000\,000}{365\,\text{Days}} = \$175\,342$$

The average day's sales have been computed to be $175 342. This number is then divided into the accounts receivable (shown on the balance sheet, Exhibit 14.2) to determine how many days it takes, on average, for accounts receivable to be collected from our customers:

$$\text{CAA Tronics Inc.'s Days Receivable} = \frac{\$5\,400\,000}{\$175\,342} = 30.79\,\text{days}$$

On average, it takes CAA Tronics Inc. 30.79 days to turn a dollar of receivables into cash. The organization would then benchmark this against its established policy, and measure it over time to ensure that the organization was not seeing an unnecessary lengthening of this period of time. Allowing the number of days receivable to increase could put short-term pressure on the organization's liquidity, as it would lengthen the cash operating cycle (cash-to-cash cycle) and require CAA Tronics Inc. to use more of its own cash to fund its operations until repayment is provided. Managers can perform the same type of calculation on key customer accounts to ensure that such customers are paying on time and there is not too much trade credit being lent to customers, thereby minimizing the risk of default. Companies desiring to speed up the payment process often provide slight discounts on invoice amounts to get customers to pay quickly (within 10 days), thereby improving the company's cash operating cycle.

Inventory Turnover   The ability of a company to turn its inventory into cash is an important activity ratio to measure. Inventory represents products that have been paid for (either purchased as a finished good or manufactured) but have yet to be sold by the company and converted into sales revenue. The longer the inventory remains unsold, the greater the concern that the company will not be able to get its full selling price for it. Also, the longer it remains unsold, the greater the strain it places on the organization's cash flow. Managers therefore look to closely monitor the number of days products sit in inventory and the number of times the inventory is turned over in a given period. Two ratios that assist in assessing the financial aspects of inventory management are as follows:

$$\text{Inventory Turnover} = \frac{\text{Cost of Goods Sold}}{\text{Average Inventory}}$$

Let's assume that the cost of goods sold for CAA Tronics Inc. is as shown on its income statement (Exhibit 14.1), or $49 500 000. Let's also assume that the average value of inventory for the current period is $4 000 000. The inventory turnover ratio would be computed as follows:

$$\text{CAA Tronics Inc.'s Inventory Turnover} = \frac{\$49\,500\,000}{\$4\,000\,000} = 12.37\,\text{times}$$

This means that CAA Tronics Inc. is turning its inventory over 12.37 times, or a bit more than once per month. In fact, we can compute the actual number of days that the organization's products sit in inventory by conducting the following calculation:

$$\text{Day's Inventory} = \frac{365}{\text{Inventory Turnover}}$$

In CAA Tronics Inc.'s situation, this would be computed as follows:

$$\text{CAA Tronic Inc.'s Day's Inventory} = \frac{365}{12.37} = 29.50 \text{ days}$$

BUSINESS in Action

Revisiting the Cash Operating Cycle

Managers spend a great deal of time conducting ratio analyses and analyzing financial statements. This information, as discussed throughout this chapter, provides them with valuable insight into the liquidity, solvency, efficiency, and capacity of their organization. In addition to monitoring these key performance indicators, managers also need to be aware of the length of time it takes for their organization to build, distribute, and sell their products, and, ultimately, receive payment from their customers. As was introduced in Chapter 9, this time period is known as the cash operating cycle (also called the cash-to-cash cycle). Understanding this cycle is critical in  assessing the working capital or cash needs of an organization. The longer it takes, the more the organization is going to have to rely on its own cash reserves or external credit facilities, such as a line of credit, to ensure that it maintains an appropriate liquidity position. Economic downturns, product obsolescence, slow-paying customers—all impact an organization's cash operating cycle (COC) and the length of time it takes to get its initial product-based cash expenditures back.

To calculate an organization's cash operating cycle, take the number of days a product spends in production and in inventory (called DIO, or days inventory outstanding), add to this the number of days it takes to receive money from the customer (called DSO, or days sales outstanding), and subtract from this total the number of days you take to pay your suppliers (called DPO, or days payable outstanding).

$$\text{Cash Operating Cycle (COC)} = \text{DIO} + \text{DSO} - \text{DPO}$$

As an example, let's assume that it takes Automaker Inc. 85 days to procure and receive the required auto parts, manufacture an automobile, and transport the automobile to a dealership. It takes another 38 days for the product to be sold to the customer (or for the dealer to pay Automaker for the automobile). Automaker Inc. pays its suppliers, on average, every 30 days. Automaker Inc.'s cash operating cycle would be computed as follows:

$$\text{Automaker Inc.'s COC} = 85 \text{ days} + 38 \text{ days} - 30 \text{ days} = 93 \text{ days}$$

It takes Automaker Inc. 93 days to receive its money for the sale of its automobiles. This means that Automaker Inc. must have sufficient working capital to fund the organization's cost base during this period of time, as it is paying its suppliers on a 30-day basis, paying employees bi-weekly, and incurring other operating expenses during this time. Should its automobiles take longer to sell, then this will elongate (and therefore deteriorate) the cash operating cycle, requiring additional working capital in order to meet Automaker Inc.'s operating expenses. In general, companies will work to shorten this cycle to as few days as possible, keeping in mind the extent to which such policies will impact the attractiveness of their products. This reduces working capital requirements and minimizes the risk that inventory will become obsolete and harder to sell. Comparing the cash operating cycle on a quarter-by-quarter basis, or a year-by-year basis, will enable managers to recognize and proactively deal with changes to the flow of cash into and out of the organization, and to the additional working capital requirements the organization will need to ensure its liquidity position is not compromised.

Leverage Analysis

Leverage refers to the amount of debt an organization uses in order to finance its asset base.

As was commented on above, **leverage** refers to the amount of debt an organization uses in order to finance its asset base. A firm whose liabilities represent a significant portion of its assets is considered to be highly leveraged. Depending on the profitability level of the firm, leverage can be interpreted as being either positive or negative. In profitable situations, where the EBIT of a firm is sufficient to cover its interest expenses, investors can realize higher percentage returns by employing debt financing to assist in the profitable growth of the organization. In situations where EBIT is not sufficient to cover the interest expense obligations of an organization, the loss that the organization incurs will be greater than if leverage were not employed. The following situation is meant to illustrate the positive and negative impact of leverage.

BENEFITS OF LEVERAGE

Assume that the ABC Corporation has total assets of $40 000 000. Now, assume two options associated with the creation of this asset base.

Option #1—ABC Corporation's asset base is created as a result of $40 000 000 being invested by its owners (shareholders).

Option #2—ABC Corporation's asset base is created as a result of $30 000 000 (borrowed at 6 percent) in debt financing and $10 000 000 in owner contributions.

Now, assume that the ABC Corporation's operation for the current year produces an EBIT of $4 000 000. With Option #1, because there is no debt there would be no interest expense; therefore, earnings before taxes would be the same: $4 000 000. Assuming a 25 percent tax rate, net income would be $3 000 000 ($4 000 000 − $1 000 000), and the return on equity (ROE), which is a measure of the return to owners (shareholders), would be as follows:

$$\text{ROE} = \frac{\text{Net Income}}{\text{Total Equity}} \quad \text{or} \quad \frac{\$3\,000\,000}{\$40\,000\,000} = 7.5\%$$

With Option #2, assume the same EBIT of $4 000 000. There is, however, $30 000 000 of debt, which requires the payment of interest expense totalling $1 800 000 (computed by $30 000 000 × .06). This means that EBT would be $4 000 000 − $1 800 000 = $2 200 000. Using the same 25 percent tax rate, the net income for ABC Corporation, in this situation, would be $1 650 000. With debt of $30 000 000, the total equity position of ABC Corporation's investors is $10 000 000. This means that the ROE for Option #2 would be:

$$\text{ROE} = \frac{\text{Net Income}}{\text{Total Equity}} \quad \text{or} \quad \frac{\$1\,650\,000}{\$10\,000\,000} = 16.5\%$$

FIGURE 14.13 Benefits of Leverage

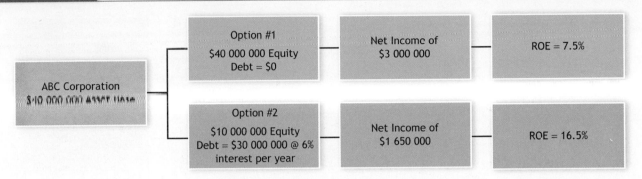

Thus, by using someone else's money (creditors), investors in the ABC Corporation can improve their returns from 7.5 percent to 16.5 percent, or from 7.5 cents for each dollar invested to 16.5 cents for each dollar invested (see Figure 14.13).

RISKS OF LEVERAGE

As shown above, leverage can benefit investors, assuming that sufficient net income is earned by the organization. What happens, however, in a situation where the organization does not earn a profit? How does this impact a firm that is using leverage as a mechanism for growing its asset base?

As will be illustrated, leverage comes with risk. If an organization chooses to use a significant level of debt financing, and the end result is an operating loss, the impact to investors would be greater than the loss that would have occurred had leverage not been utilized. Again, let's assess on the basis of a situation similar to that used above.

Assume the same two asset-base creation options as noted above:

Option #1—ABC Corporation's asset base is created as a result of $40 000 000 being invested by its owners (shareholders).

Option #2—ABC Corporation's asset base is created as a result of $30 000 000 (borrowed at 6 percent) in debt financing and $10 000 000 in owner contributions.

Now, assume that ABC Corporation suffers a loss (EBIT) of ($1 000 000). In Option #1, the negative ROE for investors would be (assume no taxes will be paid due to an operating loss):

$$\text{ROE} = \frac{\text{Net Income}}{\text{Total Equity}} \quad \text{or} \quad \frac{(\$1\ 000\ 000)}{\$40\ 000\ 000} = -2.5\%$$

In Option #2, however, the loss is much greater, as the ABC Corporation, in addition to an EBIT of ($1 000 000), would also still have to pay the interest expense on the $30 000 000 of debt, which amounts to $1 800 000. This brings the total operating loss to $2 800 000. Again, assuming that no tax payments would be required, the ROE to investors would be:

$$\text{ROE} = \frac{\text{Net Income}}{\text{Total Equity}} \quad \text{or} \quad \frac{(\$2\ 800\ 000)}{\$10\ 000\ 000} = -28\%$$

FIGURE 14.14 Risks of Leverage

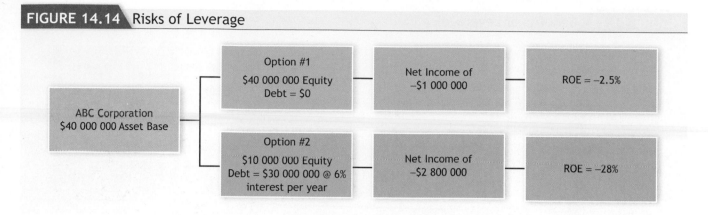

The greater losses, when assessed against a smaller equity base, result in a negative ROE of 28 percent to investors in the ABC Corporation (see Figure 14.14). In addition, as interest expense payments must be made, the ABC Corporation would either need to pay the interest expenses out of its cash reserves or seek some other external financing arrangement in order to ensure that it does not default on its debt obligations. As is illustrated, with debt financing comes an increased financial risk, particularly in situations where the organization is not driving operating margins sufficient to fund its debt obligations. As managers, we need to recognize this exposure and seek to utilize debt in a way that enhances the profitable growth of the organization versus exposing it to significant liquidity and solvency issues by carrying too much debt.

> Managers need to recognize this exposure and seek to utilize debt in a way that enhances the profitable growth of the organization versus exposing it to significant liquidity and solvency issues by carrying too much debt.

Trend or Comparative Analysis

Up to this point, we have been assessing financial statements and ratios based on a specific point in time. Although that information is valuable, to truly understand how an organization is doing managers often look to review current results against prior-year actual results and anticipated forecast results. We call this comparative or trend analysis. By comparing financial statements and ratios against targeted objectives or against historical performance, we can draw some conclusions as to whether an organization's liquidity and solvency position are being improved or compromised, and whether the organization is improving its overall operating efficiency. Figures 14.15, 14.16, and 14.17 provide some examples of such an analysis.

Figure 14.15 illustrates the operating performance of Yahoo Inc. from 2006 to 2010. A key takeaway here is that although Yahoo Inc.'s sales revenue increased from 2006 through 2008, its net income and profit margin decreased (this followed a trend that actually started in 2004). One can conclude that during this time period Yahoo's expenses were rising faster than its revenues, thus resulting in the erosion of its profit margin (chart A). This is further confirmed in chart B, which illustrates that Yahoo Inc.'s operating performance was basically at its breakeven point in 2008, earning a $0 profit for that fiscal year. Recognizing this deteriorating annual performance leading to a breakeven position in 2008, Yahoo's management team initiated significant cost reduction and efficiency strategies in 2009 and 2010 that resulted in improving the operational performance of the company, and its overall profitability, despite a reduction in sales volume.

FIGURE 14.15 Yahoo Inc.: Operating Performance

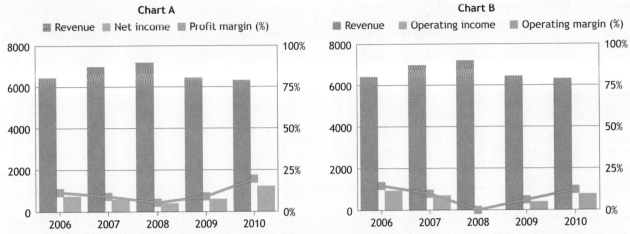

Source: googlefinance.com, June 2011; yahoofinance.com; investopedia.com; reuters.com.

FIGURE 14.16 Yahoo Inc.: Debt to Assets Relationship

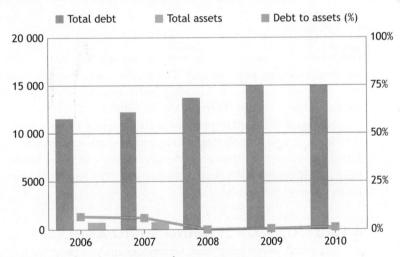

Source: googlefinance.com, June 2011; yahoofinance.com; investopedia.com; reuters.com.

> By comparing financial statements and ratios against targeted objectives or against historical performance, we can draw some conclusions as to whether an organization's liquidity and solvency position are being improved or compromised, and whether the organization is improving its overall operating efficiency.

Figure 14.16 illustrates the debt to assets relationship for Yahoo Inc. for the period 2006 through 2010. As the chart illustrates, Yahoo Inc.'s utilization of debt has been fairly constant throughout the period leading up to 2007. In 2007, Yahoo Inc. paid off $750 million in long-term debt obligations, leaving the organization free of long-term debt as of the end of fiscal year 2010.

Figure 14.17 compares Yahoo's profitability ratios against industry, sector, and the S&P 500 averages for the period ending December 31, 2010. Information provided includes both 12-month trailing averages (defines how Yahoo performed over the last 12 months against the

FIGURE 14.17   Yahoo Inc.: Profitability Ratios

Profitability Ratios (12/31/2010)

	Company	Industry	Sector	S&P 500
Gross Margin (TTM)	61.32	41.05	35.97	33.18
Gross Margin—5 Yr. Avg.	57.96	43.79	40.11	31.34
EBITD Margin (TTM)	24.57	—	—	—
EBITD—5 Yr. Avg.	18.63	25.37	21.38	19.79
Operating Margin (TTM)	13.03	28.26	19.07	—
Operating Margin—5 Yr. Avg.	8.41	22.14	16.78	15.13
Pre-Tax Margin (TTM)	16.67	28.06	18.93	15.96
Pre-Tax Margin—5 Yr. Avg.	10.91	23.08	17.40	14.68
Net Profit Margin (TTM)	12.90	20.35	13.33	11.86
Net Profit Margin—5 Yr. Avg.	6.48	17.67	12.89	10.83
Effective Tax Rate (TTM)	22.63	24.49	25.91	22.03
Effective Tax Rate—5 Yr. Avg.	40.64	22.04	26.46	25.02

TTM = Twelve month trailing average

Source: Reuters.com, June 2011

comparative figures from the industry, sector, and S&P 500), as well as comparing against the last five years (five-year average). This enables managers and analysts to assess Yahoo's efficiency and effectiveness in delivering profits in comparison to its competitive landscape and the marketplace at large (noted by the S&P 500).[4]

Managers will look to perform analyses across all ratio sectors (profitability, solvency, and debt), as well as analyzing activity ratios—such as inventory turnover, accounts payable turnover, and accounts receivable turnover ratios—in order to truly understand just how efficient their organization is and whether concerns regarding working capital and financing issues loom on the horizon.

A CAUTION CONCERNING RATIO ANALYSIS

It is important to recognize that, while ratio analysis provides many useful insights into the financial performance of an organization, ratios should not be the sole focus of the financial assessment process. As with any methodology, ratio analysis does carry with it some risks and limitations. Keep in mind that ratio analysis, by virtue of the method employed, focuses on single aspects of financial performance and, therefore, defines one performance dimension when many factors need to be, or should be, taken into consideration. As an example, computing an organization's sales growth rate from one year to the next may show solid growth overall, but excludes in the analysis the cost of capital that the organization expended to achieve this growth. The end result is that the cost of the sales growth may have exceeded the benefit. The same could hold true for a market-share calculation. Again, market share could have grown year-over-year, but at what cost? If volume is pursued at any cost, the additional market share gained could result in reduced earnings for the firm. EPS (earnings per share) could be going up, but this could be temporary and/or artificial growth in this metric. Managers may simply choose to cut or defer costs, repurchase shares, postpone projects, or take other short-term measures, all with the idea of producing greater immediate returns, which could compromise the long-term health of the organization. To compensate for this, a good guideline is not to look at a single ratio in isolation, but to view the business and its activities from a productivity, momentum, and profitable growth perspective, rather than simply the calculation of a series of ratios based on financial results. This shift in the assessment process enables managers to think of ratios as tools, not outcomes, and restructure their thought process toward questions such as Did our investments add value for our customers? Did the increased sales volume result in greater profitability for the organization? Is the return on the capital invested in support of a project sufficient to warrant the investment? and Did the decisions we have made relating to where and how to compete result in gains in long-term shareholder wealth?[5]

> It is important to recognize that, while ratio analysis provides many useful insights into the financial performance of an organization, ratios should not be the sole focus of the financial assessment process.

Absolute Analysis

Ratio analysis and assessments of percentage changes in sales levels, margins, and other barometers of operating performance are sound assessment tools for managers to use when analyzing the efficiency, effectiveness, and financial health of an organization. We must, however, recognize that managers need to assess financial strength in absolute terms as well. Absolute analysis refers to an assessment of the actual dollar amount that organizations are generating and/or have at their disposal. As an example, doubling the cash balance on the balance sheet from $5000 to $10 000 is a 200 percent increase in the cash the firm has at its disposal. Although this sounds impressive, the amount is still only $10 000. Managers must look at the dollar monetary requirements that will be necessary to support the operation and determine whether such resources currently exist and/or are obtainable from outside sources (debt or equity financing). In addition, managers must assess their organization's financial capabilities against those of their competitors. This will enable them to determine where and how to compete, especially against much financially stronger opponents. As an example, let's take a look at three companies that are competing actively with each other for market share in the Internet search engine business (see Figure 14.18).

As we can see, all three companies have fairly significant cash reserves from which to draw in the event of a need to invest in their organizations, fund new market opportunities, or weather revenue downturns that could result in operating losses. Of the three, however, Yahoo Inc. has the least cash to work with, as both Google Inc. and Microsoft have much greater financial resources at their disposal. These significant cash reserves enable Google Inc. and Microsoft greater capacity to develop products and services, make acquisitions, and invest in cutting-edge technologies that will enable them to further improve their operating performance, over the long term, when compared to Yahoo Inc.

As managers, it is important to understand the absolute dollar values we have access to, the dollar amount of debt we owe, and the future potential dollars we believe the organization

FIGURE 14.18 Absolute Analysis: Cash

	Google Inc. (03/31/2011)	Yahoo Inc. (03/31/2011)	Microsoft Corporation (03/31/2011)
Cash on Hand (millions USD)	$ 7375.00	$1619.18	$ 7021.00
Short-Term Investments (millions USD)	$24 260.00	$1169.41	$43 129.00
Total Cash and Short-Term Investments (millions USD)	$36 675.00	$2788.59	$50 150.00

Source: Googlefinance.com, annual and quarterly financial statements, Yahoo Inc., Google Inc., and Microsoft Corporation, March 2011.

can generate. An understanding of our financial resources in absolute terms, when combined with ratio analysis and using comparative (trend) analysis, gives managers the best picture of the organization's health.

> As managers, it is important to understand the absolute dollar values we have access to, the dollar amount of debt we owe, and the future potential dollars we believe the organization can generate.

Forecasting and Budgeting

Up to this point, our focus has been on analyzing and interpreting actual but historical information relating to an organization's financial performance. Although this is a valuable and necessary process in managing an organization, so too is our ability to project forward anticipated results for the upcoming quarter, year, or planning cycle period. This process, commonly referred to as **forecasting and budgeting,** challenges management teams to anticipate what the organization's financial position will be, based on an analysis of a variety of factors. These factors could include (but are not limited to) external factors such as the economic environment, market conditions, emergence of new competitors, and new substitutes for the products and/or services we offer. Also considered would be internal factors such as new product launches, new technology applications, product discontinuation, new distribution channels, new uses for our products, new pricing requirements, and anticipated changes to our cost base. The importance of forecasting and budgeting is fourfold:

Forecasting and Budgeting refers to management's ability to project forward anticipated results for the upcoming quarter, year, or planning-cycle period.

1. Forecasting and budgeting require the organization to think about what is happening in the markets within which it competes and to determine how its various products and services will perform in the upcoming period.
2. Forecasting and budgeting set specific operational parameters for the various divisions and departments within the organization (and, therefore, the organization as a whole), and subsequently become operational targets that keep the organization on track in terms of operational efficiency and effectiveness.
3. Forecasting and budgeting require managers to make decisions related to resource allocation when measured against specific outcomes, thereby providing a process under which such scarce resources can be allocated toward those projects, initiatives, and products and services that are anticipated to yield the best results.
4. Forecasts and budgets become benchmarks/targets against which actual results can be measured, thereby enabling managers to make proactive decisions relating to reinforcing or correcting business activities and tactics in the event that actual results exceed or lag behind forecast or anticipated results.

One of the most difficult aspects of forecasting and budgeting lies in determining anticipated revenue streams. This becomes particularly more challenging in periods of economic retraction or volatility. The anticipated sustainability of revenue streams is an important part of the forecasting and budgetary process. The accuracy of sales forecasts underlies decisions relating to production, inventory management, and infrastructure spending. Decisions relating to cost adjustments that the company anticipates and competitive pricing pressures will influence the price the company will charge for its goods and services, and thus its sales revenue. Changes in customer needs, wants, and desires will also influence this. Companies must consider all of these things (and many more) when making predictions about what revenue will look like in the weeks, months, and years ahead. In essence, all decisions relating to the operation will stem from its sales revenue forecasts.

The company must then assess such sales levels against anticipated expenses to determine whether the company can meet the desired profitability and growth targets expected by its internal and external stakeholders. If such targets are not met, the organization must then seek to modify its cost base and/or find alternate revenue streams to ensure that sufficient

FIGURE 14.19 Forecasting and Budgeting Process

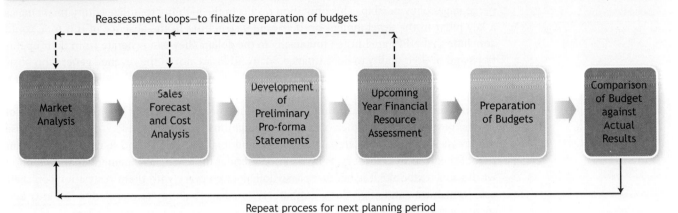

cash flow is generated and that targeted profitability and growth projections are met. The forecasting and budgetary process can be visualized as per the diagram illustrated in Figure 14.19.

> The accuracy of sales forecasts underlies decisions relating to production, inventory management, and infrastructure spending.

Utilizing the strategic planning process and the various models at their disposal (Porter's five forces, PESTEL, SWOT), organizations will conduct an external assessment of how they believe their products and services will perform for the upcoming period. Based on this assessment, along with information derived from customers and distributors, organizations will quantify this anticipated performance into a formal financial revenue (sales) forecast. While this process is taking place, organizations will also assess their cost base and their various expense lines to determine changes that they anticipate will occur (wage adjustments, changes to the cost of goods sold, changes to indirect expenses such as insurance premiums, service contracts, etc.). With this analysis having taken place, the organization's management team will then proceed to the preparation of pro forma (projected) statements to determine the organization's anticipated profitability position. Additional financial resource requirements will be brought into the picture (capital asset transactions, non-operational needs, etc.), thereby finalizing the full financial picture of the organization and resulting in the development of the financial budgets for the upcoming period. These budgets then become the benchmark against which the organization will measure its progress (actual versus forecast results) for the period the budget covers. It should be noted that, as Figure 14.19 illustrates, the process will contain a number of situations where sales and expense forecast revisions and further financial analysis will be required. These are reflected in the reassessment loops shown in Figure 14.19. Information relating to the forecast versus actual results also becomes important for the next budgetary process and planning period.

A Note Pertaining to Not-for-Profits

Like for-profit entities, managers of not-for-profit (NFP) organizations need to demonstrate the same financial analytical skills as discussed above when managing the business side of their organizations. Liquidity, solvency, and efficiency issues are as important when managing an NFP as when managing in the for-profit environment. Having said this, in guiding the NFP it should be understood that there are some notable differences to the financial landscape that will impact the ability of the organization's manager to respond to immediate and longer-term financial challenges. A good example of this lies in the balance sheets of many NFPs. Unlike for-profit entities, NFPs, by their nature, are unable to sell shares of stock or percentages of ownership. This limitation results in the inability to utilize equity financing as a key pillar in the development of their capital structure. In the absence of this, one could conclude that NFPs are limited financially to the dollars they can generate from their operations and in their ability to debt-finance. Many NFPs are not in the revenue generation business, and/or do not have a capital asset base of sufficient size that they could use as collateral for debt-financing purposes. So, how do these organizations generate the dollars needed to sustain their charitable and community-based mission? The answer lies in the receiving of grants, government subsidies, and private donations. For many NFPs, the ability to raise money via events, annual campaigns, capital (building) campaigns, and so on is an important part of their business strategy. Why mention it under the financial statement analysis section within this textbook? It is because these dollars often carry with them restrictions on their use—which can, and often does, limit an NFP manager's ability to respond to liquidity and solvency issues within the organization.

> Like for-profit entities, managers of not-for-profit (NFP) organizations need to demonstrate the same financial analytical skills when managing the business side of their organizations.

When reviewing the asset portion of a balance sheet of an NFP organization, the key focus of our analysis is on the identification of such restrictions. Donations that have been raised for the renovation of a building, for example, will often be identified as being restricted, and therefore cannot be used for funding the day-to-day operations (salaries, administrative expenses, office supplies, etc.) of the NFP. Take a university as an example. The university may have significant endowments or bequeaths identified on its balance sheet that have been set up for specific, restricted purposes. Despite this significant wealth, the university still has to raise tuition fees to cover its operating expenses, as these endowments are restricted in their use (e.g., to fund research, purchase equipment, build new learning centres). Restricted funds are funds that have been designated for specific purposes. Although they may appear as a line item in the asset section of the balance sheet, managers have to be careful—for example, when computing ratios (such as the current ratio)—that such funds are not viewed as part of the organization's current asset base. This is because, although the organization has this money, it does not have the ability to use these dollars in the same way that a for-profit organization can manage its cash, near cash, and current asset base. In the NFP setting, the focus of the analysis is on what is termed "free and clear" available money. Simply put, this can be determined by taking

Designated Restricted Assets are assets that have been earmarked for a specific purpose and that are not available for managers to support organizational operating needs.

the cash and near-cash assets of the NFP and subtracting any **designated restricted assets** (cash and near cash) in order to determine the true surplus funds available to management for the purpose of responding to the working capital needs of the NFP organization (see Figure 14.20).

Additional commentary in this regard is beyond the scope of this textbook. Just keep in mind that NFPs, although similar in their financial reporting, have significant and unique differences that require managers to assess financial liquidity, solvency, and efficiency from a

FIGURE 14.20   NFP: Available Funds

different perspective. This, coupled with its unique financial mission objective (delivery of community needs versus profitability), results in a different application of the analytical tools needed for evaluating the success of the organization.[6]

Management Reflection—Keeping Your Finger on the Pulse of the Organization

Imagine trying to manage a business without having any sense of the financial results that the organization is realizing. How would we know if the business decisions we are making are effective in achieving the business objectives set forth in our strategic plan? How would we know if top-line revenue is growing, or if profitability improvement initiatives have been successful? How would we know if we will have enough money next month or next quarter to meet the financial obligations that the organization will incur? Herein lies the importance of financial statement analysis. As Will Fang pointed out at the beginning of this chapter (From the Student's Perspective), managers must be comfortable in preparing, reading, and interpreting financial statements. The ability to do this enables managers to "keep their finger on the pulse" of the organization. Financial statement analysis is what cues managers to changes that are occurring within their organization's operations and with regard to its working capital requirements. Reviewing these statements provides us with tremendous insight into the liquidity, solvency, and financial capacity of an organization. The income statement provides us with crucial information regarding the operation. The balance sheet provides us with an understanding of the depth and strength of an organization's current financial capabilities, and the statement of cash flows enables us to sense whether the organization is generating or using cash, given its operations and capital asset transactions. Recognizing revenue trends, changes to operating efficiencies and profitability, and the breadth of our capital capacity are but a few of the key takeaways managers can derive as a result of their constant monitoring of the organization's financial statements. Actively monitoring these statements on a monthly, quarterly, and annual basis, as well as assessing comparative trends across operating periods, enables managers to truly understand their overall financial stability and potential.

Although looking at historical data is important, so too is our ability to utilize projected statements (called pro formas) to visualize what is going to happen looking forward. Assessing the results of the organization's financial performance, and proactively anticipating future results via forecasting and budgeting techniques, enables managers to effectively manage the financial needs of the organization and ensure that decisions relating to long-term profitable growth are identified and followed through with. Financial statement analysis should be thought of as a tool that, when mixed with a manager's assessment of the market environment within which the organization is competing, enables decisions to be made that contribute to the growth in the economic value of the organization and help it to achieve its vision and mission.

> Financial statement analysis is what cues managers to changes occurring within the organization's operations and with regard to its working capital requirements.

Chapter Summary

The focus of this chapter is to familiarize students with the importance of a manager's ability to analyze and interpret an organization's financial position. This is essential to making good decisions pertaining to how, and where, to deploy the organization's assets and financial resources. In support of this, the chapter provides students with an overview of the types of financial transactions that occur within an organization. The concepts of liquidity, solvency, efficiency, and financial capacity are also discussed as an essential part of assessing the financial condition of the organization and its ability to provide the necessary capital resources in support of its strategic plan. The chapter then provides an overview of the core components of the three primary financial statements—the income statement, balance sheet, and statement of cash flows—that managers analyze and interpret as a means for keeping their finger on the pulse of the organization. A further discussion is provided relating to the key ratios that managers calculate from the information presented on these financial statements, thereby enabling managers to draw conclusions relating to profitability, solvency, leverage, and operational efficiency. The use of trend and/or comparative analysis as a key component of this ratio analysis process is also discussed, as is the value in including absolute analysis as a core part of this managerial assessment approach. The importance of sales forecasting and budgeting forms part of this discussion as well. The chapter closes off with a note pertaining to a cursory overview of the differences between financial analyses of not-for-profit organizations and for-profit entities.

Developing Business Knowledge and Skills

KEY TERMS

gross profit margin *p. 386*

profitability margin *p. 386*

operational transactions *p. 388*

capital asset transactions *p. 388*

income statement *p. 390*

balance sheet *p. 394*

assets *p. 394*

liabilities *p. 395*

owners' equity *p. 395*

retained earnings *p. 396*

statement of cash flows *p. 397*

cash from operational activities, *p. 399*

cash from financing activities, *p. 399*

cash from investing activities, *p. 399*

net change in cash position, *p. 399*

ratios *p. 400*

profitability ratios *p. 400*

solvency and liquidity ratios *p. 402*

debt ratios *p. 404*

activity ratios *p. 405*

leverage *p. 408*

forecasting and budgeting *p. 414*

designated restricted assets *p. 416*

QUESTIONS FOR DISCUSSION

1. What are the two fundamental types of business transactions? How are they interconnected and how can each type of transaction affect the other?

2. What is the difference between solvency and financial capacity? How are the two interrelated?

3. Which is more relevant in determining a company's well-being: activity ratios or solvency ratios?

4. What are the advantages and disadvantages, to a business, of taking on additional leverage?

5. Which is more relevant in interpreting and analyzing a company's financial position: ratio analysis or absolute analysis? What is the difference between the two?

6. Why are forecasting and budgeting so important? What is the difference between the two?

7. How is managing the financial resources of a not-for-profit organization different from overseeing a for-profit entity? In your mind, which is the more difficult to manage?

QUESTIONS FOR INDIVIDUAL ACTION

Go online and obtain the most recent annual reports for at least three North American airlines (WestJet, Air Canada, United Airlines, Southwest Airlines, Delta Airlines, etc.). Conduct profitability, solvency, debt, and activity ratio analyses of their financial statements. Of the organizations that you have selected, which is the most profitable, and why? Which is the healthiest? Which is most at risk?

TEAM EXERCISE

As a team, go online and obtain the most recent annual reports for Research In Motion (RIM), Apple, Google, and Nokia. Conduct an absolute analysis of these companies' balance sheets. Based on your analysis, which of these companies is best positioned to move forward in the smartphone industry? What types of business decisions will these organizations have to make, and be able to make, as a result of your findings? Prepare a presentation of your research and analysis.

Case for Discussion

Based on the information provided, respond to the six questions asked about these financial statements.

SR Magnum Corporation Comparative Income Statement				
In Millions	**2009-12-31**	**2008-12-31**	**2007-12-31**	**2006-12-31**
Total Revenue	7 208.77	7 691.64	7 175.96	6 128.84
Cost of Goods Sold	4 214.37	4 027.56	3 715.06	3 316.87
Gross Profit	2 994.40	3 664.08	3 460.90	2 811.97
Selling/General/Admin. Expenses, Total	1 410.84	1 537.95	1 367.14	1 073.21
Depreciation/Amortization	778.24	700.33	629.63	560.63
Interest Expense (Income)	1 220.83	998.68	46.07	45.00
Other Operating Expenses, Total	9.65	217.29	86.02	90.00
Total Operating Expense	3 419.56	3 454.25	2 128.86	1 768.84
Operating Income	−425.16	209.83	1 332.04	1 043.13
Other Income Net	87.94	4.44	15.04	18.43
Income Before Tax	−337.22	214.27	1 347.08	1 061.56
Income After Tax	−337.22	171.42	943.02	743.09
Net Income	−337.22	171.42	943.02	743.09

With respect to the income statement for the SR Magnum Corporation, respond to the following:

1. Compute the gross profit margin percentage for SR Magnum Corporation for each of the four years shown. Has the gross profit margin percentage improved or deteriorated over the past three years? Explain what you think might be causing the changes observed.

2. Looking at the last four years, identify three other concerns that you would have about this organization's current operational performance. You may want to conduct some additional (profitability) ratio analyses to aid in your discussion.

SR Magnum Corporation Balance Sheet				
In Millions	2009-12-31	2008-12-31	2007-12-31	2006-12-31
Cash & Equivalents	295.64	416.12	452.94	377.93
Accounts Receivable	459.07	519.29	481.38	463.30
Inventory	111.50	126.94	118.46	111.83
Total Current Assets	866.21	1 062.35	1 052.78	953.06
Property/Plant	20 098.72	20 237.22	20 037.09	18 916.75
Goodwill Net	86.35	1 262.92	1 300.75	1 314.56
Intangibles Net	347.21	362.10	367.20	377.48
Equipment	4 642.86	2 482.73	1 280.69	931.15
Total Non-Current Assets	25 175.14	24 334.97	22 985.73	21 539.94
Total Assets	26 041.35	25 407.32	24 038.51	22 493.00
Accounts Payable	1 773.67	1 226.28	1 006.06	265.60
Notes Payable/ Short-Term Debt	1 047.61	0.00	0.00	0.00
Total Current Liabilities	2 821.28	1 226.28	1 006.06	265.60
Long-Term Debt	12 856.58	11 175.23	12 994.87	12 355.43
Total Liabilities	15 677.86	12 401.51	14 000.93	12 621.03
Common Stock	4 018.41	3 951.16	2 806.64	2 586.59
Retained Earnings	6 345.08	9 054.65	7 230.94	7 285.38
Total Equity	10 363.49	13 005.81	10 037.58	9 871.97
Total Liabilities & Shareholders' Equity	26 041.35	25 407.32	24 038.51	22 493.00

With respect to the balance sheet for SR Magnum Corporation, respond to the following:

3. Compute the current ratio for the SR Magnum Corporation for each of the four years shown. What has happened? What are the implications of these results for SR Magnum?

4. Identify, and explain, the two things about SR Magnum Corporation's current financial position that concern you the most.

Using both statements…

5. Compute the solvency ratio and the times interest earned ratio for SR Magnum for each of the four years shown. What has happened? Again, what are the implications of this result for SR Magnum?

6. Assume that you are a member of the board of directors of SR Magnum Corporation and that you have just reviewed these two statements. Identify three questions that you would ask the management team to respond to.

Practise and learn online with Connect. Connect resources include additional and interactive study exercises, videos, and practice quizzing, as well as additional material you won't find in the printed text.

15 Analyzing New Business Ventures

Snapshot—What to Expect in This Chapter

As identified by the learning objectives, this chapter focuses on exposing students to the basics associated with analyzing business ventures and new business opportunities. The content emphasized in this chapter includes the following:

From the Student's Perspective

How many of you have wanted to start your own business? It wouldn't be surprising if most, or all, of you have had visions or dreams of being your own boss. I know I have. The prospect of having your own hours, complete autonomy, the CEO title, and—not least of all—the uncapped earning potential is very alluring. But why is it that so very few of us go into business for ourselves?

My perspective is that in school we are not traditionally taught the ins and outs of venture analysis. A really important requirement is to have a bulletproof business plan and an irrefutable understanding of the risks. It's this knowledge that allows you to recruit more interest. And it's that growth in interest that is invaluable to growing your idea. The focus of this chapter is to provide you with the ammo you need to give yourself a shot in a business environment where venture investors are commonly referred to as sharks or dragons.

For those of you not interested in starting your own ventures, this chapter is still relevant. The business environment is profuse with venture analysis. Wherever you may work, chances are a portion of the organization's clients or suppliers—or perhaps both—will be small and/or medium-sized enterprises backed by an entrepreneur. From accountants auditing businesses, to consultants and financiers launching IPOs, to marketers evaluating opportunities in the business community, familiarity with ventures is a competitive advantage.

Ahmad Iqbal has a Pakistani background, but over the course of his life he lived in seven different countries, attending international schools before graduating with a Commerce degree in 2010. It was his range of experiences that influenced him most to forge his own path and start his own business. He has a keen interest in venture capital and hopes to establish a long-standing career in the field. Ahmad's start-up business has won several business plan competitions across Canada and he aspires to be nominated for an Entrepreneur of the Year award in the near future.

BUSINESS *in Action*

Saputo Inc.: A Case of Classic Entrepreneurship

With $500 that he had saved while working as a labourer, in 1954 a Sicilian immigrant and master cheese maker, Giuseppe Saputo, along with his wife, Maria, began making cheese in the corner of a cheese factory in Montreal. Their 17-year-old son, Lino, in the true spirit of a family operation, handled delivery of the cheese using his bicycle. Thus were the humble beginnings of one of Canada's many classic entrepreneurial success stories. Fast forward to 2010, and Saputo Inc., now publicly traded on the TSX (SAP), has sales of $5.8 billion and net income in March 2010 topping $380 million. The operation, which spent the first two years of its existence generating enough volume to be able to build its own factory, is now of international scale, with operations in Canada, the United States, Argentina, Germany, and the United Kingdom. Known in the industry as the "Mozzarella King" due to its commanding market leader position of 40 percent in the Canadian market, today Saputo Inc. is much more than just a cheese manufacturer. Through a series of well-planned organic growth initiatives coupled with timely acquisitions, Saputo Inc.'s products stretch across a number of industry sectors such as powdered and condensed milk, cheese and butter, baked goods, dairy products, and ice cream. The organization is structured around two sectors (dairy products and grocery products) and five operating divisions, Dairy Products (Canada), Dairy Products (Europe), Dairy Products (Argentina), Dairy Products (USA), and the Bakery Division. Its stable of banners includes such well-known Canadian brands as Vachon, Stella, Frigo, Neilson, and Dairyworld. Continued acquisitions, both domestically and abroad, have resulted in Saputo Inc. becoming Canada's number-one dairy group, the number-one Canadian snack-cake manufacturer, and one of North America's top three dairy processors. Its purchase in 2004 of Argentina's Molfino Hermanos SA for $51 million was its first initial action toward achieving its desire to be a global dairy industry player. Cheese production now extends well beyond mozzarella, including specialty European cheeses such as havarti, brie, feta, and goat cheeses; manufacturing stretches across three continents, with 45 production facilities and 9800 employees. Giuseppe Saputo stepped down as CEO in 1969, with Lino taking the helm and transitioning Saputo Inc. into the international player it is today. Lino (Emanuele) himself stepped away from the CEO position in 2004, but remains chairman of the board of directors. A third-generation Saputo, Lino A. Saputo Jr., serves as president and CEO as of this writing. Since the movement to a publicly traded company in 1996, the Saputo family's ownership in the company has been reduced to just under 60 percent. This percentage of ownership, however, makes this family one of the wealthiest in Canada (estimated net worth $3.5 billion). For the Saputo family and Saputo Inc., business is not just about money. The organization is an active supporter

of athletic-based initiatives in Quebec and across Canada, including a strong sponsorship position in the 2010 Vancouver Winter Olympic and Paralympic Games. The company also actively invests in the communities where its employees live, and in environmentally responsible business practices. In Montreal, the company is a driving force in the establishment of a professional soccer team (Montreal Impact), and in the construction of the $15 million Saputo Soccer Stadium.[1]

WEB INTEGRATION
Interested in learning more about Saputo Inc.? Visit **www.saputo.ca**.

Analyzing Business Ventures

L01

Entrepreneur refers to a person who starts a business and is willing to accept the risk associated with investing money in order to make money.

One of the most important skills a manager or **entrepreneur** can learn is how to analyze a business venture. Whether it is a new business opportunity or the expansion of an existing business's market space, the ability to assess the financial and market risk associated with such a venture is critical to the overall evaluation process. Recognizing that some level of risk will

FIGURE 15.1 Fishbone Diagram: Venture Assessment

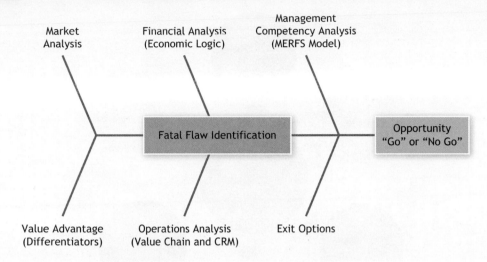

always exist, the analytical process associated with business ventures can be best thought of as a methodology for recognizing the degree of financial and market risk a potential business opportunity faces, and then, given this risk, assigning a "go or no go" to the project. This analytical process can best be described as a six-phase approach (see Figure 15.1), with each phase designed to assist in solidifying the final decision concerning the viability of the opportunity being assessed.

The six phases associated with venture analysis are as follows:

1. Market analysis
2. Value analysis
3. Financial analysis
4. Operations analysis
5. Management competency analysis
6. Exit options

A key emphasis within each of these areas is to try to define the certainty and therefore the probability of success of the venture in what is often a very uncertain and risk-laden environment. A key to this assessment approach lies in the search and identification of "fatal flaws" that could potentially derail a venture in its early stages. Examples of fatal flaws can be inadequate pricing models, undercapitalization, weak management competencies, insufficient marketing research initiatives, poor understanding of industry configuration and market segmentation, or the absence of a well-focused execution strategy (see Figure 15.2).[2] Identifying and understanding such fatal flaws enables managers to determine whether such barriers can be overcome and whether the risk associated with these barriers results in too much uncertainty to move forward with the venture. The remainder of this chapter focuses on placing risk into perspective and outlining the key analytical approach required within each of the phases identified above, thereby providing managers and entrepreneurs with a blueprint for assessing the risk and potential success of a business opportunity.[3]

A key to this assessment approach lies in the search and identification of "fatal flaws" that could potentially derail a venture in its early stages.

FIGURE 15.2   Fatal Flaw Analysis

Life in the "Uncertainty" Lane

LO2

The uncertainty associated with the commencement of a business venture is to some degree unavoidable. Despite our best efforts, success is never a certainty. The less an existing business and its structure can be leveraged in support of the new opportunity, the higher that uncertainty becomes (see Figure 15.3)—and, therefore, the greater the challenge to managers and

FIGURE 15.3   Risk and Business Ventures

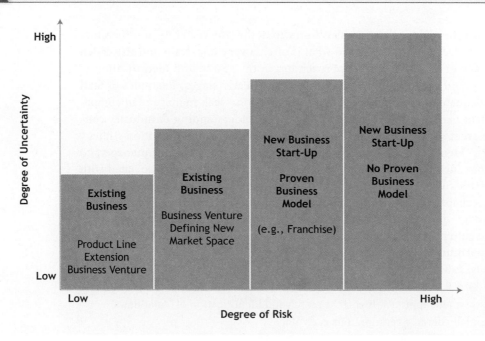

entrepreneurs to fully recognize and define the magnitude of risk presented.[4] Companies initiating business ventures built around existing product lines, or capable of leveraging an existing business's competencies and experience, have some knowledge of competitors, market dynamics (PESTEL), technology application, cost structure, and revenue potential. Despite this knowledge going in, thereby reducing the risk/certainty profile of the venture, many still do not succeed. With new businesses where these competencies and experience are lacking, the risk/certainty profile is even more forbidding. The utilization of a proven business model or turnkey operation, such as a franchise, can assist to some extent in mitigating this risk, but considerable uncertainty with respect to the probability of success remains. Entrepreneurs heading out into market space where no one has treaded before, and absent of any proven business model, expose themselves to the greatest risk and uncertainty. It is true that, in these types of ventures, with success can come considerable reward—just look at the current valuations of Facebook and Google as examples. Yet, for every couple of big winners, many more businesses simply cannot create the demand and scale to survive and, therefore, exit or cease to exist soon after they enter a given market.

BUSINESS *in Action*

Franchising

Over the past several decades, one of the most popular start-up business models has been the franchise. Just what is a franchise? It is a business model under which business owners share a common brand and operate through a defined business framework. Why are franchises so popular? For many new entrepreneurs, the franchise (in theory) provides a proven way to launch and manage a business. At their core, "best of class" franchises provide their franchisees (the purchaser of the franchise) with brand recognition in the marketplace, a proven turnkey operating plan, pre-launch and ongoing owner and staff training, purchasing power through economies of scale, regional and/or national marketing support, and new product development and operating technique improvement R&D. Starting a new business is a risky venture. The idea behind franchises is that this risk is reduced when compared to going it alone. Many entrepreneurs do not have the time, the financial resources, or the expertise to develop all aspects of the business formula required for success. Developing profile and awareness, for example, can take months and/or years for new business ventures. The franchise model ideally will bring to the new business owner immediate profile and awareness. Operating as a franchise, however, does not come without a price. Most franchise models require the business owner to pay an initial franchise fee (often several thousands of dollars) at the time of purchase, as well as ongoing royalties for the use of the franchise name and business model. Contributions to a national marketing fund are also quite common. As an example, A&W, Canada's second largest hamburger chain, requires its franchisees to pay an initial franchise fee of $50 000 (for a 20-year agreement) as well as royalties (called service fees) of 2.5 percent of net sales and a contribution to the A&W Advertising Fund of 2.5 percent of net sales. In addition to these fees, the franchisee must pay for the cost of the business. Investment in a freestanding A&W restaurant is in the $900 000 to $1.2 million range. Franchisees need to demonstrate unencumbered access to cash in the $300 000 to $420 000 range in order to qualify as a business owner. Tim Hortons' current royalty fee is 4.5 percent of gross sales, and its monthly advertising fund contribution for franchisees is 4 percent of gross sales. Currently, a Tim Hortons franchise costs between $430 000 and $500 000. Franchisees are expected to have unencumbered access to cash of approximately $200 000. Tim Hortons also reserves the right to have franchisees upgrade or refurbish their Tim Hortons location(s) at the end of each five-year franchise period.

The purchase of a franchise, however, does not mean guaranteed success. Prospective business owners need to recognize that due diligence still must be conducted for the local market to ensure that the size of the market is large enough and the competitive landscape is understood. The franchisor (the seller of the franchise model) must also be assessed in order to ensure that the level of support and expertise it is purporting to offer can actually be delivered. Finally, the franchisee needs to execute the business model in an efficient and effective manner, and meet his/her customer expectations if he/she is to be successful. Under a franchise agreement, it

WEB INTEGRATION

For more information regarding franchise business opportunities in Canada, Google "Canadian franchise opportunities" or visit the Canadian Franchise Association Web site at **www.cfa.ca**.

should also be understood that the freedom to deviate from the defined franchise model will most likely be significantly restricted. A&W Food Services Canada Inc., for example, does not permit franchisees to add items to the menu on their own. Menu items are set, and considerable market research and testing by the franchisor is required prior to the addition of any menu item. Franchisees should expect reduced control over products, services, operating hours and protocols, and advertising as part of their franchise agreement.

Franchise models are not for everyone. Each individual, based on an assessment of his/her skills and competencies, monetary capacity, and desire for control and creativity, will need to determine if this business model works best for them. For many, as indicated above, it is a desirable way to get into business while at the same time reducing the risk of going it alone. It is a personal decision. The marketplace is full of franchise opportunities. The question becomes whether it is the right way for you to become an entrepreneur.[5]

Offsetting the Uncertainty: The Business Plan

Mitigating uncertainty and risk is all about planning. By planning, organizations create a definitive path to navigate through the turbulent waters of risk and uncertainty and define, in advance, how to respond to the critical make-or-break issues that will challenge them. New venture assessment focuses on, first, the development of a business plan, and then assessing the viability of the plan to work and to meet its identified objectives. The business plan describes the business, assesses the opportunity given market and competitive conditions, defines the strategy, details the management expertise and operation-based and marketing-based tactics, provides financial validation, and explains why you will succeed (see Figure 15.4).

In reviewing the business plan, we look to assess the viability of the economic base, validate the size of the target market, assess the competitive landscape, draw conclusions on the level of saturation that already exists in the market, determine the validity of the cost estimates and capitalization requirements offered, and ensure that we understand how the business will connect with, and acquire, the necessary customers to ensure success. An easy way to think about what a business plan needs to deliver is shown in Figure 15.5, the five "rules of the road" for business plan development.

FIGURE 15.4 The Business Plan

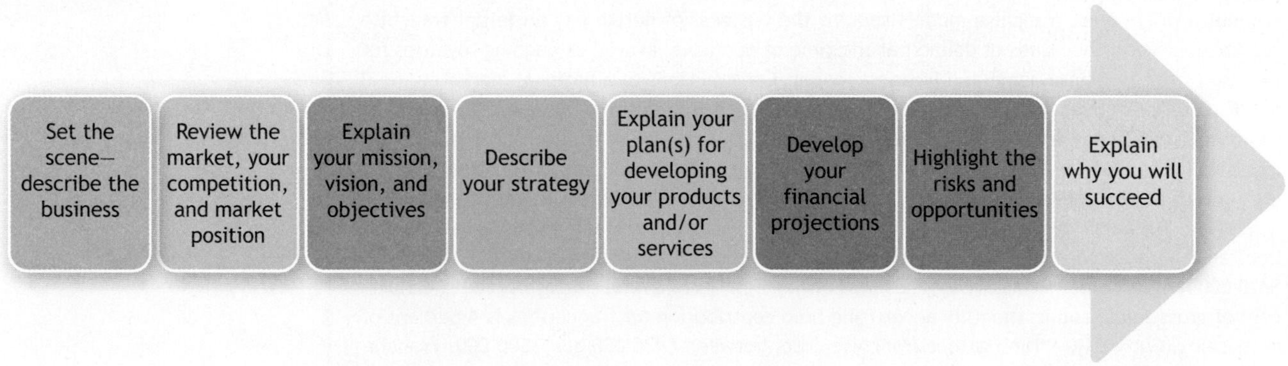

| Set the scene—describe the business | Review the market, your competition, and market position | Explain your mission, vision, and objectives | Describe your strategy | Explain your plan(s) for developing your products and/or services | Develop your financial projections | Highlight the risks and opportunities | Explain why you will succeed |

FIGURE 15.5 Business Plan: Rules of the Road

- Rule #1—Know Your Customer
- Rule #2—Know Why You Will Win
- Rule #3—Know How You Will Win
- Rule #4—Know What It Will Take to Win
- Rule #5—Demonstrate Why Others Should Believe in You

Upon reading a business plan, you should be able to determine who the customer is, why the business will be successful in reaching these customers, how the business will reach these customers, what it will take (in terms of resources) to get the job done, and why the organization or **venture capitalist** should believe in the management team and/or the entrepreneur. After all, successful ventures have three common characteristics: (1) they possess a sound understanding of their markets and competitors, (2) they create a realistic business plan that frames the strategy to be undertaken, and (3) they utilize a defined set of short-term and long-term health and performance metrics by which to assess their progress, thereby ensuring successful plan execution. This assessment process is defined by the six-phase approach illustrated in Figure 15.1.[6] Let's now look at each of these areas in more detail.[7]

> **Venture Capitalist** refers to an individual who provides capital to a business venture for start-up or expansion purposes.

> Successful ventures have three common characteristics: (1) they possess a sound understanding of their markets and competitors, (2) they create a realistic business plan that frames the strategy to be undertaken, and (3) they utilize a defined set of short-term and long-term health and performance metrics by which to assess their progress, thereby ensuring successful plan execution.

Six Phases of Business Plan Assessment   `LO3, LO4`

Market Analysis

Market analysis is focused on the assessment of the risk and uncertainty associated with entry into the targeted market space. In this assessment phase we are looking to draw credible conclusions to the validity that the proposed plan will achieve the market penetration anticipated and will obtain sufficient market reach and scale to ensure the successful sustainability of the organization. Key success factors can vary depending upon whether we are creating new market space as a first mover, looking to compete as a new entrant in an existing market, or launching a product line extension, thereby leveraging existing market competencies (see Figure 15.6).

Market analysis is all about assessing the legitimacy of the perceived opportunity that the manager or entrepreneur sees for the organization. To legitimize this opportunity, we need to assess it in four ways (see Figure 15.7). First, we need to analyze the current market environment. Is it the right time to enter into the market? Is the market's direction clear enough to ensure the sustainability of the venture, particularly in the early stages? Does our PESTEL analysis reveal any significant barriers or concerns that could impact our ability to succeed? Second, we need to look at the market sector or industry within which we will be competing.

FIGURE 15.6 Market Analysis: Key Success Factors

First Mover—New Market	New Entrant—Existing Market	Extension—Existing Market
• Need/demand identification and alignment • Profile of need solution and company • Proper deployment of capital • Driver of the consumer adoption process	• Innovation • Superior customer relationship model to target market • Disruption of consumer adoption process • Proper deployment of capital in support of the business initiative	• New revenue generation opportunity • Degree of cannibalization • Validation of segmentation stretch opportunity • Degree of channel involvement in demand stimulation • Strength of brand extension • Proper deployment of capital

FIGURE 15.7 Four Key Metrics for Market Analysis

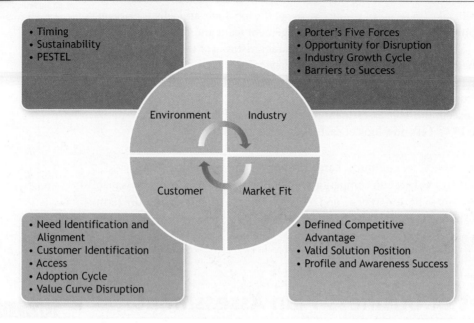

An assessment via Porter's five forces, coupled with a solid company-focused SWOT analysis and well-researched competitive analysis, should enable us to sense the overall future growth potential of the industry, and enable us to draw conclusions as to our overall company strength in comparison to that of our competitors. Third, we need to draw conclusions relating to the actual customers we hope to attract. What is the primary market for our product and/or service? Is the size of the segment we plan to attack large enough to achieve operational stability? Do we fully understand the profile of the customer we hope to acquire? What is the current adoption process for products and/or services such as ours? Do we really have a disruptive innovation that will lead customers to change their predetermined purchase order? Finally, can we conclude a true market fit? Do we feel that the products and/or services being offered provide a valid solution to the "pain" it is attempting to respond to? Will the proposed communication strategy deliver on the profile, awareness, and preference requirements that need to be achieved in order for our business to be successful? Can we conclude a definitive competitive advantage that we can build our positioning around?

> Market analysis is all about assessing the legitimacy of the perceived opportunity that the manager or entrepreneur sees for the organization.

Value Analysis

Although identified as a separate phase, the value analysis phase is closely integrated with the market analysis phase. In fact, the value analysis is really about fully understanding "market fit" and validating that we do have a definitive competitive advantage or uniqueness around which we can develop a positioning campaign. The ability to fully develop and communicate why your product and/or service is unique, why it is important in solving the target market's problems, and what its underlying value proposition strengths are, will, ultimately, determine if customers will indeed adopt it. In short, we are really attempting to draw three conclusions from our value analysis:

1. Does the business plan demonstrate that we can create a customer habit of purchasing our product and/or service?

FIGURE 15.8 Value Analysis Litmus Test

Litmus Test Component	Key Outcome
Value Proposition	What is it? What makes it unique? Where is the value?
Target Market	Who is the primary target market? What does the target market look like? Do we understand the connection between the target market and the value proposition?
Customer Profile	How does the customer behave? Are there any unique characteristics we can leverage?
Key Decision Criteria	Why does this customer buy? Where is the decision-making weight placed? Is the value proposition properly aligned to this?
Target Message Development	What do we plan to say to catch and hold this customer's attention?
Communication Delivery	What is the plan for reaching the customer? Does this fit with the customer profile ?

2. Does the business plan demonstrate that we can build an association with our targeted customer base and that our product and/or service provides a credible solution to their needs?
3. Does the business plan demonstrate that we can get customers to care more about our products and/or services than those of our competitors?

Chapters 10 and 11 of this textbook focused on the importance of being able to sense the core strengths of our value proposition and communicate them to our target audience. In assessing a business venture, we need to feel comfortable that the value proposition presented will achieve the three conclusions noted above. The way that we accomplish this is via the value analysis **litmus test** shown in Figure 15.8.

> **Litmus Test** refers to a process or something that is used to make a judgment or draw conclusions about the acceptability of an opinion.

> Value analysis focuses on fully understanding "market fit" and validating that we have a definitive competitive advantage or uniqueness around which we can develop a positioning campaign.

Financial Analysis

Equally important to the task of understanding the market that the organization plans to attack, and the value proposition around which this attack is to be formulated, is the need to assess the financial requirements required to support the business venture. To be successful, managers and entrepreneurs need to develop a valid estimate of the capital needs of the organization, the length of time needed to ensure financial stability, and the cash requirements applicable to the cash operating cycle. Defining and understanding these base fundamentals will enable those conducting the analytical process to draw conclusions relating to the actual depth of the investment required, the expected returns on this investment, and the level of affordable loss that could be absorbed should financial projections not be met as anticipated. Astute managers and entrepreneurs, in conducting such an analysis, will assess the financial potential of a venture and, consequently, the risk/reward trade-off associated with it across five key areas (see Figure 15.9).

> To be successful, managers and entrepreneurs need to develop a valid estimate of the capital needs of the organization, the length of time needed to ensure financial stability, and the cash requirements applicable to the cash operating cycle.

FIGURE 15.9   Focus of Financial Risk Analysis

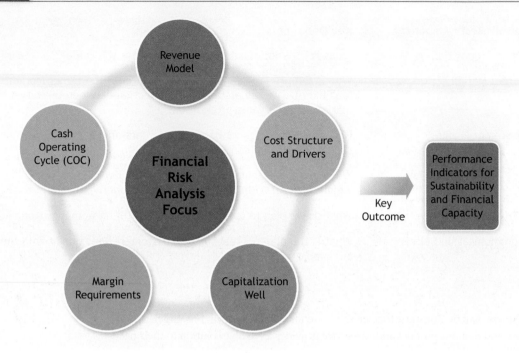

REVENUE MODEL ASSESSMENT

Assessing the revenue model of a new venture is really about validating the legitimacy of where revenue is going to come from and how it will be generated. Revenue analysis focuses on the number of potential revenue streams the organization is adding, the sources of revenue within each stream, the initial size of these revenue streams, the growth potential of this revenue looking forward, the interdependency of this new revenue source on existing revenue sources (if they exist), and the price pressure that can be anticipated on the revenue streams identified (see Figure 15.10). In essence, we are trying to determine, with an acceptable degree of credibility, the initial revenue inflow anticipated, its projected growth, and external forces that may impact such growth potential. A good approach to drawing conclusions, with respect to revenue, is to develop a potential range of outcomes, thereby defining with a higher probability of confidence the upside and downside boundaries of the level of revenue anticipated. As an example, let's assume that the ZOOM Corporation is scheduled to launch its version of a tablet computer called the Scorebook. Let's further assume that marketing has developed its forecasts for this initial year, with ZOOM expecting to sell 4 million units (realistic forecast) at an average selling price of $450. ZOOM's management team, along with analysts, however, see upside sales potentially reaching 6 million units (optimistic forecast). On the downside, however, concerns are that sales may be as few as 2 million units (pessimistic forecast). For ZOOM, the Scorebook, at an estimated average selling price of $450, will generate revenue of between $900 million and $2.7 billion, with an expected revenue stream of $1.8 billion achieved should the 4 million unit estimate be achieved. Being able to define the revenue sources and the anticipated revenue stream, particularly in the early stages of a new venture launch, is a first step in determining the financial viability of a business opportunity.

> Assessing the revenue model of a new venture is really about validating the legitimacy of where revenue is going to come from and how it will be generated.

FIGURE 15.10	Key Financial Assessment Risk Factors

Revenue	Cost Drivers	Benchmark Requirements	Cash Operating Cycle (COC)	Capitalization Well
• # of streams • Source(s) • Size of each stream • Growth potential of each stream • Interdependency of each stream • Price pressure on each stream	• Structure—fixed, semi-fixed, committed, and variable • Type—reoccurring vs. non-reoccurring • Key cost centres • Degree of control and market volatility • Source of competitive advantage • Built-in expense creep within each cost centre	• Point of positive cash flow • Breakeven point • GPM (gross profit margin) requirement and target • OM (operating margin) Requirement and target • PM (profit margin) requirement and target	• Timing and size of cash inflows and outflows • Identify key impact factors on cash flow • Define the range of movement available prior to liquidity impact • Determine the cash reserve required to fund the COC	• Total investment size • Maximum financing needs • Depth of private-equity support • Free cash reserve availability

COST DRIVER ASSESSMENT

As was discussed in Chapter 12, understanding an organization's cost base is a fundamental managerial responsibility. So, too, is this need when assessing a new business venture. The core difference, however, is that in assessing existing businesses managers have historical records to fall back on. In new ventures, particularly new business start-ups, such a history is not generally present. The end result is that cost estimates, like revenue estimates, are projected and/or anticipated. A number of key factors need to be reviewed by managers and entrepreneurs when assessing an organization's cost base (see Figure 15.10). These factors are as follows:

1. What does the overall cost structure look like? What is the relationship (to revenue) of product costs and operating expenses? What are the key cost centres that will ultimately drive a large percentage of the organization's cost base?
2. What costs are anticipated to be reoccurring versus those felt to be non-reoccurring?
3. What type of built-in expense creep do we anticipate within these cost areas?
4. Will market volatility, such as commodities, impact our expense lines? If so, by how much?
5. Do we feel that our cost base, as it is estimated, yields a competitive advantage?

Going back to our example of the ZOOM Corporation, let's assume that the organization estimates that product costs associated with building the Scorebook are estimated at 70 percent of the average selling price of $450. Fixed, semi-fixed, and committed costs are projected to be $378 million. Knowing this information, along with the various revenue ranges described above, now allows us to get a feel for the potential profitability of the Scorebook at the potential volume outcomes identified earlier. This is shown in Table 15.1.

ZOOM Corporation, based on revenue and cost estimates, is now able to determine that its upside operating profit potential (EBT) is $432 000 000, with its downside operating loss exposure being estimated at ($108 000 000). This pessimistic outcome of ($108 000 000) communicates to the management team that, should the pessimistic case outcome materialize, the organization will need to be prepared to spend an additional $108 000 000 to cover the operating loss associated with this weak market performance. This becomes part of the financial risk assessment and the decision-making process of whether to assign this project a "go" or a "no go" decision.

TABLE 15.1   ZOOM Corporation: Optimistic, Realistic, and Pessimistic Sales Forecasts

	2 Million Scorebooks Sold	4 Million Scorebooks Sold	6 Million Scorebooks Sold
Revenue @ ASP of $450	$900 000 000	$1 800 000 000	$2 700 000 000
Less Product Costs @70% of ASP	$630 000 000	$1 260 000 000	$1 890 000 000
Equals GPM	$270 000 000	$ 540 000 000	$ 810 000 000
Less Operating Expenses	$378 000 000	$ 378 000 000	$ 378 000 000
Equals EBT	($108 000 000)	$ 162 000 000	$ 432 000 000

ASSESSING BENCHMARK REQUIREMENTS

Cash Flow Positive refers to the point where cash inflows finally exceed cash outflows.

Benchmark requirements focus on an assessment of key performance indicators that will assist us in better understanding the various outcomes that could materialize given the estimates we have made and the operational efficiencies that need to be achieved (see Figure 15.10). Two key benchmarks are understanding the point at which the organization becomes **cash flow positive**, and where the initial estimated breakeven point is anticipated to be. "Cash flow positive" is that point where cash inflows finally exceed cash outflows for the organization. This is an important first step in defining how long a new venture's burn rate will last. As long as cash outflows exceed cash inflows, additional capital will be needed to offset the burn rate occurring. Breakeven point, as defined in Chapter 12, is that point in time where total revenue = total expenses and, therefore, profit = $0. Using our ZOOM Corporation example, based on the information provided the breakeven point for the Scorebook for its first year of operation is as follows:

BEP units = FC/(SP−VC)
BEP units = $378 000 000/($450−$315)
BEP units = $378 000 000/$135
BEP units = 2.8 million

> Two key benchmarks are understanding the point at which the organization becomes cash flow positive, and where the initial estimated breakeven point is anticipated to be.

Other key benchmark requirements would be, for example, striving for a gross profit margin of 30 percent, or an operating margin of 9 percent. Table 15.2 illustrates the impact that margin erosion can have on operating results if cost creep or cost inefficiencies work their way into the operating processes of the Scorebook's first-year launch results at its anticipated sales volume of 4 million units.

TABLE 15.2   ZOOM Corporation Gross Profit Margin Erosion

	4 Million Units Sold GPM = 30% and OE = $378M (Benchmark)	4 Million Units Sold GPM Erodes to 27% and OE Remains at $378M	4 Million Units Sold GPM = 27% and OE Rises to $400M
Revenue	$1 800 000 000	$1 800 000 000	$1 800 000 000
GPM	$ 540 000 000	$ 486 000 000	$ 486 000 000
Operating Exp. (OE)	$ 378 000 000	$ 378 000 000	$ 400 000 000
Operating Profit (EBT)	$ 162 000 000	$ 108 000 000	$ 86 000 000

Table 15.2 illustrates that even though 4 million units are expected to be sold, a potential rise in product costs (which negatively impacts GPM), which causes an erosion of GPM by −3%, and/or a rise in operating expenses (such as higher than expected marketing costs), will negatively impact operating profit. Just as managers and entrepreneurs need to be cognizant of ranges of outcomes in sales revenue, they must also recognize that cost estimates are just that, and that a range of potential outcomes can occur even if sales projections are made.

ANTICIPATING THE CASH OPERATING CYCLE

As discussed in Chapters 9 and 14, the cash operating cycle defines the timing and size of cash inflows and outflows. By seeking to define and anticipate estimates associated with the movement of cash within a new business venture, managers and entrepreneurs are able to identify the key impact factors on cash flow and proactively plan for it. This important metric relating to liquidity assists in ensuring that developing and maintaining adequate capital reserves is factored into the financial risk assessment process (see Figure 15.10).

DEFINING THE CAPITALIZATION WELL

Up to this point, our financial discussion has focused on assessing the financial risk associated with the new venture or new product launches operating framework. Our emphasis has been on ensuring that we understand our sales forecast and the corresponding revenue derived from it, our cost base and the key performance indicators around which we will benchmark, and the need to understand the estimated cash operating cycle of the new venture or product. This is, however, only one-half of the financial assessment equation and process. In addition to assessing the financial potential of the business, once it is operating we also need to assess the magnitude of capital asset investment and other pre-launch costs, often referred to as **start-up costs**, required to launch the new business venture and/or a new product line. In many situations, this can, and will, require a considerable capital commitment. Even for small business entities, start-up costs can run into the thousands of dollars. As an example, the start-up costs of an M&M Meat Shop are estimated to be $300 000 to $450 000. These start-up costs are needed to cover equipment, construction costs in customizing a location for the shop, legal and professional fees, grand-opening advertising, staff training, product initial inventory, and other costs associated with the use of the M&M Meat Shop name and its trademark.[8]

> In addition to assessing the financial potential of the business, once it is operating we also need to assess the magnitude of capital asset investment and other pre-launch costs, often referred to as start-up costs, required to launch the new business venture and/or a new product line.

To truly understand the magnitude of the total capital needed to launch and support a new business venture or product (start-up costs and initial operational costs), managers and entrepreneurs are advised to make use of a business model called the **capitalization well**. The idea behind the capitalization well (see Figure 15.11) is to provide a framework by which managers and entrepreneurs can assess the full capital requirements that will be needed to ensure the successful capitalization of a business venture. By doing so, managers and entrepreneurs can minimize one of the primary reasons for new venture failures, that being **undercapitalization**. Fully understanding the capitalization requirements of the organization also results in a much better outcome pertaining to "go and no go" decisions at the outset of a venture assessment process versus dealing with significant and unanticipated cash burns and cash deficiencies once a business or product launch is underway.

To fully understand the capitalization well concept, think of the process involved in drilling for oil. Our initial phase is exploring for oil. This research-based phase will require the organization to spend some capital in determining where, and with what process, we should drill for the oil we hope to find. Once a site and start date have been determined, the organization will then need to proceed with some fairly significant capital asset expenditures (start-up

Start-up Costs refers to the initial capital investment required to launch a new business or product venture.

Capitalization Well refers to a framework for assessing the full capital requirements of a business venture.

Undercapitalization is the situation where a company lacks the required funding to continue business activities.

FIGURE 15.11 Capitalization Well: Assessing Viability

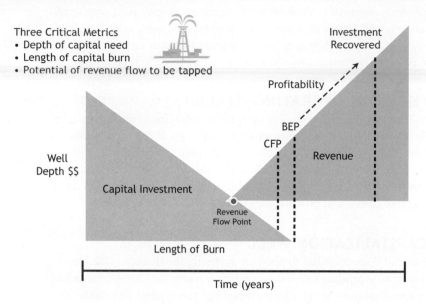

Three Critical Metrics
- Depth of capital need
- Length of capital burn
- Potential of revenue flow to be tapped

costs). This would entail purchasing and/or developing the oil rig or oil well components, shipping them, erecting them, and then testing the site and training staff to ensure that the rig or well is ready to go and that all pre-operational requirements are met. Following this start-up period is the commencement of operations. With our oil rig or oil well, this would be drilling for oil. Keep in mind that we may need to drill for a period of time before oil begins to flow. Assuming that all goes well, we will then begin to see oil pumping through our well. Again, we need to recognize that this may not be of sufficient quantity to cover our drilling costs. As our oil well continues to produce oil and we realize the revenue from it, we will eventually be able to cover our direct costs. This is where we finally become cash flow positive (CFP). This is then followed by a breakeven point (BEP) where we not only cover direct costs, but are now covering our total expense line, including non-cash transactions such as depreciation. Finally, assuming that revenue continues to grow, we begin earning profit, followed by reaching that point where our investment is fully recovered. Ideally, the well remains profitable long after the payback period is reached, and continues to generate profit for our oil company.

The same holds true for a business. We may need to spend a considerable amount of money prior to seeing any definitive revenue flow. A new business venture requires initial investment on determining the viability of the concept or idea. This could be spent on concept design and prototype development, market research such as surveys, focus groups, competitive analysis, and test marketing, to mention a few initiatives in this phase. This is then followed by investment in the capital asset base required to support the new venture. This could be a bricks-and-mortar location, manufacturing equipment, technology-based hardware and software, pre-launch marketing, recruitment, hiring and training of staff, and so on. With all of this in place, we then open our doors and commence business operations, striving to move to cash flow positive and breakeven point as quickly as possible in order to minimize our burn rate. With the burn rate eliminated, our focus is then placed on driving profitability to recoup our investment and to create long-term wealth for our stakeholders.

In assessing business plans and new ventures, managers and entrepreneurs need to define and understand three key fundamental points relating to the capitalization well:

1. What is the depth of the capital burn—in other words, how much money will we truly need?
2. What is the length of the capital burn—how long will it take to get to cash flow positive and then breakeven point?

3. What is the potential revenue that we believe can be realized? Will this enable us to achieve profitability and long-term business stability, return the investment made in the business, and contribute positively to stakeholder wealth?

In utilizing the capitalization well as a core element of the financial risk analysis of a new business venture, we are trying to conclude whether or not we have the financial capacity to create and support the business venture until such a time that its revenue stream is sufficient to ensure profit stability and long-term sustainability. Depending on the situation, this could take a number of months or even years (see Figure 15.12). For example, Amazon.com, founded by Jeff Bezos in July 1994 and launched in 1995, did not generate an operating profit until it reached a sales volume in excess of $1 billion in the fourth quarter of 2001.[9]

FIGURE 15.12   New Venture Evolution[10]

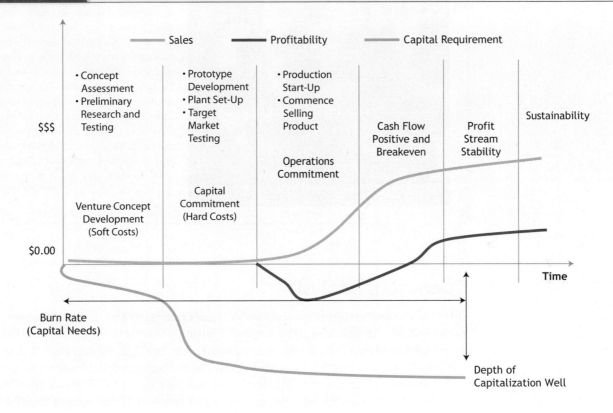

BUSINESS in Action

Success Is in the Details

What makes the difference between a merely satisfactory delivery and a great delivery of a new and innovative idea to the marketplace? Well, if you ask Richard Branson, philanthropist, entrepreneur, and founder of the Virgin Group, his response would most likely focus on ensuring that you have a structure in place that ensures definitive attention to detail. In a recent article in *Canadian Business* (February 2011), Branson discussed why attention to detail is so important and offered some tips that enable him to stay on top of the delivery of services across the many organizations that exist within the Virgin Group's portfolio. A key component of this process is to think of service delivery in conjunction with what you have identified as your company's core values, key mid-term strategic considerations, and the overall long-term vision. A second critical requirement is to continuously sample the products and/or services that your company offers, making notes on where deficiencies and improvements need to be made and then ensuring that such product and/or service delivery refinements are put into action. A core aspect of this sampling process is to take the time to speak with staff to ensure that you understand the organization's delivery model from their perspective. They are also great identifiers as to where bottlenecks are occurring and inefficiencies are creeping in. An open-door communication policy that encourages staff and customer suggestions for product and/or service improvements is

fundamental to this detail-focused approach as well. In business, profitable market share is generated one customer at a time. Don't be afraid to take the time to ensure that each customer contact receives the level of attention necessary to create a loyalty bond between you and them. Remember that value proposition development and creating customer commitment is not so much about the products and services offered, but the relationship experience that customers have with your business and you. Competitors should also be thought of as potential opportunities versus enemies. Interacting with key individuals in direct and indirect business competitors offers the opportunity to gain market knowledge and to uncover collaborative opportunities that may assist in further growing the scale and profitability of all involved.[11]

Operations Analysis

Often overlooked in light of the emphasis on market analysis and financial assessment, a key analytical area in determining whether a business venture will be successful lies in a firm understanding of the infrastructure, equipment, and value chain flow that will be needed to effectively execute the business plan and the accompanying business strategy. A well-developed business plan will demonstrate just how the business and/or its products and services will be developed, communicated, and connected to customers. Think of this as a business schematic that details the framework around which the business plan will be executed.

As an example, consider McDonald's decision to develop and offer its Big Mac sandwich to its customers. The Big Mac consists of two beef patties, special sauce, lettuce, cheese, pickles, and onions on a sesame seed bun. For McDonald's, the operational analysis would entail how to fully integrate the creation of this sandwich in the back end (kitchen and food prep areas) of its quick-service restaurant locations, and deliver it to customers at the time of purchase. This would entail a full value chain development plan (see Figure 15.13). A business plan and the business venture assessment processes look at the legitimacy of an operation as well as the efficiency and effectiveness associated with it.

> A key analytical area in determining whether a business venture will be successful lies in a firm understanding of the infrastructure, equipment, and value chain flow that will be needed to effectively execute the business plan and the accompanying business strategy.

FIGURE 15.13 Value Chain: McDonald's Big Mac

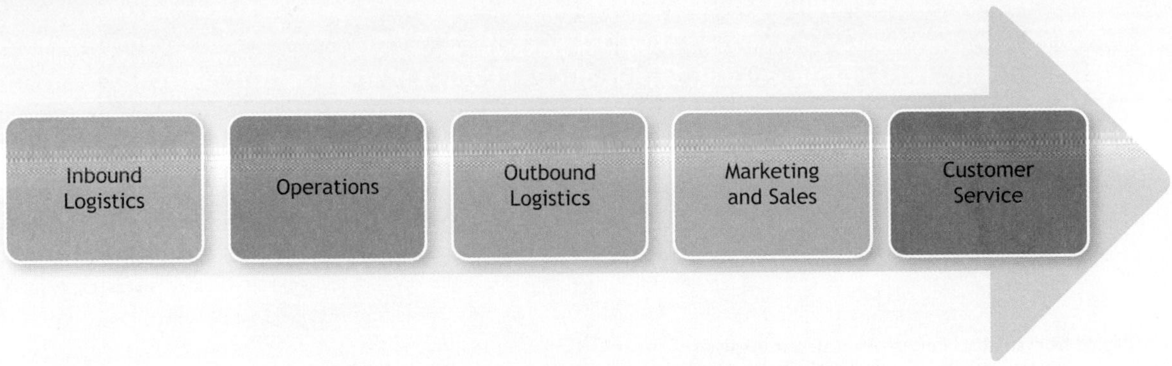

Inbound Logistics	Operations	Outbound Logistics	Marketing and Sales	Customer Service

- Product procurement
- Product storage
- Inventory levels

- Product handling and preparation
- Portion control
- Big Mac assembly flow
- Kitchen configuration
- Quality C=control
- Training

- Product packaging
- Big Mac holding, pending sale
- Quality control—shelf life

- Advertising and communication
- Pricing
- In-store promotions
- Menu board set-up
- Meal Deal packaging

- Staff delivery training
- Warming bin management
- Product quality assessment

Source: Value Chain adapted from Michael Porter—Value Chain Analysis

The plan will also detail the expertise required to staff the proposed venture, the capacity that the operation possesses with respect to the design, development, and delivery of the products and/or services, and the supporting infrastructure needed to ensure that the operation can deliver on the vision and the communication strategy commitments being made. Using an additional example, assume that a business plan indicates a new restaurant venture is projecting sales of $2 million. An analysis of the menu indicates that an average cheque amount from its customers, based on menu item pricing, is estimated to be $15. The restaurant's seating capacity consists of 10 tables, each with 4 chairs. This means that the "per seating" capacity of the restaurant is 40 patrons. The restaurant plan calls for it to be open 350 days per year, serving lunch and evening diners. The question is whether the seating capacity of the restaurant can realistically deliver $2 million in sales given an average cheque size of $15 per diner. A quick operational analysis would yield the following:

1. $2 million in sales, at $15 per diner, requires 133 334 diners per year.
2. Dividing the 133 334 diners by 350 days results in 381 diners per day.
3. Assuming 40 seats, this means that we will need to serve approximately 10 diners per day, per chair, in order to achieve the estimated $2 million in sales. Is this possible?

To achieve the results noted above would require a very high-volume-based operation. Will market demand provide 381 diners per day? Can the kitchen and serving staff handle this volume? How many tables can a single server handle? If the average person sits in a seat for 45 minutes per meal, this means that the seat must be occupied for 7.5 hours per day with diners. Given that peak-period times are between 12 p.m. and 2 p.m. for lunch, and 4:30 p.m. and 7:30 p.m. for dinner, can we realistically expect to have all chairs fully occupied all the time? These are just some of the questions that need to be asked to determine the viability of the operation in order to yield the desired sales revenue figures, given the identified price point that the restaurant realistically can achieve.

Up to this point, our two examples have focused on base-level operational issues that need to be assessed as part of our operational analysis. Keep in mind that the situation is more

FIGURE 15.14 Value Chain: Support Activities

FIGURE 15.14 Value Chain: Support Activities

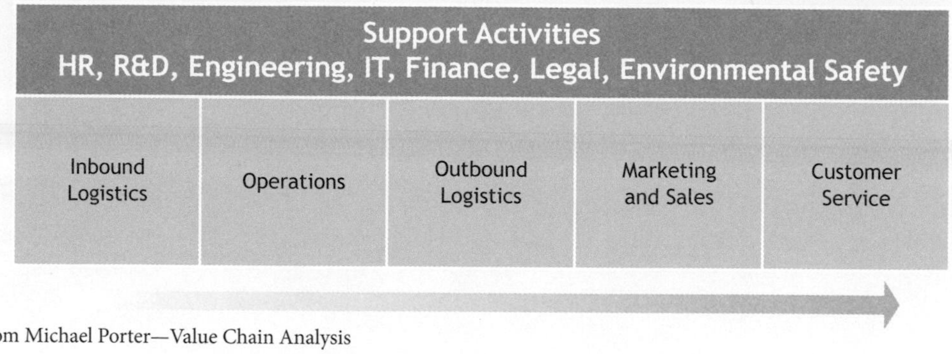

Source: Adapted from Michael Porter—Value Chain Analysis

complex than this in that technology decisions, environmental safety and compliance decisions, legal risk assessment, engineering and R&D decisions, and employee management decisions all form part of this analytical process as well. Using the value chain model identified in Chapter 9 and shown again in Figure 15.14 is an excellent way to assess the overall legitimacy of the operational model being proposed within the new venture.

Management Competency Analysis

Going back to Chapter 1, we are reminded that an organization's business system is founded on the basis of four key components: capital, assets, labour, and management acumen. In the assessment of a business venture, the ability of the management team to illustrate its competencies to successfully execute the business plan and yield the intended financial results is paramount in the eyes of private-equity companies and investors considering bankrolling the new venture. In many cases, the final "go or no go" decision comes down to this management acumen analysis. Fully assessing the overall competencies and commitment of an entrepreneur and/or a management team is never an easy task. This becomes even more critical when specialized skills are required early on to ensure successful business and/or product development. Skill requirements also may change as the venture proceeds through the various stages of development noted in Figure 15.12. In summarizing this process, however, an assessment of the overall managerial acumen and the human resource talent base required can be framed around three fundamental questions:

1. What specific competencies, skills, experience, and expertise are essential to the effective execution of the business plan?
2. Do the individuals identified as key to the business start-up demonstrate a possession of such competencies, skills, experience, and expertise? In other words, can these individuals translate the vision and the near-term objectives into specific tactical and actionable plans?
3. In addition to the operating expertise requirements noted above, do these same individuals possess the required relationships and leadership skills to successfully execute the plan?

Looking for the answers to the three questions noted above results in the need to conduct an exhaustive evaluation of the key individuals and/or management team who represent the business venture. This evaluation requirement means assessing both objective and subjective success characteristics of these individuals in order to determine the probability that they can truly deliver the projected results identified within the business plan.[12] To ensure a thorough assessment of this individual and/or management acumen, prospective investors and/or

FIGURE 15.15 Management Acumen Assessment Model (MERFS)

What management needs to demonstrate:

M = Motivation	E = Expertise	R = Relationships	F = Focus	S = Skin in the Game
• Adaptability • Realism • Durability • Desire to excel • Bulldog mentality	• Skill • Knowledge • Direct experience • Willingness to make decisions	• Customer contacts • Network with suppliers, channel partners • Advisory board • Access to specialized skills	• Strategic plan • Vision • Leadership • Rifle vs. shotgun • Funnelling	• Time • Treasure • Talent • Commitment

business plan analysts will often focus on the metrics presented in the management acumen model illustrated in Figure 15.15. An easy way to remember these success-based evaluation metrics is by the acronym MERFS.

> In the assessment of a business venture, the ability of the management team to illustrate its competencies to successfully execute the business plan and yield the intended financial results is paramount in the eyes of private-equity companies and investors considering bankrolling the new venture.

MERFS stands for motivation, expertise, relationships, focus, and "skin in the game." Each of these five categories of analytical assessment contributes to the overall determination of whether an individual and/or a management team has what it takes to successfully execute the proposed business plan.

M—Motivation refers to the overall desire to excel. The assessment process looks at whether the individuals and/or management team possess that "bulldog" mentality to carry on even when things get off track or when unanticipated barriers and challenges appear. It also seeks to assess the adaptability of the management team, the durability of their commitment, and the realism of the vision that they have initially set for the business venture in the near term.

E—Expertise focuses on the skill set, knowledge base, experience, and decision-making aptitude of the individuals and/or the management team. Is the management acumen there to ensure that good decisions will be made and that, when challenged, the willingness to make the essential decisions for success exists?

R—Relationships focus on the linkages that key individuals and managers have with key external stakeholders and that are critical to the business venture's success. This refers to customer contacts, supplier contacts, channel partners, and advisory board members, to name a few. It also refers to the ability of these individuals and/or managers to identify critical sources for specialized skills needed for the venture, and the ability to recruit, obtain, and retain such human resources.

F—Focus refers to the vision that the key individuals and/or managers have for the business venture, their leadership capabilities in communicating this vision to their employees and stakeholders, and their ability to maintain their focus and direction in pursuit of this vision. A good way to think of this is to assess whether their understanding of the market and their "fit" is effectively rifled toward definitive outcomes, or whether they are simply taking a broad shotgun approach to the market, trying to do a variety of things and hoping that something will be successful.

S—Skin in the Game refers to the overall level of commitment that individuals and/or managers have to the business venture. "Skin in the game" is assessed in three ways: What personal time commitment are they prepared to make to the venture? How much financial risk are they personally absorbing? and What responsibilities are they willing to hold themselves accountable for within the new business venture?[13]

For a business venture to be given a "go" decision, investors and decision makers need to confirm that the individuals and/or management team possess solid assessment scores across all five of these areas. A deficiency in any one area can, and often will, result in an ineffective execution of a business plan.

Exit Options

Exit options refer to whether or not there is an intended exit plan from the business and, if so, what type of conditions would trigger such a strategy. In some cases, exit options can be thought of as a "plan B" to be taken where anticipated revenue growth does not materialize. In other cases, exit options can be a formal intent of the entrepreneur to exit a business or venture via a planned sale of the business once a certain sales volume or level of profitability is achieved. Private-equity investors and stakeholders are interested in the overall long-term commitment that an entrepreneur or company has to a given product, service, or business entity. Equally important is the recognition by an entrepreneur or management team that a different skill set may be required once certain growth levels are realized. For some entrepreneurs, their focus is all about creating market space and establishing innovative solutions to new technology needs. Once a foothold has been established in a market, their interest then shifts toward moving away from the day-to-day management needs of the organization and focusing on the next new innovative ideas. In analyzing a business venture, the formal communication of an exit strategy signals to the financial supporters of the venture that the entrepreneur envisions a defined and limited involvement period. This should be assessed against the business and plan and the corresponding analysis across the other five areas mentioned in order to understand how the exit strategy integrates into the overall business model. Measuring the exit strategy against the findings resulting from a capitalization well analysis enables us to determine whether the exit strategy, as communicated, significantly impacts the overall risk of the project. This is then incorporated into the "go or no go" decision process.

LO5 Acquiring an Existing Business

Up to this point, our discussion has focused on the development of a business opportunity through the launch of a new business, the launch of a new product line, or, perhaps, an extension of an existing product line. These mechanisms for growing a business are generally referred to as **organic growth** options. Organic growth implies growing a business from within, using its existing business lines as a basis for such growth. In many cases, however, the idea of developing a new business opportunity from the ground up represents significantly greater risk than a company is willing to take on. This may be the result of an immediate need to gain access to a particular market, the length of time it may take to develop the competencies and/or capabilities internally to successfully compete, concerns over heightened competition and its potential for deteriorating margins and profitability, or the long-term capital commitment required to generate the scale needed to ensure profitability and sustainability. The alternative to growing organically is to consider the **acquisition** of an existing business that offers the entrepreneur and/or a company immediate access to a currently operating entity and, therefore, access to a desired market and an established customer base. Just as success in the start-up of a new business or business line is predicated on an organized and thorough assessment of a proposed business plan, so, too, is the case for acquiring a company. The venture assessment process identified in Figure 15.1 is still very much part of this process. Market risk and

Organic Growth refers to growth that comes from an organization's existing business portfolio.

Acquisition refers to the process of acquiring another company or operation.

financial risk "due diligence" needs to be properly conducted. A determination of the value advantage that the acquisition needs to bring to the entrepreneur and/or the company must be recognized and validated. The efficiency and capacity of the operation needs to be assessed, not only in terms of current scale and market delivery but also in terms of the forward-looking objectives of the acquiring individual or organization. If the acquiring organization intends to keep all, or part, of the existing management team, then the level of managerial competency needs to be assessed as well. In addition to this process, an acquisition also presents some additional analysis on the part of the entrepreneur or the acquiring company. This entails identifying the potential target for acquisition, determining a price to offer for the company or operation to be purchased, arranging the financing for the acquisition, and then integrating the acquisition into the business portfolio. This process is shown, in a summary format, in Figure 15.16.

> The alternative to growing organically is to consider the acquisition of an existing business that offers immediate access to a currently operating entity and, therefore, access to a desired market and an established customer base.

- **Identify the Target** refers to conducting a search as to potential candidates for acquisition. Once found, preliminary negotiations will need to take place to determine whether the acquiring company should proceed with a formal "fit" analysis.

- **Assess the Fit** takes us back to Figure 15.1 and the "due diligence" associated with our six-phase venture assessment process. Given that we are purchasing a going concern, however, it also requires additional due diligence in a number of key areas. This additional due diligence will, most likely, focus around technology and intellectual property, product and/or service offerings, capital asset infrastructure and operational efficiencies, financial capacity and debt structure, HR policies and procedures, sales and marketing approaches, culture, and overall organizational practices. Key focal points of this analysis will be to determine **operational synergies** that can be realized, cost savings that can be achieved, and the cultural fit of the two organizations.

  Operational Synergies refers to maximization of productivity and efficiency through the combining of resources.

- **Determine a Price** focuses on business valuation. At some point in the process, an offer and acceptance need to be made. For the acquiring company, the price being paid for the acquisition must not exceed the current value of the company plus the anticipated synergies to be realized. In reality, the acquiring company will strive for an agreed-upon price below this point in order to realize an immediate value for the acquisition. For the selling

FIGURE 15.16 Acquisition Process

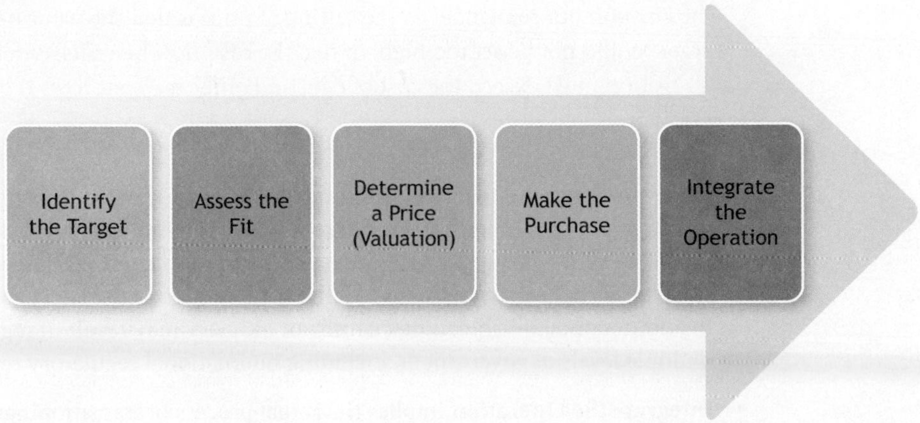

FIGURE 15.17   Acquisition Valuation Model

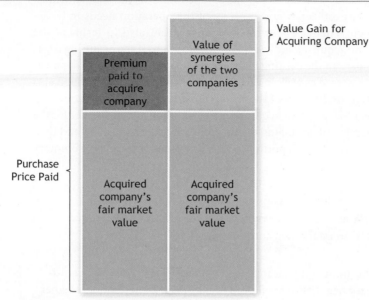

Source: "CEO's Guide to Corporate Finance, Corporate Finance Practice," Dobbs, Huyett, Koller, McKinsey & Company, *McKinsey Quarterly*, 2010, February 2011.

company, the value must be sufficient to ensure that investors view the sale of the company as being in their best interests. This will generally mean striving for a value that exceeds the immediate market value of the organization (see Figure 15.17).

The price of the acquisition can be determined in a number of ways. Valuation methods can include P/E ratios, **EBITDA** calculations, gross profit margins, revenue forecasting, market capitalization analysis, total enterprise analysis modelling, cash flow analysis, and net present value calculations coupled with weighted cost of capital (WACC) calculations. The actual valuation process is often developed by financial analysts on behalf of the companies involved in the acquisition and is beyond the scope of this textbook. In many cases, the valuation process will include a number of approaches in order to validate an acceptable purchase price range. The key point to remember in the setting of price is that the value being placed on the target should not be set too high, in that the cash flow benefits anticipated from the acquisition must exceed the cost of debt and other cash outflows required to make the purchase. Other factors that will have to be taken into consideration will be the cost of debt associated with the purchase and whether any, or all, of the target company's liabilities will also be assumed.

> **EBITDA** is earnings before interest and taxes + depreciation expense + amortization expense.

> The key point to remember in the setting of price is that the value being placed on the target should not be set too high, in that the cash flow benefits anticipated from the acquisition must exceed the cost of debt and other cash outflows required to make the purchase.

- **Make the Purchase** involves the legal steps associated with the actual purchase of the target. A key component of this phase will be a finalization of how the acquisition will be financed. Will it be an all-cash purchase? Will it be a combination of cash and shares of stock in the acquiring company? Will it include substantial short and/or long-term debt? In addition, major acquisitions within an industry may result in regulatory review at multiple levels of government, including international regulatory review.

- **Integrate the Operation** implies the actual process of transitioning business processes and protocols to and through the acquired company once the actual purchase process is completed. In many ways, this is the most challenging aspect of the purchase. This is the execution of the tactics needed in order for the objectives for the acquisition and the achievement of the anticipated synergies to be realized.[14]

Although on a somewhat smaller scale, the same process holds true for small businesses. Entrepreneurs interested in acquiring an existing business must approach it in the same manner as large corporations approach an acquisition. Great care needs to be taken in valuing the existing business and in determining an acceptable price to pay, given the anticipated additional value that the entrepreneur feels he or she can create. Paying too high a price or taking on too much debt in the purchase of the business can result in most of the benefit of the acquisition accruing to the seller. The base principle of ensuring that inflows of cash exceed the anticipated (and possibly, higher) outflows of cash, once the acquisition takes place, is a core barometer for ensuring that the newly acquired company can remain liquid and solvent.

BUSINESS *in Action*

Target Buys into Canada

So, just how does a major U.S. retail player gain access to the Canadian market? One way is to grow organically one store at a time. The trouble with this approach is that there are only so many premium commercial real estate locations in Canada. Another concern is that this approach takes time and effort to source suitable retail locations one by one, develop reach across the country's various provinces, create a distribution structure from scratch, and generate sufficient scale early on to firmly entrench in what is becoming an increasingly competitive retail landscape. A second approach to gaining market access is through acquisition. Recognizing the need to act quickly, and finding a suitable market player that possesses the premium commercial real estate locations desired, Target's entry into the Canadian retail sector has opted for this second option. Facing slower growth in the United States, Target, like many other retailers, sees international markets as an opportunity for expansion—and what better way to get your feet wet than to simply shift north, especially to a country that has weathered the economic downturn of 2008-09 better than most G7 countries? For Target, moving into Canada is something that the company wanted to do, and they wanted to take advantage of the opportunities present in Canada as quickly as possible. Following a quick assessment of potential options, Target viewed the Canadian icon Zellers, and its attractive commercial real estate holdings, as an ideal solution. Hudson's Bay Company, the parent company of Zellers, ideally would have liked to continue to invest in Zellers and turn it into its own version of Target. For HBC, however, to accomplish this would have taken considerable financial resources and considerable market risk. Recognizing the limitations of being able to turn Zellers around, HBC's management team (and its private-equity owners, NRDC Equity Partners) made the decision to entertain offers for its Zellers chain. For NRDC Equity Partners, which purchased the Hudson's Bay Co. in 2008 for US$1.1 billion, the estimated C$1.825 billion deal was simply an offer that they could not refuse. For Target, the acquisition of Zellers means immediate access to the Canadian market at a scale that enables them to become a major player. The deal provides Target with access to 220 Zellers store locations and, more importantly, the premium commercial real estate leases

(many at discounted prices) that Zellers possesses. Over the next two to three years, Target will spend close to an additional C$1 billion converting a majority of these stores to Target stores. For NRDC Equity Partners, the deal provides significant capital that the organization can use to reduce its debt load and to further invest in its other businesses, including its high-end retail operations, such as the Hudson's Bay Co. and Lord & Taylor.[15]

WEB INTEGRATION

For more information on this acquisition, Google "Target's entry into Canada," or visit Target's web site at **www.target.com**.

A Note Pertaining to Not-for-Profits

Just as for-profit entities need to seek out new business opportunities in order to grow their companies, so too do not-for-profits. Historically, many not-for-profits have relied on external funding sources, such as government, foundations, and granting agencies, to cover their operating expenses. For foundations, reduced returns on principal invested have resulted in a reduction in the dollar amount of support that they, in turn, are able to provide. Faced with budgetary deficits coupled with taxpayers demanding minimal increases in taxes, governments are reducing or withdrawing support in many non–core service areas. Transfers to non-government granting agencies are also being reduced. The end result is that not-for-profits are being increasingly challenged to create new revenue streams and business opportunities. Management teams, largely focused on administrative efficiency and service delivery, now find themselves challenged to become increasingly entrepreneurial if they are to survive and grow. A good example of this entrepreneurial transition is a recent agreement between Sunnybrook Health Sciences Centre, located in Toronto, and Sanofi-aventis, a major pharmaceutical player. Researchers at Sunnybrook have created a breakthrough compound that could help millions of people afflicted with diabetes. The agreement provides Sanofi-aventis with exclusive rights to commercialize a compound, called Vasculotide, that is designed to treat chronic wounds, a major threat to diabetics. The licensing fee, paid in the form of royalties, will return to Sunnybrook Health Sciences Centre much-needed dollars to support continued research and to fund patient care.[16] Other not-for-profits, such as the Salvation Army, the March of Dimes, and the Cerebral Palsy Association of Canada, have developed retail thrift stores as a mechanism for generating revenues to support their organizational missions and financial requirements. As has been stated earlier, the balancing act for not-for-profits seeking additional revenue through the sale of products and/or services is to accomplish this without being perceived as abandoning their mission, and without causing the for-profit sector to challenge their not-for-profit status, and the tax shield that it provides, due to perceived unfair competitive practices. Absent of the ability to seek private-equity investment, and challenged by heightened competition among NFPs for a dwindling pool of philanthropic dollars, not-for-profits increasingly need entrepreneurial ideas and concepts if they are to ensure the long-term sustainability of their organizations.

Management Reflection—The "Go or No Go" Decision

As stated earlier in this chapter, the idea of starting one's own business has tremendous appeal to many individuals. The feeling of being your own boss can be second to none. Having said that, the physical, emotional, and financial stress that it places upon an individual, and his/her family, can be challenging to say the least. An important aspect of assessing a business opportunity is the understanding of the market risk and the level of financial commitment the new business will require. The use of the "capitalization well" (see Figure 15.11), developing a strong feeling for the initial capital requirements at the time of business inception, and the ongoing required cash infusions needed to become cash flow positive and reach the break-even point are essential analytical elements to determining whether a business opportunity can attain the revenue levels required to sustain itself and whether its backers possess the capacity to provide the level of capitalization needed to ensure its formation and operational liquidity and solvency. Financial risk assessment alone, however, does not constitute a formal venture analysis. Investors and/or business analysts must look beyond the numbers and fully analyze other health and performance metrics. Reviewing the product development process, assessing customer connection tactics, critically evaluating the acumen of the management and/or entrepreneurial team, and identifying the specialized assets and employee skill sets needed for success are all fundamental to this analysis.[17] Analysts and investors also need to

FIGURE 15.18 Market/Opportunity Pyramid

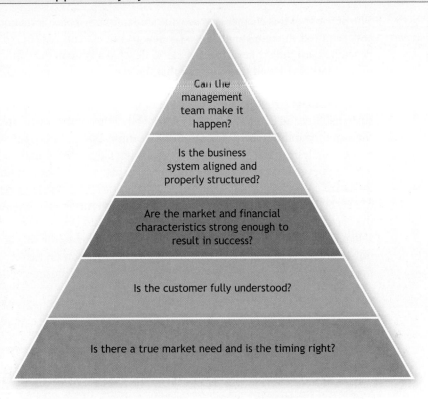

assess the operational capacity of the infrastructure being put into place in order to determine if the financials being projected can actually be realized via the value chain being developed. Venture analysis is all about validating the opportunity, placing this opportunity in context with the external market dynamics within which it will operate, and assessing the people skills on board to seal the deal and drive its execution. The core "go or no go" decision will, ultimately, come down to whether the idea being presented can achieve sufficient scale to ensure short-term initial success and longer-term sustainability. A tool to assist in the conclusion of a "go or no go" decision is what is termed the market/opportunity pyramid (see Figure 15.18). If the response to the five questions posted in the pyramid is yes, then a "go" decision would appear to be the likely conclusion reached.

Chapter Summary

The purpose of this chapter is to provide students with a base-level understanding of the process required to competently assess a new business venture. This process, which has been developed around six key phases, seeks to develop a systematic approach toward the analysis of the market risk and financial risk that the venture will be exposed to. This analytical process also assesses the internal competencies present within the management team, the proposed business structure, and the vision of the entrepreneurs behind the project in terms of sustainability and commitment, thereby enabling the reviewer to draw conclusions relating to the viability and potential success of the venture. The six phases that form this process are market analysis, value analysis, financial analysis, operations analysis, management competency analysis, and exit options. The discussion also recognizes that not all business opportunities are created organically, but that opportunities for acquiring a business form a key part of new business opportunity and growth plans. With this in mind, a preliminary discussion of the approach that individuals and/or businesses should consider when acquiring a business is also provided. The chapter closes with a note pertaining to the role of venture analysis in the not-for-profit sector, and a closing management reflection on the key components that form the decision-making process leading up to a "go or no go" business venture decision.

Developing Business Knowledge and Skills

KEY TERMS

entrepreneur *p. 424*

venture capitalist *p. 429*

litmus test *p. 431*

cash flow positive *p. 434*

start-up costs *p. 435*

capitalization well *p. 435*

undercapitalization *p. 435*

organic growth *p. 442*

acquisition *p. 442*

operational synergies *p. 443*

EBITDA *p. 444*

QUESTIONS FOR DISCUSSION

1. What is meant by the term "fatal flaws"? Why is the identification of fatal flaws so important when assessing a business venture?

2. What type of business venture offers the greatest degree of risk to the entrepreneur? Why is this so?

3. What are the six key phases of business plan assessment? Do you feel that one phase is more important than the others? Why, or why not?

4. What is the purpose of the capitalization well? Why is knowing this information so important to new venture analysis?

5. What additional factors need to be taken into consideration (beyond the six phases of business venture assessment) when considering an acquisition?

6. Why are not-for-profits taking on more entrepreneurial characteristics than ever before?

QUESTIONS FOR INDIVIDUAL ACTION

Assume that you are considering opening a College Pro painting franchise in your home town this summer. Using the six phases of new venture assessment as a guide, prepare a business plan for this potential new venture. Be sure to focus on both market risk and financial risk analysis.

TEAM EXERCISE

Choose a recent public corporate acquisition. Research both the acquiring company and the target company. What reasons were provided for the acquisition? What synergies were identified as key immediate benefits and communicated by the acquiring company to stakeholders at the time of the acquisition? What was the purchase price? How was the acquisition financed? Now, fast-forward to today. Have the synergies that were communicated at the time of the acquisition actually been realized? Is the acquisition believed to be successful in the eyes of the acquiring stakeholders? Prepare a presentation to your class summarizing your conclusions.

Case for Discussion

Knowing that you are currently taking this business course, your sister and her spouse have asked you to evaluate a potential business opportunity they have been researching. Having a strong love of coffee, ample savings, and some experience in the service industry sector, they have been searching for an opportunity that will enable them to test their entrepreneurial spirit and skills. After months of searching, they believe that they have stumbled upon the *perfect* opportunity for a café/bakery/deli-style business.

FRANCHISE OPPORTUNITY

The opportunity they are asking you to formally assess is an investment in a franchise called The Perfect Blend. Franchise marketing literature indicates that The Perfect Blend franchisers can earn upward of an annual 15 percent return on investment (ROI) and achieve annual sales volumes as high as $1.5 million. Quick at math, your sister realizes that 15 percent of an estimated $600 000 investment is $90 000 annually. Not a bad return if everything goes right.

Discussions with the franchisor (The Perfect Blend) have indicated the following franchise-based expenses:

- A one-time franchise fee of $40 000

- Annual "franchise" royalties of 6 percent of gross sales

- Annual "marketing" fund payments of 3 percent of gross sales

THE PERFECT BLEND

The Perfect Blend provides a complete line of coffee, specialty coffees, and food products. The Perfect Blend Café and Bakery franchise was started by two former executives with Tim Hortons, and now total 51 locations across central and western Canada. A product breakdown for the typical Perfect Blend Café and Bakery franchise would be as follows:

- A wide range of coffee and assorted beverages including caffe latte, cappuccino, espresso, steamers, blended teas, frozen drinks, and smoothies.

- "Perfection" sandwiches featuring power breakfast bagel sandwiches, paninis, pitas, wraps, and deli sandwiches including their famous "Montreal smoked meat" sandwich

- Fresh-baked-daily breads, muffins, cookies, pastries, and sweets

- All-natural and organically stocked soups, salads, and California nouvelle cuisine

Although it is recognized that the actual size of The Perfect Blend Café and Bakery franchise will vary by location, most stores are in the 2500-square-foot range.

As was indicated earlier, franchise store revenues for the 51 stores currently operating in Canada have hit as high as $1.5 million. Annual store revenue, on average, however, is generally around the $1.2 million level (in years two and beyond).

YOUR TASK

Excited about the opportunity, your sister and her spouse are all set to write the $40 000 cheque necessary to get their franchise awarded and to begin making their dream of being in business for themselves a reality. An initial trip to the bank, however, has doused their enthusiasm a bit, as the lender is requiring that they create a business plan prior to agreeing to lending them a portion ($350 000) of the estimated dollars needed to buy the equipment and prepare the store for opening day.

QUESTION

Based on the expense information provided below, prepare the following for your sister and her spouse:

a. A projected first-year income statement (before taxes), a cash-flow statement, and an opening day balance sheet

b. Identification of the total potential cost of the investment in year 1, including an estimate of any additional working capital needs

c. The initial BEP (breakeven point) for this venture in $$$

d. Given the bank's limit of $350 000 in financing, how much money do your sister and her spouse have to provide in order to properly finance this start-up?

e. Provide a summary assessment of the risk associated with this business venture. What concerns do you have about this investment, given the financial analysis you have conducted?

APPENDIX: EXPENSE INFORMATION
FINANCIAL CAPACITY

- Your sister and her spouse's pre-approved borrowing line from the bank (conditional upon an acceptable business plan) is $350 000. This would be repaid over 10 years and carries an interest rate of 7.5 percent on the loan. Assuming approval, the first-year loan amortization schedule would be as follows:

  –Annual interest payments in year 1 = $25 421

  –Annual principal repayment in year 1 = $24 333

FIRST-YEAR ESTIMATED SALES

- Initial *first-year sales* for The Perfect Blend franchises are typically around $1 080 000. There have been a few stores, recently, however, whose first-year sales revenue have

reached $1 200 000. Having said this, some franchise store locations have failed to reach $1 000 000 in sales in year 1, with average sales revenue of $950 000.

- The average cheque size per visit per customer is $8.

START-UP COSTS

- The initial investment for equipment, betterments, and improvements is projected to be $500 000.

- Incorporation fees and related professional fees to start the business are estimated at $3500.

- Prepaid expenses (deposits, site reconfiguration, etc.) are $20 000, payable prior to the start of business operations.

- Owner training and pre-opening expenses (at the Winnipeg head office location) are estimated at $10 000.

- Pre-opening inventory, required to be purchased prior to the commencement of operations, would be 1/12th of the annual cost of goods sold.

Operating Expenses

- Annual Direct Operating Expenses (as a percentage of sales) are typically as shown:

–Cost of Goods Sold	34%
–Total Labour	32%
–Royalties	6%
–Perfect Blend Ad Fund	3%
–Local Advertising Expenses	1%
–Misc. Expenses	7%

- Annual Indirect Operating Expenses are estimated to be:

–Lease Costs	$35.00 per square foot*
–Utilities	$ 3.50 per square foot*
–Insurance	$10 000
–Professional Fees	$ 1 500

Depreciation = 10% of total value of equipment (10-yr. straight-line depreciation schedule)

* use average store square footage of 2500 sq. ft., noted above, to project these expenses

Practise and learn online with Connect. Connect resources include additional and interactive study exercises, videos, and practice quizzing, as well as additional material you won't find in the printed text.

Glossary

Accounts Payable refers to money owed by an organization to its suppliers and other short-term service providers.

Accounts Receivable refers to money owed by customers of the organization for products or services that the organization has delivered to such customers, but has not yet received payment for.

Acquisition refers to the process of acquiring another company or operation.

Activity Ratios assist managers in assessing the efficiency and effectiveness of key components of an organization's operations.

Amortization Period refers to the length of time over which a credit facility (loan) will be paid off.

Asset-Based Expenditures are expenditures for the purchase of assets required by a firm in order to support the company's business operations, and which contribute to the firm's ability to earn a profit.

Assets refers to (1) the infrastructure and resource base of the organization; (2) the resources that the organization has at its disposal and that it can utilize in the generation of business activity and, ultimately, profit.

Balance of Trade is the relationship between imports and exports over a defined period of time. A positive balance (where exports exceed imports) is known as a trade surplus. A negative balance (where imports exceed exports) is known as a trade deficit.

Balance Sheet refers to a financial statement that provides managers with an understanding of the resources the organization has at its disposal at a given point in time, and the financial obligations the business has incurred as a result of purchasing these resources.

Black Market is the illegal market that arises within economies where goods are scarce, taxation on such goods is high, or the prices of legitimate goods are beyond the capacity of significant segments of the population to buy.

Board of Directors is an appointed or elected body of a for-profit or not-for-profit corporation that oversees and advises management on issues challenging the organization on behalf of its stakeholders and shareholders.

Bond refers to a credit facility with which an organization borrows money for a stipulated period of time. In return for the use of these funds, the organization promises to pay the holder of the bond an agreed-upon amount of interest at regular intervals (generally, semi-annually) during the period of time for which the funds are borrowed.

Breakeven Point (BEP) is the level of sales revenue or volume that is required for the organization to cover all of its costs.

BTU (British thermal unit) is a measure of heat required to raise the temperature of one pound of water by 1°F.

Business refers to the mission-focused activities aimed at identifying the needs of a particular market or markets, and the development of a solution to such needs through the acquisition and transformation of resources into goods and services that can be delivered to the marketplace at a profit.

Business-Level Strategy outlines specific objectives the organization hopes to achieve for each of its identified business initiatives and/or business units.

Business Model (System) is the operational platform or structure that a business uses to generate revenue and profit.

Buy-Sell Agreement is a written agreement among the partners that details the sale by one partner and the purchase by another of the business interest of the selling partner.

Cannibalism is the reduction in sales of an existing product/service due to the launch of a new, similarly targeted product/service offering.

Capacity refers to the maximum amount of product that can be produced, or services delivered, given facility, equipment, and process constraints.

Capital refers to the money needed by an organization to support asset-based expenditures, meet operating cash requirements, and invest in the development of new products and/or services which the organization desires to introduce into the marketplace.

Capital Asset Evaluation and Acquisition refers to an assessment by the operations management team of the state of current capital assets and a determination as to their applicability to meeting the needs of the organization.

Capital Asset Transactions are the decisions managers make with respect to investment and divestment of capital assets (buildings, equipment, business subsidiaries) that may be needed, or are no longer needed, as part of the organization's business system.

Capital Structure refers to an organization's mixture (use) of debt, internal cash reserves, and external equity-based investments in financial support of operational activities.

Capitalization Well refers to a framework for assessing the full capital requirements of a business venture.

Cash Flow Positive refers to the point where cash inflows finally exceed cash outflows.

Cash from Financing Activities refers to sources of cash flowing into the organization from non-operating activities.

Cash from Investing Activities refers to uses of cash flowing out of the organization from non-operating activities.

Cash from Operational Activities refers to adjustments to net income to reflect the actual cash provided by operating activities.

Cash Operating Cycle (COC) refers to the amount of time it takes for an organization to recover the cash (product is sold and money is received) it has paid out for the development, production, and distribution of products.

Channel Intermediary refers to an organization that assists a company in the distribution and delivery of goods or services to its customers.

Chartered Banks are financial institutions regulated under the Canada Bank Act. Their primary responsibility is to bring together borrowers and lenders by accepting deposits and lending out money—all in a manner that safeguards the interests of their customers.

Code of Conduct is the name for a statement that describes the required responsibilities, actions, and rules of behaviour of an organization's employees.

Collateral refers to capital assets or monetary assets used to secure a credit facility. The collateral would be used to pay off the lender in the event that the organization cannot meet the credit facility repayment obligations.

Collective Entrepreneurship ensures that the involvement of the community where an organization is located and the population that it serves are reflected in the formulation and implementation of the strategy.

Commercial Endeavours refers to the markets the organization serves, the products and services it offers, and the needs it professes to meet in the marketplace.

Comparative Advantage refers to the ability of a country to produce or supply goods or services at a lower cost than other countries or to possess resources or unique services that are unavailable elsewhere.

Competitive Advantage is an advantage an organization has over its competitors that enables it to generate more sales, achieve greater margins, achieve a lower cost base, or attract and retain more customers.

Competitive Emphasis refers to the extent to which the organization rewards and reinforces goal achievement, emphasizes competitiveness (internal and external), and defines its success on the basis of market superiority.

Consumer Price Threshold refers to the maximum price point that the customer is willing to pay for a product or service.

Control Protocols refers to the rigidity or flexibility associated with the application of, and adherence to, rules, policies, and procedures within the organization.

Controlled System refers to an economic system where the fundamentals of the law of supply and demand, private ownership, entrepreneurship, and wealth creation are largely restricted or absent, and the government fully controls the economic direction and activity.

Convenience Goods are goods purchased by customers on a regular basis, with minimum effort and little emotional connection.

Coordination of the Work Effort is the organization and allocation of the HR complement, and the development of the structure surrounding it, in a manner that produces the most effective and efficient business system.

Corporate Level Strategy defines what the organization intends to accomplish and where it plans to compete.

Corporate Social Responsibility (CSR) is the understanding that the purpose of an organization is to create shared value (business and society) by strategically integrating into its actions a partnership mentality with society where the objectives of both parties are met.

Corporation is a business entity that, legally, is separate and distinct from its owners.

Cost of Borrowing refers to the total sum of money over and above the principal borrowed paid by an organization as a result of incurring and repaying a debt obligation. This would include interest paid as well as costs incurred in setting up the credit facility.

Cost of Capital is the cost of company funds (both debt and equity).

Credit Facilities is a general term that describes (1) the variety of loans that could be offered to a business or a country; (2) debt that an organization has taken on in support of its business activities.

Culture defines how the individuals within the organization behave and how the organization as a whole will react to both internal and external challenges and stimuli.

Current Account is a country's net trade in goods and services (balance of trade surplus or deficit), plus net earnings from interest and investments and net transfer payments to and from the rest of the world during the period specified.

Customer Desertion occurs when customers move to a competitive offering due to a change in brand or product communication message focus.

Customer Intimacy is the term for the interactions and connectivity that organizations seek to foster with their customers in order to meet their expectations for contact, service, and support.

Customer Service refers to the support provided to customers before, during, and following the purchase process.

Debt Leverage refers to the use of debt to finance an organization's capital asset base.

Debt Ratios focus on the amount of debt an organization has taken on, the relationship of this debt value against its total asset base, and the ability of the organization to meet its debt servicing (payments) obligations.

Decision-making Control refers to the level of responsibility and decision-making authority that is actually transferred to each specific managerial position.

Degradation is the deterioration of the environment through the depletion of resources and the destruction of ecosystems.

Departmentalization refers to the process of dividing the organization's work units into defined functional areas.

Designated Restricted Assets are assets that have been earmarked for a specific purpose and that are not available for managers to support organizational operating needs.

Direct Costs See Variable Costs.

Direct Distribution refers to connecting directly with customers and handling the final sale of products and/or the delivery of services without the assistance of a channel intermediary.

Directional Lock-in is the level of financial and operational commitment an organization incurs as a result of implementing the organization's strategies.

EBITDA is earnings before interest and taxes + depreciation expense + amortization expense.

Eco-efficiency Management is the tactical shift required within our business operations to maximize the efficiency of our resource utilization and minimize or eliminate the resulting current degradation to the planet.

Economies of Scale are reductions in the cost base of an organization as a result of greater size, process standardization, or enhanced operational efficiencies.

Employee Interaction refers to (1) the level and style of interaction that occurs among employees and between work units and their management teams; (2) the value-creating skills an organization's employees bring to the marketplace. The success of many businesses lies with the specialized skills that exist within its labour force.

Entrepreneur refers to a person who starts a business and is willing to accept the risk associated with investing money in order to make money.

Environmental Stewardship is the integration of sustainability values into the managing of environmental resources.

Ethics is a reflection of the moral principles or beliefs about what an individual views as being right or wrong.

Exchange is an organization that facilitates the trading of securities, stocks, commodities, and other financial instruments. Exchanges provide a platform for selling these financial instruments to the public at large.

Exclusive Distribution refers to a decision by an organization to offer its products and/or services through a single market representative.

Expense Creep refers to the tendency for expenses associated with the organization's various cost lines to rise due to inflationary pressures, union negotiated contracts, and so on.

Facility Design and Layout refers to infrastructure layout and related facility components that will be required to house and support the processes and materials used by the organization.

Feed-in Tariffs are government payment subsidy arrangements whereby participants are paid a guaranteed premium for energy developed through the adoption of alternate energy sources.

Financial Protectionism refers to government actions or policies that restrict or restrain the outflow of funds from one economy to another.

Fixed Costs (also referred to as indirect costs) are those costs that, although not directly tied to the manufacturing of a specific product or the delivery of a specified service, nonetheless exist as a result of conducting our business and operating our company.

For-Profit Companies are organizations whose overarching objective is profitability and wealth creation on behalf of their shareholders and stakeholders.

Forecasting and Budgeting refers to management's ability to project forward anticipated results for the upcoming quarter, year, or planning-cycle period.

Foreign Direct Investment (FDI) occurs when a company or individual from one country makes an investment into a business within another country. This investment can reflect the physical ownership of productive assets or the purchase of a significant interest in the operations of a business.

Forensic Accounting is the integration of accounting, auditing, and investigative skills.

Free Trade Agreements facilitate international trade between companies that is not constrained or regulated by governments, and that is not impacted via the use of tariffs, duties, or other monetary restrictions.

G7/8 a quasi-organization comprising the world's major fully developed economies. The G7 consists of the United States, Japan, Germany, Great Britain, France, Italy, and Canada. In 2006, the G7 transitioned to the G7/8 with the inclusion of Russia into its membership. Heads of the G7/8 countries meet at least once annually to discuss major economic, political, and societal issues challenging the global marketplace. Recent meeting trends have also resulted in representatives of major developing economies (such as China) attending at least part or all of such summit meetings.

Gantt Chart is a methodology used to schedule the steps associated with a project and the time required to complete each step.

GDP (Gross Domestic Product) refers to the total market value of the goods and services (economic output) a nation produces domestically over a period of time (generally one calendar year).

Gross Profit Margin is the portion of an organization's revenue that is left over after the organization has paid the direct costs (wages, components, materials, etc.) associated with its products or services.

Harvesting is a strategy that reflects a reduced commitment to a particular market given its perceived weak future growth or profitability potential.

Hostile Takeover refers to an attempt by a company to take over another company whose management and board of directors are unwilling to agree to the merger or takeover.

Inbound Logistics refers to the management of supplier relationships relating to those parts and/or components, or finished products, that are brought into the organization in order to produce finished products for delivery to the marketplace.

Income Statement is the financial statement that responds to the question of whether our business is earning a profit as a result of the sales we have made versus the expenses we have incurred in developing our goods and services and delivering them to the marketplace.

Incorporation is the legal process of setting up a corporation.

Indirect Costs *See* Fixed Costs.

Indirect Distribution implies the use of a channel intermediary, such as a broker, wholesaler, or retailer, to facilitate the sales of a company's products and/or services to its customers.

Inflation is a rise in the level of prices of goods and services within an economy over a period of time.

Initial Public Offering (IPO) refers to the initial sale of stock, by a corporation, through a public exchange.

Integrity is honesty, reliability, ethics, moral judgment.

Intensive Distribution is a decision by an organization to distribute the product and/or service through as many locations or channel outlets as is possible.

IPO (Initial Public Offering) is the sale of a company's stock for the first time in the public marketplace with the intent to raise equity (money) to fund company operations and growth.

ISO (International Organization for Standardization) is the world's largest developer and publisher of international standards.

Joint and Several Liability refers to the liability obligation of partners as the result of a legal contract. Partners can be held individually liable for their share of the obligation (several), or fully liable for the full obligation (joint) in the event that the other parties to the agreement are unable to pay their obligations.

Junk Bonds refers to a high probability of default; commonly referred to as speculative bonds due to their potential for default on either their interest rate or principal payment obligations.

Kyoto Protocol is the 1997 (effective 2005) international agreement that binds participating nations into stabilizing and reducing greenhouse gas (GHG) emissions.

Labour refers to the human resource requirements of the business.

Law of Supply and Demand refers to the ability of the market, independent of external influences, to determine the price for which a product or service will be bought and sold.

Leverage refers to the amount of debt an organization uses in order to finance its asset base.

Liabilities are the debts or financial obligations that an organization has incurred as a result of conducting its business.

Limited Liability Partnership is a partnership that is made up of both general partners (at least one) and limited (passive) partners.

Line of Credit refers to an arrangement with a lending institution that provides an organization with a pre-arranged borrowing ceiling (maximum) that the organization can draw on at any time, and in any amount, up to the agreed-upon limit.

Liquidity refers to the cash position of a company and its ability to meet its immediate debt and operational obligations. It also refers to the ability of the company to convert existing assets to cash in order to meet such obligations.

Litmus Test   refers to a process or something that is used to make a judgment or draw conclusions about the acceptability of an opinion.

Long-Term Credit Facilities   represent debt that an organization obligates itself to repay over a time frame that exceeds one year.

Long-Term Note   refers to a credit facility under which an organization borrows a stipulated amount of money for a defined period of time (which exceeds one year), and with a defined interest rate schedule (fixed or variable).

Managerial Acumen   refers to the foresight, drive, knowledge, ability, decision-making competency, and ingenuity of the organization's key individuals—its owners or top-level managers.

Managerial Hierarchy   refers to the number of levels of management deemed necessary to effectively manage the organization, and the sequential ranking of the managerial positions in relationship to one another.

Market Capitalization Value   refers to the current market value of an organization. It is calculated by taking the number of shares outstanding multiplied by the current value of its shares.

Market Segment   is a portion of the market that is deemed to possess unique characteristics businesses can target in order to generate a preference for their products and/or services.

Marketing   is the process through which organizations design, develop, and communicate the value of their products and/or services.

Marketing Mix   refers to an organization's strategic and tactical decisions relating to its product/service offerings, pricing, distribution, and marketing communication efforts and approaches.

Marketing and Sales   refers to those activities that create profile and awareness for the organization's products, services, or brand(s), and the benefits derived from the acquisition and use of such products or services.

Mark-up   refers to the addition to the manufacturer's price that distributors add to the price of a product to ensure that their own direct and indirect costs are covered and that their profit margin is achieved.

Materials Management   refers to the management of the inputs required in order to develop the products or services that the organization is intent on delivering to the marketplace.

Message Rifling   is a focused message, driven by a well-defined and developed value proposition, that is targeted specifically at a defined audience.

Mission   defines an organization's purpose or reason for existence.

Mixed Distribution Systems   are distribution systems that incorporate both direct and indirect distribution options within their distribution strategy.

Mixed Economic System   refers to an economic system that contains components of both open and controlled systems. It includes the core principles of economic freedom, with some degree of centralized economic planning and government regulation and involvement.

Monopolistic Markets   are markets that possess a number of different suppliers of products and services, but the nature of the product or service, along with the marketing effort initiated by businesses within the sector, has enabled true differentiation to set in.

Monopoly-based Markets   are markets that are served by a single product/service supplier.

Mortgage   refers to a credit facility that is backed by real estate collateral (generally, the real estate the mortgage underwrites), and that sets forth a defined schedule of periodic payments for the full repayment of the debt owed, plus interest, over a defined period of time.

Multi-Channel Distribution   refers to the incorporation of a number of different channel connections through which customers can purchase a product and/or service.

Nature of the Work   refers to the specific tasks that need to be accomplished at the individual job level within the organization.

Net Change in Cash Position   refers to the net movement in the cash position of the organization based on operating, financing, and investing activities.

Not-for-Profit Organizations (NFPs)   are organizations whose overarching objective is not profitability and wealth creation but to deliver services to the people, groups, and communities that they serve via a model of collective interest and social goal achievement.

Offshoring   is transferring a component (operations, service, support) of a firm's business system to another country for the purpose of reducing costs, improving efficiency or effectiveness, or developing a competitive advantage.

Oligopoly-based Markets   are markets that contain a small number of suppliers that control a large percentage of market share within the market, and that compete on the basis of products and/or services that have achieved success in distinguishing themselves from their competitors.

Open System   refers to an economic system that adheres to the principles of economic freedom: the law of supply and demand, full and open access to the principles of private ownership, entrepreneurship, and wealth creation, and an absence of regulation on the part of government.

Operating Expenditures   are expenses incurred as a result of a company performing its normal business operations.

Operating Plan   is a detailed, immediate-term set of objectives and corresponding tactics designed to achieve a specific business initiative.

Operating Profits   equal total revenue minus total operating expenses.

Operational Synergies   refers to maximization of productivity and efficiency through the combining of resources.

Operational Transactions   represent the flow of money within the organization that is directly related to day-to-day business dealings.

Operations   refers to the manufacturing and/or product change processes set up to ensure that the final product the organization is manufacturing or handling is ready for the marketplace.

Operations Cycle   is the alignment of the operational tasks within an organization by its management team in order to meet the strategic outcomes defined in the organization's business strategy.

Operations Management   is the effective design, development, and management of the processes, procedures, and practices embedded within an organization's business system for the purpose of achieving its strategic intent.

Organic Growth   refers to growth that comes from an organization's existing business portfolio.

Organizational Efficiency and Structure is a reflection of the complexities of the business activities that circulate within an organization.

Outbound Logistics refers to getting the finished product to the customer via a distribution channel that is accessible, convenient, and able to minimize stockouts and other sales impediment factors.

Outsourcing is contracting out a portion of, or a component of, a firm's business system for the purpose of reducing costs, improving efficiency or effectiveness, acquiring expertise, or developing a competitive advantage.

Over-the-Counter (OTC) refers to stocks being publicly traded through a dealer network versus an exchange.

Owners' Equity represents the value of capital received from the owners of the business that is used to fund the start-up or ongoing operations of the business, as well as reflecting the value of the organization's retained earnings.

Parity means being equal or equivalent to; specifically, the value of one currency being equal to that of another.

Partnership is a business organization that is formed by two or more individuals.

Partnership Agreement is a written agreement among the partners that outlines the expectations of each partner and details how the partnership is going to work.

Payback Period represents the length of time required to recover, or earn back, the cost of an investment.

Peak Model Theories are based on the belief that resources are finite and that, at some point in time, the availability of such resources will pass their maximum production point and begin to decline.

Personal Power is the power that a manager possesses as a result of his/her leadership competencies. It is the ability to motivate, facilitate, demonstrate empathy, and collaborate with staff in order to meet organizational expectations.

PERT Chart is a scheduling methodology that focuses on task sequencing and the identification of the critical path of steps that will most greatly impact the ability to complete a project, and the length of time needed for completion.

PESTEL Analysis refers to a macro-level assessment of the political, economic, social, technology, environmental, and legal trends that can or will impact the markets within which an organization competes.

Philanthropy refers to the receipt of funds from another person or organization for the purpose of using them to enhance the well-being of others.

Ponzi Scheme is a type of investment fraud that involves the payment of purported returns to existing investors from funds contributed by new investors.

Position Power is the power that a manager legitimately holds due to the title he/she has within an organization. This power is derived on the basis of expertise, legitimacy of rank, the ability to control rewards and resources, and the obligation to assess performance.

Positioning is the ability of an organization to develop a unique, credible, sustainable, and valued place in the minds of our customers for its brand, products, and/or services.

PPP (Purchasing Power Parity) a measure that takes into account the relative cost of living and the inflation rates of each country, and adjusts the total value of economic activity accordingly.

Predetermined Purchase List refers to the ranking of products/services that purchasers develop for all the options available when making a purchase decision.

Price Dilution means that the price of existing shares of stock will decline due to the fact that a larger number of shares (which represent ownership in the company) now exist.

Price Discounting is a reduction in the price of the product with the intent to stimulate the sale of the product over a defined period of time.

Price Elasticity is the change in demand that is anticipated to occur at the various price points the organization is considering for its product and/or service.

Price Skimming refers to the utilization of a premium price strategy in order to maximize the margin return on the sale of each individual unit of a particular product.

Primary Activities relate to the specific activities through which the development and transformation of a product or service occurs as it is produced and delivered to the marketplace.

Primary Sources of Information are those that an organization develops or utilizes to generate information specific to the organization and the products and services it offers.

Prime Lending Rate refers to the base lending rate used by banks. It is also often interpreted to be the rate at which banks lend money to their most preferred customers.

Principal refers to the amount borrowed or the amount remaining on a loan separate from the cost of borrowing, as represented by the interest expense charges applicable to the credit facility (loan).

Private Corporations are corporations whose ownership is private. The shares of stock of the corporation are not publicly traded.

Private Equity refers to equity capital that is obtained by an organization from private sources (not through one of the public exchanges).

Private Label Brands are products that are created by one company for sale by another company under this latter company's own brand name.

Process Design, Layout, and Execution refers to the assessment and implementation of the tasks necessary to get the required work accomplished, and how such tasks will be grouped and sequenced to ensure that the most efficient and effective processes are utilized in the production of products and/or services.

Process Management is the design and development of the work flow and connectivity of the transformation requirements (processes) needed to ensure that an organization's products and services are efficiently produced and effectively delivered to the marketplace.

Process Simplification is the design and utilization of a minimum number of tasks when developing products and/or services.

Process Standardization is the design and utilization of common platforms and common task sequencing to produce/develop a variety of products or services.

Product/Service Management refers to the variety of activities that commence with the design and development of potential new products in R&D and extend to the post-purchase support of products/services now in the hands of customers.

Productivity Cycle includes the processes involved in transforming materials into a product or service available for sale in the marketplace.

Profit is the "bottom line" result an organization has realized for an identified, immediate period of time. In simple terms, Total Revenue − Total Expenses = Profit.

Profit Leaks are inefficiencies within an organization's marketing mix that result in margin erosion and loss of profit.

Profitability measures how well a company is using its resources over a specific period of time to generate earnings relative to its competitors.

Profitability Margin is the portion of an organization's revenue that is left after all operating expenses associated with its products or services have been paid.

Profitability Ratios focus on assessing the amount of income the organization has earned in comparison to the operating activity that has taken place and the assets that have been used to support its generation.

Prospectus refers to a legal document to be filed with the securities commission that has jurisdiction for the share issuance; it provides information relating to the current financial stability of the company and the intent of the share issuance, thereby enabling investors to make an informed decision on the risk associated with the purchase of the shares being offered.

Protectionism is the outcome of the intent of economic policies that are put in place to protect or improve the competitiveness of domestic industries via impeding or restricting the openness of a market or markets to foreign competitors through the use of tariffs, trade restrictions, quotas, artificial control of currency values, or other related activities.

Psychological Pricing is the utilization of pricing tactics that are designed to respond to the psychological tendencies of purchasers.

Public Corporations are corporations whose shares of stock are traded on at least one stock exchange or are publicly available in the over-the-counter market.

Public Equity refers to equity investments in an organization, by investors, as a result of the purchase of publicly traded shares (stock) due to an initial public offering (IPO) or an additional public offering (APO), also referred to as a secondary offering.

Purely Competitive Markets are markets that are characterized by a number of similar (undifferentiated) products or services, the absence of a dominant market leader, and few barriers to entry.

Rating Agencies refers to organizations that offer an objective and independent creditworthiness assessment of an organization's solvency, liquidity, and overall long-term organizational health.

Ratios seek to define the relationship between critical components of information found on the financial statements.

Rebate refers to a temporary price reduction offered on a product or service in order to stimulate sales. Rebates can be offered at the point of sale or on a deferred basis (example: mail-in).

Recession is a period of time that marks a contraction in the overall economic activity within an economy. A recession is typically believed to occur when an economy experiences two or more quarters of negative GDP movement.

Resource Management is the ability to actively manage existing supplies and regenerate new supplies of materials in such a way that we minimize resource depletion.

Restructuring addresses the need to change an organization's business system or desired position in the marketplace, or to make fundamental changes to the way an organization does business.

Retained Earnings refers to the dollar amount of net earnings accumulated over the history of an organization that it has chosen to hold within the organization.

Risk Allowance refers to the degree of entrepreneurship that is embedded into the organization.

Rootedness refers to the extent to which the NFP is interwoven into the fabric of the community that it serves and is supported by a broad representation of its organizations, businesses, and citizens.

Secondary Offering refers to an additional public offering of an organization's stock for the purpose of raising new capital.

Secondary Sources of Information are those that already exist and are available at no cost or on a fee basis; managers use these information sources to conduct research and draw conclusions.

Segmentation refers to determining the best way to divide the market in a manner that will result in a better understanding of potential customer needs, interests, preferences, attitudes, and behaviours.

Segmentation Stretch refers to expanding the focus of a product/service to similar and related market segments that share a positive affinity for the product/service offering.

Selective Distribution refers to a decision by an organization to sell its products and/or services through a limited number of channel intermediaries.

Short-Term Credit Facilities refers to debt obligations that an organization takes on for a short period of time, generally less than one year.

Silo Mentality refers to managerial decisions that do not take into consideration the cross-organizational impact that such decisions will have.

Six Sigma is a methodology that focuses on a philosophy of total improvement.

Sole Proprietorship refers to a business that is owned by one person and that is initiated without a requirement to create a separate legal entity.

Solvency and Liquidity Ratios analyze the financial obligations that an organization has against its financial resources in order to determine whether the organization possesses sufficient capital to meet its upcoming needs.

Solvency refers to the long-term stability of the company and its ability to meet its ongoing debt and operational obligations, and to fund future growth.

Sovereign Debt is debt issued or guaranteed by a national government.

Sovereign Wealth Funds are country- or state-owned investment funds.

Span of Control refers to the number of subordinates a manager has reporting to him or her.

Stakeholders refers to individuals, groups, or organizations that have a direct or indirect relationship with an organization, and that can be impacted by its policies, actions, and decisions. Stakeholders could include customers, suppliers, government, employees, and so on.

Start-up Costs are the initial capital investment required to launch a new business or product venture.

Statement of Cash Flows provides managers with a full understanding of the total movement of cash (from all sources) into and out of the business.

Stock is a security that represents a percentage of ownership in a corporation's assets, and entitlement to a pro-rata claim on earnings when released.

Stockholders refers to any person, company, or organization that owns at least one share of stock in a specific company.

Strategy refers to the development of plans and decisions that will guide the direction of the firm and determine its long-term performance.

Structure is the formal framework around which tasks are organized and responsibilities allocated within an organization.

Supply Chain Management is the management of the interdependencies among suppliers, manufacturers, and distributors; it seeks to develop the terms and conditions that will enable all parties to efficiently and effectively meet their obligations to one another due to their business relationships.

Supply Chain Operating Execution refers to the execution of the specific tasks necessary to ensure that key performance results are achieved.

Supply Chain Performance Evaluation refers to the critical outcomes that the supply chain must achieve in support of the organization's overall operating performance.

Support Activities are those areas within the organization that are not directly associated with the actual processes the organization uses to produce products and/or deliver services but that are an integral part of the support structure the primary activities rely on to successfully execute strategy.

SWOT stands for strengths, weaknesses, opportunities, and threats.

Tactics refers to the immediate-term actions which a firm executes in order to meet the short-term objectives set forth in the current planning cycle.

Target Marketing is the process whereby organizations determine which market segments represent the strongest clustering of potential customers who are most likely to purchase the product and who have the capacity to do so.

TQM (Total Quality Management) is a broad-based approach to managing quality within the organization.

Undercapitalization is the situation where a company lacks the required funding to continue business activities.

Value Chain is the term for the processes and initiatives needed to support and direct the product/service transformation within the organization, the creation of the value proposition applicable to such products/services, and the distribution, marketing, sales, and service in support of these products/services.

Value Maximization refers to maximizing the benefits (price/quality comparison) that an individual or set of customers will realize as a result of using a product or service.

Value Proposition is a statement that summarizes whom a product/service is geared toward and the benefits the pur-

chaser will realize as a result of using the product.

Variable Costs (also referred to as direct costs) are those costs that are directly tied to the manufacturing of a product or the delivery of a service depending on the type of business being assessed.

Venture Capitalist refers to an individual who provides capital to a business venture for start-up or expansion purpose.

Vision is a forward-thinking statement that defines what a company wants to become and where it is going.

Vitality refers to the ability of the NFP to grow and sustain its membership base and donor base.

Whistleblowing is the process through which an individual informs someone in authority of a dishonest act or the dishonest behaviour of another person.

Work Efficiencies refers to the alignment of the tasks required to support the design, development, marketing, distribution, and sale of an organization's products/services in the most efficient and effective manner possible.

Endnotes

Chapter 1

1. Gareth R. Jones, *Introduction to Business: How Companies Create Value for People,* McGraw-Hill Irwin, 2007, pp. 4–33.

2. Peter Richardson & Ken Wong, Queen's Strategy Workbook, Queen's University.

3. Research In Motion, www.rim.com/company/index.shtml, accessed June 2008; and Research In Motion, http://finance.google.comp/finance?q=TSE%3ARIM, accessed June 2008.

4. Apple Inc., http://finance.yahoo.com/q?s=AAPL, accessed June 2008; and Apple Inc., http://finance.google.com/finance?q=NASDAQ%3AAPL, accessed June 2008.

5. Brenda Welch, "Toyota Builds for a Greener Future, Corporate Caring," *Montreal Gazette,* May 10, 2008, p. A17.

6. QMI Agency, "Target Acquisition Highlights Canada's Allure for Foreign Retailers," *Toronto Sun,* January 14, 2011, www.torontosun.com; and Strauss & McNish, "With Target, Canada's Retail Landscape Set for Massive Makeover," *The Globe and Mail,* January 13, 2011, www.theglobeandmail.com.

7. Ken Wong, Queen's University, Instructional Slides, MBUS 800, Role of the General Manager, 2006–2008.

8. Tim Hortons, www.timhortons.com, accessed June 2008 and May 2010.

9. Booster Juice, www.boosterjuice.com, accessed June 2008 and May 2010.

10. The Airbus 380, http://www.airliners.net/aircraft-data/stats.mai?id=29, accessed June 11, 2008; and Nelson D. Schwartz, "Airbus: Losing Altitude," CNNMoney.com, *Fortune,* July 25, 2006.

Chapter 2

1. G7/8, http://www.g7.utoronto.ca/what_is_g8.html, July 27, 2009.

2. Foreign Affairs and International Trade Canada, State of Trade and Investment Update 2009, www.international.gc.ca/economist-economiste/performance, May 26, 2010; and Economic Research, BMO Capital Markets, June 22, 2007.

3. Michael Porter, Diamond Model, Competitive Advantage of Nations Diamond Model, http://www.valuebasedmanagement.net/methods_porter_diamond_model.html, accessed August 22, 2008.

4. Statistics Canada, Foreign Direct Investment, www.statcan.gc.ca, May 26, 2010; Foreign Affairs and International Trade Canada, State of Trade and Investment Update 2009, www.international.gc.ca/economist-economiste/performance, May 26, 2010; and Investment Partnerships Canada, Policy Group, Role of Foreign Direct Investment in Canada, accessed August 5, 2008.

5. Historical Price Charts, www.OntarioGasPrices.com, May 18, 2011.

6. Bannock, Baxter, and Davis, *Dictionary of Economics,* 7th Edition, Penguin Books.

7. Bank of Canada, About the Bank, www.bankofcanada.ca, accessed August 6, 2008.

8. TradingEconomics, Global Economics Research, Canada and USA Gross Domestic Product (GDP), www.tradingeconomics.com/economics/gdp/cad, May 18, 2011; and Gross Domestic Product, Nominal and Real of Canada, 1998–2005, http://www.sjsu.edu/faculty/watkins/canadagdp.htm, accessed August 14, 2008.

9. TradingEconomics, Global Economics Research, Canada and USA GDP Growth Rate, www.tradingeconomics.com/economics/gdp/cad, May 18, 2011.

10. Statistics Canada, Canadian Economic Accounts, First Quarter 2009, *The Daily,* June 1, 2009, www.statcan.gc.ca; and Gordon Isfeld, "Statistics Canada Corrects GDP Figures for 2010," *Financial Post,* www.vancouversun.com, May 11, 2011.

11. TradingEconomics, Global Economics Research, Canada and USA Gross Domestic Product (GDP), www.tradingeconomics.com/economics/gdp/cad, May 18, 2011; TradingEconomics,

Global Economics Research, Canada and USA GDP Growth Rate, www.tradingeconomics. com/economics/gdp/cad, May 18, 2011; and Gross Domestic Product, Nominal and Real of Canada, 1998–2005, http://www.sjsu.edu/faculty/watkins/canadagdp.htm, accessed August 14, 2008.

12. Alberta Economic Quick Facts, Alberta Finance and Enterprise, Government of Alberta, February 2010, www.finance.alberta.ca, May 26, 2010; Alberta Economic Quick Facts, Alberta Finance and Enterprise, Government of Alberta, May 2009, www.albertacanada.ca, May 2009; and 2007 Alberta Budget Report, BDO Dunwoody, April 19, 2007, http://www.bdo.ca/library/publications/tax/budgets/2007/alberta.cfm, accessed August 22, 2008.

13. Lynne Olver, Reuters, Canadian Banks Seen Hitting U.S. Acquisition Trail, Canada.com, accessed August 6, 2008; and "Scotiabank Expanding in Costa Rica," www.cbc.ca/money/story, June 13, 2006, accessed August 6, 2008.

14. Gordon Isfeld, "Statistics Canada Corrects GDP Figures for 2010," *Financial Post,* www.vancouversun. com, May 11, 2011; Economic Forecast, Table 1, Key Economic Indicators, Forecast Completed June 18, 2008, The Conference Board of Canada, p. 40; and Economic Forecast, Table 2, Gross Domestic Product, Expenditure Based, at Market Prices (2002 $millions), The Conference Board of Canada, p. 41.

15. "Food for Thought," The Chartist, *Fortune,* May 2, 2011.

16. Currency Calculator—Stockgroup.financialpost.com, accessed August 6, 2008.

17. Peter Franklin, Osler, Hoskin & Hartcourt LLP, "Canada: Wilson Report Recommends Far-Reaching Changes to Canadian Investment and Competition Laws," July 17, 2008, Mondaq, http://www.mondaq.com/article.asp?articleid+63368, accessed August 9, 2008.

18. "Stores to Reduce Energy Use (Walmart)," *Toronto Star,* Canada-Retail, August 27, 2008, p. B2.

19. Aging Workforce News, Canada: Oil Industry Facing Skills Shortage, www.agingworkforcenews. com, March 29, 2011; and David Friend, "Canadian Workforce Aging Rapidly," www.thestar.com, March 4, 2008.

20. Biz Fact, Breakdown of Canadian Businesses by Number of Employees, CFIB, Sun Media, July 7, 2009.

21. Economic Research, BMO Capital Markets, June 22, 2007; and TradingEconomics, Global Economics Research, Canada and USA Gross Domestic Product (GDP), www.tradingeconomics.com/economics/gdp/cad, May 18, 2011.

22. Michael Porter, Five Competitive Forces Model, Value Based Management.net, http://www.valuebasedmanagement.net/methods_porter_five_forces.html, accessed August 22, 2008.

23. How Many Americans Have a Passport, www.theexpeditioner.com/2010/02/17, updated January 6, 2011.

24. Currency Converter, Exchange Rates, www.bankofcanada.ca, May 2011.

25. Economic Spotlight, Alberta Finance, Budget and Fiscal Planning, June 28, 2007; Amanda Ferguson, "Alberta Budget Surplus Hits $4.6 Billion Mark," www.ctvedmonton.ca, June 24, 2008; 2007 Alberta Budget Report, BDO Dunwoody, April 19, 2007, http://www.bdo.ca/library/publications/tax/budgets/2007/alberta.cfm, accessed August 22, 2008; Government of Alberta, Budget 2009, http://alberta.ca, May 26, 2010; Government of Alberta, Budget 2010, http://alberta.ca, May 26, 2010; and Highlights of the Alberta Economy, Alberta Finance and Enterprise, Enterprise Division, March 2009.

Chapter 3

1. Lululemon Athletica Inc., www.reuters.com, May 14, 2010; Lululemon Athletica Inc., Our Company History, www.lululemon.com, August 5, 2009; and Lululemon Athletica Inc., www.googlefinance.com, May 14, 2010.

2. Wal-Mart Stores Inc., Annual Income Statement, Google Finance, www.googlefinance.com, May 19, 2011.

3. "Magna Changes Final Offer for Opel—Govt Source," www.wsj.com, July 28, 2009.

4. "The World's 500 Largest Companies," *Fortune,* Volume 160, Number 2, July 20, 2009; and Fortune Global 500, www.fortune.com, July 28, 2009.

5. Sheridan Prasso, "American Made, Chinese Owned," *Fortune,* May 24, 2010.

6. Vanderklippe and Hoffman, "China Makes Billion-Dollar Oil Patch Move," *The Globe and Mail Report on Business,* May 13, 2010.

7. Shawn McCarthy, "Canada a Quiet Powerhouse in Africa's Mining Sector," *The Globe and Mail,* May 10, 2010.

8. "American Made, Chinese Owned."

9. CAE Inc., www.cac.com; and www.Googlefinance.com, May 14, 2010.

10. Ibid.

11. Prospects for the Global Economy, The World Bank, GDP at Market Prices, http://web.worldbank. org, August 9, 2009; Stephen Poloz, Canada and the New Trade Paradigm, EDC, Global Business Session, Queen's University, August 4, 2009.

12. Jeff Immelt, "Time to Re-embrace Globalisation," *The Economist,* The World in 2009 print edition, Nov. 19, 2008.

13. The World Trade Organization...In Brief, www.wto.org, July 2009.

14. International Monetary Fund (IMF), www.imf.org, August 11, 2009; and Sharon Singleton, QMI Agency, "Hunt On for New IMF Boss," *Kingston Whig-Standard,* May 21, 2011.

15. World Bank, www.worldbank.org, August 11, 2009.

16. "In Italy's Piracy Culture, Black Market Is Thriving," *New York Times,* www.nytimes.com.

17. "Judge in Massachusetts Download Case Rules for Music Companies," *USA Today,* July 31, 2009, www.usatoday.com.

18. Trading Economics, China GDP, Exports, Imports, Government Budget, www.tradingeconomics. com, August 11, 2009; and China, CIA World Fact Book, www.cia.gov, August 11, 2009.

19. G20, www.g20.org, July 28, 2009.

20. "The Spend Is Nigh, Rebalancing the World Economy," *The Economist,* July 25, 2009 and August 1, 2009; Peter Bisson, Elizabeth Stephenson, S. Patrick Viguerie, "Global Forces: An Introduction," *McKinsey Quarterly,* McKinsey & Company, June 2010; Canada Goose—Our Story, www.canada-goose.com, May 2011; European Union, http://europa.eu/abc/index_en.htm, August 8, 2009; US GDP 2008, https://www.cia.gov/library/publications/the-world-factbook/geos/us.html; and European Union, GDP 2008, https://www.cia.gov/library/publications/the-world-factbook/ geos/eu.html.

21. "Canada Plays Catch-up in Race for Trade with China," *The Globe and Mail,* August 10, 2009.

22. Economic Development Canada (EDC), www.edc.ca, August 6, 2009.

23. "CIC, Sovereign Wealth Fund," *Globe and Mail Report on Business,* August 12, 2009.

24. "The Ambition of Geely," *The Economist,* August 1–7, 2009.

Chapter 4

1. The Conference Board of Canada, Environment, Water Consumption, www.conferenceboard.ca/ hcp/details/environment/water-consumption.aspx, March 2011.

2. Program on Water Governance, Factsheet: Water Use and Consumption in Canada, Shrubsole and Draper, *Water (Ab)uses and Management in Canada,* UBC Press, 2007, www.watergovenance.ca/ factsheet, March 2011.

3. The Conference Board of Canada, Environment, Water Consumption, www.conferenceboard.ca/ hcp/details/environment/water-consumption.aspx, March 2011; Program on Water Governance, Factsheet: Water Use and Consumption in Canada, Shrubsole and Draper, *Water (Ab)uses and Management in Canada,* UBC Press, 2007, www.watergovenance.ca/factsheet, March 2011; and Canada vs. the OECD: An Environmental Comparison, OECD Environmental Data 1999, www. environmentalindicators.com, March 2011.

4. The Sustainability Business Report, Natural Capitalism, www.sustreport.org/business, March 2011; The Sustainable Development Journey, BSD Global, www.iisd.org/business/sd_journey.aspx, March 2011; and McDonough & Braungart, "The NEXT Industrial Revolution," *The Atlantic Online,* www.theatlantic.com/past/docs/issues/98oct/industry.htm. March 2011.

5. Ben Block, U.N. Raises "Low" Population Projections for 2050, World Watch Institute, March 28, 2011, www.worldwatch.org/node/6038, March 2011.

6. "One Degree Over, Climate Change on Crop Yields," *The Economist,* Science and Technology, March 19, 2011.

7. Beinhocker and Oppenheim, "Building a Post-Carbon Economy," McKinsey&Company, February 2009, http://whatmatters.mckinseydigital.com/climate_change/building-a-postcarbon-economy, March 2011.

8. International Agencies Promote Global Revolution in Vehicle Fuel Economy, Global Fuel Economy Initiative News Release, January 25, 2011.

9. Impact of Deforestation, Atmospheric Role of Forests, Mongabay.com, http://rainforests.mongabay.com, March 2011; Deforestation, National Geographic.com, http://environmenta.nationalgeographic.com/environment/globalwarming/deforestation/overview, March 2011; and 10 Countries with Highest Deforestation Rates in the World, www.forestforclimate.org, September 2009.

10. McCartor & Becker, World's Worst Pollution Problems 2010, Top 6 Toxic Threats, Blacksmith Institute, New York, NY, USA.

11. Andrea Thompson, Pollution May Cause 40 Percent of Global Deaths, www.lifescience.com, September 2007.

12. Peter Goodchild, Depletion of Key Resources: Facts at Your Fingertips, www.culturalchange.org, January 2010.

13. Averting the Next Energy Crisis: The Demand Challenge, McKinsey Global Institute, McKinsey & Company, March 2009.

14. UNEP Warns of Fish Stock Depletion, 2010 United Press International, www.upi.com/news/resource-wars/2010, December 29, 2010.

15. Jenny Higgins, Economic Impacts of Cod Moratorium, Newfoundland and Labrador Heritage Website, www.heritage.nf.ca/society/moratorium_impacts, 2008.

16. Peter Goodchild, Depletion of Key Resources.

17. David Hopkins, Depletion of Water Resources More Serious Than Oil Reserves, www.edie.net/news, February 18, 2005; Alex Hutchinson, "Las Vegas Tries to Prevent a Water Shortage," *Popular Mechanics,* www.popularmechanics.com/science/environment, October 1, 2009; and Dan Shapley, Natural Resources Being Depleted at Record Rates, Vital Signs Report, www.thedailygreen.com, www.thedailygreen.com/environmental-news/laterst/6628, 2011.

18. Dobbs, Lund, Schreiner, "How the Growth of Emerging Markets Will Strain Global Finance," *McKinsey Quarterly,* McKinsey & Company, December 2010.

19. Dobbs, Spence, "The Era of Cheap Capital Draws to a Close," *McKinsey Quarterly,* McKinsey & Company, February 2011.

20. ExxonMobil Algae Biofuels Research and Development Program, www.exxonmobil.com/corporate/files/news_pub_algae_factsheet.pdf; ExxonMobil Plans $600M Investment in Biofuels, Environment News Service, www.ens-newswire.com/ens/jul2009; and Katie Howell, "Exxon Sinks $600M into Algae-Based Biofuels in Major Strategy Shift," *Greenwire,* www.nytimes.com/gwire/2009/07/14.

21. Canon, Ecosense Green Branding Strategy, ShareGreen Sustainable Business Practices, Case Studies, www.sharegreen.ca, April 2011.

22. Berns, Townend, Khayat, Balagopal, Reeves, Hopkins, Kruschwitz, *The Business of Sustainability, Imperatives, Advantages, and Actions,* The Boston Consulting Group, September 2009.

23. "The Colour of Money, Wyoming Hot Springs Transformation from Coins Tossed by Tourists," Dreamstime, *Toronto Star,* April 9, 2011.

24. Joe Castaldo, "Special Report: Nuclear Options," *Canadian Business,* April 11, 2011.

25. Ibid.

Chapter 5

1. PBS, 2010, "Enron: The Smartest Guys in the Room," Independent Lens, accessed at http://www.pbs.org/independentlens/enron/timeline2006.html, July 12, 2010; "Enron Chiefs Guilty of Fraud and Conspiracy," *New York Times,* http://www.nytimes.com/2006/05/25/business/25cnd-enron.html?_r=1&oref=slogin, accessed May 27, 2006; Mark Sherman, "High Court Hears Ex-Enron CEO Skilling's Appeal," Associated Press, via yahoo.com, March 1, 2010; David Teather, "Skilling to Report to Prison," *The Guardian,* http://business.guardian.co.uk/story/0,,1971179,00.html, accessed December 13, 2006; and K. Eichenwald, *Conspiracy of Fools: A True Story* (New York: Broadway, 2005).

2. David Voreacos, "Madoff Criminal Charges: Summary of the 11 Counts Against Him," Bloomberg, March 11, 2009; Diana B. Henriques, "Madoff Sentenced to 150 Years for Ponzi Scheme," *New York Times,* June 30, 2009; "Madoff's Victims," WSJ Reporting: The Associated Press, *The Wall Street Journal,* March 6, 2009; and Anthony Destefano, "Prosecutors Reduce Madoff's Ponzi Scheme Total to $13B," Newsday.com, June 19, 2009.

3. Nortel Accounting Scandal, Meng, Galler, Still, Deloitte & Touche LLP, Auditors Nortel Networks Corporation, http://baf3motoday.com/uex/Fraud%20Project/Nortel%20Accounting%20Scandal.pdf; Tyler Hamilton, "Yet Another Delay at Nortel," *Toronto Star*, November 12, 2004; J. Edward Ketz, The Accounting Cycle, Nortel's Accounting Scheme, http://accounting.smartpros.com, July 2008; and Jacquie McNish, "Nortel, A Year Later: How The Liquidation Was Done," *The Globe and Mail*, January 12, 2010.

4. Ingrid Peritz, "Jones Enjoyed Lavish Lifestyle at Investors' Expense, Trustee Says," *The Globe and Mail*, August 19, 2009.

5. Oliver Moore, "Dozens of Charges Laid in Nova Scotia Legislature Expenses Scandal," *The Globe and Mail*, February 14, 2011; Leblanc and Sher, "Quebec Corruption Probe Reaches From Hard Hats to High Rise Offices," *The Globe and Mail*, December 3, 2010; Jordana Huber, "Integrity Czar to Review Agency Expenses, McGuinty," *National Post*, Canwest News Service, September 1, 2009; and Rod Mickleburgh, "Trial's End Lets Campbell Liberals Off the Hook," *The Globe and Mail*, October 18, 2010.

6. When Your Calendar Is a Moral Document: A Conversation with Reverend Jim Wallis, CEO, Sojourners, *McKinsey Quarterly*, McKinsey & Company, January 2010.

7. Felton, Hudnut, Witt, "Building a Stronger Board, Corporate Governance," *McKinsey Quarterly*, McKinsey & Company, 1995, Number 2; and Felton and Watson, "Change Across the Board," *McKinsey Quarterly*, McKinsey & Company, 2002, Number 4.

8. Barry Shaw, Bill 198—Sarbanes-Oxley Comes to Canada, BRS Management Consulting, www.itprojecttemplates.com/WP_SEC_BillC198.htm, 2005; and Stephanie Ben Ishai, Associate Professor, Osgoode Hall Law School, "Sarbanes-Oxley, Five Years Later: A Canadian Perspective," *Loyola University Law Journal*, June 2008, www.luc.edu.

9. News Release, Financial Accounting Standards Board, January 28, 2011, www.fasb.org/cs/; and International Accounting Standards Board, ISAB and FASB update to G20 Leaders, June 2, 2010, www.ifrs.org.

10. P. Beard, "In Defense of Wal-Mart," *Capitalism Magazine*, October 2, 2004, accessed July 21, 2010, http://www.capitalismmagazine.com/markets/business/3957-Defense-Wal-Mart.html; S. Greenhouse, "Workers Assail Night Lock-Ins by Wal-Mart," *New York Times*, January 18, 2004, accessed July 21, 2010 from http://www.nytimes.com/2004/01/18/us/workers-assail-night-lock-ins-by-wal-mart.html; S. Maich, "What the Numbers Say about Wal-Mart," *Maclean's*, May 28, 2008, accessed July 21, 2010 from http://www.macleans.ca/columnists/article.jsp?id=3&content=20080528_54437_54437; Steven Malanga, "The Tort Plague Hits Wal-Mart," *City Journal*, accessed July 21, 2010 from http://www.city-journal.org/html/eon_06_24_04sm.html; Jeff M. Sellers, "Women Against Wal-Mart," *Christianity Today*, April 22, 2005, accessed July 21, 2010, from http://www.christianitytoday.com/ct/2005/aprilweb-only/52.0b.html; Walmart, 2010 Annual Report, accessed July 21, 2010, from http://walmartstores.com/sites/annualreport/2010/corporate_responsibility.aspx; and Wendy Zellner, "No Way to Treat a Lady," *BusinessWeek*, March 3, 2003, accessed July 21, 2010 from http://www.businessweek.com/magazine/content/03_09/b3822067_mz021.htm.

11. Corporate Social Responsibility Branding Survey, Penn, Schoen & Berland Associates, LLC, 2010.

12. Bonini, McKillop, Mendonca, "What Consumers Expect from Companies," *McKinsey Quarterly*, McKinsey & Company, 2007.

13. Bonini, Brun, Rosenthal, "Valuing Corporate Social Responsibility: McKinsey Global Survey Results," *McKinsey Quarterly*, McKinsey & Company, 2009; and Bonini, McKillop, Mendonca, "What Consumers Expect From Companies," *McKinsey Quarterly*, McKinsey & Company, 2007.

14. "Six Tiny Treasures: The McGhee Sextuplets," *The Oprah Winfrey Show*, February 21, 2011.

15. Health Charities Coalition of Canada (HCCC), Award of Distinction 2010, Mac Voisin, M&M Meat Shops, www.healthcharities.ca/hccc-award-of-distinction, February 24, 2011.

16. Neil Edmunds, P. Eng., Impacts and Mitigations of In Situ Bitumen Production from Alberta Oil Sands, Submission to XXIst World Energy Congress, Montreal 2010.

17. B. Ross and J. Rhee, "Are You Playing Rental Car Roulette? Federal Study: Major Rental Agencies Rent Out Cars That Have Been Recalled for Defects," ABC News, www.abcnews.com, February 25, 2011.

18. Diane Jermyn, "The Top 50 Greenest Employees," *The Globe and Mail*, April 22, 2010; Keys, Malnight, van der Graaf, "Making the Most of Corporate Social Responsibility," *McKinsey Quarterly*, McKinsey & Company, December 2009; and Bonini, Brun, Rosenthal, "Valuing Corporate Social Responsibility: McKinsey Global Survey Results," *McKinsey Quarterly*, McKinsey & Company, 2009.

19. The Business of Giving, Special Advertising Section, Fortune Magazine in partnership with CECP, *Fortune,* February 7, 2011.

20. L. Burkitt, 2010, Companies' Good Deeds Resonate with Consumers, Forbes.com, May 27, 2010, accessed from http://www.forbes.com/2010/05/26/microsoft-google-apple-ford-cmo-network-most-inspiring-companies.html on July 12, 2010; and McDonald's Corporation, 2009, Worldwide Corporate Responsibility Online Report: The Values We Bring to the Table, accessed from http://www.aboutmcdonalds.com/mcd/csr/report/community.-RightParaContentTout-43872-ReportsLinkList-81999_File1.tmp/mcd052_2009report_v6.pdf, July 12, 2010.

21. David Bruser, "Game Over For Shady Charity," *Toronto Star,* March 8, 2011.

22. Number of Canadians Concerned about Charity Fraud up Considerably, www.newswire.ca, February 2011.

23. www.bombardier.com/files/en/supporting.../CODE_EN_2005.pdf.

24. Ministry of Government Services, 2007. Consumer Protection in the Payday Lending Sector. Ontario, Accessed from http://www.ontla.on.ca/library/repository/mon/17000/273096.pdf, August 2010.

25. Canadian Western Bank Group, http://www.cwbank.com/ August 2010.

Chapter 6

1. Calvin Leung, "How Wal-Mart Canada Plans to Thrive in Tough Times," *Canadian Business,* March 2, 2009.

2. Kevin P. Coyne, "Sustainable Competitive Advantage," McKinsey & Company, www.mckinseyquarterly.com, 2000.

3. Boston Pizza International Mission Statement, www.bpincomefund.com, August 17, 2009; and Walmart's Mission Statement, www.walmartstores.com/investors/7614.aspx, August 17, 2009.

4. Hudson's Bay Co. Sells Credit Card, Financial Services Arm for $370 Million, http://agoracom.com/ir/agoracom/forums/discussion/topics/76409-hudson-s-bay-co-sells-credit-card-financial-services-arm-for-370m/messages/447177, August 17, 2009.

5. Avon Distribution Restructuring Leads to Closures, www.cosmeticsdesign.com, January 2007; and Avon Moves to Enhance Presence in China, www.chinadaily.com, March 2004.

6. Kevin P. Coyne, "Sustainable Competitive Advantage"; Roberto Buaron, "New Game Strategies," McKinsey & Company, www.mckinseyquarterly.com, 2000; Richard N. Foster, "Attacking Through Innovation," McKinsey & Company, www.mckinseyquarterly.com, 2000; and Amar Bhide, "Hustle As Strategy," *Harvard Business Review,* McKinsey & Company, www.mckinseyquarterly.com, 1986.

7. Anupreet Sandhu Bhamra, "B.C. Lottery Corporation Raises Weekly Play Limit to $10,000 from $120," *The Globe and Mail,* August 20, 2009, p. A9.

8. The following resources have influenced this section of the text: Kevin P. Coyne, "Sustainable Competitive Advantage," McKinsey & Company, www.mckinseyquarterly.com, 2000; Roberto Buaron, "New Game Strategies," McKinsey & Company, www.mckinseyquarterly.com, 2000; Richard N. Foster, "Attacking Through Innovation," McKinsey & Company, www.mckinseyquarterly.com, 2000; and Amar Bhide, "Hustle As Strategy," *Harvard Business Review,* McKinsey & Company, www.mckinseyquarterly.com, 1986.

9. Merck & Co., 2008 Annual Report, www.merck.com, August 2009; Merck & Co., investor relations, www.merck.com, August 2009; and Jonathon D. Rockoff, "Merck to Buy Rival for $41 Billion, Schering-Plough Deal Is Latest Bid to Diversify," *Wall Street Journal,* March 10, 2009, www.wsj.com.

10. The work of Dr. Peter Richardson, Queen's University, with respect to planning cycles and strategic turnarounds was a general resource for the discussion in this section of the text.

11. Sony Corporation (ADR) Financials, www.googlefinance.com, August 21, 2009; USD to Japanese Yen, $1 (USD) equals 94 Yen, www.googlefinance.com, August 21, 2009; and Richard Siklos, "Sony: Lost in Transformation," *Fortune,* www.fortune.com, June 26, 2009.

12. Interview, Elwin Derbyshire, Canadian Tire Centre—Cataraqui, Kingston, Ontario, September 3, 2009.

13. Guide for Analysis of Social Economy Enterprises, Réseau d'investissement social du Québec, 2005, ISBN 2-923253-01-9.

14. Ibid.

15. Joe Castaldo, "Wireless Wonder Boy," *Canadian Business,* September 14, 2009.

Chapter 7

1. March Davis, Management Strategies from a Top CEO, SFGate.com, March 16, 2010; Biography, Jack Welch, The Welch Way, official website of Jack and Suzy Welch, www.welchway.com, May 14, 2010; and Management in Action, Jack Welch, The Welch Way, official website of Jack and Suzy Welch, www.welchway.com, May 14, 2010.

2. George Ambler, 25 Lessons from Jack Welch, Practice of Leadership.net, www.thepracticeofleadership.net, May 14, 2010.

3. Notes from *Mission Critical Marketing*, Ken Wong, Queen's University School of Business, May 2010.

4. Organizational Structure, www.referenceforbusiness.com/ob-or/organizational-structure.html, May 10, 2010; and Organizational Structure, www.npd-solutions.com/orgstructure.html, May 10, 2010.

5. Alex Taylor III, "Fixing Up Ford," *Fortune,* Volume 159, May 25, 2009; Ford Motor Company, Googlefinance, www.googlefinance.com, May 13, 2010; and Biography, Alan Mulally, www.media.ford.com, May 13, 2010.

6. Geert Hofstede, Hofstede's Cultural Dimensions Model, www.geert-hofstede.com, May 2011.

7. Organizational Culture, Mikander, Human Resource Development, www.mikander.fi/en/culture.php, May 2010.

8. The following resources have influenced this section of the text: Saxby, Parker, Nitse, Dishman, "Environmental Scanning and Organizational Culture," *Market Intelligence & Planning,* Volume 20, MCB UP Ltd., 2002; and Mikander, Organizational Culture, Human Resource Development, www.mikander.fi/en/culture.php, May 2010.

9. Eastman Kodak, Annual Report 2000, www.kodak.com, May 14, 2010; Ben Dobbin, "Questions Intensify as Kodak Tries to Complete Turnaround," *New York Times,* January 29, 2008, www.nytimes.com; William Symonds, "Kodak Rewrites the Book on Printing," *BusinessWeek,* September 4, 2006; and Eastman Kodak, Google Finance, www.googlefinance.com, May 13, and June 29, 2010.

10. Stuart C. Gibson, How to Make Restructuring Work for Your Company, 2001, HBS Working Knowledge, Harvard Business School, http://hbswk.hbs.edu/cgi-bin/print?id=2476, May 2010; and Richard Heygate, "Immoderate Redesign," *McKinsey Quarterly,* February 1993, www.mckinseyquarterly.com, May 2010.

Chapter 8

1. Elizabeth G. Chambers, Mark Foulon, Helen Handfield-Jones, Steven M. Hankin, Edward G. Michaels III, "The War for Talent," *McKinsey Quarterly,* 1998, Number 3; and Elizabeth Axelrod, Helen Handfield-Jones, Tim Welsh, "War For Talent, Part II," *McKinsey and Company,* 2001.

2. The following resources have influenced this section of the text: Matthew Guthridge, Asmus B. Komm, Emily Lawson, "Making Talent a Strategic Priority," *McKinsey Quarterly,* 2008, Number 1; and Gurdjian, Triebel, "Identifying Employee Skill Gaps," *McKinsey Quarterly,* May 2009.

3. Betsy Morris, "Steve Jobs Speaks Out (Management Style and Finding Talent)," *Fortune,* 2008.

4. The following resources have influenced this section of the text: Matthew Guthridge, Asmus B. Komm, Emily Lawson, "Making Talent a Strategic Priority," *McKinsey Quarterly,* 2008, Number 1; "Motivating Employees When Budgets Are Tight," *McKinsey Quarterly,* www.mckinseyquarterly.com, May 2010; and Dewhurst, Guthridge, Mohr, "Motivating People: Getting Beyond Money," *McKinsey Quarterly,* November 2009.

5. Moskowitz, Levering, Tkaczyk, "The 100 Best Companies to Work For," *Fortune,* February 8, 2010; *Financial Post*'s Ten Best Companies to Work For in 2010, Yerema and Caballero, Mediacorp Inc. (staff editors), November 2009; www.eluta.ca/top-employer, April 2010; and Dewhurst, Guthridge, Mohr, "Motivating People: Getting Beyond Money," *McKinsey Quarterly,* November 2009.

6. ACCEL Team Development Practices, www.accel-team.com, April 23, 2010. Excerpts from a Supervisor's Guide to Employee Motivation.

7. Gurdjian, Triebel, "Identifying Employee Skill Gaps," *McKinsey Quarterly,* May 2009.

8. Where Are You on the Journey of Good to Great? Diagnostic Tool, Individual Worksheet Packet, Release Version 1.0, Jim Collins, www.jimcollins.com, April 30, 2010.

9. Hsieh and Yuk, "Leadership as the Starting Point of Strategy," *McKinsey Quarterly,* 2005, Number 1, McKinsey & Company, www.mckinseyquarterly.com.

10. Derek Sankey, "Managing Staff Gets Personal," *Financial Post,* May 3, 2010.

11. Kmazur Kewich, "Goalposts Set for Success," *Financial Post,* May 3, 2010; Derek Sankey, "Managing Staff Gets Personal," *Financial Post,* May 3, 2010; and "The Things That Keep Business Owners Awake," www.BizLaunch.ca, *Toronto Star,* April 24, 2010.

Chapter 9

1. Toyota Production System, Toyota Vision and Philosophy, www2.toyota.co/jp/en/vision/production_system/, 1995 – 2010 Toyota Motor Corporation.

2. Hitt, Black, Porter, Gaudes, *Management,* Canadian Edition (Pearson Custom Publishing, 2009).

3. Andrew Vanacore, "Research Firm Puts $499 iPad Costs at $259.60," *The Globe and Mail,* www.globeandmail.com, April 7, 2010.

4. Michael Porter, Value Chain Model Framework, Value Based Management.net, www.valuebasedmanagement.net, May 25, 2010; and Michael Porter, The Value Chain, QuickMBA Strategic Management, www.quickmba.com/strategy/value-chain/, May 25, 2010.

5. Doris Burke, "Planet Wal-Mart, Fortune 500: No. 1," *Fortune,* May 3, 2010; and Walmart Website, Walmart Corporate, www.walmart.com/aboutus, May 27, 2010.

6. Nickels, McHugh, McHugh, Cosa, *Understanding Canadian Business,* 6th edition (McGraw-Hill Ryerson, 2007); and Hitt, Black, Porter, Gaudes, *Management, Canadian Edition,* (Pearson Custom Publishing, 2009).

7. Toyota Production System, Toyota Vision and Philosophy, www2.toyota.co/jp/en/vision/production_system/, 1995–2010 Toyota Motor Corporation.

8. Walmart Website, Walmart Corporate, www.walmart.com/aboutus, May 27, 2010.

9. Tony Van Alphen, "800 New Toyota Jobs for Ontario," *Toronto Star,* December 11, 2009.

10. Steve Arnold, "Harvey's Puts Fresh Ideas into Operation," *The Hamilton Spectator,* January 8, 2008.

11. Demand Drives, Optimizing Inventory-to-Cash Conversion to Drive Financial Performance, Executive Report, SSA Global, January 2006; and Constantine, Ruwadi, and Wine, "Management Practices That Drive Supply Chain Success," *McKinsey Quarterly,* McKinsey & Company, February 2009.

12. Putten and MacMillan, *Unlocking Opportunities for Growth* (Wharton School Publishing, July 2008).

13. Tide Laundry Products and Accessories, www.tide.ca, June 2010.

14. Jessica Mintz, "Apple Profit Skyrockets on Sales of iPhone," *Toronto Star,* www.thestar.com, April 21, 2010.

15. International Organization for Standards, About ISO, www.iso.org/iso/home, May 2010.

16. Six Sigma, Aveta Business Solutions, www.sixsigmaonline.org/six-sigma-training-certification-information, May 2010; and Lean Sigma Institute Six Sigma Methodology, www.sixsigmainstitute.com, May 2010.

17. Total Quality Management, Business Excellence, www.beexcellence.org/Total-quality-management, May 2010.

Chapter 10

1. Jessie Hempel, "Facebook's Friend in Russia," *Fortune,* October 18, 2010.

2. Kenneth Wong, Marketing for Profit: The Mission Critical Approach, AMBA Mission Critical Marketing, Queen's University, 2007.

3. Francois Legarde, Social Marketer, Marketing and Positioning Presentation, YMCA of Ontario, CEO Conference, February 2006.

4. Marc Gunther, Marilyn Adamo, Betsy Feldman, "3M's Innovation Revival," *Fortune,* September 2010, www.fortune.com, December 2010.

5. Starbucks Corporation, Fiscal 2009 Annual Report, form K10, www.starbucks.com, January 2011; "Give Me Venti Brew: Seattle Starbucks Serves Beer," Associated Press, October 18, 2010; Brand Evolution FAQs, www.starbucks.com, January 2011; "Starbucks Climb Isn't Over Yet," Fortune Finance, www.CNNMoney.com, December 3, 2010; and Julie Jargon, "Starbucks Looks to Juice Bars to Squeeze Out More Profits," *Globe and Mail Report on Business,* November 11, 2011.

6. Ansoff Matrix, QuickMBA Strategic Management, www.quickmba.com/strategy/matrix/ansoff, July 2010.

7. Canadian Tire Retail, Facts and Stats, Canadian Tire Corporation, http://corp.canadiantire.ca/en/media/factsandstats/pages/canadiantireretail.aspx, July 2010; and Canadian Tire Annual Report 2009, http://canadiantire.ca/en/investors/financialreports, July 2010.

8. Population by Year, Province, and Territory, Summary Table, Statistics Canada, www.statcan.gc.ca, November 2009.

9. Jeremy Caplan, "Google Acquisitions Binge: Why It Bought Picnik," *Time,* www.time.com, March 2010.

10. Tata, Leadership with Trust, www.tata.com, June 2011.

11. The following resource was a key contributor to the thoughts in this section of the text: Court, Elzinga, Mulder, Vetvik, "The Consumer Decision Journey," *McKinsey Quarterly,* 2–9, Number 3, December 2010.

12. Court, Elzinga, Mulder, Vetvik, "The Consumer Decision Journey," *McKinsey Quarterly,* 2–9, Number 3, December 2010.

13. Humane Society of Canada, www.humanesociety.com, January 2011; and Kingston Humane Society, www.kingstonhumanesociety.com, January 2011.

14. Ibid.

15. Kenneth Wong, Marketing for Profit: The Mission Critical Approach, AMBA Mission Critical Marketing, Queen's University, 2007.

16. Mattel, 2009 Annual Report at http://files.shareholder.com/downloads/MAT/998102199x0x362364/DE3C1DC8-EDD4-41AD-81E5-2D8251DB8E5D/Mattel_Annual_Report_As_Printed1.pdf, August 2010; and MGA Entertainment, 2010. Bratz. Accessed at http://www.bratz.com/, August 2010.

Chapter 11

1. Can FreshDirect Revive U.S. Online Grocery Market? Reuters, 2010, http://www.reuters.com/article/idUSTRE6381NM20100409, August 2010; and J. Wuorio, "These Online Grocers Got It Right," *BusinessWeek,* 2009, <http://www.businessweek.com/magazine/content/09_66/s0906023658729.htm, August 2010.

2. "Companies We Love, Special Report," *Canadian Business,* June 13, 2011; and Kristian Gravenor, "The French Connection," *Canadian Business,* June 13, 2011.

3. Authorized Distributors, www.coach.com, January 2011.

4. K. Allison & C. Nuttall, "Dell to Sell Computers through Walmart," FT.com (*Financial Times*), May 24, 2007.

5. Sears Opens Pop-Up Store at McMaster University, CNW, http://cnw.ca/en/releases/archives/september2008/10/c3241.html, January 2011; P. Levy, Sears Hopes New Brand Strategy Will Jump-Start Sales, www.marketingpower.com, Library Resources, March 2010; and Sears Holdings Corporation, Our Brands, http://searsholdings.com/about/brands/htm. January 2011.

6. Sofame Technologies Inc., www.sofame.com, August 2010; and Sofame Technologies Inc.: Sparking Growth in a Mature Manufacturing Company, Case Study, Ken Mark, Ivey Publishing 9B09M070, 2009.

7. Boaz, Murnane, Nuffer, "The Basics of Business-to-Business Sales Success," *McKinsey Quarterly,* McKinsey & Company, May 2010; and Davie, Stephenson, Valdivieso de Uster, "Three Trends in Business-to-Business Sales," *McKinsey Quarterly,* McKinsey & Company, May 2010.

8. David Edelman, "Four Ways to Get More Value from Digital Marketing," *McKinsey Quarterly,* McKinsey & Company, March 2010.

9. Social Media Opportunities for Public Companies, Case Study: Players Network, Inc., Pojunis & Small, NewMediaPlus, www.newmediaplus.com, June 2011.

10. Michael Oliveira, "Facebook Not Just For Friends Anymore as Businesses Makes Its Marketing Network," *Canadian Business,* March 23, 2011, www.canadianbusiness.com.

11. Ibid.

12. http://www.facebook.com/timhortons, June 21, 2011.

13. http://www.facebook.com/lululemon, June 21, 2011.

14. Keep on Trucking, Economist 2010, http://www.economist.com/node/16595179?story_id=16595179, August 2010; S. McCarthy & N. Vanderklippe, "As Oil Nears $100 Mark, Threat to Recovery Grows," *The Globe and Mail,* www.globeandmail.com, January 18, 2011; and J. Wohl &

N. Zieminski, "Costs Put New Pressures on Manufacturers in 2011," www.nationalpost.com, January 13, 2011.

15. Full List of Brands, Frito Lay, www.fritolay.com/our-snacks/full-list-of-brands.html, January 2011.

16. The BCG Growth-Share Matrix, NetMBA Business Knowledge Center, www.netmba.com/strategy/matrix/bcg/, January 2011.

17. Marina Strauss, "Quebec Retail Mainstay Set to Head West," *The Globe and Mail Report on Business,* January 20, 2011.

18. Dana Flavelle, "Joe Fresh Goes to the Mall," *Toronto Star,* January 20, 2011.

Chapter 12

1. Air Canada Fourth Quarter Results and 2009 Highlights, February 10, 2010, Air Canada website/investor relations, http://www.aircanada.com/en/about/investor/rep_info.html, May 2010.

2. Richard Stutely, *The Definitive Business Plan,* 2nd Edition (Prentice Hall, 2007).

3. Layton and Penttinen, "A Better Way to Cut Costs," *McKinsey Quarterly,* McKinsey & Company, October 2009.

4. Marn, Roegner, Zawada, "Pricing New Products," *McKinsey Quarterly,* McKinsey & Company, 2003; and Dolan, Gourville, Principles of Pricing, Harvard Business School, 9-506-021, April 3, 2009.

5. The Forzani Group Ltd., Investor Presentation, April 28, 2009, www.forzanigroup.com, May 2010; Forzani Group Q4 Sales and Earnings Dip on Warm Weather, SportsOneSource, April 7, 2010; Forzani Group Ltd. Q4F10 Web Presentation, April 6, 2010; Marina Strauss, "Canadian Tire Acquires a New Set of Customers," *The Globe and Mail,* www.globeandmail.com, May 9, 2011; and "Canadian Tire Spends $771 million to Snap Up Forzani Group," CTV.ca News Staff, www.ctv.ca, May 9, 2011.

6. Marn, Roegner, Zawada, "Pricing New Products," *McKinsey Quarterly,* McKinsey & Company, 2003; and Dolan, Gourville, Principles of Pricing, Harvard Business School, 9-506-021, April 3, 2009.

Chapter 13

1. Alexei Oreskovic, "Revenue Tops $800 Million for Facebook," *Toronto Star,* June 19, 2010; Benn Parr, Facebook Could Surpass $1 Billion In Revenue This Year, http://mashable.com, March 2, 2010; Facebook Marketing Statistics, Global Audience, www.CheckFacebook.com, June 2011; and Facebook Use Drops In Canada, U.S., CBC News, www.cbc.ca, June 13, 2011.

2. Ontario Securities Commission, www.osc.gov.on.ca, June 15, 2010; and Autorité des marchés financiers (AMF), www.lautorite.qc.ca/autorite/a-propos.en.html, June 15, 2010. In addition, the following resources have influenced this section of the text: Holly Crosgrey, "Registering a Sole Proprietorship in Canada," Resources for Canadian Business Owners, The Free Library, May 28, 2009; Partnerships FAQ, LEANLEGAL.COM, www.leanlegal.com/faq_partnerships.asp, June 14, 2010; and Limited Partnerships & Limited Liability Partnerships, Lohn Caulder Chartered Accountants, Topical Library, www.lohncaulder.com, June 2010.

3. Lululemon Athletica Inc., Advent International, www.adventinternational.com/investmentdata, June 15, 2010; Lululemon Athletica Inc. IPO, www.123jump.com, Yordanka Bahchevanska, August 1, 2007; Lululemon Receives $195 Million Infusion, Sporting Goods Business, January 1, 2006, AllBusiness, a D&B Company, www.allbusiness.com, June 2010; and Lululemon Athletica Inc., SEC Filing, Form S-1A-EX 3.5, Amended and Restated Certificate of Incorporation, www.secinfo.com, June 30, 2010.

4. Sequoia Capital, www.sequoiacap.com, June 16, 2010; and Sequoia Capital, Crunch Base Profile, www.crunchbase.com/financial-organization/sequoia-capital, June 16, 2010.

5. Investment and capital structure terms were validated via a check against the Investment Dictionary, www.investopedia.com, June 2010.

6. DBRS Ratings and Other Processes, www.dbrs.com, June 16, 2010.

7. President's Choice Financial, Mortgage Calculator, www.pcfinancial.ca/a/tools/mortgagecal.ams, June 16, 2010; and Vorton Financial Power Tools, Loan Calculations, June 2010.

8. Lululemon Athletica Inc. IPO, www.123jump.com, Yordanka Bahchevanska, August 1, 2007.

9. Mae Anderson, "Toys R Us Says It Plans to Go Public Again," Associated Press, *Kingston Whig-Standard,* May 29, 2010.

10. General Maritime Corporation Announces Pricing of Common Stock Offering, General Maritime Corporation, www.stockhouse.com/news, June 17, 2010.

11. Scott Deveau, "Porter Drops Plans for IPO," *Financial Post,* www.financialpost.com, June 1, 2010.

12. Barrie McKenna, "How Apple Became the New Tech King," *The Globe and Mail,* www.globeandmail.com, May 26, 2010; and Ravi Nagarajan, Apple Leads Microsoft in Market Cap Race, Rational Walk, www.rationalwalk.com, May 26, 2010.

13. Shaw Announces Acquisition of a Restructured Canwest for $2.0 Billion, Shaw News Release, Shaw Investor Relations, www.shaw.ca, June 2010; Dana Flavelle and John Spears, Shaw Buys Control of Canwest Global, www.thestar.com, February 12, 2010; Canwest Global Communications Corporation, Company History, www.canwestglobal.com, June 2010; Calvin Leung, "The Good, The Bad and the Ugly: Canwest Global Communications," *Canadian Business,* March 30, 2009; Dana Flavelle, "Canwest CEO Opposed Bankruptcy Decision," www.thestar.com, January 11, 2010; Debt Tests Canadian Media Giant Canwest, New York Times DealBook, Edited by Andrew Ross Sorkin, February 27, 2009; Canwest's Dance With Debt, Business Canada, CBC News, www.cbc.ca/money/story/2009/02/24/f-canwest.html, April 23, 2009; and Susan Krashinsky, "Canwest Newspapers to Sport New Name," *The Globe and Mail Report on Business,* www.theglobeandmail.com, July 2, 2010.

Chapter 14

1. Timothy Koller and Jonathan Peacock, "Time for CFOs to Step Up," *McKinsey Quarterly,* 2002.

2. Dobbs, Leslie, Mendonca, "Building the Healthy Corporation," *McKinsey Quarterly,* 2005; Circuit City to Lay Off 3500 Employees, AP News Wire, www.foxnews.com, March 28, 2007; Stephanie Armour, "Circuit City's Plan to Fire 3400 Employees Will Have Ripple Effect," AP News Wire, *USA Today,* www.usatoday.com, 2007; and Circuit City to Liquidate U.S. Stores, www.msnbc.com news service, January 16, 2009.

3. The following resource supports the commentary across this section of the text and was also used to check the accuracy of the formulas provided: Introduction to Financial Ratios and Financial Statement Analysis, William Bruns, Harvard Business School, Rev. September 13, 2004. The following resource was also used to check the accuracy of formulas: Definitions Verification, www.investopedia.com, January 2010.

4. Googlefinance.com, annual and quarterly financial statements, Yahoo Inc., Google Inc., and Microsoft Corporation, June 2010.

5. Bennett Stewart, EVA Momentum: One Ratio That Tells the Whole Story, EVA Dimensions, *Journal of Applied Corporate Finance: A Morgan Stanley Publication,* Spring 2009.

6. Guide for Analysis of Social Economy Enterprises, Réseau d'investissement social du Québec, 2005.

Chapter 15

1. Dedicated Everyday, 2010 Annual Report, Saputo Inc., February 2011; Saputo Inc., Company Profile, www.saputo.ca/investorsandmedia/companyprofile, February 2011; Saputo Inc., Company History, www.fundinguniverse.com, February 2011; The Rich 100: Canada's Wealthiest People, www.canadianbusiness.com, February 2011.

2. Saras D. Sarasvathy, New Venture Performance, Darden Business Publishing, University of Virginia, UV0811, 2006.

3. The following resources provided a general reference to comments made throughout this chapter: Course Notes, MBUS 981, Management of New Ventures, Dr. Elspeth Murray, School of Business, Queen's University, February 2011; Richard Stutely, *The Definitive Business Plan,* Revised 2nd Edition, FT Prentice Hall, 2007; and Peter J. Capezio, *Manager's Guide to Business Planning,* Briefcase Books (McGraw-Hill Ryerson, 2010).

4. Richard Stutely, *The Definitive Business Plan,* Revised 2nd Edition, FT Prentice Hall, 2007.

5. The A&W Franchise Opportunity, A&W Food Services of Canada, Inc., www.awfranchise.ca, June 2011; and Tim Hortons Canada Franchise Information, www.timhortons.com, June 2011.

6. Saras D. Sarasvathy, New Venture Performance, Darden Business Publishing, University of Virginia, UV0811, 2006.

7. Richard Stutely, *The Definitive Business Plan,* Revised 2nd Edition, FT Prentice Hall, 2007.

8. Franchise Package, M&M Meat Shops, www.franchise.mmmeatshops.com, February 2011.

9. 2003 Annual Report, Notes to Consolidated Financial Statements, p. 78, Amazon.com/investor relations/annual reports and proxies, February 2011.

10. The following resource was used as a general reference for the creation of Figure 15.12 and the discussion in this section of the text: Milestones for Successful Venture Planning, Block Macmillan Harvard Business Review, Reprint 85503.

11. Richard Branson, "Good Delivery Relies on Attention to Detail," *Canadian Business,* February 28, 2011.

12. Hamermesh, Heskett, Roberts, A Note on Managing the Growing Venture, Harvard Business School, 9-805-092, August 2005.

13. Dr. Elspeth Murray, Course Notes, MBUS 981, Management of New Ventures, School of Business, Queen's University, February 2011.

14. The following resource was used as a general resource for the discussion in this section of the text: Note on Valuation for Venture Capital, Teddy Rosenberg, Richard Ivey School of Business, Ivey Management Services, 9B09N009, March 2009.

15. Financial News Release, Target Corporation to Acquire Interest in Canadian Real Estate from Zellers Inc., a Subsidiary of Hudson's Bay Company, for C$1.285 Billion, www.target.com/investornews, January 13, 2011; and Strauss & McNish, "With Target, Canada's Retail Landscape Set for Massive Makeover," *The Globe and Mail,* www.globeandmail.com, January 13, 2011.

16. Lisa Priest, "Diabetes Discovery Brings Out Hospital's Entrepreneurial Side," *The Globe and Mail,* February 15, 2011.

17. Dobbs, Leslie, Mendonca, "Building a Healthy Organization," *McKinsey Quarterly,* McKinsey & Company, 2005, Number 3, February 2011.

Photo Credits

Chapter 1

Page 3: Photo courtesy of David Waugh; page 9: BlackBerry®, RIM®, Research In Motion®, SureType®, SurePress™ and related trademarks, names and logos are the property of Research In Motion Limited and are registered and/or used in the U.S. and countries around the world; page 12: © DIEGO AZUBEL/epa/Corbis; page 19: © Tracy Leonard, used with permission of Booster Juice; page 21: Used by permission of EADS; page 22: © ANDY RAIN/epa/Corbis.

Chapter 2

Page 27: Photo courtesy of Jay Oduwole; page 28: The Canadian Press/Darryl Dyck; page 35: The Canadian Press Images/Bayne Stanley; page 40: © Government of Alberta; page 41: (left) The Canadian Press/Mario Beauregard, (right) The Canadian Press/Kevin Frayer.

Chapter 3

Page 59: Photo courtesy of Gemma Gadher; page 60: (top) © Christopher Morris/Corbis, (bottom) The Canadian Press/Bayne Stanley; page 62: Iain Masterton/GetStock.com; page 63: Alex Segre/GetStock.com; page 66: The Canadian Press/Andy Rain; page 69: Bloomberg via Getty Images; page 70: AFP/Getty Images; page 76: Used with permission from Canada Goose; page 77: Used with permission from Canada Goose.

Chapter 4

Page 89: Photo courtesy of Kimchi Hoang; page 90: Kelly Ann Tierney/Getty Images; page 102: The Canadian Press/Gene J. Puskar; page 103: Hubert Raguet/Look at Sciences/Science Photo Library; page 108: © Tracy Leonard.

Chapter 5

Page 117: Photo courtesy of Joanna Pleta; page 118: (top) James Nielsen/Stringer/Getty Images, (bottom) Dave Einsel/Stringer/Getty Images; page 127: © Tracy Leonard; page 136: © Tracy Leonard.

Chapter 6

Page 143: Photo courtesy of Margaret Walsh; page 144: © Tracy Leonard; page 160 © Action Press [2004] all rights reserved./The Canadian Press; page 161: Used with permission of Canadian Tire Corporation and Jac Jacobson; page 162: Used with permission of Canadian Tire Corporation.

Chapter 7

Page 169: Photo courtesy of Noel Chow; page 170: The Canadian Press/Teru Iwasaki; page 178: AFP/Getty Images; page 179: The Canadian Press/J. Scott Applewhite; page 186: The Canadian Press/Damian Dovargames; page 187: © Action Press [2004] all rights reserved/The Canadian Press.

Chapter 8

Page 195: Photo courtesy of Katharine Berger; page 196: Digital Vision/Getty Images; page 201: The Canadian Press/Marcio Jose Sanchez; page 203: The Canadian Press/Don Denton; page 206: H. Armstrong Roberts/Getty Images.

Chapter 9

Page 219: Photo courtesy of Hyuk-tae Kwon; page 220: Christian Science Moniter/Getty Images; page 228: © Tracy Leonard; page 237: © Tracy Leonard.

Chapter 10

Page 251: Photo courtesy of Rachel Zimmer; page 252: AFP/Getty Images; page 261: (top) Bloomberg via Getty Images, (bottom) The Canadian Press/Ted S. Warren.

Chapter 11

Page 277: Photo courtesy of Bram Warshafsky; page 278: (top) Getty Images, (bottom) © Karen Huntt/CORBIS ; page 284: (top) The Canadian Press/Ryan Remiorz, (middle) The Canadian Press Images/Darryl Dyck, (bottom) The Canadian Press/Bayne Stanley; page 288: Used with permission from YMCA; page 306: (top) AFP/Getty Images, (bottom) Don Hammond/DesignPics/getstock.com.

Chapter 12

Page 315: Photo courtesy of Niklas Elofsson; page 316: © Bettmann/CORBIS; page 324: Thomas Barwick/Getty Images; page 335: The Canadian Press/Larry MacDougal.

Chapter 13

Page 351: Photo courtesy of Heather Hawks; page 352: AP Photo/Paul Sakuma, File/The Canadian Press; page 361: (all three logos) Photo Edit/getstock.com; page 376: (top) © SCANPIX Photos Limited (2004) all rights reserved/The Canadian Press, (bottom) The Canadian Press/Paul Sakuma.

Chapter 14

Page 385: Photo courtesy of Will Fang; page 386: Thomas Barwick/Getty Images; page 390: © Frances Roberts/getstock.com; page 407: gerenme/Getty Images.

Chapter 15

Page 423: Photo courtesy of Ahmad Iqbal; page 424: The Canadian Press/Ian Barrett; page 438: The Canadian Press/Reed Saxon; page 445: Getty Images.

Index

 STUDENTS...

Want to get **better grades**? *(Who doesn't?)*

Prefer to do your **homework online**? *(After all, you're online anyway...)*

Need **a better way** to **study** before the big test? *(A little peace of mind is a good thing...)*

 With **McGraw-Hill's Connect,**™

STUDENTS GET:

- **Easy online access** to homework, tests, and quizzes assigned by your instructor.

- **Immediate feedback** on how you're doing. (No more wishing you could call your instructor at 1 a.m.)

- **Quick access** to lectures, practice materials, eBook, and more. (All the material you need to be successful is right at your fingertips.)

- A Self-Quiz and Study tool that **assesses your knowledge** and **recommends** specific readings, supplemental study materials, and additional practice work.